Asset Protection and Security Management Handbook

OTHER AUERBACH PUBLICATIONS

The ABCs of IP Addressing
Gilbert Held
ISBN: 0-8493-1144-6

The ABCs of TCP/IP
Gilbert Held
ISBN: 0-8493-1463-1

Building an Information Security Awareness Program
Mark B. Desman
ISBN: 0-8493-0116-5

Building a Wireless Office
Gilbert Held
ISBN: 0-8493-1271-X

The Complete Book of Middleware
Judith Myerson
ISBN: 0-8493-1272-8

Computer Telephony Integration, 2nd Edition
William A. Yarberry, Jr.
ISBN: 0-8493-1438-0

Cyber Crime Investigator's Field Guide
Bruce Middleton
ISBN: 0-8493-1192-6

Cyber Forensics: A Field Manual for Collecting, Examining, and Preserving Evidence of Computer Crimes
Albert J. Marcella and Robert S. Greenfield, Editors
ISBN: 0-8493-0955-7

Global Information Warfare: How Businesses, Governments, and Others Achieve Objectives and Attain Competitive Advantages
Andy Jones, Gerald L. Kovacich, and Perry G. Luzwick
ISBN: 0-8493-1114-4

Information Security Architecture
Jan Killmeyer Tudor
ISBN: 0-8493-9988-2

Information Security Management Handbook, 4th Edition, Volume 1
Harold F. Tipton and Micki Krause, Editors
ISBN: 0-8493-9829-0

Information Security Management Handbook, 4th Edition, Volume 2
Harold F. Tipton and Micki Krause, Editors
ISBN: 0-8493-0800-3

Information Security Management Handbook, 4th Edition, Volume 3
Harold F. Tipton and Micki Krause, Editors
ISBN: 0-8493-1127-6

Information Security Management Handbook, 4th Edition, Volume 4
Harold F. Tipton and Micki Krause, Editors
ISBN: 0-8493-1518-2

Information Security Policies, Procedures, and Standards: Guidelines for Effective Information Security Management
Thomas R. Peltier
ISBN: 0-8493-1137-3

Information Security Risk Analysis
Thomas R. Peltier
ISBN: 0-8493-0880-1

A Practical Guide to Security Engineering and Information Assurance
Debra Herrmann
ISBN: 0-8493-1163-2

The Privacy Papers: Managing Technology and Consumers, Employee, and Legislative Action
Rebecca Herold
ISBN: 0-8493-1248-5

Secure Internet Practices: Best Practices for Securing Systems in the Internet and e-Business Age
Patrick McBride, Jody Patilla, Craig Robinson, Peter Thermos, and Edward P. Moser
ISBN: 0-8493-1239-6

Securing and Controlling Cisco Routers
Peter T. Davis
ISBN: 0-8493-1290-6

Securing E-Business Applications and Communications
Jonathan S. Held and John R. Bowers
ISBN: 0-8493-0963-8

Securing Windows NT/2000: From Policies to Firewalls
Michael A. Simonyi
ISBN: 0-8493-1261-2

Six Sigma Software Development
Christine B. Tayntor
ISBN: 0-8493-1193-4

A Technical Guide to IPSec Virtual Private Networks
James S. Tiller
ISBN: 0-8493-0876-3

Telecommunications Cost Management
Brian DiMarsico, Thomas Phelps IV, and William A. Yarberry, Jr.
ISBN: 0-8493-1101-2

AUERBACH PUBLICATIONS
www.auerbach-publications.com
To Order Call: 1-800-272-7737 • Fax: 1-800-374-3401
E-mail: orders@crcpress.com

Asset Protection and Security Management Handbook

POA Publishing LLC

AUERBACH PUBLICATIONS

A CRC Press Company
Boca Raton   London   New York   Washington, D.C.

Library of Congress Cataloging-in-Publication Data

Asset protection and security management handbook / POA Publishing LLC.
    p. cm.
Includes bibliographical references and index.
ISBN 0-8493-1603-0 (alk. paper)
    1. Private security services--United States--Handbooks, manuals, etc. 2. Corporations--Security measures--United States--Handbooks, manuals, etc. I. POA Publishing.

HV8291.U6 A87 2002
658.4′7—dc21
                                        2002030545

This book contains information obtained from authentic and highly regarded sources. Reprinted material is quoted with permission, and sources are indicated. A wide variety of references are listed. Reasonable efforts have been made to publish reliable data and information, but the author and the publisher cannot assume responsibility for the validity of all materials or for the consequences of their use.

Neither this book nor any part may be reproduced or transmitted in any form or by any means, electronic or mechanical, including photocopying, microfilming, and recording, or by any information storage or retrieval system, without prior permission in writing from the publisher.

The consent of CRC Press LLC does not extend to copying for general distribution, for promotion, for creating new works, or for resale. Specific permission must be obtained in writing from CRC Press LLC for such copying.

Direct all inquiries to CRC Press LLC, 2000 N.W. Corporate Blvd., Boca Raton, Florida 33431.

Trademark Notice: Product or corporate names may be trademarks or registered trademarks, and are used only for identification and explanation, without intent to infringe.

Visit the Auerbach Publications Web site at www.auerbach-publications.com

© 2003 by POA Publishing, LLC
Auerbach is an imprint of CRC Press LLC

No claim to original U.S. Government works
International Standard Book Number 0-8493-1603-0
Library of Congress Card Number 2002030545
Printed in the United States of America 1 2 3 4 5 6 7 8 9 0
Printed on acid-free paper

Contents

1	**Introduction to Assets Protection**	1
	The Management Function	1
	Asset Protection — A Historical Perspective	1
	Definition of Assets Protection	2
	Basic Considerations	4
	Countermeasures Planning	4
	Management Support	5
	Communicating the Plan	8
	Statutory and Regulatory Requirements	8
	The Systems Approach	8
	Countermeasures	9
	People	9
	Hardware	10
	Software	11
	The System Test	13
	Selected Bibliography	14
	Appendix A: Self-Inspection and Protection of Assets Check Sheet	15
	Protection of Assets Scoring Sheet	17
2	**Security Vulnerability**	19
	Introduction	19
	Defining the Problem	19
	Loss Event Profile	19
	Loss Event Probability or Frequency	21
	Probability Factors	23
	Historical Experience	24
	Application of Probability Factors Analyses	25
	Checklists	26
	Risk Matrix	26
	Probability Ratings	27
	Rating Symbols	28

ASSET PROTECTION AND SECURITY MANAGEMENT HANDBOOK

Loss Event Criticality	29
The Criticality Concept	29
Kinds of Costs to Be Considered	30
Permanent Replacement	30
Temporary Substitute	31
Related or Consequent Cost	31
Lost Income Cost	31
Cost Abatement	32
A Cost-of-Loss Formula	32
Criticality Ratings	33
Rating Symbols	34
Alternative Approaches to Criticality	34
Establishing Priorities	35
Preparing A Solution	36
Threat Analysis	36
Leverage	37
Network Design	38
Solving the Problem	38
Countermeasures	38
Countermeasures Criteria	39
Systems Evaluation Technique	40
Component Selection	41
Keeping the System Current	41
Risk Management	42
Economic Justification of Security	42
Cost Avoidance	43
Cost Avoidance in Loss Control	44
Asset Recoveries	46
Measuring Return on Expenditures	47
Selected Bibliography	48
Appendix A: Basic Security Survey	49
Part 1: Geography and Climate	49
Part 2: Size and Configuration	49
Part 3: Social and Political Environment	50
Part 4: Internal Activity	51
Part 5: Physical Safeguards	52
Part 6: Fire and Disaster	52
Part 7: Controls	53
Part 8: Indemnity	53
Appendix B: Basic Matrix	54
3 **Structural Barriers**	55
Introduction	55
Barrier Categories	56

	Building Surfaces.	57
	Roofs, Floors and Walls	57
	Roofs	57
	Exterior Walls	57
	Concrete Structures	58
	Floors	58
	Interior Walls	58
	Ceilings	60
	Evaluation of Building Surfaces	60
	Building Openings	62
	Doorways	62
	Windows	65
	Other Openings	66
	Concrete Block Barriers	67
	Bomb Protection	70
	Vehicle Barriers	75
	Selected Bibliography	77
4	**General Locking Concepts**	**79**
	Introduction	79
	Basic Lock Grouping	79
	Mechanical Locks	79
	The Warded Lock	80
	The Lever Lock	81
	The Pin Tumbler Lock	81
	The Wafer Tumbler Lock	84
	Dial-Type Combination Locks	86
	Electronic Dial-Type Combination Lock	89
	Master Keying Mechanical Locks	89
	Master Keying the Lever Lock	90
	Master Keying the Wafer Lock	90
	Master Keying the Pin Tumbler Lock	90
	Security Vulnerabilities of Mechanical Locks	92
	Attack by Force	92
	Surreptitious Attack	93
	Picking	93
	Attack by Impression Making and "Try" Keys	94
	Rearranging Mechanical Locks	94
	Rotation of Cylinders	94
	The Interchangeable Core	95
	A Caution on Combination Schemes	96
	Door Locks	97
	Office Function	100
	Classroom Function	100

Storeroom Function	100
Institution Function	100
Corridor Function	100
Electrified Locking Mechanisms	100
Electric Deadbolt	101
Electric Latch	101
Electric Strike	102
Stairtower Lock	103
Electric Lockset	104
Exit Device	106
Electromagnetic Lock	106
Shear Lock	108
Access Control during an Emergency	109
Selected Bibliography	110

5 Alarm Sensors — 111

Sensor Applications	111
Security Applications	111
UL Standards	113
ASTM Standards	114
Other Standards and Specifications	115
Categories of Sensors	116
Passive Infrared (PIR) Sensors	116
PIR Design	117
Application and Installation	118
Glass Break Sensors	120
Acoustic Sensors	121
Shock Sensors	122
Dual-Technology Sensors	123
Electromechanical Sensors	123
Foil	123
Magnetic and Mechanical Switches	124
Wire and Screen Detectors	125
Pressure Mats	125
Ultrasonic Sensors	126
Microwave Sensors	127
Capacitance Sensors	128
Shock and Vibration Sensors	128
Audio Sensors	128
Photoelectric Sensors	129
Other Sensors	130
Closed-Circuit Televsion	130
Balanced Pressure Sensor	130
Chemical Sensors	131

	Alarm Transmission and Control Panels.............	131
	Combinations Of Sensors	131
	Sensors For Fire Detection.............................	132
	Stages of Fire.....................................	133
	Sensor Types and Selection	134
	Fixed-Temperature Sensors	135
	Rate-of-Rise Sensors...............................	136
	Smoke or Combustion Product Sensors	136
	Water Flow Indicators	137
	Emerging Technology	138
	Selected Bibliography	139
	Appendix A: Federal Specification Components for Interior Alarm Systems	140
6	**Systems Considerations**	153
	Introduction...	153
	Alarm Termination	153
	Local Alarm Termination...........................	153
	Central Station Termination	154
	Reliability	155
	Direct Police or Fire Department Termination.........	156
	Proprietary Termination	157
	Termination Combinations	158
	Systems Design	158
	Cost Reduction and Protection Improvement.............	158
	Protection Enhancement............................	160
	Patrol Reduction...................................	160
	Closed-Circuit TV and Personnel Reductions	161
	The Automated Security System........................	163
	Centrally Controlled Systems.......................	163
	Systems Computer Applications	164
	Control Center Equipment	164
	Costs	165
	Personnel Control	165
	Identification	165
	Physical Control at Access Points..................	167
	Other Security System Tasks	170
	Monitoring of Sensors..........................	170
	Supervision of Protection Personnel	170
	Time and Attendance Recording..................	170
	Programming the System	171
	System Expansion and Flexibility....................	172
	The Control Center	172
	Emergency Power	172

ASSET PROTECTION AND SECURITY MANAGEMENT HANDBOOK

Standby and Continuous Emergency Power	172
Standby Power	172
Continuous Power	173
Selected Bibliography	176
Appendix A: Glossary of Frequently Used Security Terms	177
Appendix B: Glossary of Frequently Used Fire Terms	182

7 Access Control ... 187

Basic Access Control Objectives	187
Granting/Denying Entry	187
Locks	187
Push-Button Locks	187
Touchpads	187
Telephone Entry Systems	188
Turnstiles	188
Pedestrian Passageway	188
Exit Control	188
Exit Hardware	189
Delayed Exit	189
Authorized Access Control	190
Large Systems	190
The Access Control Sub-System	191
Operational Requirements	191
Equipment Requirements	192
Durability	192
Maintainability	192
Coded Card Technology	193
Magnetic Stripe Cards	193
Watermark Magnetics	193
Barium Ferrite	194
Wiegend Wire	194
Proximity/Contact Readers	194
Resonant Circuits	195
Radio Frequency Readers	195
Biometric Technology	195
Dielectric Readers	196
Embossing Readers	196
Hollerith Readers	196
Optical Character Readers	196
Smart Card	197
Smart Card Encryption	198
Distributed Intelligence Systems	198
Special Access Features and Applications	198
Anti-Passback	198
Two-Man Rule	199

Mantrap	199
Sally Port	200
Gatehouse	200
Vehicle Parking Garages	201
Limit Operating Hours	201
No Guard Placed at the Entrance	201
User-Friendly Entry and Exit	201
Accommodating Visitors and Contractors	201
Accommodating Car Pools	202
Traffic Control	202
Excluding Unauthorized Pedestrians	202
Controlling Garage-to-Building Access	202
Emergency Alarms	202
CCTV in Garages and Parking Lots	203
Mixing Employee and Public Parking	203
Campus Parking	203
Elevator Control	203
Janitor's Privileges	204
Other Miscellaneous Applications	204
Office Equipment	204
Tools and Inventory	204
Personal Equipment at Work	204
Personal Safety	205
Monitoring Prisoners	205
Hotels and Motels	205
Dressing Rooms at Performing Art Centers	205
Weapons and Contraband Screening	205
Physical Configuration	206
Screening Policies and Procedures	206
Metal Detectors	206
X-Ray Inspection	208
Explosives Detectors	209
X-Ray Machines	209
Combination Systems	209
Vapor Detectors	209
Particle Detectors	209
Canines	209
Selected Bibliography	210
Periodicals	210
Organizations Associated with Smart Cards	210
8 Emergency Planning	**211**
The First Step	211
Advance Planning	211

Objectives of Emergency Planning and Crisis Management	212
Stages of an Incident	212
Types of Threats and Contingencies	213
Types of Contingency Plans	214
Planning Formats	214
Development of the Plan	215
Planning Process	216
Special Planning Needs	216
Components of an Emergency Plan	217
Planning Issues and Considerations	217
Priorities	217
Planning Assumptions	218
Command/Management and Control	219
Crisis or Emergency Management Team	219
Alternate Designations	220
Management/Command Succession	221
Continuity of Operations (COOP)	222
External Liaison and Coordination	223
Planning Liaison	223
Emergency Response Agencies	224
Mutual Aid	225
Public Affairs/Media Relations	225
Family/Victim Support	226
Emergency Medical Services	227
Security and Fire Protection	228
Alert and Warning System	230
Emergency Evacuation	230
Emergency Shutdown and Restoration	231
Resources and Logistics	233
Transportation	233
Other Considerations	234
After the Plan Is Written	234
Training, Drills and Exercises	234
Keeping the Plan Up-to-Date	235
Selected Bibliography	238
Appendix A: Company Disaster Control Program Policy	240
General	240
Procedure	243
Appendix B: Resources and Logistics Equipment and Services	244
Equipment to Consider:	244
Services to Consider:	245

Contents

9 Information Systems Security: An Overview 247
    Introduction 247
    Encoding Digital Data 247
    Processing Digital Data 248
    A Typical Central Processing Unit 249
    The Impact of Large-Scale Integration 251
    A Typical Information System 252
        The Computer and Network Hardware 253
        Computer System Software 253
        The Application Programs 253
        Physical Facilities 253
        An Operating Staff 253
        Operating Procedures 254
        User Training 254
        Activity Monitoring 254
    Classes of Computers 255
        Mainframe Computers 255
        Minicomputers 256
        Personal Computers 256
        Laptop Computers 258
    The Evolution of Information Systems 258
        The 1960s: Batch Processing Mainframe Systems 258
        The 1970s: Online Information Processing Systems ... 260
        Local Area Networks 262
        Wide Area Networks 264
        Internet: The Public Network 265
        Distributed, Three-Tier Information Systems 267
    What Is Information Systems Security? 269
    Is Information Systems Security Important? 269
    The Evolution of Information System Risks 270
        Batch System Risks 270
        Online Information Systems Risks 271
        Local and Wide Area Network Risks 272
        Internet Risks 272
        Distributed Systems 273
    Management of Information Systems Security 273
    Functional Definition of Information Systems Security 274
        How Risks, Potential Losses and Security Measures
           Are Related 275
        Selected Bibliography 276

10 Information Systems Security 279
    Introduction 279
    Roles and Responsibilities 279

xiii

ASSET PROTECTION AND SECURITY MANAGEMENT HANDBOOK

  Senior Management 280
  Information Systems Security Program Management ... 280
  Information Systems Operational Management 281
  Supporting Functions............................. 283
  Users 285
Information Systems Security Policies, Procedures and
  Standards 285
  Policy Implementation............................ 286
    Standards 286
    Procedures 287
    Documentation and Distribution of Policy,
      Procedures and Standards. 287
Information Systems Security Program Management 287
  Risk Management 287
    Risk Assessment Techniques 288
    Threat Occurrence Rate Estimates 289
    The Spectrum of Expected Losses. 290
    The Spectrum of Risk Management Actions. 291
    Why Cost-Benefit-Based Risk Management Often
      Fails 291
    Four Reasons for Adopting a Security Measure. 292
    How to Address Low–High Risks 292
    Reducing the Magnitude of High Single Occurrence
      Losses 293
    Reducing the Occurrence Rate of High Single
      Occurrence Losses......................... 293
Information Systems Security and Planning 293
  Initiation... 294
  Development and Acquisition...................... 294
  Implementation................................... 295
  Operation and Maintenance 295
  Disposal 295
Operating and User Controls 295
  Staffing 296
    Job Descriptions 296
    Work Schedules 296
    Personnel Selection 296
  Personnel Reassignment or Termination 296
Audit Trails and Transaction Logs 297
  Audit Trail Integrity 298
  Operational Use of Audit Trails 298
The Internet 299
  Confidentiality and Authentication 299
  Reliability and Response Time 299

Using a Value-Added Network	300
Hacker Attacks	300
Making Wise Use of the Internet	301
Selected Bibliography	301

11 Investigations: General Comments ... 303
- Public- and Private-Sector Investigations ... 303
- Investigations — In General ... 304
- Qualities of An Effective Investigation ... 305
  - Objectivity ... 305
  - Thoroughness ... 306
  - Relevance ... 306
  - Accuracy ... 306
  - Timeliness ... 307
  - Investigative Resources ... 308
  - Cost Elements ... 309
  - Sources of Information ... 310
  - Online Investigations ... 312
- Legal Guidelines ... 312
  - Local Licensing Statutes ... 313
  - Civil and Criminal Suits and Actions ... 313
    - Defamation ... 313
    - False Imprisonment ... 314
- Investigative Reports ... 314
  - Types of Reports ... 314
    - Initial Report ... 315
    - Progress Report ... 315
    - Special Report ... 315
    - Final Report ... 315
  - Parts of the Report ... 315
    - Administrative ... 315
    - Summary ... 315
    - Narrative ... 316
      - Style ... 316
      - Objective ... 317
      - Factual ... 317
      - Chronological ... 317
      - Comprehensive and Relevant ... 317
    - Conclusions and Recommendations ... 318
    - Enclosures ... 318
  - Report Distribution ... 318
  - Selected Bibliography ... 318
- Appendix A: Selected Internet Investigative Resources ... 319
- Appendix B ... 320

Summary of Consumer Rights as Prescribed by the
Federal Trade Commission 320
A Summary of Your Rights under the Fair Credit
Reporting Act 320

12 Security and Protective Lighting 325
Introduction 325
Lighting and Lighting Definitions 325
Lighting Systems 329
Lighting Economics 329
Starting and Re-Strike 332
Security Lighting Applications 333
    Perimeter Fencing 333
    Site Landscape and Perimeter Approaches 333
    Building Facade. 333
    Parking Structures 333
    Open Parking. 334
    Loading Docks. 334
    Security Control and Monitoring Rooms. 334
    Guard and Gate Houses 334
Security Lighting and Closed-Circuit Video Systems 336
Standards for Security Lighting Levels 337
    Selected Bibliography 338

13 Crime Prevention through Environmental Design: CPTED 341
Introduction 341
    CPTED Fundamentals. 342
Understanding CPTED: Theory, History and Practice 344
Basic Crime Prevention Assumptions 346
Contemporary Thinking on Crime and Criminals 347
    Target Selection 348
    Concept of Capable Guardian 349
    Criminal Choice 349
    Situational Crime Prevention 350
    Potential Offenders' Perspective 352
    Defensible Space. 353
    Tim Crowe and CPTED. 354
    CPTED Survey 355
Concepts of Risk Management. 357
Reducing Crime through Physical Design 359
    Introduction to Planning the Building 359
    The Architectural Planning Process. 360
    Effective Access Control 362
Site Development and Security Zoning. 363
    Privacy versus Security 366

Security Design Criteria for Parking Facilities............. 367
Design Considerations for Industrial Buildings 372
Design Considerations for Office Buildings............... 374
    Asset to Be Protected: People 374
    Asset to Be Protected: Information 376
    Asset to Be Protected: Property..................... 378
        Offices and Office Buildings. 379
Special Considerations Regarding U.S. Federal Buildings ... 382
    The General Services Administration (GSA) Security
    Standards 382
    Application of GSA Security Standards to All Building
    Types... 383
Graphics and Signage for Crime Prevention and
Environmental Security 385
Summary 386
    Selected Bibliography 387

14 United States Criminal Law 389
Introduction.. 389
Federal and State Constitutions 389
Statutory Law 389
Definition and Classification of Crimes 390
    Federal Criminal Law.............................. 390
    Definition of Federal Crimes 391
    Definition of State Crimes 391
    The Essential Character of a Crime 391
    Criminal Intent 392
    Establishing Guilt for Crime 393
    Formal Charge.................................... 394
    Arraignment 394
    Trial 395
    Sentence 395
    Confinement 398
Case or Decisional Law................................. 398
    Federal and State Constitutions..................... 399
Relevance to Asset Protection........................... 399
    Crimes Based upon Unauthorized Entry or Presence.... 400
    Crimes Based upon Theft or Larceny 401
    Crimes Based upon Force or Threats of Force against
    Persons 402
    Permissible Use of Force........................... 403
    Crimes Based upon Damage or Threat of Damage to
    Property 405
Important Procedural Considerations 406
    Arrests 406

ASSET PROTECTION AND SECURITY MANAGEMENT HANDBOOK

Federal or State Law	407
With or Without a Warrant	407
By a Police Officer or Private Person	408
Interviews and Interrogations	409
Searches and Seizures	410
Entrapment	412
Specific Criminal Statutes of Security Interest	412
The Economic Espionage Act	412
Eavesdropping Statutes	413
Pertinent Federal Law	414
Summary of Federal Law	414
State Laws	416
Number of Government Interceptions	416
Deception Detection Instruments	416
Federal Polygraph Legislation	416
Broad Interpretations of the EPPA	417
Definitions	417
Prohibitions	417
Exemptions	418
Government and National Security Exemptions	418
Ongoing Investigations Exemption	418
Security Services Exemption	419
Drug Security Exemption	420
Restrictions on Exemptions	421
Rights of the Examinee	422
Qualifications of Examiners	423
Disclosure of Information	423
Enforcement	423
Admissibility of Polygraph Results in Evidence	424
Admissibility of the Lie Detector	424
State Laws	424
Federal Jurisdiction	424
The National Labor Relations Board	425
The Military	425
Labor Arbitrators	425
Voice Stress Analyzer	425
Conclusion	426
Selected Bibliography	426
Periodicals	427
15 The Civil Law	**429**
Definition	429
Major Branches	429
Statutory Law	430

Federal Statutory Law	430
State Statutory Law	430
Important Areas of Statutory Law	431
Administrative Law	431
Civil Common Law	433
Major Areas of Civil Common Law	434
Contract Law	434
Express Contract	435
Implied Contract	435
Some Precautions	436
Warranties	438
Limitations of Liability	439
Agency	440
How Agency Is Determined	441
The Significance of an Agency	443
Vicarious Liability	443
The Earlier Questions	444
Question 1	444
Question 2	444
Question 3	444
Question 4	445
Torts In General	445
Willful Torts	445
Specific Willful Torts	446
Negligence	447
Gross Negligence	447
The Area of Civil Rights	448
Civil Rights at Common Law	448
Civil Rights under Statute	448
The Civil Rights Act of 1964 (42 U.S.C. 2000e)	448
State Anti-discrimination Statutes	449
The Test for Discrimination	449
The Trend in Civil Rights	450
Discrimination Based on Disability	450
Selected Bibliography	451

16 Security as a Management Function ... 453

Introduction	453
Developing the Organization	453
Who Is the Customer?	453
Definition of Responsibilities	454
Program Implementation	455
Top Management Responsibility	455
Involvement of Others	457

Communications 458
Staffing the Protection Organization 458
    Compensation 460
    Reporting Level 460
Program Management 461
    Planning 461
    Training 462
    Delegation 463
    Relationships: Internal and External 463
    Selected Bibliography 464

17 Ethics in the Security Profession 469
Introduction 469
What Are Professional Ethics? 469
    The Need for Professional Ethics 469
    Professional Responsibility Matches Professional
        Recognition 470
The Security Profession 470
The Professional Society 470
The Code of Ethics of the American Society for Industrial
    Security 472
    Official Commentary on the Early ASIS Code of Ethics ... 472
The Practical Application of Professional Ethics 472
    The Former ASIS Code as a Practical Guide 476
        Article I 476
            Rule A 476
            Rule B 477
        Article II 478
        Article III 478
        Article IV 478
            Rule A 479
        Article V 479
            Rule A 479
            Rule B 479
            Rule C 480
            Rule D 480
            Rule E 481
            Rule F 481
        Article VI 482
            Rule A 482
            Rule B 482
            Rule C 484
        Article VII 485
        Article VIII 486

	Rule A	486
	Rule B	486
	Rule C	486
	Rule D	487
	Rule E	487
	Rule F	487
	Rule G	487
	Article IX	488
	Rule A	488
	Rule B	488
	Article X	488
	Selected Bibliography	488
18	**Detecting Deception in Interviews and Interrogations**	**491**
	Introduction	491
	Different Types of Responses	491
	Some Preliminary Cautions	492
	Verbal Responses	492
	Verbal Profiles	494
	Nonverbal Responses	494
	Activities Suggesting Deception	495
	Comparative Postures	495
	Eye Contact	496
	The Behavior Analysis Interview	496
	What Is a Behavior Analysis Interview?	497
	Behavior-Provoking Questions	497
	The Reid Nine Steps of Interrogation	499
	The Positive Confrontation	499
	Theme Development	499
	Handling Denials	500
	Overcoming Objections	500
	Keeping a Suspect's Attention	500
	Handling a Suspect's Passive Mood	500
	Presenting an Alternative Question	500
	Having the Suspect Relate Details	501
	Converting an Oral Confession	501
	Selected Bibliography	502
19	**A Plan for Threat Management**	**505**
	Overview	505
	The Concept of Threat Management	506
	The Focus of a Threat Management Program	506
	Liability and Legal Considerations	507
	The Psychological Dynamic of Workplace Violence	508
	Pre-Employment Screening	509

ASSET PROTECTION AND SECURITY MANAGEMENT HANDBOOK

Physical Security	510
Access Control	510
Employee and Visitor Identification	510
Lighting	510
Closed-Circuit Television (CCTV)	511
Furniture and Equipment Configuration	511
Policy Statement and Reporting Procedure	511
The Incident Management Team (IMT) and Supporting Resources	512
The Incident Management Process	513
Notification of a Potential or Actual Problem	513
Assessment Phase	514
Initial Information Collection by the DMR	514
Initial Contact	514
Additional Interviews	515
Decision to Interview in Person or by Phone	515
Selection of the Interview Site	515
Decision to Secure the Interview Site	515
Development of an Offender and Incident Chronology	516
Analysis of Initial Information	516
Extensive Background Investigation of the Offender	516
Location of Any Prior Relevant Data	516
Information Sources	517
Law Enforcement Liaison	518
Decision to Interview the Offender	518
Securing the Interview Site and Assessment Personnel	520
Site Selection	520
Site Preparation	520
Site Security	520
Hostage Contingency Plan	520
Training of Interview Participants	520
Summary Assessment and Plan for Further Action	520
Plan in Event of Termination	521
Company Personnel Selected for Interview	521
Site Selection and Preparation	522
Time of the Interview	522
Planning Communications with the Offender	522
Plan for Exit of Offender from Company Property	522
Extended Security and Incident Monitoring	523
Sizing Up the Threat	523
Establishment of the Reaction Response Plan	523
Protective Team's Responsibility	523

Establishment of Continuing Communications 524
   Contact between Offender and the Company 524
   Offender Contacts with Other Employees of the
      Company 524
   Communication within the Protective Team 524
   Public Emergency Services Personnel 524
Plan for Situation Reassessment 525
Phased Withdrawal of Protective Personnel 525
Selected Bibliography 526
   Periodicals 526
   Other Resources................................. 527
Appendix A: Model Policy for Workplace Threats and Violence 527
Appendix B: Minimum Qualifications for Outside Consulting Team Members 528
Appendix C: Normal Incident Assessment/Resolution Process... 530

Index 531

1
Introduction to Assets Protection

THE MANAGEMENT FUNCTION

Protecting the assets of any corporation, institution or public interest today is a daunting task — such efforts transcend traditional brick and mortar security concerns to include securing vital intellectual property used in e-commerce and Internet applications in a global economy. Clearly, the Web is redefining how we live our lives and how we need to secure the assets entrusted to employees. In fact, the definition of what constitutes an employee is also changing and evolving at a rapid rate. Temporary workers, contractors and joint venture employees are required to have significant access to information, resources and various other tools previously reserved for full-time employees — exploding previous concepts of protecting assets and people. The role of the security professional is rapidly changing in this environment and requires a combination of strategic thinking, process management and the ability to implement programs and initiatives in increasingly shorter periods of time to match the incredible pace of today's business.

Macroeconomics teaches us that resources in any given situation are limited; thus, choices must be made regarding the trade-off between the resources necessary to generate products, profits and market share, and the assets required to protect them. The successful security practitioner strikes the appropriate balance between these competing demands. It is the goal of the *Asset Protection and Security Management Handbook* to assist the security professional in achieving this difficult but essential equilibrium in determining the appropriate level of acceptable risk in any given situation and the investment required to mitigate those risks.

Asset Protection — A Historical Perspective

From the earliest of times, humans have recognized the need to protect themselves, their family and their property. Individuals or small groups living together provided the protection until loosely organized tribes developed into more formal groups. As civilization began to trace outlines of government in the sense that we would recognize it today, the need for forces to maintain order was recognized. These forces were usually created to deal with the threat of attack from other groups and not with problems of order within the primary group itself. The raising of armies and their deployment to territorial borders was the initial method of establishing group defense.

As local communities were further removed from the seat of central power and as more individuals in those communities were strangers to each other, rather than close relatives, the need became clear for some form of local order. This was done to preserve peace and enforce laws made at distant regional or central capitals. Primitive forms of night watch and patrol were developed, again to protect the community against outside attack. The idea of public protection for purely private property did not take hold until after the industrial revolution and even today is a concept of limited application. The proprietor of a private enterprise or the owner of private assets is and always has been largely self-dependent for adequate protection against all but major threats to the public peace.

There are a number of excellent discussions tracing the parallel development of law enforcement and formal private security programs in the U.S. and elsewhere to which the reader may refer for more detail.[1] A review of the history of security and its relationship with law enforcement will help the reader better to understand the real need for private security resources. The hazards faced by every industrial and business enterprise, as well as by private and public institutions, have continued to multiply over the years. There is ample anecdotal evidence that the viability of the enterprise is frequently threatened by the loss of financial, human and physical assets. As a result, the protection of the assets of every organization has continued to increase in importance, and the state of the art of the protection field has become far more sophisticated. Table 1 illustrates the shift in required skill-sets of the protection professional from the 1980s to the new millennium to demonstrate this point.

For that very reason, this manual is entitled *Asset Protection and Security Management Handbook,* a broader title than "security" because it more adequately describes the full range of functions required to protect the modern enterprise against pure risk losses. The term is intended to include all the traditional security countermeasures, such as security officers, investigations, locks and alarms, fire protection, emergency planning, etc., but it also refers to such functions as risk management, computer, network and Internet security among others. In other words, it includes the larger spectrum of risk management as it relates to the complete protection of assets.

DEFINITION OF ASSETS PROTECTION

Generally, we consider money, accounts receivable, physical and intellectual property, proprietary information and claims or rights of action as assets. But the employees of the enterprise may also be considered among

---

[1] For example, Purpura, Philip P., *Security and Loss Prevention, An Introduction,* 1998, Butterworth-Heinemann.

Table 1. Required skill sets in the protection of assets field.

1980s	2000 and Beyond
High School, Associate's or Bachelor's degree in police science	Master of Business Administration degree or equivalent law or related education
Police or military background	General business background
General investigative experience	White-collar and computer crime prevention/investigation skills
Knowledge of government security programs and requirements	Understanding of Internet, e-commerce, network and computer security best practices
Physical security requirements	
General understanding of business	
Strike and labor disturbance mitigation	Knowledge of global economics, finance and cultures
Senior executive security requirements	
Protection of intellectual property (paper and some data precautions)	Protection of employees against workplace violence, travel and expatriate security requirements
General written and verbal skills	

the most valuable assets. Without a skilled workforce, other assets may be useless in accomplishing business purposes. The next chapter of this handbook deals in detail with the problem of vulnerability and risk analysis; however, a short discussion here of the scope of the hazards to be considered in designing an assets protection program will set the stage for the detailed treatment that follows.

The hazards faced by every organization may be divided into two general categories: human and catastrophic. *Human problems* are generally caused by two classes of individuals:

- Those who have a right or license to be inside the organization or facility, such as employees, contractors, temporary employees, visitors and customers.
- Outsiders who intend to cause harm, such as burglars, robbers, vandals, rioters and industrial spies, whether their intention is to enter the facility physically or electronically. The hazards introduced by these individuals pose unique considerations when attempting to protect assets on a global basis.

Catastrophic problems result from such events as fires, explosions, earthquakes, hurricanes and floods. They typically occur as natural catastrophes or workplace accidents.

Losses resulting from the misbehavior of people, both inside and outside the enterprise, can have a broad range of causes. Some of the more common are:

1. Dishonesty
2. Substance abuse resulting in safety problems or trafficking in drugs on company property

3. Fraud and conflict of interest, which are destructive to the interrelationships of employees, organizational trust and potentially the reputation of employees and the firm itself
4. Emotional problems and related issues resulting in violence in the workplace;
5. Antisocial behavior, including making threats, engaging in sexual harassment, etc.
6. Gambling
7. Rioting, particularly in countries engaged in social unrest
8. Sabotage, criminal damage, etc.
9. Computer, network and related abuse
10. Theft of intellectual property

Although recent trends show a modest decline in the index of property crime in the U.S.,[1] the amount of property crime remains high and is roughly four or more times the amount of crime against the person.[2] There is no precise data regarding the magnitude of white-collar crime. In 1974, the U.S. Chamber of Commerce estimated the annual cost of white-collar crime at no less than $40 billion while other estimates have indicated that white-collar crime may cost more than $200 billion annually. Crime in other countries is difficult to establish as reporting mechanisms are not as precise or aggregated on a country-wide basis.

Losses from catastrophic problems have also been increasing annually. Fire is a particularly serious problem. It is estimated that about half the businesses struck by fire do not resume operation or are out of business within six months. In some years, flood damage exceeds $1 billion and hurricanes have been known to cause tens of billions of dollars in damages. As an example, the 1989 San Francisco earthquake alone caused damage estimated at $5.6 billion.

BASIC CONSIDERATIONS

There are two factors that determine the quality of an assets protection program: an adequate and active prevention plan to prevent and limit losses and top management's understanding and support of the program.

Countermeasures Planning

Rather than formulate and implement a comprehensive prevention plan, some organizations adopt protection measures in bits and pieces, reacting to problems as they occur. In fact, in some cases the problems are avoided until they become so serious that they can no longer be ignored. For example, when an organization receives a bomb threat, the facilities are often

---

[1] *Uniform Crime Report 1995–1997,* FBI, Department of Justice, Washington, D.C.
[2] *Crime Victimization Survey,* U.S. Department of Justice, 1997 (http://www.ojp.usdoj.gov/bjs/abstract/cv97.htm)

evacuated immediately and the matter is typically referred to law enforcement. When additional bomb threats are received and production is seriously affected, the organization develops plans to cope with that hazard because it is perceived as the most urgent. By reacting in this way, the organization overlooks a wide variety of other potential emergency situations just as destructive as bombs or the threat of bombs. With very little more effort or expense, a complete plan could be developed to include all types of emergencies, instead of coping with only one situation.

Other organizations have adopted only one countermeasure instead of a complete program. An illustration of this is the organization that attempts to limit losses of materials by hiring security officers for each exit. The losses may decrease somewhat due to the use of security officers. But large losses may continue because the bulk of the material is not being removed stealthily through exits but it is being diverted through a conspiracy between inside employees and delivery drivers.

Avoidance of loss or prevention of loss is important in the design of the complete plan. Some security programs have been based almost entirely on after-the-fact responses to events that have already occurred. This is appropriately described as "crisis management." An example is the enterprise that depends entirely upon arrest and prosecution to deter dishonesty. While fear of detection will discourage some individuals, others will conclude that the risk of discovery is small and they will take a chance.

When a loss does occur, every organization has the right to make a criminal complaint and to initiate civil action to recover damages, when appropriate. The goal of the criminal complaint is a conviction with an order of restitution. In a civil action, judgment for the organization will result in an order for restitution. But those orders may be of little economic value if it is impossible to recover anything. This often happens, and firms have been forced out of business because they were unable to recover their losses. The fact that an individual is convicted and sentenced to jail will be of little benefit to an organization that has been damaged. This explains why *private security is more interested in loss prevention than in loss detection and prosecution.*

Although many potential losses can be avoided by effective security controls, others, such as natural disasters (for example, earthquakes and floods) cannot be prevented. But developing adequate emergency plans in advance to cope with all such problems can help mitigate the damage to property, even when some losses are inevitable.

Management Support

Some protection programs have been ineffective because the second basic factor, the need for *complete management support*, has not been efficiently stressed. When senior management delegates complete protection responsibility to lower-level managers without top-level backing, the results are usually unsatisfactory. The protection program must be fully understood and supported at the top level in the enterprise and senior management must be interested enough to ensure that all personnel follow the established requirements. The example, good or bad, set by senior executives in complying with requirements will permeate the organization. It is incumbent upon the asset protection professional to establish a well-defined strategy and communications program to ensure all levels of management and employees understand the goals of the security organization.

Neglect or a lack of appreciation for adequate protection can also result in personal liability for corporate officers and directors — the stockholder's suit. Top officials of a company may be personally involved in legal actions if stockholders become aware of losses that could have been prevented by a prudent asset protection program. Additionally, two statutes also provide criminal penalties for "controlling persons" in corporations under certain conditions.

The Foreign Corrupt Practices Act (FCPA)[1] applies to any company that has a class of securities registered pursuant to Section 12 of the Securities Exchange Act of 1934 and any company that is required to file reports pursuant to Section 15 (d) of that act. One segment of the FCPA makes it a criminal offense to offer a bribe to a foreign official in order to obtain or retain business. The segment of the FCPA that is most pertinent to our discussion requires that the company devise and maintain a system of internal accounting controls sufficient to provide reasonable assurances that the following four objectives are met:

1. Transactions are executed in accordance with management's specific or general authorization.
2. Transactions are recorded as necessary to:
    a. permit preparation of financial statements in conformity with generally accepted accounting principals or any other criteria applicable to such statements, and
    b. maintain accountability for assets.
3. Access to assets is permitted only in accordance with management's general or specific authorization.
4. The recorded accountability for assets is compared with the existing assets at reasonable intervals and action is taken with respect to any differences.

The penalties for failure to maintain these internal controls include a fine of not more that $10,000 or imprisonment for not more than five years, or both. These internal control requirements might appear to be solely within the purview of the accounting department. However, the assets protection

---

[1] 15 U.S.C. § 78dd-1

Introduction to Assets Protection

organization should make a significant contribution to attaining the third objective concerning control of access to assets.

It should also be noted that in January 1998, that the Organization for Economic Cooperation and Development (OECD) adopted a "Convention on Combating Bribery of Foreign Public Officials in International Business Transactions." The OCED consists of 29 member nations, and an additional five non-member nations (Argentina, Brazil, Bulgaria, Chile and the Slovak Republic) that also ratified this approach. The convention requires all signatory countries to enact legislation in their countries similar to the requirements of the FCPA in the United States. When this legislation is complete, a corporation will be required to adhere to the provisions of the FCPA and also meet the tenets set forth by each specific country in which it does business. These requirements subject the corporation to potentially multiple prosecutions in the event a bribe to a government official is discovered.

The second statute is the Federal Organizational Sentencing Guidelines. The purpose of these guidelines was to stiffen the penalties imposed on corporations when their employees violate federal criminal statutes. They apply to antitrust, securities, tax, bribery, ERISA, fraud, money laundering and environmental violations. The guidelines substantially increased the penalties for businesses that do not make any effort to deter, detect and report crime. The penalties were significantly decreased for those businesses that do.

The deterrent aspects of the guidelines provide that every company must make restitution to any party injured by criminal conduct and must pay a non-tax-deductible fine. A criminal violation that results in a $20 million gain for the company can result in a fine ranging from $1 million to $80 million. The amount of the fine is determined by the application of a table of multipliers based on aggravating and mitigating factors to arrive at a "culpability score."

A compliance program designed to deter and detect criminal conduct can result in a significant reduction in the "culpability score" and the fine. An effective compliance program must meet seven requirements:

1. The company must establish compliance standards that are reasonably capable of preventing criminal conduct.
2. High-level management must have specific responsibility to oversee the standards.
3. The standards must be communicated to the employees and training in compliance issues should be offered.
4. The company should test the system by monitoring, auditing and other systems designed to detect criminal conduct.
5. The company must exercise due care to ensure that discretionary authority is not delegated to individuals with a propensity to engage in illegality.

6. The compliance standards must be enforced through appropriate disciplinary procedures that include provisions that individuals will be disciplined for failing to detect or report an offense.
7. After an offense is detected, all reasonable steps must be taken to prevent a future similar offense.

A simple self-inspection checklist and scoring plan for assessing the level of your current security program is found in Appendix A to this chapter.

Communicating the Plan

Top management support of the plan will be based on a solid understanding of the value of the effort. The plan must, therefore, be couched in terms that will be readily understood by top management. Business is ultimately conducted in financial terms and the prudent assets protection professional will communicate in those terms. Senior management will usually embrace an assets protection plan that is cost-effective and, if possible, provides a return on the investment made.

Statutory and Regulatory Requirements

The conduct of many of the activities in the assets protection plan will be regulated by federal or state agencies or by statutes. For example, the Fair Credit Reporting Act provides requirements for the conduct of certain personnel investigations in most organizations operating in the U.S. Some segments of commerce and industry are governed by specific statute or regulation. For example, security requirements in the banking industry are specified in the Banking Act while the requirements for nuclear power generating stations are found in the regulations of the Nuclear Regulatory Commission. The specific requirements are addressed in other chapters of this handbook.

Senior management will understand the need to comply with the statutory and regulatory requirements. The assets protection manager must be aware of the requirements and include them in the assets protection plan. The innovative assets protection professional will meet the requirements in a cost-effective manner and, where possible, simultaneously fulfill other needs of the enterprise.

THE SYSTEMS APPROACH

To be effective, the design and implementation of an assets protection program incorporates the systems approach, defined as *a comprehensive solution to a total problem*. This is an orderly and rational method of problem solving and, when properly carried out, should ensure a sound program.

There are three general steps in the systems approach:
1. A vulnerability analysis
2. Selection and installation of countermeasures
3. A thorough test of the operating program

The following chapter deals in detail with the first step, the risk or vulnerability analysis. In this chapter, we consider the other two.

COUNTERMEASURES

Countermeasures apply to people, hardware and software. All three must be interrelated in the system design to ensure an effective, integrated protection program. For the purposes of this discussion, the term "software," in addition to electronic systems programming instructions, will refer to all directives and instructional or training material, written and verbal, needed to make an assets protection program operate as intended.

People

People are the most important and generally the most expensive of the three types of countermeasures. During system design, particular attention should be given to the substitution of automated functions for people wherever possible and to deriving optimal return on the investment when people must be used. This is referred to as shifting from a *labor-intensive to* a *capital-intensive* approach.

For maximum efficiency, assets protection procedures can specify that operating employees and managers in areas other than protection perform certain protection checks and controls as part of their own regular duties. Assets protection personnel can conduct spot-checks or detailed inspections to ensure that the operating personnel are performing the functions assigned to them. In an automated environment, the performance of some of the checks can be reported electronically to the assets protection control station.

Assets protection personnel may be employees of the enterprise or contract employees, or a combination. Organizations of sufficient size normally assign responsibility for administration of the program to a full-time executive. This official usually has a number of employees and may have, in addition, contract personnel such as security officers. Smaller organizations, not able to justify the cost of a full-time executive for the protection function, may rely on other employees to administer the program on a part-time or added-duty basis. In such situations, contract personnel can be utilized extensively. The current trend in both large and small organizations is to out-source many of the assets protection functions that have historically been performed by company employees.

Regardless of whether the enterprise is large or small, it is essential that a skilled administrator be delegated the authority and direct responsibility for the security system on at least a part-time basis. The individual selected should be of sufficient stature in the organization to operate as an acknowledged member of responsible management. Some organizations make the mistake of assigning this task to a security officer supervisor with limited supervisory skill and management experience. When this is done, the protection program will almost certainly be less than optimal; it may even fail, mainly due to a lack of executive access by the assigned supervisor.

If contract security service personnel are utilized, the contribution each service provider will make to the complete assets protection system must be carefully assessed. Some contract service providers offer a wide range of security services; however, the claim that a provider has the solution for every security problem must be viewed with skepticism until proven. Many contract security companies provide only one service, such as security officers. The contract service representative may be a salesperson whose knowledge of the protection field is limited to his own company's service. If that company were a guard company, for instance, the objective would probably be to urge the use of as many security officers as possible. The contract security service provider may not have the capability to evaluate the overall protection needs of the client enterprise.

For the management representative who is not comfortable deciding what type of contract service is necessary, there are reputable, ethical consultants available who can objectively review each organization being examined. They are able to recommend practical and cost-effective solutions to the complete assets protection problem because they are not profiting from any particular type of service. The consultant fee will normally be more than recouped by an efficient assets protection system.

Hardware

Some examples of hardware items (the second element of countermeasures) are locks, fencing, safes, vaults, lights, turnstiles, closed-circuit television and other electronic devices. When properly utilized, these can make a significant contribution to the protection of a facility. As with the other two countermeasures categories, people and software, each item of hardware must be carefully planned to ensure that it interrelates with the system and economically increases the protection of the facility.

A lock, for instance, has traditionally been regarded as an effective security measure; however, a lock should not be expected to provide complete protection. A door secured by a lock might be penetrated without ever touching the lock by using a pry bar or jimmy, or by cutting the latch bolt with a torch or saw. To make a lock effective, procedures should be established defining how and when it is to be used, to arrange for a periodic inspection by a security officer or other individual, and to provide alarm coverage and adequate response in case of a penetration. So planned, all three countermeasure categories are involved. A lock is the hardware element. Software is represented by procedures providing for the activation, inspection and response to an alarm. And the third element, people, are needed to inspect and respond in case a penetration is signaled.

Electronic access control and intrusion detection systems are effective in raising the level of protection and simultaneously reducing costs. Fully integrated electronic systems include command and control functions involving security, fire, safety, and utilities. Because of the importance of electronics in the systems approach, several later chapters are devoted entirely to that subject.

Software

In this discussion, the term "software" refers to electronic system programming instructions and to all directives and instructional or training material, written and verbal, needed to make an assets protection program operate as intended.

A basic item in any assets protection system is a written policy statement issued by the top management of the enterprise establishing the program. This statement, and others that may be released, set the tone for the complete program, indicate the interest of top management and are the basis for implementing material.

Other procedures, practices and directives usually define in detail the controls that are being established throughout the enterprise and the responsibilities all employees must assume. Such material should be designed so that it can be easily understood and followed by employees at all levels in the organization. It is usually not adequate simply to issue directives or procedures and expect them to be followed without explanation.

The material should take into consideration that all employees in the organization must participate and assist in the program to make it operate successfully. It should be stressed to supervisors at all levels that they must ensure the compliance of all employees under their supervision. The cooperation and assistance of all employees is necessary because the assets protection organization, regardless of its size, cannot protect the enterprise alone. Therefore, general employee reaction and attitude are important.

An assets protection program necessarily imposes controls and limits on people and their activities. A natural antagonism may develop if the program is not implemented properly. Employees resent controls that seem arbitrary; thus, the assets protection program should be designed for the least possible disruption of normal operations. If the need for controls, the benefits to the employees and the method of operation of the assets protection program are reasonably explained, most employees will accept the program and help to make it work.

An educational effort reduces resistance and enhances cooperation. The educational effort should be implemented when planning for the assets protection program is started. This will reduce the normal human resistance to unexpected change. Employees should be advised, in positive manner, of the projected operational changes in the implementation of the assets protection program.

Employees are often not aware that losses must be deducted directly from the profits of the organization. They must be shown that losses that might at first appear very small could have far-reaching effects on profitability and might even have an adverse effect on staffing. Employees can be informed that prevention of a loss will avoid a decrease in net profit, and that the success of the organization, largely measured in profit, will enhance personal security for them in terms of future employment. Losses resulting from dishonesty can also have a serious impact on profits. A $100 theft loss in a business earning a 2 percent net profit requires that sales increase $5000 to offset the loss. A 0.5 percent theft loss in a business with $100 million in sales at a 5 percent profit margin would require another $10 million in sales to offset it. Actually, losses are *never* actually offset unless directly indemnified. No matter how much sales increase, the original loss remains.

Employees also take a greater interest in the assets protection program and are more willing to make a contribution to its success if they understand that the program has been designed for their own protection as well as the protection of the enterprise. The fact that a complete assets protection plan has been designed to cope with all types of emergencies, including those threatening employees — for example, fires, explosions, workplace violence and natural disasters — should be explained. Employees need to be reminded of how the plan benefits them by safeguarding their lives and welfare.

In addition to policies, procedures and directives, a variety of other means can be utilized to inform employees of the operation of the program and the contributions they are expected to make to it. Some of the methods for instructing employees are:

- Publication of a protection manual
- Articles in the company newsletter
- Bulletins and posters
- Awareness presentations
- Discussions in staff or other types of meetings

Each organization will determine its own best means of communication with employees. The education process must be a continuing one so that employees are constantly reminded of the importance of the assets protection program.

Methods of dealing with employees who violate or ignore procedures must be established. Violation of an assets protection practice should be handled in the same way that the infraction of any other major company practice is handled. The problem should be referred to the appropriate level of supervision for corrective action. As part of the educational effort, employees and supervisors should be informed of the standards and procedures that have been established for addressing instances of nonconformance.

A different, but equally important type of training material is needed for the employees and supervisors in the assets protection organization, including uniformed security officers, investigators and clerks. Once procedures or practices for use within the assets protection organization are developed, the protection employees must be given appropriate instruction so they are familiar with the detailed operation of the program. For example, guidelines for conducting pre-employment investigations should be established to ensure that all information needed by the organization to make a hiring decision is obtained. A guide as to who reviews the information and who makes the hiring decision must also be provided.

THE SYSTEM TEST

For several reasons, tests of the operating program are essential in the implementation of the assets protection system. Tests should result in the following:

- Risks or hazards still existing are identified and system deficiencies are revealed.
- System changes required to accommodate facility or organization revisions become apparent.

Checks or tests can be performed by the regular workforce as part of their normal work assignments, as well as by the employees operating the assets protection system. Arrangements should be made to test the system frequently.

Selected employees can be asked to make suggestions for the improvement of the protection program. If the education effort mentioned earlier has been effective, the response will usually be positive. General employee comments and suggestions also give some indication of how well the protection system is operating and what changes, if any, should be made. The comments and suggestions will frequently involve modifications to make compliance with the assets protection program more convenient to the employees. If these suggestions can be implemented without sacrificing the security of the assets, the employees, feeling that they have contributed to the plan, will usually cooperate more readily with the program.

Procedures can be established requiring supervisors at all levels to make regular checks to ensure that employees comply with system requirements. Supervisory personnel can also be prepared to perform other tasks, such as inspections of areas and periodic audits of transactions, and to report any discrepancies to the executive responsible for the operation of the system.

Security officers are normally assigned inspection duties as part of their regular duties. All members of the assets protection organization can be required to remain alert to any deficiencies in the system operation. In addition, they can be assigned specific inspection responsibilities to be performed periodically.

Errors can be inserted purposely into the system to determine if they are noted and reported. Test exercises can also be designed and conducted to determine how the system reacts. For example, a controlled test might involve the report of a bomb in the facility to check the reaction of people responsible for taking action in such a situation. Of course, trained personnel must carefully supervise such exercises so that undesirable reactions and results are prevented.

Selected Bibliography

Books

Burstein, Harvey; *Introduction to Security;* 1995; Prentice-Hall Career & Technology.

Crime in the United States; a Uniform Crime Report for the U.S. by the FBI, Washington, D.C., U.S. Government Printing Office, annual.

Fischer, Robert J. and Green, Gion; *Introduction to Security, 6th ed.;* 1998; Butterworth-Heinemann, Boston, MA.

Kelly, Raymond W., Ed.; *CRP's Guide to Workplace Security;* 1994; Conflict Resolution and Prevention, Inc.

Purpura, Philip R.; *Security and Loss Prevention, An Introduction, 3rd ed.;* 1998; Butterworth-Heinemann, Boston, MA.

Schaub, James L. and Biery, Ken D.; *The Ultimate Security Survey;* 1994; Butterworth-Heinemann, Newton, MA.

Simonsen, Clifford E.; *Private Security in America, An Introduction;* 1998; Prentice-Hall, Upper Saddle River, NJ.

Periodicals

Access Control and Security Systems Integration; PRIMEDIA Intertec, Atlanta, GA.
— Nolan, John; Six Laws for Choosing a Security Consultant; August 1996.
— Richardson, Bill; Increasing Employee Acceptance Boosts Success of Access Control Systems; October 1997.

Information Security; International Computer Security Association, Carlisle, PA.
— Burge, Theresa; Policing Your Security Policy; June 1998.

Security Management; American Society for Industrial Security, Alexandria, VA.
— Cole, Richard B.; Seeing Beyond Security; April 1995.
— Freimuth, Kenneth C., CPP; Checking Security's Customer Compass; September 1996.
— Golsby, Mark J.; Four Steps to Success; September 1992.
— Harne, Eric G., CPP; The Politics of Protection; August 1997.
— Hayes, Richard D.; Charting Security's Service Renaissance; April 1997.
— Kaloustian, Diane H., CPP; Selling Security In and Out; December 1998.
— Kohr, Robert L.; Putting Security to the Test; December 1994.
— Kovacich, Gerald L.; Six Secrets of a Successful Survey; September 1993.
— Lebo, Fern; Know the Code; June 1997.
— Pearson, Robert L.; Cutting Costs Through Consolidation; December 1996.
— Sutherland, Garrell E.; Answering the Question — What Is Security?; July 1992.

Security Technology and Design; Locksmith Publishing Corp., Park Ridge, IL.
— McNaughton, Donald; Management Audits; May 1998.

APPENDIX A
SELF-INSPECTION AND PROTECTION OF ASSETS CHECK SHEET

1. Do you audit your cash accounts periodically at unscheduled times? Yes _____ No _____
2. Do you have your accounts audited regularly by either a disinterested employee (other than the one who keeps the records) or a firm of certified public accountants? Yes _____ No _____
3. Are employee exits monitored by supervisors or security officers? Yes _____ No _____
4. Are stationery supplies, small tools, expendable supplies, raw materials, stock stores and small merchandise stores under inventory control and an employee charge-out system? Yes _____ No _____
5. Are employee parking lots, shipping and receiving areas or loading docks, and general work or display areas separated from each other by physical barriers or by controlled entrances? Yes _____ No _____
6. Do you have a plan for handling emergencies such as bomb threats, explosions, fires, hurricanes, floods and earthquakes? Yes _____ No _____
7. Have all supervisors and management personnel been properly briefed within the past year as to their security responsibilities? Yes _____ No _____
8. Are visitors, salespeople, vendors and contractors escorted by responsible personnel while in the facility? Yes _____ No _____
9. Have you changed the combinations of safes and vaults since the termination or retirement of an employee who knew the combination? Yes _____ No _____
10. Are all employees who handle or control money or other valuable assets placed under a fidelity bond? Yes _____ No _____

11. Can you account for all keys and access cards to your buildings and storage, equipment and supply areas? Yes _____ No _____
12. Are all employment applicants required to complete an application form covering at least the past ten years of employment and residence, and do you verify the information prior to employment? Yes _____ No _____
13. Are your vital records stored in a safe place such as a fire- and burglar-resistant file, safe or vault? Yes _____ No _____
14. Are your bank drafts, checks and airline tickets and your check-writing machine properly controlled and locked when not in use? Yes _____ No _____
15. Are procurement personnel forbidden to negotiate sole-source purchases without review by appropriate management-level personnel? Yes _____ No _____
16. Do you have an effective compliance program designed to deter and detect criminal conduct in place and have you determined that it is functioning properly? Yes _____ No _____
17. Do you have a program for the protection of sensitive company information against inadvertent release or industrial espionage? Yes _____ No _____
18. Have you determined whether any of your personnel have business interests that conflict with the interests of the firm? Yes _____ No _____
19. Do you conduct a security survey of your firm and its operations at least once each year? Yes _____ No _____
20. Are the telephone numbers of your local police, fire and other emergency services displayed prominently in key locations throughout the premises? Yes _____ No _____
21. Have you determined that your premises are not being used by your personnel to carry on a private business venture? Yes _____ No _____
22. Do you have a firm company policy prohibiting kickbacks, bribes and gratuities, and are employees aware of the policy and the penalty for violations? Yes _____ No _____
23. Have personnel been assigned specific responsibilities for locking all internal storage areas and exterior doors to the premises at the close of business each day? Yes _____ No _____
24. Have you examined your insurance coverage to determine whether you have adequate coverage for all risks to which the organization may be vulnerable? Yes _____ No _____
25. Do you have a program for protection of your information services equipment and networks and the information processed there? Yes _____ No _____

Introduction to Assets Protection

Protection of Assets Scoring Sheet

Score four (4) points for each "Yes" answer above.[1]

0–100 Management is aware of the basic problems and apparently has a common-sense security program. If your score was slightly less than 100, the obvious deficiencies can be corrected using countermeasures indicated by the questions you answered incorrectly.

50–80 Management is only partially aware of its potential loss factors and should take action immediately. A survey and vulnerability analysis is the first logical step, with countermeasures keyed to the operational and financial requirements of the business to follow as soon as possible. Keep in mind that overzealous safeguards can be as much a problem as the losses when determining proper safeguards for the company's interests.

0–50 Your firm is still in business by extraordinary luck, which may fail to protect you at any moment. Present the results of this quiz at your next management meeting and take action immediately to protect your firm's interests in the future.

---

[1] **A word of caution if your score was fairly high.** More than 60 percent of the management officials who were asked these basic questions by industrial security consultants were surprised to learn that their "Yes" answers were based only on assumptions and they had no specific knowledge about what was really being done.

2
Security Vulnerability

INTRODUCTION

A basic precept of assets protection is that *an effective security plan or program must be based on a clear understanding of the actual risks it faced.* Until the actual threat to assets is assessed accurately, precautions and countermeasures — even those of the highest quality, reliability and repute — cannot be chosen, except by guesswork. The value of a security program depends as much upon the relevance of resources as upon their high quality. *First* understand the problem; *then* consider solutions.

DEFINING THE PROBLEM

Defining a security problem involves an accurate assessment of three factors:

1. The kinds of threats or risks affecting the assets to be safeguarded
2. The probability of those threats becoming actual loss events
3. The effect on the assets or on the enterprise responsible for the assets if the loss occurs

The first can be called *loss event profile*, the second *loss event probability* or *frequency*, and the third *loss event criticality*.

The relationship among these three aspects of a loss event is fundamental in any system of countermeasures. Each aspect increases or decreases in significance in the light of the other aspects. For example, if a loss event probability or frequency is high, then even relatively low loss event criticality becomes significant because of the probable repeated events. A single loss event with a criticality that, considered alone, would have only a slight impact would require different assessment if that loss event were to occur hundreds of times in any one year.

LOSS EVENT PROFILE

Recognizing individual loss events that might occur is the first step in dealing with asset vulnerability. It requires clear ideas about the kinds of loss events or risks as well as about the conditions, circumstances, objects, activities and relationships that can produce the loss events.

A security countermeasure should be planned if the loss event has the following characteristics:

- The event will produce an actual loss, measurable in some standard medium such as dollars.
- The loss is not speculative in the sense that nonoccurrence of the event would result in a gain.

The kind of event that may produce either a loss or a gain is often called a business or conventional risk. If a product can be sold profitably, it will result in net income to the seller. Whether or not this is possible depends upon many factors, including:

- Controlling manufacturing costs
- Securing a suitable share of the available market
- Being price competitive
- Maintaining quality levels

To the extent that these contingencies are properly managed, sales are profitable. Loss results from failure to manage them correctly — for example, by misjudging the cost or availability of raw materials, or the time needed to manufacture the final item, or the actual market demand. *This loss is not the kind of loss being described here.* The individual events of manufacture, distribution and sale could have produced either a gain or a loss. Properly gauging the profit and loss potential is the task of conventional business management.

But if the anticipated profit were not realized because of some event that could only cause a loss, the situation would call for positive assets protection and loss prevention measures. The kinds of events that are loss-only oriented and that involve so-called *pure risks* include crime, natural catastrophe, industrial disaster, civil disturbance, war or insurrection, accident, conflicts of interest and maliciously willful or negligent personal conduct. Table 1 lists a number of such pure risk loss events.

Recognizing a particular loss event in any given enterprise is not necessarily a matter of simple common sense. It often demands the special skill of an experienced security professional to perceive that a given exposure is present. For example, there may be a vulnerability to loss of market share through industrial espionage or competitive intelligence. But there may be no risk of loss by forced or surreptitious entry or theft because adequate gates, fencing, locks and alarms exist. The casual assessment might identify only the physical safeguards. The professional assessment would involve an analysis of the procedures and would identify the weakness in or lack of control over information assets. The professional assessment is necessary if countermeasures planning is to have any value. But the recognition of even obvious risks implies some estimate of the probability that the risk will actually produce a loss. To the extent that the risk itself is concealed, the task of estimating probability of occurrence is more difficult.

Security Vulnerability

Table 1. Pure risk loss events.

Event	Example
War	
Natural catastrophe	Earthquake, flood, hurricane, tidal wave, tornado, typhoon, volcanic eruption
Industrial disaster	Explosion, fire, major accident, environmental incident, structure collapse
Civil disturbance	Insurrection, riot
Crime	Common crimes against the person (murder, rape, assault) and crimes against property (larceny, arson, vandalism)
Conflicts of interest	Bribery, disaffection, espionage, kickbacks, sabotage, competitive intelligence, unfair competition
Workplace violence	Acts of revenge, disaffection, personal grudge
Terrorism	Bombing, extortion, kidnapping, assassination with political or militant activist overtones
Other risks	Disturbed persons, personnel piracy, traffic accidents

LOSS EVENT PROBABILITY OR FREQUENCY

We know from elementary statistics that probability is measured as the number of ways in which a particular event can result from certain activity, divided by the number of all events which could occur from that activity. Stated as an equation, this is:

$$P = \frac{f}{n}$$

where:

P = the probability that a given event will occur
f = the number of outcomes or results favorable to the occurrence of that event
n = the total number of equally possible outcomes or results

As a practical example, what is the probability that in two throws of a coin it will come up heads at least once? The total events possible in two throws of a coin are:

1. First throw, heads — second throw, heads
2. First throw, heads — second throw, tails
3. First throw, tails — second throw, heads
4. First throw, tails — second throw, tails

Thus, there are four equally possible outcomes for two throws of a coin. Of the four (n = 4), three would produce at least one head in two throws (f = 3). Thus, substituting in the formula, the probability of at least one head in two throws of a coin is P = 3/4, or P = 0.75.

Although this simple statement illustrates the most direct way to calculate probability mathematically, it is not enough for practical application for a number of reasons. First, not all simultaneously possible events will be equally probable. Second, an event may occur more than once. Such recurrence is actually its *frequency*. But some events will only occur once, and the reaction will so change the environment that the theoretically probable further occurrences will be prevented. For example, a theft might so change the method of protecting the asset stolen that future thefts would be much less likely.

To be able to predict probability of security loss events, we must generally settle for something considerably less than the precision of the classic equation. Even if efforts were made to apply the equation, such attempts would be impractical because of the amount of time and data needed to determine the nature of the relationship between contributing events and their individual and combined probabilities of occurrence.

But we *can* employ a basic concept: *the more ways a particular event can occur in given circumstances, the greater the probability that it will occur.* For example, suppose that the asset at risk is finished goods inventory. Suppose also that the particular loss event to be evaluated is pilferage. Now add to the facts some particular circumstances that could lead to or result in pilferage. One circumstance could be that there is no record of control or accurate count of the inventory. Another might be that the inventory is not physically separated. A third might be that there are few or no controls on access to the place in which it is kept. A fourth might be that the inventory items are of high unit value, in general demand and useful anywhere in the world. A fifth might be the absence of any identification to distinguish one item from a similar item.

Although it may not be easy to say precisely how much each factual situation would increase the overall probability of pilferage — or to state the relative probabilities of each as a cause of pilferage — it is easy to say that the more there are, the greater the probability. In other words, the finished goods inventory is more likely to be pilfered if two sets of favorable circumstances are present than if only one is present. Pilferage would be still more likely with three sets of circumstances, and so on. With each added circumstance, the likelihood of pilferage increases, not only of a single loss but also of repeated acts of pilferage. Increased probability for a repeatable event means increased frequency.

For effective assessment of probability, as many as possible of those circumstances that could produce the loss must be known and recognized. We must emphasize the earlier statement that common sense alone is not an adequate basis or yardstick for identifying risks. Specialized knowledge is required; and the larger or more complex the enterprise or loss environment, the greater the need for such expertise.

Security Vulnerability

Probability Factors

The conditions and sets of conditions that will worsen or increase asset exposure to risk of loss can be divided into major categories. The categories are as follows: (1) physical environment, (2) social environment, (3) political environment, (4) historical experience and (5) criminal state-of-art.

Tables 2, 3 and 4 list items to be considered in evaluating the various categories.

Table 2. Physical environment factors.

Composition	Material, mass, weight, volume, density
Climate	Temperature, range and mean; relative humidity, mean and range; rainfall; snowfall; onset and end of freezing; storm cycles or seasons
Geography	Latitude, longitude, elevation
Location	Neighboring exposures; sheltered or unsheltered environment; controlled or uncontrolled
Conditions of use	Times, processes, procedures

Table 3. Social environment factors.

Ethnic identity	Population mix and distribution
Age groups	Children, adolescents, young adults, middle adults, aging, old and infirm
Income levels	Impoverished, unemployed, blue collar, white collar, affluent, wealthy
Neighborhood	Percent residential, business, industrial, institutional, recreational, undeveloped, deteriorated
Social history	Peaceful, local incidents, major disturbances; chronology of significant events
Planning	Reconstruction, rehabilitation, extension, rezoning
Crime	High crime, moderate crime, low crime; types of crime, organized or random; police relations, amount and frequency of patrol

Table 4. Political environment factors.

Government unit	City, town, village, unincorporated hamlet
General tone	Conservative, liberal, major parties, minor parties, mixed, apolitical
Attitudes	Tightly organized, loosely organized, no neighborhood organization, competitive organizations, dominant group(s)
Political arena	Single election or congressional district, multiple districts, identities and affiliations of federal, state and local legislators

Historical Experience

A special problem exists with regard to historical experience: there are usually not enough historical data in usable form within most enterprises to permit accurate forecasting. This problem has two aspects: the availability of information about past losses or suspected losses, and the organization of that information into a format that permits statistical processing. Most enterprises maintain some loss data, chiefly in connection with insured losses. These losses are described in various claim notices and proof-of-loss reports to the insurance carrier. Most insurance departments maintain loss records in a database and have the capability to produce reports of losses in various formats. Some organizations maintain only the paper documents and the files will not yield useful history except through extensive rearrangement of data. A note of caution: the database may only contain information as of the date of inception of the database; prior records may not have been entered.

In other enterprises, where the risk of loss is either ignored (no insurance or other risk management measure) or assumed (self-insurance or very large deductibles in commercial policies), the records may not exist. That is, in many organizations, if a loss is not insured and does not come within the dollar coverage limits of the policies, records of the loss are transitory and may not be accessible over time.

Accurate historical information about losses or loss events can be among the most useful information kept by an enterprise. First of all, sufficient information permits forecasting future occurrences. From the science of statistics we know that frequency of occurrence suggests probability of future recurrence. A distribution curve based on the number of times various kinds of events have occurred among other similar events indicates which events have a high probability of occurring again.[1] Along with the other facts developed in the probability factors evaluation, this can be used to arrive at an overall statement of likelihood of occurrence.

Predictions are of secondary importance but their accuracy increases with the accumulation of historical data. It is a principle of probability theory that *the larger the number of actual cases or events of the kind that includes the predicted event, the greater the agreement between the predicted pattern and the actual pattern of occurrence.* For a very large enterprise, such as a commercial or industrial organization with multiple locations or a retail chain with many outlets, the volume of data available from internal collection alone could be sufficient to allow quite accurate predictions.

The second aspect of the historical loss information problem concerns the organization of the information. It is not unusual to find assets protection

---

[1] For extended discussions, see Walsh, James et al., *Risk Management Manual,* Vol. 1, Exposure Identification, POA Publishing LLC, Los Angeles, CA.

departments that keep incident or other suspicious event reports dating back many years. In the past, each report consisted of one or more sheets of paper that had to be studied individually to yield any data.

The modern assets protection department utilizes a database to record incidents. These databases range from complex incident management systems purchased from specialized software vendors to relatively simple database software that is provided with most computers. In many instances the information is keyed into a report screen in the database by the investigating security personnel. If manual incident report forms are used to collect the information, they are designed to simplify the input of the information into the database. As such, codes are frequently used to denote the type of incident or the method of operation. The database fields usually include, as a minimum:

1. Date of occurrence
2. Time of occurrence
3. Place of occurrence (pinpointed as precisely as desired, even to the post-and-column intersection of a given building area)
4. Nature of the event under a general head such as crime or accident
5. Description of the specific event, such as fire, larceny by stealth, forced entry, mysterious disappearance, etc.
6. Method of operation or mode of occurrence, if known (such as padlock hasp removed with pry bar, window used for entry and exit, or fictitious person named on requisition)
7. Number for the distinctive event, to serve as the general locator for the incident and unite all files, reports and log data
8. Value of the assets involved and value of damage

The database reporting software usually provides for retrieval of the information in any desired order. The data can be viewed on the screen in detail or in summary format or the information can be printed out.

Later chapters of this handbook discuss the contribution such information should make to overall programs of risk management. The point to note is that the information has real value in vulnerability assessment. Every professionally competent asset protection or loss prevention staff should have a system for collecting incident data suitable for the size and complexity of the enterprise.

Application of Probability Factors Analyses

The practical value of vulnerability analysis depends upon the skill and thoroughness with which the basic risks to an enterprise are identified. This is the first and most important step in the entire process. Every aspect of the enterprise or facility under review must be examined to isolate those conditions, activities and relationships that can produce a loss. For an effective analysis, the observer must take into account the dynamic nature of the enterprise on each shift and between daylight and darkness. The daily routine must be understood, because the loss-producing causes can vary from hour to hour.

An actual situation illustrates the point. An enterprise conducts background investiations of its employees, carries fidelity insurance on all employees, and employs strict access control to sensitive areas during normal working hours. After normal working hours, the doors to all administrative offices are to be locked. The housekeeping tasks in the buildings are conducted by a contract firm whose employees are subjected to criminal records checks prior to hire but the enterprise fails to ensure that the records checks are conducted. The turnover in the contract custodial staff for the facility ranges from 150 to 200 percent annually. The housekeeping contract requires the custodial firm to carry general liability insurance but does not address the subject of general crime coverage. The housekeeping tasks are performed after normal working hours. Two contract custodial supervisors are issued access cards and master keys for the buildings at the beginning of the custodial work shift and return the cards and keys at the end of the shift. Each supervisor has a crew of six to eight custodians. To facilitate access for the custodial crews, the supervisors unlock all doors at the start of the shift and relock them after inspecting the work of the crews. As a result, during the seven- or eight-hour contract custodial shift, access control to the sensitive and administrative areas is essentially nonexistent. Furthermore, contract personnel whose criminal and personal histories are unknown roam free while conducting their custodial duties.

Checklists

Every enterprise differs from every other, and general recommendations must always be modified to meet local needs. Consult the appendices to this chapter for forms and checklists to use in the initial gathering of loss event data. *Note that these checklists must be modified to perform a comprehensive survey at a particular facility.* The items in the appendices relate to the probability factors discussed earlier and should help in avoiding mistakes of omission or oversight.

Risk Matrix

After the first-level analysis has identified the specific threat or risk, it will be necessary to describe individually the details that make occurrence of each event more or less probable. The method suggested is a grid or matrix description, arranged either by asset or by type of risk, and setting forth all the factual statements that are relevant to probability. (In Appendix B to this chapter, a model matrix is presented.) In effect, matrices describe the particular situation with respect to each of the risks identified in the general fact gathering by relating the risk to the asset involved. For

Security Vulnerability

example, a first-level survey might tell an observer that fire was a significant risk to the entire enterprise or to some specific assets contained in it. The matrix analysis would relate fire to the threatened assets by factual statements about the probability of fire occurring. These would describe the sources of ignition, combustibility of the asset, the fire detection and extinguishment resources available and the skill with which such resources would be used. As larger and more combustible assets become involved, or there are more sources of ignition, or less resources for detection and extinguishment, the probability of fire occurring and producing a loss would vary.

Probability Ratings

When all the available data has been gathered concerning each risk and its factual circumstances, it is proper to assign a probability rating. Ratings will not consider any precaution or countermeasure that may later be taken to reduce or eliminate the risk. A primary purpose of such unconditioned ratings is to allow for later priority scheduling in the selection of countermeasures.

As mentioned earlier, it will usually be impossible to arrive at simple probability by the classic equation route; but it should be fairly easy to make estimates with some objective basis. For purposes of security and protection planning, it may be enough to be able to say that event X is more probable than event Y. To be able to say this about entire series or categories of events, it must be possible to assign each to some class that can then be compared with other classes to arrive at a conclusion of "more likely" or "less likely."

We will establish five categories of probability because five is easy to use and easy to remember. We will assign these categories the names indicated in Table 5. With the amount of information available concerning each risk, plus the skill of the protection specialist in assessing the effect upon probability of the factual circumstances surrounding it (by using a matrix analysis), it should be possible to assign one of the five ratings. Let us define the ratings as follows:

    A. *Virtually Certain.* Given no changes, the event will occur. For example, given no changes, a closed intake valve on a sprinkler riser will prevent water flow in the event of fire.
    B. *Highly Probable.* The likelihood of occurrence is much greater than that of nonoccurrence. For example, unprotected currency lying visible on a counter is very likely to be taken.
    C. *Moderately Probable.* The event is more likely to occur than not to occur. Mathematically, this category lies somewhere between the probability ratios of 0.333 and 0.749, or from between one-to-two and three-to-one odds.

D. *Improbable.* The event is less likely to occur than not to occur. This does not imply impossibility, merely improbability.
E. *Probability Unknown.* Insufficient data is available for an evaluation.

Obviously, this approximate system of ratings contains wide latitude for error. Two observers could assign different probabilities to the same risk, based upon their different evaluations of the circumstances. But an advantage of this technique is that precision is not important. If the correct general label can be attached, it does not matter that a highly probable risk has a ratio of 0.751 or 0.853. What is important is to be able to segregate all risks of virtually certain probability from all others, and to make similar distinctions for each other general class. It is also recognized that even competent professionals disagree on what is highly probable and what is moderately probable. But the greater the detailed information available about each risk, the less the disagreements in rating.

To compensate for inexactness, *it is recommended that if a rating is in doubt after all available information has been gathered and evaluated, then the higher of two possible ratings be assigned.* Even with errors, a security vulnerability analysis based on systematic procedures such as those discussed in this chapter will be of greater value than one that is purely subjective or nonsystematic.

Rating Symbols

To save time and space, the five levels of probability can be assigned the symbols A, B, C, D and E, ranking downward from Virtually Certain to Probability Unknown. These symbols will later be combined with symbols representing criticality in the development of priority lists. It should be noted that the probability rating E, or Probability Unknown, is merely a temporary rating pending the development of all relevant data. In the construction of threat logic patterns, E ratings will be replaced by one of the definite ratings.

The second step in vulnerability analysis is completed when the particular risk, identified in the first level of the survey through the use of forms and checklists, has been assigned a probability rating based on the data developed through application of the matrix technique. No standard recording system is in universal use and each protection organization making a survey must set up its own recording system to be sure that each risk, once identified, can readily be found again in the growing volume of survey data. A simple method for doing this is to assign a distinctive number to each risk classified. It will be necessary to locate and identify each risk to add a later criticality rating, to rank the rated risk in a table or priority list, and to plot it in a threat logic tree based on relative priorities. Each of these terms is explained later in this chapter.

Table 5. Probability ratings.

Rating	Risk Potential
A	Virtually Certain
B	Highly Probable
C	Moderately Probable
D	Improbable
E	Probability Unknown

LOSS EVENT CRITICALITY

Highly Probable risks may not require countermeasures attention if the net damage they would produce is small. But Moderately Probable risks require attention if the size of the loss they produce is great. Obviously, the correlative of probability of occurrence is severity or criticality of occurrence. Assessing criticality is the third step in vulnerability assessment. Criticality is first considered on a single event or occurrence basis. For events with established frequency or high *recurrence* probability, criticality must also be considered cumulatively.

The Criticality Concept

Loss impact can be measured in a variety of ways. One is the effect on employee morale; another is the effect on community relations. But the most important measure overall is in dollars. Because the money measure is common to all ventures, even not-for-profit enterprises, the seriousness of security vulnerability can be most easily grasped if stated in monetary terms.

When the trade-off decisions are being made as part of the risk management process, the only useful way to evaluate security countermeasures is to compare cost of estimated losses with cost of protection. Money is the necessary medium.

It should be mentioned that security professionals often have difficulty in achieving the degree of credibility or acceptance with enterprise management that they consider essential to the development of an adequate program. One of the chief reasons for lack of acceptance is the absence of quantitative evaluations of the security effort. Although social responsibility in a broad sense is a recognized part of enterprise management, it is quite accurate to say that most managers and senior executives still set goals and measure results in financial terms, either of profit achieved or of costs reduced.

To fit easily into a typical manager's frame of reference, security and assets protection programs must be cost justified. Ignoring or underplaying cost implications while emphasizing the need for security will predictably generate low-grade programs. *Cost justification means not spending more than the benefits derived are worth.*

Kinds of Costs to Be Considered

Costs of security losses are both direct and indirect (see Figures 1 and 2). They are measured in terms of lost assets and lost income. Frequently, a single loss will result in both kinds of costs.

Permanent Replacement. The most obvious cost is that involved in the permanent replacement of a lost asset. If a building is destroyed by fire, finished goods lost through diversion or a laptop computer stolen from an office, the lost asset must be replaced. If the asset is a product, the proprietor may elect not to replace but to absorb the cost of production and the unrealized profit that would have been earned. Although a viable option, this course is not the one that a healthy business would choose, because failure to offer a product that could have been sold tends to have an impact on share of market. If the asset is a tool of production, its replacement is even more important because it is essential to the continued activity of the enterprise.

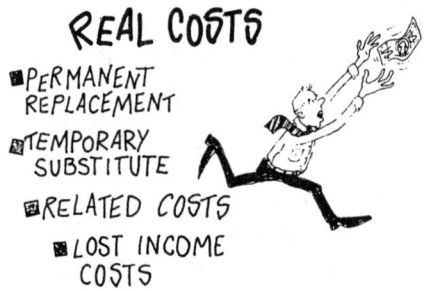

Figure 1. Real costs of losses.

DIRECT COSTS	INDIRECT COSTS
• MONEY	• REPUTATION
• NEGOTIABLE INSTRUMENTS	• GOODWILL
• PROPERTY	• LOSS OF EMPLOYEES
• INFORMATION	• MORALE OF EMPLOYEES

Figure 2. Two types of costs: direct and indirect.

Permanent replacement of a lost asset includes all of the cost to return it to its former location. Components of that cost are:

1. Purchase price or manufacturing cost
2. Freight and shipping charges
3. Make-ready or preparation cost to install it or make it functional

Note that a lost asset may have cost significantly less when it was first acquired than a replacement would cost now. Conversely, a replacement computer might cost less than the original.

Temporary Substitute. In regard to tools of production and other items making up the active structure of the enterprise, it may be necessary to procure substitutes while awaiting permanent replacements. This may be necessary to minimize lost sales and profit and to avoid penalties and forfeitures often encountered when a contractor fails to deliver. The cost of the temporary substitute is properly allocable to the security event that caused the loss of the asset. Components of temporary substitute cost might be:

1. Lease or rental
2. Premium labor, such as overtime or extra shift work to compensate for the missing production

Related or Consequent Cost. If other personnel or equipment are idle or underutilized because of the absence of an asset lost through a security incident, the cost of downtime is also attributable to the loss event. This happens most often when an activity is idle whose output becomes the input of another activity. Loss of discounts in paying bills due to failure of a computer and delay in completing the accounts payable cycle is an example.

Lost Income Cost. In most enterprises, cash reserves are held to the minimum necessary for short-term operations. Remaining capital or surplus is invested in varying kinds of income-producing securities. The larger the enterprise, the more important these investments are. If cash that might otherwise be so invested must be used to procure permanent replacements or temporary substitutes or to pay consequent costs, the income that might have been earned had it remained invested must be considered part of the loss. If income from investment is not relevant to a given case, then alternative uses of the cash might have to be abandoned to meet the emergency needs. In either case, the use of the money for loss replacement will represent an additional cost margin, which we call *lost income*. To measure total loss impact accurately, this must also be included. The following formula shows how that could be done:

$$I = \frac{i}{365} \times P \times t$$

where:

    I = income earned
    i = annual percent rate of return
    P = principal amount (in dollars) available for investment
    t = time (in days) during which P is available for investment

Example: What would be the income earned from $1000, invested at 10 percent per annum for a period of 90 days?

$$I = \frac{10}{365} \times \$1000 \times 90$$

$$= \$24.66$$

Cost Abatement

Many losses are covered, at least in part, by insurance of some kind. Indeed, in some enterprises, it is still the practice to consider insurance as the only factor in risk loss protection. Fortunately, this unenlightened approach is becoming less common and is being replaced by modern risk management techniques. Risk management is an overall designator applied to the combined functions of loss prevention, loss control and loss indemnification, typified in older business organizations by the use of engineering, fire, and security and insurance departments.

Some insurance coverage, usually far from total, is available for many losses. To the extent it is available, that amount should be subtracted from the combined costs of loss enumerated above. But even where insurance is available, there is usually a purchase cost or allocable premium share connected with the particular assets for which the insurance claim is made. For precision, that cost or share should be subtracted from the available insurance before the insurance is, in turn, used to offset the cost of loss.

A Cost-of-Loss Formula

Taking the worst-case position and analyzing each security vulnerability in light of the probable maximum loss for a single occurrence of the risk event that should occur under typical circumstances, we can use the following equation:

$$K = (C_p + C_t + C_r + C_i) - (I - a)$$

where:

    K = criticality, total cost of loss
    Cp = cost of permanent replacement
    Ct = cost of temporary substitute
    Cr = total related costs
    Ci = lost income cost

I = available insurance or indemnity
a = allocable insurance premium amount

The assets protection staff does not usually have this information immediately available and must work with the financial and insurance organizations to develop it. But an enterprise with extensive insurance coverage probably has accumulated much of the information in the course of preparing schedules of coverage. It is not unusual to find extensive criticality data in an insurance department and some form of loss-risk probability data in the assets protection or security department. Far less often is this data systematically combined. Logically, however, it must be combined for either aspect of the risk management scheme to fulfill its intended purpose.

Criticality Ratings

When the cost data has been collected, a decision can be made as to the proper criticality rating to be applied to the loss under consideration. If the same general technique is used here as was used in assigning probability ratings, we can achieve an effective—although rough—grading or separation. It is suggested that the ratings in Table 6 be used, and interpreted as follows:

1. *Fatal.* The loss would result in total recapitalization or abandonment or long-term discontinuance of the enterprise.
2. *Very Serious.* The loss would require a major change in investment policy and would have a major impact on the balance sheet assets.
3. *Moderately Serious.* The loss would have a noticeable impact on earnings as reflected in the operating statement and would require attention from the senior executive management.
4. *Relatively Unimportant.* The loss would be covered by normal contingency reserves.
5. *Seriousness Unknown.* Before priorities are established, this provisional rating is to be replaced by a firm rating from one of the first four classes.

The nature and size of the enterprise determines the dollar limits for each of these classes. For a small proprietary company, a $10,000 loss might be fatal; although in a large industrial conglomerate, the same loss

Table 6. Criticality ratings.

1	Fatal to the Enterprise
2	Very Serious
3	Moderately Serious
4	Relatively Unimportant
5	Seriousness Unknown

might be relatively unimportant. *The value of the rating system is in its relevance to the enterprise. The terms used are not intended to have any absolute significance.*

Rating Symbols

We can assign symbols to criticality ratings as we did with the probability ratings. Using the numerals 1 through 5 for each class from *Fatal* to *Seriousness Unknown,* each risk that was identified in the first step and rated as to probability in the second, is now also rated as to criticality. This completes the third step in vulnerability assessment.

ALTERNATIVE APPROACHES TO CRITICALITY

There are other ways in which the weighted importance of a probable risk event can be measured. One is when a historical frequency can be identified. For example, natural catastrophes such as floods and earthquakes occur a *stated number of times per year,* based upon the number of actual past occurrences. Other events may also have a reliable rate of recurrence. When a frequency rate is known, the single event criticality can be multiplied by the number of events expected during the period considered, normally the calendar or fiscal year. Thus, if K = \$10,000 for an event, and it has a frequency rate of once a year, the weighted impact would be \$10,000 × 1. If the same event had a frequency rate of once every three years, the weighted impact would be \$10,000 × 0.333 or \$3333. If it had a frequency of three times a year, the weighted impact would be \$10,000 × 3, or \$30,000.

Another technique, useful to convert the symbolic rankings to simple numerical statements, is to assign an agreed real numerical probability to each of the four categories below. Thus:

A. *Virtually Certain* might be assigned a numerical probability of 0.85;
B. *Highly Probable* might be assigned 0.65;
C. *Moderately Probable* might be assigned 0.50; and
D. *Improbable* might be assigned 0.20.

Next, the criticality of any single loss event would be multiplied by the agreed value of the probability. Thus, a \$10,000 criticality for a Moderately Probable event would be \$10,000 × 0.50 = \$5000. Note that this is used hypothetically to arrive at an overall picture of exposure. If the loss occurs at all, it will cost \$10,000, not \$5000. But to permit ranking before loss so as to expedite countermeasures, the technique would preserve the weighted differences.

Another method to present overall risk is to use a *scatterplot.* This is a method of plotting each risk on a graph whose axes are cost and frequency. Figure 3 shows a number of such risks plotted that way. First, the criticality

Security Vulnerability

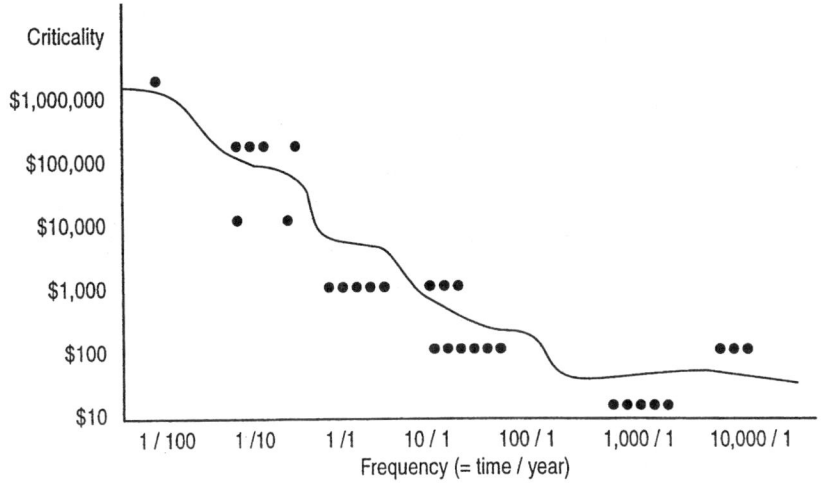

Figure 3. Vulnerability/criticality scatterplot.

or cost impact is located on the vertical axis. Then, moving right in a straight line, a dot or mark is placed above the frequency rate for that event shown on the horizontal axis. When all the risks have been plotted on the graph, a smooth curve (a line passing through the areas of highest concentration of dots) can be drawn. This would indicate the approximate distribution of expected losses for the planning period. The countermeasures program would be designed to lower that line as much as feasible.

Establishing Priorities

The next step is to arrange the entire body of rated risks into a sequence of priority for countermeasures attention. This ranking requires that the more serious risks be listed first, followed in descending order of importance by the others until all the risks have been listed. The listing should identify each risk and indicate the combined probability-criticality rating that has been assigned.

Such an approach would produce a list of all the risks in each of the various rating classes, as follows: A1, A2, A3, A4; B1, B2, B3, B4; C1, C2, C3, C4; D1, D2, D3, D4. Precise positioning of the middle levels B3 and C2 depends upon whether probability/frequency or criticality is given the greater weight. It is suggested that criticality be given the greater weight.

Thus far we have discussed the accomplishment of all of the tasks manually. In a small facility this might be acceptable. In most facilities, a software program is used to assemble the information and assess the risks.

ASSET PROTECTION AND SECURITY MANAGEMENT HANDBOOK

When the risks have all been ranked, the formal task of vulnerability assessment is completed. The enterprise now has a documented schedule of security and protection problems in the most probable order in which they should be addressed. The next stage, countermeasures planning, indicates that although several problems have been separately stated, a single countermeasure may neutralize them all. This is because a number of risks all depend upon a common cause or condition precedent. Arranging risks to highlight these connections produces a *threat logic* pattern that suggests not only the interrelated risks but also the most appropriate place at which to interpose a countermeasure. The work of planning the logic pattern is considered *threat analysis*.

PREPARING A SOLUTION

Threat Analysis

For each security risk identified as a primary vulnerability (Figure 4), certain events or conditions are necessary before it can occur. Some of these events and conditions must exist simultaneously, some in a stated sequence, some individually and some individually, but not in the presence or line of sequence of others.

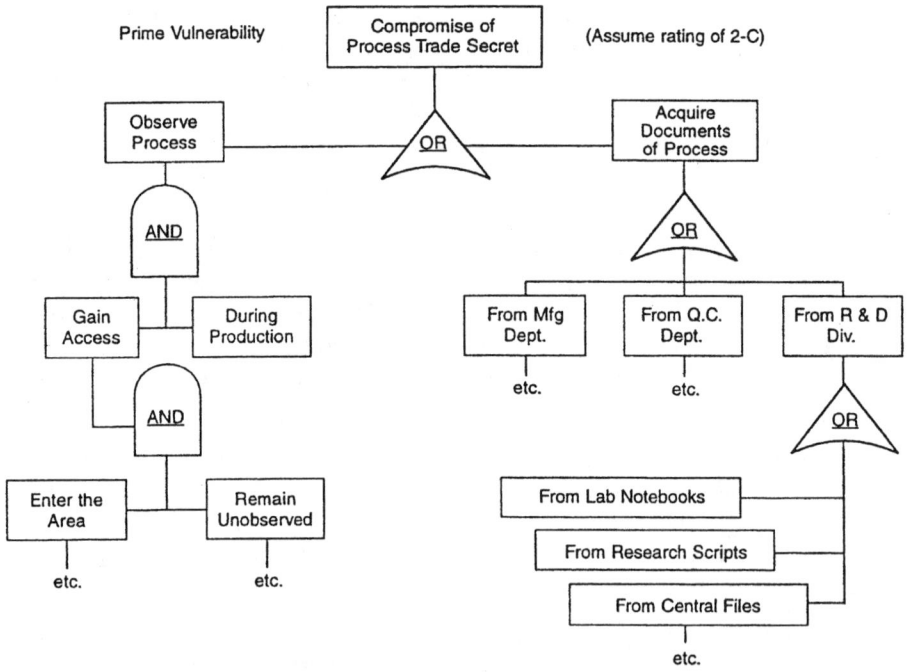

Figure 4. Threat model.

Security Vulnerability

Logically, these combinations can be represented by the following terms:

1. *AND* — simultaneous existence
2. *AND, but X before Y* — all must exist but in a stated sequence or with a stated priority
3. *OR* — any one alone must exist
4. *OR, but if X then not Y* — any one alone but not together or in a stated sequence

These categories are mutually exclusive, logical alternatives. Before any event can occur, it must be preceded by a set of conditions and events falling into one of the alternative sets. For example, consider the case of a fire. Before a fire can occur, there must be fuel *and* oxygen *and* ignition. All three must exist together; the absence of any one will prevent combustion.

Now consider the case of a theft from finished goods inventory. This theft might occur from manufacturing *or* from quality control *or* from distribution and transportation *or* from a warehouse. Because a theft at any one of these locations would be theft of an item of finished goods inventory, each area must be adequately protected to neutralize the threat of finished goods theft.

But there will be combinations of logical alternatives in most threat models. That is, of all the required facts and conditions, some may be in the "*and*" group, some in the "*or.*" Figure 4 illustrates the compound nature of most threat models.

In addition to the compound nature of the threat model, there are also common, or class, or threshold vulnerabilities from which other vulnerabilities develop. For example, a typical common vulnerability is unauthorized access to a building, room, area, storage facility, etc. Once unauthorized access has been achieved, the person gaining it is free to do a variety of things to one or more assets. Any exposure that would exist after a threshold vulnerability has been actualized should be considered an active threat as long as the threshold threat exists. This is consistent with the worst-case approach used in arriving at criticality.

Leverage

It is apparent that if a common vulnerability exists and if it can be neutralized, all subsequent or related vulnerabilities may also be fully or partly neutralized. *Note that it does not necessarily follow that eliminating a common vulnerability will eliminate all related vulnerabilities. Careful analysis of the threat logic pattern must be conducted to be sure such related vulnerabilities could not also be actualized in other ways.*

If it is possible to neutralize a common vulnerability by applying a countermeasure to some "*and*" set, thus breaking a necessary chain, the application of a single countermeasure at the appropriate place may neutralize many threats. We call this the *principle of leverage*, because, as with the lever, a small force correctly applied can accomplish a large task. The most important factor in making programs of security countermeasures cost-justifiable is the recognition and application of this principle of leverage.

NETWORK DESIGN

The final step in preparing the discovered and rated vulnerabilities for direct application of countermeasures is to arrange them so that the interrelationships of those with common or threshold risks are clear. This arrangement can take the form of a network in vertical layers (as in Figure 4), each layer representing a separate set of conditions or circumstances necessary to create the level above. The top level is the primary security vulnerability or threat to be dealt with, from the list of threats developed during the vulnerability analysis phases. Each such threat is coded for its combined vulnerability/criticality ratings, and each lower level of fact situations represents the logical series of events that could or must occur for the main event to occur.

This process can be carried to as many levels as desired, right down to what might be called the entry point — that is, the first event or set of conditions to bring the threat to life. For example, in many situations, this event is the arrival of some potential aggressor at the facility boundary. Thereafter, all the things he could or might do or conditions he would or might encounter along the path to his objective constitute intermediate facts. The final fact is the occurrence of the loss event, such as theft or sabotage. In practice, the threat network for each threat model studied can be stopped at the point where it is obvious that there are already countermeasures options indicated.

When the network has been carried as far as desired, all leverage points described earlier are marked so that even a visual inspection of the whole network indicates immediately the places at which productive countermeasures should be inserted.

SOLVING THE PROBLEM

Countermeasures

Each leverage point indicates a possibility for a countermeasure, although it does not immediately suggest which countermeasure to use. As shown in Figure 4, the trade secret can be lost either through observation of the process or securing its documentation. Because either of these would cause the loss event, both must be neutralized. To observe the process, however, one must gain access to the production department while production is in process. Furthermore, to gain access, one must both enter the area and remain unchallenged.

Security Vulnerability

To neutralize the risk of unauthorized observation, the first point of leverage is at the "*and*" set. *Either* entry is effectively denied *or* challenge is assured. This suggests several countermeasures, including (1) area access control at point of entry, (2) area surveillance on a continuing basis, and (3) area access control only during periods of production. The network or threat model is not extended to a logical conclusion in Figure 4, so it does not indicate a similar leverage point in regard to record security. Even if it were extended, it might not show any. To protect records, it might be necessary to apply specific countermeasures at each location where a record was available.

Countermeasures Criteria. To complete the countermeasures options development, we must look at each leverage point in the overall threat model network. We should list or catalogue each countermeasure that might be appropriate at that point. In our example, we show three. For each countermeasure, four factors should be determined and listed:

1. *Validity.* This determines whether the countermeasure does what it is supposed to do. For example, does a water flow alarm register the flow of water in a sprinkler riser? If *actual detection of fire* were the requirement, then a products-of-combustion or ultraviolet flame detector would be more appropriate.
2. *Degree of reliability.* Reliability is defined as the consistency with which the countermeasure achieves its functional objective over a large number of similar cases. For example, in 1000 cases in which ambient temperature actually reaches 165°F, how many times will a fixed temperature thermostat for that rated capacity operate? If it operates 1000 times, it is 100 percent reliable. Any lower percentage reduces its reliability proportionately.
3. *Approximate cost* to put it into effect.
4. *Delay* or elapsed time required to put it into effect. If this is significantly longer than for other available countermeasures, that fact should be underscored.

Cost is listed above as the third item to consider in selection. It is evident that among countermeasures of equal or approximately equal validity and reliability, the least expensive measure should be chosen. This principle, applied throughout the selection process, will produce an appropriate system at optimal cost. In regard to cost, it should be noted that there is some point at which the cost of loss and the cost of countermeasures are proportionate. Before that point, the amount spent would not buy adequate protection. After that point, increased expense would not buy added protection of equal value. Figure 5 illustrates this relationship.

With the rapidly advancing technology now characterizing the protection of assets field, the task of knowing the appropriate countermeasures will grow increasingly complex. Later chapters of this *Manual* assist in the

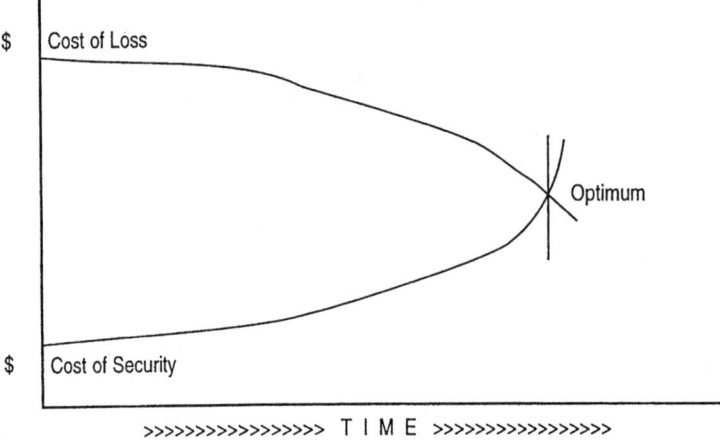

Figure 5. Optimum security resourcing.

choice and evaluation of countermeasures by describing the strengths, weaknesses, availability and applications of many of them. But each professional in the field should have other sources and inputs to assure that he or she remains current. The principal sources are professional, commercial and standards literature, each of which is growing. The bibliography at the end of this chapter identifies a number of such sources.

Systems Evaluation Technique

A system is defined as *a regular and orderly arrangement of parts and components in an interrelated and integrated whole.* The system is different from a simple group or aggregation in that it is integrated by design. Every part is present and functions in terms of its relationship to every other part. A system requires planning so that there are no unintended surplus parts or unanticipated absences of necessary parts. In applying the systems technique to security countermeasures planning, it is first necessary to select individual countermeasures that will support or be supported by each other. *Each resource in the properly designed system plays a unique and indispensable role.* This type of design tends to reduce the total number of countermeasures and to optimize performance of those that are used.

Next, the system is assembled and tested. This can be done either theoretically, such as through computer analyses or other parameter-varying model techniques, or physically, such as through the operation of mechanical, electric and electronic components. A system also involves the application of procedures and human actions and reactions, which can be tested by the command post exercise or simulated emergency.

Component Selection. We noted earlier that reliability of each countermeasure should be evaluated. When each risk in the threat network is considered for neutralization, an important point is the degree of reliability required of the countermeasure. In access control at facility entries, for example, an error rate of one improper admittance in every 100 might be sufficient. An error rate of one in 20 might also be acceptable. In the former case, we would assume that very few other countermeasures are in effect, and hence the door check has to be very effective. In the latter case, there may be sufficient other precautions that the door check can be relaxed. In the first case, 99 percent reliability would be required, a very high requirement for that kind of countermeasure. In the second case, 95 percent would be required. The 4 percent reduction could avoid large dollar expenditures. If 95 percent is acceptable, there is no need to spend to achieve 99 percent.

In another case, zero error may be demanded, as with a fire detection subsystem in a major computer installation. In that case, even with a very high reliability rate in a single sensing device, we might require two or three devices to provide redundancy. The likelihood that several highly reliable devices will fail simultaneously is calculated as the product of the separate probabilities of each device involved. Thus, if we used two thermostats, each with a probability of failure of 0.01 (99 percent reliable), the probability that both would fail simultaneously would be 0.01×0.01 (i.e., 0.0001), or 9999 to 1. Adding one more device would raise the odds to 999,999 to 1.

For achieving very high levels of reliability in security systems, it will generally be much less expensive to design complex redundant countermeasures than to seek a single countermeasure of the required level. In the fire scenario, we might use a fixed temperature thermostat *and* a rate-of-rise thermostat *and* a products of combustion detector. Each would operate in a different domain (detect a different aspect of fire) as well as multiply the detection devices. Also, standard models of multiple different detectors cost less than super-reliable models of a single detector.

Keeping the System Current

There are three main reasons for security losses:

1. Failure to recognize vulnerabilities
2. Failure to use the proper countermeasures
3. Failure to consider change

The change can be in the vulnerability or in the relevance of the countermeasure. Vulnerability changes can involve change in either probability of occurrence or criticality of impact, or both.

The assets protection professional must use the tools of vulnerability assessment in such a way as to maintain a current posture. This means remaining very close to ongoing processes and activities within the enterprise and modifying the threat models or the priority lists, as required.

These practices lead to the best possible posture of defense and they are essential to good risk management.

Risk Management

The trend is toward closer integration of the three functions of risk management; loss *prevention,* loss *control* and loss *indemnification.* This trend, in itself, is a testimonial to system techniques. The practical implication for assets protection professionals is that greater familiarity with and understanding of the other functions are needed. Many enterprises combine the functions under a single executive called the risk manager. In later chapters of this handbook, loss prevention and loss insurance are discussed. But these discussions are primarily intended to clarify the main issue: loss control. Wide and continued reading in the areas of prevention and insurance is strongly recommended.

ECONOMIC JUSTIFICATION OF SECURITY

It was noted earlier that security expenditures must be cost justified because they imply diversion or application of enterprise assets or resources that might be better used elsewhere. For example, a security program costs $250,000 each year but cannot demonstrate in any quantitative way that it is returning any of that sum by way of losses avoided or minimized or assets recovered after losses. The argument could be made for simply investing the $250,000 at 10 percent annually, thus not only conserving the $250,000 but earning an additional $25,000.

If, instead of investing the $250,000 each year, however, it were spent in each of the next five years on security, at the end there would be a net cumulative expenditure of $1,250,000. Invested at 10 percent compounded each year for five years, the same amount would be worth $1,5826,275 at the end. That amount (the expenditure plus the lost income) would be the net cost to the company for the security program. Security must show some equivalent value to justify such lost income opportunity.

In many cases some results of security operations are not directly quantifiable but are, nonetheless, necessary. Maintenance of order and prevention of violence in the workplace are clearly necessary, despite lack of cost justification. But because security programs are not equivalent to law enforcement, they cannot rationally be justified purely in law enforcement terms. To achieve an allocation of enterprise capital, the security function should establish, to the maximum achievable extent, that its return on that capital is as good as any other element in the organization. How can this be done?

Cost Avoidance

One way to establish economic justification is to show that the losses which would (or probably would) have occurred without the security

Security Vulnerability

program did not occur at all or did not occur to the extent expected. Then show that the avoided costs of those losses that were expected but did not occur would have been greater than the costs of the program instituted to prevent them. In other words, the costs of the program were less than the costs of the losses that would have occurred without the program.

This approach, although it seems heavily theoretical, is often used by risk management specialists in determining how much risk an enterprise retains and how much it insures. For this application, the costs of insurance premiums and claims administration are compared to the costs of the expected loss. A position is sought at which the amount of retained risk is not likely to produce a larger amount of loss than the added expense that would be required to provide commercial insurance protection. Many factors are considered in this determination in addition to the relative amounts of cost of loss and cost of insurance. The present value of future earnings (or expenses) must be calculated if the determination is to spend X amount in the beginning of a year for a premium or to risk spending Y amount later in the year on a retained risk loss. At an annual rate of interest of 10 percent or higher for borrowed funds, or at a 10 percent rate of return on invested funds, the larger the amount in question, the more important the time interval.

In using the avoidance approach for security justification, it is the costs of the proposed loss prevention program that are considered in the light of expected losses. For a complete analysis of the risk management posture of any enterprise, the costs of the assets protection program should also include those costs appropriate to the insurance phase of the program. That is, the total costs relevant to the assets protection or risk management program include:

- The costs of losses that occur despite the program and are not insured or indemnified
- The costs of the loss prevention or control program, aside from insurance costs
- The costs of insurance premiums and claims administration

If the total of these three types of costs is less in any given year (or over any longer appropriate time span) than the costs of losses that probably would have occurred without the prevention and control program, then the risk management efforts are successful.

Cost Avoidance in Loss Control

Although there has been long experience with estimating risk management efficiency for risk retention purposes (i.e., costs of loss versus the costs of insurance), there has not been very much experience with such estimating when applied to loss control. Loss control — the prevention or minimizing of losses — is the specific function of the security and assets protection program. It is therefore necessary, if security cost justification is to be demonstrated, to apply this technique directly to the security program. If the weighted impact of an identified security loss event has been established, then that quantity should go into the total of all such quantities for all such loss risks.

Refer for a moment to an earlier example of a $10,000 single occurrence loss amount and an annual frequency of 0.333. The weighted impact of $3333 should be included in the probable or expected losses for the following year. If the same $10,000 event had been rated D4 and the suggested conversion of 0.20 were substituted for D4, it would have a weighted impact of $2000. Note that there is a difference, but that the relative posture of the risk is about the same. As both approaches are predictive, both could be wrong. Either, however, is reasonable given the amount of information available about similar past losses or about the probability factors, if there is no known history. *Every significant loss exposure identified in the vulnerability analysis would be given its weighted impact value and all of those values would constitute the total expected or probable loss for the year under study.*

Note carefully that total loss is calculated before considering any proposed security countermeasures. It is the condition of the enterprise without a security or assets protection program. Even that statement is subject to some clarification. If we are considering the fire loss risk in a building that already has a complete sprinkler system, it would be pointless to calculate the loss exposure as if there were no sprinklers. The fire loss will be the fire loss estimated in a sprinkler-protected facility.

But if in addition to the sprinklers, there are sprinkler alarms, a full-time security officer or fire warden force, a volunteer plant brigade, early detection devices, and the like, the cost of those optional elements would also be considered. The probable cost of a fire with the sprinklers *but without* the other options would be compared to the probable cost of a fire with all the options in place. The critical question is whether the marginal, increased cost of the options significantly reduced the probable cost of a fire, at the least by an amount equal to the cost of the options.

When countermeasures are proposed or implemented, a second estimate is needed of the losses that may occur notwithstanding the countermeasures. For example, it might be estimated that there would be probable losses of $100,000 in thefts from finished goods inventory if there were no specific security controls. But a security program involving CCTV surveillance, intrusion alarms and patrol guard response might be proposed. The probable effect of such a program on inventory theft might be estimated to reduce the losses with the program to $10,000. The difference between losses estimated without the program ($100,000) and those probable with the program ($10,000) is $90,000. This amount would be considered the loss avoided.

The differences or losses avoided for every significant loss exposure would all be totaled to derive an overall loss avoided amount. This amount would then be used in an equation to justify the security expenditure. The better the security system design, the more likely that it will withstand such analysis.

It is important to note that the prediction of losses, either with or without a security program, is only that — a prediction. When used as such, it is a good preliminary guide to approving security budget requests. If one cannot even predict a positive return from some proposed security expense, there is serious reason not to approve it. But the most valuable application of these loss avoidance formulas will be after the fact. At the end of the year (or period of years), has the amount actually expended on security produced a measurable avoidance or reduction in losses?

Consider the following cases:

1. A company driver has an automobile accident with a non-employee in the course of the business day. The non-employee sues the company, alleging negligence by the company driver and vicarious liability of the company. The claim is for $500,000. A skillful investigation by the security department, under the guidance of company counsel, establishes that the plaintiff had been drinking heavily just prior to the accident and, in fact, had been refused further bar service and warned not to drive by the bartender. Counsel for the company estimates that a settlement offer of $10,000 might be quickly accepted by the plaintiff and that there would be a very good chance that the company would prevail if the case were tried. If it were tried, the costs of the trial counsel would probably be $20,000.
2. A company has had experience with persons employed as department managers who later proved unsatisfactory and were terminated because of dishonesty. There has been an average of three per year throughout the company of such terminations and the amounts of loss involved in the acts of dishonesty that led to the terminations ranged from $100 to $25,000, with an average value of $5000 over the five-year period. This year, background investigations of potential new managers by the security department identified two potential employees who had histories of prior dishonesty but who had concealed that information in their applications. The two individuals were not hired.

Cleary, well-performed security tasks or properly functioning security countermeasures have direct financial consequences. In these two examples, an obvious loss was avoided. In one case, the potential liability was reduced from $500,000 to $10,000. In the other, the prevention was of two probable losses of $5000 average value.

Asset Recoveries

There is a second element to the economic justification exercise. It involves identifying and evaluating actual recoveries made solely as a result of having a security program. Some examples of recoveries include:

1. A hijacked truck is located and recovered because of prompt and effective investigation. The truck contained finished goods bound for a distributor with a value to the enterprise at that point of $85,000.
2. An employee is stopped by a security guard on the way out of the facility because the employee is carrying a box but does not have a proper pass. The box is opened after the employee's supervisor is called and is shown to contain $200 worth of company-owned components from a manufacturing process. The employee has no acceptable explanation.
3. There is an inventory variance in the raw materials inventory of $175,000. Packaging materials purchased from a local vendor cannot be found in physical inventory. Inquiry by the security department produces a confession from a receiving clerk that over a six-month period he had colluded with the supplier to acknowledge receipt of the packaging material when, in fact, it was not shipped and the clerk knew it was not. The clerk admitted receiving $2500 from the vendor. The company has a blanket fidelity bond with a deductible of $5000 and a ceiling of $10 million. A claim was made on the fidelity carrier for $170,000 as a result of the investigation by security.

It should be clear that there are many situations in the course of a year in which recoveries are made solely as a result of security efforts. The actual or agreed value of these recoveries represents part of the return on the security expenditure.

Note that in the cases of the hijacked truck, the inventory variance and the employee stealing company property, there was no doubt about real value. But there could be a dispute as to agreed value or recovery amount. Is the depreciated book value of an asset the correct value? The original acquisition cost? The current replacement cost? The answer depends upon enterprise policy and should not be difficult to come by. The recovery value is that value agreed to or arrived at by the consistent application of enterprise policy. That value, for each recovery made, is added to all other recoveries, and the total for the year is also used in the equation that follows.

Measuring Return on Expenditures

Based on the preceding discussion, a return on the expenditures made for security in any one year can be measured by the application of the following equation:

$$\text{ROE} = \frac{\text{AL} + \text{R}}{\text{CSP}}$$

where:

ROE = return on expenditures
 AL = avoided losses
  R = recoveries made
CSP = cost of the security program

To represent the costs of the security program (CSP), it is necessary to include:

1. Personnel expense (salaries, wages and benefits).
2. All other expense items such as telephone, mail, travel, memberships, purchased services, etc.
3. The allocable portion of capital costs. For example, if a security alarm system is installed at a capital cost of $150,000 and has an asset cost recovery period or useful life of five years, then in each of those five years, 1/5 or $30,000 will be included in expense as depreciation or asset cost recovery.

The goal is to achieve an ROE as large as possible. An answer equal to 1 means that security is at least paying for itself. An answer less than 1 means it is not, and greater than 1 means it is adding value that would not accrue to the enterprise without the security program.

It is important to distinguish the elements of the program attributable to different levels of the organization and the loss avoidance or recoveries claimed by those levels. If one were measuring the ROE of a corporate security staff that conducted investigations, proposed standards and policies, and made local audits but did not actively direct or manage local physical security programs or personnel at plant and other facilities, then the costs to consider would be only those directly incurred by the corporate staff. They would probably exclude the capital costs of local physical security programs. Similarly, the recoveries attributed to the corporate staff would probably come mostly from the investigations and audits and not from application of local loss prevention techniques or physical countermeasures.

It is not a good idea to carry an attempt to assess efficiency on a unit or departmental basis too far. If the corporate staff proposes the standard under which a local alarm system is installed, and if that alarm system effectively prevents a theft, is the avoided loss creditable to the local security program or to the corporate program? The better approach would be to attempt an integration of all the security efforts and results and a presentation of an overall picture. Taken together, do the security expenditures in a given year for the organization produce an acceptable return?

It is important that security costs and benefits be quantified to the degree possible. Without such quantitative assessments, many enterprises eliminate known security costs without realizing that they may be losing far greater benefits.

Selected Bibliography

Books

Barefoot, J. Kirk and Maxwell, David A.; *Corporate Security Administration and Management;* 1987; Butterworth-Heinemann, Newton, MA.

Broder, James F.; *Risk Analysis and Security Survey;* 1984; Butterworth-Heinemann, Newton, MA.

Dalton, Dennis R.; *Security Management: Business Strategies for Success;* 1995; Butterworth-Heinemann, Newton, MA.

Fischer, Robert J. and Green, Gion; *Introduction to Security, 6th ed.;* 1998; Butterworth-Heinemann, Newton, MA.

Purpura, Phillip P.; *Security and Loss Prevention, 3rd ed.;* 1998; Butterworth-Heinemann, Newton, MA.

Schaub, James L., and Biery, Ken D., Jr.; *The Ultimate Security Survey;* 1995; Butterworth-Heinemann, Newton, MA.

Sennewald, Charles A.; *Effective Security Management, 3rd ed.;* 1998; Butterworth-Heinemann, Newton, MA.

Simonsen, Clifford E.; *Private Security in America: An Introduction;* 1998; Prentice-Hall, Upper Saddle River, NJ.

U.S. Marshal Service and a federal interagency task group; *Vulnerability Assessment of Federal Facilities;* 1995; U.S. Government Printing Office, Washington, D.C.

Walsh, James et al.; *The Merritt Risk Management Manual;* 2001; POA Publishing LLC, Los Angeles, CA.

Periodicals

Information Security; International Computer Security Association, Norwood, MA.
 — Corby, Michael J.; Top-Down Risk Assessment; January 1999.

Security Management; American Society for Industrial Security, Alexandria, VA.
 — Schultheiss, Robert A.; Evaluating Corporate Exposures; January 1996.

APPENDIX A
BASIC SECURITY SURVEY

NOTE: This form may be used to gather basic risk data for any facility or enterprise. It can be augmented by additional data-gathering forms appropriate for specialized occupancies.

Part 1: Geography and Climate

1. Name of facility: _____

2. Street address and Zip: _____

Security Vulnerability

   3. Telephone: _____

   4. (a) Latitude _____ (b) Longtitude _____ (c) Elevation _____

   5. Nearest large body of water: _____

   6. (a) Elevation of body of water _____ (b) Distance from facility_____

   7. Nearest river: _____

   8. (a) Distance from facility _____ (b) Average depth _____

      (c) Maximum depth _____ (d) Date of last flood_____

   9. Rainfall: (a) Average _____ (b) Record max. _____

      (c) Date of (b) _____

 10. Month snow (a) Starts _____ (b) Stops_____

 11. Average annual snowfall: _____ (inches)

 12. Maximum recorded snowfall: (a) Amount _____ (b) Date_____

Part 2: Size and Configuration

 13. Total acres or square feet in plot: _____

 14. Number of structures: _____

    (a) Structure name _____

    Construction: ( ) Concrete or masonry ( ) Steel ( ) Wood
              ( ) Mixed construction

    Total square feet structures: _____ Number of stories:_____

    Structure used for: ( ) Manufacturing ( ) Research
                    ( ) Administration ( ) Storage
                    ( ) Sales ( ) School or other assembly
                    ( ) Residence

    (b) Structure name _____

    Construction: ( ) Concrete or masonry ( ) Steel ( ) Wood
              ( ) Mixed construction

    Total square feet structures: _____ Number of stories:_____

    Structure used for: ( ) Manufacturing ( ) Research
                    ( ) Administration ( ) Storage ( ) Sales
                    ( ) School or other assembly ( ) Residence

    (c) Structure name _____

ASSET PROTECTION AND SECURITY MANAGEMENT HANDBOOK

Construction: ( ) Concrete or masonry ( ) Steel ( ) Wood
( ) Mixed construction

Total square feet structures:_____ Number of stories: _____

Structure used for: ( ) Manufacturing ( ) Research
( ) Administration ( ) Storage ( ) Sales
( ) School or other assembly ( ) Residence

(d) Structure name _____

Construction: ( ) Concrete or masonry ( ) Steel ( ) Wood
( ) Mixed construction

Total square feet structures:_____ Number of stories: _____

Structure used for: ( ) Manufacturing ( ) Research
( ) Administration ( ) Storage ( ) Sales
( ) School or other assembly ( ) Residence

(Continue on separate paper as required.)

15. Number of structures interconnected:

    (a) At grade level or higher_____ (b) Below grade _____

16. Total working population on:
    (a) Day shift_____ (b) Afternoon shift_____ (c) Night shift_____

17. Estimated number daily visitors:_____

18. Number of automobiles parked daily:_____

Part 3: Social and Political Environment

19. Facility is in a ( ) City ( ) Town ( ) Incorporated village ( ) Rural area

20. Estimated percentage of neighboring area: (a) Residential_____
    (b) Commercial_____ (c) Industrial_____ (d) Agricultural_____
    (e) Undeveloped_____

21. Estimated percentage of (a) One family homes_____

    (b) Multiple dwellings_____ (c) High-rise multiple dwellings_____

22. Estimated value range of one family private homes: $_____ to $_____

23. Ethnic mix of residents: _____

24. Police department having jurisdiction:_____

25. Total police personnel in that department: _____

26. Average interval between call to police and arrival time at facility:
    _____

Security Vulnerability

27. Usual police resources making response: _____
28. Is area separately reported in Standard Metropolitan Statistical Area section of Uniform Crime Reports? _____
29. If 28 is yes, what are most recent indexes for:

    (a) Total crime____ (b) Violent crime____ (c) Property crime____
    (d) Rape____ (e) Murder and manslaughter____ (f) Robbery____
    (g) Car theft____ (h) Aggravated assault____ (i) Burglary____
    (j) Larceny over $50____

30. Nearest fire department: _____
31. Travel time for fire department to facility:_____
32. "First due" fire response: _____
33. Equipment available for second and subsequent alarms: _____
34. Is there a mutual aid agreement with other fire departments? _____

Part 4: Internal Activity

35. Products manufactured or services rendered: _____
36. Approximate dollar total of annual production, sales, or services:
    _____
37. Is activity on a 5, 6 or 7-day basis? _____
38. Is activity on a 1, 2 or 3-shift basis?_____
39. What is busy season? _____
40. What is slack season?_____
41. Number of ( ) Vaults ( ) Safes in facility
42. Approximate total dollar value of safe and vault contents: _____
43. Largest cash balance in facility:_____ When?_____
44. Estimated value of (a) Gemstones_____ (b) Precious metals_____
    (c) Negotiable securities_____
45. Are there ( ) controlled substances ( ) dangerous drugs?
46. Approximate total amount of controlled substances or dangerous drugs: _____
47. Is there trade secret or other confidential proprietary information at the facility? _____
48. Is there classified defense information at the facility?_____

ASSET PROTECTION AND SECURITY MANAGEMENT HANDBOOK

Part 5: Physical Safeguards

49. Is there a perimeter fence? _____ Fence material ____ Height _____
50. Is there any form of access control on: ( ) Pedestrians ( ) Vehicles
51. Are intrusion or other security alarms in use? _____
    If yes, are alarms: ( ) Central station ( ) Local ( ) Proprietary
    ( ) Directly connected to police
52. Is there a building access control system? _____
    If yes, is the system: ( ) Key locks ( ) Magnetic Stripe ( ) Weigand
    ( ) Proximity ( ) Biometric
53. Is there a formal program of key control?_____
54. Date of last total or major lock recombinating: _____
55. Is there a guard or patrol force? _____
56. Total officers: (a) Day shift _____ (b) Afternoon shift_____
    (c) Night shift_____
57. Security force profile mean and median: (a) Age ____/____
    (b) Years formal education ____/____
    (c) Years service at facility ____/____
58. Percentage of security force assigned to limited duty: _____
59. Current pay range (per hour) of security force personnel:
    $_____ per _____
60. Are officers ( ) Agency supplied ( ) Employed by facility ( ) Both
61. Are guards armed? _____

Part 6: Fire and Disaster

62. How many structures have (a) Complete sprinkler protection _____
    (b) Partial sprinkler protection_____ (c) No sprinkler protection_____
63. Show other fixed extinguishment systems (a) Building _____
    (b) Location _____ (c) Type system _____
64. How many buildings have automatic fire detection and alarm system? _____
65. Is there an on-premises fire brigade? _____ If yes, number of fire personnel on (a) Day shift_____ (b) Evening shift _____
    (c) Night shift _____
66. How frequently does brigade hold training sessions? _____
67. Dates, nature and amount of fire losses for past 12 months
    (a) Date_____ (b) Nature_____ (c) Amount_____

Security Vulnerability

Part 7: Controls

68. Is there a property pass system? _____
69. Are inbound and outbound parcels and packages inspected? _____
70. Are inbound and outbound vehicles inspected? _____
71. At the last inventory was book value over or under actual and by what amount for:
    (a) Finished goods _____ (b) Work-in-process _____
    (c) Materials _____ (d) Central supplies _____
72. Is there a formal information security program? _____
73. Are new employees investigated before being hired? _____
74. Is there a security awareness or training program? _____

Part 8: Indemnity

75. Is there fire insurance? _____ If yes, what is the:
    (a) Total coverage _____ (b) Deductible _____
76. Is there business interruption insurance? _____ If yes, what is the:
    (a) Total coverage _____ (b) Deductible _____
77. Is there fidelity or comprehensive crime coverage? _____
    If yes, what is the:
    (a) Total coverage _____ (b) Deductible _____
78. What is 12-month claim history on all coverages? _____

ASSET PROTECTION AND SECURITY MANAGEMENT HANDBOOK

APPENDIX B
BASIC MATRIX

This matrix is designed to gather probability data in all cases in which a specialized matrix is not indicated. In appropriate cases, it will be supplemented or replaced by another. For each asset under review, identify every location at which it will be found. Answer each question for each location using "Yes," "No" or the required numeral or information.

ASSET: (name or type)	LOCATIONS (identify each)							
	1	2	3	4	5	6	7	etc.
1. Quantity or amount?								
2. Is area physically segregated?								
3. Is working access controlled?								
4. Locked after hours?								
5. Formal key control?								
6. Alarm protection?								
7. Guard or other surveillance?								
8. Accountability records?								
9. Frequency of inventory or audit?								
10. Date of last audit?								
11. Each quantity change fully documented?								
12. Each quantity change involves at least two people?								
13. Any loss history?								
14. Most recent loss date?								
15. Fire hazard rating? (Light–Ordinary–Extra)								
16. Fixed extinguishment in area?								
17. Portable extinguishment in area?								
18. Fire detection and alarm protection?								
19. Fire loss history?								
20. Most recent loss date?								

3
Structural Barriers

INTRODUCTION

A barrier is a natural or manufactured obstacle to the movement of persons, animals, vehicles or materials. It defines physical limits to and delays or prevents penetration of an area. A basic security concept is to design a series of layers, or concentric circles, so that highly protected assets are within a configuration of multiple barriers.

Barriers are commonly utilized to discourage three types of penetration: accidental, by force and by stealth. A properly installed barrier should clearly warn a potential intruder to "Keep out!" either explicitly or intuitively. An exception or adjunct to this rule might be when stealth is incorporated into the overall physical safeguards. An example of this is the placement of the "sensitive" facility or operation in a location that would be considered the last place one would expect to find anything of value. A major corporation in New York located its backup computer operations in what appeared to be a run-down warehouse. This outer shell did not broadcast its contents. Of course, standard protective safeguards were also employed. There should be no accidental or inadvertent penetration. The type and construction of barriers to resist force will depend upon the nature and extent of the force expected.

If a barrier is being penetrated by *stealth*, an attempt is usually made to go over, under, around or through it without being detected. In these situations, supplemental countermeasures such as surveillance and alarm sensors are required. In the field of intelligence and counterintelligence, covert penetration of a target is generally the objective, versus a break-in, which would allow the opposition to know you have gained access to a particular piece of information. Knowing the keys to the target's codes, without them being aware of this capability, has proven to be one of the most valuable capabilities of any government.

Do not overlook the fact that barriers also play an important role in keeping people and property within a given area. Barriers keep prisoners within the confines of the correctional institution. Barriers prevent or at least impede the removal of corporate assets by dishonest employees or others that have penetrated the barrier system.

BARRIER CATEGORIES

Barriers may be divided into two general categories: natural and structural. Natural barriers include bodies of water, mountains, marshes, deserts or other terrain difficult to traverse. Structural barriers are man-made and include ditches, fences and walls. A structural barrier physically and psychologically deters or discourages the undetermined, delays the determined and channels the flow of authorized traffic through entrances.

Structural barriers may be made from a wide variety of material, such as wood, metal, masonry, plastic or glass. The types of physical barriers most often used can be grouped into three general categories:

1. Building surfaces
2. Metal, including drawn wire
3. Masonry walls

It is impossible to build a barrier that cannot be compromised. If enough time, money, personnel, planning and imagination are used, any structural barrier can be penetrated. Rather than establish physical protection with a single barrier, a series of barriers are usually included in an effective physical protection plan. The objective is to design each barrier so that it will cause as much delay as possible. With some time, a situation may be controlled or an attempted penetration discouraged. As this handbook frequently stresses, no one countermeasure or control can be relied on for effective protection. Each must be integrated with others. This is also true for barriers. In addition to the proper choice and construction of barriers, some means of determining when a penetration has been made should be provided, such as an alarm system. Timely response to any penetration should also be planned.

Security in depth is a traditional designation of a series of barriers in a protection plan. *Compartmentation* is another term that describes the use of barriers to segregate and physically protect valuable material or information. In addition to preventing physical penetration, barriers may be used to prevent visual access or the introduction of clandestine listening devices. In this day and age, access to the most vital corporate assets — information — does not even require gaining access to a company Web site. Intruders can now gain access to a company's computer system from a site anywhere in the world.

Barriers can work well in controlling movement in either direction — in or out. For example, theft can be controlled if barriers are designed to prevent those on the inside from conveniently throwing material out or removing it through an opening.

A factor that should be considered in planning barrier protection is the prevention of surreptitious entry. If an intruder is forced to leave evidence

Structural Barriers

of a penetration, prompt action can be taken to assess the damage, and plans made to neutralize the effects of the entry. Damage may be immediately apparent if property has obviously been removed. However, if an entry has been effected and a valuable formula or other sensitive data copied or photographed, there may be no evidence that anything has been taken, and it may never be known that there has been a compromise and penetration. Therefore, the physical protection plan should be designed so that if an intruder does succeed in gaining entry, some evidence of that fact will be left.

When barriers are installed outdoors, clear zones should be established on both sides to provide an unobstructed view of the barrier and adjacent terrain. Clear zones should be kept free of weeds, rubbish or other material capable of offering concealment or assistance to an intruder attempting to breach the barrier. A clear zone of 20 feet or more should separate a perimeter barrier from exterior structures, parking areas and natural features. A clear zone of 50 feet or more should separate a perimeter barrier from structures within the protected area, except when a building wall constitutes part of a perimeter barrier.[1]

BUILDING SURFACES

Although the surfaces of buildings — walls, ceilings, floors and roofs — are not constructed primarily as security barriers, they do deter penetration. An exterior surface is normally at least two layers thick, because it is designed to protect against rain and wind. The following discussion of the construction of building surfaces and their vulnerability will help the reader to design and install more appropriate countermeasures.

Roofs, Floors and Walls

Roofs. The roof usually has sheathing placed over the rafters, often horizontal wooden boards placed flush on the rafters. Sheathing may be covered with felt or other insulating material, and these foundation layers covered with shingles, metal sheet, tar paper, tile or other weather-resistant material.

Exterior Walls. Exterior walls may be similarly constructed, with sheathing placed diagonally on vertical studs and covered with sheathing paper. This is usually topped with an exterior material such as stucco, or siding composed of overlapping horizontal boards or vinyl siding. Exterior surfaces of buildings constructed of such materials as brick, concrete block, stone block, cinder block or reinforced concrete offer greater resistance to penetration than those made of wood.

---

[1] *Physical Security,* FM 19-30, Department of the Army, Washington, D.C.

Concrete Structures. An ordinary concrete building wall, because of its rugged and formidable appearance, may give the impression that it offers good protection against penetration, but may not. Standard poured concrete or concrete block walls are utilized to support structural loads, or are used as curtain walls to enclose spaces between load-bearing walls, but are not normally designed to prevent or delay penetration. Concrete walls that are six inches or less in thickness are vulnerable to penetration with hand tools and small amounts of explosives. For example, bolt cutters can be used to cut the small-size reinforcing bars (rebar) — usually number four or less — sometimes used in four-inch-thick concrete walls. Four-inch concrete walls are not load bearing, are used principally to curtain spaces between columns, and offer little protection against even moderate force.

Eight-inch-thick, reinforced concrete walls are found in all types of structures. They are load bearing and cannot easily be penetrated with hand tools alone. However, small amounts of explosive, supplemented by hand tools can quickly penetrate them. Walls thicker than eight inches are usually found in vault construction.

Standard concrete block walls, without reinforcing material, are easily penetrated with hand tools, power tools or explosives. The strength of these walls can be increased materially by filling the hollow cores with concrete or by installing rebar.

It takes as little as 45 seconds to batter a 12×15-inch hole through an eight-inch, mortar-filled concrete block wall with a ten-pound sledge hammer, and only 55 seconds for a five-inch, mortar-filled concrete block wall with 0.5-inch steel reinforcing rods. Modern tools such as cutting torches and high-speed drills significantly reduce the penetration time. Also, the thermal lance or burning bar may be used to penetrate the most substantial construction. This tool consists of a length of pipe connected to pressurized acetylene and oxygen supplies. The interior of the pipe is packed with small welding rods that raise the burning temperature of the bar to a level that allows it to penetrate concrete and metal vault type construction.

Floors. Wooden floors normally have flush sheathing covering the joists diagonally. This surface may then be covered with building paper and flooring such as tile, cork, rubber, linoleum or wood. Floors may also be constructed of poured concrete, which may be reinforced with steel rods. A concrete floor may be used without any covering or may be covered with wood, tile, linoleum or carpet. The floor may be a concrete slab poured directly onto the ground, or it may be on a foundation, raising it above the ground and leaving a space underneath for an intruder to penetrate the floor surface.

Interior Walls. Interior walls and ceilings may be constructed of lath and plaster. However, prefabricated sheets and panels of material such as

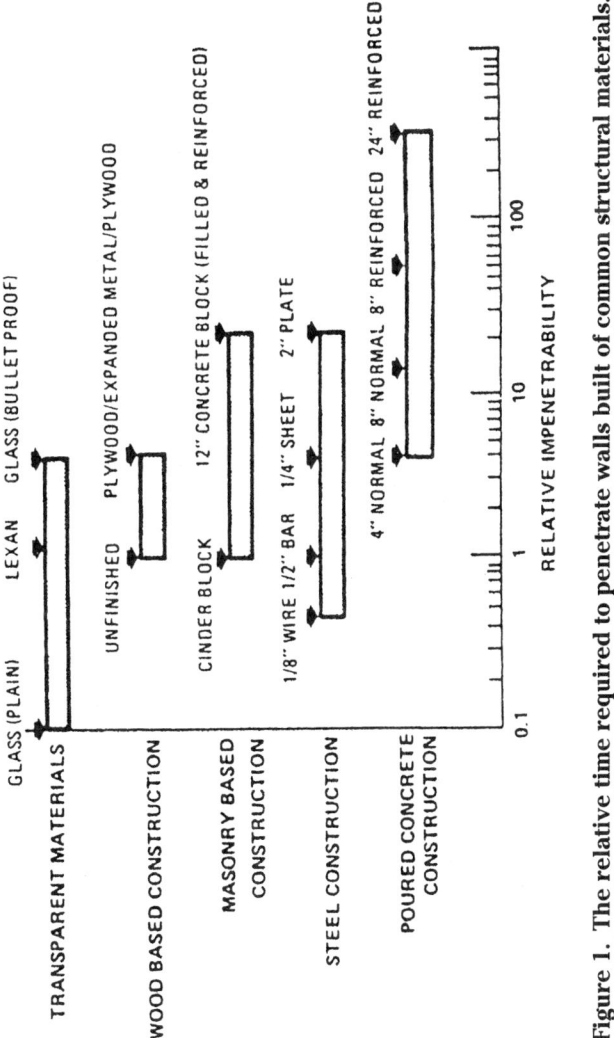

Figure 1. The relative time required to penetrate walls built of common structural materials.

Table 1. The relative time to surreptitiously neutralize standard locking devices.

Type of lock	Average time delay
Warded	0 seconds
Disk/wafer	3 minutes
Pin tumbler	10 minutes (most common lock in use)
Super pin tumbler	30 minutes per mushroom or serrated pin
Lever	30 minutes

Note: The times specified are average time taken to pick this type lock. The figures do not take into consideration other bypass techniques which will neutralize a lock within seconds or a fraction of the above times. High-security locks are often not vulnerable to the types of attacks upon which these times are based.

Combination locks are vulnerable to an attack that will compromise the combination within a period of 20 minutes.

plasterboard have become, in recent years, a popular method of interior wall and ceiling construction. The joining edges of the material are sealed with paper or fabric tape and are then sealed with a plaster covering. After installation, surfaces constructed of such material resemble plaster. Plywood or other types of wooden paneling may also be used and are usually attached to the studs or rafters. The vertical joining edges may be covered by narrow wooden strips.

The inner surfaces of the exterior walls and roof may also serve as the interior walls and ceilings. These surfaces may be finished by applying plaster to form a sealed surface.

Ceilings. Ceilings may be covered with acoustic or decorative tile. It is a common modern building technique to construct ceiling plenums that do not have security barriers between rooms and areas. As a result, an intruder who can gain access to the plenum space can work from there to achieve access to rooms or spaces below.

EVALUATION OF BUILDING SURFACES

Interior and exterior building surfaces should be evaluated for effectiveness as structural barriers. This appraisal can best be accomplished using two techniques: a physical inspection of the structure and a study of architectural and engineering drawings. The study of drawings is essential and critical because construction details that might affect security are often not apparent from a physical inspection but are immediately evident in prints.

A heavy room entry door with a combination lock might suggest that the entire area was constructed of cement block or other resistive material, but a review of drawings might reveal that the walls were not designed to give the same protection as the door and were constructed only of metal lath and plaster. For example, a lockout of a vault door of a pharmacy was quickly and easily overcome when the plans showed that the walls were actually cinder block.

A review of drawings will reveal not only the construction of all surfaces, but also the amount of space between walls, below floors and above ceilings, and any hazards created by ventilation ducts. New construction or changes will also be revealed. Only up-to-date prints with current information should be used. Original or *as-built* prints may be completely out-of-date because of changes or additions normally made to most structures over a period of time. Although security has little to do with the maintenance of blueprints, the lack of up-to-date prints when budgeting for a security construction project can have a major impact on completing the project. An example: a construction crew hired to add a vent through the interior wall of a Sensitive Compartmented Intelligence Facility (SCIF) estimated — based on the original plans for the building — the project would take less than three hours. Because the plans were not up-to-date, the SCIF was shut down for 31 days while the construction crew completed the project.

Any weakness revealed by the review of drawings should be checked during a physical inspection. Such an inspection may also reveal hazards not noted during the print review. All surfaces should be inspected, including the roof and the basement or underside of the structure if there is any accessible space underneath. In addition to the evaluation of the surfaces, consider what possible threats may be found on the opposite side of these surfaces and what safeguards need to be considered.

In the analysis of surfaces, the amount of time each structure or area is unoccupied each day or week must be considered, because privacy and time are valuable to an individual attempting penetration. Large losses have occurred on weekends when areas have been unoccupied for 24 hours or longer, allowing intruders time to cut through roofs, floors or walls. The vulnerability of a roof should not be overlooked, especially in high-rise buildings. Every roof, regardless of height, must be considered a potential point of penetration — even high-rise structures, which can be reached by helicopter. However, it is not always the roof that is targeted. In one case, a group in Los Angeles targeted safe deposit vaults in several banks. Using advance tunneling techniques and heavy but portable equipment, they bore a hole in the floor of the vault to gain access. Because the time lock on the vault door precluded opening the door until Monday morning, the theft was not discovered until then. The important thing to remember is that each room or area has *six sides* to be considered and protected.

BUILDING OPENINGS

Openings in buildings provide means of entrance and exit, access for utilities and delivery, and permit use of natural illumination and ventilation. But the gaps in the barriers provided by the building surfaces may constitute security hazards. As building openings are designed to provide some type of access, potential intruders can be expected to attempt to locate one that will allow them to gain entry.

A report by the Small Business Administration noted that 92 percent of entries were accomplished through doors and windows. Any openings less than 18 feet above the ground or 96 square inches or larger invite penetration.[1] Openings should be protected so they are as difficult to penetrate as the building surfaces.

Doorways

Doorways, including the frame, jambs and stops, are constructed of either wood or metal. Doorways are of two general applications: personnel and vehicular.

Personnel doorways, in both outer and inner building walls, may be single or double. They are usually fastened by hinges to the door jamb on one side and equipped with a latch and perhaps a lock on the other side. Sliding doors and folding doors may also be used. Folding personnel doors are ordinarily installed in the interior of a building and are often intended to deny visual rather than physical access.

Vehicular doorways may also serve as entrances and exits for personnel. Double doors are often used because of the size of the openings. They may be hinged on the outside on jamb edges and secured with a locking device where the inner edges of the doors meet in the center. Sliding or rolling doors, single or double, may also be used. They may move horizontally or vertically on tracks or rollers. Folding doors that fold in hinged sections are another option. Regardless of the design or the size, doors have weaknesses.

A door is often much weaker than the surface into which it is set. Sometimes, the door is hollow core, or constructed of comparatively thin wooden or glass panels between the rails and stiles, and the panels may be easy to remove. For more on lock hardware, turn to Chapter 4. Figure 2 illustrates the penetration times for a standard industrial pedestrian door.

The door frame may also be a weak spot if it is not properly installed. If the frame is wood, it is usually installed by nailing the doorjamb to the wall studs, after which the doorstop is nailed to the jamb. If this installation is

---

[1] *Installation and Classification of Mercantile and Bank Burglar Alarm Systems,* UL 681, Underwriters' Laboratory, Inc., Northbrook, IL.

Structural Barriers

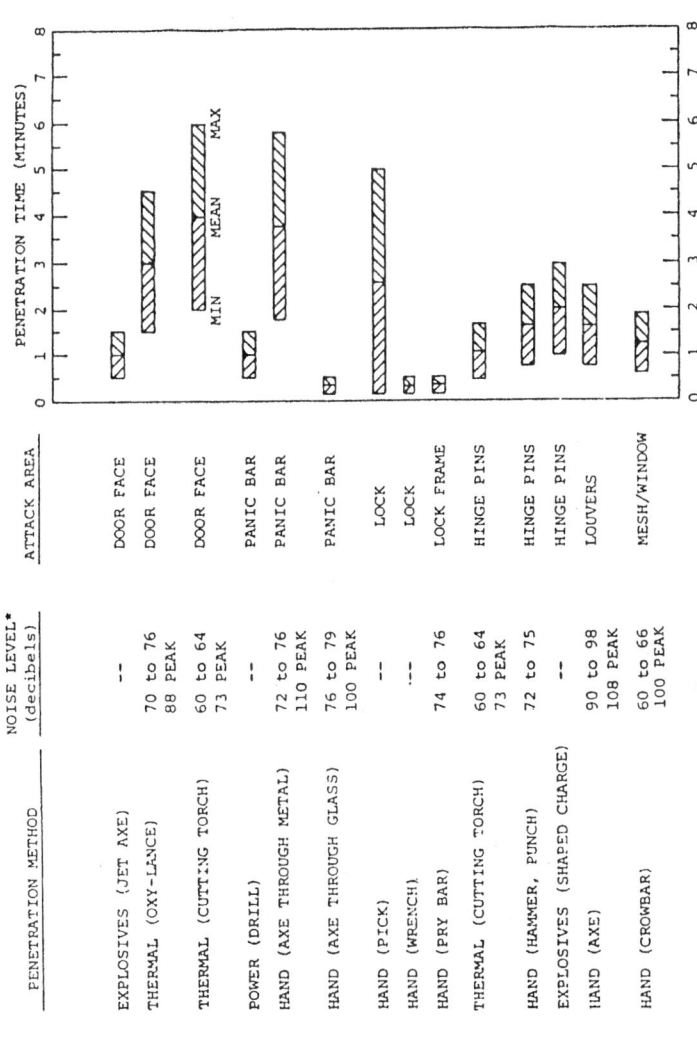

Figure 2. Penetration times for standard industrial pedestrian door. (From *Barrier Technology Handbook*, prepared by Sandia Laboratories, Albuquerque, NM.)

not correctly done, the piece-by-piece construction may allow thin shims or levers to be inserted so that the lock bolt can be disengaged. In addition, most doors are installed by a carpenter, not a locksmith. Carpenters are generally more concerned with the swing of the door rather than the effective function of the locking mechanism. An all-metal door does not cause such a problem if properly installed. However, the door frame must be of sufficient strength that it will not allow the door to be pried out of the frame or allow the bolt in the lock to be released.

If not correctly installed, hinges may contribute to the weakness of a door. For example, if hinges are surface mounted so the mounting screws or hinge pins are exposed on the exterior surface of the area being protected, intruders can quickly remove the screws or pins and gain entrance by opening the door from the hinged side and replace the door as they leave. There would be no evidence of penetration if the removal and replacement were done carefully. Hinges should be installed so that the screws are concealed and the hinge pins are on the interior. The hinge pins can also be welded or flanged to prevent removal. Surface-mounted hinges are sometimes installed with bolts extending through the door. Removal of these bolts is possible even from the bolt head side if sufficient pull is exerted. The threaded end of the bolt can be peened to eliminate this hazard.

Another way to prevent unauthorized removal of the pin is to drill a small hole in the inactive side of the hinge while the door is open. (The hinge pin where the hole has been drilled should be notched.) Then a small steel pin can be inserted, flush with the frame, into the hole drilled in the inactive side of the hinge and protruding into the notch in the pin. This prevents removal of the hinge pin from the outside, yet allows removal of the steel pin by authorized individuals (see Figure 3).

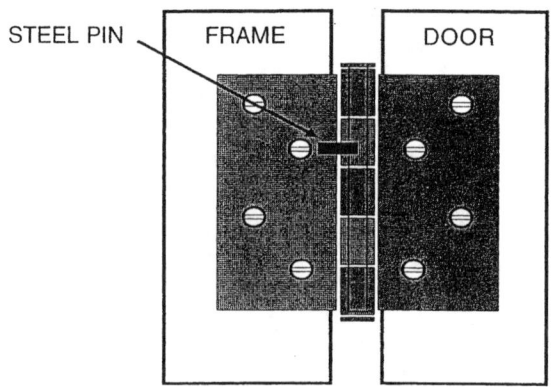

Figure 3. Method to prevent hinge pin removal.

Windows

Windows are designed to provide ventilation, natural illumination or visual access through a wall, or any combination of the three. Most windows are equipped with clear glass and can often be opened to provide access. Other windows, in areas where it is necessary to deny visual access, are glazed with frosted, pebbled or other opaque or translucent glass. Picture windows or those installed in air conditioned buildings are permanently fixed in place. While they allow illumination and visual access, they do not open to provide ventilation. Windows, classed according to construction, are:

- *Double-hung windows.* This type of window is divided into upper and lower sections that slide vertically past each other. They may be counterweighted with sash weights or spring balances to hold them at a desired open position. They also may be completely free-sliding, requiring some means of holding them open, such as a stick or a spring-loaded bolt.
- *Casement windows.* This type of window has one or two movable panels hinged at the side to the frame to provide a complete opening of the window.
- *Awning windows.* This window is made of a series of sections of glass, enclosed by sashes, that swing outward from either the top or the bottom. The sections are sometimes controlled by a permanent or removable rotating crank handle and may be controlled simultaneously or separately.
- *Jalousie windows.* This window is similar in operation to awning windows, but is made entirely of glass with no sash around the individual sections.
- *Projected windows.* These windows have movable ventilators, which project outward or inward, hinged on one horizontal side. Usually, one section swings outward while a second section swings inward.
- *Horizontal sliding windows.* In this type of window, the movable sash, or the glass itself in some cases, slides in a horizontal direction.
- *Picture windows.* A picture window is a large, heavy glass pane fixed in the window frame. The pane, usually plate glass, may be made with two layers.

The weakest area in a window is usually the glass. An intruder can easily cut out a section with a glass cutter, or the glass may be covered with tape so it can be broken without the broken pieces falling and causing noise. Because of the innate vulnerability of glass to penetration, two products have been developed to discourage forcible entry. One type, a polycarbonate, is constructed of plastic material, while the other has a special plastic laminate sandwiched between two pieces of glass. Both products are highly resistant to impact. Versions of these products are listed by Underwriters Laboratories as "bullet resistive."[1] Both give the appearance of ordinary glass. However, the laminated glass is about twice the cost of tempered glass; the plastic is a bit less costly than the laminated.

Window glass is installed in one of three ways: (1) with putty, (2) molding may be nailed to the window frame to hold the glass in place, or (3) the window frame may be grooved so that the glass can be inserted in the grooves and then clamped into place with elastic glazing compound. The first two methods allow removal of the entire pane by removing the putty or molding and replacing the glass, leaving no evidence of an intrusion. The molding removal and replacement is probably the easiest to accomplish because, if care is taken in the removal, the same material can be used to replace the glass. If a pane installed with putty is removed, the new putty used to replace the glass has to be colored to match the putty around other panes.

If they are not strengthened, standard windows may be the weak link in the barrier protection in a structure. (Figure 4 illustrates comparative window penetration times.) Because most standard windows can be penetrated with hand tools in less than a minute, additional protection, such as protective coverings, grills or mesh, may be required for proper protection.

Security window film can improve the ability of existing glass to mitigate the impact of explosive force, windblown debris and seismic stress. The primary function of the film is to hold firm the broken glass, thereby preventing the broken glass from becoming lethal projectiles.

Security window film is made of polyester film (from four to 15 mils thick) that can be adhered to the interior surface of existing glass. More than 3700 windows at FBI headquarters and 2700 windows at the Pentagon are now protected by window film.

The cost of laminated glass is approximately $20 per square foot. Security window film costs approximately $3 to $4 per square foot. However, several factors can increase the basic cost of installation of security window film, but it has become the option of choice in enhancing a structure's ability to protect occupants and withstand damage from explosions, windblown debris and seismic stress.

Other Openings

In addition to doors and windows, a wide variety of other openings in the roof, walls and floor may require consideration. These include openings for shafts, vents, ducts or fans; utility tunnels or chases for heat, gas, water, electric power and telephone; sewers and other types of drains; and other small service openings.

---

[1] U.L. 752, Bullet Resistive Equipment.

Structural Barriers

Various techniques and material can be used to give added protection to surface openings. Expanded metal, wire fabric and fencing may be utilized.

Steel bars or grills may be used to protect glass-paneled windows or doors. Such bars should be spaced no more than five inches apart. If they are round, their diameter should be at least 1/2 inch; if they are made of flat steel, they should be at least $1 \times 1/4$ inch in size. Steel grills that have $1/8 \times$ 2-inch mesh offer good protection. Both bars and grills must be securely fastened so they cannot be pried loose; and if possible, they should be installed on the interior surface.

If a door needs to be strengthened, it can be covered on the inside with 16-gauge sheet steel, attached with screws. Sound-reducing baffles can be installed in ducts to protect a room or area from unauthorized listening.

Wire mesh, expanded metal or metal grills can be used to secure chases and tunnels, locked in place to permit removal, if necessary.

Concrete Block Barriers

Concrete blocks can be utilized effectively in the construction of barriers. This type of barrier construction is usually less expensive than cast-in-place concrete, which requires forms and is more costly. Hollow concrete masonry units, which can be used without forms, are a balanced building product engineered to offer all of the desirable qualities of any building material. The method of manufacture, the choice of raw materials and the design of the units all combine to provide an adaptable construction product. The basic material, Portland cement, is strong, durable and rigid. It is immune to rot, vermin, oxidation and fire, and, depending upon thickness, offers poor to moderate protection against penetration.

When lightweight aggregate is used in block, the weight of the concrete is reduced by more than a third. The strength of the foundation can be reduced a similar amount. Because the blocks are easier to work with, labor costs are also reduced.

The construction of the blocks and the airspace in the hollow units provide good sound absorption and low sound transmission. The surface texture of blocks has exceptional sound absorption qualities, and the hollow masonry resists impact sound transmission. This quality may be of little or no value in outdoor installations. However, in interior areas or rooms where sensitive work is being done and where it is necessary to keep the transmission of sound to a minimum and prevent surreptitious listening, the noise insulation qualities of concrete block are valuable.

Reinforced concrete blocks can also be utilized in the construction of fire-resistant barriers for vaults and file rooms. Standards for this type of construction are outlined in *National Fire Protection Association Standard,* No. 232, Protection of Records.

ASSET PROTECTION AND SECURITY MANAGEMENT HANDBOOK

TYPE OF WINDOW	PENETRATION TOOL	PENETRATION TIME (MINUTES)
GLASS		
1/4-IN TEMPERED	FIRE AXE	0.05 TO 0.15
1/4-IN WIRE	FIRE AXE	0.015 TO 0.45
1/4-IN LAMINATED	FIRE AXE	0.30 TO 0.90
9/16-IN SECURITY	SLEDGEHAMMER AND FIRE AXE	0.75 TO 2.25
PLASTIC		
1/4-IN LEXAN®, LUCITE®, OR PLEXIGLAS®	FIRE AXE	0.05 TO 0.15
	DEMOLITION SAW	0.15 TO 0.45
1/2-IN LUCITE® OR PLEXIGLAS®	FIRE AXE	0.05 TO 0.15
	DEMOLITION SAW	0.35 TO 1.05

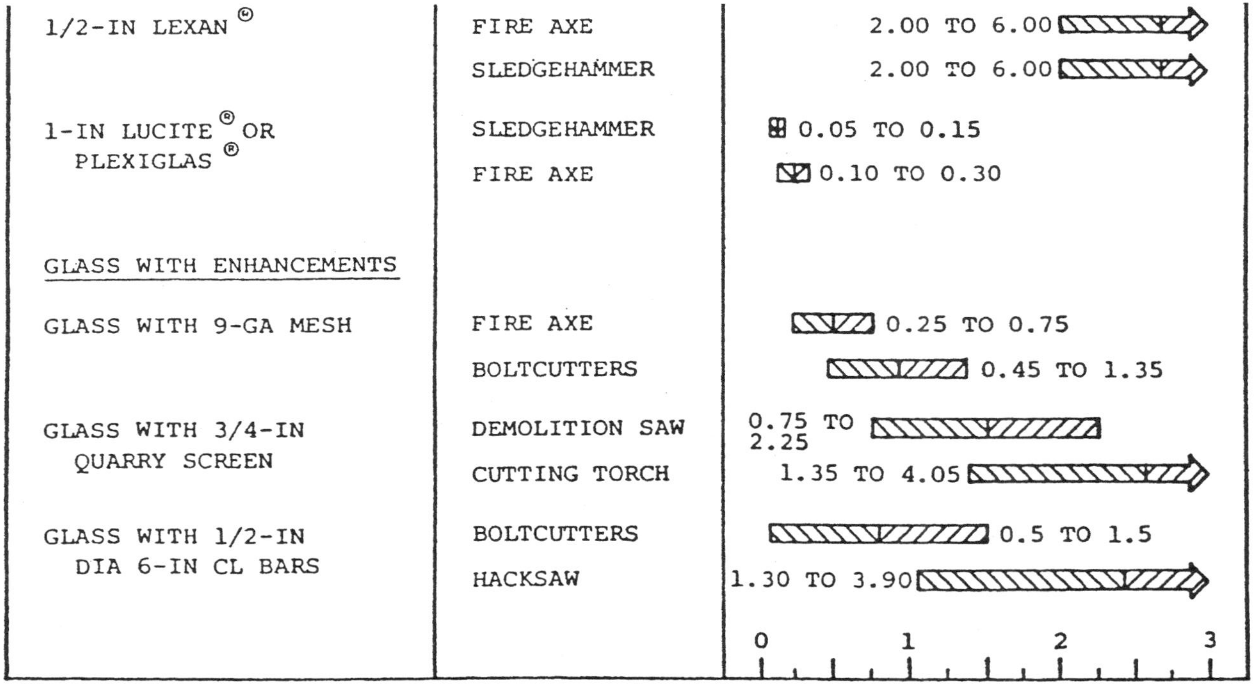

Structural Barriers

Material	Tool	Time (minutes)
1/2-IN LEXAN®	FIRE AXE	2.00 TO 6.00
	SLEDGEHAMMER	2.00 TO 6.00
1-IN LUCITE® OR PLEXIGLAS®	SLEDGEHAMMER	0.05 TO 0.15
	FIRE AXE	0.10 TO 0.30
GLASS WITH ENHANCEMENTS		
GLASS WITH 9-GA MESH	FIRE AXE	0.25 TO 0.75
	BOLTCUTTERS	0.45 TO 1.35
GLASS WITH 3/4-IN QUARRY SCREEN	DEMOLITION SAW	0.75 TO 2.25
	CUTTING TORCH	1.35 TO 4.05
GLASS WITH 1/2-IN DIA 6-IN CL BARS	BOLTCUTTERS	0.5 TO 1.5
	HACKSAW	1.30 TO 3.90

Figure 4. Comparative window penetration times. (From *Barrier Technology Handbook*, prepared by Sandia Laboratories, Albuquerque, NM.)

Because blocks are available in such a wide variety of shapes, sizes, colors and textures, the design opportunities are virtually unlimited (see Figure 5).

Units with relief designs may be used, or different blocks may be combined to offset one another, to create sculptured effects throughout a wall, with a customized concrete block face different from all others. Thus, concrete unit masonry can be architecturally adapted to any building or site treatment.

Barriers constructed with solid-face blocks are sturdier and more difficult to penetrate because they can be reinforced better than open-face screen-type blocks. Cement blocks may also be combined with other types of material in the construction of barriers. For example, blocks may be used to construct a portion of a barrier, with chain-link fence and barbed wire at the top of the blocks.

Design criteria for building surfaces are ordinarily specified in local building codes. However, outside wall construction may not always be included in code specifications. For that reason, a short discussion of some of the design criteria that should be considered in the construction of outside walls is included here.

Three types of foundations may be used in the construction of a wall designed to act as an outside barrier: (1) continuous footings, (2) pad footings under the pilasters, and (3) post-hole footings (see Figure 6).

Post-hole footings are usually used when the barrier is on the property line or when the ground slopes away from the wall, as on a hillside. Because of the spacing of the holes, it is easier to tunnel under a fence using post-hole footings than under either of the other two types of foundations. The soil under the foundation should be compacted, have a minimum bearing capacity of 1000 pounds per square foot and a lateral capacity of 200 pounds per square foot. If wall is used to retain earth, construction specifications for retaining walls must be followed.

Concrete block cells that contain reinforcement should be filled solidly with grout. The grout should be a mix of one part cement, three parts sand and two parts pea gravel. If additional strength is desired, every cell may be reinforced and filled with grout. The mortar mix should consist of one part cement, one-half part lime and four and one-half parts sand. Table 2 outlines additional design criteria that should be considered.

BOMB PROTECTION

Bombs and other explosives cause heavy damage, as evidenced in Oklahoma City and the Middle East. Thus, in critical situations or in areas targeted by bomb terrorists, it may be desirable to utilize special barrier construction.

Figure 5. Examples of the variety of shapes and sizes of concrete blocks available.

ASSET PROTECTION AND SECURITY MANAGEMENT HANDBOOK

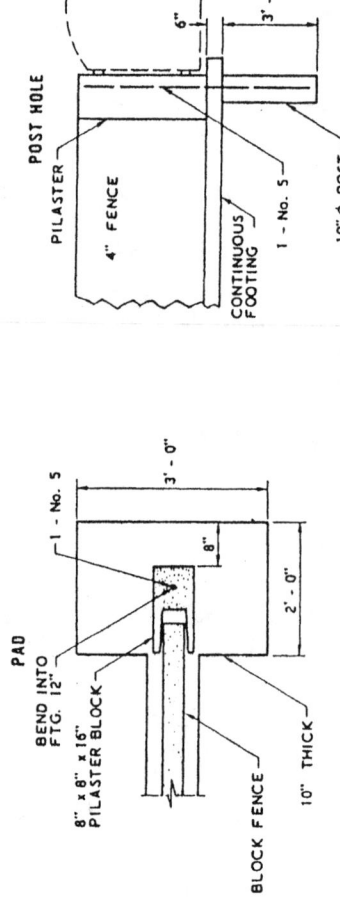

Figure 6. Foundation and gate post design: four-inch block fence foundation and gate post design (assume four-foot wide gate).

Table 2. Concrete block wall design criteria.

Allowable soil bearing	1000 psf
Foundation concrete	2000 psi
Hollow concrete masonry	675 psi
Reinforced steel	20,000 psi
Joint reinforcing	30,000 psi
Weights of Material	
Concrete (poured)	150.0 pcf
4-inch Block	22.5 psf
6-inch Block — grouted 48 inches o.c.	50 psf

Note: psf = pounds per square foot; psi = pounds per square inch; pcf = pounds per cubic foot.

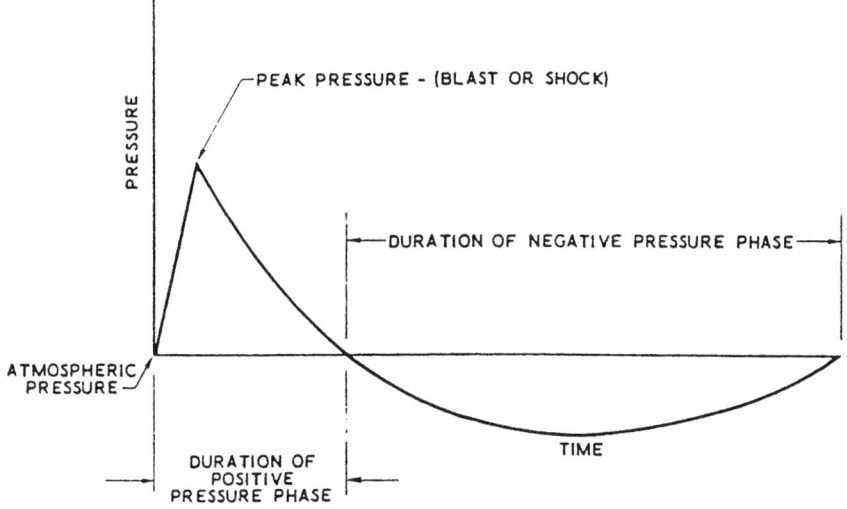

Figure 7. Phases of a blast wave showing the positive and negative pressure forces.

A bomb produces three kinds of damage: incendiary, blast and fragmentation. The high temperatures that accompany an explosion frequently cause fire to break out, particularly if flammable materials are close to the explosion. Blast damage is caused by two forces: a positive pressure force and a negative pressure or suction force (see Figure 7).

During the positive pressure phase, compressed air moves outward and is bounded by an extremely sharp pressure wavefront less than 0.0001 inch thick, which abruptly increases the pressure to far above normal. The pressure wavefront moves outward with an initial velocity greater than the velocity of sound at sea level, which is 1088 feet per second at 32°F. This front applies a sudden and considerable thrust or push against any obstacle in its path. The positive pressure phase has a duration measured in fractions of a second, after which the pressure rapidly decreases to a point lower than normal.

The negative pressure phase is not as great as the positive phase but has a more extended duration. The period during which the pressure is subnormal is the suction phase of the blast effect. This phase can be severely damaging, as most enclosed structures are designed and constructed to withstand an inward rather than outward thrust of force. This must be considered in designing a barrier to protect against blast.

To illustrate the relative resistance to blast from explosions of various kinds of structural walls, the following list is arranged in the approximate order of resistance, beginning with the most resistant.

- Thick, reinforced concrete walls
- Thick brick or concrete
- Thin, reinforced concrete walls
- Thick, earthen barricades
- Steel-frame building walls
- Well built, wooden-frame building walls
- Thin brick walls
- Wire-reinforced glass windows
- Unreinforced glass windows

It is difficult to determine with accuracy the blast damage that an explosive device will cause. The intensity of explosives is expressed in brisance, or shatter power, and is related to the time during which the explosion takes place. The most brisant explosives are the most destructive. The very brisant or rapid explosives include dynamite, TNT, nitroglycerin and high-explosive military munitions. Slower and less brisant explosives, sometimes called low explosives, include black powder and other propellant powders used in firearms. They explode more slowly, pushing rather than shattering the immediate surroundings.

Improvised or homemade explosives can be manufactured from chemicals found in a wide range of products that are in everyday use. The easy availablility of these potentially explosive chemicals is compounded by the fact that information on making bombs is readily available from a variety of sources, including thousands of sites on the Internet. The intensity of these improvised explosives varies widely with the materials and formula used.

Fragmentation results when the expanded gases of a bomb explosion cause the bomb's case to disintegrate. About half the energy produced by an explosion may expand the case and propel the fragments.

Structural Barriers

Table 3. Minimum thickness based on 500-lb. bomb at a distance of 50 feet.

Material	Inches
Steel	1½
Reinforced concrete	12
Brick wall	13½
Unreinforced concrete	15
Earthen barricades between wooden walls	24
Earthen walls	30

Table 4. Wall thickness required to protect against missiles.

Distance from explosion (feet)	Missile velocity (feet per second)	Wall thickness (inches of concrete)
100	2000	12
225	2000	10
500	1500	7
900	1000	5
2350	500	2½

Flying objects may penetrate soft materials that do not break up into fragments. If the material gives without being torn (baled cotton, for example), the missile is brought to a stop gradually and remains embedded in the material, often being deformed by the process. This principle is used in the design of some bullet-resisting vests, in contrast to light steel body armor which depends on its strength to prevent perforation. A metal fragment weighing 1⅓ ounces with a velocity of nearly 4000 feet per second can be stopped by a steel plate 9/10 of an inch thick.

Table 3 is based on a British paper entitled "Aircraft Bombs and Their Effects."

Table 4 is a typical velocity/distance/thickness table showing how the wall thickness required to protect against missiles decreases as the distance from the explosion increases.

VEHICLE BARRIERS

Light vehicles can penetrate most ordinary fences by ramming them at high speeds. Heavier vehicles can be used to breach more substantial barriers. If a breaching vehicle is so severely damaged in such an attempt that it is no longer usable, a second vehicle can be driven through the opening after the ramming vehicle has been removed. Table 5 illustrates that light

Table 5. Light vehicle penetration of barriers.

Barrier	Vehicle	Barrier Results	Vehicle Results	Occupant Results	Comments
Chain-link fence	3/4-Ton pickup	Full penetration	Paint scratched	No injury	Vehicle used to breach barrier
Double swing gate	3/4-Ton pickup	Full penetration	Slight dents	No injury	Vehicle used to breach barrier
Chain-link with 3/4-inch cable	3/4-Ton pickup	Full penetration, vehicle stopped, cable held	Extensive front-end damage	Risk of injury	Vehicle used to breach barrier
Concrete media barrier	3/4-Ton pickup	No penetration	Major damage	Risk of injury	Vehicle used as breaching aid
Tires	3/4-Ton pickup	No penetration	Major damage	Risk of injury	Vehicle used as breaching aid

(From *Barrier Technology Handbook,* prepared by Sandia Laboratories, Albuquerque, NM.)

vehicles can penetrate most fences and some heavier barriers by ramming them at high speeds.

Standard highway metal guardrails can be used as vehicle barriers. Most barriers of this type are designed to be effective at impact angles of less than 30°. Penetration with a light vehicle is possible but the vehicle can be expected to be extensively damaged.

Concrete vehicular barriers or bollards are more effective. Such barriers can be cast in place and anchored into the ground so that removal would be difficult. Concrete blocks with four-foot sides, concrete cylinders that are four feet in diameter and four feet high, or concrete tetrahedrons that are four feet high, with five-foot square bases may all be constructed as vehicle barriers.

Another effective concrete barrier that can be utilized is the standard concrete highway median barrier. This median is known as the "New Jersey Bounce" because it was first used on the New Jersey turnpike as a median barrier to prevent head-on collisions. This barrier is about 32 inches high, 24 inches wide at the base and six inches thick at the top. As indicated in Table 5, this barrier can be penetrated with a 3/4-ton pickup. In the test that was conducted, a 3/4-ton pickup sustained major damage when it struck the barrier traveling perpendicular to the median at approximately 50 miles per hour. Yet, the barrier remained intact.

Heavy equipment tires can also be employed to construct an effective vehicular barrier. The tires should be seven to eight feet in diameter and should be half-buried in the ground. The earth around them should be tamped solid to hold them rigid. Table 5 indicates that a 3/4-ton pickup was

Structural Barriers

unable to penetrate this type of barrier as well. In the test that was conducted, the vehicle was stopped abruptly, thrown backward for a short distance, and sustained major damage.

Metal posts or railroad ties partially embedded below ground in concrete also make a formidable vehicular barrier. Such posts should be angled outward in the direction of a possible penetration at a 30 to 45° angle and should be spaced four feet apart. A vehicle attempting to penetrate this type of barrier at high speeds would sustain major damage and any occupants could expect to be severely injured.

Also commercially available are hydraulic impact barriers consisting of plates, bollards and wedges. These can be remotely or locally actuated or can be erected in response to the speed of a vehicle, sensed through photo-optical sensors or loop detectors. These barriers can be deployed in less than two seconds and have successfully stopped heavy trucks traveling at 50 miles per hour.

Selected Bibliography

Books

Fennelly, Lawrence J.; *Handbook of Loss Prevention and Crime Prevention, 2nd ed.*; 1989; Butterworth-Heinemann, Stoneham, MA.

Berger, David L.; *Industrial Security, 2nd ed.*; 1999; Butterworth-Heinemann, Stoneham, MA.

Physical Security; Field Manual 19-30, Department of the Army, Washington, D.C.

Physical Security of Door Assemblies and Components; U.S. Department of Justice, NILECJ, Standard #0306.00.

Periodicals

Security magazine, Cahners Publication, Des Plaines, IL.
— Bomb-blast Demonstrations Show Benefits of Glazing, Film; January 1998.
— Bomb Blast Drape Combines Aesthetics, Safety; January 1999.
— Bombing Reiterate Need to Protect Windows; September 1998.
— From Bullets to Bombs, Glazing Is a System Approach; May 1999.
— Gates, Operators Office Wide Variety of Options; July 1999.
— Help Wanted: Experienced Terrorists; April 1997.
— Size, Precision, Automation Improve Bomb/Metal Tech; October 1997.
— Special Report — Airport Security: 10 Years after Lockerbie; December 1998.
— Terrorism, Theft Concern Prompt Barrier Popularity; December 1998.
— Vehicle Barriers Offer a Wide Range of Choices, Applications; August 1997.

4
General Locking Concepts

INTRODUCTION

The most widely used method of controlling physical access is the lock. Locks are used on doors at home, on vehicles, for offices, hotels and safes, and in desks, cabinets, files, briefcases, display cases and jewelry boxes. Locks are also one of the oldest of security devices and to this age is owed the technical jargon that has grown with the locksmith's craft.

This chapter demystifies the terminology by describing the different types of locking mechanisms and their relative strengths and weaknesses. Special attention is given to the application or use of different locks (and locksets), and to the most common types of electrified locks used in automated access control systems. The chapter does not attempt to teach the craft skills needed to work with locks — installation, repair, service, manipulation and compromise — as this discipline requires considerable study and years of experience. However, readers will develop an understanding of locks, their benefits and limitations, and the specific locks to use for particular applications.

BASIC LOCK GROUPING

Locks can be divided into two very general classes: (1) those that operate on purely *mechanical* principles and (2) those that are *electrical* and combine electrical energy with mechanical operations and are commonly associated with automated access control systems.

Mechanical Locks

A mechanical lock utilizes some barrier arrangement of physical parts to prevent the opening of the bolt or latch. In such a lock, the functional assemblies of components are:

1. The bolt or latch that actually holds the movable part (door, window, etc.) to the immovable part (jamb, frame, etc.).
2. The keeper or strike into which the bolt or latch fits. The keeper is not an integral part of the lock mechanism but provides a secure housing for the bolt when in a locked position.

ASSET PROTECTION AND SECURITY MANAGEMENT HANDBOOK

3. The tumbler array, which constitutes the barrier or labyrinth that must be passed to move the bolt.
4. The key or unlocking device, which is specifically designed to pass the barrier and operate the bolt.

In most mechanical locks, the bolt and barrier are found in the permanently installed hardware or lockset, and the key or unlocking device is separate. However, in some mechanical locks that use physical logic devices, the entire lock is a single assembly. Examples of these would be locks with integral digital keypads, which mechanically release the bolt if the correct sequence is entered, and dial type combination locks.

The Warded Lock. The mechanical lock longest in use and first developed is the warded lock. Figure 1 illustrates a typical warded lock. This lock is exemplified by the open, see-through keyway and the long, barrel-like key. In the illustration, six different keys are shown plus a master or skeleton key that will open all six locks. Still found in older homes and farm buildings, and even in older inns, the warded lock, as used in the U.S., is a very simple device.

The greatest weaknesses of this type of lock are its vulnerability to spring manipulation by any key that is not stopped by the wards, and corrosion due to weathering and age. A well-planned, modern locking program does not include warded locks. In any installation where extensive warded

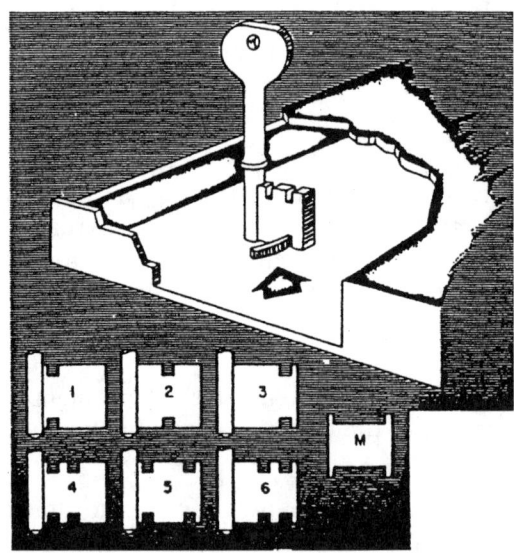

Figure 1. Cutaway of a typical warded lock and the principle of operation of the warded lock key.

locks are already present, phased replacement or augmentation with other locks is recommended.

The Lever Lock. A significant lock improvement after the warded lock came in the 18th century with the perfection of the lever principle. (Terminology note: a *lever lock* should not be confused with a *lever handle* on a lockset.) Figure 2 illustrates the operating principle of lever locks. Note that the lever tumblers are flat pieces of metal held to a common pivot and retained in place inside the lock case by the tension of spring wire. Each lever is cut on the edge opposite the pivot to accommodate a lug or appendage attached to the bolt and is designated as a *fence*. When all the levers are positioned so that the fence slides into the spaces cut into the levers, the bolt can be withdrawn.

By varying the position of the cut in each lever, it becomes necessary to lift the levers to different heights to bring the cuts into proper alignment for insertion of the fence. This is accomplished by designing the lever lock key so that the cut or bit depth for each lever tumbler is matched to the fence cut on that tumbler. When inserted in the keyway, the flat key is turned and, as it rotates, the varying depths of the tumbler cuts lifts those tumblers until the fence cuts are all aligned. Continuing the key rotation then draws the fence into the aligned cuts and withdraws the bolt. In locking, the action is reversed and the bolt is thrown until the fence leaves the recess.

Returning the key to the original entry position allows the lever tumblers to drop into their home positions, retained by the spring tension, and disarranges the fence cuts, thus preventing the bolt from being withdrawn.

The lever lock offers more security than the warded lock. Moreover, by placing two or more fence cuts on each lever tumbler, it is possible for two or more keys, cut to different dimensions, to operate the lock. This permits "master keying," which is discussed later in this chapter.

The lever lock finds continued application today in such varying situations as desk, cabinet and locker installations, bank safe deposit boxes, and U.S. mail boxes. Although the lever lock is inherently susceptible to picking, it can be designed to provide a high degree of lock security through resistance to picking.

The Pin Tumbler Lock. The most important development in the history of mechanical locks to date has been the invention of the pin tumbler in the 19th century by Linus Yale, an American who also developed the dial-type combination lock. The pin tumbler is probably the most widely used lock in the U.S. for applications such as exterior and interior building doors. A number of very useful refinements have been added to the basic pin tumbler in recent years so that now a very high level of lock security can be achieved with many models.

ASSET PROTECTION AND SECURITY MANAGEMENT HANDBOOK

EXAMPLES OF SINGLE KEY LEVERS

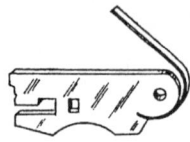

1. Levers with one gate.

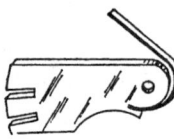

2. Levers with two gates.

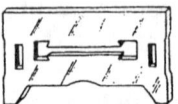

3. Levers with the gate in the center of the lever.

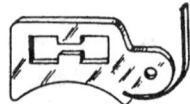

4. Double-acting levers — levers that lock the bolt in both the open and closed positions. These levers have the gate in the center of the lever or one edge — see illustration of one gate and double-acting levers.

THE MOST POPULAR METHODS OF MASTER–KEYING LEVERS ARE:

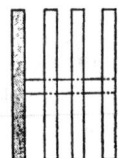

1. Carrier lever with a pin extending through the free lever.

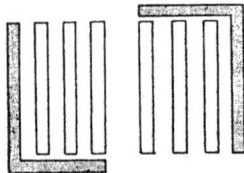

2. Carrier lever with a bar extending under the free lever.

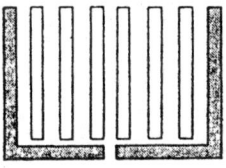

3. Two carrier levers with a "split" bar extending under the free levers — half of the levers for each carrier and bar.

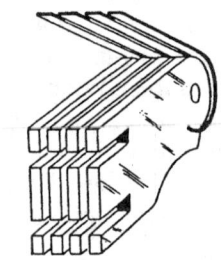

4. Levers with two gates — one for the change keys and one for the master key.

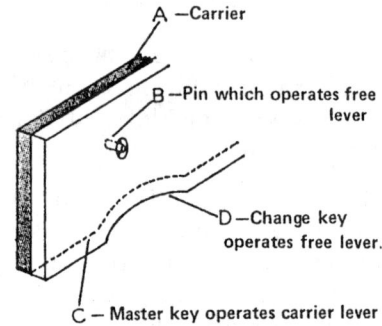

A — Carrier
B — Pin which operates free lever
D — Change key operates free lever.
C — Master key operates carrier lever

5. Paired levers — one lever in each pair is a carrier for the other lever of the pair. The carrier is operated by the master key; the other lever is operated by the change key.

Figure 2. Various lever tumblers with single key and master key applications.

The pin tumbler is illustrated in Figure 3. It consists of the same basic elements as all mechanical locks: the bolt moving device, the maze or labyrinth, and the keyway. It is in the maze or obstacle segment that it is different from the others.

General Locking Concepts

CONVENTIONAL CYLINDER
A conventional cylinder always has its key pins equally spaced in one row only. When masterkeying is employed, split pins are introduced, and the number of key changes is greatly reduced. Conventional cylinders usually contain only 5, 6 or 7 pins.

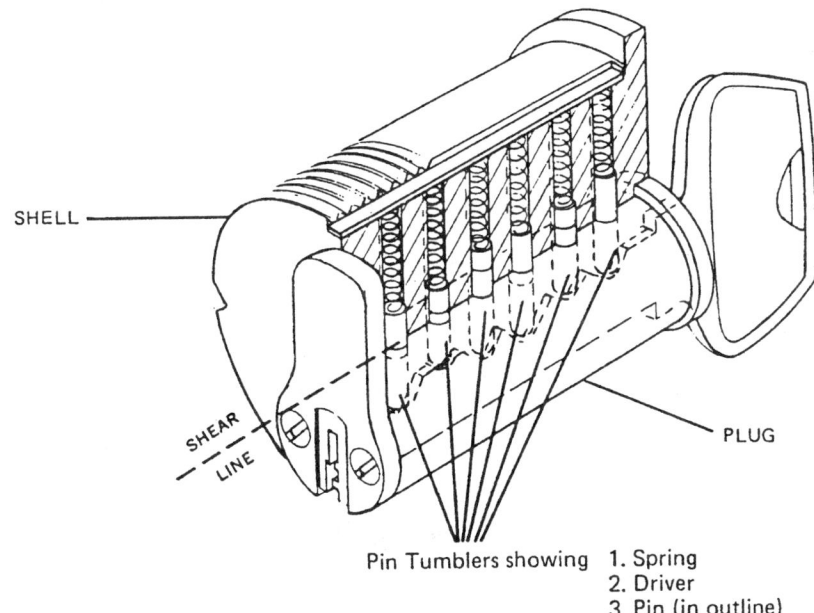

Pin Tumblers showing 1. Spring
                                    2. Driver
                                    3. Pin (in outline)

Figure 3. Conventional pin tumbler lock.

The pin tumblers are cylindrical metal sections that fit into matching cylindrical holes in two complementary parts of the lock. The first part, called a *plug,* rotates with the key when properly actuated and permits the bolt to be thrown or drawn by that rotary action. The second part is the *shell* or immovable housing into which the plug is fitted. Because the pin tumblers extend from the shell into the plug, they prevent the plug from turning. The pin tumbler cylinder lock operates on the principle that the pin tumblers must be manipulated into a position in which they are entirely contained in the plug, leaving no interference with the free turning of the plug.

Figure 3 shows that each pin tumbler actually consists of at least three elements: (1) the pin, (2) a driver or separate metal cylinder, and (3) a spring. The spring provides tension against the driver, which in turn pushes against the pin, forcing it down from the shell into the plug. The pin is retained in the plug and prevented from falling into the keyway by the fact that the keyway is narrower than the diameter of the pin.

When a properly designed key is inserted into the keyway, each pin is raised so that the line at which the pin and driver meet is brought exactly even with the edge of the plug. When this is done for each pin tumbler, a *shear line* is created between the plug and the shell and the plug is free to turn. To complete the bolt or latch action, the plug usually makes a complete revolution so that when the key is removed, the plug is locked into the shell, with the bolt in either the locked or unlocked position. Unless a separate device is present on the particular cylinder lock, it is necessary to use a key both to lock and unlock the bolt.

To enhance security in some models of pin tumbler locks, the pins and driver are interlocked so that random movement of the pins by lock picks or keys not specifically coded for the lock will not properly align the pins and drivers. In such locks, although the individual pins might be aligned at a shear line, the interlocking feature on the driver will prevent the plug from turning in the shell (see Figure 4). In this type of lock, the keys are cut at precise angles, as well as depths, so that when inserted into the plug, the key will both raise the individual tumbler array of driver and pins to a shear line and, at the same time, turn each pin so that the interlocking mechanism is positioned to pass through a special groove at the base of the plug, thus permitting the entire plug to rotate enough to move the bolt. Figure 4 illustrates the operating principles involved, as exemplified in the Emhart (Corbin) high-security cylinder.

A variant of this principle is found in the Medeco high-security cylinder. In the Medeco lock, instead of grooves at the bottom of the plug through which the interlocking feature of the pins pass, a side bar is moved into a cutout housing in the shell or withdrawn into grooves in the pins. The side bar or fence would otherwise prevent the plug from turning. In some locks, the pin tumblers are not interlocked but are "mushroom" shaped so that failure to align them correctly will cause them to bind in the housing, again preventing the plug from turning. In both types of high-security locks, the keys are specially cut at specific angles, as indicated in Figure 4, thus making routine duplication of keys quite difficult, except on special equipment used by the manufacturer.

Another variant of the pin tumbler lock utilizes multiple tumblers on different axes and requires an entirely different type of key. In locks of this type, the spacing between the pins and the lengths of the pins are both varied to establish the individual lock coding. In Figure 5, the multiple-axes-tumblers technique is illustrated in the Sargent Maximum Security System.

The Wafer Tumbler Lock. A fairly late development, the wafer tumbler lock utilizes flat tumblers fashioned of metal or other material to bind the plug to the shell. A properly designed key raises the wafers out of the lower portion of the shell until they are all contained within the plug, thus creating a shear line, with the plug free to turn inside the shell. Spring tension keeps each wafer locked into the shell until lifted out by the key. By varying

General Locking Concepts

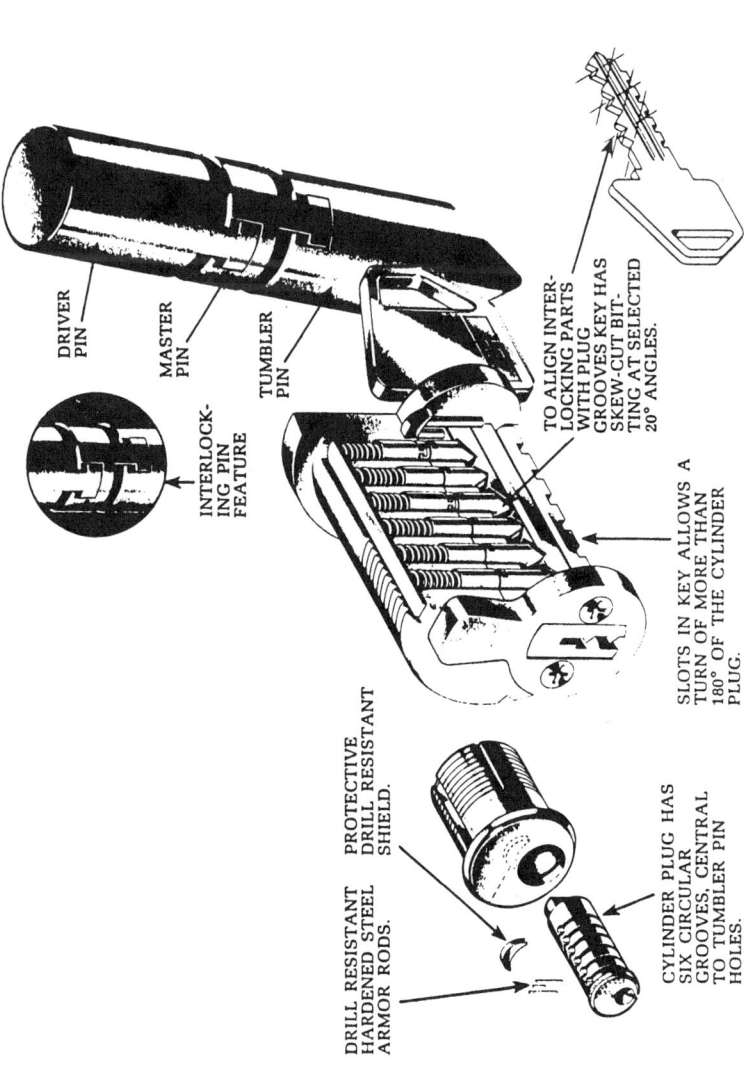

Figure 4. Pin tumbler cylinder lock with interlocking pins.

85

ASSET PROTECTION AND SECURITY MANAGEMENT HANDBOOK

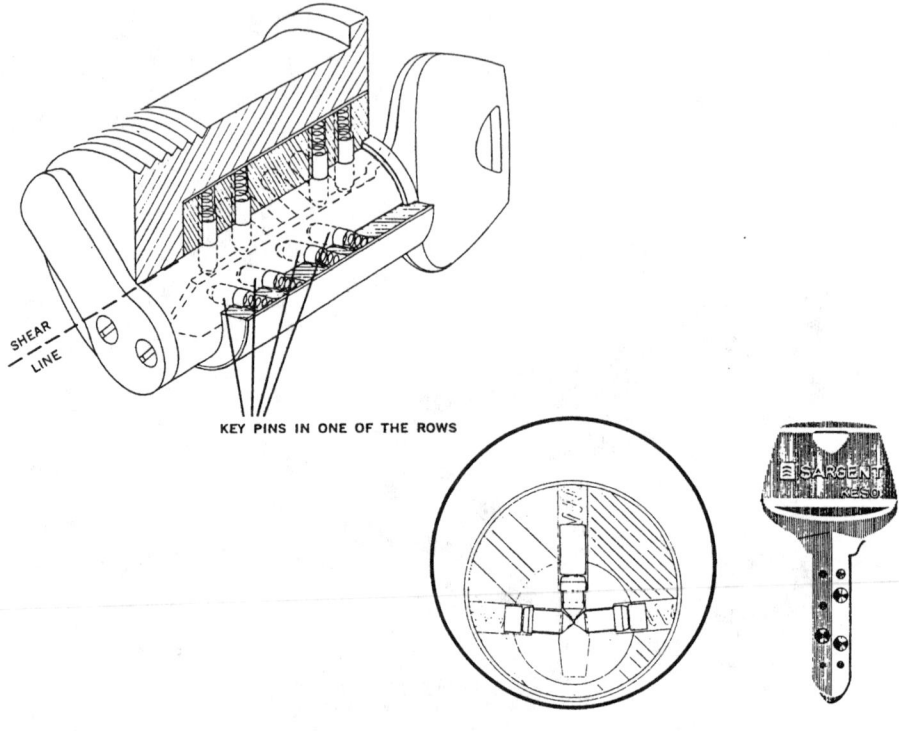

Figure 5. Pin tumbler lock with multiple tumbler axes.

the height of the central hollow portion of the wafer through which the key passes, withdrawal of the wafer from the shell can be matched to varying key bit depths. Figure 6 illustrates a typical wafer tumbler assembly.

If the hollow center is divided in half, with the left and right sides being of different heights, keys can be designed to operate on either side of the wafer tumbler, raising it to different positions. This permits master keying of wafer tumbler locks by using one side of the wafer for the master key bit position and the other side for the operating or change key bit position.

Wafer tumbler locks may be designed for double-bitted keys by spring loading some wafers to protrude *upward* into the shell and others to protrude *downward*. The key, cut on both sides, will draw all wafers back into the plug, irrespective of which way they protrude.

Dial-Type Combination Locks. Dial-type combination locks, while not employing a key, resemble the lever tumbler lock in many respects. They operate by aligning gates on tumblers to allow insertion of a fence in the

General Locking Concepts

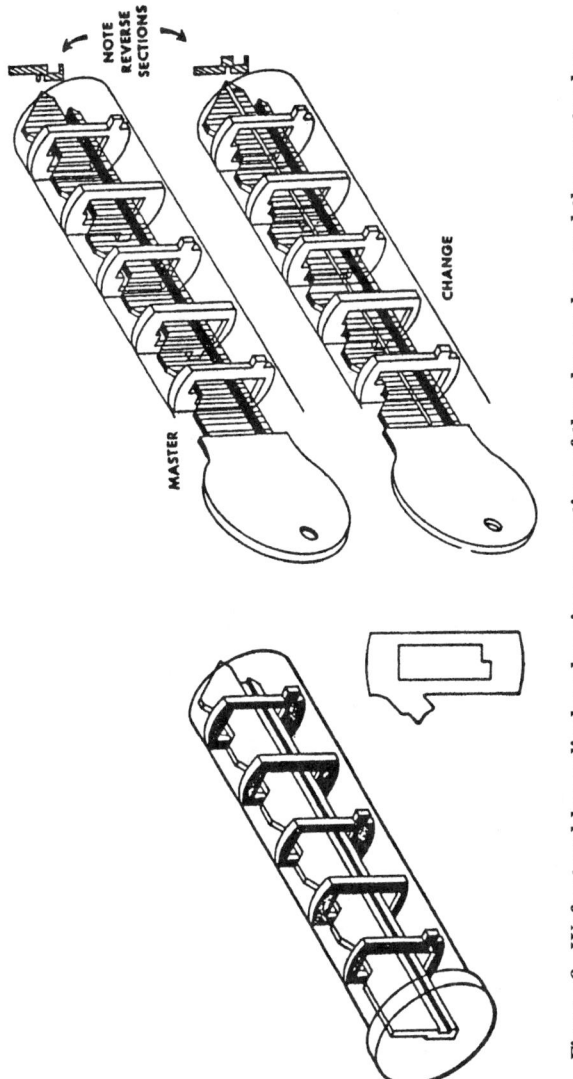

Figure 6. Wafer tumbler cylinder showing operation of the change key and the master key.

bolt. However, the tumblers are fully circular and are interdependent; that is, moving one results in moving the others. This makes the order of movement important and is really why these are true combination locks rather than permutation locks.

The number of wheels or tumblers in a combination lock determines the number of elements in the combination. For example, a combination of Right-10, Left-25, Right-9, Left-0 to open would indicate a three-tumbler lock. Dialing the first three numbers in the correct sequence would align the gates on each of the three wheels. Dialing to "0" at the end would move all aligned wheels to a position at which the fence would fall into it. The "gate" and "fence" mechanisms are quite similar to those discussed previously for the lever lock. The primary difference is that in a combination lock, the tumblers are circular and are not restrained by steel spring pressure.

To unlock a combination dial-type lock, the first tumbler to move is the one furthest away from the dial. This is designated as a "driver" tumbler and is the only one actually turned by the spindle. From it will protrude a drive pin or dog that will engage a stop on the next tumbler nearer to the dial.

That tumbler also has a drive pin that will engage the next nearer tumbler, and so on, until all tumblers have been engaged and moved to the correct opening position. The *direction* of movement alternates to permit picking up successive tumblers and moving them into proper alignment. This makes it clear why it is recommended practice when locking a combination type lock to scatter the combination by dialing randomly in several directions at least as many times as there are tumblers. This effectively changes their relative alignment so that no two tumblers will have their gates aligned.

With combination locks, the theoretical maximum number of combinations is the base number of positions on each tumbler (typically 100 on a good-grade lock), raised to the power of the number of tumblers. Thus, a 4-tumbler combination lock, each of whose tumblers has 100 numbers of dial positions, would have a theoretical maximum of 100^4 or 100,000,000 changes. A three-tumbler lock with 100 numbers to each tumbler would have a maximum of 100^3 or 1,000,000. The theoretical maximum is not really available, however, as it is generally wise not to utilize the numbers immediately adjacent to the opening number on any single tumbler or to repeat the same number twice in a single combination. In a three-tumbler lock, the reduction in combinations would be from 1 million to 912,673 (97^3) when the opening number and the two numbers adjacent to the opening number on each tumbler are dropped. Even so, when reduced, the available maximums are still very formidable to an attacker.

Most important in the use of combination locks are procedures for the selection and maintenance of the numerical combination. The selection should allow those who must know and use it to memorize it without having to write it down. One suggestion that is included in Defense Investigative Service training manuals (for the protection of classified government materials), is to select a six-character word that can easily be remembered; the characters are transformed into numbers by looking at a telephone keypad. For example, the word "S-E-L-E-C-T" transforms into 73-53-28. For more or fewer tumblers, a longer or shorter word can be used. Procedures should also be in place for changing the combination, usually whenever a person who knows it is terminated or no longer requires access, or if there has been some form of compromise. In any event, the code should be changed at least once every one to two years.

Electronic Dial-Type Combination Lock. Recently, electronic combination locks have been developed as direct replacements for dial combination locks on safes and secure document cabinets. These devices are powered by the user turning the dial; the combination numbers are displayed via an LCD rather than by gradations on the dial. The display is viewable only from a limited angle and the number being dialed bears no direct relationship to the position of the mechanical dial. Additional features include a time-out of a specified number of seconds between each number dialed, and a two-person rule where two numbers must be dialed before the lock will open. As each user is assigned an individual number, an audit trail of which combinations were used to open it and when it was opened is available. The lock can memorize the number of unsuccessful attempts to open. Because of the electronic precision of the system, there is no reduction in the number of combinations due to the unavailability of adjacent numbers. These locks are claimed to be immune from all the typical defeat modes of a regular mechanical combination lock, as well as from electrical and magnetic attacks.

MASTER KEYING MECHANICAL LOCKS

The principle of master keying is that a single lock may be operated by more than one key by designing various different keys to engage or work upon different tumblers or different aspects of the same tumblers. Master keying is utilized to provide a hierarchy of access to groups of locks, from access to only one lock through access to increasingly larger groups of locks, and, finally, to access to all locks in the population. Master keying is defended and advocated on the theory that in large locking programs involving hundreds or thousands of individual locks, it would be totally unworkable to require those persons with broad or variable access requirements to carry a separate key for each lock. Thus, master groupings are developed within which a single key opens all the locks in that group.

Three major security difficulties are presented by the master keying technique and they must be balanced against the alleged need for the master key convenience.

The first difficulty is that very effective master key accountability must be maintained. The loss, compromise or unauthorized use of such a key exposes all the locks in that group. Restricted-access key cabinets and software running on personal computers are products that will assist the security professional in achieving adequate key accountability.

The second difficulty is that in any manipulation of the lock, additional positions or possibilities are presented for surreptitious unlocking by the creation of multiple shear lines or gate openings.

The third problem is that for cylinder locks, the additional parts required in the lock core create the need for additional maintenance. In some types of master keyed mechanical locks, there is frequent difficulty with locks binding or sticking because additional master key elements, often very frail, become disarranged or break and necessitate a mechanical disassembly and removal of the involved lock.

Master Keying the Lever Lock

A lever lock may be master keyed by cutting several gates at the end of the tumbler opposite the pivot. Another and more widely used technique is to select one lever, the master lever, and attach to it a bar that raises all the other levers when the master lever is raised. Raising only the master lever with a master key designed to engage only at that one point will bring the other levers into proper alignment to accept the fence by means of the bar. However, if one or more other levers are raised at the same time as the master lever by a key, which would engage the master and other lever tumblers at the same time, the gates will be out of alignment and will not accept the fence. A single lever master key would be easier to duplicate than a multi-lever key, and is therefore more vulnerable to compromise. (Both the multiple gate and master lever techniques are illustrated in Figure 2.)

Master Keying the Wafer Lock

Wafer tumblers have a hollow center, usually rectangular in outline, to permit the body of the key to enter the keyway and pass through each wafer. By notching the keyway to receive two different shaped keys, it is possible to use keys that contact the wafer either to the right or to the left of the center of the hollow rectangle. The rectangle is then altered in shape so that one side is higher or lower than the other, thus requiring a different bit depth cutting to withdraw that wafer into the plug. Keys for one side are the master keys, and keys for the other side are the normal operating keys. The keyway will accept either key blank.

Master Keying the Pin Tumbler Lock

The conventional pin tumbler lock utilizes multiple pins in each tumbler to achieve mastering. The smaller pins are sometimes referred to as *master*

General Locking Concepts

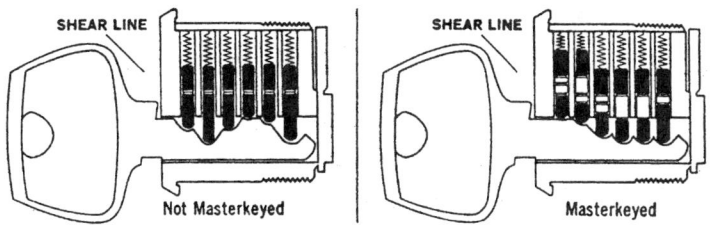

Figure 7. Master keying of a pin tumbler cylinder.

wafers, and are inserted in the tumblers between the lower pin and the driver. The effect is to create several positions or arrangements within the tumbler that produce a shear line (see Figure 7).

The theoretical maximum number of keys that can be cut to totally different combinations or bitting arrangements within any lock utilizing the same tumblers for both master and operating purposes is greatly reduced by the introduction of master and sub-master combinations. Because this primarily affects the pin tumbler lock with a single aligned set of tumblers — the conventional type — the security professional should be aware of the significance of this fact.

The actual limit of combinations (really *permutations,* but the term "combination" is so generally used to describe the arrangement of pins in a pin tumbler lock that we will regard both terms as interchangeable) is determined by raising the number of bitting positions possible in each tumbler to an exponent or power represented by the number of tumblers in the lock. In a fairly common cylinder lock with five tumblers, each of which could contain pins set to any one of ten bitting or key notch positions, the total theoretical number of changes would be 10^5 (100,000), or ten depth positions raised to the power of the total number of tumblers.

However, when we introduce a single level of master keying using a master key position in each tumbler, we eliminate one depth or bitting position from those available for different operating keys. This has the effect of reducing the base number in the normal formula by one, which for our five-tumbler lock immediately reduces 100,000 to 59,049, a reduction of almost one half. In a fairly typical locking system that would utilize one grand master, one master, one sub-master, and operating combinations, the formula would be 7^5, and we would get a theoretical maximum of 16,807 change combinations.

In addition to the loss of different operating combinations, master keying a conventional pin tumbler cylinder makes the lock more vulnerable to surreptitious entry because it creates additional shear line positions to which the pins in any tumbler can be manipulated, permitting the plug to rotate.

SECURITY VULNERABILITIES OF MECHANICAL LOCKS

Mechanical locks are subject to a variety of attacks that can result in their failure or compromise. Some types of attack require a high level of skill; others are almost invited by the mere appearance of the lock.

Attack by Force

Force can separate the door or movable element from the jamb or immovable element without a direct attack on the lock. If the bolt is short or does not engage the bolt keeper in a positive way, simply spreading the door frame or jamb with a hydraulic jack, or jimmying the bolt out of the keeper with a pry bar or large screwdriver, will do. This vulnerability is overcome by using long bolts (one-inch minimum), bolts with flanged edges or that engage the keeper vertically (the burglar- or jimmy-proof type of lock), and by assuring that the door and its frame or jamb are strong or reinforced.

Using a deadlocking latch instead of a deadbolt will increase vulnerability to attack by force because of the shorter length of the latch. This vulnerability can be reduced by adding an astragal (a metal plate that covers the gap between the door and the frame in the region of the deadbolt or latch) and by ensuring that the door frame is specified as being sufficiently rigid to prevent spreading. It should be mentioned here that the door, and the walls on either side of the door, should be constructed of materials sufficient to match the penetration delay afforded by the lock. There is no rationale for installing an expensive, high-security lock when an intruder can "walk" through adjacent drywalls.

Another way force can be used is to remove the lock from its housing and expose the bolt to manual manipulation. With cylinder locks this is often done by applying torque to the cylinder with a pipe wrench, snapping the retaining screws, and unscrewing the cylinder from the lock case. This vulnerability can be reduced by covering the entire lock face with a hardened reinforcing plate, fastened through the door to the inside, with no screws, bolts, or rivets on the outside surface. For cylinder locks not flush with the door, another precaution is the *slip ring,* a spinning metal collar that covers the cylinder portion protruding beyond the door surface. A wrench or other torque tool merely spins the collar without turning the cylinder.

Force can also be used on pin tumbler cylinders to snap the pin tumblers and turn the plug freely. This weakness is reduced by using good grade metal pins and by using every tumbler (i.e., putting pins in each tumbler to add to the total amount of metal resisting the force). High-security cylinders that utilize multi-axial tumblers or side bars are also more resistive to this attack.

General Locking Concepts

Surreptitious Attack

Picking. Picking or manipulating the tumblers through the keyway is the common surreptitious approach to opening a lock. But, TV crime shows notwithstanding, this method is not easy for the unskilled and requires not one but several tools. In lever-type locks, tension is applied to the tumblers with a tool that reaches through them and fits into the bolt grooves. By turning it in the opening direction, the bolt is thus tightened against the tumblers. If each tumbler is then manipulated with a pick, minute imperfections in machining found in almost every conventional lock cause the tumblers to bind or tighten with varying force. As the tightest is manipulated into the normal opening position, the fence moves slightly into its gate, thus easing the tension and allowing the next tightest tumbler to move into a still tighter position. The process is repeated until all the tumblers are aligned and the lock opens.

The skill required is to maintain adequate tension (not too much or too little), and at the same time successfully manipulate each tumbler. A popular method for defeating picking of lever tumbler locks is to fashion serrations on the tumbler edge above or below the normal gate position. When tension is applied and that tumbler is manipulated, it may lock one of the serrations on the bolt instead of allowing the fence to move into the gate. The feeling is the same to the manipulator, except that the lock does not open. To undo the false gate effect, tension has to be released, and then all the tumblers return to their home positions.

In pin tumbler locks, the same theory applies as with lever locks, except that tension is applied to the *plug* while the pin tumblers are picked. Machining differences again allow the plug to turn slightly (not noticeably to the eye but palpably to the skilled hand) when the tightest binding tumbler has been picked to the shear line. Because master keyed pin tumbler locks offer multiple shear lines in each tumbler, it is much easier to manipulate such a lock.

Techniques for defeating or preventing pin tumbler manipulation include *mushroom-shaped pins,* which bind in the tumbler if not lifted straight up; the addition of a *side bar* to the tumbler set; and the use of *notched, rotating pins* to form a gate for the spring-loaded side bar when the proper key is introduced. This modification of conventional pin tumbler operations offers increased security. If the side bar is not withdrawn into the plug, it offers the same resistance to turning the plug that usual pin tumblers do — even more, because it is a solid piece of metal protruding into the shell along most of the length of the plug. Picking the pins to their own shear line is not enough, for each pin must be positioned so that the notch in it is properly presented to receive the side bar. Although it is theoretically possible to manipulate this cylinder, the difficulty is much greater than with conventional pin tumblers.

Other innovations in pin tumbler lock security include:

1. The use of multiple banks or sets of pins, inserted at different angles and requiring keys with bitting impressions on more than one surface (as shown in Figure 5)
2. The use of magnetic pins and complementary magnetic inserts on the key by which like or unlike polarity in the facing magnets causes attraction or repulsing of the pins
3. The use of the side bar and non-spring-loaded rotating disc tumblers, somewhat similar in operation to the lever lock

Attack by Impression Making and "Try" Keys. If a blank designed for the particular keyway can be introduced into the lock before any bitting cuts have been made, it may be possible, by applying turning pressure, to make faint marks on the key blank. This requires that the blank be conditioned in some way so that the slight markings made will be visible. The blank is then carefully filed down at each place where markings show until the markings do not show. The technique of picking up the markings in the first place and then filing the key blank to the proper bitting depths varies with different types of locks, but it is applicable to warded, lever, wafer, and pin tumbler locks. It is, of course, a slow process and requires unchallenged access to the lock in question for a considerable period of time, plus the skill to take the impression. However, such access is often possible in locking programs that are not augmented by patrol, surveillance or alarm safeguards.

"Try keys," or "jingle keys" as they are sometimes called, are nothing more than key blanks correctly milled to fit the particular keyway and contain random bitting. Insertion in the keyway and combined turning/raking movements may cause the lock to open. Particularly with pin tumbler locks, the two-phase movement of the try key simulates the effect of a tension tool and rake pick. With lever locks, the movement will not be effective, but the random cutting may match the actual tumbler combination of the lock. The added security problems of master keying pin tumbler locks are again emphasized with the try or jingle key because of the multiple shear line possibilities.

Rearranging Mechanical Locks

Rotation of Cylinders. Periodically, an installed locking system requires changes in the lock tumbler arrangement because of changes in authorized personnel, compromise of the system, loss or unaccountability of keys, or major changes in occupancy. There are several ways in which the tumbler change or the equivalent effect can be achieved. One is the simple relocation of the lock. Door locks may be rotated among doors,

General Locking Concepts

cabinet locks among cabinets, and so forth. For security benefits to accrue from simple relocation, there should be no identification on the lock that would permit a former key holder (perhaps still in possession of the key) to recognize the lock in its new location.

A serious attempt should be made to recapture outstanding keys at the time of the rotation to reduce the problem of accidental discovery of the relocated lock. Furthermore, if the system involves master keying, the rotated locks must remain within their original level in the hierarchy or the master keys will not operate properly. Nevertheless, in some applications such as hotels, temporary office suites, and other high-turnover occupancies, periodic rotation of existing locks reduces the likelihood of unauthorized access by former users or occupants.

The second and more effective way is to rearrange the actual tumblers within each lock to a new combination. With lever and wafer tumblers, this means disassembly of the lock and a change in the order of the tumblers. The same tumblers, however, may be used many times in such changes. With pin tumbler locks, the same thing can be done; that is, the same pins can be used but in different tumblers. However, in master keyed pin tumbler lock systems, this does not work, and new pins must be placed in the tumblers so as to preserve the master combination not intended to be changed. The flexibility of pin tumbler cylinder locks in changing combinations is what makes them so popular. It is possible to change the operating combination only, the sub-master or master combination only, or any group of some or all of them. It is also possible to take all the master and sub-master pins and wafers out of a particular lock, leaving only the operating pins. This is known as "taking a lock off the master system."

The Interchangeable Core. The convertible or interchangeable core is a design feature available from some manufacturers of pin tumbler locks that makes possible the very rapid redistribution of combinations. Figure 8 illustrates this type of lock, in which the entire plug or core is removable with a key. It can be replaced on the spot by another core already arranged to the desired new scheme. The core is retained in the shell of such locks by retaining pins or lugs that are retractable into the plug by the action of a *control* combination scheme. This is a set of pins in the tumblers that will not create an opening shear line, but a shear line to allow the retaining lug to be withdrawn into the plug and the plug to be withdrawn from the case.

Using interchangeable cores, the labor time and skill level required to make large-scale changes are reduced sharply. To change a conventional pin tumbler combination requires removal of the cylinder from the lockset, removal of the core from the cylinder by disassembly, changing the pins in the tumblers, reassembly of the cylinder and installation of the cylinder in the lockset. The combined labor time at the lock location and in the shop

ASSET PROTECTION AND SECURITY MANAGEMENT HANDBOOK

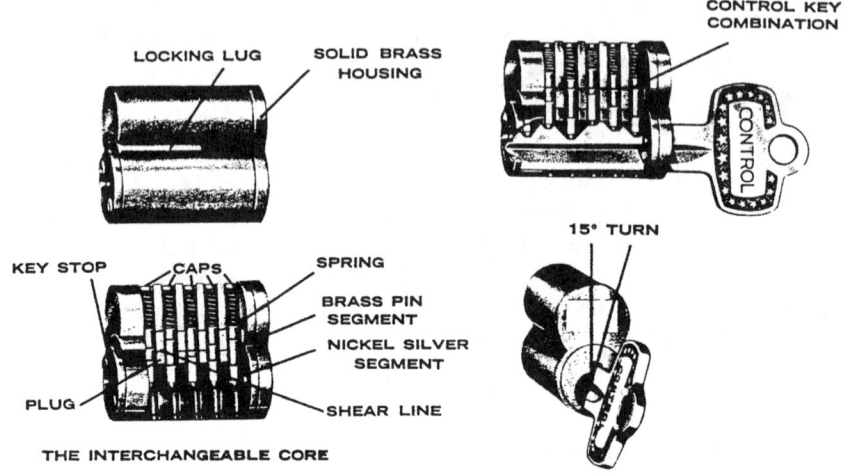

Within the interchangeable core are columns of small brass segments of various lengths. A core may have five, six, or seven barrels to house these columns of segments. The segments are put into each barrel according to a mathematical plan called Masterkeying. After the proper segments are in the core and the core is sealed, a key is cut to fit the combination.

The keyway revolves within the core housing. The point of contact between the plug and housing is called a shear line. The lock opens when the segments in each barrel separate at the shear line, permitting the key to be turned. One barrel out of line keeps the lock from opening. Segments may be inserted in a core so they shear properly according to many different combinations. This means that the same core may contain different combinations for the Control Key, Grand-Master, Master, Sub-Master, and Operating keys.

Figure 8. A typical interchangeable or convertible core pin tumbler cylinder lock.

can run from 15 to 45 minutes. In comparison, the time required to replace an interchangeable core cylinder is five to ten seconds and requires only that one core be removed and another inserted. The replacement core will already have been arranged to the desired scheme. At a convenient time, the replaced core can be fitted with a new combination or, in some cases, returned to the manufacturer for a replacement.

The savings in labor time in large locking programs, when measured over a reasonable useful life of the combination (in any case, not more than five years), is approximately equal to additional hardware cost of interchangeable core locks. Viewed this way, the total cost is approximately the same, although with the interchangeable core lock a larger initial investment is required.

A Caution on Combination Schemes. *The use of a single grand master combination for any mechanical locking system is not a sound security practice.*

The larger the system, the less sound the use of a single grand master. Loss or compromise of the grand master key, or loss of a fully combined cylinder, could compromise the entire lock network. It is doubtful that any locking system actually requires a single grand master combination. Most systems can be broken down into multiple masters.

For example, consider a high-rise office building of 50 stories. Such a building would normally be served by at least three banks of elevators, the low-rise, mid-rise, and high-rise, each covering approximately one-third of the building. At the very least, such a building could be divided into three master systems, one for each building section. Each section in turn could be divided into the necessary sub-masters by individual floor, or function, or occupancy, or any appropriate plan. The separate master systems would assure that a lost or compromised master key in one section did not expose the locks in the other two. It is virtually as easy for the relatively limited number of persons who legitimately require total access in the building to carry three master keys as to carry a single grand master. Within each master system, the key blank milling could be different, so that keys from one system would not even pass in the other systems' keyways.

In actual practice, single grand master schemes place the grand master key into the hands of many persons, such as porters, maintenance personnel, and other service employees. The access required by such persons, while broadly regarded as access to the entire facility, usually can be managed on a sectional basis. Multiple masters add to security indirectly as well as directly, making it possible to restrict access by such personnel to one major area at a time.

The exposure caused by loss or compromise of a grand master key also exists, within interchangeable core systems, through loss or compromise of the *control* or core removal key. For the same reasons that multiple master systems are recommended, so are multiple control systems. Generally, the control and master system can be co-extensive in such cases.

It should also be noted that in a mastered interchangeable core system, the loss of a fully combined core also exposes the system to compromise. A skilled person can remove the pins and springs to a lock layout board in the same order that they are arranged in the cylinder. By then cutting keys to all the possible shear lines, one of the keys produced would be the highest level master in the system. In a large system with many levels, this could be quite time consuming. However, if two cores from the same system were obtained by the attacker, finding the combinations common to both would much more quickly identify the master levels.

Door Locks

Although locks are used for many control applications, the most common usage is for doors. There are two major types of door locks — cylindrical and

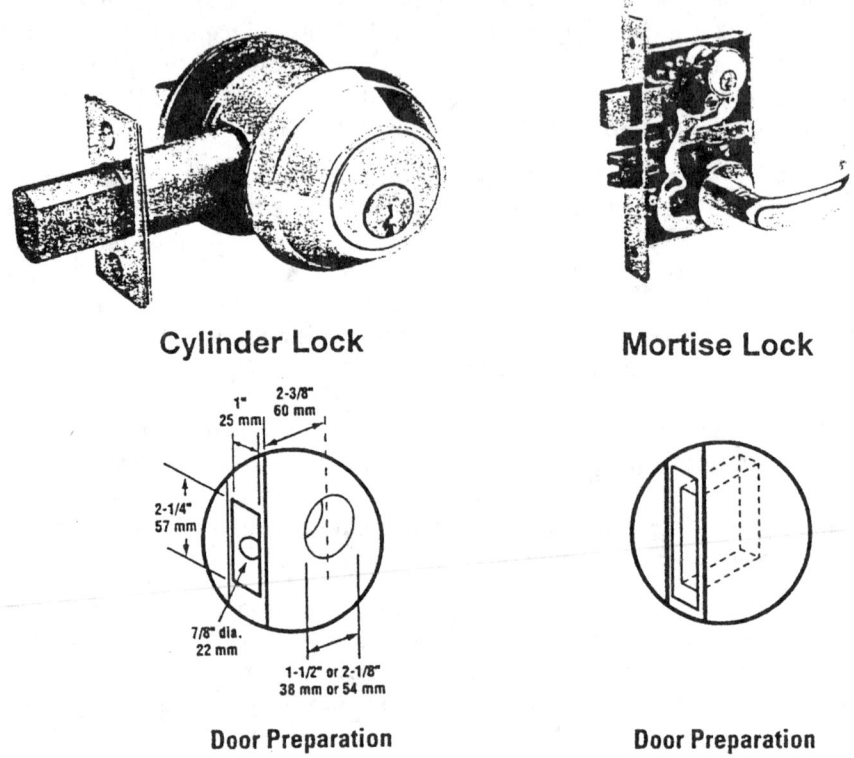

Figure 9. Cylinder and mortise locks with typical door preparation.

mortise — as shown in Figure 9. The names are taken from the type of hole that is cut into the door to receive the lock. A cylindrical (or key-in-the-knob) lock requires two circular holes in the door at right angles to each other, as shown in Figure 9. The mortise lock requires a single rectangular hole, or mortise, to be cut into the door to accept the lock case. Although knobs are still the most prevalent type of handle on doors, all new installations required to meet the Americans with Disabilities Act (ADA) will have lever handles.

Locksets are specified by the functions they perform. The standard functions listed below are not exhaustive but cover most applications. Readers should be careful not to be confused by the name given to various lockset functions. For example, a common application of an electrified "storeroom function" lockset is for automated access control in a passageway or at an entrance door. For reference, the labeled cutaway drawing below in Figure 10, illustrates the parts of a typical Schlage mortise lock.

General Locking Concepts

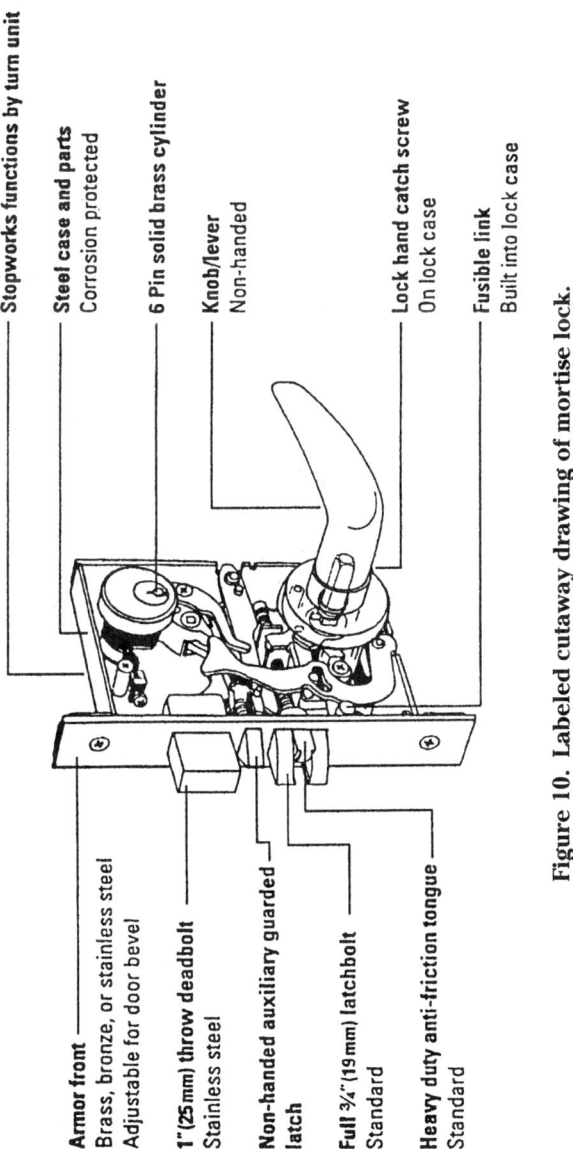

Figure 10. Labeled cutaway drawing of mortise lock.

Office Function. The latchbolt is retracted by the handle from either side unless the outer handle is made inoperative, using a key on the outside or a thumbturn on the inside. The auxiliary latch deadlocks the latchbolt when the door is closed. Note that a *latchbolt* is the spring-loaded, triangular-shaped component that is pushed into the lock case by the strike plate as the door closes and springs into the hole in the strike plate once the door is fully closed. A *deadbolt* is rectangular or cylindrical in shape and must be slid into and out of the strike plate by the user.

Classroom Function. The latchbolt is retracted by the handle from either side unless the outside handle is made inoperative using a key on the outside. The function is the same as above except that there is no inside thumbturn — egress is always free. The auxiliary latch deadlocks the latchbolt when the door is closed.

Storeroom Function. The latchbolt is retracted by a key outside or a handle inside. The outside handle is always inoperative — egress is always free. The electrified version of this lock allows the outside handle to operate when electrically unlocked. The auxiliary latch deadlocks the latchbolt when the door is closed.

Institution Function. The latchbolt is retracted by the key from either side. Handles on both sides are inoperative. The auxiliary latch deadlocks the latchbolt when the door is closed.

Corridor Function. This operates the same way as the "office function" except that the outside key or inside thumbturn throws or retracts a deadbolt. To ensure free egress, the inside handle retracts both the deadbolt and the latchbolt.

ELECTRIFIED LOCKING MECHANISMS

Electrified locking mechanisms allow doors to be locked and unlocked by a remote device. The device may be a simple electric push button or a motion sensor, or may be a sophisticated automated access control device such as a card reader or digital keypad. In addition, many access control systems allow the use of Boolean logic to augment the control of electrified devices. Boolean logic relates to the combination of conditions; for example, "if door A is locked *and* door B is locked *then* door C can be unlocked."

This is useful in the design of mantraps and other high-security operations. When considering failure and defeat mechanisms for locks, the addition of remote-control devices requires that these other devices be included in the analysis.

Before describing the different types of electrified locking mechanisms, it is useful to clearly define two important terms: *fail safe* and *fail secure*.

General Locking Concepts

These terms are usually applied in reference to fire/life safety codes and relate to doors in the path of egress from an occupied space that are required to be unlocked either at all times of occupancy or only during a detected fire emergency. Codes also state that the means of egress must be by a single action that requires no special knowledge, although there are some exceptions for banks, jewelry stores, and other high-security applications. Turning a door handle or pushing an exit device (panic bar) are allowable single actions. Pressing a button, turning a key, using a card reader, or keying a number on a digital keypad *before* turning the handle do not constitute single actions. Local fire codes vary by municipality and the reader should refer to them when specifying any door locking mechanisms.

A fail safe locking mechanism is one that will unlock under any failure condition. The failure mode most commonly considered is loss of power, but failure of the mechanism itself and any connected control device need to be considered also. Most, but not all, locks related to code-required egress are fail safe to ensure that they provide free egress if a power failure occurs at the same time as a fire emergency. Note, however, that the lock for a door that normally provides free egress simply by turning a handle or depressing the exit bar from the secure side does not need to be fail safe. For example, an electrified exit device (panic bar) will mechanically unlock its door when pushed, regardless of whether or not the lock is electrically energized.

A fail secure lock is one that will remain locked when power is lost or other failure occurs. As noted above, a fail secure lock may be used on a door in the path of egress provided that free egress is available regardless of the state of the lock's power or other control mechanisms.

Electric Deadbolt

The electric deadbolt is the oldest and simplest of all electrical locking devices. A solenoid (electro-magnet) moves a deadbolt, typically mounted on a door frame, either into or out of a strike plate on a door (see Figure 11). The mechanism can be either fail safe, automatically unlocking on the removal of power, or fail secure, remaining locked on the removal of power. The electric deadbolt is not normally recommended for application to doors required to be unlocked automatically in response to a fire alarm signal. This is because the bolt may bind in the strike plate if pressure is on the door when power is removed. This can occur in a panic situation when people are pressing on the door before the lock is de-energized. Some deadbolts are designed with tapered bolts to prevent binding but the reader should check the local building and fire codes before specifying this type of device for fire egress doors.

Electric Latch

Somewhat similar to an electric deadbolt is the electric latch, illustrated in Figure 11. It is also solenoid activated, mounts on the door frame, and

ASSET PROTECTION AND SECURITY MANAGEMENT HANDBOOK

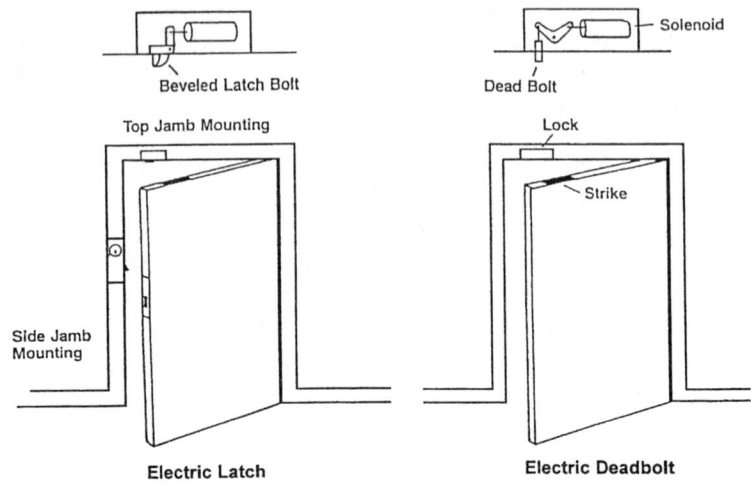

Figure 11. Electric deadbolt and electric latch.

uses a strike plate in the door. Instead of a deadbolt, a beveled latch is used. It has an advantage over the deadbolt because the latch does not need to be withdrawn for the door to close since it is pushed into the lock mechanism against spring pressure as it rides up and over the strike plate.

Electric Strike

The electric strike operates as an adjunct to any standard mechanical lock. The operating principle is simple: electrical energy is delivered to a solenoid that either opens or closes a mechanical latch keeper or strike plate. (Note that the electric strike is not a lock but operates with a lock to hold the door closed or to permit it to be opened.) Such devices have been used for many years in apartment houses, business offices, commercial installations, and occupancies in general. Figure 12 illustrates a typical electric strike.

A typical application of the electric strike is to control passage in one or both directions. The lockset handle is fixed (i.e., will not turn) on the side(s) from which passage is to be controlled. The only means of access becomes remote, unlocking the electric strike by a button or switch within the secure space, or by an automated access control device, such as a card reader or digital keypad. If the knob or handle on the secure side of the door remains operational (i.e., it will turn), then egress can be free. If the knob or handle is fixed on both sides, egress can be achieved by the same types of devices described for access. Additionally, if the mechanical lockset is equipped with a lock cylinder on one or both sides, the door can be unlocked with a key.

General Locking Concepts

Figure 12. Typical electric or breaking strike.

A problem arises when electric strikes are used to control doors for re-entry from fire stairs to an occupied floor. Fire code may permit re-entry to be restricted, except at times when there is a fire emergency. At such times, code requires that doors be equipped with locks that are fail safe and unlock automatically for re-entry on a signal from the fire alarm system. (Some codes require re-entry to be gained only on every fourth floor or "nth" floor of high-rise office buildings.) However, the doors must *remain latched* to prevent from being blown open by expanding fire gases and thus permit smoke to enter the stairway. A fail safe electric strike will not keep the door latched when power is withdrawn. A solution is discussed below.

Stairtower Lock. To meet the specific fire codes related to stair doors, both for new construction and retrofit on older multi-story buildings, a special hybrid electric locking device, known as a stairtower lock, was developed. The arrangement is illustrated in Figure 13. The mechanism consists of a frame-mounted electric solenoid device that does not protrude beyond the frame but controls the dead-locking mortise latch bolt of a regular mortise-type door lock. Removal of power to the device releases the dead-locking latchbolt mechanism to allow the door handles to operate. One of its advantages is that drilling the door for electrical wiring, which could negate the door's fire certification, is not required.

103

ASSET PROTECTION AND SECURITY MANAGEMENT HANDBOOK

Figure 13. Stairtower lock.

Electric Lockset

The electric lockset is simply a regular mortise lockset that has been electrified to control the ability to turn the handle. As the lock is contained within the door, the door must be drilled to allow power wiring to be fed to the hinge side. The cabling must then be fed either through or around the door hinge. Figure 14 shows an electric lockset and different types of electric hinges and an armored cable door loop.

This type of electric lock is becoming increasingly popular for automated access control applications. The normally fixed, unsecure side handle of a storeroom function electric lockset is controlled by an access control device (e.g., a card reader), while the secure side handle remains operational at all times for unimpeded egress. Some models offer an option of a sensor switch in the lock that is activated when the inside handle is turned. This provides a request-for-exit signal to the access control system to automatically shunt any magnetic switch or local horn associated with the door so that alarms are not sounded for a valid egress. It should be noted that

General Locking Concepts

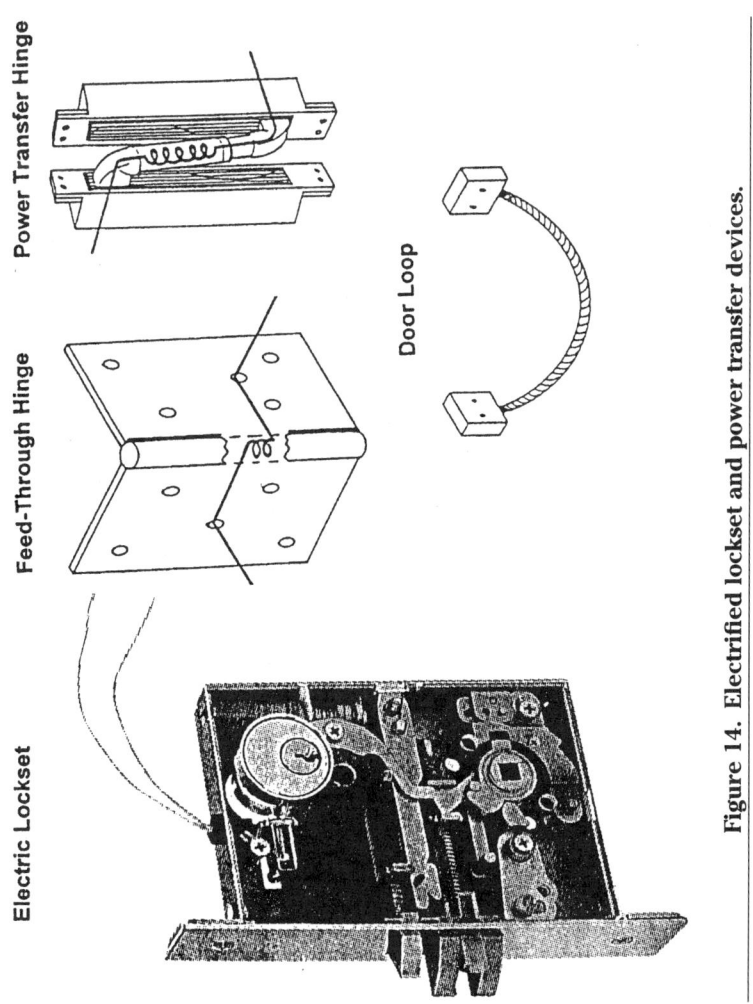

Figure 14. Electrified lockset and power transfer devices.

this option will require the specification of a four-wire (instead of two-wire) transfer hinge to accommodate both the lock power and the sensor switch cabling.

Exit Device

Also known as a panic bar or crash bar, the exit device is commonly used on doors in the path of egress from structures with high occupancy. Figure 15 illustrates some of the types. The rim-mounted device requires little modification to the door, as it is surface mounted. The mortice-mounted device requires the locking mechanism to be mortised into the edge of the door in the same manner as a regular mortise lock. Vertical rod devices are used on doors with double leaves where there is no fixed frame or mullion to accept a latchbolt. The rods, which move into holes or strike plates in the frame header and floor to restrain the door, can be surface mounted or concealed within a hollow door.

Exit devices can be electrified to permit remotely controlled re-entry via a push button or card reader/keypad. One special application of this type of hardware is the *delayed egress* locking system. Developed as a compromise between safety and security, this system is usually applied to doors intended to be used only for emergency fire egress. Instead of allowing immediate egress when pushed, activation of the bar starts a 15- or 30-second *delay*, after which the door will unlock. Special signage is required to inform users of the delay, the system must be connected to the fire alarm system, and the delay must not occur in the event of a fire or other defined life safety emergency. Although it will not usually provide enough of a delay to permit interception of an escaping thief, the system will sound a local alarm and report that alarm condition to a central monitoring location. A CCTV camera can be used to identify the perpetrator and any articles being carried, and to record the incident.

Much controversy has surrounded the delayed egress system. Readers intending to use them should carefully check with their local building officials and fire marshals as some communities require application for a special variance before they can be installed, and some communities have banned them completely.

Electromagnetic Lock

The electromagnetic lock, also known simply as a magnetic lock, utilizes an electromagnet and a metal armature or strike plate. When energized, the magnet exerts an attractive force upon the armature and thus holds the door closed. Figure 16 illustrates this type of locking mechanism. Although the lock is usually mounted at the head of the door, it can be mounted on the side. This location, while reducing the door passage width, provides a considerably more secure door.

General Locking Concepts

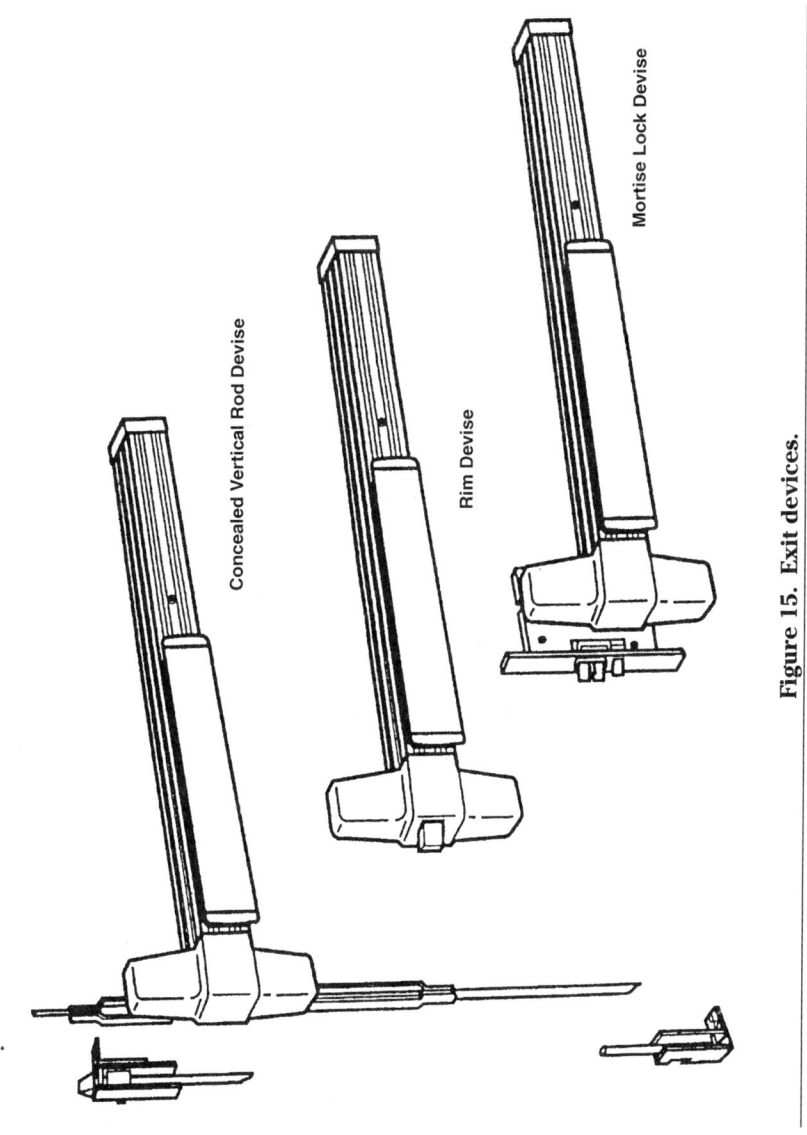

Figure 15. Exit devices.

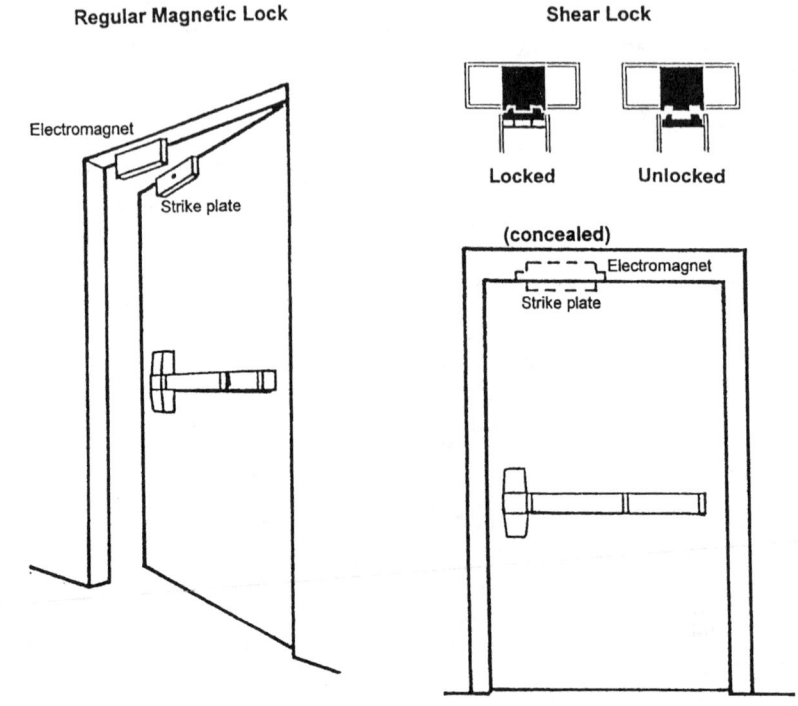

Figure 16. Electromagnetic lock.

Magnetic locks are rated by the pounds of force required to separate the armature or strike plate from the electromagnet, and are available from 500 to 2000 pounds. Although most applications will need only a single magnetic lock installed on a door, multiple locks can be used for high-security requirements.

Shear Lock. An adaptation of the electromagnetic lock is called the *shear lock*. The electromagnet is concealed in the header of the door frame and the armature is mounted in a channel in the top of the door. The plane of both pieces is horizontal, in contrast to the regular type where it is vertical. The armature "floats" up and down on vertical pins so that it can be "sucked" up to the magnet when energized. The face of the armature rests in an indentation in the magnet to prevent the two faces from sliding or shearing when the door is pushed. Although the shear lock is considerably more attractive than the regular magnetic lock because it is totally concealed, it is not very forgiving to installation variances between the door and the frame. As little as a 1/8-inch sag after installation or door distortion due to wedges being used to keep the door open will render the lock inoperative.

General Locking Concepts

Manufacturers are continually trying to make design improvements to counteract the poor installation and usage of doors, but shear locks have had to be replaced with the regular type in a number of situations.

A very valuable feature of regular electromagnetic locks is that they involve no moving parts and are much less maintenance sensitive than mechanical or electromechanical devices. As long as the surfaces of the magnets and the armature are kept clean and in alignment, and provided there is assured electrical power, the devices will operate as intended. Better electromagnetic locks have built-in switches to monitor the bonding of the magnet and armature and to monitor the door position. These sensors are important to void the simple defeat mechanism of placing a nonmetallic sheet between the magnet and the strike plate to reduce the bonding power.

Electromagnetic locks are intrinsically fail safe because removal of power will release the strike plate. In high-security applications, backup power should be used to ensure that the lock fulfills its function in the event of a power failure. It is possible to use electromagnetic and electric bolt or strike plate locks in combination. For example, consider an area under ingress and egress access control that must remain secure against unauthorized entry but permit free egress during a defined emergency.

These types of locks are also used in delayed egress systems as described above for egress devices. A switch in the magnet senses that the door has been pushed and starts the required countdown. The same caveats as described above should be observed.

Access Control during an Emergency. An electromagnetic lock, used in conjunction with in and out card readers and an auxiliary electromagnetic bolt or latch, can maintain security, even during life safety emergencies. Normally, all ingress and egress is via card reader when the door is locked against both entry and exit, except via card readers that control the electromagnetic lock. In an emergency, the electromagnetic lock fails safe (permitting free movement in both directions). However, an electric latch or deadbolt, installed on the same door and normally unlocked, fails secure but can be retracted by turning an inside (secure side) handle or lever. This lock permits free egress but prevents re-entry from the unsecure side, even to those with approved cards, because the electric latch or bolt is not connected to the card readers. Upon termination of the emergency, the latch is restored to the unlocked state, the magnetic lock is restored to the secure state and normal traffic resumes. If access to the secure space from the outside might be required during an emergency, a key-operated cylinder can be incorporated in the deadbolt or latch to operate from the outside.

Accountability for egress would be lost during the emergency mode but could be addressed by installation of one or more CCTV cameras and recorders to monitor movement through the door.

ASSET PROTECTION AND SECURITY MANAGEMENT HANDBOOK

Selected Bibliography

Books

Allen, Sam; *Locks & Alarms;* 1984; Tab Books.

Ellis, Raymond C. Jr.; *Security and Loss Prevention Management;* 1986; American Hotel and Motel Association — Security Committee.

Healy, Richard J.; *Design For Security, 2nd ed;* 1983, John Wiley & Sons, New York (see especially Chapter 9).

James, J.D.; *Locks & Lock Picking: How Locks Work and How to Pick Them: A Basic Guide for Law Enforcement, Security, Military;* 1987; R & R Publishing.

Mayers, Keith A.; *Dictionary of Locksmithing;* 1979; Mayers.

Mele, Joe A., Edgar, James M. and McInerney, William D.; *The Use of Locks in Physical Crime Prevention;* 1987, National Crime Prevention Institute, Butterworths Publishing Co., Stoneham, MA.

Roper, Carl A.; *The Complete Handbook of Locks & Locksmithing;* 1976; Tab Books.

Schum, John L; *Electronic Locking Devices;* 1988; Butterworths Publishing Co., Stoneham, MA.

Steed, F.A.; *Locksmithing;* 1982; Tab Books.

Periodicals, Monographs, and Standards

Burglary Resistant Electric Locking Mechanisms; Standard 1034; Underwriters Laboratories, Inc., Northbrook, IL.

Key Locks, Standard 437; Underwriters Laboratories.

Key-Locked Safes (Class KL), Standard 786; Underwriters Laboratories.

Locksmith Ledger [The]; Nickerson & Collins, Co., Des Plaines, IL.

Security Management; American Society for Industrial Security, Arlington, VA.
 — Channell, Warren T.; Electronic Locks: Finding the Right Fit; January 1996.
 — Cytryn, Jay.; A Primer of Locks for All Occasions; May 1985.
 — Dunckel, Kenneth D.; Electronic Safe Locks: A New Current; November 1991.
 — Dunckel, Kenneth D.; Safekeeping for Safe Combinations; November 1990.
 — Hall, George P.; The Key to Electronic Locks; January 1996.
 — Miehl, Frederick; The Ins and Outs of Door Locks; February 1993.
 — Roland, Fred W.; Inns and Outs; November 1986.
 — Spargo, Robert C.; Smart Locks Balance Safety and Security; November 1986.

5
Alarm Sensors

SENSOR APPLICATIONS

Applications for sensors extend to every phase of business, industrial and scientific activity. This chapter discusses alarm sensors found in security, fire and life safety systems.

Sensors are the basic ingredients of an alarm system. They detect the condition or event indicating a security or fire problem. All logical discrimination, transmission, processing, display and recording activities that occur subsequent to initial detection have meaning because of what sensors see, hear, feel or otherwise sense with optical, electronic, electromechanical or mechanical capabilities. If the sensor is inappropriate or inadequate for the task, the output of the entire system will be severely limited, becoming a greater burden than benefit. Indeed, when the National Burglar and Fire Alarm Association (NBFAA) is striving to reduce false alarms to one a year for each system, device selection is paramount.[1]

In early intrusion and fire systems, sensors were typically mechanical or electro-mechanical devices directly connected to some fairly simple display and recording equipment. Sensors were either individually enunciated, or grouped in "zones" (clusters) and enunciated in some form of common signal. A permanent record, if provided, might have been a paper tape or single line printer with coded messages.

The state of the sensor and of alarm systems has since developed dramatically. 1996 Electronic sensors report changes in their status over multiplexed circuits to central or distributed controllers that process the data in logical fashion. These sensors utilize stored memory programs that display and record results, then give instructions to human operators or non-human elements of the system to change or reconfigure the device. Much takes place without human intervention.

Security Applications

The use of alarms for security purposes began around the turn of the 20th century with the installation of electrically operated alarms to protect banks and retail establishments against burglary. The installations were recognizable because of the bell boxes installed on the outside of the facilities being protected. Frequent false alarms were characteristic of such

---

[1] Jay Velgos, NB&FAA, Bethesda, MD, March 1996.

ASSET PROTECTION AND SECURITY MANAGEMENT HANDBOOK

ITEM	DEVICE	APPLICATION	EFFECTIVENESS					ENVIRONMENT						UTILITY		
			DETECTION CONFIDENCE	RESISTANCE TO DEFEAT	DIFFICULTY TO OBSERVE	OPERATING RELIABILITY	FREEDOM FROM FALSE ALARMS	IMMUNITY TO AIR TURBULENCE	IMMUNITY TO NOISE – ACOUSTIC	IMMUNITY TO NOISE – VIBRATION	IMMUNITY TO NOISE – ELECTRICAL MONOCHROMATIC	IMMUNITY TO NOISE – ELECTRICAL IMPULSE	IMMUNITY TO TEMPERATURE CHANGES	EASE OF INSTALLATION	EASE OF CALIBRATION	EASE OF MAINTENANCE
1.	MECHANICAL SWITCHES (all types)	DOORS, WINDOWS	H	L	L	H	H	H	H	H	H	H	H	H	H	H
2.	MAGNETIC SWITCHES (unbalanced)	DOORS, WINDOWS	H	L	L	H	H	H	H	H	H	H	H	H	H	H
3.	MAGNETIC SWITCHES (balanced)	DOORS, WINDOWS	H	L	L	H	H	H	H	H	H	H	H	H	H	H
4.	BREAKWIRE	DOORS, WINDOWS, OPENINGS	H	L	L	M	H	H	H	H	H	H	M	L	H	M
5.	BREAKWIRE	WALLS, CEILINGS, FLOORS	H	H	M	H	H	H	H	H	H	H	M	L	H	M
6.	BREAKWIRE	CONTAINERS	H	L	H	M	H	H	H	H	H	H	M	L	H	M
7.	ACOUSTIC MOTION ULTRASONIC	SPACE	H	H	L	M	L	L	M	M	H	H	H	M	L	M
8.	MICROWAVE MOTION DETECTOR	SPACE	H	H	L	M	M	M	H	M	H	H	H	M	L	M
9.	CAPACITIVE DETECTOR	PASSAGEWAYS	M	M	M	M	M	H	H	M	M	M	H	L	M	M
10.	CAPACITIVE DETECTOR	SPACE	M	M	M	M	L	H	H	L	L	L	H	L	M	M
11.	CAPACITIVE DETECTOR	CONTAINERS	H	M	M	H	M	H	H	H	H	M	H	M	H	M
12.	VIBRATION DETECTOR	WINDOWS, WALLS, CEILINGS, FLOORS	M	L	L	M	M	H	H	L	H	H	H	M	L	M
13.	VIBRATION DETECTOR	CONTAINERS	M	L	L	M	H	H	H	L	H	H	H	M	L	M
14.	ACOUSTIC DETECTOR (microphone)	WINDOWS, WALLS, CEILINGS, FLOORS	M	L	L	M	L	M	L	M	H	H	H	M	L	M
15.	ACOUSTIC DETECTOR (microphone)	SPACE	L	L	L	M	L	M	L	M	H	H	H	M	L	M
16.	ACOUSTIC DETECTOR (microphone)	CONTAINERS	M	L	L	M	L	M	L	M	H	H	H	M	L	M
17.	INFRARED BREAK BEAMS	DOORS, WINDOWS, OPENINGS	H	L	M	M	H	H	H	M	H	M	H	M	H	M
18.	INFRARED BREAK BEAMS	PASSAGES	H	L	M	M	H	H	H	M	H	M	H	M	H	M
19.	INFRARED BREAK BEAMS	CONTAINERS	H	L	M	M	H	H	H	M	H	H	H	M	H	M
20.	THERMAL DETECTOR	CONTAINERS	M	L	M	M	H	H	H	H	H	H	H	M	H	M
21.	CHEMICAL SNIFFER	SPACE	M	H	H	M	L	H	H	H	H	H	M	M	L	L
22.	MOTION DETECTING TV	SPACE	M	M	L	M	M	H	H	M	H	H	H	L	M	L
23.	PASSIVE INFRARED	SPACE OR POINT	H	L	H	M	M	H	H	M	H	H	H	M	M	M

Evaluation: H = HIGH, M = MEDIUM, L = LOW

Figure 1. The application and evaluation of various sensors.

installations because many factors other than intrusion attempts caused alarms, and there was no effective way to collect and distinguish irrelevant events from genuine ones.

Modern sensors and detectors available for security applications, when properly selected and installed, make a much more useful contribution to the protection of an enterprise (see Figure 1).

Designed to report the presence of persons attempting to enter or move about in protected areas, intrusion detectors can be divided into three general classes, based on what they are intended to detect and the location of the installation: (1) perimeter or point of entry, (2) general area, and (3) object (see Figure 2).

Alarm Sensors

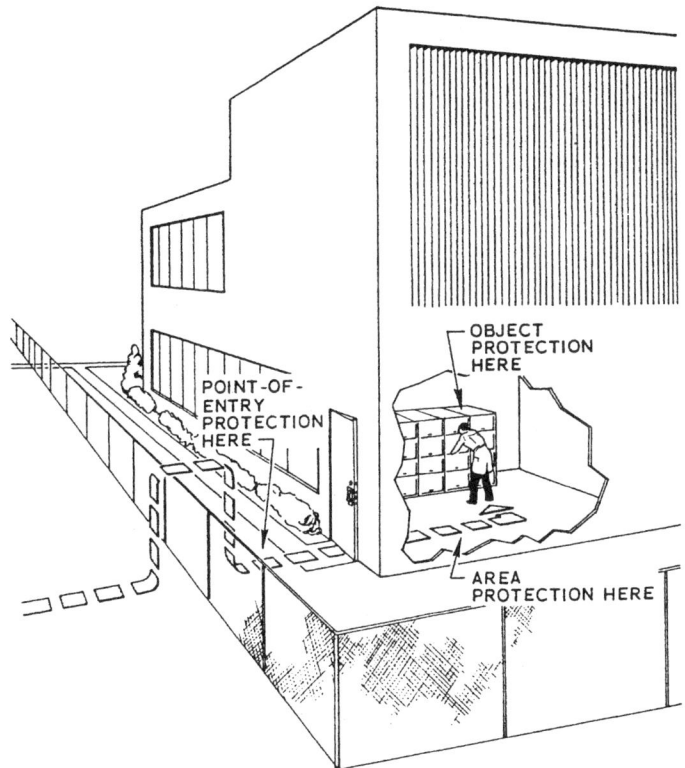

Figure 2. Three general categories of security sensors.

UL Standards. There are many manufacturers of the various types of sensors now available and it is important that users have standards upon which to judge the quality and appropriateness of each application. While there is no single source of standards covering alarm sensors, there are authoritative bodies that provide guidance. Perhaps the best known of these is Underwriters Laboratories (UL), headquartered in Northbrook, IL, with other locations in the U.S. and abroad.

UL prepares standards primarily as a guide to device manufacturers, and then certifies whether devices submitted to the laboratories for approval meet those standards. The standards themselves are developed in response to broad feedback from the public, the insurance industry, government, academic bodies, inspection authorities, consumer organizations and end users. The laboratories have often stated that while their standards are publicly available, they would prefer that the public (the users of approved devices) be guided by the periodic Directories. These are listings of specific devices (and their manufacturers) that have been

Table 1. UL standards.

Std. No.	Name
365	Police Station Connected Burglar Alarm Units and Systems
606	Linings and Screens for Use with Burglar Alarm Systems
609	Local Burglar Alarm Units and Systems
611	Central-Station Burglar Alarm Systems
634	Connectors and Switches for Use with Burglar Alarm Systems
636	Hold-Up Alarm Units and Systems
639	Intrusion Detection Units
681	**Installation and Classification of Mercantile and Bank Burglar Alarm Systems**
1037	Anti-Theft Alarms and Devices
1076	**Proprietary Burglar Alarm Units and Systems**
1610	Central Station Burglar Alarm Units
1635	Digital Burglar Alarm Communicator Units
1641	**Installation and Classification of Residential Burglar Alarm Systems**

Note: Each of these UL standards has also been designated a "national standard" by the American National Standards Institute (ANSI).

submitted, tested and certified by UL as meeting the requirements of a particular standard. (The Directory that lists security devices is the "Automotive, Burglary Protection and Mechanical Equipment Directory," which is distributed annually in October and revised annually six months later.)

For asset protection professionals and other sophisticated users, however, a more detailed knowledge of the standard is important so that the full effect of UL approval can be appreciated. It often happens that UL approval is a requirement found in specifications for security systems and in municipal building and fire codes.

A complete current catalog of UL Standards for Safety can be obtained by writing the Underwriters Laboratories, 333 Pfingsten Rd., Northbrook, IL, 60062. Individual standards are available by purchase from the same source. UL has promulgated numerous standards that apply to fire and security systems, most relevant to the engineering and manufacture of alarms and related controllers. Of the security system standards listed in Table 1, those in **bold type** are especially relevant for installers and users because they specify the manner of installation and/or operation.

ASTM Standards. The American Society for Testing and Materials (ASTM), in Philadelphia, has established a committee to deal with security standards.[1] The scope of the committee as defined by ASTM is:

---

[1] ASTM Committee F-12 Security Systems and Equipment.

"To develop and standardize nomenclature, definitions, test methods, specifications, classifications, and recommended practices for security systems and equipment and promotion of knowledge as it relates to security systems and equipment for security of property and safety of life. This work will be coordinated with other ASTM Technical Committees, organizations and individuals in this area."

ASTM standards have not yet been developed for security alarm systems or sensors. However, ASTM did publish a hardcover text in June 1981, entitled *Building Security*, which was described as a "publication to establish a reference base for the evaluation and performance of building-related security systems, components, and equipment."[1] One section of the text is devoted to devices and is entitled, "Design Considerations for High Security Interior Intrusion Detection Systems."

Other Standards and Specifications. The U.S. General Services Administration (GSA) first published a specification for alarm system components in 1969. That specification, then known as Interim Specification WA-0045A, was twice revised, once in 1973 (Interim Spec. WA-0045B) and again in 1990. The latest revision, W-A-45OC/GEN, is a regular rather than interim document. Its full text is set out in Appendix A to this chapter, and is current as of early 1996.

In 1976, a comprehensive report was issued by Sandia Laboratories, Albuquerque, NM, entitled, *Intrusion Detection System Handbook*.[2] The material was prepared by members of the Sandia Laboratories staff, under the sponsorship of the former ERDA Division of Safeguards and Security (DSS). It was based on data obtained from evaluation programs, conducted at various laboratories, sponsored by DSS, the ERDA (now Department of Energy), Division of Military Application, the Department of Defense (DoD), and other governmental agencies, and on information provided by commercial security equipment suppliers. The original publication has undergone several revisions and is now released as separate volumes covering: Intrusion Detection System Concepts; Considerations for Sensor Selection and Subsystem Design; Exterior Intrusion Sensors; Interior Intrusion Sensors; Alarm Assessment Systems; Alarm Reporting Systems; and Intrusion Detection System Integration. Although not intended to be used as specifications or standards for devices, the handbook does cover various aspects of the use of intrusion detection devices in useful detail.

The National Fire Protection Association (NFPA) publishes detailed standards for municipal, central station, proprietary, and local fire alarm systems. Previously released as separate documents, NFPA Codes 71, 72A,

---

[1] *Building Security*, John Stroik, Ed.; 1981; American Society for Testing and Materials, Philadelphia, PA; Publication Number STP 729.
[2] *Intrusion Detection System Handbook*, SAND 76-0554, Information Systems Department, Sandia Laboratories, Albuquerque, NM 87185; 1976, Revised October 1977 and July 1980.

72B, 72C, 72D, 72E, 72F, 72G, 72H and 74 were consolidated in 1993 into a single NFPA 72, *National Fire Alarm Code*. The NFPA also publishes the *National Fire Alarm Code Handbook*, an explanatory text to assist in interpreting and applying the formal language of the Code.

CATEGORIES OF SENSORS

Sensors of all types should be designed to initiate alarms under any of the following conditions:

1. Occurrence of the event or condition being monitored (penetration of protected area, rise in temperature, presence of smoke, etc.)
2. Loss of electrical power
3. Opening, shorting, or grounding of the device circuitry
4. Failure of the sensor itself
5. Tampering with the sensor's enclosure or distributed control panels (transponders)

Units for indoor use should be capable of operating in a temperature range of 32°F to 120°F. Units to be installed outdoors or in unheated structures should be capable of operating in temperatures ranging from –30°F to +150°F. All units should be capable of operating at 90°F and 95 percent relative humidity.

Passive Infrared (PIR) Sensors

Passive infrared sensors, commonly referred to simply as PIRs, are the most widely used intrusion detectors today and are highly versatile. PIRs "see" the invisible, bold colors of thermal or infrared (IR) energy. Because there is no beam, they are called passive. This energy, like heat from the sun, has no visible color or light. Just as a camera takes in light, a PIR sees warm, infrared images against a cooler background (Figure 3). It must distinguish between heat from a heating vent, office space-heater, lights and others sources, and the infrared image of a human intruder. Temperature operating ranges are from –40°C to +50°C (–40°F to +120°F), with some units able to discriminate to within 1°C.[1]

PIRs are actually able to detect objects that are either warmer or cooler against (or when compared to) background temperature. Effectiveness diminishes as background temperature approaches that of the intruder. Because human intruders in temperate climates are usually warmer than the background, the requirement here is for a PIR to detect warmer objects. This perspective changes in warmer climes, where room temperatures may be hotter than intruders. The cooler temperature of a human (98.6°F) is what the PIR should see here. In environments where temperatures are not artificially regulated — such as unheated, non-air-conditioned

---

[1] Product Catalog 1995; Sentrol, Inc., Tualatin, OR.

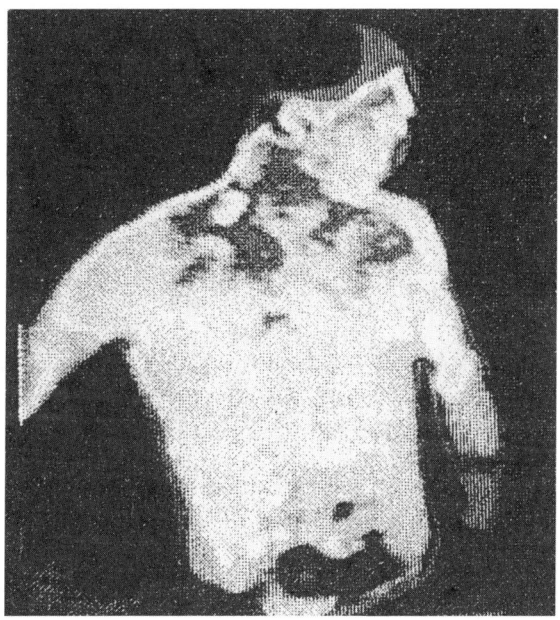

Figure 3. What the PIR sees.

warehouses or vacant vacation homes — or where the ability of the PIR to discern temperature variations is particularly critical, automatic temperature compensation is an essential feature. A unit is needed that expands the temperature range at which it can see an intruder. Design and installation of PIRs are key to avoiding sources of false alarms.

PIR Design. A working understanding of modern PIR design can be gained from knowing how two essential components work together. First is the *fresnel lens*. The lens focuses IR images onto a pyro-electric sensor. Much like a magnifying glass focuses the sun's heat, the fresnel lens creates a sharper image. By concentrating otherwise scattered energy, the PIR improves detection of heat sources differing from background temperatures. Newer fresnel lenses are made up of concentric circles that are spaced closer together as they reach the edge of the lens. In older designs, these rings were equally spaced. Most often, these rings are molded into the interior side of the lens. By masking the lens, it is possible to block out areas the PIR would normally see (such as a heater).

Another component of most PIRs permits incoming signals to be shaped or concentrated in different patterns. Standard coverage patterns, such as those depicted in Figure 5, can be shaped as a curtain to protect openings like doors and windows, or artwork hung on a wall. Fresnel lenses filter out white light and gather signal energy more effectively than older mirror-based PIRs.

The second thing to know is that the *pyro-electric sensor* (simply, pyro) *produces an electrical output when subjected to a change in IR energy.* If the sensed changes are typical of a human signature in terms of mass, shape and intensity, a signal processing unit in the PIR alarms. For the PIR to "see" it as human, the image must pass across (in front of) two pyro elements, one negative and one positive. Units should be specified whose design electrically connects both pyro elements. Greater false alarm immunity is afforded by PIRs utilizing quad element pyros because small targets, like birds and rodents, will only be detected by one pair of elements while larger targets, such as humans or vehicles, will be picked up by both pairs (see Figure 4). An integrated circuit called an ASIC (application-specific integrated circuit) is the brains of the PIR. The ASIC operates much like a dedicated computer, constantly monitoring signals generated by the pyro until it identifies a human or other specified signature. This signal would in turn be transmitted to the alarm control panel.

Application and Installation. Proper installation is a primary consideration in avoiding false alarms. Ideally, a PIR should be mounted in such a location that an intruder would pass *across* its field of view. PIR designs suitable for wall or ceiling mounting are available. Because of their versatility, PIRs can be installed so as to protect perimeters, areas and objects. Installed directly behind a valuable painting, a PIR would alarm if the painting were removed. Installed in all four corners of a room with focus directed toward an adjoining corner, the entire perimeter of a room can be protected. Electrically connected peripheral devices — CCTV cameras, video recorders, lights, heating and ventilation controls, door openers and local alarms — can all be activated when a PIR is triggered. PIRs may be suitable for building openings, such as air-conditioning vents, manhole covers and skylights, where alarm screens were previously the only option. PIR detection paths should not be blocked with partitions, furniture or doors (see Figure 5).

Radio frequency interference (RFI), a common source of false alarms, requires RFI filtering. This vulnerability should be kept in mind when specifying PIRs for certain applications. Drafts and insects are other common sources of false alarms. Air from vents and other sources of drafts should not flow directly on the unit. Well-sealed housing can guard against this problem. Direct sunlight can cause false alarms, so it is important to avoid mounting a PIR where it will see a bright window or direct sunlight in its field of view. Conditions where the PIR may see rapid changes in temperature should also be avoided.

Wired or wireless detectors are available for PIR as well as other alarm sensor technologies. Wireless systems are often used in residential applications where building codes are less stringent and complicated retrofitting would be costly and aesthetically unpleasant.

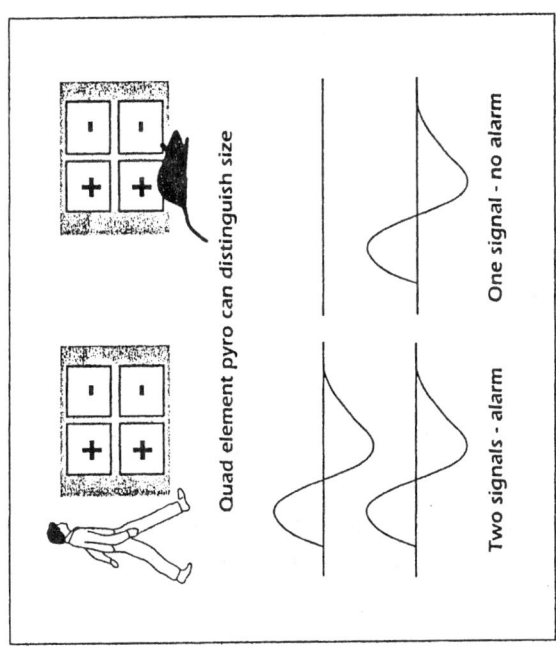
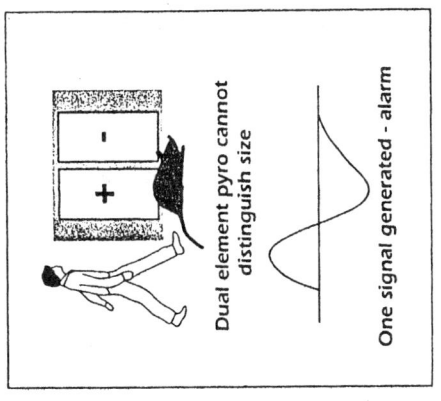

Figure 4. PIRs utilizing quad element pyros.

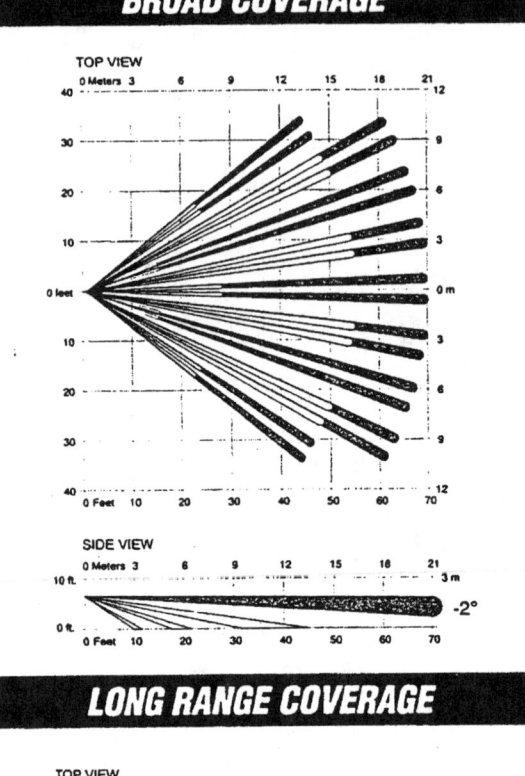

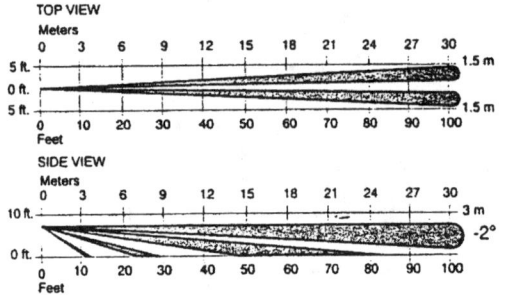

Figure 5. Typical PIR detection patterns.

Glass Break Sensors

Glass break sensors have largely replaced foil (discussed briefly later) in most applications. They offer the advantage of sounding an alarm while an intruder is still outside. Breaking glass produces unique sound wave frequencies (3–5 kilohertz, or kHz) that glass break sensors "hear," and seismic shock frequencies (200 hertz, or Hz) that they "feel" (see Figure 6). Built-in

Alarm Sensors

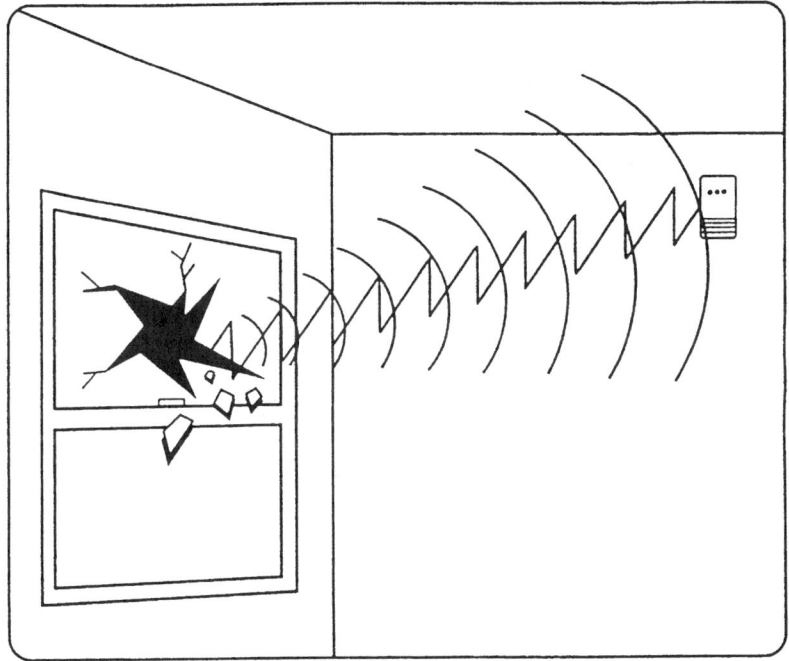

Figure 6. Glass break sensors.

microprocessors enable the devices to react to these sounds and ignore others that cause false alarms.

Acoustic Sensors. While several designs of acoustic sensors are available, they are often configured as a rectangular box the size of a light switch, with two small LED status indicator lights. Acoustic sensors may have the capability of sensing one or both of the acoustic and seismic frequency ranges. Those that simultaneously listen and feel are more reliable and less susceptible to false alarms. Microprocessors make it possible to differentiate between the sound of breaking glass and other sounds that cause false alarms. This is because detectors equipped with microprocessors analyze sound wave shapes (pattern or signature) rather than amplitude (the loudness of a sound). Early designs that merely listened for the loud sound of breaking glass (in the 4–6 kHz range) frequently false alarmed to the sound of clashing metal or barking dogs. Detectors designed and tested to listen across a wide spectrum of frequencies are better able to discriminate between the sounds of breaking glass and other sounds that can cause false alarms (see Figure 7). A detector that is UL listed for protecting all types of glass, whether plate, laminated, tempered or wired, is preferable.

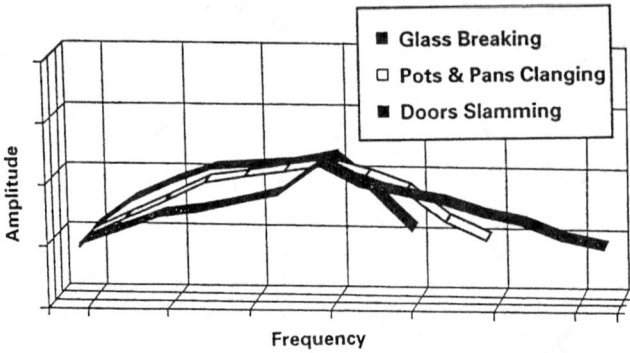

Figure 7. Acoustic glass break sensors.

Acoustic glass break detectors can be installed on walls or ceilings. Detection is best when installed on a wall *opposite* protected glass, because sound waves need not then reflect off an opposing wall before reaching the detector. Their range depends on the room being protected. Rooms with bare floors and few furnishings reflect sound better than those filled with furniture, partitions, and draperies. Assume the worst-case scenario when installing sensors. When selecting and installing glass break sensors, consideration should be given to their susceptibility to false alarms from radio frequency interference.

Shock Sensors. Glass break shock sensors "feel" the shock wave generated by breaking glass and signal an alarm. Attached directly to a protected pane of glass or adjoining window frame, they are an appropriate choice for protecting glass in loud, occupied rooms where acoustic sensors may be prone to false alarms. Designs vary but devices are approximately one to two inches square and are mounted with adhesive tape in the corner of the protected pane of glass. This installation also provides a visible deterrent to intruders. Corner mounting is optimal because shock waves are concentrated in that location, improving detection. Shock sensors are most effective when used to protect a single pane of glass, but the technology permits otherwise in some applications.

Shock sensors operate by one of two methods. The most common design can be compared to a disc-like mechanism that sits on two electrical contacts, completing a circuit. The shock of breaking glass causes the disc to move (jump) off the contacts, breaking the circuit and initiating an alarm. This principle permits sensors of this type to detect shock waves traveling into adjoining window frames, allowing for protection of several panes. Another method utilizes an electrical element called a piezo, which operates like a bias switch. The piezo creates its own electrical current as it bends or flexes to the frequency of breaking glass. This feature virtually eliminates false alarms because the device cannot alarm without generating its own electricity. The greatest limitation of piezo technology is the fact that devices utilizing it can assuredly protect only one pane of glass, leading to higher equipment and installation costs.

Dual-Technology Sensors

Dual-technology PIR/microwave detectors initiate an alarm upon simultaneous activation of two alarm technologies working in concert (communicating) with one another. Both technologies must process and signal to initiate an alarm. Internal microprocessors require a specific signature and timing of signals. Modern pattern recognition technology is capable of identifying and ignoring repetitive false alarm sources. Dual-technology sensors are better able to distinguish between signals caused by human intruders and those of small animals, such as cats or rodents, than the best single-technology detectors. Units with supervised circuitry provide continuing protection from the PIR alone if the microwave fails.

Devices are available that combine PIR with glass break technology. This innovation has solved the problem of arming glass break sensors in occupied buildings. Because glass break sensors are prone to false alarms caused by noises other than breaking glass, such as banging mop buckets and noisy janitorial crews, it was often impractical to arm glass break sensors until buildings were totally vacant. By combining technologies, the glass break sensors can be relied upon to ignore noise that might otherwise generate an alarm whenever the PIR sensor "sees" someone (like a janitor) inside the room.

Electromechanical Sensors

Electromechanical devices are relatively simple and provide stable, reliable service. Included in this category are such items as foil, wire and screen detectors, pressure mats, and mechanical or magnetic contacts. Foil, wire, and screen detectors and pressure mats have been largely replaced in many applications by PIR, glass break and dual-technology sensors. Wired electromechanical devices may be costly to install and, because of their simplicity, easily circumvented by a knowledgeable intruder. This type of sensor is designed to place a current-carrying conductor between an intruder and an area to be protected. The current keeps a holding relay (switch) in an open position. A cessation of the electrical current releases the relay, allowing contacts to close, and activating an alarm circuit.

Foil. This type of detector was formerly widely used on glass windows. Breaking the glass would presumably cause foil to be severed, interrupting the electrical current and initiating an alarm. Foil is a thin, current-carrying metallic tape typically applied with adhesive to the secure side of the surface

ASSET PROTECTION AND SECURITY MANAGEMENT HANDBOOK

being protected. Use of foil is considered obsolete by most installers and it has been replaced by glass break sensors.

Magnetic and Mechanical Switches. Accessible openings such as doors, windows and skylights may be protected with either mechanical or magnetic intrusion switches. This type of sensor is composed of a two-part electrical contact. One is installed on the opening surface, the other installed on the fixed surface. When the opening surface, typically a door, is in a closed position, the two contacts provide a closed circuit and a continuity of electrical current. When the opening surface is moved, separating the contacts, the circuit is broken and the interruption in current activates an alarm. The switch is usually installed so that it operates when the leading edge of the movable surface is opened.

The switches may be either mechanical or magnetic, recessed or surface mounted, wired or wireless. They should always be installed on the protected or secure side. While surface mounted switches are cheaper to install than those that are recessed, they may be more susceptible to damage and compromise. Surface-mounted switches may not be aesthetically suitable for office or residential applications (see Figure 8).

Two examples of mechanical switches are the plunger and the lever. They are activated by the movement of the surface upon which they are mounted. The plunger switch may be recessed mounted, while the lever switch is usually surface mounted. Mechanical switches are prone to malfunction when exposed to freezing or wet weather and heavy, repeated use.

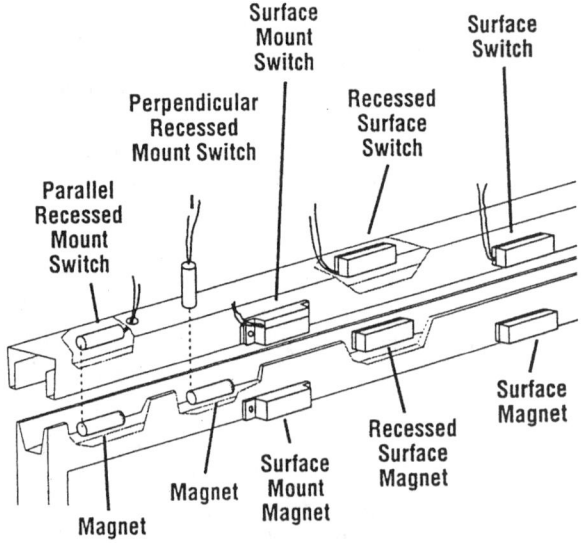

Figure 8. Magnetic switch options.

Alarm Sensors

They also accumulate dirt from the environment, and without regular maintenance will often stick.

A magnetic switch has two parts. One part is the magnet, generally mounted in a nonferrous housing or bracket; the other part is the switch assembly consisting of a ferrous lever attached to an actuator. When the magnet is properly oriented and mounted on the opening surface adjacent to the switch, metal reeds within the switch are opened. When the alarmed door is opened, moving the magnet, the reed switches close — energizing an electrical circuit and activating an alarm. For higher security, a bias switch should be used. Biased (or dual-magnet) switches are designed with a small magnet on the reed switch. If exposed to an increase or decrease in the magnetic field, or if substitution of an external magnet is attempted, the polarity of the switch is quickly reversed. The switch should also be electrically protected so that a sudden surge of voltage from lightning strikes or other sources does not cause an alarm.

Wire and Screen Detectors. Fine, hard-drawn breakwire may be utilized in various configurations to fabricate window screens, grids and lacing for installation on openings and barriers to detect forcible penetration. Prefabricated screens are commercially available. Such an installation should be designed so that an alarm is initiated if the current-carrying wire is cut, broken, grounded or spread enough to allow an opening of 96 square inches or more. This method of protecting building openings is not as widely used today as other technologies.

Wire "strain gauges" may also be used on fencing. For example, a single strand of wire can be installed along a barrier, such as a chain-link fence. If the tension of the wire is disturbed by an intruder attempting to climb the fence, an alarm is initiated. In newer systems utilizing optical fiber, flexion or stress on the fence modifies the light path through the fiber to cause an alarm.

Pressure Mats. This type of intrusion detection device is virtually obsolete and has been replaced by other technologies — principally PIRs. New installations are extremely uncommon, although they may still be in place in some facilities. Mats were typically installed under carpeting near doors, on stair treads or in other strategic locations. Operation involved initiation of an alarm when a weight from 5 to 20 pounds per square foot was applied to the mat surface.

A version of the mat is still used, in conjunction with other detectors, to screen the numbers of persons or gross permissible weight through a portal. In these cases the mat or pad is actually a weight transducer and can be used at a remote card or keypad-controlled entry point to ensure that no person exceeding a programmed weight can gain access. When combined with distributed databases and unique PINs or cards, the authorized holder's actual weight, plus or minus a set margin, can be stored. When the PIN is entered in the keypad or the card inserted in the reader, the transducer-detected weight will be processed by the software entry algorithm.

Ultrasonic Sensors

The operation of ultrasonic sensors is much like that of more technologically advanced and popular passive infrared detectors. Based on the Doppler effect, microwaves or sound waves are disturbed when movement changes signal frequency between transmission and receipt. As long as the return pattern being received is the same as that being transmitted, a stable condition exists. When a distortion of the wave pattern caused by movement is detected, an alarm is initiated.

Discriminator logic (intelligence) can be designed into sensors so that the amplitude of the disturbance can be determined. The discriminator can be adjusted so that the movement of a bird or small animal would be disregarded, while movement of a human would signal an alarm. Discriminators should be set so an alarm is initiated when an intruder walks through a wave pattern at the rate of one step per second. For area coverage, a sensor should initiate an alarm as the result of an intruder walking not more than four consecutive steps, at a rate of one step per second.[1]

The ultrasonic sensor employs sound waves at a frequency higher than the human ear can detect. The waves travel between transmitter and receiver at about 1130 feet per second, at a frequency of about 19.2 kHz. Transmitted sound waves are integrated with other sound waves in the area and are returned to the receiver. Samples of the transmitted and received signals are fed to a microprocessor for comparison. When there is no movement in the protected area, the signals received directly from the transmitter and those reflected from stationary objects remain unchanged. Because signal frequencies reflected from a moving object differ, a comparison of the two patterns causes initiation of an alarm (see Figure 9). This type of sensor is usually limited to indoor applications where types of movements are less varied than those found in typical exterior environments.

Like PIRs, the range of an ultrasonic detector is limited. In larger rooms it may be necessary to use more than one transmitter and receiver. Construction and contents of a room also affect the size of an area that a single unit is capable of filling with sound waves. Empty rooms without structural obstructions attenuate sound waves far less than do rooms with heavy drapes, soft furniture, rugs, etc., which absorb or muffle sound.

An ultrasonic sensor is not influenced by exterior audio noise. Because it reacts only to movement within a protected area, movement beyond

---

[1] *Installation, Classification and Certification of Burglar Alarm Systems;* UL 681, 12 ed.; Underwriters Laboratories, Inc., Northbrook, IL

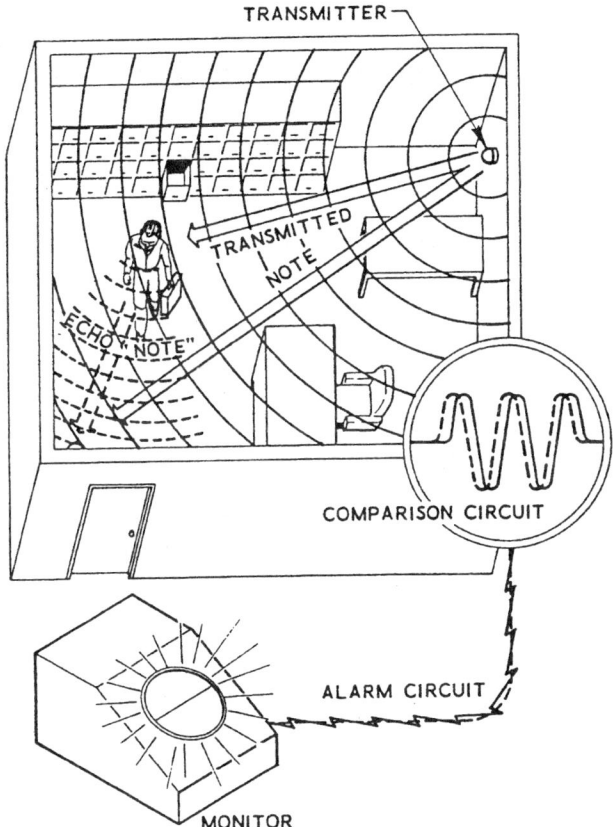

Figure 9. A diagram demonstrating the operations of an ultrasonic sensor.

walls of the protected area will not cause an alarm. Sensors can be adjusted so that movement of air caused by a fire will activate an alarm, but other air currents, such as those from air conditioning, may cause false alarms. As with a PIR, an ultrasonic detector would detect a "lock in" or concealed intruder by that person's movement. It does not alarm if cabinets or containers placed flush against a wall are penetrated through the wall, because there is no movement in the path of the sound waves.

Microwave Sensors

The microwave sensor operates on generally the same principle as the ultrasonic sensor. The difference lies in the type of wave or signal used. The ultrasonic sensor uses a high-frequency sound wave, whereas the microwave sensor utilizes much higher frequency electromagnetic energy. The microwave transmitter sends a signal that is reflected back to an antenna. A comparison circuit compares the transmitted and reflected signals. If there is no movement in the area, the waveform remains constant. When the signal is reflected from a moving object, the waveform changes, initiating an alarm.

Microwave sensors may be utilized in outdoor applications as well as indoors, because they are not generally affected by heavy fog, rain, snow, sleet, air turbulence, drafts, noise, temperature extremes, or atmospheric disturbances. When utilized for area protection, the wave pattern is designed to flood a room or area being protected. When used for perimeter protection, a narrow beam is directed around the area or zone to be protected. An interruption of this beam causes an alarm. Installed in this way, microwave sensors are identifiable by the thick, round disc-like device mounted on a short pole.

A microwave beam can be blocked or diverted by metal objects, so any movement behind metal objects in a room or area will not be detected. The waves do penetrate common nonmetallic construction material, such as plaster walls, and detect movement outside the protected area. False alarms may result if this factor is not considered in planning a microwave installation.

Capacitance Sensors

A capacitance sensor is a large electrical condenser that radiates energy and detects change in the capacitive coupling between an antenna and a ground. In a typical installation, a capacitance sensor wire is connected to an object to be protected, such as a safe or file cabinet. An intruder who touches the object absorbs some of the electrical energy, disturbing the circuit and causing an alarm. Newer technologies, such as PIRs, detect an intruder long before he or she reaches a protected object and have replaced many capacitance-type devices. However, if it is critical to limit the field of detection just to the protected object (safe or file cabinet for example), the capacitance device may still be the preferred protection.

Shock and Vibration Sensors

Utilizing the same technology as glass break shock sensors for object protection, these alarms detect vibrations caused by an intruder's forced entry tools as they attempt to penetrate the wall of a room, enclosure, vault, control panel, safe or filing cabinet. An alarm discriminator may be included in the sensor and adjusted so that vibration outside the protected space or surface is disregarded.

Audio Sensors

Microphones capable of receiving sound in the audible range (from 20 to about about 20,000 Hz) are inconspicuously installed inside an area to be

Alarm Sensors

protected. An amplifier is also part of the installation so that intrusion sounds can be transmitted and activate an alarm. As audio sensors have become more sophisticated, their use has increased in specialized applications. A typical use may be inside a specialty retail store in a busy shopping mall. Central station operators monitoring sensor output can actually listen in on the protected space, recording sounds and voices of intruders, later to be used as evidence. Fences may also be protected by audio sensors that "listen" to the sound of cutting or climbing as it travels through fencing material. Audio sensors may allow for greater discrimination between genuine forced entry or climbing attempts and false alarm sources such as wind or accidental impact.

Photoelectric Sensors

Photoelectric sensors operate based on modification of a light level, or interruption of a light beam protecting an area. In the first application, an ambient light threshold is established in a protected area. When an intrusion alters this light level, the sensor initiates an alarm. A basic concept of beam interruption is that the wavelength of light being transmitted is compatible with receivable frequencies. Most light sources cover essentially all of the visible spectrum and are richer in infrared rays of lower frequency. The receiver operates by receiving light and converting it with a photoelectric cell into electrical energy. This energy is used to establish a reference value from which variations can be measured. Variation in the amount of light received by the photoelectric cell when the light beam is interrupted changes the reference value and causes an alarm.

If the light beam is visible, it can be avoided. For this reason, infrared filters are usually placed over the light source so only invisible light is transmitted. Because photoelectric cells are sensitive to infrared, no modification to the receiver is necessary. Over distances longer than normal 500- to 1000-foot operating ranges, light sources or receiver strength may need to be amplified. To counteract the possibility of circumventing the device by introducing an outside light source such as a flashlight, receiver frequencies may be designed to modulate, thereby being unpredictable.

Photoelectric detection devices can be used both indoors and outdoors. Exterior units are designed with protection against the elements. Some are equipped with self-contained heaters to maintain a reasonably constant operating temperature. Extremes of weather involving snow or heavy fog can affect or even disable exterior photoelectric devices. In a typical application protecting multiple doors such as at a loading dock, a single straight beam of light may be zigzagged using mirrors or multiple beams may be tiered, making avoidance difficult. Each mirror shortens the effective range by about one third.

Other Sensors

Closed-Circuit Televsion. Closed-circuit television (CCTV) use as a motion alarm sensor has grown in recent years. Measurement of a change in the scene under CCTV surveillance is the basis for this technology. The scene is stored and compared to the real-time signal during the next frame. Such systems are capable of detecting and comparing motion on multiple video signals, generating hardware or software alarms. Parameters of motion detection algorithms — such as for the sensitivity of detection — are under user control. While these devices prove useful in many applications, the generation of a video alarm alone cannot determine whether the "intruder" appearing in the image is a "good guy" or a "bad guy." With digitized imagery it is possible to develop TV motion detection even further in that any number of screen "bits" can be selected for change (movement) monitoring. Irregular patterns of a screen display can thus be studied without being affected by status changes elsewhere in the scene being viewed.

Balanced Pressure Sensor. A balanced pressure sensor has been developed for outdoor applications. This sensor consists of liquid-filled hoses spaced about four feet apart. A differential pressure sensor is connected at one end of each hose or tube. Intruders are detected by sensing slight changes in differential pressure on soil as intruders walk or crawl over ground where hoses are buried. When a momentary pressure differential is sensed, an alarm is generated. The hoses can be buried to conform to the contour of the ground along fence lines or across open spaces. Hoses are buried about 12 to 15 inches deep and depend on the elasticity of soil around lines to transmit detection pressure. Anything reducing this elasticity, such as rock or frozen soil, reduces device sensitivity. Because there are two tubes, the pressure sensing can be directional because of a time differential between activating the first and second tubes.

For an intruder to be detected, he must exert pressure almost directly over the line. It is possible to bridge the sensor with planks or stiles if the location of the line is visible in the soil. Extraneous vibration caused by nearby heavy traffic or by trees bending in the wind can cause the sensor to false alarm. Considerable difficulty may be experienced in burying the sensor in rocky, frozen or clay soil.

A better buried detector utilizes coaxial cable whose shielding has been stripped or perforated at measured intervals. This "leaky coax" radiates an electronic signal that creates a standing pattern through the soil and to a height of several feet above the surface. Movement through the signal causes an alarm. Discrimination logic can be used to screen out insignificant movements like blown leaves or small animals.

Chemical Sensors. Chemical sensors designed to take samples of air in a protected area have also been developed. If human effluvia is detected, a meter records the change and triggers an alarm.

Vapor trace analyzers are another form of chemical detector, used chiefly for explosives or inflammables detection but applicable, in theory, to other substances such as drugs. Sample air is drawn into a tube and analytically compared to a retained exemplar of the suspect substance. If the two are identical within a set variation range, an alarm or display is activated.

Alarm Transmission and Control Panels

Methods for transmitting alarm signals, like the technology of devices themselves, are advancing rapidly. No longer must alarm and control points be wired together. RF, microwave, laser, cellular telephones and satellites are but a few of the alternatives now available. Cellular telephone transmission has vastly improved flexibility because the availability of telephone lines is no longer an issue. Cellular transmission also makes redundancy possible in the event phone lines are cut or fail. Digitized cellular can be even more effective because the transmissions are not subject to degradation or garble from atmospheric interference like random RFI or EMI (electromagnetic interference).

Control modules are intended for collecting, processing and reporting data from various detection devices that are part of an intrusion system. System controllers do not detect anything themselves; rather, they collect and process intelligence from the actual sensors. Choosing a controller that offers features you will need and use (while avoiding flashy but unnecessary bells and whistles) is critical to overall functionality of an alarm system. As a marketing tool, manufacturers may offer features like "duress code" that are of little real value and a frequent cause of false alarms. System controls range from simple electronic keypads resembling handheld calculators typical of many residential applications, to sophisticated computer-based equipment found in larger commercial installations.

Combinations Of Sensors

False alarming of sensors is a frequent problem. A former solution was to require input from two or more detectors. The development of sophisticated dual-technology sensors permits a combination device to replace these redundant or multiple devices, although their use remains a viable option. Integrated, redundant devices must react at the same time to cause an alarm. When utilizing redundant sensors, it is necessary that the units be carefully selected to ensure that their response time is approximately the same (see Figure 10).

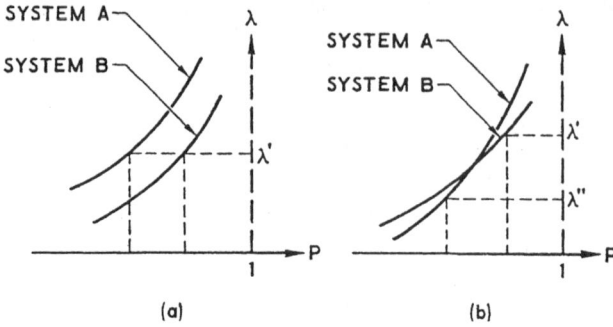

Figure 10. The two curves (a) and (b) illustrate how two sensors might be used in combination so that they compensate for the false alarm tendencies of each other.

SENSORS FOR FIRE DETECTION

As with alarm sensors for security applications, fire alarm systems have also become more "intelligent" and addressable. Modern sensors are intelligent ("smart") detection devices that provide two-way communication and sophisticated graphical user interfaces. Communication software employs protocols that contain both digital and analog signals, allowing each sensor to communicate its individual address, sensor type, and an analog value. System controllers analyze the analog signal to measure the sensitivity of each sensor and to communicate its status. Normal, pre-alarm, alarm and trouble conditions are differentiated. Operators are able to "observe" changing conditions of the sensor and environment at an alarm's point of origin.

Normal status indicates that sensors are operating within design parameters, and that conditions of the environment being monitored present no cause for alarm. A pre-alarm condition may indicate that conditions are favorable for a fire, or that one is underway in its early stages. Pre-alarms often indicate non-fire conditions, such as smoke from welding or soldering, which, if allowed to continue, would activate fire safety systems and cause unnecessary building evacuations. During pre-alarm status, operators can observe data indicating the percent of obscuration (concentration of smoke) at a specific sensor as it changes. If pre-alarm conditions worsen, and an alarm is initiated, operators can determine the precise type and location of the device activated. Activation of more than one device in the same area is generally an indication of a real fire. In the event of an actual fire, an operator's first indication may be activation of a smoke detector. If followed by a fire alarm pull station, another smoke detector, and then a water flow indicator, the system tracks and reports the fire's path and involved area. Trouble status indicates a need for maintenance, ground-faults in wiring, or dirty devices.

Such systems and component devices are referred to as *smart*, or *intelligent*, because of their ability to process data logically using microprocessors and system software. Addressable systems provide information on the status of each device by way of an LCD (liquid crystal), computerized graphic, or other display. Addressable systems operate on a communication loop known as an intelligent loop interface circuit or signaling line circuit (SLC) — commonly referred to as a "loop." Connected to the circuit are sensors, monitors and supervisory devices of various types (smoke, heat, water flow switch, pull station, etc.). Each device is assigned a unique address when the system is programmed. These in turn are connected to a transponder that collects data from devices within a specified area and reports it to head-end equipment at the central station or on-site control center.

Each sensor is scanned continuously by the system, requiring only a fraction of a second to check or pole each device. Users are able to inquire about or observe the status of any device on the system through the graphical interface — typically a personal computer and display terminal. Alarm parameters for each device can be set, adjusted to new thresholds, or deactivated. Devices can be taken offline, or out of the loop with a few keystrokes or clicks of a mouse. In less expensive and less complicated systems, a coded message similar to those used in early intrusion detection systems may be used. Programming options may be more limited. Larger systems can be thought of as a local area computer network (or LAN), with each transponder serving as a small computer, all connected to a system host computer or server.

Stages of Fire

Data suggests that under some circumstances an incipient or smoldering fire can erupt into a full-blown conflagration in under five minutes.[1] Detecting a fire at a very early stage is critically important if it is to be controlled. Selection and application of the proper fire sensors effectively accomplish that objective. Almost invariably it takes a fire longer to develop through the first two stages than the last two. Records indicate that although incipient and smoldering stages can exist for hours or even days, once the flame and heat stages are reached, fires develop at a very rapid rate. Sensors that detect fire or fire precursors as early as possible should be selected because (1) an early alarm permits safe evacuation of a building or facility, (2) the fire can be extinguished while small, and (3) destruction of facilities and material can be prevented.

[1] *NFPA Fire Protection Handbook, 17th ed.,* 1991, Section 10, Chapter 6.

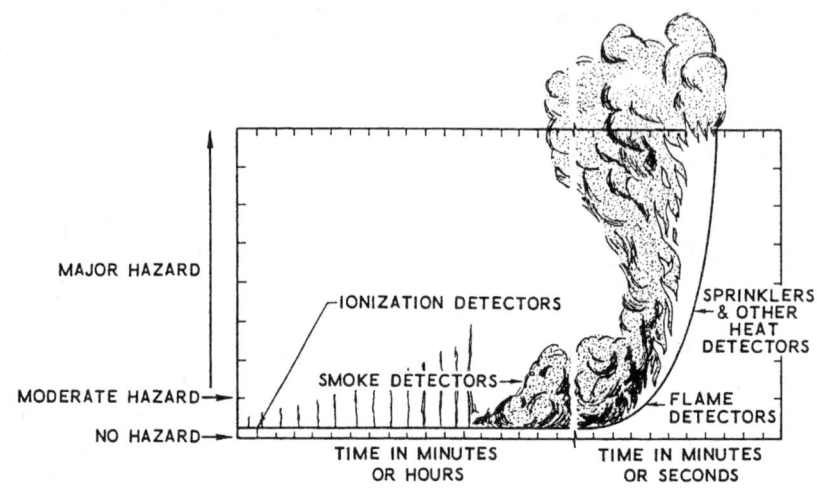

Figure 11. The stages of a fire.

The four stages of fire are:

1. *Incipient stage.* Invisible products of combustion are given off and no visible smoke, flame or appreciable heat is yet present.
2. *Smoldering stage.* Combustion products are now visible as smoke, but flame or appreciable heat is still not present.
3. *Flame stage.* The actual flames of a fire now exist; and while appreciable heat is still not present, it follows almost instantaneously.
4. *Heat stage.* Uncontrolled heat and rapidly expanding air are characteristic of a fully involved fire (see Figure 11).

Sensor Types and Selection

Types of fire sensors include thermal (heat), smoke (photoelectric), flame (ultraviolet), products-of-combustion or ionization, fusible element devices, and water flow indicators. Two types of thermal detectors are available. A fixed-temperature type responds when detection elements reach a predetermined temperature, and a rate-of-rise type responds to an increase in heat at a rate greater than some predetermined value. Some sensors combine both the fixed-temperature and rate-of-rise principles. Still others integrate smoke and thermal detection capabilities.

Smoke sensors are designed to activate an alarm when obscuration in a test chamber is caused by smoke accumulation in the air. Flame detectors alarm when the spectral field reaches the predetermined color, usually in the ultraviolet range. Invisible products-of-combustion detectors respond

Alarm Sensors

to the very early change in ionization (electrical charge in the air) typical of early combustion. Fusible element devices involve frangible materials or those with very low melting temperatures. When the ambient temperature causes the frangible element (often liquid inside glass) to break, or the low melting point link to melt, a contact is opened or closed and an alarm transmitted. Water flow indicators are installed in sprinkler system risers and mains and when water flows in the system at a faster than preset rate (typically ten gallons per minute or more), electrical contacts are closed and an alarm initiated.

The following five factors should be considered when selecting fire sensors:

1. *State and local fire codes.* A careful study must be made to ensure that sensors meet all applicable code requirements. Underwriters Laboratories' or Factory Mutual listing and compliance with NFPA Codes and National Electrical Manufacturers Association standards alone may not suffice.
2. *Local fire authorities.* Consulting fire authorities during the planning of fire detection and alarm systems is an effective way of ensuring that sensors conform to applicable codes. Local fire authorities who help plan changes in local codes can often advise on the best practices in matters such as evacuation plans and connection to municipal systems. Rural areas and municipalities in some states may be governed by state codes. Consult the office of the state fire marshal or equivalent.
3. *Type of occupancy.* Type of occupancy includes typical use, types of material stored or processed, and human occupants. Considering such characteristics of the place to be protected when selecting appropriate detection devices becomes a logical process.
4. *Physical considerations.* Size and layout of a building or facility, whether single or multi-story, and interior configuration determine the types of sensors required and their location.
5. *Number of buildings.* In larger structures and multi-building complexes, sensors of various technologies are typically used, with alarms transmitted to a central station or on-site operations center.

Fixed-Temperature Sensors

The most widely used fixed-temperature sensor employs a thermostat. If the thermostat exceeds a preset limit (e.g., 135°F), an alarm is sounded. The bimetallic strip thermostat is common. It uses differing coefficients of expansion of two eutectic metals. When heated, the resulting bending movement closes electrical contacts. The bimetallic strip operates against a fixed contact, with the distance between the strip and contact determining the detector's temperature rating. A variant of this technique is the snap disc, which is snapped or pulled by the rising temperature. It is more positive in operation than the strip and is generally preferred to the strip sensor. Some thermostats of this type utilize movable stops in the sensor so a wider range of temperatures can detected. Sensors used in Great Britain employ this principle, but in the U.S., most sensors are not adjustable, initiating alarms only at the single temperature for which they are rated.

Other types of fixed temperature sensors use fusible links and quartzoid bulbs. A fusible link holds an electrical switch open until a particular temperature is reached, thereby "fusing" the link and initiating an alarm. The same type of link is often designed to melt and separate at a predetermined temperature. When separation occurs, electrical contacts close, initiating an alarm. The same general technique is used with the quartzoid bulb thermostat. The small glass, fluid-filled bulb is broken when the temperature reaches a set point, closing an electric switch and sounding an alarm. Fusible links are typical design components of sprinkler heads and kitchen exhaust hood systems.

Rate-of-Rise Sensors

The rate-of-rise sensor initiates an alarm when the rate of temperature increase exceeds a preset number of degrees per minute — 15° per minute is common. This type of sensor is a more efficient detector than the fixed-temperature sensor for a number of reasons. It operates more rapidly, and is effective over a broader range of ambient temperatures, making it useful in low-temperature as well as high-temperature areas. In addition, rapid recycling keeps it available for continued service, and it tolerates slow rises in ambient temperature without alarming. The usual sensor is an air- or inert gas-filled copper tube in which the air expansion caused by rising temperature causes contacts to close. There are two disadvantages to this type of sensor: (1) its susceptibility to false alarms when a rapid increase in ambient temperature occurs due to normal phenomena not associated with combustion, and (2) it may fail to initiate an alarm if a fire evolves slowly. Detectors are available that integrate rate-of-rise technology with the reliability of a fixed-temperature sensor.

Smoke or Combustion Product Sensors

Fires that smolder for long periods, then quickly burst into flame may overcome fixed-temperature or rate-of-rise sensors. A smoke sensor gives an early warning that fire is present, as it is sensitive to fires that start by generating little heat.

Smoke detectors are of either the photoelectric or ionization type. In a photoelectric sensor, a combined sender and receiver is used. When a

Alarm Sensors

change in current between the two results from smoke partially obscuring the photoelectric beam (measured in percent of obscuration per foot), an alarm is sounded. Ionization detectors identify a fire in its incipient stage before any smoke is visible. It operates on the principle that air is made conductive by means of alpha particles emitted from a minute radioactive source, in this case a fire. The alpha particles ionize the air molecules into positive and negative ions. When a voltage is applied across an ionization chamber, a minute electrical current is caused to flow. When invisible products of combustion (usually generated in advance of any visible evidence of fire) enter the chamber, they also become ionized. Due to their relatively large size, they move more slowly, thereby reducing current flow.

The current that exists is extremely small, and in order to complete an alarm circuit, it must be amplified. This is achieved using dual unipolar chambers. With the outer chamber open to the air and the inner chamber virtually sealed, any reduction of current in the outer chamber increases the voltage at the trigger electrode, causing it to activate relays that initiate an alarm (see Figure 12). P-O-C (product of combustion) detectors often react more quickly than other types, including smoke detectors, particularly if they are near the area of the fire.

The ionization sensor is of particular value for installation in concealed spaces where a fire might smolder for a long period. It is ideal for the protection of electrical equipment in control rooms, switch gear rooms and generator areas. Computer systems can best be protected by this type of sensor because an immediate alarm makes possible an early attack on the fire before serious damage occurs. Time is critical in a computer fire because sustained temperature in excess of 140°F can cause malfunction of components and data corruption or destruction.

Water Flow Indicators

Water flow valves in sprinkler systems have been used for many years to signal the activation of sprinklers due to fire or malfunction. Early types of alarm check valves were unreliable. Also, such valves were not responsive to small flows of water. Improvement has mainly been in mechanical and electrical design rather than operating principle. Some of the earliest devices, made before 1890, used the movement of a water clapper to actuate an electric switch. Grooved check valve seats and pilot valves to admit water to water-motor gongs were early developments. A typical water flow indicator is the paddle or vane type.

It consists of a movable, flexible vane of thin metal or plastic inserted through a circular opening in the wall of a sprinkler supply pipe and extending into the waterway. The vane is deflected by any movement of water flowing to opened sprinklers. Motion of the vane operates an electric

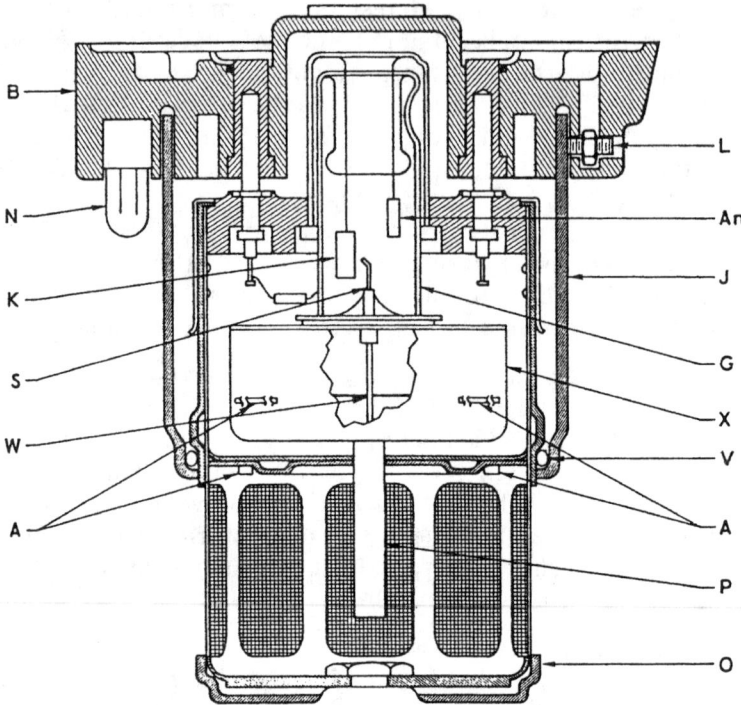

Figure 12. An ionization sensor: A — alpha source; An — anode; B — detector base; G — gas discharge tube; J — locking shell; K — cathode; L — locking screw; N — neon lamp; O — out chamber; P — control pin; S — starter electrode; V — O ring; W — inner chamber electrode; X — inner chamber.

switch. A mechanical, pneumatic or electrical time delay feature in the detector prevents false alarms due to transient flow caused by fluctuating water pressures (see Figure 13).

Emerging Technology

As of early 1996, an emerging fire detection technology was VESDA — for Very Early Smoke Detection Apparatus. VESDA uses pneumatic tubing to draw in air samples that are analyzed for oxygen content and minute components of combustion with the precision of scientific laboratory equipment. Presumably, this technology will be particularly suitable for clean-room environments, where any component of combustion could destroy sensitive production materials. Vapor detection for fire safety applications is also in early developmental stages, but not yet in production.

Alarm Sensors

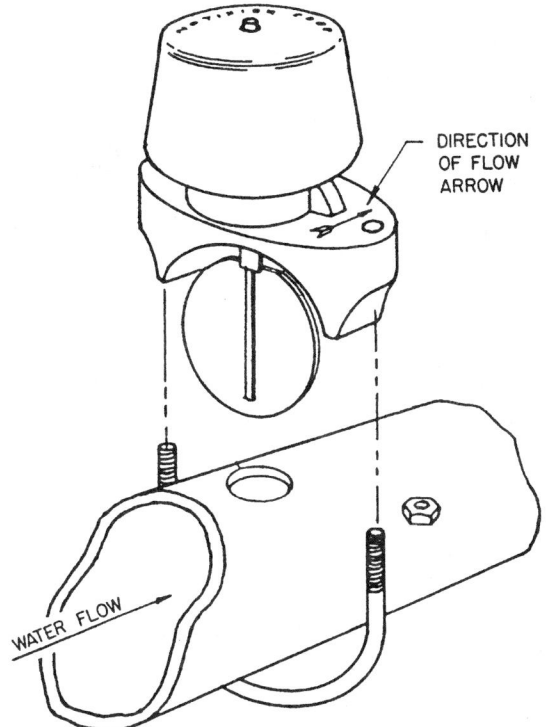

Figure 13. A paddle or vane type water flow sensor.

Selected Bibliography

Books

Barnard, Robert L.; *Intrusion Detection Systems;* 1988; Butterworth Publishers, Stoneham, MA.

Capel, Vivian; *Security Systems and Intruder Alarms;* 1989; Butterworth-Heinemann Publishing; Stoneham, MA.

Cumming, Neil; *Security: A Guide to Security System Design and Equipment;* 1992; Butterworth-Heinemann, Woburn, MA.

Fire Protection Handbook, 17th ed.; 1991; National Fire Protection Association, Quincy, MA.

Healy, Richard J.; *Design for Security;* 1983; John Wiley & Sons, New York; see especially Chapter 4.

Honey, Gerard; 1996; *Electronic Protection and Security Systems — A Handbook for Installers and Users;* Butterworth-Heinemann, Woburn, MA.

Sanger, John; 1988; *Basic Alarm Electronics;* Butterworth Publishers, Stoneham, MA.

Sentrol, Inc.; *GlassBreak University;* 1995; videotape; Tualatin, OR.

Sentrol, Inc.; *PIR University;* 1995; videotape; Tualatin, OR.

Trimmer, H. William; *Understanding and Servicing Alarm Systems;* 1990; Butterworth Publishers, Stoneham, MA.

Walker, Philip; *Electronic Security Systems: Better Ways to Crime Prevention;* 1988; Butterworth Publishers, Stoneham, MA.

ASSET PROTECTION AND SECURITY MANAGEMENT HANDBOOK

Periodicals

Security Management; American Society for Industrial Security, Arlington, VA.
— Griffiths, Barry D.; Detecting Intrusion with Fiber Optics; July 1992.
— Ohlhausen, Peter E.; Sandia: Putting Sensors to the Test; September 1988.
— Sentell, Ronald J.; On the Line with Data Transmission; November 1992.
— Skiffington, Barbara; Catching Intruders in a Neural Net; February 1994.
— Thomas, Ronald C.; Technology Meets the Alarm Industry; September 1992.
— Trimble, Mike; Sensors Communicate for Better Protection; April 1987.
— Vitch, Martin L.; The Importance of IDS Inspection; March 1993.
— Vitch, Martin L.; Sensing Your Way to Security; July 1992.

APPENDIX A
FEDERAL SPECIFICATION COMPONENTS FOR INTERIOR ALARM SYSTEMS

W-A-450C/GEN
August 28, 1990
SUPERSEDING
Int. Fed. Spec. W-A-00450B
January 16, 1974

This specification is approved by the Commissioner, Federal Supply Service, General Services Administration, for the use of all Federal agencies.

1. SCOPE AND CLASSIFICATION

1.1 SCOPE. This specification covers intrusion detection equipment which when deployed as an intrusion detection system, is designed to include, but not be limited to detection of intrusions and to assist in protection of national security information, sensitive information and equipment, high dollar items, and weapons. The intrusion detection equipment, when selectively assembled, provides interior detection capabilities specifically designed for security application.

1.2 CLASSIFICATION

1.2.1 UNITS AND TYPES. Intrusion detection system components shall consist of at least one of the following units:

Unit 1 — Detector (see 1.2.2 and 3.5)

Unit 2 — Annunciator (see 3.6 through 3.6.4)

Unit 3 — Signaling Technology (see 1.2.3 and 3.7)

Unit 4 — Control Unit (see 3.8)

1.2.2 DETECTORS (UNIT 1). Detectors furnished under this specification shall be one of the following types:

Alarm Sensors

Type I — Balanced Magnetic Switch

Type II — Foil

Type III — Breakwire

Type IV — Light Threshold Motion Detection

Type V — Infrared Beambreak Detector

Type VI — Passive Infrared (PIR) Detector

Type VII — Vibration Detector

Type VIII — Proximity Detector

Type IX — Ultrasonic Motion Detector

Type X — Microwave Motion Detector

Type XI — Pressure Mat Detector

Type XII — Closed Circuit Television (CCTV) Motion Detector

Type XIII — Glass Breakage Detector

Type XIV — Flexible Cable Detector

Type XV — Infrasonic

Type XVI — Sound Discriminator (Sonic)

1.2.3 **CIRCUIT SUPERVISION.** The supervised alarm transmission means shall be of the classes specified in 3.7 and 3.7.1.

2. APPLICABLE DOCUMENTS

2.1 **GOVERNMENT PUBLICATIONS.** The issues of the following documents, in effect on the date of invitation for bids or solicitation for offers, form a part of this specification to the extent specified herein.

FEDERAL SPECIFICATIONS:

PPP-B-601 — Boxes, Wood, Crated-Plywood

FEDERAL STANDARDS:

Fed. Std. No. 123 — Marking for Domestic Shipment (Civil Agencies).

(Activities outside the Federal Government may obtain copies of the Federal Specifications, Standards and Handbooks as outlined under General Information in the Index of Federal Specifications and Standards and at the prices indicated in the Index. The Index, which includes cumulative monthly supplements as issued, is for sale on a subscription basis by the Superintendent of Documents, U.S. Government Printing Office, Washington, D.C. 20402.)

(Single copies of the specification and other Federal Specifications required by activities outside the Federal Government for bidding purposes are available without charge from Business Service Centers at the General Services Administration Regional Offices in Boston, New York, Washington, D.C., Atlanta, Chicago, Kansas City, MO, Fort Worth, Denver, San Francisco, Los Angeles, and Seattle, WA.)

(Federal Government activities may obtain copies of Federal Specifications, Standards, and Handbooks and the Index of Federal Specifications and Standards from established distribution points in the agencies.)

MILITARY STANDARDS:

MIL-STD-105 Sampling Procedures and Tables for Inspection by Attributes

MIL-STD-129 Marking for Shipment and Storage

MIL-STD-461 Electromagnetic Emission and Susceptibility Requirements for the Control of Electromagnetic Interference

MIL-STD-462 Electromagnetic Interference Characteristics, Measurements of

MIL-STD-810 Environmental Test Methods and Engineering Guidelines

(Copies of military Specifications and Standards required by contractors in connection with specification procurement functions should be obtained from the procuring activity or as directed by the contracting officer.)

2.2 **OTHER PUBLICATIONS.** The following documents form a part of this specification to the extent specified herein. Unless a specific issue is identified, the issue in effect on date of invitation for bids or request for proposal shall apply.

AMERICAN SOCIETY FOR TESTING AND MATERIALS.

ASTM D3951 Standard Practices for Commercial Packaging.

(Application for copies should be addressed to the American Society for Testing and Material, 1916 Race St., Philadelphia, PA 19103.)

3. **REQUIREMENTS**

3.1 **GENERAL.** The annunciator units, control units, and the line supervision under this specification shall be products that meet

Alarm Sensors

the minimum specifications required herein and that have been tested and passed the tests specified herein. The detector units offered under this specification shall be units which are qualified for listing on the applicable qualified products list.

3.2 **PARTS AND MATERIALS.** Parts and materials for components shall be as specified herein. Those not specified shall be equivalent to and interchangeable with the corresponding parts, materials or processes in the manufacturer's normal commercial product and shall be subject to all provisions of this specification. Normal commercial product shall be interpreted to mean an end item acceptable under this specification.

3.2.1 **CUSTOM TOOLS.** Any custom tools required for the adjustment or maintenance of products specified in this specification shall be provided with each unit shipped.

3.3 **EQUIPMENT ENCLOSURES.** All enclosures for equipment supplied under this specification shall be protected against tampering. Enclosures shall be equipped with tamper switches or triggering mechanisms electrically compatible with the alarm system. Such tamper switches or trigger mechanisms shall be capable of being disabled when the enclosure is opened for service. Tamper switches shall be armed automatically when the enclosure is reclosed. Internal wiring of equipment shall be such that the tamper switches and triggering mechanisms are not bypassed though the detector itself is operating in the "ACCESS" mode. All controls that affect the sensitivity of the units shall be located inside the tamper-resistant enclosure. If the contract specifies that the enclosures be metal they shall be constructed of sheet steel and shall be not less than No. 16 U.S. Standard Gauge. Enclosures shall not have prepunched knockouts. Where doors are mounted on hinges with exposed pins, the hinges shall be tack welded to prevent easy removal. The tamper switches shall be located so that activation occurs when the door or cover is moved as little as 5 mm (0.2 inches) from its normally closed position (unless otherwise specified.) Movable covers and doors shall have flange edges at least 5 mm (0.2 inches) in width and shall be equipped with high security locks at the latch edge.

3.4 **ELECTRONIC COMPONENTS.** To the extent practical all electronic components shall be the solid-state type.

3.5 **DETECTORS.** All detectors shall initiate an alarm signal under any of the following conditions: (1) When sensing a stimulus or condition for which it was designed to react; (2) primary power fails and secondary power does not take over properly; (3) a tamper switch or triggering mechanism is activated. Terminals shall be located within the detector enclosure and shall be readily accessible to permit wiring connections to be made.

3.6 **ANNUNCIATOR UNITS.** Annunciator units shall be so designed that when connected with the ancillaries into a detection circuit they provide the means to remotely monitor the condition and control the operation of the detection circuit. A tamper alarm shall be generated when the line between the annunciator and the detector is opened, shorted, or grounded. Annunciator units shall be electrically compatible with the detector and circuit supervision equipment described herein and shall be of modular design capable of being installed with other annunciators in a rack, console, or cabinet. When specified (see 6.2), individual annunciator units shall be furnished in appropriate enclosures. To the extent practicable, equipment related to the annunciator such as standby-battery, power supply, battery charging equipment, audible alarm, and circuit supervisor functions, shall be contained in the same enclosure.

3.6.1 **ANNUNCIATOR ACCESS/SECURE AND RESET SWITCHES.** The annunciator panel may have an access/secure switch and shall have an alarm resets switch. An alarm shall create a lock-on condition to be displayed by both audible and visual means, which shall require a manual restoration and controls shall be provided to reset the system. A received alarm shall cause the visual device to operate in a pulsing or flashing mode, or other visual indication. The annunciator shall have a means of silencing the audible signal from a particular zone during prolonged alarm conditions. However, the visible signal shall remain illuminated on the annunciator panel or CRT display until the system is restored to normal operation, except that the visual signal shall be changed from pulsing/flashing to a steady mode. CRT displays will continue to show an alarm until all areas are secured. The silencing control shall be so connected that the audible alarm signal shall be activated upon receipt of an alarm from another zone. When a detection circuit is conditioned for authorized entry into the protected area (Access Mode), annunciators shall continue to indicate alarms if circuit supervision limits are exceeded or any tamper switches are disturbed.

3.6.2 **ANNUNCIATOR READOUT.** The annunciator shall be equipped with a readout of the type specified in 3.6.2.1 or of the type specified in 3.6.2.2.

3.6.2.1 **ELECTRONIC TYPE.** This type of readout shall have either a Cathode Ray Tube (CRT) (MTBF of 40,000 hours or greater), or a light

Alarm Sensors

emitting diode (LED) (MTBF of 50,000 hours or greater) or liquid-crystal display (LCD) type of display and a printer, if used, for recording alarm conditions. The display, as a minimum, shall display any location that has a change of status and show the present status of that location. The printer, if used, shall print out a location that has a change of status, the present status of that location, and the date and time of day the change occurred.

3.6.2.2 COLORED SIGNAL LIGHTS TYPE. This type shall indicate, by duplicate colored signal lights (MTBF of 20,000 hours of greater), the following conditions:

(1) That the detector(s) and circuits are in the secure condition (green light);
(2) That a detector in the protected area is in an alarm condition, or that circuit supervisor limits have been exceeded. If the detector provides an indication of component failure, this also should be annunciated (red lights);
(3) That the system is operating in an access condition (yellow amber lights);
(4) That the detector(s) in the protected area is operating on standby power (white lights).

In addition to the visual signal lights, an audible signal shall be annunciated whenever the system changes from one condition to another. However, the audible signaling device need not be part of each individual module.

3.6.3 ANNUNCIATOR CONSTRUCTION. Individual annunciator modules of a given manufacturer shall be interchangeable to facilitate maintenance. Plug and sockets shall be used to the extent possible. All parts of the annunciator shall be easily identified and readily accessible to authorized maintenance personnel. All controls required for normal operation shall be permanently and conspicuously marked. All controls not required for operation of the system shall not be readily accessible to the operator when the equipment is installed in a rack or console.

3.6.4 ANNUNCIATOR CONNECTIONS. The annunciator shall be provided with terminals for all required external connections.

3.7 CIRCUIT SUPERVISION UNITS. The circuit supervisors shall provide security to the communication link between the detector and the annunciator. The circuit supervisors shall be classed according to relative security as specified herein.

3.7.1 LINE SUPERVISION CLASSES. The circuit supervisors shall provide security to the communication link between the individual control units in the protected areas and the monitor display. The level of security provided to the data information on the communication lines between the protected areas and the monitor are designated as follows:

Class A — Compromise would require the application of national level computer analysis before the attempt to attack. A collection of encrypted data from the communication lines to be compromised must be available for the analysis. Special equipment or software is necessary and it would require professional engineering skills and experience to implement.

Class B — Compromise would require the use of a microprocessor and prior computer analysis. The compromise will require significant competence of the technical personnel and working samples of the equipment.

Class C — Compromise would require the use of special logic circuitry, without requiring the use of prior computer analysis.

Class D — Compromise would require the use of active analog circuitry including transistors and tape recorders.

Class E — Compromise would require the application of a combination of passive or active components such as filters and phase shifters.

Class F — Compromise would require only the insertion of a single passive or active component.

3.8 **ACCESS CONTROL UNITS.** The premises control unit shall be so designed that when operated it permits access to a protected area without activating an alarm signal. The unit shall consist of circuitry installed in a metal enclosure, the cover of which shall contain a two or more position, key-operated switch. The positions shall be labeled ACCESS and SECURE plus whatever other labels are required to denote the functions designed into the unit submitted for qualification. Turning the switch from SECURE to ACCESS shall alter the signal(s) to the annunciator and shall deactivate the detection device; however, the tamper switches shall continue to be monitored. Turning the switch from ACCESS to SECURE shall alter the signal(s) to the annunciator and shall activate the detection device to enable monitoring of alarm and tamper signals.

3.9 **PRIMARY POWER REQUIREMENTS.** The alarm systems shall operate on 115 or 220 volts (±10%), as specified, and shall operate on either 50 or 60 Hz (±5%) or as specified (see 6.2).

Alarm Sensors

3.9.1 **STANDBY BATTERY.** A standby-battery source for use in the event the primary power source fails shall be provided. The standby-battery power source, when fully charged, shall be capable of maintaining full operation of the alarm system for not less than four (4) continuous hours at temperatures from minus 30°C (−22°F) to plus 49°C (+120°F). Switch-over to battery power shall be instantaneous and automatic upon failure or restoration of the primary power source and shall not create alarms on annunciator modules. However, loss of primary power shall be noted by separate indication.

3.9.2 **BATTERIES.** Batteries shall be float charged and so arranged that they are fully charged at all times when primary power is available. Charger shall be of ample capacity to recharge the batteries from a fully discharged state to not less than 85% of capacity within 24 hours. Controls shall provide monitoring to preclude overcharging, or the circuit and battery combination shall intrinsically provide the feature.

3.9.3 **VENTILATION.** Power supplies shall be vented or otherwise protected against excessive heat.

3.10 **IDENTIFICATION MARKINGS.** Each major component furnished under contract or order shall have the manufacturer's name and address, unit model and serial number, year manufactured, and the symbol, W-A-450, indented or embossed on a metal plate that shall be firmly affixed in such a place to identify the unit without removing the cover.

3.11 **TECHNICAL MANUALS AND OPERATOR INSTRUCTIONS.** Manufacturer's installation recommendations/instructions, applications guides, equipment limitations, specifications for operation as listed in section 3, technical manuals, and operator and maintenance instructions, shall be complete and comprehensive and delivered with the equipment, as specified (see 6.2). The manual shall include schematics and wiring diagrams for all components and complete electrical values and ratings as well as a section containing the theory of operation of all portions of the total system, i.e., specific technical descriptions relating to respective circuit schematics. All production run changes or component modifications, and revisions to technical information, shall be reported to the recipient installation security office for 36 months following date of system acceptance by that security office.

3.12 **WORKMANSHIP.** All components shall be manufactured and finished in such a manner as to meet specification requirements. Circuit wiring shall be neat with good electrical connections that

3.13 **SPARE PARTS.** Spare parts, as required by the procuring activity, shall be furnished as specified (see 6.2).

3.14 **ELECTROMAGNETIC RADIATION INTERFERENCE.** Alarm system units shall be designed to minimize susceptibility to external electromagnetic fields and to minimize adverse effects on electronic equipment in the unit's vicinity, in accordance with the latest revision of MIL-STD-461 and MIL-STD-462. Equipment shall comply with all relevant FCC regulations pertaining to licensed or unlicensed transmitters, as appropriate.

3.15 **LIGHTNING PROTECTION.** The annunciator and ancillary devices shall be protected against lightning-induced power surges that would damage the equipment. The protection device shall be of unit construction and shall not include fusible elements that will require replacement.

4. **QUALITY ASSURANCE PROVISIONS**

4.1 **INSPECTION RESPONSIBILITY.** Except as otherwise specified herein, the supplier is responsible for the performance of all inspection requirements as specified herein. Except as otherwise specified, the supplier may use his own or any other inspection facility or services acceptable to the Government. Inspection records of the examinations and tests shall be maintained by the manufacturer for at least one year, and shall be available for Government inspection. The Government reserves the right to perform any of the inspections set forth in this specification where such inspections are deemed necessary to assure that supplies and services conform to prescribed requirements.

4.2 **COMPONENTS AND MATERIAL INSPECTION.** In accordance with 4.1, the supplier is responsible for insuring that components and material used are manufactured, tested, and inspected in accordance with the requirements of referenced subsidiary specifications and standards to the extent specified, or if none, in accordance with this specification.

4.3 **INSPECTION FOR ACCEPTANCE.** Units to be offered for acceptance on the GSA schedule may be inspected by a Government Inspector at any time during manufacturing processes to assure that the units function as intended, that parts and material are complete and as specified, that parts and components are properly located, that mechanical and electrical connections are

Alarm Sensors

secure, that soldered connections provide good electrical conductivity, that component enclosures are protected against tampering, and that all workmanship details are of good quality. When specified (see 6.2), acceptance inspection shall be performed at the destination after equipment is installed and ready for use.

4.3.1 TESTING FOR ACCEPTANCE. To ensure continued compliance with specification requirements relating to operation performance, the Government reserves the right to purchase from the manufacturer's regular production samples of alarm system components for testing. The testing shall be performed by a facility designated by the Government and shall be at no cost to the manufacturer. Failure to meet testing requirements shall provide reason to suspend GSA listing of the manufacturer's product. Once the testing requirements have again been successfully met as per this document, the manufacturer must resubmit an application to be placed on the GSA schedule again.

4.4 INSPECTION OF PREPARATION FOR DELIVERY. An inspection of preparation for delivery shall be made in accordance with ASTM D3951.

4.5 QUALIFICATION. In accordance with 3.1, products submitted for qualification shall be inspected for workmanship as specified in 4.3 and subjected to the tests in the individual product specifications. Failure to meet requirements for GSA listing shall be considered as failure to meet requirements for GSA listing.

4.5.1 TESTING AGENCY. Qualification testing shall be performed by an independent laboratory of the manufacturer's choice, at his expense. Requests for authorization to submit products for qualification testing shall be in accordance with Management Regulation (FPMR) 101-29.

4.5.2 TEST COSTS. All costs entailed in the qualification testing of proposed products shall be borne by the supplier.

4.5.3 TEST SAMPLES. The samples submitted for qualification testing shall consist of all components required by this specification and individual product specifications, necessary for complete working unit of the type the supplier proposes to furnish. Included with the product shall be a complete set of technical manuals, wiring diagrams and schematics for use during testing.

5. PREPARATION FOR DELIVERY

5.1 PRESERVATION, PACKAGING, PACKING, AND MARKING. Preservation, packaging, packing, and marking shall be in accordance with ASTM D3951. The level of preservation and packaging shall be A or C, and the level of packing shall be A, B, or C, as specified (see 6.2).

5.2 **CIVIL AGENCY MARKING.** In addition to any special marking (see 6.2) required by the contract or order, the interior packages and shipping container shall be marked in accordance with Fed. Std. No. 123.

6. **NOTES**

6.1 **INTENDED USE.** Intrusion detection systems constructed with components qualified under this specification are intended to notify protection personnel (e.g., response force) whose responsibility is the protection of areas requiring special security measures. Properly assembled systems are highly resistant to neutralization or compromise. Guidance in selecting a particular item covered by this specification for a particular situation is not intended and is beyond the scope of this document.

6.2 **QUALIFICATION.** With respect to products requiring qualification, awards will be made only for products which are, at the time set for opening of bids, qualified for inclusion in the applicable qualified products list whether or not such products have actually been so listed by that date. The attention of the supplier is called to this requirement, and manufacturers are urged to arrange to have the product they propose to offer to the Federal Government tested for qualification in order that they may be eligible to be awarded contracts or orders for the products covered by this specification. The activity responsible for the qualified products list is the General Services Administration, Federal Supply Service, Furniture Commodity Center, Engineering Division, Washington, D.C. 20406, and information pertaining to qualification of products may be obtained from that activity.

6.3 **ORDERING DATA.** Purchaser should exercise any desired options permitted herein and include the following information in procurement documents:

(a) Title, symbol and date of this specification
(b) Type of detector unit and number required (see 1.2.2)
(c) Number of annunciators required (see 1.2.1)
(d) Type of annunciator readout required (see 3.6.2)
(e) Enclosure for single annunciator required (see 3.6)
(f) Class of circuit supervision unit required (see 1.2.3 and 3.7)
(g) Number of premise controls desired (see 3.6)
(h) Power requirements (see 3.9)

Alarm Sensors

(i) Spare parts required (see 3.3)
(j) Destination inspection required (see 4.3)
(k) Level of packaging and packing required (see 5.1)
(l) Whether special marking required (see 5.1.1)

6
Systems Considerations

INTRODUCTION

Individual sensors do not provide security protection unless they are integrated into a system that transmits the individual signals to one or more monitoring locations. When sensors are configured into a meaningful and functional array, it is called *sensor integration* and is the basic task of security system design. Systems that maximize the common control of a variety of sensors and field devices are called *integrated systems*.

Sensors and their array are one part of a protection system. Two other elements, software and personnel, are necessary to complete it. But a good system greatly depends upon the suitability and quality of its sensors. These, in turn, are optimally useful only if they are properly integrated.

ALARM TERMINATION

Proper termination of alarms ensures response to signals. There are four methods of alarm terminations: (1) *local*, (2) *central station*, (3) *direct connection* (to police or fire), and (4) *proprietary* termination in a business or industrial facility. These methods can be used individually or in combination.

Local Alarm Termination

Local alarm termination utilizes a sound-generating device — usually a bell, horn or klaxon on the exterior wall of the protected area — to call attention to a violation.[1] The installation can be designed so that lights are turned on both inside and outside the protected area, and other presumed deterrents are activated. In this type of installation, it is anticipated that the police hear an alarm, or that a passerby, hearing the alarm, alerts the police. However, there is a tendency for the average person to disregard such an alarm; and in a remote area, no one may be near enough to hear the alarm signal. This type of termination is inexpensive to install, but is relatively easy to defeat because of its simplicity. Some local sounders rely on battery power that requires frequent testing and increases maintenance costs. It is recommended that all such devices be connected to a power

---

[1] Underwriters Laboratories Standard 609, Local Burglar Alarm Units and Systems.

supply supported by both main power and short-term battery backup to cover main power blackouts and brownouts.

One positive feature to an alarm is that an intruder knows his entry has been detected, and therefore he might leave immediately without causing any damage. However, this does not always occur. Reports indicate that the police usually do not respond immediately to local alarms because of their heavy workload and shortage of personnel. An experienced intruder might be aware of this factor and might:

1. Estimate the amount of time available before a police response could be expected.
2. Disregard the sound of the alarm.
3. Quickly accomplish the mission.
4. Escape before the police arrive. There is little chance that police will apprehend a criminal on the scene unless a response occurs within a few minutes of the crime or attempt.

Local alarm sounders may be used simply to embarrass or frighten a possible perpetrator. For example, horns can be installed on doors leading to stair towers in order to discourage usage where the door, nevertheless, must remain unlocked for emergency egress.

Local alarm advantages and disadvantages are summarized as follows:

Table 1. Advantages and disadvantages of local alarms.

Advantages	Disadvantages
Psychological deterrent — intruder knows entry has been detected	Easy to defeat
	Intruder might not be apprehended
Damage will be minimized	Intruder may disregard alarm because of normal response delay
Cheap to install	May be expensive to maintain

Local alarms are inadequate if any real value is exposed.

Central Station Termination

Alarm termination at a commercial central alarm station is sometimes referred to as a silent alarm installation because there is usually no signal at the protected location. Intruders may not know they have been detected. In some applications, however, a local alarm may also be combined with this application so that the local signal deters intruders before they have an opportunity to penetrate. In this situation, the central station feature ensures that, even if the attackers are deterred by the local alarm, a timely response to the facility occurs to check for possible damage. The response also secures any entries that might have been breached.[1]

---

[1] Underwriters Laboratories Standard 611, Central Station Burglar Alarm Unit and Systems.

Protected premises with such an installation are normally connected by dedicated telephone lines to the central station that is staffed continuously. Radio transmissions to the central station are also permitted,[1] as are digital communicators utilizing the telephone-switched network.[2]

A company offering central station service ordinarily makes a one-time charge for installation and charges a monthly fee that includes the costs of monitoring, leased lines and maintenance of equipment. When an alarm signal is received at the central station, a present employee is responsible for dispatching a "runner" and/or calling the police. Some alarm companies offer the additional service of patrolling guards who check the protected areas periodically.[3] In case of an alarm, both the police and the guards patrolling the general area are alerted, and both respond to the alarm.

The central station may receive signals from protected premises by one of four methods:

1. *Direct wire:* a dedicated enunciation device or switchboard at the station for that single subscriber.
2. *Common transmitter:* serves multiple subscribers but involves a higher level of vulnerability because failure or compromise of the common transmitter imperils all users and may leave all of them without alarm protection, at least temporarily.
3. *Multiplex circuits:* transmit simultaneous or sequential signals over a common communication channel with a means for positively identifying each signal.
4. *Digital communicator:* provides for the connection of protected premises to the central station via the telephone-switched network. Communicators must use either (a) two switchable telephone lines, or (b) one line that sends a signal at least once every 24 hours.

Direct wire, common transmitters and multiplexed systems may utilize leased telephone lines, microwave or radio frequencies, or a combination.

Reliability. When considering this type of installation, examine the reliability of a central station company. A subscriber trusts all the assets of the protected facility to the personnel operating the central station. The careless handling of an alarm signal or the failure of a sensor or communication line might result in great damage.

This is not an academic problem, for there have been recorded instances of serious losses caused by equipment malfunction or by lack of the correct response to an alarm. Because most central station alarm con-

---

[1] Underwriters Laboratories Standard 611, Central Station Burglar Alarm Unit and Systems.
[2] Ibid.
[3] U/L 611 requires a central station operator to maintain and dispatch alarm investigators (runners) for all alarms. For an installation to be certified under U/L 611, the station operator must comply with this requirement.

tracts contain limitation of liability clauses, an alarm company is generally not liable for damages, irrespective of the size of the client's loss resulting from an alarm installation failure (except for a nominal amount indicated in the limitation). Nor will the central station be liable beyond the liquidated damages provision for simple negligence in failing to properly respond to an alarm actually received. The exception is if the alarm company is grossly negligent, which is usually difficult to prove.

Carefully select a central station service company, particularly if the service includes alarm investigators assigned to check a protected facility since they must have keys to gain access. That access must be recognized as a potential risk.

Although a central station alarm termination makes a significant contribution to the protection of an enterprise, inherent risks require some control on the performance of the service organization. For example, periodically checking the quality of service and the adequacy of personnel training ensures that effective protection is actually being received.

Direct Police or Fire Department Termination

Some jurisdictions allow alarms to be terminated at police or fire headquarters. In these cases, the municipal dispatcher or another individual monitors alarm signals received and initiates a response. As with the central station termination, a leased telephone line is usually used to transmit signals between the protected area and the facility receiving the alarm. Even if there is no charge for this service by the police or fire department, they may impose heavy fines for responding to false alarms. In some instances, false alarms happen too often for monitoring and response services. Central station companies that do not have facilities in some areas will often provide "direct connect" police or fire service if permitted by local authorities.

The owner of the enterprise being protected must arrange for a vendor to install the necessary equipment, which is either purchased or leased. If leased, the same costs outlined in the discussion of the central station installation apply, with the exception of the fee for monitoring alarms at the central location. If the equipment is purchased, the owner of the enterprise must arrange for installation, maintenance and for the leased telephone line.

Instead of leased lines, automatic digital dialers are now widely utilized to connect a protected area with a police or fire department headquarters. When a sensor is activated, the dialer automatically dials the number of the termination headquarters. The use of this type of device is attractive from a cost standpoint, for it eliminates the monthly leased line charge. A problem here is that when not transmitting an alarm, there is no active telephone connection or circuit to the monitoring site. Loss of the alarm unit at the protected premises would not be apparent to the monitoring site.

One partial solution is periodic test transmissions, even when there is no alarm condition. Some police agencies object to this type of arrangement because of the increased signal traffic. Note the U/L requirement, noted earlier, for 24-hour testing of single line digital communicators.

A large number of automatic dialers have been marketed, some by unreliable manufacturers and sold by unethical representatives. Many were not well designed and the quality control was so poor they did not operate properly. Some initiated an excessive number of false alarms. Police officials in some jurisdictions tend to view automatic dialers with suspicion and some local ordinances prohibit their use. In many communities, the dialer must dial a special number so as not to tie up main police lines with false alarms.

Although reputable manufacturers offer automatic dialers, dedicated lines are more reliable for a number of reasons — in addition to the attack vulnerability. First, if it is not possible to provide line security because dialers use the regular telephone switch network. Second, if the number being dialed (to signal a penetration) is busy, the signal may not get through, although later models will redial for a set period or number of tries. Also, if an extension telephone connected to the dialer line is being used, or if the phone is off the hook, an alarm signal will not go through. Likewise, a simultaneous incoming call may block the dialer line. Finally, if a switch network error rings an incorrect number and it picks up, the dialer will not repeat and the alarm may be lost.

Using a central station alarm termination may result in an insurance rate reduction. However, the insurance company must approve this central station in order for this to happen. This usually requires certification that the system meets Underwriters Laboratories (U/L) or Factory Mutual (FM) requirements.

Some high-security facilities (e.g., commercial jewelry vaults) require two redundant systems, each complete with its own sensors, wiring and alarm transmission equipment, reporting to separate U/L-approved central alarm stations.

Proprietary Termination

A proprietary alarm termination is designed so that all alarm signals in a facility terminate at a central point within the protected enterprise (see Figure 1).[1] This type of installation is similar to the central station but, instead of a commercial central station monitoring alarms, personnel in the protected facility, or otherwise under control of the owner of the facility, perform that task. An adequate number of security officers must be employed to monitor the console where the alarms terminate and to respond to alarm conditions.

---

[1] Underwriters Laboratories Standard 1076, Proprietary Burglar Alarm Units and Systems.

Many disadvantages listed for the other type of alarm terminations are eliminated when an enterprise is of sufficient size to justify installation and operation of a proprietary alarm system.

Termination Combinations

The use of local sounding devices in conjunction with other alarm annunciation methods has already been discussed above. The use of proprietary systems combined with central station communication is common where the facility is not large enough, or has a sufficiently high enough security need, to justify on-site personnel to monitor systems during nighttime hours or on weekends. This combination is also employed where an integrated proprietary system is used for automated access control during business hours and is used to transmit to a central station when closed during off-hours.

SYSTEMS DESIGN

The integration of all sensors and devices utilized in a modern protection system is a complex design task. Electricians and technicians can install devices and equipment, but qualified security systems designers should handle the overall design and supervision of the installation. Otherwise, the results may not be what the owner anticipated.

Before systems can be designed, it is necessary to analyze both security needs and operating constraints. Inexperience in security operations or in the application of security technology may result in expensive installations that do not meet security needs and/or irritate users. If experienced protection personnel are not available in the facility, a qualified consultant can be retained to prepare the analysis requirements. The same consultant may also be qualified to take responsibility for the technical design.

The integration of electronic sensors is related to the overall protection system as outlined in Chapter 1. Proper personnel, software, and other hardware is included in the design of the electronic portion of the overall protection system. For example, when planning the utilization of *personnel,* adequate employed or contract staff are included in the plan, not only to operate the central control center, but to respond timely to signals of violations and abnormal situations. *Software* includes complete instructions and directions for the persons operating the central control center and those responding to alarms. *Other hardware items,* such as locks, doors, windows and barriers, complement the integrated electronic sensor plan so that all such items support each other and constitute a protection system.

COST REDUCTION AND PROTECTION IMPROVEMENT

The use of electronic systems and components can result in two advantages: cost reduction and improvement of protection. Major cost reduction

Systems Considerations

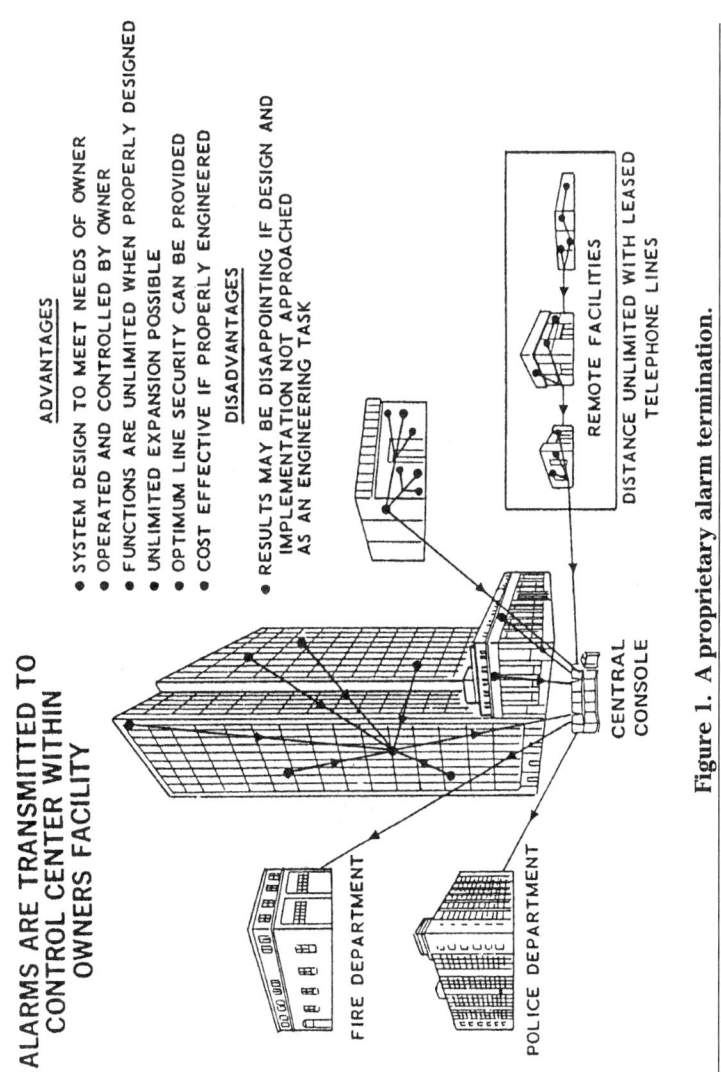

Figure 1. A proprietary alarm termination.

is often possible because electronic techniques and equipment can be substituted for personnel. For example, the average cost of one guard in the United States is currently estimated to range between $15,000 and $40,000 a year.[1] This includes contract as well as proprietary guards. A guard post that requires 24-hour coverage costs between $67,500 and $180,000 per year, excluding supervision. If the electronic system is properly designed, personnel can usually be eliminated or reduced in two areas — patrol inspections and entry control. Past experience indicates possible reductions of as much as 50 percent of pre-system personnel costs. The cost of the installed system would be amortized over its estimated useful life and the net expense decrease would be the achievable saving.

Protection Enhancement

Better protection usually results when reliable sensors are properly installed and maintained. If electronic sensors are not utilized, the only way to ensure continuous protection is to assign spot personnel to observe the area or item. Because such an arrangement is costly, personnel on patrol are often assigned to check periodically instead — perhaps every hour or two. However, a fire, penetration, or other problem might develop immediately after an inspection, and an enormous amount of damage can result before the next inspection. The individual responsible for an inspection might overlook an area, either intentionally or out of neglect, and a loss could occur due to an unchecked problem in the area. An appropriate device, continuously monitored, is more effective than sporadic or inattentive human inspection.

Patrol Reduction

Some patrol inspection can be eliminated or reduced with electronically supervised sensors. This reduces the total number of personnel needed and results in lower personnel costs. However, some patrol personnel are usually required to perform tasks that cannot be accomplished with electronics alone.

Electronic techniques can also enhance supervision of such personnel. For example, each individual can be equipped with a portable radio or cellular telephone in regular communication with the central control. Also, a system of checkpoints, such as guard patrol supervisory stations, can be established throughout the patrolled areas and tied into the control center. When a station is activated, the time and location are recorded and audible or visible signals, or both, are displayed at the control center. Missed, out of sequence, or off-schedule stations cause an alarm. The control center operator can then dispatch other patrolling personnel to investigate. The combination of checkpoints and mobile communication makes it possible

---

[1] Hourly Security Officer Compensation in Selected U.S. Metropolitan Areas, *Security Letter,* XXVI(18), Oct. 15, 1996.

Systems Considerations

for the control center operator to know where the patrolling personnel are located at all times. In the event of patrol tour delinquency, injury or other exceptions, other nearby stations can respond. In general, the more effective the personnel, the fewer personnel needed.

Closed-Circuit TV and Personnel Reductions

A variety of techniques can reduce the number of personnel assigned to control entrances. In small areas with few individuals to be controlled, a local device, such as a biometric sensor or a lock activated by a coded card, a personal identification number (PIN), or a combination of these, might be effective. Personnel otherwise assigned to monitor the area entrance could be eliminated. However, the application of such simple local control is limited because it works effectively only with low-density personnel movements. It is less satisfactory with large numbers, particularly if they move in dense queues over short time periods. For more dense populations and where higher security levels are indicated, consider positive access control techniques (i.e., identification and control of access to one individual at a time, such as credential reader controlled turnstiles).

When integrated into a complete electronic scheme, closed-circuit television is also effective at personnel entrances. The control center operator is responsible for remotely controlling entrances with the aid of CCTV cameras and for remotely unlocking them. Properly designed, this arrangement can result in the elimination of spot personnel at individual entrances. The number of entrances a single console operator can control depends on the amount of traffic through them. Because of this limitation, this type of control is best planned for times and at entrances where little traffic is expected. Where there is heavy periodic traffic, this type of control can be put into operation after the heavy traffic has diminished. For example, an entrance might have constant heavy traffic during a day shift. However, if the traffic after that shift consists of only a limited number of individuals, the control center operator can handle it during that usage period. When CCTV is used to control access during low-traffic periods, a reduction in personnel normally assigned that task is possible.

A variety of CCTV control methods may be utilized. When a minimal number of individuals need to be controlled, the simplest method employs one camera and one monitor and relies upon personal recognition when few individuals are to be controlled. In such an arrangement, the control center operator must recognize all persons allowed access at that point. (See Chapter 7 for a discussion of personal recognition.)

Another technique, useful when too many individuals must be controlled for the control center operator to be able to recognize all of them, is to utilize two cameras: one to observe the individual seeking admittance and the other to check a picture badge presented by that individual. The control center operator can observe both the individual and the picture badge on two monitors, or on a single monitor designed to show a split image. An access list of those authorized to enter an area would also permit the control center operator to determine whether that particular individual is allowed access.

Such a control system may be further automated to require more positive control. An individual could be required to input a specific code before being allowed entry. In a fully automated system, the ID card would be coded for specific data/time/gate entry, and would be checked by the central processor. The CCTV camera would serve as a backup should the individual be identified as unauthorized or encounter difficulty during entry. This further reduces console workload since it demands operator intervention only for exception or problem cases.

In addition to closed-circuit television, other control equipment is necessary in such an installation. For instance, a method of signaling the control center operator can be a simple button at the portal actuating a bell or a light at the control center. This informs the operator which of several entrances is used. A method of voice communication is also generally installed between the portal and the control center. In addition, an electric locking device permits remote automatic or manual door opening.

In planning a CCTV access control installation, two limiting factors must be considered:

1. Sufficient light must be provided and the camera must be close enough to the observed object so that an identifiable picture is transmitted.[1]
2. A CCTV picture image cannot be transmitted without some delay on a transmission wire that is also used for voice; dedicated optical fiber or coaxial cable should be used.[2] Time-delayed CCTV images transmitted over regular telephone lines were not normally acceptable in a personnel access control situation because of the lack of real-time surveillance. However, new technology and software enhancements for video compression and transmission have improved the quality and speed of telephone line CCTV transmission to near-real-time. With the use of dedicated phone lines, and even with switched lines, this medium is becoming more and more acceptable.

---

[1] An exception would be an infrared-sensitive TV camera and an infrared illuminator at the surveillance point. This would not illuminate the entrance itself, as the area would still appear dark locally.

[2] An exception would be wire connections over an Integrated Services Digital Network (ISDN) whose broadband capability permits multiple mode, simultaneous transmission. ISDN networks will become much more common in the future.

Systems Considerations

THE AUTOMATED SECURITY SYSTEM

In all the applications of electronic equipment and techniques discussed so far, an operator at a central console must be constantly alert to all signals received. In such an arrangement, the operator must perform both routine and nonroutine tasks.

Current technology has changed the role of a central console operator through the use of digital microprocessors and digital computers. The microprocessor is steadily shrinking in size and growing in capabilities.

Another development has been the widespread use of multiplex signal distribution, substituting a single multiplex trunk cable and clusters of field devices for the former hard-wired circuits. Such devices are known as transponders, multiplexers, data gathering panels and intelligent field panels (IFPs). IFPs contain considerable data processing power and memory and, in addition to transmitting alarm data to a central monitoring location, they are capable of remotely activating security devices such as horns and lights in response to alarm inputs.

For example, a hold-up alarm at a cashier or teller position can be connected to a local IFP that receives, stores and transmits an alarm. In addition, the IFP could directly initiate a surveillance camera to begin filming the area for a timed period or activate a local CCTV recorder.

Centrally Controlled Systems

Alarm data received from a remote IFP at a central location is processed by a digital computer. Most computer-based security systems on the market utilize personal computers (PCs) as the central processing unit. Added to the computer are the typical direct access storage devices, such as hard drives, and floppy, Zip or compact disks. The disks store large amounts of user-programmable data that is referenced during system operations, and also store a history, or log, of all transactions that occur within the system.

Most of the multi-user systems (with multiple alarm annunciation or administration stations) are Unix or Microsoft NT-based, with the ability to use available LANs (local area networks), WANs (wide area networks), GANs (global area networks) for communications between workstations, IFPs and, in some cases, CCTV cameras and card readers.

When processing is done centrally, the system is vulnerable either to the failure of the computer or to the loss of communication links to IFPs. In most security and life safety systems, the single computer vulnerability is overcome by adding a second computer to function in one of several standby modes. Failure of the master computer causes all or a designated part of system function to be taken over by the slave. Failure of the computer or the IFP communication circuit can be substantially offset by redundant circuits that function simultaneously or only in the event of primary communications failure.

The optimum configuration utilizes intelligent field panels to the maximum extent, employs redundant IFP transmission paths and uses redundant digital computers at the central console location. In addition to the trunk redundancy, the display and recording devices at the central console should also be duplicated for redundancy.

Systems Computer Applications

The major application of the digital computer is to permit variable programming, reference to large amounts of stored data, and the development of a transactional database. The database allows retrieval of stored information that can contribute to planning and analysis. For example, patterns of entry and exit in an automated access program can be studied, as can the frequency and distribution of various alarm signals. In addition, system operator comments or analyses can be generated simultaneously with events occurring in the system and stored for later review.

The variable programming option permits system parameters to be changed from the control console or other system processors without the need to physically modify field sensors or devices. This allows changes in times and modes of operation of various field devices, such as intrusion alarms, card readers, lights, door locks and the like. Such changes can be instituted in a number of ways:

1. By the operator console or a systems administrator via keyboard input
2. Automatically where the security system database is linked to that of another system (e.g., a human resources database)
3. Automatically by a time schedule

Control Center Equipment

The following items are typical of those found in the control center of an integrated security system:

1. An operator console
2. A principal video display terminal with keyboard and pointing device (e.g., mouse)
3. A high-speed logging printer
4. A redundant visual display, such as a graphic display terminal, showing site maps

In addition to these basic items, various systems will also include CCTV monitors and controls, access controls, gate controls, telecommunications equipment and radio equipment. Figure 2 shows examples of system elements.

Costs

Considering only the costs of the computer and display devices, a medium-sized integrated security system can range from $5000 to $30,000. When the other possible peripherals are added, and when field devices and installation are considered, the total cost for such a system can reach $1,000,000 or more. A rule of thumb: when estimating the cost of digital systems, consider each separate digital point (or "zone" under the old hard-wire terminology) to cost $1000, installed. This is only for rough estimating, however. (Table 2 shows typical costs for selected integrated security system components.)

Personnel Control

The control of personnel at entrances and within the facility is one task a security system can perform.

It was pointed out earlier that closed-circuit television can help reduce personnel access control costs, but only during low-traffic periods, because an individual at the control console must identify each individual and then take admittance action. An automated controlled access system does not have this limitation because it is able to process data and respond in microseconds. Because there is no significant time delay in automated identification and response, such a system can control a large number of personnel. When a security system is used for access control, it is possible to eliminate more personnel than with closed-circuit television or other manual systems because the computer is faster, more accurate and records transactions.

Another benefit is that the access database can be modified whenever a status change occurs for a user, even if the access card is not retrieved. In distributed systems, the changed database is downloaded from the computer to the field panels whenever necessary.

An automated system's signals can be transmitted on voice-grade lines — either proprietary or leased. Hence, there is no distance limitation on such an installation.

In addition to reduction of costs, more positive identification and control of personnel is achieved with automated systems because the human error factor, present in every control system requiring identification by a human being, is greatly reduced or eliminated.

Identification. Positive identification of individuals at access points is an essential element in an access control system. (For a detailed discussion of identification and access control systems, see Chapter 7.) A simple method uses coded cards and card readers, with or without a keypad for the input of a personal identification number (PIN), at all access points.

ASSET PROTECTION AND SECURITY MANAGEMENT HANDBOOK

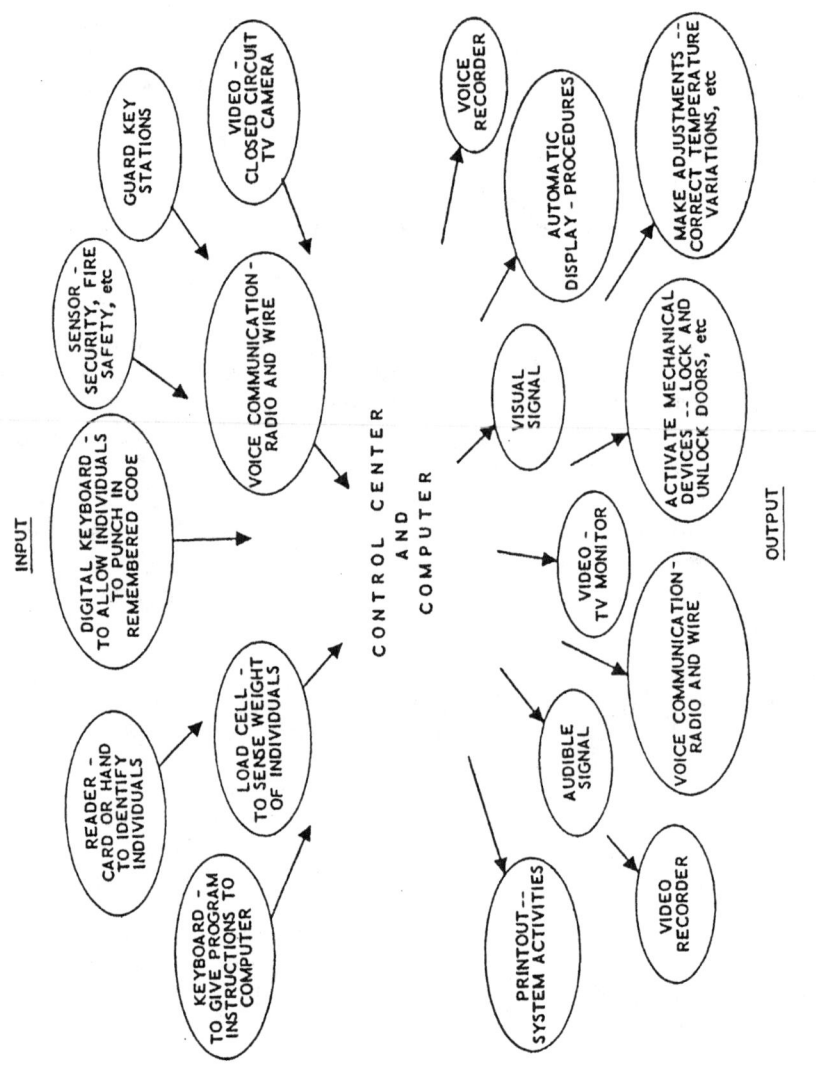

Figure 2. Some examples of input and output devices.

Table 2. Typical costs for selected integrated security system components.

Device	Performance capability	Cost
Personal computer	Including display, storage, keyboard, etc.	$2000–$75,000
Software	For access control/alarm monitoring	$1000–$100,000
Impact printer	For transaction log: 100–500 cps[a]	$100–$600
Laser printer	For report printing: 6–20 pages/min.	$300–$1000
Keyboard	Extended, multiple function buttons	$150
Digital photo badging	(Integrated w/access control)	$3000–$35,000

[a] cps — characters per second.

This technique ensures positive identification of the card and code and is generally more effective than depending on guards or other personnel to identify individuals through the use of badges or personal identification media. However, an individual without authorized access could obtain a card and code voluntarily from an authorized individual or by theft and watching a PIN being entered. (This is called *shoulder-surfing*.)

There are other methods of positive personal identification, unique to each individual, for higher security applications. Biometric systems measure such unique features as: voiceprint, fingerprint, hand geometry, signature analysis, retinal scans and facial recognition. A discussion of these techniques is contained in Chapter 7.

Physical Control at Access Points. Positive physical control at access points must also be considered. When automated monitoring is substituted for manpower at access points, the system design must include a reliable method of access control. One method of accomplishing an effective control is to utilize a "mantrap" or double-door booth arrangement (see Figure 3).

The identification reader is installed inside the booth. An individual enters through the exterior door of the booth and performs the established identification routine. The second or inner door remains locked until this is complete. The system then reacts by locking the outer door and unlocking the inner door. The booth can be designed so that both doors of the booth lock as soon as an individual enters. However, emergency egress from the booth to a recognized exit path must be provided under most local life safety codes.

An audio intercom link from the booth to the control center is also desirable so that an individual in the booth can converse with the control center operator when necessary. A closed-circuit TV camera installed in the booth can allow the control center operator to observe the booth on a monitor in case of an alarm or other problem, and can inspect property

ASSET PROTECTION AND SECURITY MANAGEMENT HANDBOOK

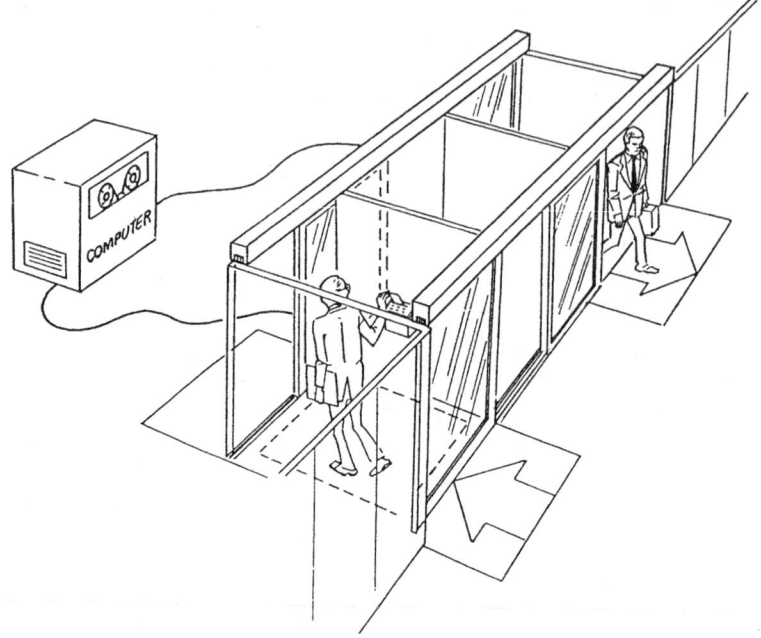

Figure 3. An example of a mantrap or double-door booth control.

carried by persons in the booth. Intrusion alarm sensors should be installed in the booth so that the control center operator is alerted to any difficulties or attempted unauthorized transactions.

"Tailgating" or multiple entries can be a problem. To counteract this, a load cell might be installed in the floor of the booth to weigh each person upon entry. This is not an identification feature, so the weight of each individual, within 50 to 75 pounds, is programmed. Prefabricated mantrap booths with a variety of such features are available for purchase and installation.

A turnstile might be used instead of the booth. All the control elements described above could also be incorporated into the design of a turnstile (see Figure 4).

A time range between three and seven seconds is required for each individual to be processed through an entrance point. An analysis of traffic through each access point is necessary to determine the number of booths and/or turnstiles needed at each location. The traffic analysis should include parameters that define the acceptable queuing time at each entry point. Redundant units should be considered to ensure adequate traffic flow if one unit fails.

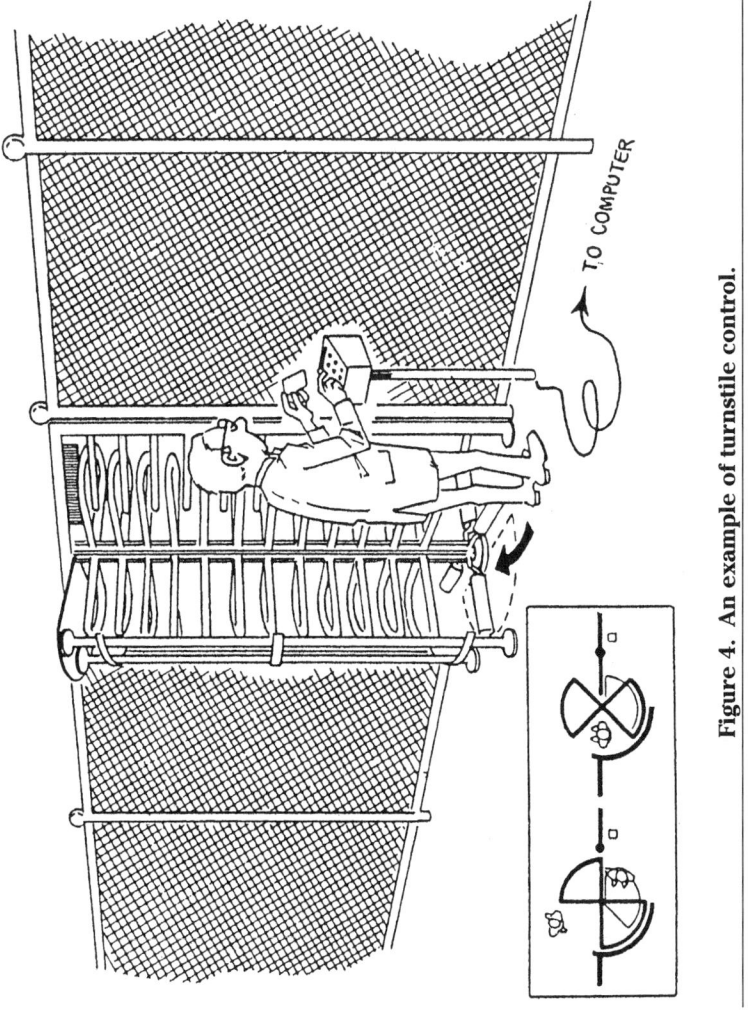

Figure 4. An example of turnstile control.

It is necessary to design the booths and turnstiles so that they can be adjusted to control traffic in either direction — in or out. During the time of heavy entering traffic, the majority of booths and turnstiles can be programmed to accommodate this need. During heavy exit traffic, the majority can be reversed to accommodate those leaving. The identification routine for those leaving could also be simplified. For example, if both a card and PIN are required for entrance, either the card or the code could be specified for exit. Safety, ADA, and fire code issues must also be considered in the design; additional conventional access and/or egress portals may have to be added for special use.

Other Security System Tasks

A few of the other everyday functions that might be controlled by a computer-based security system are discussed below to indicate the wealth of applications that might be incorporated into a system.

Monitoring of Sensors. Any device capable of initiating a signal on a pair of wires can be monitored. The system can be programmed so that only irregularities, exceptions or violations in the system are signaled at a central control point. Routine data can be recorded to disk and all routine outputs or system responses can be automatically initiated. For example, in case of a signal from a fire sensor, the fire department is called. Or in case of an indication of a penetration, the police department is called. The alarm event and the fact of the call are recorded and displayed on the operator's terminal for acknowledgment and further action.

The system can also be programmed to perform functions and to make automatic adjustments or corrections against the clock or calendar. Some of the timed functions the system might perform automatically are:

1. Lock and unlock doors at specifically programmed times.
2. Turn lights off and on as required.
3. Start and stop certain machinery at predetermined times.
4. Automatically activate and deactivate sensors.

Supervision of Protection Personnel. The use of key or card reader stations for the supervision of patrolling personnel was discussed earlier in this chapter. The system software is designed to automatically check the activation of each station to ensure it meets the requirements of the patrol tour program's user-defined parameters. Any variance immediately results in an alarm signal being activated at the control center. Variances include: (1) station visited out of order, (2) time delinquency (station visited too early or late), (3) station repeated, and (4) station skipped.

Time and Attendance Recording. The security system can record attendance of employees and can be programmed to compute time for payroll purposes. If an access control system is in operation, it is relatively simple to add time and attendance (T&A) control to the access control program.

It should be noted that most access control system manufacturers provide somewhat simplistic T&A software that processes access and egress transaction data to be passed to a payroll system. The transmission may be via a serial data line, LAN or physically carried on a removable magnetic medium such as a floppy disk. A careful analysis of operating requirements, exceptions (e.g., sickness and vacations) and collective bargaining contract requirements should be made before T&A software is considered as an addition to an access control system. Purpose designed T&A systems are considerably more sophisticated and may be more appropriate.

Programming the System

The capabilities of a computer to perform control functions for which it has been properly programmed are almost endless. A computer does not exercise judgment so it can only perform those tasks that it has been specifically instructed to carry out.[1] Each organization ordinarily has its own protection requirements because of various factors such as size, location, number of employees, value of tools, equipment and inventory, type of work and sensitivity of work. Therefore, standard programs require their databases to be customized to meet specific requirements. Many off-the-shelf applications are of the fill-in-the-blanks type and can easily be customized.

Typical database input (included in the process of commissioning) for a sensor might include such information as the text to be displayed if the point goes into alarm mode, operator instructions for alarm response, and output points (e.g., lights) to be switched on or off as a result of the alarm. The data would also include a definition of those times of the day during which the point should be in access mode (i.e., the alarm signal is ignored) or of any signal that should be sent to a CCTV switcher to display an associated camera view. The importance of good commissioning cannot be overemphasized. The best and most expensive hardware, software and peripheral equipment cannot give satisfactory results if the system has not been properly commissioned as a database.

Development of custom software is time-consuming and extremely costly to write, debug and maintain. For usability and reliability, in addition to budgetary concerns, it is advisable to use standard, off-the-shelf software packages whenever possible.

---

[1] It should be noted that with artificial intelligence (AI) or fuzzy logic, computers can be programmed to draw inferences, i.e., in a primitive way to act rationally. This means that the computer could derive a new rule or action from the combination of past events when such action was not anticipated by the program designer. Such programs, as of this writing, are not commercially available for security applications.

System Expansion and Flexibility

When a protection system is being designed, the possibility of future expansion and changes in modes of operation should be considered because not all eventualities can be predicted during the initial design stage. Flexibility of both capacity and capability ensures that changes can be accommodated inexpensively and quickly and that the system will not become prematurely obsolete.

The Control Center

A control center for an automated protection system performs essentially the same functions as any electronic control center, except that many of the tasks handled by a control center operator are automatically performed by the system. The system automatically processes routine events in accordance with its programmed instructions without alerting anyone in the control center. However, the operator is immediately notified of exceptions or violations in the system by visual and audible signals, as well as by printouts and displays. The system can also be programmed to print or display instructions for the operator to follow in situations that can be anticipated in advance, such as building emergencies. Access to program or data files for changes or edit functions should be reserved to a specified hierarchy of authorized persons by means of passwords or restricted IDs.

EMERGENCY POWER

Security systems are completely dependent on a continuous power supply; an interruption of power can jeopardize an entire facility. Normal power sources fail occasionally, so an emergency power system must become part of the system design.

The wiring network influences the emergency power plan. If a common circuit is utilized, with every component obtaining power from one source, a single emergency power source can provide energy to the complete system. If a random circuit system is used, components are connected to the most convenient power source. Because each sensor may be on a separate circuit, a source of power for each component may be required (see Figure 5).

If possible, an underground installation for any outside wiring network should be provided. The emergency wiring will then have better protection from the hazards that might disable conventional power distribution.

Standby and Continuous Emergency Power

Standby Power. Employing the standby concept is the most effective method of providing emergency power (see Figure 6). A relay device constantly monitors the normal supply of power. If this fails, the relay switches to an emergency source.

Systems Considerations

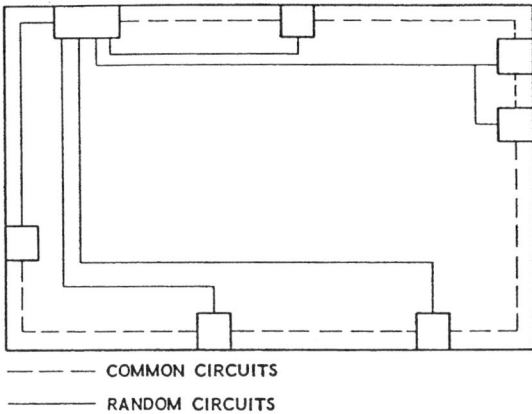

— — — COMMON CIRCUITS
———— RANDOM CIRCUITS

Figure 5. Common and random circuit systems.

A standby generator is the typical emergency power source. This unit can be used exclusively for the security system, or used for other purposes as well. With an exclusive unit, it is merely necessary to size the load of the system and ensure that the generator can handle that load. However, even a large protection system is unlikely to require more than 10 KVA, which is usually insufficient to justify a dedicated generator. With a generator that also serves other functions, ensure that power for the security system is always available. The use of the power source should be checked frequently to make certain that other demands do not overload the generator. Emergency generators must also be properly maintained and regularly tested.

An alternative to a generator is a standby system based on batteries. If the security system requires alternating current, typically 120 VAC, inverters are used to convert the low-voltage DC battery supply, typically from 24 VDC to 120 VAC. A battery charger is also included in the design to maintain the battery at full charge in its standby condition and to recharge it after it has supplied power to the security system. Transfer relays and other accessories are needed to complete the system. For small loads, battery standby packages are available. In larger systems, the emergency power components must be designed for the specific job.

Continuous Power. A more sophisticated power support system is the uninterruptable power supply (UPS), which uses batteries to provide continuous power. Power is constantly furnished to the security system, whether or not normal power is available (see Figure 7).

If the system requires 120 VAC, the UPS system usually employs an inverter. Normal power feeds a battery charger that maintains a low-voltage

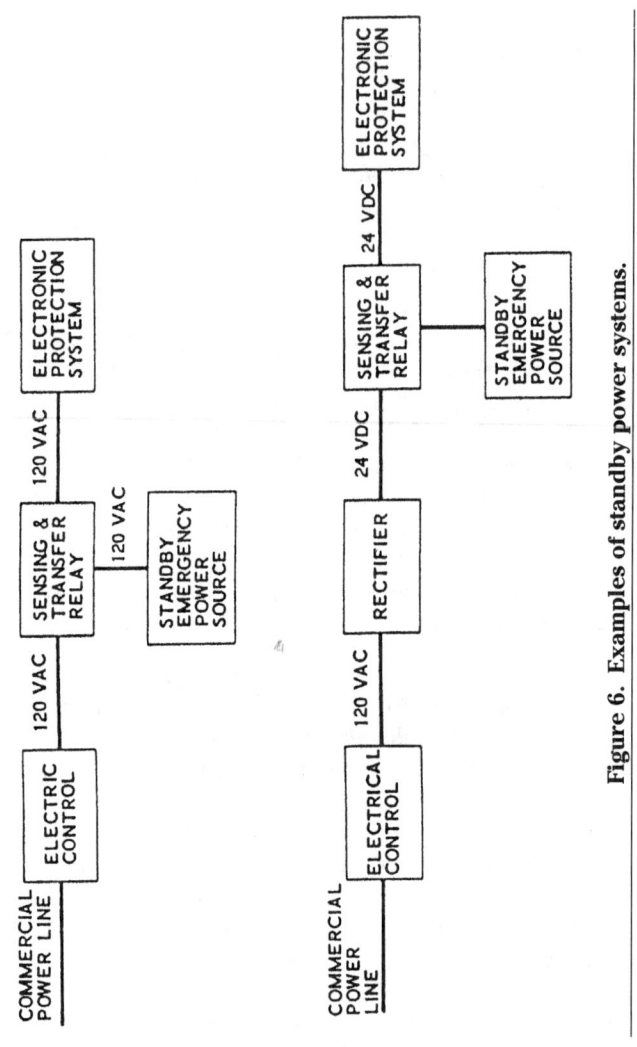

Figure 6. Examples of standby power systems.

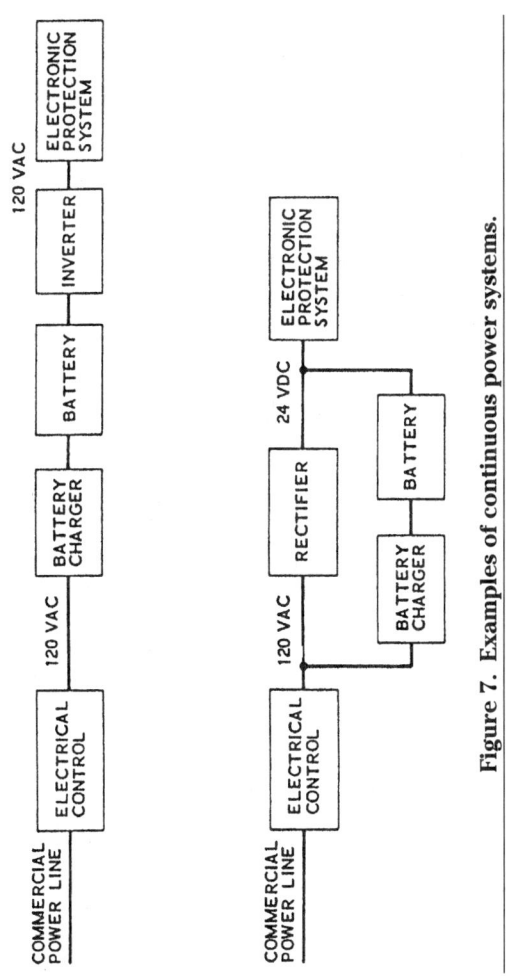

Figure 7. Examples of continuous power systems.

DC battery. The battery supplies low-voltage DC to the inverter, which converts it to 120 VAC and supplies the system. In the event of a commercial power failure, the charger ceases charging and the batteries continue to supply the inverter until their energy is depleted. When commercial power is restored, the charger again charges the batteries and the cycle continues.

If the security system requires low-voltage DC, typically 12 or 24 VDC, the continuous system requires a battery, a charger and a rectifier. Normal power is supplied to the rectifier, which converts it to a DC and supplies that to the system. At the same time, one or more batteries are "floated" on the supply wiring. In the event of a power failure, the rectifier ceases operating, but the batteries already on the line continue to supply the protection system until they are depleted. A generator can be added to this array, to switch in automatically upon failure of commercial power and switch out automatically upon its restoration.

One of the major advantages of battery support systems is that they reduce the possibilities of regular power surges or dips and those that occur when changing between regular and standby power.

It is important with both standby and continuous power supplies that their status and condition be monitored by the security system. If main power failure is isolated to a dedicated circuit breaker used by the system, an alarm signal annunciating that support power has been engaged may be the only indication of the off-normal condition. Similarly, a low-battery-voltage alarm is useful to indicate that an orderly shutdown of the system and, perhaps the deployment of additional security staff, are required. The low-battery alarm will also indicate a failure in either the charging circuit or in the batteries themselves.

Selected Bibliography

Books

A Practical Guide to Fire Alarm Systems; 1995; Central Station Alarm Association.

An Insurance Guide to Selecting a Burglar Alarm System; 1994; Central Station Alarm Association.

Barnard, Robert L.; *Intrusion Detection Systems;* 1988; Butterworth-Heinemann, Woburn, MA.

Cumming, Neil; *Security: A Guide to Security System Design and Equipment Selection and Installation;* 1992; Butterworth-Heinemann, Woburn, MA.

Honey, Gerard; *Electronic Protection & Security Systems;* 1996; Butterworth-Heinemann, Woburn, MA.

Sanger, John; *Basic Alarm Electronics;* 1988; Butterworth-Heinemann, Woburn, MA.

Trimmer, H. William; *Understanding and Servicing Alarm Systems;* 1990; Butterworth-Heinemann, Woburn, MA.

Walker, Philip; *Electronic Security Systems: Better Ways to Crime Prevention, 2nd ed.;* 1988; Butterworth-Heinemann, Woburn, MA.

Periodicals

Security Management; American Society for Industrial Security, Arlington, VA.
— Bowman, Erik; Security Tools Up for the Future; January 1996.
— Cottman, Lawrence; Out of the Showroom and into the Manufacturing Plant; 1972.
— Griffiths, Barry D.; Detecting Intrusion with Fiber Optics; July 1992.
— Sentell, Ronald J.; On the Line with Data Transmission; November 1992.
— Skiffingtion, Barbara; Catching Intruders in a Neural Net; February 1994.
— Thomas, Ronald C.; Technology Meets the Alarm Industry; September 1992.
— Trimble, Mike; Sensors Communicate for Better Protection; April 1987.
— Vitch, Martin L.; Sensing Your Way to Security; July 1992.

APPENDIX A
GLOSSARY OF FREQUENTLY USED SECURITY TERMS

Access control: Control of traffic through entrances and exits of a protected area. Control may be as simple as having a guard posted at these locations, or using voice identification over an intercom system with verbal approval to enter or exit; or it may be a more complex system for centrally controlling the locking and unlocking of doors and/or gates. It may even include closed-circuit television for monitoring and identification purposes.

Alarm discriminator: A device used to minimize or eliminate the possibility of false alarms caused by extraneous sounds or vibrations. It can be adjusted to provide alarm discrimination under any job conditions. It may be either a special circuit incorporated in a detector or a device that is added to a system.

Alarm line: A wired, electrically supervised circuit used for the transmission of alarm signals from a protected area to a central receiving point such as in a remote station system, proprietary system or central station system. The term is synonymous with the terms "reporting line," "security line" and "security loop"; all are used interchangeably.

Alarm receiver: An annunciator that also provides supervision of the alarm line and may or may not include an audible alarm device. Various circuit and contact arrangements are usually available to provide auxiliary functions upon receipt of an alarm signal.

Alarm signal: An audible and/or visual signal indicating an emergency, such as intrusion, fire, smoke, unsafe equipment conditions, equipment failure, reporting line tamper or failure and so forth, that requires immediate action. In general, all signals are treated as alarm signals, although alarm signals are sometimes differentiated from circuit fault or trouble signals.

Annunciator: A visual indicator that shows from which of several zones or buildings an alarm signal has originated. It may incorporate an audible signal common to all zones as an alert that a signal is being received on the annunciator. Annunciators can be mechanical (drop flags), electrical (lamps), electronic (LCDs or LEDs), or video display systems.

Area detection: A technique for detecting an intruder's presence anywhere within a specifically defined, protected area, as opposed to detection at a specific point such as a door.

Audible alarm device: The term applies to any noise-making device used to indicate an alarm condition or a change in state or a device or component in the security system (access to secure, alarm reset, etc.).

Audio detection: An arrangement of microphone, audio amplifier and sound-actuated relay used to detect noises made by an intruder in a protected area and to transmit an alarm signal. Also known as a sound threshold or "scream" alarm.

Audio monitoring: An arrangement of microphone, audio amplifier and receiver that permits a guard at a remote central location to listen for abnormal sounds in a protected area.

Authorized access control switch: A device for switching a detection system on and off, sometimes referred to as a day-night switch or subscriber's unit (U/L term). It may be a double-pole, single-throw switch, usually key operated.

Break alarm: An alarm signal produced by opening or breaking an electrical circuit, sometimes referred to as an open-circuit alarm. Trouble signals are generally open or break alarms.

Building security systems: A completely integrated system to protect against intrusion, espionage, vandalism, theft, smoke, fire, unsafe or faulty equipment operation, and any other condition or act that might endanger an installation, which includes the control of traffic and operation of doors and/or gates from a remote location. Use is made of human guards, or mechanical, electrical, and electronic devices, or combinations thereof, in sufficient quantities and varieties to assure the desired degree of protection.

Capacitance detection: A means of producing an alarm signal by making use of the capacitance effect of the human body or other large mass in a tuned electronic circuit. Less expensive systems operate on an increase in capacitance only; more sophisticated systems operate on an increase or decrease in capacitance.

Central station system: A system in which the alarm signal is relayed to a remote panel located at the facilities of a privately owned protection service company staffed by personnel employed by the protection company.

Clear zone: An unobstructed area on both sides of a perimeter barrier. A clear zone is kept free of rubbish, weeds, bushes, trees or other material that might conceal anyone attempting to climb, tunnel or cut through a perimeter barrier.

Contact device: Any device that, when actuated, opens or closes a set of electrical contacts, such as a door switch or relay.

Contact microphone: A specially constructed microphone attached directly to an object or surface to be protected. This type of microphone is generally insensitive to ambient room noises, responding only when the protected object or surface is disturbed.

Control cabinet or panel: A centrally located assembly containing all power supplies, relays, amplifiers and any other equipment required to receive and interpret alarm signals from a protected area via reporting lines and to supervise these lines.

Cross alarm: An alarm signal produced by crossing or short-circuiting an electrical circuit.

Detector: Any device for detecting intrusion, equipment failure or malfunction, unsafe equipment operation, presence of smoke or fire, or any other condition requiring immediate action. Detectors include a means for translating the detected abnormal condition into some form of alarm signal — either a local or remote alarm, the latter over a reporting line, with or without electrical supervision.

Double-drop: A method often required in central station systems whereby a reporting line is first opened to produce a break alarm and then shorted to produce a cross alarm. In such a system, all signals are treated as alarm signals.

Dual-technology motion detector: A sensor that utilizes two technologies (e.g., microwave and infrared) in a logical combination to reduce false alarms.

Electronic vibration detector (EVD): An extremely sensitive detection device employing a contact microphone. The device is used to protect such objects as vaults, safes, file cabinets and works of art. Walls, floors and ceilings can also be kept under surveillance through the use of EVD devices.

End-of-line resistor: A resistor used to terminate an electrically supervised line. The resistor is used to make the line electrically continuous, and also to provide a fixed reference for current and/or resistance against which to measure changes that produce an alarm signal. It is effective when installed at the alarm device location.

Field panel: (or intelligent field panel, IFP). A microprocessor-based unit to which multiple alarm and security devices can be connected. It transmits status changes to the security system server on a trunk line. When used with access control systems, the IFP stored on a downloaded database allows it to determine the validity of a credential presented at a credential reader.

Impedance matching: The circuit arrangement required to adjust the impedance of an alternating current load to the value recommended for the proper operation of a given device. In security systems, this generally relates to speaker impedance adjustment relative to the impedance of the input and/or output circuit of an amplifier. Impedance in an AC circuit is the apparent resistance to current, equivalent to actual resistance in a DC circuit. It is measured in ohms.

Inside perimeter: A line of protection adjacent to a protected area and passing through points of possible entry into the area, such as doors, windows, skylights, tunnels or other points of access.

Line amplifier: An audio or video amplifier used to provide pre-amplification (increased strength) of an audio or video signal before transmitting the signal over a reporting line. Use of a line amplifier permits extending the transmission distance between two points.

Local alarm system: A system in which the alarm signal is heard and/or seen only in the immediate vicinity of the protected area. However, some local systems do have provisions for simultaneous transmission of an alarm signal to a remote station, central station or control center of a proprietary system.

Matching network: The equipment and circuit arrangement required to couple an audio signal to a reporting line. Generally, a combination of transformer and capacitor is arranged so that audio signals can be transmitted while any direct current used for line supervision is blocked; i.e., prevented from passing into the audio portion of the circuit.

Microwave motion detection: A means for detecting the presence of an intruder through the use of radio frequency generating and receiving equipment operating in the range of 1 GHz to 300 GHz. This type of device is one in a family of radio frequency motion detection devices, which are classified according to frequency. This is an area detection type of system.

Monitoring station: A term used to indicate the remote area at which guards or other personnel monitor the security system annunciators or alarm receivers.

Motion detection: Detection of an intruder by making use of the change in location or orientation in a protection area as the intruder moves about. (*See* sonic, ultrasonic, radio frequency and video motion detection.) When used in reference to video motion detection, this term means changes in key parameters of a viewed scene from a recorded reference image of that scene.

Object protection: A form of protection for objects such as safes, files or anything of value that could be removed from a protected area.

Outside perimeter: A line of protection surrounding but somewhat removed from a protected area, such as a fence.

Percent(age) supervision: The ratio of the change in current or resistance to normal operating current or resistance in a supervised line required to produce an alarm signal, expressed as a percentage.

Perimeter barrier: Any physical barrier used to supplement the protection of an inside or outside perimeter.

Physical barrier: Any physical means to impede, delay or prevent intrusion into a protected area. Barriers may be natural, such as rivers, cliffs, canyons, seas or other natural features; or structural, such as fences, floors, walls, grills, roofs, bars, barbed wire, other structures resisting penetration, or combinations thereof.

Systems Considerations

Police station unit: An alarm receiver that can be placed in operation at a police station to receive alarm signals from protected premises.

Portable detector system: A complete detector system, easily transportable from one place to another. The system normally has provisions for a local alarm device, alarm lines, and automatic or manual resetting.

Proprietary system: A system in which the alarm signal is relayed to a central location that is owned, manned and operated by the building proprietor (owner) or his agents. This term is also used to describe a system, component, technology or software package supplied by only one manufacturer.

Protected area: The specific area being protected by a security system or the area under surveillance.

Radio frequency motion detection: A means for detecting the presence of an intruder through use of radio frequency generating and receiving equipment. Generally, it is an area detection type of system, where the area under protection is saturated with a pattern of radio frequency waves, any disturbance of which initiates an alarm signal. (*See also* sonic and ultrasonic motion detection.)

Remote detector panel: A detector located at the monitoring station rather than at the protected area. The device provides supervision of the wiring between the two locations.

Remote station system: A system where the alarm signal is transmitted to a remote location manned and operated by an independent party, such as a police headquarters.

Reporting line: Synonymous and interchangeable with alarm line.

Security line: Synonymous and interchangeable with alarm line.

Security loop: Synonymous and interchangeable with alarm line.

Security monitor: A device that provides supervision of the alarm line and associated equipment. It can be adjusted to provide the desired degree of supervision for any system.

Sonic motion detection: A system using audible sound waves (20 Hz–20 kHz) to detect the presence of an intruder or any other disturbance of a sound pattern generated in a protected area. (*See also* motion detection, ultrasonic motion detection, and radio frequency motion detection.)

Subscriber's unit: A term used by U/L that is synonymous and interchangeable with authorized access control panel.

Supervised line: A wired circuit under supervision.

Supervision: In building security systems, a term used to describe electrical protection of any wired circuit between two points. A break, cross, increase or decrease of current and/or resistance on such a circuit is immediately translated into a distinctive signal different from an alarm signal.

Surveillance: Monitoring of building equipment conditions such as temperature, pressure, motor speed, or other equipment conditions, which, if not correct or operating properly, could cause damage in an installation. In general, a separate field of technology to ensure safe and correct operation of all mechanical and/or electrical equipment associated with an installation, but often included as part of an overall building security system.

Trouble signal: In some building security systems, a differentiation is made between a break alarm and a cross alarm. Generally, the cross alarm is used to indicate intrusion or a dangerous condition; the break alarm indicates trouble, such as a broken line — more often found in fire alarm systems. Generally used to describe internal problems with the system, not a security alarm event.

Type I Installation; Type II Installation; Type III Installation: These terms are synonymous with the Underwriters' Laboratories classifications: "Installation No. 1; Installation No. 2; and Installation No. 3," which set forth certain minimum standards that must be observed in protecting mercantile premises, stockrooms and stock cabinets. The requirements are contained in the Underwriters' Laboratories publication, *Standards for Safety, Installation, Classification, and Certification of Burglar Alarm Systems*, U/L 681.

Ultrasonic motion detection: A system using inaudible sound waves (above 20 kHz) to detect the presence of an intruder or other disturbance of the inaudible sound pattern. The sound waves are of a higher frequency than in a sonic motion detection system and are inaudible to the human ear, but they are far lower than those of a radio frequency detection system.

Video motion detection (VMD): A system for detecting changes in the field of view of a CCTV camera, based upon changes in contrast or in the light levels created by movement. In digital motion detection, the monitor screen (CCTV scene) can be divided into individual pixels (picture elements) and any combination of one or more pixels can be defined as an alarm zone. In this way, all or only a defined part of the scene viewed can be sensitive to movement.

APPENDIX B
GLOSSARY OF FREQUENTLY USED FIRE TERMS

Alarm indicating device: Any audible or visual signal used to indicate a fire condition.

Alarm initiating device, automatic: Any device, such as a fire detector, smoke detector or water flow switch, that automatically transmits an alarm signal when a condition indicative of a fire occurs.

Alarm initiating device, manual: A fire alarm station that transmits an alarm signal when manually operated.

Annunciator: An electrically operated signaling device having one or more target or lamp indications.

Auxiliary fire alarm system: A system maintained and supervised by a responsible person or corporation and having alarm initiating devices

Systems Considerations

that, when operated, cause an alarm to be transmitted over a municipal fire alarm system to the fire station, or to the fire headquarters for retransmission to the fire station.

Bell, single-stroke: A device whose gong is struck only once, each time operating energy is applied to the bell.

Bell, vibrating: A device that rings continuously as long as operating power is applied to the bell.

Buzzer: A vibrating reed device in which an armature is continuously vibrated as long as operating power is applied to the buzzer. The vibrating reed or armature is usually adjusted to strike the magnet core or the housing of the device to amplify tone output.

Chime: A single-stroke, audible signal with a soft, pleasing tone, ordinarily used in pre-signal systems to advise selected personnel of a fire condition before an evacuation alarm is sounded.

Coded system: A system in which not less than three rounds of coded alarm signals are transmitted, after which the fire alarm system may be manually or automatically silenced.

Detector, thermal fire: Heat-responsive devices such as tubing, cable or thermostats.

Double supervised system: A system in which the source of power for the trouble signal is supervised by a second trouble signal, which is actuated by the main power supply in the event of loss of the trouble power supply.

Horn, vibrating: An electrically operated horn in which the action of a vibrating armature working against a metal diaphragm produces a signal.

Local fire alarm system: An electrically operated system producing signals at one or more places at the premises served, primarily for the notification of the occupants.

Local non-interfering coded station: A fire alarm station which, once actuated, transmits not less than four rounds of coded alarm signals and cannot be interfered with by any subsequent actuation of that station until it has transmitted its complete signal.

Master coded (MC) system: A system in which a common coded alarm signal is transmitted for not less than four rounds, after which the fire alarm system may be manually or automatically silenced.

McCulloh type system: An arrangement of apparatus and wiring that enables an alarm initiating circuit to function despite a single or open or ground, or a simultaneous open and ground; may be manually switched (Manual McCulloh) or automatically switched (Automatic McCulloh).

Non-breakglass station: A manual fire alarm station in which the operation of the station does not require the breaking of a glass plate or rod.

Non-coded system: A system in which a continuous alarm signal is transmitted for a predetermined, minimum length of time, after which the fire alarm system may be manually or automatically silenced.

Positive non-interfering and succession coded station: A fire alarm station that, once actuated, transmits not less than three rounds of coded alarm signals without interference from any other station on the circuit. One or more of these stations, if subsequently operated, transmits not less than three rounds of their coded signals without interference with each other or with the first station actuated.

Pre-signal system: A system in which the operation of an automatic detector or the first operation of a manual fire alarm station actuates only a selected group of alarm indicating devices for the purpose of notifying key personnel. After investigation of the condition, a general alarm may be sounded on these same indicating devices and on an additional group of devices from any manual station to warn all occupants.

Proprietary fire alarm system: A system with supervision by competent and experienced observers and operators in a central supervising station at the property to be protected. The system is to include such appliances as to permit the operators to maintain, test and operate the system and, upon receipt of a signal, take such action as shall be required under the rules established for their guidance by the authority having jurisdiction.

Remote-station fire alarm system: A system of electrically supervised devices employing a direct-circuit connection between alarm-initiating devices or a control unit in protected premises and signal-indicating equipment in a remote station, such as fire or police headquarters or other places acceptable to the insurance rating organizations having jurisdiction.

Selective coded system: A system in which each manual fire alarm station and each group of automatic detectors has its own individual one-, two-, three- or four-digit code, which sounds on all alarm indicating devices in the system when the manual station or automatic detector is actuated.

Shunt non-interfering coded system: A coded system in which the fire alarm station, once actuated, transmits not less than three rounds of coded alarm signals without interference from any station electrically further away from the control unit.

Single supervised system: A system in which the source of power for the trouble signal is not supervised.

Station, fire alarm: A manually operated alarm-initiating device that may be equipped to generate a continuous signal (non-coded station) or a series of coded pulses (coded station).

Supervised system: A system in which a break or ground in the wiring that prevents the transmission of an alarm signal actuates a trouble signal. A separate source of power shall be used to operate the trouble signal.

Time limit cutout: A time limit cutout, when used, shall limit the maximum duration of the alarm signal to not less than three minutes nor more than 15 minutes. This device shall provide either a fixed or adjustable time interval and shall be of either the automatic or manual-reset or replaceable type. The operation of the time limit cutout shall operate a trouble signal until the device has been reset (or replaced) and the system restored to normal.

Trouble signal: A signal indicating trouble of any nature, such as a circuit break or ground, occurring in the devices or wiring associated with a fire alarm system.

Zoning: The process by which a protected building is divided into areas or zones. Any alarm-initiating device in a given zone can be arranged to sound an identifying code and/or indicate on an annunciator the area of the fire.

7
Access Control

BASIC ACCESS CONTROL OBJECTIVES

Access control programs are instituted to:

- Permit or deny entry to or presence in a given place
- Increase or reduce the rate or density of movement to, from or within a defined place
- Protect persons, materials or information against unauthorized observation or removal
- Prevent injury to people or damage to material

It is important to be clear what objective is sought, because that influences the type, degree of reliability and cost of access control equipment.

GRANTING/DENYING ENTRY

There are a variety of techniques to employ in granting or denying access to a given place. These techniques — some as simple as a deadbolt on the door, others as sophisticated as coded card access systems — are addressed in the following pages.

Locks

In its simplest form, access control imposes a physical restraint to be overcome or bypassed in order to gain entry. Doors with locks are the basic means of applying this restraint. With the help of today's technological advances, there are a myriad of modern, unconventional locks available, some of which include push-button locks, touchpads and telephone entry systems. (For an extended discussion of locks, refer to Chapter 4.)

Push-Button Locks. A lock can also utilize mechanical push buttons. Push-button locks are mechanical and are mounted directly on the door. This will speed entry and eliminate the need for keys.

A typical application of a push-button lock is to separate public and private space. For example, in an office complex, push-button locks can control entry into storage rooms and restrooms.

Touchpads. Electrical and electronic touchpads are mounted on the wall and work in conjunction with an electrical strike or electrical lock set on the door.

Touchpads are primarily used on perimeter doors to control entry into office buildings. At the entry, there is a touchpad and telephone. After entering the proper code, it triggers the control station to unlock the door. The door is locked against entry with an electric strike or lockset, but the mechanical exit hardware is still active.

Telephone Entry Systems. Telephone entry systems are most commonly used at apartment buildings and condominiums. Located outside the building, they consist of a panel installed with a handset and touchpad. Each tenant has a special entry code that a visitor dials. Once the tenant answers, the tenant releases the door lock by pressing a designated key on the residence phone. For added security, some systems add a CCTV camera in the entry lobby with small monitors provided to each occupant.

Turnstiles. Turnstiles are used for high-traffic areas to control entry. There are two types of turnstiles: low profile and full-height. The most common is low profile, used primarily in subway stations and sports arenas. They operate in one direction and can maintain a count of the users. Low-profile turnstiles are also used in subway stations in which entry is granted using a fare or coded card.

Full-height turnstiles are used to ensure that only one person passes through in any single authorized entry transaction, and defeats any attempt to jump over — as can happen with low-profile turnstiles.

Pedestrian Passageway. In 1975, architect Philip Johnson designed the AT&T headquarters building in New York City with pedestrian passageways to control egress of employees. Rather than conventional turnstiles, Johnson used passageways — built of the same material used throughout the lobby — to channel the employees.

A card reader placed at the entrance and motion sensors installed within the passageway ensure that only one person, moving in the correct direction, can pass on a single authorized card.

Pedestrian passageways are now referred to as optical passage. Mechanical barriers are now included in the passageway to physically prevent passage until the card is validated.

Exit Control

The NFPA Life Safety Code 101 requires that emergency exit from a building be unobstructed. This collides with proper security goals to prevent unauthorized entry and exit through exit doors that remain open. Large losses can occur due to material or merchandise being carried through unguarded fire exits.

Access Control

To combat this problem, special hardware is used to control the exit. The hardware used is tailored for different businesses. In retail establishments and restaurants, for example, alarms are installed to sound when the exit door is opened. In office buildings where employees are in a secure area, the exit door needs to be screened because it bypasses normal security checks.

Exit Hardware. Exit hardware allows egress when the exit bar is pushed to unlock the door. Exit doors are usually double. The inherent problem with double exit doors is the ease with which they can be opened unlawfully. A coat hanger can be stuck through the space between the doors from the exterior, hook the panic bar and open them.

A padlocked chain wrapped around the panic bar is sometimes used to thwart illegal entry, but this is a direct violation of the fire code. It is also a common cause of life loss in buildings in which this method is employed. This particular method should not be tolerated.

There are a number of supplemental locks for doors that swing out. These locks rest on the door jamb at each side of the door, providing a greater resistance than a lock. When the release bar is pushed, the assembly will drop. This enables the door to open.

Delayed Exit. The other option available to secure double exit doors is an electromagnetic lock. This lock holds a door locked against exit for 15 or 30 seconds after the panic bar has been pushed, without interruption of the cycle. A horn or bell sound emits after the bar is pushed. There are new models that make a voice announcement instructing the person to keep pushing the door and it will open within the allotted time. With these newer models, the time-delay countdown is digitally displayed on the lock.

The intent of the time delay is to allow a guard ample time to arrive at the door and observe the situation. Currently, the maximum accepted locking time is 15 seconds.

The downside to this method, however, is that its use requires acceptance by the authority that has jurisdiction, even though Underwriters Laboratories has listed the equipment and NFPA lists the operation in Life Safety Code 101.

Most people are unaware of delayed egress locks on the emergency exit doors. Even with the appropriate emergency training, knowing about the 15-second time delay will not assuage a person's reaction in wanting to flee the premises as quickly as possible. Also, there are very few buildings in which the guard can get to the appropriate exit door within the alloted time. These are inherent problems with a time-delayed egress door.

However, if the building fire alarm has been activated, whether or not someone has used the exit hardware, the door will release immediately for fail-safe exiting. This is an invaluable asset in public buildings because it accommodates the hearing and sight impaired, and any verbal instructions can be tailored for specific requirements or recorded in more than one language.

The other alternative for exit door control is to simply leave the approved exit hardware in place. This will allow anyone to exit at anytime. Security is heightened by providing magnetic switches and installing CCTV cameras to view the doors and corridor. Magnetic switches will be activated when the door is opened, automatically instructing the camera to monitor the scene and record it, and notify the alarm center. This method does not prevent the exit, but it does instigate an investigation of the incident and identify the person who left the premises.

AUTHORIZED ACCESS CONTROL

Every business depends on some sort of controlled entry onto the premises. Usually, this begins with identification of the person entering. Authorized access control is simply an extension of people identification.

The identity of employees or visitors can be determined by a human or a computer. There are three basic types of identification verification and access control:

1. *Guards:* to make a personal recognition or inspect identification — such as a badge — of the employee or visitor, and then formulate a judgment of that person's validity.
2. *Card reader systems:* to compare the coded card[1] with the computer records for authorized personnel verification.
3. *Biometric readers:* use of a person's physical property — such as retinal pattern, hand geometry or fingerprint — to gain entry. These readers also verify the date and time of entry.

Large Systems

The larger access control systems that include operators' terminals perform the following functions:

- Admit or reject cards for entry
- Alarm if an unauthorized entry or exit attempt is made
- Alarm when penetration is made without using a card
- Make a permanent transaction record
- Print real-time events and historical logs

---

[1] *Editors note:* The term "coded cards" is used throughout this chapter in reference to any authorized entry device.

Access Control

Frequently, these functions exist as a sub-system of the security system as a whole and require interfacing with other security features — such as CCTV switching, intercoms, watch tours, fire alarms, ventilation, and heating and air conditioning (HVAC) monitoring. Every function of the entire security system is interrelated. Therefore, it is vital that their interfacing occurs as smoothly as possible; for example, operator terminals controlled by a computer can be programmed to perform these functions without a console operator.

The operator terminal is the center of the security system but it will not display certain security functions — such as employee use of valid coded cards. This is because no operator response is required. The console terminal will display an alarm if a card is tried in a door for which it is not programmed. In addition, it will automatically activate CCTV coverage to videotape the event.

Whatever the situation, there are complex and elaborate access systems available to accommodate almost every condition that requires restricting personnel or material flow.

The Access Control Sub-System

A major benefit of the large access control systems is one sub-system feature of recording each event that transpires. This is a function of the console terminal, an invaluable feature in theft investigations for determining the people who had access to stolen materials at or about the time of theft. Compounded with CCTV tape recordings, the records will indicate each door that was opened, whose card was used to gain entry, the exact time, and the route used to enter and exit the premises.

The advantages the access records generate may be enough to justify the investment in control programs.

For example, the need for timekeepers and certain administrative personnel can be eliminated and substituted with a time and attendance program for payroll. This program includes issuing unique identification badges that serve as the input media for computer-controlled data functions. A program of this type requires the purchase of identification and encoding devices, identification readers and data storage equipment.

Operational Requirements

To merit confidence, a mechanized or automated identification system must pass a number of performance tests. One is to have very few misreads — excluding entry to authorized cards or allowing entry to unauthorized cards. The modern card reader systems are incredibly reliable and exhibit few errors. The following performance requirements define what a modern card reader system should embody:

1. *Validity.* The system must establish the identity of the individual person involved. For example, it must recognize John Jones as John Jones, not Tom Smith.
2. *Reliability.* The system must correctly identify an individual each time the individual is presented. This proves the system is consistently valid.
3. *Ease of Use.* This is a relative concept because the level of difficulty acceptable in one situation may be intolerable in another. Generally, however, the system should be as simple and uncomplicated as possible.
4. *Tamper-Resistance.* As more and more systems are becoming automated, the possibility of surreptitious substitution or counterfeiting increases dramatically. The system employed must be as tamper-resistant as possible.
5. *Longevity.* Once set up, the system should remain functional over appreciable periods of time. This requirement applies both to identification cards and card readers.

The automatic and remote operation of mechanized systems is further discussed at length in this chapter.

Equipment Requirements

Durability. System components should be physically adequate to resist predictable attempts of force or manipulation. This can be a highly resistive design — such as a steel-lined, reinforced concrete constructed vault — or a less resistive design — such as securing a boardroom of drywall or plaster with a deadlock latchbolt on the door.

Whatever the level of resistivity, the key is to determine the predictable penetration probability. A careful analysis of the vulnerability of the asset to be protected will indicate the level of physical integrity required of the access control mechanism.

In a bank, for example, an unguarded vault in a remote area with long periods between observation is an inadequate deterrent to a determined attacker. On the other hand, if the vault is located in a busy corridor and in a well-lit structure, a locked room can be a sufficient deterrent for the attacker.

The identification system hardware must provide consistency and quality. Partitions, doors, and locking hardware should also have the same high quality and reliability as the computer system. If not, the inadequacy of one can totally defeat that of the other.

Maintainability. Components must have a satisfactory service life and replacements, when needed, should be readily available. At most locations,

Access Control

the best method of maintenance is an annual service contract from the installation company.

CODED CARD TECHNOLOGY

Coded cards search the identification medium used for key information, encoded in a way that is readable by the processor. The most popular card readers today read magnetic coding, sometimes in combination with a PIN from a keypad. A summary description of the different types of technology will illuminate their distinctive differences.

Magnetic Stripe Cards

The market for magnetic stripe card technology is thriving. As a result, features demanded by users — such as reliability, durability and security — are being taken to new heights through improved manufacturing techniques, high coercivity encoding and sophisticated data protection schemes. By far, the most popular coded card in use is the worldwide credit card.

How do magnetic readers work? The readers sense the magnetic energy present in, or absent from, a minute field within a medium capable of receiving magnetic energy. Magnetic tape is the most common example. The presence of a field on the tape, or the strength of the field, is detected by the reader. In presence/absence detection, the magnetic charge may be of either digital or non-digital characters — its presence or absence being what is significant. The complete pattern of the presence/absence character in the magnetic medium yields a datum that has some logical function — for example, in opening or closing an electrical control circuit.

In the strength-of-field readers, the impressed magnetic energy is converted to different readable frequencies by causing voltage oscillations in an electrical current in the reader. The varying voltages then perform a logical task. With digital characters, the total pattern may be an input for some computer-based discrimination.

Watermark Magnetics

This card differs from the magnetic stripe card in that it has enhancements that make it extremely difficult to defeat. The base material is passed through a coating trough where a magnetic slurry is applied. The particles are set at alternating angles by an alignment magnet that is the width of the tape, while the iron oxide slurry is still wet. Spacing of the binary structure of this computer-generated pattern is then oven-cured permanently into the magnetic oxide to create unalterable watermark magnetics in 10 or 12 digit code — numbers.

This is comparable to the watermark process used on paper, wherein it is possible to type over the paper and still read both the watermark and the typed message. The magnetic stripe has a permanent number, but it can also be encrypted with an additional code.

In order to read these cards, a special watermark magnetics verification track needs to be added to an existing conventional magnetic reader head. What is actually read is the stripe and data content and the original watermark magnetics coded card number. Watermark magnetic cards cannot be duplicated because the watermark code number is different for every card. The combination of the card's watermark coded number and the changeable magnetic stripe data make this card unique.

Barium Ferrite

Barium ferrite is another form of magnetic coding. It positions magnetic fields throughout the card, with alternating north and south poles. This technology was used in the early design stages of coded cards but is not in wide use today due, in part, to its vulnerability to sabotage.

A new barium ferrite application is the "touch card." It operates by placing the card on a reader with no aperture or slot — as with conventional magnetic readers. This makes the reader much less vulnerable to sabotage or misreads due to the failure to align the card within the reader.

Wiegend Wire

Wiegand cards are more secure than magnetic stripe cards. Weigand cards are named after its inventor, John Wiegand, who discovered the technology in the late 1970s. First licensed by Sensor Engineering, it is now owned by HID Corporation.

The code is developed from bits of ferromagnetic wire positioned on strips of plastic in specific patterns that are embedded into blank or customer-logo cards. Any attempt to reach the code strip destroys the card. These cards are not affected by magnetic fields, and work outdoors as well as indoors. They are able to work outside because the readers are weatherproof — there are no exposed or moving parts.

Due to the wide acceptance by the security industry, the 26-bit Wiegand-reader output code has become a standard that many other readers try to match. The only major problem with this card is they are extremely difficult to reproduce.

Proximity/Contact Readers

Proximity and contact readers are compatible for people who have disabilities that prohibit them from being able to use an insertion or swipe reader. Of the two, the proximity reader has a wider application because it will operate with the card at a greater distance from the reader.

Access Control

These readers also conform to the Americans with Disability Act. It is predicted that the proximity reader will take a large share of the market in the future.

Resonant Circuits

Integrated, resonant micro-circuits have both coded card technology and an access control function. Presently, its access control functions are used for electronic surveillance of merchandise and stock control.

Resonant circuit devices are passive modulators that receive a generated energy pulse and modulate it so that the modulated signal — when picked up by a receiver — triggers a switching function. This function is to either sound an alarm or proceed to the next logical step in the ID or access control routine. The function works because the micro-circuit chip is impressed into the ID device at the time of preparation.

U.S. manufacturers are currently marketing systems that use an active transmitter at the controlled door and a passive modulator in the ID device, as well as personal device transmitters and passive modulators located at the controlled doors.

Radio Frequency Readers

Radio frequency (RF) readers are considered long-range proximity readers. The most common applications of an RF reader are:
- Electronic article surveillance in retail stores
- Receiving the signal from a keyring push-button transmitter that locks
- Unlocking a car
- Automatic vehicle ID devices that identify a vehicle traveling at speeds up to 35 mph

Biometric Technology

The areas of law enforcement, banking, and welfare organizations are recognizing that reliable personal identification is a key requirement to the success of their programs. This has spurred the continued growth of biometric technology throughout the world in a wide range of applications.

These devices take unique physical data about the person, convert them to an electronic information format, and then compare critical parameters of the viewed information with previously stored information. Biometric devices measure hand geometry, read retinal patterns, compare single fingerprints, and record and compare voiceprints or signatures. Currently in development is a face scanner that uses an infrared camera; but availability is still a few years away.

Hand geometry readers and retinal scanners are used in situations in which identification of an individual is required in addition to the verification of data encoded on a card. The high cost of these devices and the slower entry and exit time they generate are factors that should be considered with biometric applications.

Dielectric Readers

A dielectric medium is one that allows an induced electrical current to pass through it from one conductor to another. Varying the character of the dielectric medium varies the induced current, and the variations can be keyed to perform logical tasks.

Contact has to be made through an exposed terminal strip on the side of the card to connect the circuit in the card to the reader. This causes the mechanical connection to be a source of trouble, thus limiting its application. Consequently, dielectric readers may not be the most viable reader option.

Embossing Readers

These involve a matrix or field throughout which micro-switches are distributed in some pattern. The embossing on the card activates the switches to pass current through control circuits. The operation of the reader is determined by the precise location of the switches within the matrix — if the switches are "cancel" types (for example, if the presence of embossing will prevent or abort the function) — and by the thickness or tolerance required to make switch contact.

Embossing readers are purely electromechanical in that switch closure can or will not occur. Thus, no information is processed.

Hollerith Readers

Hollerith readers embody hollerith punching. This is most commonly associated with punching seen on standard, paper data or time cards. The presence of the punch permits the momentary closure of electrical contacts when the card is inserted into a reader. Distribution of the punches determines the logical output.

Cards featuring hollerith punching have a major security vulnerability. If the punched code is solely relied upon to control access or establish identity, it can be easily duplicated and an unauthorized or substitute device produced. This can be solved by including other critical requirements in the reading process or including one or more logical steps in addition to the card reader.

Optical Character Readers

Optical character readers are magnetic ink character readers (MICR) or conventional optical character readers (OCR). They can read information recorded on a card, such as a person's complete medical history or service

Access Control

manuals for products shipped internationally. The data is impressed in a certain configuration that enables the OCR devices to read the data directly.

Being able to download information without retyping it is the ultimate convenience of OCR devices. In 1995, Canon developed the Optical Memory Card (OMC). It can store up to 3.4 megabytes of information on a standard size card. This enables highly classified information to be carried on a card and encrypted for security.

Smart Card

The smart card is a personal identification device. It is similar to a credit card or conventional ID card in that it contains an integrated circuit (IC). The card stores all the information needed to identify and permit access to the card bearer in its chip memory. The advantage of using a smart card is that the device validates itself when used in conjunction with the security system as a whole.

The card can only be read by a smart card reader and the user must enter a personal identification code (PIN). The smart card will recognize the PIN, and signal the local or central controller to perform the access control function. At the same time, the ID information in the IC on the card is processed by the central or local processor memory, and makes a recording of the transaction. This system eliminates the need for central files to retain a "lookup" or reference entry on any particular ID device.

The IC-based smart card features programmable memory. The programmable memory is entered onto the card chip in RAM and PROM so that two different functions can be performed on the card. RAM is used to permit revisions or updates of the data contained within the card chip, and PROM is used when the card requires processing or modification. Smart cards originally had a bump in the card where the diode was located in the circuit. Modern cards are flat and smooth on both sides and almost as thin as a magnetic strip card.

Smart card applications have been expanding throughout the U.S. as well as the world. France has been using smart cards for many years. In French restaurants, the wireless card readers are brought directly to the table to read the card and print a bill. The patron, therefore, never has to surrender his card. The U.S. Department of Defense has even contracted French-developed smart cards.

The U.S. Department of Defense is considering replacing soldier ID tags — or dog tags — with smart cards. They can carry the soldiers' complete medical and military service records. This eliminates the need to produce and carry medical records and travel orders.

In Hawaii, all people entitled to welfare are issued a smart card. This prevents most forms of welfare fraud. Smart cards are also being used as debit cards in the broad point-of-sale and bank card markets; but, when being used as a debit card, it must treated with the same care as cash.

Smart Card Encryption. Cryptography and smart cards are closely linked. Cryptography provides the basic mechanism for security and confidentiality in smart cards, and the smart card provides the mechanism to make cryptography secure, portable and personal. From Internet commerce to the privacy of health and financial records, cryptography has become so vitally important that computer users need it to access their accounts.

DISTRIBUTED INTELLIGENCE SYSTEMS

Distributed intelligence systems are security systems that incorporate control and discrimination logic, which is programmable from either the console at the control center or other operator's terminals — such as guard posts in remote buildings.

Information on card access is recorded in the host computer at the control center and downloaded to every card reader panel where the card is authorized. With the availability of relatively inexpensive microchips, each card reader control panel can store all the information necessary to control entry at that point. If the host computer fails, operation can continue intact at each card reader location. Both the host computer and the local control panel would have to fail in order for the card readers to malfunction. When the card reader is in degraded mode, it releases the door for any card with a facility code.

If the central processor is offline, local transaction information will be retained in a buffer at the local control panel. When the central processor is functional again, all the stored transactions will be transmitted for permanent recording.

Multiple levels of authorization can be divided among overlapping time periods and, dependent upon various contingent events, authorize or deny entry. The basic function of distributed intelligence systems is for all programs to achieve one or more of the four access control objectives.

SPECIAL ACCESS FEATURES AND APPLICATIONS

Using a card to release a door, gate or turnstile is simple to observe and understand. However, there are other access control applications that need to be addressed.

Anti-Passback

The following example is used to demonstrate the effectiveness of the anti-passback feature. A large business complex has a high-value area,

Access Control

such as a research laboratory. Employees authorized to enter the high-value area must pass through a door that has an anti-passback feature in addition to the normal card reading access control measures. Once inside the restricted area, the card can be used only on other readers within the area, or to exit.

When using a card to exit, the anti-passback feature automatically returns the system to the general facilities mode and immediately blocks further use inside the area, unless the card is first used for re-entry. This prevents unauthorized personnel from entering a restricted area if one of the cards were passed out.

Two-Man Rule

Some businesses have high-security areas in which a person cannot be in the area alone, such as the reserve currency vault of a bank or classified information storage vault. To control entry, two employees with valid coded cards must use their cards in sequence — within 45 seconds of each other — to unlock the door for entry or exit.

If only one employee attempts entry or exit, it will be denied, an alarm will sound, and a permanent record will be made of the attempt. The locking feature can be designed to fail safe if life safety requirements dictate that the exit should not be impeded under emergency conditions.

In this instance, egress will be free but the database will not recognize their exit — they will still be listed as being in the area. A correction to the database is required after any emergency event.

Mantrap

A mantrap is used where a high degree of access control is required and egress is low. It is typically a vestibule with card reader controlled doors on both ends so that when one door is open, the other automatically locks.

For example, a person uses a card to enter, shuts the entry door — which automatically locks — and uses the card a second time to open the other door. If the card is not authorized, the user is held in the mantrap. An intercom between the mantrap and the guard post and/or the alarm console is usually included.

Frequently, separate mantraps are used for entry and exit. Mantraps can also use the anti-passback feature. Note that just as with the two-man rule, a fail-safe provision needs to be instituted for use during life safety emergencies.

There are several manufacturers that offer the entire mantrap as an access control booth. These models range from a simple two-door vestibule to a truck-size enclosure with features for card reading, PIN keypad, metal detection, bomb detection, weight feature, occupant count, biometric sensors, voice instructions, and backup power — all built-in.

Sally Port

A sally port is similar to a mantrap except it is large enough for a truck to drive into. At military posts, they are built of heavy reinforced chain-link fencing or masonry. At a federal reserve bank, they are interior and are built to withstand a bomb.

There are two operational requirements for a sally port:

1. It should provide a safe and isolated location to inspect the vehicle.
2. It should provide a sheltered access to a nearby safe room in which the driver is interviewed.
3. A sally port should also have the following safeguards:

   — CCTV cameras to inspect the vehicle. A common camera placement is to have one camera mounted on an articulated arm to inspect underneath and inside the truck.
   — An enclosed, bullet-resistant corridor around the top of the sally port to provide the guards with the ability to view the situation and use fire power, if necessary.
   — Intercoms placed throughout the corridor for easy communication.
   — An interview room located adjacent to the sally port. Thus, the driver parks the truck in the sally port and enters a bullet-resistant interview room for further identification and processing.

Gatehouse

Construction of a gatehouse must include roads that have the capacity to handle rush-hour traffic, with enough lanes to screen employees and visitors. Ideally, the gatehouse should be in the center of the road so the guard is adjacent to both the incoming and outgoing traffic lanes.

Every lane around the gatehouse should have curbs on both sides and a traffic arm. Entry for employees can be reader controlled with an intercom at each card reader for communication between the driver and security. To exit, the vehicle drives over a loop in the driveway, automatically raising the traffic arm. A detection loop should be present in all lanes to sense when the vehicle has cleared the arm so that it can automatically lower it.

More control is required to accommodate business visitors and employees who forget their passes. If entry is made during normal business hours, the guard stationed in the gatehouse can handle the identification process. After normal business hours, the transaction needs to be accomplished remotely from the control console, which could be a mile or more away. The entrance lane next to the gatehouse can be used for this purpose.

Access Control

For after-hours entry, a custom-built vehicle access control unit is mounted on the side of the gatehouse facing the incoming traffic lane. Inbound drivers stop outside the traffic arm and push a button on the face of the unit. This alerts the alarm console operator, sets up the intercom, brings up two CCTV cameras in the control unit, and turns on lights in the control unit. The driver then places his or her driver's license on the control unit to be viewed at the console. A second camera, positioned on the driver's face, can also be viewed at the console. A third camera is positioned to read the rear license plate. If the driver is authorized to enter, the console operator can raise the traffic arm. A fourth camera should be placed to have a general view of the entire gate area, including incoming and exiting lanes and traffic arms. (*Note:* Generally, optical fiber circuits are used for the transmission of all signals.)

The brightness of the lights in the access control unit can be automatically adjusted for daytime or evening light. There should also be enough space left outside the traffic arm for a vehicle to turn around into the exit lane. If vehicles of varying heights are expected during after-hours remote control entry, the vehicle access unit can be installed on a vertical track and raised and lowered by the alarm console operator.

Vehicle Parking Garages

There are many options to control egress of vehicle parking lots or garages. The basic measures use a card reader and intercom to control entry, and closing loop detectors to control the exit. More detailed access control methods are described below.

Limit Operating Hours. Securing a parking garage at night requires extra control measures. The entire perimeter must be enclosed with a chain-link fence or another ornamental architectural treatment, and gates with locks must be positioned at the vehicle and pedestrian portals. Vehicles that are not removed by closing time will stay in the structure until the next day.

No Guard Placed at the Entrance. The entire vehicle control operation must be controlled from the control console 24 hours a day, every day.

User-Friendly Entry and Exit. Every entry portal must have proximity readers with long-range capabilities, and an intercom and CCTV camera. The employee ID card is the access medium of choice because placards or ID devices that are affixed to the vehicle force the driver to use the same vehicle for egress. A loop detector at the exit can provide the employee with a "free out."

Accommodating Visitors and Contractors. The alarm control operator needs to screen all drivers without a valid badge. (Refer to the earlier section titled "Gatehouse" for more information on this topic.)

Accommodating Car Pools. Special software programs are available that accept any single badge from the car pool, and automatically block the others of the group for that day. This is a valuable feature to control overcrowding in the garage because it will block other family members of the car pool groups from using the card.

Traffic Control. Traffic lights can be placed on the parking lot ramps to control traffic flow on the ramps. Card readers can control the traffic lights. Lights can also be placed at the vehicle exit to protect pedestrians crossing in front of the driveway. The exiting vehicle causes the signal to light and emit an audible alarm to alert the pedestrians. (Check with your municipality to install a "permit" traffic light in the garage exit. This will control the street traffic.)

Excluding Unauthorized Pedestrians. To detect and prevent an unauthorized person from walking through the vehicle entrance, use a combination of vehicle detector loops in the driveway and passive infrared (PIR) motion detectors.

This system works because each system is triggered by weight. So, an entering vehicle will activate only the detector loop, thus canceling the PIR detectors, and vice versa for the pedestrian. When the PIR detectors are activated, the proper exit instructions can be provided via an intercom from the control operator, loudspeakers, or a guard. A further safeguard is CCTV monitors to videotape the event.

Controlling Garage-to-Building Access. To control building elevators or the building street entrance requires the use of a valid card to operate the elevator or door entrance. The most effective configuration for the elevator is to have the elevator from the garage discharge at the lobby level, where a guard or receptionist is stationed.

Also, make the separate stairways from the garage empty only into the lobby. This will make it necessary for people to enter directly into the lobby from the garage.

Emergency Alarms. Intercoms should be available in the garage, spaced at intervals no greater than 60 feet. For easy recognition, the intercoms should be mounted on posts painted a bright color — such as yellow or orange — with a floodlight, and a sign signifying the intercom — such as "security intercom."

The intercom is activated by pressing a large button on the intercom, which then sends an alarm to the security console. The alarm initiates the intercom circuit to monitor sounds in the garage and then sends a signal to indicate the alarm signal has been received — such as sounding a chime or displaying "help coming" on the intercom window.

CCTV in Garages and Parking Lots. CCTV coverage can be limited in its scope but can still provide satisfactory coverage. Cameras placed at the main entrance, at all exit control points, guard booths, cashier booths and elevator lobbies on every floor will ensure more than adequate security.

It is impossible for cameras to provide a complete view of the parking garage due to the slope and ramping of garage floors. For best coverage, position the cameras to view the parking ramps and driveways as well as the intercom stations.

Mixing Employee and Public Parking. Mixing employee and public parking presents a serious security vulnerability, especially in a high-profile organization. It is prudent to forego whatever revenue might be generated through paid public parking and close the parking area to the public.

Public access to underground parking is what made the 1993 bombing at the World Trade Center in New York City possible. If mixed parking cannot be avoided, separate entrances should be provided for public and employee use; and the two areas should, at the minimum, be separated by sturdy partitions.

Campus Parking. A school campus is well-suited for multi-coded card applications, but a single card must meet all the requirements of the campus. Currently, hundreds of campuses have replaced the earlier card systems to accommodate magnetic stripe, bar code, and optical readers, all of which can be activated with the same card. Some have even started using smart cards.

Some of the card functions required of school campuses include the following:

- Parking
- Entrance into teaching buildings and dormitories
- Small purchases at campus stores
- Use of the gym
- Computer access
- Library book release
- Dining room charges
- Telephone service
- Banking transactions

Elevator Control

The use of coded cards to control elevators requires special card readers. There are also the hidden costs of traveler cables for each elevator cab reader and the lobby call button.

The lobby call button will not prevent a person from making an unauthorized floor call from within the cab, but it will lessen the likelihood of an unauthorized person initially gaining cab access. To combat this security loophole, it is necessary to install a reader in the cab that is interconnected with the car calling system.

The use of proximity cards for elevator control is inadequate because, when several people are in the cab, the card reader cannot determine which badge to read. Careful coordination of defining access control and selecting the appropriate card technology and readers is vital to comprehensive elevator control. This should even be considered during the building design — such as having separate elevators for sensitive floors to allow the access control system to operate from lobby readers.

Janitor's Privileges

Some programs allow special privileges for janitorial crews that clean after-hours. The janitors are issued cards or PIN numbers that inactivate all alarms and make a record indicating that a janitor is on site. When the janitors depart, all alarms are reactivated and a signal is sent to the central station indicating the janitor has left the building.

Other Miscellaneous Applications

Office Equipment. Access to computers, shredders and copiers in sensitive offices can be controlled by applying a card reader to the machine. The alarm system will record the time, date and the person who used the machine each time it is employed. This system will also prohibit unauthorized personnel use.

Tools and Inventory. Bar code tags and cards can be used to track all tools in use and work-in-progress. At each tool crib, a card reader records each tool drawn and who has it on loan. As products are being manufactured, they can have the bar code read and their location can be recorded as they move through the production line. The advantage of bar code tags and cards for inventory is that inventory reconciliation can be performed at any given time.

Personal Equipment at Work. Office equipment can be tagged with a proximity device or one that uses electronic article surveillance (EAS) with readers positioned at the exits. This causes an alarm to sound if the equipment is carried near or through the exit.

Personal computers, cameras, and other valuable equipment brought into the office by employees can also be tagged. When the employee leaves the building carrying personal equipment, the reader will detect both the employee's badge and equipment badge. The program will recognize the combination as acceptable and no alarm will sound.

Personal Safety. Wrist proximity badges are effective for hospitals and nursing homes. The wrist badge is attached to a patient's wrist, and signals an alarm if they attempt to exit the area.

Monitoring Prisoners. With prisons becoming so overcrowded, other alternatives are being considered. One such consideration is confining prisoners to their homes with an electronic monitoring device. The prisoner wears an ankle-strap radio transmitter that is monitored by a local receiver. If the receiver fails to read the transmitter, it uses the phone line to transmit the report to a central station or probation officer's pager. This will notify the monitors that the prisoner has vacated the premises.

Hotels and Motels. Very few hotels currently issue traditional room keys to their guests; coded cards are issued instead. Coded cards provide hotels with better security, are more cost-effective than the traditional room key, and provide acute detail of room egress.

Constantly replacing traditional room keys and the cylinders is more of a financial hindrance to hotels than the equipment necessary for coded cards. Coded cards require a nonwired, battery-operated card reader on every room door. The readers retain the last 50 operations and a report can be printed out using a portable handheld printer. Hotel staff have separate codes that allow room access, yet also record the time, date and who entered.

As a result of coded card use, security directors have reported less incidents from both patrons and staff.

Dressing Rooms at Performing Art Centers. Performing art centers have similar problems to hotels regarding key use — the keys are not returned and it presents a security risk. Coded cards are not a viable option for these centers because some costumes do not have pockets. To compensate, push-button locks are used instead. Push-button lock combinations can be changed daily as well as record the previous 50 operations.

WEAPONS AND CONTRABAND SCREENING

Screening before air travel has long been accepted as a necessary precaution. Screening prior to entry into commercial and governmental facilities is also accepted as routine. The acceptability of the process is partially contingent on equal treatment of all potential entrants to the restricted areas. The efficiency of the operation and the involvement of courteous, well-trained employees are also major factors in acceptance of the process.

In the air transport industry, checked baggage is screened by x-ray machines, explosives detectors and with the use of canines trained to detect explosives and drugs. Many organizations routinely use x-ray machines to screen incoming mail and certain other shipments for explosive devices.

Physical Configuration

For an effective screening operation, the screening equipment and personnel must be configured to ensure that all persons and/or shipments entering the area are screened. An unprotected entry point will render the screening ineffective. Persons with disabilities are subject to the same security requirements as all other entrants. Screening personnel should examine any assistive devices that they believe may conceal a weapon or other contraband.

Signs should be posted, in the appropriate language(s), notifying potential entrants that screening is a prerequisite for entry into the area. This provides legal notice to potential entrants and will deter some persons from attempting to enter the area with weapons or contraband.

Screening Policies and Procedures

All policies and procedures for screening should be written, reviewed and approved by legal counsel and disseminated. Federal Aviation Administration (FAA) Regulation 108, Airplane Operator Security, while specific to the air transport industry, provides a sample of screening policy and procedures.[1] Some basic considerations in formulating screening policies and procedures include:

- Identification of the personnel who will enforce the screening rules
- Training and periodic testing of the screening personnel
- Determination of the situations in which law enforcement personnel will participate in the screening process
- Action to be taken when an individual objects to screening
- The disposition of weapons and contraband found, including legal and illegal weapons

Metal Detectors. Metal detectors are used to find buried treasure, to find land mines and to screen entrants to all public and private spaces. The two basic types of metal detectors are *walk-through* and *handheld* instruments.

Metal detectors function by generating an electromagnetic field. If a metal object capable of conducting electricity is introduced into the electromagnetic field, it disrupts the pattern of the field. The disruption is announced by sound and/or other indicators.

The metal detectors used by the military to detect buried mines in World War II are crude instruments when compared with the instruments

---

[1] http://www.tisco.com/aviation/FAA/far-108/index/shtml.

available today. Early models required frequent adjustment and intensive training for efficient operation. Current models incorporate solid-state electronics and the functions are controlled by microprocessors. The sensitivity adjustment ranges from the detection of a minute piece of metal to detection of a metal mass that might approximate that of a weapon. More efficient and effective metal detectors continue to be developed. One sophisticated model displays the position of a weapon on a person, using light-emitting diodes (LEDs), as the person passes through the detector. Another model includes a signal analysis system that is reported to be able to distinguish between a weapon and a cellular telephone.

Manufacturers of metal detectors advertise, and should certify, that the equipment is in compliance with the requirements of the Americans with Disabilities Act (ADA) and is harmless to pacemakers, life support systems, pregnant women and magnetic media.

Walk-through detectors are most commonly used in fixed positions with hard-wired electrical power. Portable units that can be set up and made operational in a matter of minutes are also available. An important feature for either type of walk-through unit is the ability of the unit to function on battery power. The failure of commercial power should never translate into a failure of the screening operation. In addition, it may be difficult or impossible to connect the portable units to commercial power at a temporary location.

The basic ground rules for metal detector screening include the following:

- Adjust the sensitivity of the units to detect weapons and contraband and periodically test the sensitivity of the units.
- Train the personnel who are to operate the equipment and test their ability to detect weapons and contraband.
- Ensure that all hand-carried items, such as handbags, are screened by hand or by x-ray machines.
- Ensure that metal items deposited in trays, thus bypassing the metal detector, are inspected.
- Require that all alarms be investigated by handheld metal detectors or by physical search.

The number of metal detectors and personnel required for an efficient operation is a function of:

- The number of anticipated entrants to the area
- The weapons or contraband to be excluded
- The effective "pass through" rate of the metal detectors;
- The x-ray or other supplemental equipment available
- The physical configuration of the operation

For example, a larger number of personnel will be required to hand-search hand-carried items if x-ray screening of those items is not conducted.

X-Ray Inspection

The basic x-ray machine transmits an x-ray beam through an object and displays a black-and-white image of the object on a monitor. The penetrating power of the x-ray is dependent on the power of the delivered beam and the size and density of the object being screened. An available color enhancement can allow an operator to better evaluate a suspicious item. The varied densities of items are displayed in different colors on the monitor.

A more sophisticated dual-energy machine aids in distinguishing between organic and inorganic materials by transmitting two x-ray wavelengths through a package. Organic materials such as leather or paper are displayed on a screen in red or orange. Inorganic materials such as metal are displayed in green or blue. A dual-energy machine has one monitor to display the basic black-and-white image and a second monitor to display the dual-energy color image.

A third type of machine uses backscatter technology to allow the operator to identify items that are packed in front of other items. Items in the front of the package are displayed on one screen while a second screen displays items packed behind the first object. Note, however, that extremely dense items may absorb a significant part of the x-ray and hide items packed behind them.

Persons carrying unprocessed photographic film are frequently concerned about x-ray damage to the film. The typical airport-screening machine produces a very low x-ray dosage. A major film manufacturer[1] advises travelers carrying unprocessed film with a speed of 1600 or higher, and those carrying highly sensitive x-ray or scientific film, to request that a visual inspection be performed. Additionally, the effect of x-ray exposure is cumulative and unprocessed film that is subjected to x-ray screening more than five times may be damaged.

X-ray security scanners are in common use for applications other than the screening of personnel and hand-carried objects. Security x-ray scanning of incoming mail and screening of receiving dock shipments is a routine procedure in some organizations. Screening larger and denser objects requires larger machines with higher energy x-rays than the typical airport screening machines. The state-of-the-art in large-format, high-energy inspection is a machine that is capable of inspecting a 60-foot tractor-trailer combination in as little as two minutes. The machine incorporates a precise motion control system and a computer-assisted image analysis. Pan, zoom, contrast and color equalization controls allow the operator to examine any area of the cargo.

---

[1] http://www.kodak.de/global/en/service/faqs/faq0014.shtml.

The ability of a functional x-ray machine to detect weapons and contraband is wholly dependent on the ability of the operator to identify the items. Training and periodic testing is essential. Note that the training provided by the manufacturer of the machine focuses on the operation of the machine. Specific training tailored to the working environment must be provided by the user organization.

Explosives Detectors

X-Ray Machines. A dual-energy x-ray machine displays organic explosives such as dynamite and TNT. However, inorganic explosives such as black powder and sodium chlorate will not be readily identified as explosives.

Combination Systems. Newer explosives detection systems use a combination of x-rays and computerized axial tomography (CAT) to detect minute amounts of explosives. Some machines can determine the presence of explosives at ultratrace levels, including plastic explosive taggants that are difficult to detect using conventional x-ray machines. The process is relatively slow and expensive.

Vapor Detectors. Vapor detectors use a vacuum to collect vapor samples as the vacuum is passed over an object. The machine analyzes the samples to detect vapors generated by certain explosives. Vapor detectors will not detect plastic or black powder explosives. They should not be used as the only explosives detection system at a facility.

Particle Detectors. Particle detectors detect trace amounts of chemical compounds that may be found in some explosive devices. A vacuum hose, a swipe pad or a card is used to collect the sample. The sample is inserted into the machine particle detector, which then compares the sample with the chemical signatures of certain explosive compounds. The results are displayed on a monitor. Note, however, that a particle detector may not detect explosives that are sealed in a package wiped clean after sealing.

Canines. A dog's ability to detect scents and odors is more than 100 times greater than that of humans. The detection reliability of a well-trained dog is very high and the ability of a dog to rapidly search an area is invaluable. For example, a 50-yard corridor filled with lockers can be searched for explosives in about two minutes. Trace odors left by substances, as well as the actual substances, can be detected by a trained dog. An explosive detection dog should be able to recognize smokeless powder, C-4 plastic explosive and commercial dynamite both in gelatin form and trinitrotoluene (TNT).

ASSET PROTECTION AND SECURITY MANAGEMENT HANDBOOK

Selected Bibliography

Argus Business/Argus, Inc.; *Access Control: 1996 Buyers' Guide Issue;* 1996; Argus Business/Argus, Inc.

Bowers, Dan M.; *Access Control and Personal Identification Card Technology, 5th ed.;* The Bowers Report, Randallstown, MD, 19092.

Burke, Harry E.; *Automating Management Information Systems;* 1990; Van Nostrand Reinhold.

Carlson, Reinhold A. and DiGiandomenico, Robert A.; *Understanding Building Automation Systems;* 1991; R.S. Means Company, Inc.

Galaxy Control Systems; *Reference Guide to Access & Security Management;* 1996; Galaxy Control Systems.

Intertec Publishing Corporation; *Access Control & Security System Integration;* monthly publication, Intertec Publishing Corporation, P. O. Box 5111, Pittsfield, MA 01203-9830.

Personal Identification News; *PIN Newsletter;* 1997; 7101 Wisconsin Avenue, Bethesda, MD 20814; tel: (301) 654-0018.

Simonsen, Clifford E.; *Private Security in America: An Introduction;* 1998; Prentice-Hall, Upper Saddle River, NJ.

Rusting Publications; *The Parking Security Primer;* 1995; Rusting Publications.

Periodicals

Security Management, American Society for Industrial Security, Alexandria, VA.
— Giusti, Christopher, CPP and O'Hara, Shaun M., CPP; Mail Center Security, November 1998.

Security Technology and Design, Locksmith Publishing Group, Park Ridge, IL.
— Bjorkholm, Paul; X-rays in Modern Security Applications; October 1997.

Organizations Associated with Smart Cards

Biometric Consortium for governmental agencies on the Internet at: http://www. biometrics. org8080/~BC.

National Association of Campus Card Users; provides assistance in developing campus card-based systems; telephone: (919) 403-2273.

Personal Computer Memory Card Industry Association; sets worldwide standards for PC card technology; telephone: (408) 433-2273.

Smart Card Forum; development of open systems based on smart card technology; telephone: (813) 286-2339.

8
Emergency Planning

THE FIRST STEP

Unexpected emergencies and contingencies occur with dismaying regularity. When a disaster or other emergency strikes, many decisions must be made while the event is still unfolding and the true dimensions of the situation are usually unknown. While some decisions will affect the health of the organization for many years, some may have an immediate effect on its ability to survive. An emergency can overwhelm those who have done no planning or preparation.

Even with planning, it is necessary to improvise and remain flexible when a disaster or other emergency strikes. The varieties of emergencies make planning for every conceivable contingency impossible; however, general planning and resource allocations are feasible. Adequate planning makes the difference between recovery and the demise of the organization. For most commercial, industrial and government enterprises, the need to rapidly resume normal operations is as great as the need to control potential damage.

The logical beginning of emergency/contingency management is the development of a sound plan that accomplishes the following:

1. Defines emergency in terms relevant to the organization
2. Establishes an organization with specific tasks to function immediately before, during and after an emergency
3. Establishes a method for utilizing available resources and for obtaining additional resources at the time of an emergency
4. Provides a means for moving normal operations into and back out of the emergency mode of operations

ADVANCE PLANNING

Planning in advance of an emergency is essential. During an emergency, expect confusion and an interruption of communication links. Conditions may become chaotic. An emergency plan should enable those responsible for recovery to focus on solving major problems. They should not attempt to immediately bring complete order out of the chaos. If an enterprise considers all predictable and routine procedures in the plan, those responsible for actions during an emergency will be able to handle any unpredictable or unusual situations that develop. Because coping with an emergency situation as it begins to develop may prevent it from evolving into a substantial loss, an emergency plan should provide the basis for orderly actions and for making decisions that minimize loss.

Objectives of Emergency Planning and Crisis Management

There are three primary objectives in emergency planning and crisis management. The first is to minimize the probability of a threat or emergency. This may be possible with human or accidental threats; however, it is not achievable with natural threats, such as hurricanes, tornadoes and snowstorms. Therefore, the second objective is to mitigate the impact if the event occurs, so that the resulting loss and damage is limited. The final objective is equally important as the first two: recover from the emergency and resume normal operations. Normalcy after an emergency will be quite different among victims.

Stages of an Incident

In emergency planning, one must consider the stages of an incident. While different planners may use different terminology, the stages are essentially as follows:

1. Planning
2. Pre-event action
3. Event
4. Response
5. Recovery

The planning phase is distinguished from the pre-event action phase in that the former involves those actions taken to *plan* for the emergency, while the latter involves those taken to *implement the plan* before the emergency event occurs. In some instances, such as an approaching hurricane, there may be sufficient warning time so as to allow significant pre-event actions, including mass evacuation. In other instances, such as a tornado, there may be only sufficient warning to enable individuals in the threatened area to seek shelter in a protected part of the building. Some actions can be planned for but cannot be fully implemented until the event occurs and the response phase begins. An example is snow removal; crews and equipment are prepositioned but the actual plowing and removal cannot begin until the snow is on the ground. The nature of an emergency determines how much of a plan is implemented before the event and how much is implemented during or after the event. The last phase is the recovery and return to some degree of "normal" operations. Again, this phase will vary in scope and duration, depending on the nature of the emergency. For example, in the event of a civil disorder, the recovery phase may involve removing barricades and terminating special police patrols, which may take one or two days. Conversely, the recovery phase after a hurricane, earthquake or major flood could take years.

Emergency Planning

Types of Threats and Contingencies

The emergencies or contingencies for which plans may be developed can be grouped into three major categories: natural, human (either internal or external) and accidental threats. Natural threats include all weather-related emergencies, such as hurricanes, tornadoes, floods, winter storms and fires caused by lightning, as well as non-weather natural events such as earthquakes and volcanic eruptions. Human threats are *deliberate* adverse actions and events, including terrorist activity, arson, civil disorders and barricade/hostage situations, among others. Accidental threats encompass *non-deliberate* adverse actions and events, and can range from hazardous material spills to telecommunications and computer outages. The various types of threats can translate into a range of contingencies for which planning is appropriate.

It should be noted that emergency/contingency plans are not intended to cover those situations that are dealt with in the normal course of business or government operations. For example, if a key individual is sick, on vacation or traveling, someone else will take over that person's responsibilities in accordance with the organization's normal operating procedures. However, if the bulk of the workforce is unable to reach the work site due to a major weather emergency, or if a hurricane or tornado seriously damages the facility, a nonroutine situation exists, for which preplanning is essential.

Contingencies for which planning is appropriate include, but are not limited to:

- Fire
- Explosion
- Water outage
- Power outage
- Computer system failure
- Telecommunications failure
- Fuel leak
- HAZMAT incident
- Bomb incident
- Civil disorder
- Armed attack
- Barricade/hostage incident
- Severe weather
  — Tornado
  — Hurricane
  — Thunderstorm
  — Flood
- Other natural occurrences
  — Earthquake
  — Volcano

Types of Contingency Plans

The contingencies listed above can then be translated into the types of emergency plans shown below. Not every organization needs all of these plans; it depends on the nature of the organization's activities, the organization's criticality, its attractiveness as a target, its location and the types of facilities it occupies, among other considerations. Furthermore, the "all hazards" approach to planning should be employed to the maximum extent. This approach recognizes that many planning requirements are going to be similar, whether the planning deals with a natural threat, a human threat or an accidental incident. For example, an evacuation plan is necessary whether prompted by fire, bomb incident or HAZMAT spill. While specific signals, routes and exits may vary, primary and alternate exits, routes and assembly points will play a pivotal role. We address such evacuation issues later in this section. The various types of emergency plans can include, but are not limited to:

- Occupant emergency plan (OEP) — used within federal facilities managed by the General Services Administration
- Bomb incident plan
- Fire plan
- Medical emergency plan
- Workplace violence/trauma plan
- HAZMAT response plan
- Utility outage plan
- Computer system failure plan
- Telecommunications failure plan
- Severe weather plan
- Continuity of operations plan (COOP)
- Barricade/hostage plan

Planning Formats

While the specific emergency planning format used in a given organization depends on the nature of the organization and the organization's policy, there are several possible formats. One involves preparing a basic security plan with an annex covering actions for security upgrades, in addition to the appropriate emergency/contingency annexes. A variation of that format, which embodies the "all hazards" approach, is a basic security plan with generic annexes, such as emergency call lists, and specialized annexes for relevant emergencies/contingencies. A third format provides a basic security plan and separate supplemental/supporting plans. The fourth format involves developing separate stand-alone plans for each relevant emergency/contingency. Regardless of the format, the plan should be developed in the simplest way possible, with outlines of the specific responsibilities for those assigned to emergency response. This ensures an effective response to any extraordinary situation.

There are two significant considerations when choosing a planning format. The first pertains to the dissemination of the plan and the second relates to maintaining and updating the plan. A plan is of little value if it is not readily available to those whom it affects. Therefore, the format should facilitate the distribution of the plan to all individuals and organizational elements that have designated responsibilities under the plan. To achieve this objective, any sensitive or classified information should be published, to the maximum extent, in a separate annex or attachment that can be distributed, controlled and secured away from the main plan. This enables relevant people to have access to the primary plan even if they do not have access to the restricted portions.

The second consideration, relating to the maintenance of the plan, is equally important. To be effective, every emergency/contingency plan should be reviewed and updated on a regular basis. The planning format directly impacts the updating process. For example, if an organization uses the first or second formats described above, it is a relatively simple process to update and disseminate information common to multiple contingencies, such as emergency contact numbers. On the other hand, if an organization has chosen to publish a series of stand-alone plans in order to facilitate its dissemination and use, that organization will have to update every plan each time common points of contact or emergency numbers change.

Development of the Plan

The development and implementation of an effective plan to cope with possible emergency situations is a time-consuming process. A practical approach should be taken and a sufficient period of time allotted to complete the plan. Software tools, especially those based on a relational database system, can significantly reduce administrative tasks in capturing the dynamic information necessary to document the plan. Emergency planning consultants can also help ensure a complete plan. However, neither the software nor the consultants can reduce the need for responsible participation by the organization's management team in plan preparation.

The first step is to appoint a coordinator to assume responsibility for the plan. The coordinator should be capable of dealing effectively with management and employees at all levels in the organization. To be most effective, this appointment should be documented in an organizational policy statement, which outlines the coordinator's responsibilities and authority. As with any other critical assignment, the top management of the enterprise must give complete support to the program and to the individual selected to organize it. There should also be a designated alternate, by name or position, so there will be no gap in plan maintenance.

The individual who holds responsibility for developing the program should provide coordination and general direction within the organization.

Therefore, he or she should prepare appropriate policy and administrative directives to be issued by management to properly establish the program.

A committee of representatives from key departments or divisions should be appointed to assist and advise the coordinator in organizing the plan. Departments usually represented on such a committee include legal, personnel, medical, transportation, public relations, facility engineering and security. A totally new organization should not be developed to handle emergency situations. The existing organization, temporarily reconfigured, and those operating executives responsible for the day-to-day operation of the enterprise, should also handle emergency problems. One operating official should be designated as the organization's emergency coordinator to ensure that physical department boundaries do not impede a smooth disaster response. The coordinator should be someone regularly responsible for handling emergencies, such as the head of the security or engineering department.

The purpose of an emergency plan is to highlight the types of problems executives will encounter, and require them to consider, in advance, how to react when an emergency develops. Appendix A to this chapter provides an example of how the normal elements of an industrial organization can be reconfigured to deal with an emergency.

Planning Process

The planning process is critical and an often misunderstood aspect of emergency planning. Far too often, if plans are developed at all, they are put on the shelf and forgotten. For a plan to be effective, it must reflect the requirements of the organization to which it pertains. Furthermore, all those tasked with responsibilities must clearly understand their tasks and must be appropriately trained to fulfill those responsibilities. In addition, the plan and the people must practice on a regular basis and revise the plan as a result of the testing. An exercise or an actual implementation of the plan can result in not only revisions, but also reassignment of responsibilities and retraining of personnel, after which the plan should be retested and the whole process repeated. The most important thing to remember about the planning process is that it is a *continuing* process that is never finished as long as the plan exists.

Special Planning Needs

Some facilities have special planning requirements as a result of their particular missions, vulnerabilities, layout and clientele. These facilities can include child care centers, schools and hospitals, among others. For example, in developing an emergency plan for a child care center, the issue of emergency evacuation is one of the most critical elements, particularly as it

Emergency Planning

relates to moving, safeguarding and accounting for large numbers of children of varying ages. Since the shooting at Columbine High School, the internal layout of schools, emergency communications capabilities, and the procedures for getting response teams in and students out in an emergency situation have become much more important than they may have been in the past. With hospitals, the combination of large numbers of visitors, controlled substance storage and high levels of tension and anxiety in emergency rooms results in a variety of concerns that an emergency plan must consider.

Remember: Recognize any special, unique or unusual requirements that may apply to an organization or facility when developing a plan. Those requirements can then be appropriately addressed in the planning process.

Components of an Emergency Plan

The components of an emergency/contingency plan varies, depending on the planning format in use, the emergency/contingency for which the plan is being developed, and the needs of the organization to which the plan pertains. A plan may include all of the elements shown in Table 1, and may include additional specialized or organization-specific components, as required. In a stand-alone plan, many of these elements will be in the form of annexes to the plan itself. If there is a basic plan with contingency annexes, many of the listed elements that are common to multiple emergencies/contingencies will probably be part of the basic plan and those that pertain to a particular emergency or contingency will be included in the relevant contingency annex. In the final analysis, the plan needs to fit the contingency. For example, there is no need for a Family/Victim Support Annex in a Telecommunications Failure Plan, but there is a need for one in a plan to deal with barricade/hostage situations.

PLANNING ISSUES AND CONSIDERATIONS

Priorities

In constructing a plan, the relative importance of different types of activities must be recognized. There must be an *advance determination of priorities*: otherwise, resources will be wasted. Each organization must set its own priorities. The following is an acceptable list:

1. Protect human life
2. Prevent or minimize personal injury
3. Reduce the exposure of physical assets
4. Optimize loss control for assets whose exposure cannot be reduced
5. Restore normal operations as quickly as possible

In setting priorities, certain time-tested principles should be applied in regard to *protection of life*. Those principles include:

- *Evacuation and shelter.* Move all persons not needed in disaster operations to places of safety.
- *Personal protection.* Ensure that those persons who must remain in a threatened area are as well protected as possible, given the nature of the threat.
- *Rescue and relief.* Provide a ready means of support and assistance for exposed persons who may be injured.

For prevention or minimization of injury, the guiding principles should include:

- *Design safety.* Eliminate in advance things that increase the likelihood of injury given the nature of the emergency and the character of the organization or facility.
- *Training.* Prepare those who will deal with the disaster so that they will not increase their exposure through ignorance or ineptitude.

To *reduce exposure of physical assets,* utilize the application of good housekeeping and keep valuable materials or equipment from being needlessly concentrated in high-hazard locales. (For example, redundant or backup computers should not be located in the same fire zone as the primary computers.) Given sufficient warning time, valuable items can be relocated if provisions have been made for a relocation site and means of transportation.

To *optimize loss control,* there must be emergency response systems (people, equipment and procedures) that can rapidly deploy to threatened locations and be supported operationally. To restore normal operations quickly, it may be necessary to relocate some groups or functions, to initiate special resupply schemes for raw materials and equipment, and to revise previous schedules and programs. The data needed to make such determinations must be current and easily accessible. It should be relatively simple to maintain such information in a database, *provided there is a plan for acquiring and regularly updating the information.*

Planning Assumptions

Planning assumptions can be either supporting or limiting. Supporting assumptions are those that describe conditions that must exist for a plan to be valid as written. Supporting assumptions reduce the number of what-ifs; however, in assuming away certain problems or issues, it presupposes conditions that may not, in fact, exist. Therefore, supporting assumptions should not be developed arbitrarily. An example of a supporting assumption is: there will be sufficient vehicles available to support an emergency relocation of the headquarters. This assumption tells everyone there is no need to make any special provisions for relocation transport.

Table 1. Components of a typical emergency plan.

Purpose
Priorities
Planning assumptions
Impact
Operational tasks and procedures
    Pre-event
    During event
    Post-event
Command/management and control
External liaison and coordination
Public affairs/media relations
Family/victim support
Medical services
Emergency evacuation
Emergency shutdown and restoration
Resources and logistics
Notifications and communications
Records and reports
Training and testing
Appendices

Source: Prepared by David H. Gilmore, CPP. Used with permission.

A limiting assumption, on the other hand, sets forth the parameters under which the plan was developed and identifies issues that must be taken into account by planners. A limiting assumption is: at any given time on a business day, at least 40 percent of the assigned vehicles will be in use off-site or will be unavailable for dispatch due to maintenance. This assumption puts everyone on notice that, for planning purposes, there are a finite number of vehicles (no more than 60 percent of the total assigned). Another example of a limiting assumption: upon notification of a suspicious device, it will take the bomb squad up to 45 minutes to reach the facility. This assumption indicates a condition over which the organization has no control, namely the speed at which the bomb squad can respond. It alerts everyone involved to plan on *at least* a 45-minute interval before the bomb squad reaches the facility and begins to deal with the device.

Command/Management and Control

Crisis or Emergency Management Team. As previously indicated, an organization should avoid establishing a totally new organization to handle most emergency/contingency situations (an exception can occur in certain extremely sensitive situations). The organization's crisis management team (CMT), or similarly designated team, may include representatives from all of the following components of the organization, depending on the nature of the emergency/contingency:

- Senior management
- Plans and operations
- Public affairs
- Human resources
- Facilities engineering
- Security
- Safety and occupational health
- Legal counsel
- Resource management
- Logistics
- Chaplain (if available)
- Employee union

Just as the composition of the CMT varies depending on the type of incident, so do the responsibilities of the CMT. Those duties can include, but are not necessarily limited to, the following:

- Coordinating implementation of appropriate contingency plan(s)
- Coordinating resources and support needed by responding agencies
- Coordinating with internal and external agencies, as required
- Developing alternative courses of action for presentation to the decision maker(s)
- Preparing appropriate press releases regarding the incident
- Maintaining contact with victims and family members, as appropriate
- Evaluating intelligence regarding potentially violent employees
- Reviewing and responding to terrorist demands

While some of the duties listed above are common to a number of contingencies, others are only applicable to certain types of contingencies. In the case of a normal winter weather emergency, the first three duties, and perhaps the fourth, need to be addressed but the remainder do not apply. However, in a barricade/hostage situation, the CMT may be involved in all of these functions to one extent or another. As with the composition of the CMT, the responsibilities of the CMT need to be tailored to the particular emergency being addressed.

Alternate designations. One of the most important considerations in developing an emergency management structure is to provide for alternates to the primary decision maker, and for anyone in the organization who is charged, by name or position, with a particular responsibility under the plan. If possible, designate more than one alternate for each primary individual. It is equally important to brief, train and test the primary and alternate individuals on the performance of their assigned duties. These constitute some of the most significant aspects of the entire planning process, but they are also some of the most challenging for the emergency planner to fulfill because proper training and testing are both time and resource intensive and are often not given a high priority by management. Nonetheless, training and testing need to occur *before* an incident.

Management/Command Succession. An emergency can occur at anytime under any operating conditions. The plan must ensure that a senior management representative is always available to take charge. A management succession list, including the home or other telephone numbers where key executives may be reached, is vital. Without such delegation of authority, available executives will normally attempt to do what they think is appropriate. Because no one is coordinating and directing their efforts, they may pull in different directions, increasing confusion and possible damage to the facility and personnel.

In some private-sector organizations, emergency succession lists are sealed and stored in a safe place, opened only in a major emergency. In others, the succession lists are recorded in the written emergency plans and those involved with the plan know who is in charge at all times. Some board resolutions provide that the chief executive officer is responsible for the preparation and revision of succession lists to ensure that a management representative is always available to make decisions during an emergency. *Emergency succession* provisions do not necessarily need to reflect the anticipated normal management succession.

The boards of directors in some corporations have established a management succession list for the corporate level as well as for subsidiaries. The board decisions may take the form of resolutions. If alternates are named to the board who have not been formally elected by the shareholders, the plan should be reviewed by counsel to ensure that actions taken in an emergency are lawful.

Some organizations ensure that the board can function even if a large-scale disaster incapacitates so many board members that a quorum is no longer possible. The bylaws of such companies provide a means of returning the board to full strength. One method is for board vacancies to be filled by the remaining board members.

Some states have passed special statutes to facilitate emergency planning by corporate organizations. Where available, such provisions should be utilized.

Within government organizations, it is important to ensure that at all times, members of the organization are aware of their individual chain of command/supervision and the name or position of the individual who will succeed their supervisor or manager. At the organizational level, it is essential that the management succession be determined and available to key personnel in the event of an emergency.

Continuity of Operations (COOP). Continuity of operations (or COOP) can have more than one connotation. Some consider COOP to apply solely when a facility becomes untenable and the organization must relocate to another location. However, COOP can also apply to those measures employed to keep an organization in operation in the face of an emergency, even if it does not entail relocation. Some planners call these latter measures emergency "work-around" rather than COOP activities. For the purposes of this chapter, COOP pertains to those procedures implemented in situations that involve the temporary or permanent relocation of personnel and/or functions. Therefore, COOP can apply to a major snowstorm in which employees are shifted to alternate work locations for two days, as well as to a fire that destroys most of a building and necessitates a long-term relocation of a substantial number of personnel. In developing COOP, there are a number of issues to be addressed, including those in Table 2.

The emergency plan should list the location of the alternate headquarters and operating locations and define who should report to them and under what conditions. Reporting centers might also be arranged so that employees can signify their availability for work.

Communications necessary to maintain operations should be considered in establishing the emergency headquarters. Many disasters damage or destroy normal communications resources when the enterprise needs it most. Radio (both CB and other licensed bands), cellular telephone, satellite telephone and pagers present practical solutions.

Plans for the storage of duplicate records might be integrated into the alternate headquarters planning. To avoid what has been described as organizational amnesia, records considered vital and essential for the resumption or continuation of operations may be stored at the emergency headquarters. Table 3 lists some of the vital records that might pertain to an organization, particularly a commercial enterprise. Government agencies need to tailor the list to their particular requirements, and need to include key operating regulations and directives. The media in which the records are maintained are less important than ensuring that sufficient data and retrieval equipment is easily available. Many organizations utilize distributed data processing methods and much of the vital data may already be available at multiple locations.

If the alternative headquarters is not adequate for the storage of duplicate records, arrangements might be made with a commercial storage company. A number of companies have storage facilities in protected, remote locations, which are environmentally stable and have security and fire protection. The vaults of banks might also be used if their protection is

Table 2. Continuity of operations (COOP) issues.

What functions are time-sensitive?
What will be required to restore those functions?
What will be required to restore non-time-sensitive functions?
What conditions will necessitate a relocation?
Who can order a relocation?
What personnel and/or functions will be relocated?
Where will they be relocated?
At what point will a long-term relocation facility be required?
Does the relocation facility have provisions for the following, as appropriate?
    Communications
    Computer support
    Copiers
    Facsimile support
    Furniture
    Emergency power
    Emergency lodging
    Food service
    Sanitary facilities
    Security
    Parking
    Briefings and conferences
Is the same facility available for both short-term and long-term use?

Source: Prepared by David H. Gilmore, CPP. Used by permission.

sufficient. This alternative presents problems, however, if the enterprise needs access to its records during non-banking hours.

Arrangements should be made for the availability of emergency funds at the alternate headquarters. The funds should be sufficient to assure the organization's ability to get back into operation without delay. In addition, arrangements for lines of credit and procedures for obtaining additional funds should be developed in advance.

External Liaison and Coordination

Planning Liaison. A wide range of agencies and individuals need to be taken into account when developing an emergency plan. They can include, but are not necessarily limited to, emergency response personnel (law enforcement, fire, emergency medical services, explosive ordnance disposal and emergency management agency); senior management and department heads in the organization(s) to which the plan applies; other employees; victims, survivors and family members; elected officials; other government officials; media; neighboring private and public sector organizations and community groups; and protesters or activists. Information

Table 3. Some examples of vital records.

Accounts payable	Constitutions and bylaws
Accounts receivable[a]	Contracts
Audits	Customer data[a]
Bank deposit data	Debentures and bonds
Capital assets list	Engineering data[a]
Charters and franchises	General ledgers
Incorporation certificates	Purchase orders
Insurance policies	Plans: floor, building, etc.
Inventory lists	Receipts of payment
Leases	Sales data
Legal documents	Stockholders' lists
Licenses	Stock transfer books
Manufacturing process data[a]	Tax records
Minutes of directors' meetings	Service records and manuals, machinery
Notes receivable	Social security receipts
Patent and copyright authorizations	Special correspondence
Payroll and personnel data[a]	Statistical and operation data
Pension data	Stock certificates
Policy manuals	

[a] These records are indispensable for resumption of any level of normal activity.

obtained from other organizations can be of great value in developing the emergency plan; such contacts can help obtain assistance and coordinate planning for dealing with emergency situations.

Emergency Response Agencies. For each emergency response agency that is available to respond to incidents at the affected facility, these questions need to be answered:

- Where is it?
- What support can it provide?
- Under what conditions will it respond?
- How fast can it respond?
- What does it need from you?
- How can it be contacted?
- Is there a written agreement between your organization and the agency?
- Have representatives from the agency visited your facility?

The last question is emphasized because it is one of the most important considerations in coordinating emergency support. As demonstrated by the issues raised by the Columbine shooting incident, it is imperative that emergency response agencies be aware of the layout and peculiarities of the major facilities to which they may have to respond.

Mutual Aid. A mutual aid association is a cooperative organization of industrial firms, businesses and organizations united by a voluntary agreement to assist each other by providing materials, equipment and personnel for effective disaster control during emergencies.

The purpose of the association is to establish a workable emergency management organization that minimizes damage and ensures the continued operation or early restoration of damaged facilities. The association benefits the community as a whole because its emergency plan is part of the community's total emergency plan. In forming an industrial mutual aid association, the following steps are usually taken:

1. Obtain the advice, assistance and guidance of the local government representative responsible for disaster planning.
2. Invite local industries, utilities and businesses to send representatives to an organizational meeting.
3. Arrange to have the group addressed by a qualified person who is experienced in the operation of an industrial mutual aid association.
4. Elect association officers and appoint a coordinator.
5. Appoint committees to develop plans and procedures for various aspects of mutual aid operations, such as membership and bylaws, traffic and security control, fire protection, communications, etc.
6. Schedule periodic meetings.

Government agencies often use interagency support agreements or memorandums of understanding to delineate the support provided among agencies in particular contingency situations.

Public Affairs/Media Relations

Disasters and other emergencies are fodder for the media and news representatives, who ask for information immediately. To avoid confusion, the emergency plan should provide for the orderly release of information, preferably through a single source in the organization. The existing public or community relations division may perform this function. Procedures should ensure that the public relations director and alternates are regularly updated on developments by the corporate or plant disaster coordinator.

The Crisis Communications Creed stipulates that an organization that deals with a crisis in a forthright manner emerges stronger in the public eye. As soon as news representatives make contact, they should be told what has occurred through prepared press releases and verbal briefings. Avoid the "no comment" response. If the media gains the impression that the organization is not cooperative and is not releasing adequate information, they may contact individuals far removed from the actual situation who have little or no information. This could lead to rumors, conjecture and speculation. A public impression that the organization is hiding something could produce a lasting, unfavorable public reaction.

Press representatives usually cooperate if they understand why the enterprise must limit their attempts to obtain information. For example, safety considerations might make it necessary to limit access to the disaster area. If so, the problem should be explained, and individuals who have been in the area should be available for interviews. The names of those who have been killed or injured should be released as soon as possible. (However, press representatives understand that relatives must be informed before such information is released to the public.) The handling of information concerning casualties is an important aspect of internal human relations as well as public relations. The method of handling this information should be defined and included in the written disaster plan.

Organizations should be prepared for media requests for interviews with subject matter experts on specialized issues. In addition, in an ongoing incident, such as a barricade/hostage situation, one should expect the perpetrator(s) to be monitoring the local and national media. Organizations also have to be prepared to deal with media logistics in the event of an extended incident. This can range from providing a media briefing and filing center to setting up tours of the incident scene, to issuing media credentials and establishing media access control points. It can also include providing an area for parking microwave remote vehicles.

Photographic coverage of the disaster scene is important for insurance purposes or to support legal claims. Photographs and videos can be taken by company photographers or arrangements can be made to obtain copies of photographs taken by news photographers.

Family/Victim Support

The welfare and morale of employees and their families can pose a serious problem in an emergency. (A basic function of the American National Red Cross is to provide disaster relief; Red Cross officials are available to assist with welfare planning. Guidance is also available from the Federal Emergency Management Agency (FEMA).)

Not all emergencies entail provisions for family/victim support; but for those that do, such as a barricade/hostage incident or a building collapse with trapped victims, the organization needs to be prepared to deal with fearful or distraught or angry victims and family members. There should be a designated organizational point of contact for family members and victims. This individual should ensure that family members and victims are informed of the efforts taken to resolve the incident. The organization also needs to plan for family/victim logistics, which can include establishing a family/victim support center, situated away from any media facilities; providing food, beverages and temporary lodging; providing counseling/pastoral support; and providing transportation to the incident site, if appropriate. As major aviation accidents have graphically illustrated, the manner in which family members and victims are treated attracts media scrutiny. Consequently, any missteps in this area can have an extremely negative effect on the public opinion and perception of the organization.

Emergency Medical Services

Immediate and short-term care of the injured may have to be accomplished utilizing the medical personnel, if any, who are already present in the organization. While some industrial facilities and many military installations have in-house medical support, most public and private-sector facilities do not have any (except perhaps an occupational health nurse). Even where on-site support exists, the medical personnel may not be available every day or at all times of the day. Furthermore, if there is full-time medical support, these personnel may not have an emergency transport capability. Therefore, in developing the medical services portion of an emergency plan, planners need to first ascertain the type and capabilities of any in-house medical support. This is best accomplished by asking those personnel to define the limits of their capabilities and the conditions under which they can be called upon to provide emergency support. For organizations with in-house medical support, adequate medical supplies must be provided to properly treat the injured. The plan should include provisions to obtain additional supplies from local medical supply houses or from other facilities in the area.

Some organizations have selected personnel who are trained to administer basic first aid, including cardiopulmonary resuscitation (CPR), pending the arrival of emergency medical personnel. Other organizations rely solely on local emergency medical services (EMS). If an organization chooses to have some trained employees, it is necessary to determine the scope of training administered, the employees to train and the medical equipment to maintain on hand. In doing so, the organization should consult its supporting legal counsel regarding applicable liability, licensing and certification issues that need to be addressed. (Excellent training can be obtained from the American National Red Cross and its local affiliates.)

Hospitals should be contacted to determine the number of emergency patients each can accommodate and the types of treatment available. Not every hospital has complete treatment facilities for every type of illness or injury. For example, burn victims require special treatment and only a limited number of hospitals have facilities to treat serious burn cases. The hospital administration should know the number of shift employees and the contact telephone numbers of key management personnel. The hospital authorities should know of chemicals and other materials used in the facility for them to determine the type of injuries that might happen. In large and especially hazardous locations, the plan should include on-site triage facilities where medical personnel can make initial assessments of injuries.

Transportation of victims to hospitals or treatment centers must be considered. The number of ambulances available in the area should be determined and arrangements for their use made with ambulance company representatives. Because the available ambulances might not be able to handle all of the victims or might not be able to get to the facility, plans should be made to utilize organizational vehicles to transport the injured.

For any mass casualty situation, space needs to be designated for a triage operation, where trained medical personnel can evaluate the injured and prioritize them for treatment. Temporary hospital facilities within the enterprise may have to be provided for victims whom local hospitals cannot accommodate or for those who cannot be moved because of the nature of their injuries. Sufficient space for such emergency medical facilities should be earmarked in the emergency plan. Under favorable climatic conditions, tents can be erected in large open areas, such as parking lots, and used as temporary medical facilities.

In planning for an outside emergency medical response to a facility with multiple points of entry, planners should consider the most appropriate points of ingress and egress and most direct routes within the facility. For example, if a school or a hotel or an industrial plant has multiple wings and multiple entry points, it will save time if the responding personnel can be directed to the closest entry point. Within the facility, the movement of gurneys needs to be considered, particularly in multi-story buildings. Therefore, planners need to take into account the location of public, staff and freight elevators in developing medical emergency plans.

Security and Fire Protection

It should not be assumed that local police and fire services will assist with every emergency. Police and fire organizations might not be able to respond because of impassable roads or insufficient personnel to assist all organizations in need. The emergency plan should provide for additional employees who can assist those regularly assigned to security and fire protection duties. Total self-sufficiency may be required, at least for a limited period. However, with regard to fire and rescue operations, a distinction needs to be made between industrial and nonindustrial facilities. Industrial facilities may very well have a volunteer in-house fire and rescue operation; however, nonindustrial facilities, particularly office buildings, operate on a totally different basis. Their occupants are typically instructed to identify the problem, notify the appropriate authorities and evacuate the affected area.

Because fire is the single greatest destroyer of property and accompanies almost any disaster, it is important that an emergency fire protection group be organized and trained so it can help to limit damage in an emergency. Local fire organizations usually have personnel capable of conducting training classes and are willing to provide such services. Valuable training material is available from the National Fire Protection Association (NFPA) in Quincy, Massachusetts.

Local fire department personnel may agree to inspect the facility to identify hazardous conditions that might result in increased losses during an emergency and to recommend corrective actions. Local fire officials should also visit the facility to become intimately familiar with the layout and the location of any hazardous materials. They should also be provided with contact telephone numbers of key management personnel and periodically updated floor plans for training purposes.

The police department should be invited to participate in a tour of the facility and provided with a drawing that shows entrances and exits. They should be advised of the location of safes and vaults, especially valuable material, equipment and cash. They should also be provided with the contact telephone numbers of key management personnel.

Normal physical security features, such as fences and walls, may be destroyed or damaged in an emergency. Looting by employees and outsiders is also a hazard that must be considered because spectators are attracted to any disaster scene. Hence, additional personnel should be trained to maintain security and protect the assets and personnel of the organization. It is important not to involve all security personnel in disaster or fire control activities so that a sufficient number remains to protect assets and personnel.

Control of personnel is difficult, regardless of the number of employees assigned to perform security duties. Badges or passes to identify employees and others authorized in the area can assist in the control of personnel. The value of different types of identification in an emergency should be considered when organizational identification cards are specified. Simple arm bands or brassards can be quickly issued to emergency auxiliaries and should be considered.

The telephone numbers of police and fire departments, as well as those of all other emergency services, should be readily available at all times to avoid delay in calling them. In an emergency, the telephones of emergency services may be jammed with calls from other organizations and individuals seeking information or help. For this reason, private line numbers should be obtained so they can be used in emergencies. "Smart" telephones should be programmed to store these numbers and dial them with a limited number of digital inputs. Because an emergency results in many persons simultaneously trying to place telephone calls into or out of the affected location, it is useful to have one or more "FX" or foreign exchange lines available to the disaster response team. These are lines that are separate from the local central telephone office that normally services the facility.

Alert and Warning System

The emergency plan should provide a method of warning those occupying the facility when an emergency condition exists. The method used should be sufficient to alert individuals as quickly as possible to a dangerous condition so that appropriate action can be taken (for instance, evacuating an area of the facility). Many local building or fire and safety codes require emergency warning and communications systems in high-rises and other specific structures.

Ambient noise and distances must both be considered in planning a warning system. Outdoor as well as indoor warning systems must be provided because individuals might be outdoors during an emergency. Existing communication systems — a public address system or the telephone system — may be utilized for indoor warnings.

Outdoor warning systems may utilize bells, whistles, sirens or public address systems. A visual signal, such as a flashing light, might be utilized indoors as well as outdoors where noise prevents effective audible warning. Placement and visibility or audibility requirements of the Americans with Disabilities Act (ADA) must also be met by covered employers.

All those occupying the facility should know what the warning signals are and what actions they must take when a warning is given. The warning system should be tested periodically when employees are in the facility to actually experience and become familiar with the warning.

Emergency Evacuation

In planning for a contingency that will (or might) entail a partial or full evacuation, such as a fire, hazard material (HAZMAT) spill or bomb incident, planners need to think well beyond simply sounding an alarm and asking the building occupants to move to the nearest emergency exit. Table 4 provides some of the questions that need to be considered in this aspect of emergency planning. Note that for purposes of this listing, "short-term" is defined as less than one hour and "extended" is defined as more than one hour. This is based on the view that after about one hour, if not before, employees standing or sitting at an evacuation assembly point, particularly one outdoors, are likely to become restless and will seek some kind of resolution.

In evacuation planning, as in other aspects of planning, organizations must consider alternates; that is, alternate exits, alternate routes and alternate assembly points. Furthermore, use of these alternates needs to be practiced on a regular basis. One way to do this is to block the primary exit for a different floor or part of a building for each fire drill. This can be done with a sign reading "EXIT BLOCKED DUE TO SMOKE" or "EXIT BLOCKED DUE TO FIRE" or by having a monitor positioned at the exit to tell evacuees that it is not

Table 4. Evacuation issues.

Where are the primary exits?
Where are the alternate exits?
Will you use the same exits for emergencies *other* than fires?
How will you notify occupants to evacuate in an emergency *other* than a fire?
How will you evacuate individuals with disabilities who require assistance?
Where will you evacuate occupants for a *short-term* emergency (<1 hour)?
Where are your alternate short-term evacuation areas?
What will you do if the evacuation lasts for an *extended* period (>1 hour)?
Where are your alternate *extended* evacuation areas?
What will you do in the event of inclement weather for either a *short-term* or an *extended* emergency?
How will you establish accountability after evacuation for employees? For contractors/vendors? For visitors?
Who will keep evacuees informed of the status of the incident?
How will you transport occupants to a temporary evacuation area if it is not easily reached on foot by a large group of people?
What will you do if occupants' personal/company vehicles are inside the security perimeter and therefore not accessible to their drivers?

Source: Prepared by David H. Gilmore, CPP. Used with permission.

available. This forces the evacuees to use the alternate exit(s). Only through practice will people know what to do when the primary exit is blocked.

In addition to planning and practicing alternate procedures, keep in mind that in multi-story buildings, in which employees typically depend on elevators to move between floors, the use of *any* fire stairs, whether primary or alternate, is going to be a new experience for some employees. This again points to the need for regular drills.

A final point regarding evacuation: practice evacuations and drills prepare the employees to react in the event of a real emergency. If, in the event of real fire, employees move across the street, down the block or to the far end of the parking lot, then that is exactly what they should do in a drill, and the elapsed time for the evacuation should continue until all of the occupants have reached the designated assembly points. To do otherwise is to reinforce a "fill the square" mentality among all involved in the drill. The same rationale applies in a test of an organization's bomb incident plan or HAZMAT plan. The actual evacuation distances, which are likely to be considerably greater than those used in a fire, should be adhered to in conducting all tests and drills.

Emergency Shutdown and Restoration

If not shut down properly, certain machinery, utilities and processes may greatly increase the hazards of the disaster condition. Heat-treat furnaces, gas generators, stills, boilers, high-pressure cylinders and rapidly rotating flywheels are items that could add to the damage of the facility. Allowing them to continue operating without supervision after the facility has been evacuated could cause serious damage to the area or ruin the equipment, even if the expected disaster condition did not materialize.

Assign specific responsibility for shutdown in the emergency plan. The actual shutdown should be assigned to people familiar with the process. Shutdown of some equipment may take several hours, but a flood, fire, explosion or earthquake may not permit this much warning. This task needs immediate attention when a warning is sounded. The shutdown crews may be the last to leave the plant when evacuation is ordered, and they may even have to stay in the plant. (The model policy in Appendix A requires cognizant operational heads to designate shutdown priorities.)

When this condition exists, maximum protection should be planned for these people, including a shelter that gives good assurance of survival. Crews should be kept as small as possible and drilled in fast shutdown procedure. Simulating shutdown and tagging controls develops speed in training. Careful shutdown procedures greatly benefit and speed the recovery operation.

Restoration procedures should also be included in the emergency plan (see Table 7). If restoration has been planned, recovery is less difficult and more efficient. The protecting equipment needed for rescue, recovery and emergency repairs after the emergency is very important. Often, such items are more valuable in an emergency than under normal circumstances. A list of key recovery items simplifies emergency operations.

Efforts should not be wasted on areas or equipment that cannot be saved. It is better to concentrate efforts and save something than to spread the forces too thin and lose everything. This is sometimes a painful decision, but it must be made. Therefore, the emergency plan should concentrate on recovery, as well as on controls during the disaster. A pre-emergency review with cognizant managers and supervisors of the various physical assets within any area can help establish a salvage priority scheme. The procurement or replacement cost of the individual asset should be evaluated, as well as the cost impact of its absence when attempting to restore normal operations.

Machine tools and other heavy machinery are seldom damaged beyond repair by flood, fire, wind or blast. However, the repairs necessary to make them usable may be extensive, because motors, controls and bearings are subject to damage from heat and water. In addition, damage is sometimes hidden and may not be apparent until the machinery has been back in operation for some time. While the basic machines may not be seriously damaged, overestimate it in the early consideration to minimize further damage. Even a little first aid can simplify future repairs.

Table 5. Resource and logistics issues.

What equipment/services are required?
In what quantity?
In what time frame?
For how long a period?
What sources are available?
Can the source provide required support at all times?
How long will it take the source to respond?
How much will it cost?
How is the source contacted during normal hours?
How is the source contacted during other hours?
Will the source transport equipment to user?
If not, how will it get to the user?
Who will maintain/repair leased equipment?
Who has authority for emergency procurement/lease?
What documentation is required?
How often will the source list be reviewed/verified?

Source: Prepared by David H. Gilmore, CPP. Used with permission.

The emergency plan should give first priority to the facility structure after the emergency ceases to exist. The facility engineering crew should survey the building and grounds, particularly the building structure. At least one crew member should be technically competent to recognize structural weaknesses.

Resources and Logistics

Depending on the nature of the incident and the type of organization, equipment and other logistical support may be provided in a number of different ways. Some organizations may have some equipment available that is set aside for emergency use only and other equipment that is in regular use but also designated for use in emergency situations. Other equipment may need to be procured either from pre-identified commercial sources or from other organizations through mutual aid or interagency support arrangements.

Appendix B provides a listing of the kinds of equipment and services that may be needed in support of various contingency plans. Table 5 indicates some key questions that need to be addressed when planning for logistical support, particularly for equipment and services that must be procured from outside the organization.

Transportation

Responsibility for the control of vehicles used during an emergency should be assigned to an individual with a designated alternate. All of the vehicles available in the organization should be inventoried and included in the disaster plan.

Arrangements in advance might also be made to obtain additional vehicles from leasing companies or garages. Also, the use of vehicles owned by employees might be included in the plan and arrangements made to pay for their use. In an emergency, vehicles may be needed to haul supplies and debris, to transport personnel and to carry out rescue operations.

Other Considerations

Table 7 contains a number of other issues to consider in a disaster recovery plan.

AFTER THE PLAN IS WRITTEN

Plan implementation involves more than exercising the plan during an emergency. The plan should be integrated into company operations; personnel should be trained; and the plan should be evaluated and modified as needed.

Training, Drills and Exercises

All employees and some visitors require some form of training. This includes periodic employee discussion sessions to review policies, technical training in equipment use for professional emergency response crews, evacuation drills and full-scale exercises. Consider the training and information needs of persons regularly on the premises, including employees, contractors, visitors, managers and emergency response crews. Training can include:

- *Orientation and education sessions.* Regularly scheduled discussions to provide information, answer questions and identify needs and concerns.
- *Tabletop exercises.* Members of the emergency management group meet in a conference room setting to discuss their responsibilities and how they would react to an emergency scenario.
- *Walk-through drills.* The emergency management group and response teams perform their emergency response functions.
- *Functional drills.* Tests of specific functions such as warning and communication procedures and equipment, medical response or emergency notifications.
- *Evacuation drills.* Personnel walk the evacuation route to designated areas where procedures to account for all personnel are tested. Participants are to note potential hazards, such as stairwell congestion.
- *Full-scale exercises.* An emergency situation is simulated as closely as possible. The exercise includes company personnel and community response organizations.

Emergency Planning

Emergency planning tests and exercises are conducted for many reasons, ranging from checking the workability of a plan or a part thereof, to determining the level of staff awareness and training, evaluating the adequacy of emergency communications, and identifying shortcomings in evacuation procedures, to name a few. Not every part of a plan needs to be checked at one time; however, each exercise should be designed to evaluate one or more aspects of the emergency plan and its implementation.

Security tests and exercises are rehearsals for the real thing and, subject to safety concerns that are discussed in more detail later in this section, they should be keyed to the actual security plan to the maximum extent possible. A rehearsal for a play uses the same script as an actual performance; a security exercise should be no different. One of the least desirable outcomes of emergency planning exercises is to create a mindset that embodies such ideas as: this is only a test; or we simulate doing X, Y and Z when we do a drill. The rule should always be: train to the plan and exercise the plan.

There are a number of considerations in developing and conducting exercises of emergency plans, as shown in Table 6. Safety and controls on the use of force should be the overriding factors in any exercise. Exercises need to be planned so that people are not put at risk. In this regard, the use of force by armed security personnel and by any role players needs to be carefully controlled. There are examples of exercises that were poorly planned and controlled, with the result that employees brought multimillion dollar lawsuits against the organization alleging that the employees were traumatized by individuals playing the role of perpetrators.

Another important consideration involves notifying external agencies. Emergency response agencies outside the organization should *not* be contacted during an exercise unless the agency is involved in the exercise. This helps prevent inadvertent emergency responses that could unnecessarily put emergency responders and bystanders at risk. An alternative is to have exercise players log the external contacts they would make or, alternatively, describe them to an exercise controller or umpire.

Keeping the Plan Up-to-Date

Organizations continually change; the disaster plan must mirror the organizational changes. A formal audit of the plan should be conducted at least annually. In addition, the plan should be evaluated and modified, as required, after the following:

- After each training drill
- After each emergency
- When personnel or their responsibilities changed
- When the physical design of the facility changes
- When policies or procedures changed

ASSET PROTECTION AND SECURITY MANAGEMENT HANDBOOK

Disaster planning software and some off-the-shelf related database programs can help facilitate incorporating the changes into and disseminating the amended plan.

Table 6. Exercise planning issues.

Safety and use of force are primary controlling factors.
Exercise can deal with one part of a plan rather than the entire plan.
Train to the plan and then exercise the plan.
Develop the scenario based on the plan, or part thereof, to be tested.
Control communications to external agencies.
Have a plan to deal with real-world incidents during the exercise.
Keep exercises as realistic as possible within safety limits.
Exercise alternate decision makers, alternate exits and alternate routes.

Source: Prepared by David H. Gilmore, CPP. Used by permission.

Table 7. Items to consider in planning for disaster recovery: the do's and don'ts.

—— DO ——

- Set up *emergency headquarters* as quickly as possible after a disaster.
- Provide *briefing for employees returning to work.* Advise them of danger zones, special safety requirements, compensation, and provisions for eating, personal comfort and first aid.
- Make an effort to *return from emergency operation to normal procedures and practices.* You will minimize extraordinary responsibility on personnel, simplify the supply system and limit the establishment of precedents that are difficult to overcome.
- Consider *emergency-work pay plan for employees.* Decide, based on the company policy, company resources and prevailing practice in your area.
- Accelerate efforts to *make locker rooms, service rooms and toilets usable.*
- *Keep employees informed* of conditions and extent of recovery. Tell them when you expect to call them back and on what basis. When recalling them, advise of shift hours, pay rate, type of clothes to wear and whether to bring lunch.
- *Guard remote areas* to prevent hazards, pilferage, looting, and the natural tendency for crowds to gather at a colorful operation such as bulldozing or blasting. Use a pass system to determine who will enter the area.

- *Encourage imagination.* Only real ingenuity will solve many of the problems. Think of similarities, differences and substitutions between objects that might serve an emergency purpose.
- *Check all grinding wheels and other high-speed, rotating, equipment* prior to using it after exposed to heat or water. If in doubt, turn to the manufacturer.
- Keep *close control on internal and external temperature* when drying electrical equipment. Insulation may break down above 190 to 200°F.
- Weigh the cost of *unwrapping all packages, boxes, etc. for cleaning, drying, testing and inspection* against a superficial estimate that only rewrap is necessary. Think about how this might affect operations and customers later on.
- Send as much *damaged equipment as possible back to the manufacturer for repair* or send it to a service shop. You will need all of your availability, talent, and space for things that cannot be sent out.
- Tell employees the true extent of your *insurance coverage.* Minimize strange notions that insurance covers everything and nobody loses.
- *Assign responsibility beyond the immediate emergency.* Make sure that temporary

Table 7. (Continued) Items to consider in planning for disaster recovery: the do's and don'ts.

- Make *one person responsible for the health and sanitary conditions;* tag drinking fountains, toilets and washbasins approved for use.
- Have a person, perhaps your safety engineer, *supervise safety practices.* Make this a full-time job. Unusual tasks plus excitement and fatigue create unusual hazards.
- *Maintain routine records.* You will need them to settle insurance claims, tax deductions, legal questions, payroll arguments. Assign people to gather the required data and take photos. Also decide about out-of-pocket expenses and whether or not that will apply.
- Judge people by what they accomplish, not by display of activity alone.

repairs are redone to permanent specifications as soon as possible. Audit your condition as soon as you are in full operation, then again in 90 days. For example, a heating system will not be missed until the first freezing day of fall.
- Take time out after the first crisis to *evaluate your situation and briefly plan the next phase.* List the jobs you want done, chart your temporary emergency organization, and compare the two so as to overlook anything or assume that "someone is taking care of it."
- *Put someone of authority in charge of night activities* as important decisions must be made then as well. Use more than enough guards and be specific about what you want watched.
- Try to *help employees at home.*

—— DON'T ——

- *Jump to conclusions* based on hearsay. If time does not permit thorough checking, at least get some facts before making important decisions.
- *Be overly critical of people and work.* All of you will be anxious, tired and tense. Exercise self-control, show appreciation for effort and give clear instructions. Many tasks will be new and unusual to the workers.
- *Waste time trying to reclaim unsalvageable items or items cheaper to replace than reclaim.* This includes wet cardboard, stationery, contaminated oil, some softened cutting tools and instrumentation.
- *Forget the danger of spontaneous combustion.* Wet rags, paper, etc. can start to burn within 24 hours if ignored and conditions are right. Remove from dark, damp corners, any paper stores, rag bins and adjacent combustibles.
- *Wait too long for local services and supplies.* Place orders outside of your geographical area. Ask your suppliers to help you locate sources.
- *Lift emergency precautions too soon.* Recovery to 100 percent-safe condition takes longer than you think.

- *Spend time on routine clean-up* until key jobs and critical situations are under control. There will be plenty of time to scrub floors later.
- *Believe lightning cannot strike twice.* Protect against recurrence — tomorrow, perhaps. For instance, flood silt raises river bottoms and makes the danger of recurring floods even greater.
- *Quibble with the union over small change* during initial stages, but get policy back to normal quickly. Most unions cooperate in recovery.
- *Be overcautious.* Use good judgment. Weigh the cost/risk of a system shutdown against its value if it works with slight damage.
- *Work crews over 12 hours* to regain production loss. Use two or three shifts instead. Provide time off and vacations as soon as people can be spared for relaxation after the ordeal and recovery effort.
- *Ignore your own health.* The road ahead needs strength, courage and vitality.

ASSET PROTECTION AND SECURITY MANAGEMENT HANDBOOK

Selected Bibliography

Books

Albrecht, Steve; *Crisis Management for Corporate Self-Defense*; 1996; American Management Association.

American Society for Industrial Security; *Disaster Emergency Planning Handbook;* 1995; American Society for Industrial Security, Alexandria, VA.

Armenante, Piero M.; *Contingency Planning for Industrial Emergencies;* 1991; Van Nostrand Reinhold.

Arnell, Alvin; *Handbook of Effective Disaster Recovery Planning;* 1990; McGraw-Hill.

Auf der Heide, Erik; *Disaster Response: Principles of Preparation and Coordination*; 1989; C. V. Mosby Company.

Broder, James F.; *Risk Analysis and the Security Survey, 2nd ed.*; 2000; Butterworth-Heinemann, Woburn, MA.

Building Owners and Managers Association International; *Emergency Planning Guidebook;* 1994; Building Owners and Managers Association International.

Devlin, Edward S., Emerson, Cole H. and Wrobel, Leo A.; *Business Resumption Planning;* 1994; Auerbach Publishers Inc.

Doswell, Brian; *A Guide to Business Continuity Management;* 2000; Perpetuity Press, Ltd.

Drabek, Thomas E. and Hoetmer, Gerard; *Emergency Management: Principles and Practice for Local Government;* 1991; International City Management Association.

Educational Institute, American Motel & Hotel Association; *Security and Loss Prevention Management, 2nd ed.*; 1999; American Motel & Hotel Association.

Erickson, Paul A.; *Emergency Response Planning for Corporate and Municipal Managers;* 1999; Academic Press.

Facility Management Development Company*; Basic CEP: Manual for Composing a Company Emergency Plan;* 1999; Facility Management Development Company, Inc.

Federal Emergency Management Agency; *Are You Ready?;* 1993; Federal Emergency Management Agency.

Federal Emergency Management Agency; *Emergency Management Guide for Business & Industry;* 1993; Federal Emergency Management Agency.

Federal Emergency Management Agency; *Federal Emergency Management Agency Publications Catalog;* 2000; Federal Emergency Management Agency.

Federal Emergency Management Agency; *Risks and Hazards: A State by State Guide*, FEMA 196; 1990; Federal Emergency Management Agency.

Gigliotti, Richard J. and Jason, Ronald C.; *Emergency Planning for Maximum Protection;* 1991; Butterworth-Heinemann, Woburn, MA.

Gillis, Tracy Knippenburg; *Emergency Exercise Handbook: Evaluate and Integrate Your Company's Plan;* 1996; PennWell Publishing Co.

Ginn, Ronald D.; *Continuity Planning: Preventing, Surviving and Recovering from Disaster;* 1989; Elsevier Science Publishers, Ltd.

Gist, Richard and Lubin, Bernard; *Psychosocial Aspects of Disaster;* 1989; John Wiley & Sons, New York.

Hanna, James A.; *Disaster Planning for Health Care Facilities;* 1988; Canadian Hospital Association.

Kletz, Trevor; *Learning from Accidents, 2nd ed.;* 1994; Butterworth-Heinemann, Woburn, MA.

Levy, Louis and Toulmin, Llewellyn M.; *Improving Disaster Planning and Response Efforts: Lessons from Hurricanes Andrew and Iniki;* 1993; Booz Allen & Hamilton Inc.

Lundgren, Regina and McMakin, Andrea; *Risk Communication, 2nd ed.;* 1998; Battelle Press.

Lykes, Richard S.; *Are You Ready for Disaster? A Corporate Guide for Preparedness and Response;* 1990; Manufacturers' Alliance for Productivity and Innovation.

Mitroff, Ian I. and Pearson, Christine; *Crisis Management: A Diagnostic Guide;* 1993; Jossey-Bass Inc.

Myers, Kenneth N.; *Manager's Guide to Contingency Planning for Disasters: Protecting Vital Facilities and Critical Operations, 2nd ed.;* 1999; John Wiley & Sons, New York.

National Fire Protection Association; *Fire Protection Handbook, 18th ed.;* 1997; Quincy, MA.

National Research Council; *A Safer Future: Reducing the Impacts of Natural Disasters;* 1991; National Academy Press.

Nudell, Mayer and Antokol, Norman; *The Handbook for Effective Emergency and Crisis Management;* 1988; Lexington Books.

Overseas Security Advisory Council; *Emergency Planning Guidelines for American Businesses Abroad;* 1990; U.S. Dept. of State, Bureau of Diplomatic Security.

Pinsdorf, Marion K.; *Communicating When Your Company Is under Siege: Surviving Public Crisis;* 1987; Lexington Books.

Rainey, Kathy; *Disaster Resource Guide – 2000 Edition;* 2000; Kathy Rainey.

Reynolds, Simon and Toft, Brian; *Learning from Disasters: A Management Approach, 2nd ed.;* 1997; Perpetuity Press, Ltd.

Rothstein, Philip Jan, Ed.; *Disaster Recovery Testing: Exercising Your Contingency Plan;* 1994; Rothstein Associates, Inc.

School of Criminal Justice, Michigan State University; *Critical Incident Protocol: A Public and Private Partnership;* 2000; Michigan State University.

Sikich, Geary; *Emergency Management Planning Handbook*; 1996; McGraw-Hill.

Sikich, Geary; *It Can't Happen Here;* 1993; PennWell Publishing Co.

U.S. Department of Labor, Occupational Safety and Health Administration; *How to Prepare for Workplace Emergencies;* 1995; U.S. Department of Labor, Occupational Safety and Health Administration.

Wold, Geoffrey H. and Shriver, Robert F.; *Disaster Recovery (Planning Manual for Financial Institutions);* 1990; Bankers Publishing Co.

Wrobel, Leo A.; *Disaster Recovery Planning for Telecommunications;* 1990; Artech House, Inc.

Periodicals

Contingency & Planning Management; Witter Publishing Corporation, Flemington, NJ.

Disaster Recovery Journal; Systems Support, Inc., St. Louis, MO.

Security Management; American Society for Industrial Security, Alexandria, VA.
— Bernstein, Jonathan; The 10 Steps of Crisis Management; March 1990.
— Burns, Steve; Have You Backed Up Your Data Today?; November 1999.
— Carlton, Yvonne A.; The Plan's the Thing; August 1987.
— Coleman, Randall; Six Steps to Disaster Recovery; February 1993.
— Ginn, Ronald D.; The Case for Continuity; January 1989.
— Glorioso, John E. Sr. and Mattocks, Gerald B.; Teaming Up Against Crises; October 1989.
— Hawkes, Kenneth Gale and Neal, Jim; Command Performance; November 1998.
— Hinman, Eve E.; Lessons from Ground Zero; October 1995.
— Jenkins, Alan; Bomb Threat Preparedness: Defusing an Explosive Situation; November 1991.
— Joyce, Eugene J. and Hurth, Lawrence L.; Booking Your Next Disaster; November 1997.
— Lukaszewski, James E.; Good News about Bad News; December 1990.

- McCourt, Michael; Emergency! Stress in Security!; August 1991.
- Mitroff, Ian, Pauchant, Terry C. and Shrivastava, Paul; Crisis, Disaster, Catastrophe: Are You Ready? February 1989.
- Mitroff, Ian; Programming for Crisis Control; October 1989.
- Murphy, Joan; Taking the Disaster Out of Recovery; August 1991.
- Myatt, Paul B.; Going in for Analysis; April 1999.
- Newman, William F.; Sky-High Disaster Management; January 1994.
- Plat, John; Putting out the Fire of Disaster; January 1992.
- Ray, David L.; Business amid the Minefields; November 1997.
- Sanford, Donald C.; How to Survive and Succeed; January 1991.
- Schmock, Leo F.; Are You Ready? We Are.; July 1991.
- Viera, Diane L.; Model of Disaster Management; August 1991.

APPENDIX A
COMPANY DISASTER CONTROL PROGRAM POLICY

The Company shall conduct continuous planning to minimize the danger to life, health and property from emergencies or disasters; shall cooperate with public bodies and agencies charged with disaster control; and shall take necessary and prudent steps to assure continuity of operations and restoration of production activities as quickly as possible following an emergency, or a disaster.

General

I. Scope
   A. This SPI establishes the Company Disaster Control Program and assigns responsibilities for the implementation of the program.
II. Basis for Company Disaster Control Program
   A. The Company Disaster Control Program is based upon:
      — Department of Defense "Standards for Physical Security of Industrial and Governmental Facilities"; and the National Industrial Security Program Operating Manual (NISPOM);
      — Applicable standards of the Underwriters Laboratories;
      — The National Fire Protection Association; the American Insurance Association; and
      — State and local laws.
III. Definitions
   A. *Disaster* — Any occurrence or condition involving serious and widespread threat to life, health or property. Disasters may result either from natural or human causes.
   B. *Emergency* — A situation, actual or imminent, involving unusual conditions and hazards which, if not corrected or prevented, could lead to a disaster.
   C. *Sector* — A building area so designated, and separated by walls or other physical barriers from adjacent areas. All sectors shall be distinctively numbered for reference purposes.

Emergency Planning

IV. Disaster Control Organization
   A. In the event of a disaster, all control and rescue operations shall be under the direction of the Disaster Control Organization, which is a temporary organization consisting of the vice president, the Disaster Council (all Code E positions, the security manager, the director of building services, and the senior resident military representative) and the positions specified below with their usual subordinate organizations and resources:
      1. Building services manager
      2. Materials handling and traffic manager
      3. Chief security officer
      4. Personnel services manager
      5. Medical director
      6. Security supervisor
   B. The Disaster Control Organization shall be under the operational direction of the Security Manager during and immediately following a disaster.
   C. A chart of the Disaster Control Organization is contained in Appendix I to this SPI.
V. Responsibilities
   A. The director of building services shall:
      1. Include necessary disaster control devices, such as pumps, sprinkler systems, standpipes, fire walls and doors, protected fuel storage, standby electric power, explosive dust filters, etc., in all new and modified company facilities.
      2. Independently, or in cooperation with public authorities, assess shelter capabilities of current and future company facilities and allocate suitable space in designated shelters for the secure storage of survival supplies.
      3. Arrange for the conspicuous marking of building sectors designated by the Security Manager.
      4. Arrange for the heavy-duty rescue and damage control equipment required in a disaster situation.
      5. Prepare operating procedures to assure maximum availability during emergencies of disaster control resources regularly under his cognizance.
      6. Coordinate all post-disaster restoration and repair activities.
   B. The security manager shall:
      1. Evaluate the company's disaster vulnerability on a continuing basis, revising plans and resources as necessary.
      2. Determine sector boundaries, evacuation routes, assembly points and other traffic and area disaster controls.
      3. Develop general instruction for the guidance of all persons under emergency and disaster conditions.

4. Prepare and publish detailed operating instructions for the Disaster Control Organization.
5. Coordinate disaster control plans and procedures with local Emergency Management, fire and police agencies, cognizant military agencies and all resident government and commercial representatives.
6. Prescribe safeguards for operations involving serious risk of disaster such as oxy-fuel, open flame, paint spraying, combustibles storage, etc.
7. Provide an alarm system commensurate with the type and severity of emergency or disaster hazards.
8. Provide and train a full-time fire force and assure adequate fire protection.
9. Recruit and train required security auxiliaries from among qualified volunteers for use in disasters and emergencies.
10. Assure an inter-plant communication capability for use during emergency conditions or failure of normal facilities.
11. Consult with the Director of Building Services regarding fire and disaster control aspects of plant construction and maintenance.
12. Stock and distribute Shutdown Priority markers.
13. Establish a Disaster Control Center for direction of Disaster Control activities and notify the heads of Disaster Control Organization Units of the location, as required by the specific emergency or disaster.
14. Assume operational direction of the Disaster Control Organization upon the occurrence of a disaster, upon the sounding of an alert or take-cover warning, or upon direction by the vice president or his alternate.

C. Each division manager (or Head of other Company unit) shall:
1. Prepare for all unit operations, a shutdown procedure comprising a checklist of actions required to stop operations, halt processes and place equipment and machinery in an off or safe position. This checklist shall be prioritized to first discontinue those operations or processes that offer the greatest disaster hazard. Operations that offer extraordinarily high hazard (those utilizing explosive fuel, very high electrical voltage, open flame, etc.) shall be specially designated as warranting shutdown priority.
2. Assure that shutdown priority markers are affixed to those items of equipment designated in the shutdown procedure deemed hazardous.
3. Assure that employees who are assigned tasks under the shutdown procedure are familiar with the procedure and with their individual responsibilities under the procedure.

Emergency Planning

Procedure
VI. Alerting the Disaster Control Organization
    A. The security manager shall:
        1. Notify the head of each operating unit of the Disaster Control Organization, by means of a notification code (Condition One, Two or Three) of the probable degree of a potential disaster.
        2. Direct the head of each operating unit of the Disaster Control Organization to initiate the action specified in section B below.
        3. In the event of a Condition Two or Condition Three emergency, notify the Disaster Council.
    B. The head of each operating unit of the Disaster Control Organization shall, upon receipt of notice from the Security Manager, take the action specified below according to the type of notice received. (Condition One, Two or Three.)
        1. Condition One. (Possible emergency. No immediate danger, with estimated three hours or more lead time.)
            a. Notify all personnel having disaster assignments.
            b. Check status of emergency equipment that may be needed.
        2. Condition Two. (Probable emergency. Danger apparent, with estimated lead time less than three hours.)
            a. Notify all personnel having disaster assignments.
            b. Check status of emergency equipment likely to be needed.
            c. Begin indicated protective measures such as tie-down, movement and securing of aircraft, vehicles, etc.
            d. Begin phased discontinuance of routine operations.
        3. Condition Three. (Immediate emergency. Disaster imminent, with little or no lead time.)
            a. Notify all personnel having disaster assignments.
            b. Discontinue all routine operations.
            c. Move all assigned persons to designated locations with required supplies and equipment.
            d. If indicated, have operating divisions begin shutdown procedure.
            e. Have all Disaster Control Organization Units stand by to switch to Disaster operations.

NOTE: When a Condition Three notice has been issued by the security manager, the Disaster Control Organization shall be under his operational control from the time he issues the notice until a determination has been made by him or by the vice president that individuals assigned to the Disaster Control Organization may be released to salvage and restoration duties or to normal responsibilities. Disaster Control Organization Units shall be released from disaster control service as quickly as possible.

ASSET PROTECTION AND SECURITY MANAGEMENT HANDBOOK

VII. Post-Disaster Restoration
   A. After disaster control and rescue operations have been completed or have reached a point at which repair and restoration activities may also be conducted, such repair and restoration activities shall be started under the direction of the director of building services. Problems concerning priorities, availability of utilities, etc., arising in divisions or headquarters groups shall be referred to the Director of Building Services.
   B. The Disaster Control Council shall function during restoration activities to the extent determined necessary by the vice president.

APPENDIX B
RESOURCES AND LOGISTICS
EQUIPMENT AND SERVICES

Equipment to Consider:

   Lighting
   Pumps
   Generators
   Heaters
   Air-conditioning units

   Cots
   Blankets
   Rations
   Bottled water
   Plastic cups and plates
   Plastic utensils
   Portable toilets
   Portable showers
   Tents/tarps/canopies
   Shelters
   Trailers
   Radios
   Cellular telephones
   Portable telephone switch
   Cameras/video equipment
   CCTV
   Bullhorn/PA system
   Portable alarms
   Laptop/notebook computers
   Facsimile machines
   Reprographics equipment

Emergency Planning

Barriers
Traffic cones
Safety vests
Warning tape
Flares
Signs
Rope
Tape
Padlocks
Bolt cutters
Axe
Pry bar
Other assorted tools

Riot control equipment
Gas masks/face masks
Protective clothing
Chemical/biological detection equipment
Decontamination equipment
Replacement clothing
Gloves
Goggles
Hard hats
Brassards or arm bands
Firefighting equipment
Medical supplies

Shovels/brooms
Salt/sand
Absorbent material
Foam disbursing equipment
Containers/bags

Vehicles

Services to Consider:

Emergency repair of equipment
HAZMAT operations
Restoration of utilities
Communications/computer support
Cleaning
Removal of debris
Demolition
Emergency construction/structural work

ASSET PROTECTION AND SECURITY MANAGEMENT HANDBOOK

    Snow removal
    Labor pool
    Food service
    Emergency relocation

Source: Prepared by David H. Gilmore, CPP. Used with permission.

9
Information Systems Security: An Overview

INTRODUCTION

Through the 1990s, the use of computers was commonly referred to as electronic data processing (EDP). Now it is more common to hear terms such as Management Information Systems (MIS), Information Technology (IT) and Information Systems (IS). The term "information systems" (IS) will be used in this chapter to refer to computer-based information processing systems.

This chapter presents an overview of how information systems work, the functions of key personnel, and how information processing tasks are performed. The overview focuses on those aspects of IS that concern the security director.

Computers enable us to perform fairly simple tasks, like making an airline reservation or charging a purchase on a credit card, and more technical tasks, such as composing newspapers or controlling complex pilot training simulators. The varied applications of computers make them appear to be some mysterious mechanism — too complex to understand. As a result, many security directors are reluctant to get involved in protecting their organizations' IS. But, with an understanding of information processing technology, security directors can grasp the security implications of information processing and make an important contribution to the information systems security program. The following pages present the essential elements of IS as the basis for understanding the security implications of information processing.

ENCODING DIGITAL DATA

Digital computers are the central element of information systems. Computers are called "digital" because they represent data with digits. For technical reasons, the digits are more easily stored electrically as binary numbers — made up of ones and zeros. Each one or zero is called a bit (of data). A bit represents the smallest unit of data. To make data easier to process internally, data is most often processed in groups of eight bits. These groups are called bytes (a play on the word bite) — a bite of bits. If a byte has eight bits (a common size), a given byte can take 256 possible forms, such as 00000000, 00000001, 00000010, 00000011, etc.

By adopting a coding scheme, we can use bytes to represent letters and numbers. For example, the American Standard for Computer Information Interchange (ASCII, pronounced ask-key) uses seven-bit bytes. An "A" is represented as 1000001, "B" as 1000010, "C" as 1000011, etc. Alternatively, bytes can be used to represent numbers. One eight-bit byte can be used to represent the integer numbers from zero (00000000) to 255 (11111111). Two bytes can represent the integers from zero to 65,535, etc.

Sounds and graphic images can also be represented through the use of ones and zeros. To do this, a suitable data encoding standard is used. For example, to encode sound, if the highest frequency is 5000 Hz (cycles per second), a computer must sample the loudness of the input sound 20,000 times per second and store the loudness as a number from zero to 65,535. In essence, a two-byte number is stored 20,000 times per second or 40 kB (kilobyte) of data per second of input sound. An output device is also needed to generate an electric signal with a value that tracks the loudness value at the 20,000-Hz rate. This is done by passing the electric signal to a loudspeaker. There, the sound will be reproduced.

To encode a graphic image, the system must reduce the image to individual picture elements or pixels. An image is stored as a series of pixels from the upper left to the lower right of the image. Each pixel is encoded with numbers that represent the brightness and color. To increase the fidelity of the stored image, increase the number of pixels and the number of bytes per pixel. For example, one bit for each pixel could be represented as black (1) or white (0). This would work for an incoming fax but not a color photograph. To encode color, three bytes (24 bits) are used for each pixel to represent about 16 million different colors. At the beginning of the file, the system will include information about how many pixels there are in a row across the image, and the number of rows from top to bottom. The more pixels are stored, the better the quality of the image. There are a number of sound and graphics codes that have been adopted by the computing community.

PROCESSING DIGITAL DATA

All information systems consist of two kinds of hardware: (1) a *central processing unit* (CPU), and (2) *peripheral units,* such as tape drives, printers, disks, display monitors, etc.

Digital computers also have two central characteristics: (1) stored program computing, and (2) the ability to place branches in program instruction sequences.

Information Systems Security: An Overview

All current CPUs share a common design concept, referred to as *stored program* computing. This means, instead of having a fixed mode of operation like a telephone answering machine or a microwave oven, a modern digital computer stores a program in its *main memory*. When commanded to do so, it executes the instructions in the program. The program controls the operation of the computer hardware to cause it to read data from input peripherals, perform logical operations on the data, generate output data and send it to output peripherals. By changing the program, the functioning of the computer can be changed. In this way, it is possible for the same information system to perform the weekly payroll function in the morning and calculate rocket trajectories in the afternoon.

A second important characteristic is the ability to place branches in program instruction sequences. For example, a computer program can say to the computer hardware: "If the result of this operation is a number larger than ten, then execute the next instruction in memory, otherwise go to the memory location and continue execution from there." Unfortunately, this capability can be used to support a fraud. In a sample scenario, the account number currently being processed equals ⟨my account number⟩ then add $1,000,000 to the account balance. An actual fraud would not be quite this easy to perpetrate, but the ability to program a computer to respond in a special way to a particular record is the essential feature of many computer frauds.

A TYPICAL CENTRAL PROCESSING UNIT

Although there are many details, the actual concept behind stored program computers is quite simple. (Figure 1 illustrates the workings of a typical CPU.) Think of it as an electronic version of a post office letter rack with many pigeon holes. Each pigeon hole can store one byte and has a unique address. The main memory stores both data bytes and program instructions encoded as bytes.

Assume, for example, a program and some data have been loaded into the main memory and the *instruction decoder* has been initiated to fetch the first program instruction byte from memory and decode it. (The program instruction bytes are stored sequentially in memory.) The instruction decoder sends a command to the main memory to call up the contents of the first program pigeon hole, and it instructs *gate #1* (a special kind of electric switch) to pass the byte to the instruction decoder. The instruction decoder examines the byte and, based on its bit pattern, decides what to do next.

In some instances, instructions the decoder has loaded may cause it to copy two data bytes from specific memory addresses into the logic unit, add them together, and place the resulting sum at another location in main

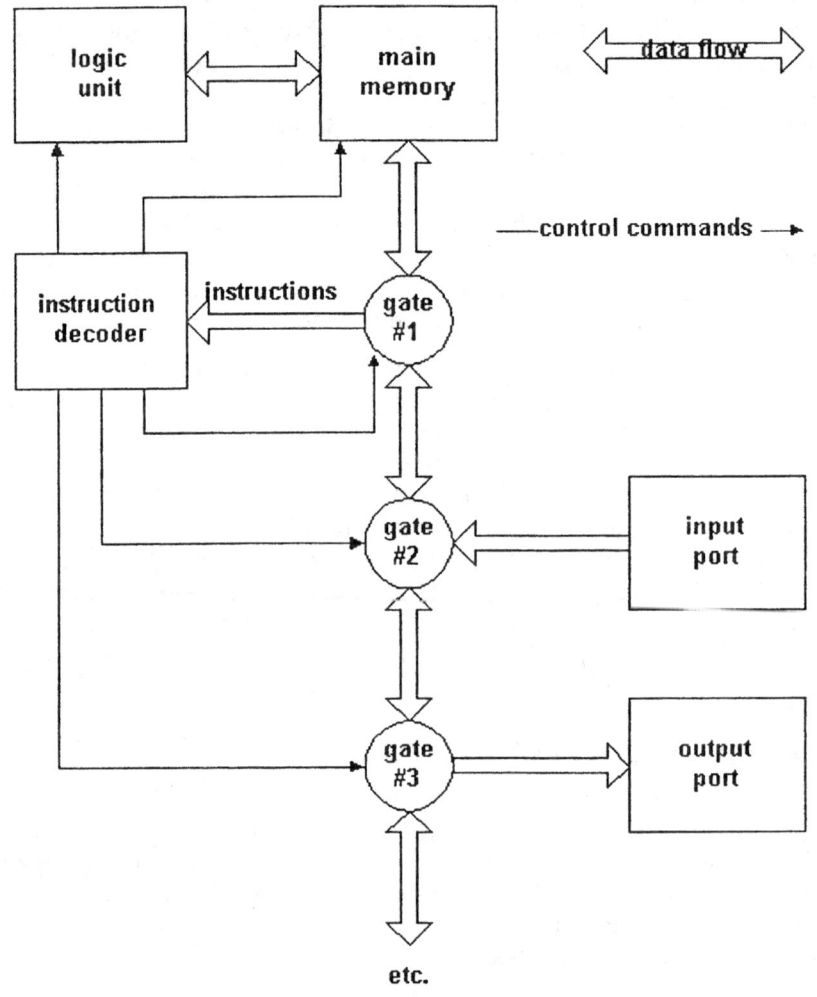

Figure 1. A typical CPU.

memory. In other words, the instructions enable the computer to add two numbers and save the result.

The typical logic unit has hardware that can add, subtract, multiply and divide numbers, compare the relative size of two numbers, and perform other functions deemed by the CPU designers as useful to computer programmers. Other instructions may cause the instruction decoder to send commands to the gates and *input/output ports* to read data from an input device, and move the bytes into main memory locations for processing, or to send data from memory to an output device. Collectively, these possible actions are referred to as the CPU's instruction set.

Information Systems Security: An Overview

The arrangement of a central processing unit is representative of the basic concept of stored program computers, but there are variations in the details. For example, computers in the 1960s had small main memories in the 8- to 32-kB range, and data moved slowly through those machines. Over the years, CPU memory size, processing speed, and data transfer rates have increased steadily. In the 1990s computers had hundreds of MBs (megabytes) of main memory storage capacity, so the number of the ports and data transmission speeds have also increased.

The instruction set of a CPU is another important factor in the variation between old and new computers. In some instances, a CPU designer may choose to have a small set of instructions, which can be processed rapidly but must be grouped together to perform common functions. These are called RISC (reduced instruction set chip) computers. If a larger set of more powerful instructions is chosen, it will require more time to decode and execute.

THE IMPACT OF LARGE-SCALE INTEGRATION

In 1970, a new transistor manufacturing process called Large Scale Integration (LSI) came into widespread use. Out of many technological advances, this was the most important factor in making computers economically practical.

LSI refers to a process in which many transistors could be created on a postage stamp-sized silicon chip, complete with interconnecting wires. This enables a complete CPU to be placed on a single chip rather than making a CPU on a printed circuit board using individual transistors and other electrical components. Similarly, chips could be designed to store data and control peripherals. (LSI production uses a highly refined photolithography process and — with each passing year — the number of transistors on a chip increases geometrically. In 1997, chips with several million transistors were common.)

What made LSI such an important factor in making computer use economical was once the initial investment in a chip fabrication plant had been made, the actual cost per chip was quite low. To use a comparison, computer chips that are now selling for a few hundred dollars have far exceeded the capacity of computers that cost a million dollars in the 1970s.

The impact of LSI as a technological development cannot be overstated. LSI has enabled powerful computers and huge computer networks to become economically feasible. As more and more organizations are upgrading performance using these networks, competitors follow suit, and the dependence on computers grows commensurately. As a result, business functions that did not exist 30 years ago have become critical to survival today. Because the evolution of LSI technology has had a profound effect on IS design and operation — and the associated security issues — security directors are faced with a new and important asset protection duty.

Although not as revolutionary as LSI, the development of lasers based on light-emitting diodes (LEDs) was another important development. Laser LEDs are essential to fiber-optic data transmission cables, so their development enabled the cost of data transmission to drop. When fiber-optic cable was combined with cheap, powerful computers, packet switched networks — such as the Internet — became economically and technically feasible. (They are also used in CD-ROMs to read the data encoded as microscopic bits on CDs.)

These developments have caused a huge evolutionary change in the composition of information systems, and the evolutionary process seems to be accelerating.

A TYPICAL INFORMATION SYSTEM

Computers are powerful business tools because they can be adapted (programmed) to perform a wide range of functions, unlike mechanical machines that are designed to perform a single function. An information system is comprised of two major parts:

1. Hardware — which accepts, stores, and processes data; and
2. Software, or programs.

It also has two types of programs:

1. Those that control the operation of the hardware (system software); and
2. Those that perform specific functions (applications programs).

The information processing concepts are simple, but the details are complex. No one person can possibly know everything about computer technology. Security directors must understand enough of the details to be able to recognize security concerns, ask the right questions, and contribute effectively to the information systems security program of their organizations.

There are three basic operations that an IS performs:

1. An information system "reads" input data. Data may be in the form of keystrokes, data stored on a diskette, data transmitted over a network, or images from an optical scanner;
2. An information system processes input and stored data; and
3. An information system produces "output." The output may appear on a display screen, be printed, stored on a diskette, or transmitted over a network.

As a rule, an information system has a store of information to which it refers as a part of the processing cycle. This stored information is updated

Information Systems Security: An Overview

based on the input data. The computer and communications hardware, stored data, and programs are configured to perform specific information processing functions.

In summary, the elements of a typical information system are listed as follows.

The Computer and Network Hardware. This is the physical embodiment of an information system — the screens, keyboards, processors, printers, etc.

Computer System Software. Multiprocessing computer hardware (multiprocessing means the computer can handle more than one service request at the same time) will require a control program, also referred to as a system software or operating system, to coordinate different functions. The control program manages the flow of data between the CPU, the data storage devices, and the data terminals. The control program also switches control between the subprograms that are processing user tasks. Typically, the system control program is developed and supplied by the hardware manufacturer. Some common operating systems are Windows, MS-DOS, MVS and UNIX.

The Application Programs. A typical information system application consists of a number of different subprograms developed specifically to perform the desired functions. In most cases, this software is developed by third parties called "software houses" or by in-house programmers.

Physical Facilities. It is necessary to provide floor space, electric power, air conditioning and other supporting facilities for the computer and network hardware and workstations. Office facilities need to be provided for the computer programmers and operators, data entry clerks, technicians and end users. Physical security measures to control access to key areas, protect the hardware, air conditioning, electric power, telephone circuits, etc., are very much a part of the physical facility.

An Operating Staff. A complex information system will not run itself. People with the appropriate skills must be recruited and trained for each of these functions: computer operators, data entry clerks, systems and applications programmers, technicians to maintain the computer hardware and network, management, and administration. Operating staffs will have broad powers to control the operation of the information systems, and to affect their reliability and integrity. Consequently, it will be important to have screening procedures that will maximize the trustworthiness of staff members, and means to insure compliance with control procedures.

Operating Procedures. Most current information systems are complex combinations of hardware, software and people. Procedures are needed to control operations. Many of these procedures relate to security issues. Following are some examples of questions that must be dealt with:

1. Who is authorized to add, access, change or delete data in a database? How are authorized users to be identified?
2. How will attempts at unauthorized access to the system be discovered and resolved?
3. How reliable should the system be — available 90 percent of the time, 99 percent, etc.?
4. How will unauthorized changes to the database be detected and prevented?
5. What action is to be taken if a report cannot be validated or is found to be completely false?
6. If an operator or data entry clerk does not report for work as scheduled, who will take that person's place?
7. If system hardware is destroyed in a fire or other calamity, how will timely operation be maintained until the hardware can be replaced?
8. How quickly should service be restored after a worst-case disaster?

It is not unusual to find that many of these issues are not explicitly addressed by technicians. Computer system designers tend to be optimists who only anticipate the most obvious problems. This is an area in which the security director can make an important contribution by thinking about how a sensitive system operates, what might go wrong, and how problems can be addressed in the design phase.

User Training. An information system is like any other complex device — operators, data entry clerks, and end users will all need training before they can use the system successfully. A training program and good documentation for operators and users are essential elements.

Activity Monitoring. Because computer staff members, particularly programmers, operators, and LAN administrators, may have unlimited access to the computer system, it is important to take steps to ensure full personal accountability. One way to do this: use a password system to control access to programs and data. Another way is to use activity monitoring programs.

For example, an automatic activity log could record the commands each operator enters from the console keyboard. Another could record the changes each programmer makes to programs, and a third could record access by individuals to records or data files. In the event any wrongdoing or unexplained anomalies occur (such as a record entered the day before was missing), these activity logs would be extremely helpful in an investigation. However, the logs must be trustworthy (secure against tampering) and any examination must be done by a party with sufficient technical knowledge to be completely independent of the information processing staff in order for this system to work properly.

This discussion emphasizes the fact that computer systems are made up of a number of tangible and intangible elements, all of which must be present and in good working order if the systems are to perform satisfactorily. Shortcomings can result in unsatisfactory operation and security breaches.

CLASSES OF COMPUTERS

Computers are divided into four classes: *mainframe computers, minicomputers, personal computers (PCs)* and *laptop PCs*. The categories loosely define their technical characteristics and the ways in which they are installed and operated.

Mainframe Computers

The term "mainframe" is commonly applied to large-scale computers that cost between $1 million and $10 million. The name originated from the fact that because of the computer's large physical size, its components needed to be installed in cabinets with frames to support the components. The central processor was often referred to as the "main" frame, later contracted to mainframe. Mainframes accounted for almost all computer sales during the 1950s and 1960s.

Because of its raw computing power (measured in terms of the millions of instructions it can execute in one second, or MIPS), a mainframe is used to process applications that have extremely large files (for example, the customer base of a large electric utility or the depositor records of a big city bank). Since 1965, mainframe systems have stored data files on direct-access disk drives. Technically, these are the same as the "hard disks" found on contemporary PCs. Magnetic tape reel and tape cartridge drives are used to make backup copies of disk drive files, and to exchange data between computers.

Because of the large amount of data stored in mainframes, the machines have high-volume printing requirements. Also, with the growth in telecommunications mainframes, computers can also be linked by high-speed data circuits.

All of these factors mean that the typical mainframe is surrounded with disk and tape drives, printers, and other supporting units. Computer experts refer to these items as *peripherals*.

The hardware needed to run a mainframe consumes hundreds of kilowatts of electric power and occupies substantial floor space. This requires the computer to be installed in a separate room — often tens of thousands of square feet in size. A massive air-conditioning system, with a capacity of hundreds of tons of cooling, is required to dissipate heat generated by the mainframe. This requires a substantial amount of electric service. Some mainframes also have hundreds of remote terminals, which may be hundreds or thousands of miles away. These "remotes" are usually connected to the mainframe through telephone or satellite circuits.

Mainframes are commonly used by hundreds or thousands of end users simultaneously. This means that the computer must have hardware and software facilities that protect the programs and data files against damage or unauthorized access or modification. End users commonly use customized programs developed specifically for a company or organization. All these factors translate into a requirement for teams of technical specialists to develop and maintain the software and operate the hardware.

Because of the relatively large staff, critical functions can be divided among staff members to ensure proper separation of duties.

A mainframe computer represents a substantial investment. The cost to buy and install a mainframe can run $1000 or more per square foot, as compared to $100 to $150 per square foot for the contents of ordinary office space. These physical assets are at risk — but the potential for loss associated with the stored data, and the business impact costs resulting from computer service interruptions, outweigh the cost of exposing the physical computer assets.

Minicomputers

In the 1970s, minicomputers came into wide use. LSI technology made it possible to build powerful computers that were relatively small in size and cost, and did not require a dedicated computer room with special air conditioning. Minicomputers are often installed in ordinary office space close to the end users and do not require a large team of technically trained staff members like those assigned to mainframe computers. These factors tend to increase risks, but the fact that minicomputers are dispersed means the loss of a single minicomputer is typically less damaging than the loss of an organization's single mainframe.

The major differences between a minicomputer and a mainframe are in scale and the more casual minicomputer operating environment.

Beginning in the 1980s, the LSI-fueled spurt in PC capabilities shrunk the role of mainframe and minicomputers. Many minicomputer-based information systems have migrated to local area networks (LANs) that are based on PCs.

Personal Computers

By the end of the 1970s, as LSI technology continued to develop, components continued to shrink in size and cost, and grow in power. It was possible to cram a CPU onto a single silicon chip. This ushered in the era of the microcomputer or, as it is now known, the personal computer.

Information Systems Security: An Overview

The concept was to package all the components of a computer system into a single, desktop-sized box with a display monitor sitting on top. Initially, data was stored on "floppy diskettes." (Floppies got their name because the storage medium was a flexible mylar disk in a protective plastic sleeve, rather than the rigid aluminum disk of early days.) The storage capacity of floppies was much lower than that of a magnetic tape, but it was adequate for basic business use. And the cost was nominal. By adding a low-cost printer, a PC could perform the same functions as a mainframe — but on a smaller scale.

Low-cost, high-capacity fixed hard disks became available later and are now installed on all PCs.

Spreadsheet programs, such as Visi-Calc, Lotus 1-2-3 and Excel launched PCs into widespread business use. Business people, in need of a quick financial analysis, liked the immediate turnaround these applications offered. Previously, in order to use a mainframe or minicomputer, the user had to enlist the services of a programmer. A request for information could take weeks or months to complete because the programmer had to analyze the user's requirements and then design, code, test and debug a custom program. This process obviously made changes difficult to make. In contrast, the PC spreadsheet program was designed so that a non-programmer could define an analysis, "code" it into the PC and see immediate results.

In the early 1980s, IBM introduced the IBM-PC, followed in the next few years by the enhanced PC/XT and PC/AT versions. When IBM made the technical details public, a host of "clones" (PCs that mimicked the performance of the IBM PCs) were developed and the basic design quickly became a worldwide standard. At the same time, the Intel Corporation developed a series of increasingly powerful CPU chips — the 286, 386, 486, and Pentium — that yielded orders of magnitude growth in processing power. With these new developments, prices declined sharply. In the late 1990s, there were an estimated 250 million IBM-compatible PCs in service.

Two other developments also spurred increased use of PCs: high-capacity hard disks and software with graphic user interfaces (GUIs, pronounced gooies).

In 1968, a 20-megabyte (abbreviated MB; it is 1,048,576 bytes) hard drive was about the size of a washing machine and cost $50,000. In 1997, a 1.6-gigabyte (abbreviated GB; it is 1024 MB) hard drive could be purchased for $250. Within 30 years, the cost of online storage has dropped from $2500 per megabyte to 16 cents per megabyte — a decrease of 99.994 percent!

Until recently, most computer systems had very crude user interfaces. Users had to compose and enter obscure commands. Errors as small as an upper case letter when a lower case letter was expected would cause the command to fail. In the 1980s, Apple Computer's operating system introduced the concept of GUIs. Valid command options are presented on the screen using graphic symbols (icons). The user selects an option with a "pointing device" (a mouse) that is used to control the position of a graphic indicator (the cursor) on the screen. In the 1990s, Microsoft Corp. followed suit with the Windows and, more recently, Windows 95 operating systems, which also use GUIs.

Laptop Computers

The PC development further expanded in 1990 with the introduction of the "laptop" PC. (It got its name because it was small enough to be used by a seated person.) The main advantage of the laptop is that it is small enough to be used while traveling. Most laptops fit into a briefcase and include a 500 or more megabyte fixed disk storage unit. The video display unit uses a color graphic display, which is comparable to a desktop PC's monitor, built into the lid. It can operate for several hours on a built-in, rechargeable battery.

Currently, laptop prices range from $1800 to as much as $7000, making them attractive targets for theft.

From a security standpoint, PCs represent an extension of the trend started by minicomputers. With the introduction of PCs, the number of computers in use in most organizations has increased, creating more points at which data and hardware are exposed to risk. As a rule, a single person performs all of the information processing functions for each PC, thus eliminating the separation-of-duties control. Controls over physical access may be weak or nonexistent.

On the other hand, each PC represents a relatively minor part of the organization's computing resources.

THE EVOLUTION OF INFORMATION SYSTEMS

The following figures illustrate the evolution of information security systems and how they have evolved concurrently with technological advances.

The 1960s: Batch Processing Mainframe Systems

The earliest information systems looked more or less like the system shown in Figure 2.

The batch processing systems of the 1960s were simply configured. The CPU had a small main memory, sometimes as little as 8 kB, and limited processing speed and power. One or two punched card readers could read the data stored on punched cards. Programs and data files were stored on

Information Systems Security: An Overview

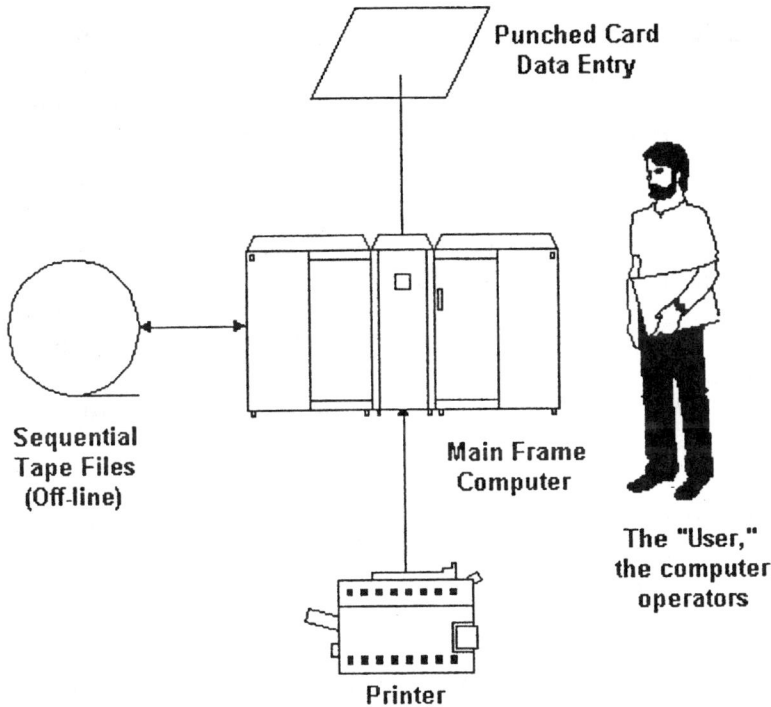

Figure 2. Early information systems.

magnetic tape. Output data was sent to printers, card punches, and magnetic tape. (There was no connection to the "outside world," and no "users" in the current sense of the term.)

These systems were called batch systems because data was processed in batches. Only one program could be run at a time. Thus, accounting data would be encoded using punched cards. Control cards would start the accounting program, read the input data cards, and data from the previous processing cycle stored on magnetic tapes, create new tape records, and print reports. When the program had completed its tasks, the operator would start another program.

Data was stored as "sequential" records written onto magnetic tapes. If an application had records for employees #001, #002, #004, #012, for example, the individual employee records would be written on the tape in the same order.

It was not practical to attempt to process records out of sequence. For instance, payroll input data would be sorted into employee order, and then processed the same way. The record for employee #001 was read from the tape file into memory and the input data applied to the record. Then, the

259

updated record for employee #001 was written to a new tape. The new tape was referred to as the "son," the previous tape as the "father," etc. (The collection of tapes for the payroll system was called a "generation" data set.) This data storage technique had the advantage of conceptual simplicity, but required processing to follow a rigid sequence.

As already mentioned, hardware for information systems was usually installed in a specially built room. A false floor, raised 12 to 24 inches above the building floor, provided space for interconnecting cables and a plenum for distributing cooling air. Because there were no users, there were no user IDs and passwords. Programs processed batches of data, with each program running at a previously scheduled time (once a day, week, etc.), depending on the function. If the data for a program was not available at the scheduled runtime, the operators could run another job while waiting for the missing data.

Printed output reports were delivered to the end users as they became available. Because end users did not expect to get a continuous flow of data from the information processing system, delays of a day or more before the output reports were received were not significant.

The 1970s: Online Information Processing Systems

The new decade launched the development of faster, more powerful computers, random access storage devices (currently called hard drives) and low-cost video display units (monitors). It became feasible to convert most programs from batch to online processing. (See Figure 3 for an illustration of a 1970s online processing system.)

Two new hardware elements were added to the 1970s systems: (1) An online, random access storage device and (2) "dumb" terminals. A dumb terminal provided the user with a keyboard to send a character stream to the computer, and a video screen that could display characters transmitted to it by the computer. The term "dumb" was used because the terminal had no internal storage or processing capability — it could only receive and display characters, and accept and transmit keystrokes.

The hard drives made it possible to process records out of sequence. Tables stored on a hard drive would tell programs where each record was stored, so a program could immediately retrieve a specific record.

The 1970s computers were enhanced to support multiprocessing. A master program, or operating system (OS), managed execution of the worker programs (applications).

For example, under the command of the operator, the OS would load and start application #1. After 50 milliseconds, the OS would interrupt the execution of app1 and store its current state in memory. App2 would be

Information Systems Security: An Overview

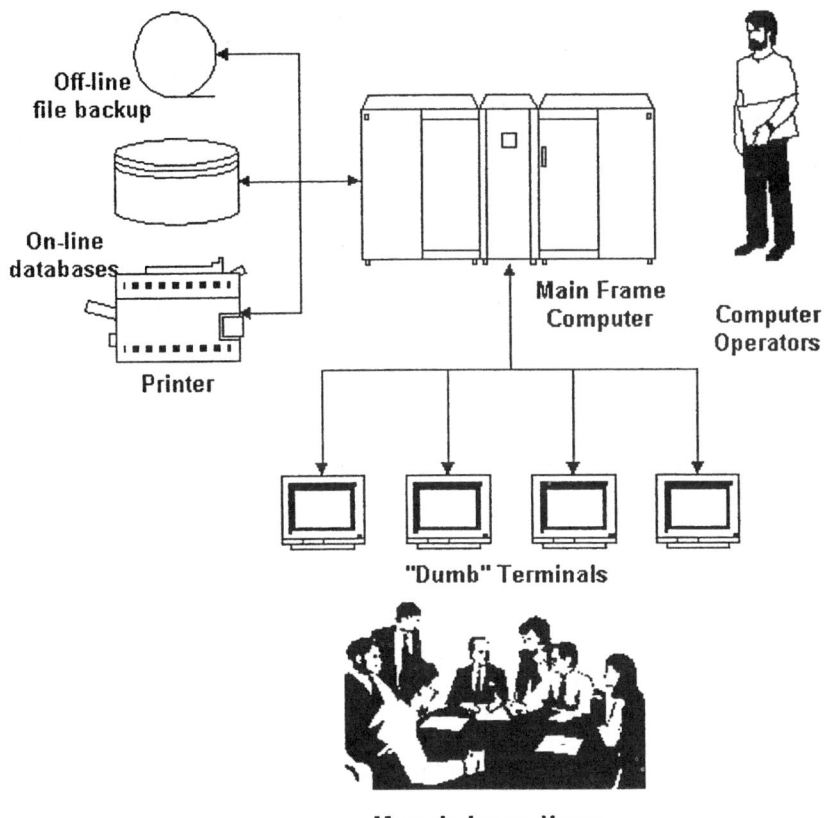

Figure 3. A 1970s online processing system.

started and run for 50 milliseconds. Then app1 would be restarted, etc. Within a second after a user had entered keyboard data, the OS would give his/her application a time slice to process the input. If the user wanted to access an employee record, the computer would pull the record from the hard drive, put it into memory, and display it on the user's terminal. After the user had modified the record, the computer would transfer it to the hard drive. These two techniques made it appear to the user as if he/she had dedicated access to the computer.

Multiprocessing and the ability to store more records online provided end users with direct access to data. It was now possible, for example, for airline reservation clerks to search for a flight requested by a caller, quote the fare, sell a ticket, and reserve a seat. Bank officers could verify an account balance, and adjust an entry to correct an error. These modifications in data were processed as received and not sequentially in batches. This flexibility led to the term "real-time."

ASSET PROTECTION AND SECURITY MANAGEMENT HANDBOOK

Within the computer industry, this was the first time the concept of the user became important. Now that users could modify data from a terminal, the use of terminals needed to be controlled. Terminals were no longer concentrated in a single location, so physical access controls alone could not be depended upon. Thus, user IDs and corresponding passwords had to be issued to end users before they could interact with the computer.

Local Area Networks

In the mid-1970s, PCs started to be used commercially as stand-alone desktop computers to perform word processing, financial analysis, and graphic processing. Each PC was a 1970s style online processing system with a single display unit and a single user — the owner of the PC. For end users, this was more convenient, but there were practical problems. For instance, it was difficult to share data with others and PC users did not always back up important data.

As PCs became more powerful, it became practical to interconnect them so users could share data. This was referred to as local area networks (LANs) because the hardware units were close together, usually in the same building or office area. They were interconnected by a powerful PC with a high-capacity hard disk designated as the file server. Other PCs (referred to as workstations) were connected to the file server via network interface cards installed in the workstations, and cables that connect the cards to the server. Special network software installed on the file server and workstations made it possible for workstations to access defined portions of the file server hard disk just as though these portions were installed on the workstations. File backup could be performed at the file server without depending on individual users.

It is estimated that, in the late 1990s, there were more than 100 million PCs operating as LAN workstations connected to about 4 million file servers. The most recognized network operating systems (NOSs) are Novell NetWare and Microsoft NT (New Technology) and its successors.

Presently, most LANs are implemented with the Ethernet protocol, which uses 10-BaseT UTP (unshielded twisted pair) wiring. UTP wire looks like heavy duty telephone wire, and uses an RJ-45 plug-in jack. Each workstation and the file server have a network interface card (NIC). A UTP wire runs from each NIC to a "hub."

The illustrated network (Figure 4) includes a dial-up modem connected to a dedicated telephone line. This enables remote users to dial into the modem and log on to the LAN. This is a great convenience to LAN users who are traveling or working at home. But it creates a new security risk.

NOS software provides for user-IDs and passwords, and selective authority to access file server data and program files. A workstation user

Information Systems Security: An Overview

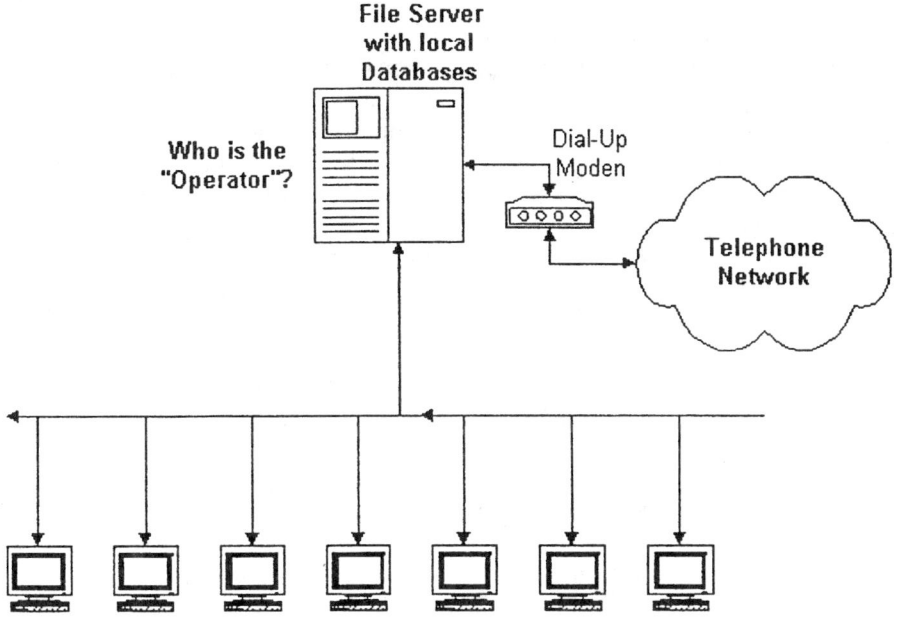

Figure 4. Illustration of a LAN.

logs in to the LAN by executing a file server log-in program. The program prompts the user to enter an ID and password. If the log-in program concludes that the ID and password are valid, it consults an access control table to determine what data and programs the user may access.

Access is defined as read-only, execute-only, create, modify, and/or delete with respect to individual files and groups of files. The access control table is maintained by the LAN administrator using a utility program. The effectiveness of the controls depends on the care taken by the administrator; therefore, in some circumstances, controls may be weak. It is essential to protect the ID and password of the LAN administrator because, if it is compromised, the entire access control system is lowered.

The absence of separation of duties is often a significant LAN security weakness.

Superficially, a LAN appears to be the same as a 1970s mainframe with remote dumb terminals. Technically, the differences between the two systems are as follows:

- *User programs on the LAN workstation are running on the workstations, not the file server; whereas a dumb terminal operator used programs executed on the mainframe.* To the user at a workstation or remote terminal, the

263

two situations appear to be the same. From a security standpoint, there are significant differences. The mainframe program software stays on the mainframe and cannot (under normal conditions) be altered during execution. A LAN program executed on a workstation can be altered — by a user or computer virus or other input. As a rule, mainframe remote terminals cannot download and save files. But workstations usually have a floppy diskette drive. Thus, it is much easier to copy data at a workstation than at a remote terminal.

- *The character of the connection between the computer and the terminals.* Each dumb terminal had a dedicated connection to its mainframe and could only receive data directly to it. A LAN operates more like a set of radio transmitters sharing a common frequency, the network of NIC-to-hub wiring described above. The file server and the workstations take turns "broadcasting" messages. Each message includes a "header" block that identifies the intended recipient. Thus, every network node (which includes the file server and the workstations) on a LAN receives all messages. Under normal circumstances, a node ignores messages not addressed to it. However, it is technically feasible for a workstation node to run a modified version of the NOS that allows it to capture all messages. A workstation with a modified NOS could identify all log-in messages and record the user-IDs and passwords. In this way, the workstation operator could gain complete access to the LAN's data and facilities.

- *The operating environment.* A mainframe had to be installed in a separate room and managed by a staff of skilled technicians. A LAN file server can be installed in ordinary office space and managed by a part-time LAN administrator (who may not be adequately trained). Consequently, the LAN has a higher exposure to tampering, sabotage, and theft. But, if a mainframe were disabled, many business functions would be interrupted, whereas the loss of a LAN file server would only interrupt a single function.

Wide Area Networks

With LANs growing in popularity, the idea of interconnecting LANs emerged. This network of networks was called a wide area network or WAN (see Figure 5 for an illustration of a WAN).

WAN technology has made it feasible to link LANs together with telecommunications circuits. So, a user of a marketing LAN could have access to files on the engineering LAN.

It was expensive to do this with 1970s online systems because all data would have to be transmitted over the network. Because processing and most data used by a workstation would be on its local LAN, a WAN network would be less expensive. Low-traffic LANs could be linked using dial-up

Information Systems Security: An Overview

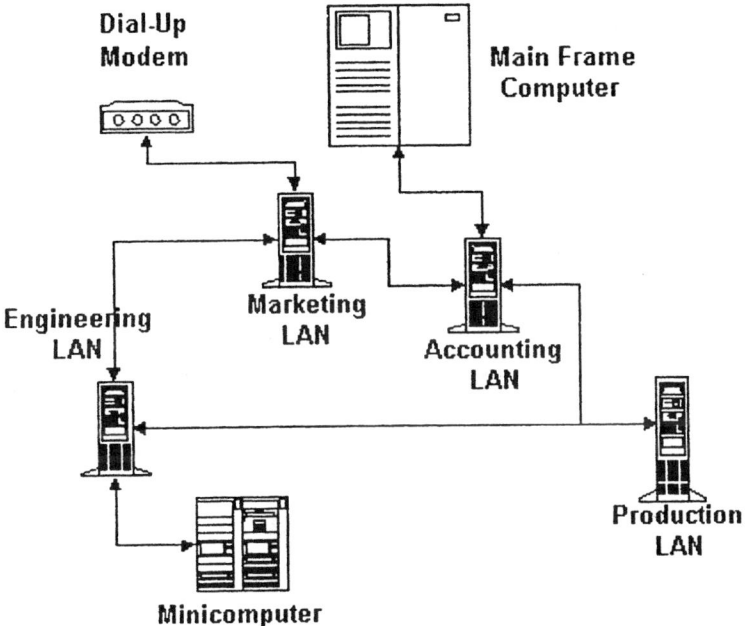

Figure 5. An illustration of a WAN. Four LANs are interconnected. Note also that two of the LANs have access to mainframe and minicomputer files and processing capabilities.

access at a minimum cost and major LANs could be linked with high-speed dedicated circuits for best performance. Apart from dial-up access, network traffic flowed over private networks.

Internet: The Public Network

The Internet is a connection of many LANs, originally designed for the decentralized interaction of American military information systems. It offered several important advantages as a source of networking:

- Low cost
- Connections available locally in most industrialized countries
- When adopting the Internet protocol, TCP/IP, one becomes instantly compatible with all other Internet users
- The World Wide Web technique made it easy for anyone to access data

As a result, almost overnight the Internet became the key to global networking (see Figure 6 for an illustration).

The Internet is operated by Internet Service Providers (ISPs) that operate Internet-compatible computers with both dial-up and dedicated access. A large ISP can offer access locations (referred to as Points of Presence, or

ASSET PROTECTION AND SECURITY MANAGEMENT HANDBOOK

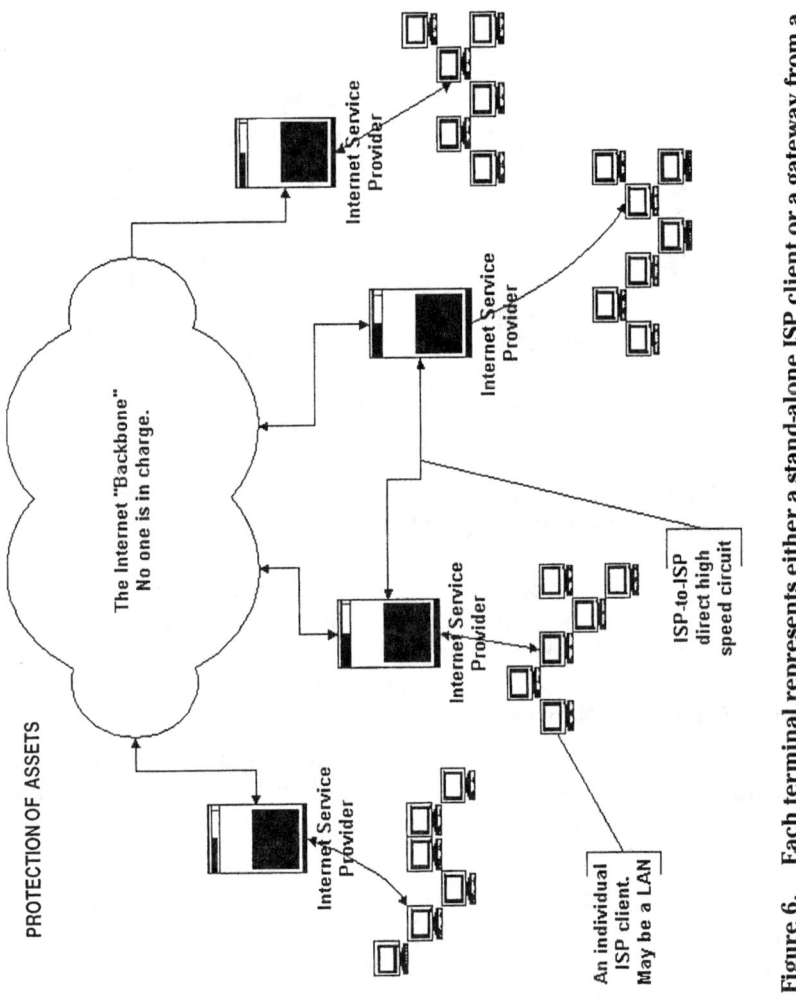

Figure 6. Each terminal represents either a stand-alone ISP client or a gateway from a client's LAN or WAN.

POPs) to many cities interconnected by its own network. Links can then be established with one another and through the four Network Access Points (set up by the National Science Foundation when the Internet was commercialized). ISP routers read the packet headers and automatically move packets from source to recipient through the interconnected ISPs.

The unfettered access provided by the Internet created new opportunities for organizations to communicate with clients. A company could implement a Web server with a full-time connection to an ISP, and open it to the public. A potential customer could access the Web site, download product information and software updates, ask questions, and even order products. The downside is that the user is alone in his or her surfing — if a connection cannot be established with another Internet user, there is no one to call for help.

Distributed, Three-Tier Information Systems

In the mid-1990s, hardware and software developments led to the adoption of *distributed* processing systems based on the *client/server* concept. (Distributed means that each data processing task is performed by more than one computer.) The user's workstation became the client, and the networked computer that responded to commands from the workstation, became the server (see Figure 7 for an illustration).

In this configuration, each workstation had its own Web browser program executing on it. Users could enter the address of the desired Web site and the browser would connect the workstation to the Web site server through a network, most likely the Internet. The Web server (see Figure 7) would send a menu of choices to the user's workstation and the user would choose from the available list of files. This request is sent to an application server (see Figure 7) by the Web server.

The application server responds by obtaining a copy of the available files list from the database server (see Figure 7) and passes the list back to the user through the Web server. This process is an illustration of a three-tier system because there are three computers between the client and the database.

Distributed, multi-tier information systems provide definite advantages:

- As the work load grows, more computers can be added. This is an extremely important characteristic referred to as *scalability*. Unless a system can be scaled up as work load grows, an expensive redesign and redeployment would be required.
- Single points of failure can be eliminated or minimized.

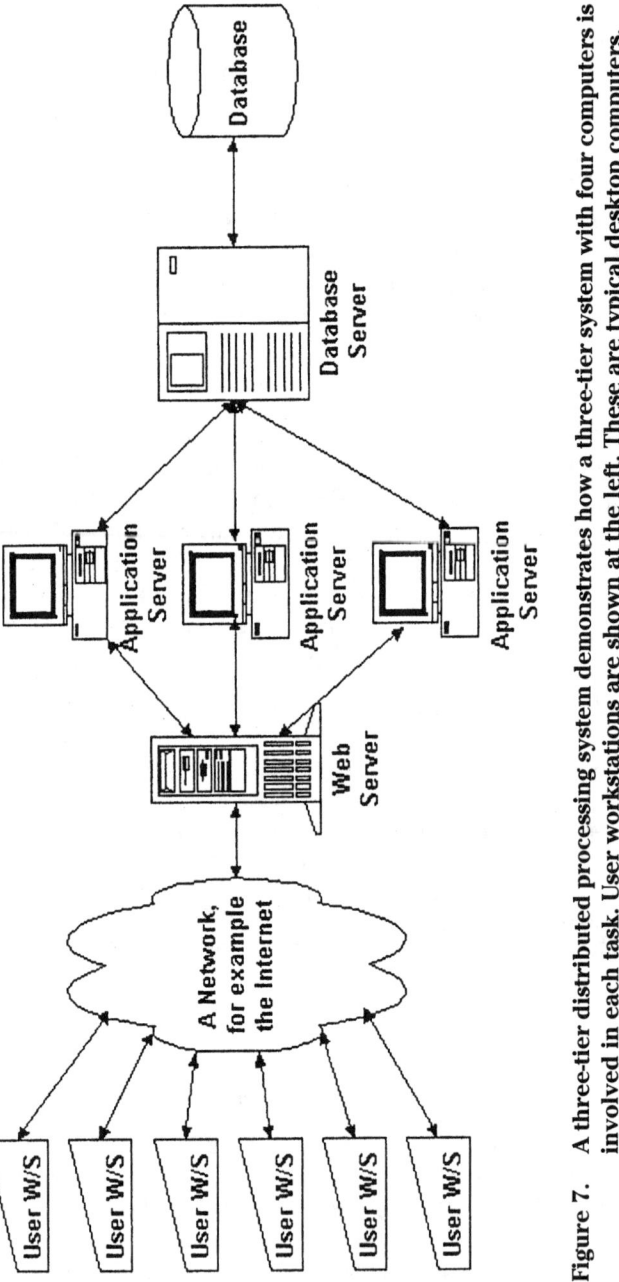

Figure 7. A three-tier distributed processing system demonstrates how a three-tier system with four computers is involved in each task. User workstations are shown at the left. These are typical desktop computers.

WHAT IS INFORMATION SYSTEMS SECURITY?

As a definition, there is no accepted meaning for information systems security. For this reason, specialists define it in terms of the portion of computer operations with which they are familiar, or "data security." For computer system software specialists, security means controlling access to the database and programs.

An example: Insurance managers might focus on the risk of damage to high-value hardware and employee infidelity. Operations managers might concentrate on having a reliable operation and disaster recovery planning, but might be indifferent to short-term outages that are disruptive to end users. Auditors might be concerned about exposures to computer fraud and unauthorized disclosure of information in the computer. (Auditors concentrate on controls over balance sheet data and may overlook extremely critical nonmonetary data.)

A comprehensive security program must consider all of these concerns.

IS INFORMATION SYSTEMS SECURITY IMPORTANT?

To determine whether information systems security is an important issue, ask this question of yourself: Is it a proper area of concern for the security director? In almost every case, the answer will be yes. The following reasons explain why:

1. *System outages.* Increasingly, information systems have become an integral part of daily operations. Consequently, a significant system outage can have a major impact on operations and trigger serious losses. However, attempting to have 100 percent reliability can be very expensive. It is important to optimize reliability and have an economically sound contingency plan.
2. *Fraud.* Many information systems control or account for significant assets, such as money, goods, services, or entitlements. For this reason, they have become targets for fraud. Automation has also created new fraud scenarios. For example, this author created the term "salami swindle" to refer to the type of fraud in which an embezzler steals a small amount (a thin slice of salami) from each of thousands of accounts with the hope that no one will notice the tiny individual discrepancies. By tampering with accounting programs, this kind of fraud is quite feasible — but it would be utterly impractical if account records were maintained on ledger cards. The discovery of losses in the tens of millions of dollars makes it clear that computer fraud is a serious exposure.
3. *Theft of information.* Computerized databases differ fundamentally from paper records in that the exposure to theft or unauthorized

disclosure of information is much higher. This is true for many reasons — but most notably because electronic data takes up so little space. For example, one can copy a data file the size of a big city telephone directory onto a magnetic tape in a matter of minutes. A CD-ROM can store the equivalent of 80,000,000 telephone directory entries. Because a digital copy of stolen data can be put to use immediately on another computer without the huge expense of keying in the data, digital data is much more valuable than the equivalent paper copy.
4. *Damage to valuable property.* Computer and network hardware and software are both expensive and fragile. It is not unusual to find that the hardware contents of a computer room or network control center are worth $2000 or more per square foot of floor area. By contrast, typical office contents are likely to be worth about $100 per square foot. Fire, water leaks, corrosive gases, and sabotage can lead to major casualty losses, as well as system outages.
5. *Theft of hardware.* As more people have their own computers at home, computer hardware and supplies are becoming increasingly attractive targets for theft. Note that the victim must not only pay for the replacement parts, but will also likely suffer the expense of the system outage or data disclosure caused by the theft. In some cases, the data stored on a stolen laptop computer may far exceed the value of the computer.
6. *Attacks on the organization.* Determined outsiders or insiders may attempt to sabotage or damage an organization by attacking its information systems. This risk applies expecially to disgruntled former employees who, in earlier times, might have first bad-mouthed management or stolen a few supplies. Today, with a few keystrokes, they can seriously cripple an organization.

THE EVOLUTION OF INFORMATION SYSTEM RISKS

The risks associated with information systems have evolved concurrently with its technological advances. As a consequence, it is important for security managers to understand how the risk environment has changed.

Batch System Risks

As Figure 2 demonstrates, batch system configurations and system operations were both conceptually quite simple. All the hardware and data could be located in one room or several adjacent rooms. Consequently, access to hardware and data could be controlled by controlling physical access to the "computer room." End users did not have direct access to data — only seeing the output on reports or punched cards.

Information Systems Security: An Overview

System operators soon realized that backup copies of data should be stored at another location to protect against fires or other accidents — and this was easy to do. At the same time a tape file was being updated, a copy of it could be created for offsite storage.

There were only a few significant risks associated with batch computer systems:

- Accidental physical damage to the hardware and data tapes caused by fires, roof leaks, etc.
- Fraud based on introduction of invalid input data, or program tampering
- System processing interruptions caused by hardware failures, software bugs, or environmental failures, such as electric power failures
- System sabotage by means of physical attack on the hardware, program tampering or theft of data tapes

The information systems were configured and installed by the hardware vendors. Once in place, they were usually operated by inexperienced people. This made it difficult to detect a loss until it occurred. Each loss event would trigger corrective action but, as a rule, information system security programs were not based on comprehensive assessments of risks leading to rational, cost-effective risk management actions.

Online Information Systems Risks

The trend toward online systems brought new and more complicated risks:

- Users will sometimes take the ID and password of another user to access data, obtain access to restricted information, or conceal the author of a sabotage or data-tampering attack.
- Because programs are stored online, it is more difficult to protect programs against tampering.
- Because of the increasing dependence on real-time processing, the end-user service interruption losses are greater. At the same time, the information system has more failure modes.
- Data backup becomes more complicated because databases change continuously during the processing day. Offsite backup tapes can only be a "snapshot" of a database taken at a single point in time.
- Because data is processed continuously, out-of-balance conditions, perhaps fraud-related, can only be detected after the fact when the books are closed.
- Because an individual user may be able to access all of the records of a database, software sabotage (systematic corruption all the records) of a database becomes feasible.

Local and Wide Area Network Risks

The risks associated with LANs and WANs:

- Management of user-IDs and passwords becomes more complex when an individual user must have access to more than one computer.
- The "broadcast" characteristic of networks creates an opportunity to capture and misuse IDs and passwords.
- LAN file servers may not be installed in a physically secure environment, thus increasing the risk of physical damage, loss of stored data, and prolonged service interruptions. If a person can gain unsupervised physical access to a file server, he or she can compromise its file access controls. Physical access may also make it possible for a potential intruder to add a hidden workstation to a LAN — which is basically an automated wiretap.
- Because typical workstations have local storage and floppy diskette drives, it is much easier for a user to make unauthorized copies of data. Note that banning diskette drives will not protect against this kind of information theft. The thief can easily connect a portable diskette drive to a workstation through its parallel port.

There are some saving graces, however. A typical LAN runs on relatively simple and low-cost hardware with most data stored locally, so it is easier to restore service to the LAN's users after a calamity. (This presupposes that backup data is being sent off-site with appropriate frequency.)

Internet Risks

Depending on the degree to which in-house information systems have access to the Internet, the following risks will arise:

- Intruders may be able to gain access to private data, alter Web site contents, or sabotage in-house systems.
- In-house users may publish inappropriate material at other Internet sites, causing embarrassment or liability to their organizations.
- Embezzlers may be able to circumvent payment for online purchases.
- Intruders may be able to capture and alter packets — or capture the connection to another Internet site and masquerade as an organization's user. (This latter deception is a favorite tactic of mischevious hackers.)
- Web pages may include active elements (mini-programs) that, when downloaded, delete data on the target workstation much like a computer virus.
- Word processing and spreadsheet files attached to e-mail messages may include so-called macro viruses that damage files on the target workstation.

Distributed Systems

Distributed systems can reduce the exposure of critical real-time systems to catastrophic failure and simplified disaster recovery because many relatively simple computers are used instead of a single mainframe. Yet, as with any system, there are associated risks.

- Because there are many processors, end-user access control becomes more complex; each computer in a processing chain must be sure that it is processing a valid, properly authorized transaction. A complex authentication system will probably be required using a dedicated "authentication" server to monitor access to individual computers by transaction.
- Configuration control becomes more complex. Program tampering can be used to support some kinds of computer fraud. Because a distributed system has many computers, assuring the integrity of the individual computers is more difficult than with mainframe information systems.
- The transactions pass both ways over a network where they are exposed to interception and tampering. Bear in mind that it is relatively easy to intercept computerized transactions. As computers become cheap and powerful, it becomes feasible to program a computer to look at all packets passing over a network, and select the packets of interest.

MANAGEMENT OF INFORMATION SYSTEMS SECURITY

Information security systems have been in existence since the 1960s, yet management of the systems are often rudimentary. This is partly due to:

- Compensation plans for middle managers may stress short-term financial results, discouraging expenditures for long-term protection.
- Information technology people tend to concentrate on technical matters and often exhibit the attitude that "it can't happen here."
- In many cases, no effort has been made to quantify the size of potential losses and make a systematic assessment of threats as the basis for selecting an optimum security strategy. Instead, information systems security managers tend to react to events rather than anticipate them. For example, the time to install a backup electric power system is one month before a two-day blackout, but most are purchased one month after.

Numerous security measures can be applied to these basic exposures; so how does one determine which is best? The essential management question to ask is: *Which specific security measures are optimum for a given information processing system?* The choice is dependent upon the risks to which the information processing system is exposed and the assets and processes subject to loss, damage, and interruption. What is right for one facility will not be for another.

FUNCTIONAL DEFINITION OF INFORMATION SYSTEMS SECURITY

Before a functional definition of information systems security could be given, an adequate basic knowledge of it needed to be understood. It can be defined in the following way:

> Information systems security comprises collectively all those measures taken to minimize the overall risk cost (cost of security measure plus risk losses) of an information system.

The basic objective of any security program must be to optimize the overall performance of the organization. This means that *the cost of security programs must be related to the effect that they have on security losses*. Obviously, spending $1 million to avoid a $10 loss is not practical, but neither is leaving an organization exposed to a $1 million loss that could have been abated with a $10 effort. The security program must be balanced in the same way — do not go overboard in one area and leave another completely uncovered. (A clear sign of unprofessional security management is to stress the effectiveness of a particular security measure while ignoring a serious weakness in another area. An enemy will always attack at the weakest point, not the strongest.)

Information systems are complex and the relationship between a security exposure and the losses it generates are not always obvious. For example, the cost of service outages cannot be determined by examining the computer system itself. End users must be asked who will suffer from the outages. Likewise, the connection between weak controls over changes to applications programs or an exposure to a major fraud that depends on program tampering may not be obvious.

Furthermore, some security measures can be costly, particularly backup standby fees, emergency electric power, and elaborate fire safety. For these reasons, information systems security needs special attention and careful analysis (see Figure 8).

In the upper left portion of Figure 8, the external environment, the building, the staff, and the information system itself collectively determine the characteristics of the significant threats (frequency of occurrence and impact on functions and physical elements). In the upper right, it demonstrates how the physical assets of the computer system (some of which are associated with the stored data, and the processes supported by the computer system) determine the potential losses that could occur.

A threat/loss potential pair is only significant if the threat and loss potential are connected by a vulnerability. Collectively, the threats, loss

Information Systems Security: An Overview

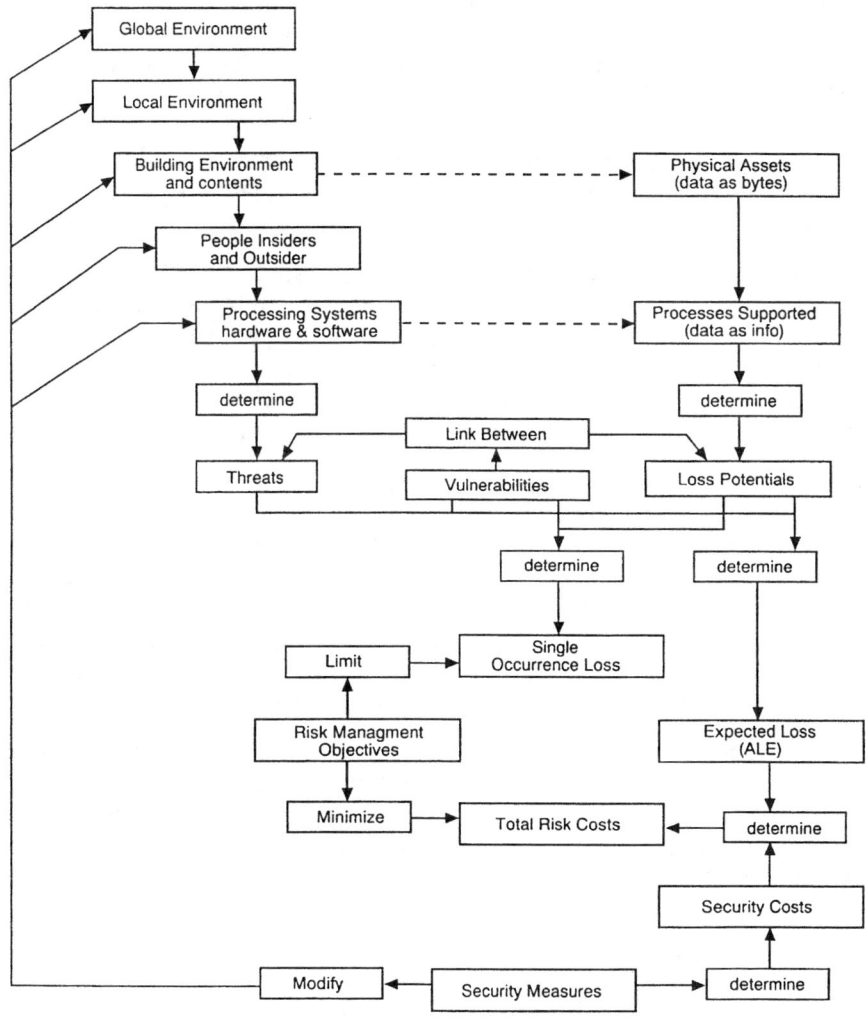

Figure 8. How risks, potential losses and security measures are related.

potentials, and vulnerabilities will determine the *expected loss*, sometimes called *Annualized Loss Expectancy* (ALE). ALE is an estimate of the losses that can reasonably be expected to occur, expressed as an average rate, often in dollars per year.

How Risks, Potential Losses and Security Measures Are Related

Loss potential and vulnerability, with respect to a given threat, are used to estimate single occurrence loss (SOL). SOL is the loss that can reasonably be expected to result from a single occurrence of the threat in question.

An example: Vandalism is expected to occur once every ten years. A file server has a replacement cost of $5000. The file server's vulnerability is estimated to be 50 percent of necessary functionality. The ALE is 1/10 × 50% × $5000, or $250. This does not mean the organization will experience a loss of $250 each year. The assumptions indicate it will experience a single occurrence loss (SOL) of $2500 about every ten years. ALE estimates are particularly useful for evaluating relatively frequent loss events. SOL is useful for evaluating rare but highly damaging events.

Referring back to Figure 8, the security measures taken to protect the computer system and their effects are listed at the bottom. (Recognize that there are costs to implement and maintain security measures. These are depicted in Figure 8 as Security Costs.) Optimally, security measures will alter the threats, loss potentials, and vulnerabilities to reduce ALE and SOL. The objectives of risk management are to minimize risk costs (such as ALE plus Security Costs) and limit SOL exposures to an acceptable level through the skillful choice of security measures.

These measures can also be used as a template to discover information about your own organization's information processing facility and the kinds of services provided to end users. This information will suggest the computer risks to which the organization is exposed and the kinds of losses that could result from security breaches. The nontechnical risks to the hardware and software are the concern of the security director.

Other questions to ask yourself include: How would your organization respond to a security breach? How would the breach be detected? If a crime has occurred, how would it be investigated and by whom? What kind of evidence would be available? What steps should be taken to ensure that the value of the evidence is not lost through mishandling?

Selected Bibliography

Stephenson, Peter; *Investigating Computer-Related Crime*; 1999; CRC Press, Boca Raton, FL.

Cheswick, William R. and Bellovin, Steven M.; *Firewalls and Internet Security: Repelling the Wily Hacker;* 1994; Addison-Wesley, Reading, MA.

Data Security Management; 1984 and continuing; Auerbach Publications, Boca Raton, FL.

Federal Fire Council, *Fire Protection for Essential Electronic Equipment;* 1969; Federal Fire Council, Washington, D.C.

Healy, Richard J. and Walsh, Timothy J.; *Principles of Security Management;* 1981; Professional Publications, New Rochelle, NY.

Bosworth, Seymour and Kabay, M.E., Editors; *Computer Security Handbook,* 4th ed.; 2002; John Wiley & Sons, New York.

Jackson, Keith; *Secure Information Transfer/PC Encryption;* 1990; ISBN: 0-8493-7711-0, CRC Press, Boca Raton, FL.

Jackson, Keith and Hruska, Jan; *Information Systems Security Solutions;* ISBN: 0-8493-7706-4, CRC Press, Boca Raton, FL.

Information Systems Security: An Overview

Tipton, Harold F. and Kraus, Micki, Editors; *Information Security Handbook, 4th ed.;* 2003; Auerbach Publications, Boca Raton, FL.

Jacobson, Robert V. et al.; *FIPS Pub No. 31, Guidelines for Automatic Data Processing Physical Security and Risk Management;* 1974; National Bureau of Standards, Washington, D.C.

Krauss, Leonard; *Safe-Security Audit and Field Evaluation;* 1972; Firebrand, Krauss & Co., East Brunswick, NJ.

Lavelle, Laurie G.; Detecting Fires before They Start; May/June 1992; *NFPA Journal,* National Fire Protection Association, Quincy, MA.

Moeller, Robert; *Computer Audit, Control and Security;* 1989; John Wiley & Sons, New York.

Perry, Robert et al.; *Computer and Data Security;* 1990; Bureau of National Affairs, Washington, D.C.

Ralston, Anthony and Reilly, Jr., Edwin D.; *Encyclopedia of Computer Science and Engineering;* Van Nostrand and Reinhold, New York.

Reed, Alan and Watt, Steve; *Computer Risk Manager;* 1989; ISBN: 946395-47-0, Elsevier Advanced Technology.

Watt, Steve; *Information Systems Security Manager;* 1989; ISBN: 946395-48-9, Elsevier Advanced Technology.

Video Cassettes

Commonwealth Films, Inc., 223 Commonwealth Ave., Boston, MA. A series of twelve information systems security cassettes. Average length, 20 minutes each.

Information Security, Inc., 1001 Spring St., Silver Spring, MD 20910. *Into Thin Air,* 19-minute video cassette.

Professional Security Television Network, 1303 Marsh Lane, Carrollton, TX 75006-9977.

10
Information Systems Security

INTRODUCTION

Information security specialists have a wide range of tools available to implement information systems security. Chapter 9 discussed some techniques and how they relate to information systems. This chapter addresses the management issues and the questions that must be answered to ensure that the security program will perform as expected.

The purpose of information systems security is to protect an organization's information assets and related functions that depend on information systems. Well-thought-out and developed security procedures are implemented to protect important assets and thereby support the overall mission of the organization.

The following is a list of essential characteristics of an effective information systems security program (ISSP):

1. Senior management recognizes the need for an ISSP and provides appropriate resources.
2. The ISSP is cost-effective. (*Cost-effective* is defined as the level of protection that will maximize the performance of the organization, taking into account the cost of the ISSP and the reduction in losses it is expected to achieve.)
3. Responsibility and accountability for all aspects of an ISSP are explicit and are defined in written policies and procedures.
4. ISSP performance and requirements are reviewed and appropriate adjustments made at regular intervals, and whenever there is a material change in the mission or risk environment.

ROLES AND RESPONSIBILITIES

In this section we discuss key roles and responsibilities, including those of the security director. By understanding his or her role in properly supporting the ISSP, the security director can play an effective part in obtaining the required managerial and employee participation to ensure the ISSP operates effectively.

Senior Management

Senior management has ultimate responsibility for the security of an organization's information systems. Shareholders routinely look to management to safeguard corporate assets and taxpayers expect responsible, effective conduct from government officials. Senior management provides two essential elements of every ISSP:

1. Definition of the organization's policy for protection of information systems, and approval of procedures to implement the policy. (Information systems managers within an organization should not be setting policy but, rather, recommending policy to senior management.)
2. The resources — such as people, money, and accountability — required to effectively implement the policy.

Similar to other staff functions, the ISSP competes for resources. Thus, senior managers make an effort to prudently allocate finite resources while at the same time choosing between a risk exposure that may occur and other operational requirements — such as new product rollouts. This dilemma can force senior managers to deliberately accept a risk.

Information systems security professionals have the obligation to present credible risk assessments and cost-justifications for proposed security measures, and to advise management against unacceptable business risks. As with other resource-allocation proposals presented to senior management, the assessments and recommendations must be credible and well-thought-out in order for the rationale to be effective.

Information Systems Security Program Management

There are three fundamentally different aspects of ISSP management:

1. *Performance of daily operational tasks,* such as administration of a user's physical and logical access controls, data backup operations, detailed implementation of technical measures, procedures to control development and operation of systems, etc.
2. *Assessment of ISSP performance,* such as auditing for compliance with internal controls, reviewing of logs and journals, investigation of suspicious events, etc.
3. *Overall management of the ISSP,* such as determining the requirements and recommendations of policies and procedures presented to senior management, selecting specific strategies to implement the procedures, etc. (Every ISSP must have a responsible manager. In a small organization this may be a part-time job but one individual must still have ultimate responsibility and accountability.)

As a rule, the first set of tasks will be assigned to information systems managers in an organization. However, the second and third aspects of ISSP management involve assessment of the performance of information systems and the impartial determination of the requirements. For this reason, these responsibilities should not be under the control of information systems managers so as to ensure objectivity and proper separation of duties.

Information Systems Operational Management

Information systems managers are the managers who — with the support of technicians — design and operate information systems to support one or more end-user applications. One primary responsibility is to implement and operate technical security measures to ensure policy objectives are achieved. Information systems managers must also be familiar with the cost and performance of available technical security hardware devices, software, and related security techniques.

IS management may appoint a system security manager who has direct responsibility for daily security operations. Typically, the system security manager is responsible for issuing and maintaining user-IDs and passwords. User access software should protect passwords using a one-way encryption scheme. This technique encrypts the password entered by the user, and then compares the result with a table of encrypted passwords to determine if it is valid.

The term "one-way" means that there is no feasible way to work the process backward and discover a password from knowledge of the encrypted list. Thus, access to the encrypted password list will not be beneficial to an intruder.

In effect, this technique also enables system security staff to masquerade as other users. To provide a check against abuses of this ability, many systems include an audit trail of system security staff actions. The audit trail is reviewed at irregular intervals by an independent audit group to look for suspicious activity. Knowledge of this audit capability will help deter wrongdoing by the systems security staff.

It is essential to provide automatic links between an entity's personnel system and the user access control system so that the latter automatically receives notice of all changes in job status. A common exposure occurs when an entity fails to disable a user's ID/password immediately after reassignment or termination.

System software can include features to help detect attempted intrusions. For example, the typical log-in system allows a user three attempts to enter the correct password and, after the third failed attempt, locks the account under the assumption that the failed attempts represent an intrusion attack. The system can also be programmed to send a message to the system security staff in real-time. This feature makes it possible for the system security staff to detect a systematic attack while in progress.

Other similar trip wires can be installed. Some banks provide a feature to allow tellers to use their computer terminals to alert the system security staff when they suspect that a current customer may be attempting a fraud. This real-time monitoring can be extremely effective — but should be properly coordinated with the "help desk" functions described below.

If the systems security manager has responsibility for generation of off-site storage of backup media, a vital aspect of that duty is the development, implementation and testing of business resumption plans (BRPs). BRPs are provisions taken in advance to facilitate recovery of information system operations following a natural or other disaster. Depending on the time-urgency of information systems applications, this may be a critically important function. In addition, the systems security manager will also be responsible for dealing with violations of security procedures.

Systems programmers and computer operators are an important part of information systems management. The organization depends on these people to comply with a wide range of controls and procedures — some of which may be a bit onerous — to maintain the integrity and reliability of information systems.[1] When problems arise, managers can put great pressure on these technicians to get results by cutting corners, causing security compliance to suffer. For example, both systems programmers and computer operators may share passwords — thereby defeating attempts to provide personal accountability.

These technicians must, by the very nature of their work, have unlimited access to systems and application software and data files. It is unlikely that technical measures can be depended upon to monitor their actions. Systems programmers can most likely circumvent audit trails by disabling the event logging during the time they want to conceal their actions.

Experience suggests two kinds of protective actions:

1. Take great care in the selection and management of systems programmers and computer operators. Every effort should be taken to select honest, conscientious individuals and to ensure attentive, alert management.
2. Provide good physical access controls and monitoring of critical work areas.

---

[1] Larger organizations can establish a separate element to provide telecommunications services, some of which may support one or more information systems. In this structure, the telecommunications services manager will also have important security responsibilities. To a lesser extent, telecommunications technicians also have unsupervised access to data because they observe and sometimes record data transmission. They also have the physical access and technical know-how to install wiretaps. The same controls used for system operators should also be applied to the telecommunications technicians.

Information Systems Security

Most information systems have a help desk function — a function designed to respond to end-user trouble reports received by telephone. Problems may simply be a request for information, but also usually include reports of systems software or hardware failures. Some help desk personnel are also responsible for responding to workstation faults, correcting software problems and replacing defective hardware. This means that they can access data stored on workstation local drives. As a rule, workstation access should be monitored by the user, and relevant activity should be logged by the help desk.

The larger help desk operations use a software system to log trouble reports, creating a numbered "ticket" for each report. The software then draws on its historic records of problems and their resolution to suggest a fix for current trouble reports. Typically, software will also allow the help desk to assign a ticket — via an e-mail message — to another part of the organization for resolution.

Because the help desk is a central trouble reporting point, it can act as the first point of reporting potential wrongdoing and other security incidents. Consequently, help desk procedures need to be designed to support security objectives. The systems security manager needs to review help desk records regularly to ensure that security incidents are being handled correctly.

Supporting Functions

The entity's security director plays an important role in support of the ISSP. The assertions made about the performance of technical and logical controls for information systems are based on the assumption that physical access to information systems hardware is properly controlled. It is well-known that the logical access controls of a popular local area network operating system can be easily defeated if one can gain unsupervised access to the file server. Consequently, it is essential that the security director be aware of all information systems vulnerabilities as the basis for implementing an appropriate physical security program as a part of the ISSP. Furthermore, the security director should be assigned responsibility for investigation of suspected security breaches.

Larger organizations may use a guard force to protect facilities. The security director should include appropriate guidance to the guard force regarding information systems. The following topics should be covered:

1. The actions guards shall take if information systems hardware — normally turned off at night — is powered-up after regular hours.
2. Computing hardware that may be removed from a facility by employees, visitors and contractors. It is important that guards are trained to identify the different types of common portable computing hardware.

3. Special measures required to protect information systems properly in the event of a fire, air-conditioning breakdown, flooding, etc.
4. Clear emergency instructions and a current list of home telephone numbers for IS staff members.

Beyond these traditional functions, the security director can take the initiative to interact with the other responsible managers to ensure that the ISSP is complete, that all responsibilities have been explicitly assigned, and that the most appropriate physical security techniques are being employed.

The human resources manager and security director need to coordinate on matters such as pre-hire screening, conducting internal investigations and monitoring personnel actions to ensure that the interests of both the organization and its individual employees are given proper consideration.

To ensure that every individual in an organization understands the requirements imposed by the ISSP, an explicit security training program is an essential part of an effective ISSP. This may include written affirmation by individuals that training, particularly with regard to the organization's policies, has been received and that they will comply. These signed statements often become important when resolving employee misconduct.

Internal auditors are responsible for examining information systems to verify proper operation, including accuracy and completeness or performance, especially with respect to record keeping and verification of compliance with control procedures. Consequently, internal audit has an important part in every ISSP. Some IS managers employ quality assurance programs to improve the quality of the products and services they provide to their end users. Because security failures can degrade quality — sometimes even catastrophically — the quality assurance group should help define ISSP requirements.

Many for-profit organizations have risk managers who are explicitly responsible for identifying and addressing potentially catastrophic risks. Traditionally, this function has focused on acquiring and managing insurance coverage for risks such as public liability, workers' compensation, employee fraud and property damage. More recently, risk managers have devoted more attention to quantitative assessment of risks and selection of other risk management techniques in addition to insurance. The ISSP manager should take full advantage of risk management expertise and coordinate information system risk management requirements with overall organizational requirements. The security director should also coordinate closely with the risk management in the assessment of risks and selection of risk reduction measures, particularly those relating to physical security and criminal activities.

Larger organizations may also have facilities managers responsible for the operation and maintenance of the premises and physical facilities, including electrical power and environmental controls. This position has a very important role in providing a safe reliable environment in which information systems can properly operate. A complete risk assessment will include facility considerations and may call for improvement in the reliability of the operating environment. For these reasons, the facility manager will have an explicit role in the success of the ISSP.

Users

Ultimately, information systems support individuals in the conduct of their responsibilities. These individuals are referred to by information systems people as "users." Users interact directly with information systems by entering data, accessing data, and generating output products — such as payment checks, billing statements, credit reports, etc. As noted above, these users need to know what is expected of them with regard to security policies and procedures. Recurring training and clear statements of policy and procedures are essential to achieving user understanding.

Inevitably, some users will carelessly or willfully attempt to circumvent controls. Therefore, activity monitoring is essential to detect these instances of noncompliance. On the other hand, it is important to configure a user-friendly security environment that avoids placing unreasonable demands on users. Thus, user requirements must be considered when security procedures are designed.

End users may not have direct contact with information systems hardware, but may depend heavily on the systems to carry out organizational requirements. It is essential to consult directly with these users when assessing the cost impact of security failures, information systems service interruptions, loss or corruption of stored data, manipulation of stored data to effect a fraud, or improper disclosure of information.

Experience suggests that information systems managers cannot evaluate these security losses because their understanding is incomplete or incorrect. For this reason, additional review by professional security personnel is required. However, there is no substitute for loss of potential information coming directly from end users. This information is a key part of the assessment of risks and the development of effective business resumption plans.

INFORMATION SYSTEMS SECURITY POLICIES, PROCEDURES AND STANDARDS

The definition of policy is *a principle, plan or course of action pursued by an organization.* In this context, a policy statement is a written affirmation by an organization's senior management of a specific compliance goal. For example, the following statement might be adopted as policy by an organization:

> Only authorized persons assigned to the accounting and personnel departments are permitted to enter or modify information stored in the payroll processing system.

Notice that the statement does not say how the policy objective is to be accomplished, merely that this is the position that senior management has adopted. Line managers are assigned responsibility for developing and implementing procedures to ensure achievement of policy goals.

Policy should always be determined by senior management. An information systems security practitioner may identify a situation where a policy statement is required and may draft a recommended policy statement for senior management review. But ultimately, the responsibility for adoption rests with the organization's senior management. Information systems security managers should recognize that such policy proposals are an effective tool for educating senior managers in the need for appropriate security measures.

In general, there are three kinds of information systems security policy statements:

1. *Program policy* is used to create or modify an organization's information systems security program (for example, assignment of security management responsibilities).
2. *Issue-specific policies* address specific information systems security issues of concern (for example, classification of data sensitivity or the employment of cryptographic protection).
3. *System-specific policies* focus on protection of a particular information processing system (for example, rules for access to a specific database).

Procedures and standards are used to describe how these policies will be implemented within an organization.

Policy Implementation

As well as policies to define management goals, an organization must develop standards and procedural guidelines to support the achievement of these goals. Standards define the techniques and methods used to implement various security measures. Procedures apply to the accomplishment of specific tasks; for example, how to enroll a new user in an access control system. Standards and procedures are discussed in greater detail below.

Standards. An organization may adopt compulsory or recommended internal or external standards to define specific technologies, parameters or procedures to be used in defined circumstances. Some examples of external standards include American National Standards, Federal Information

Processing Standards published by the National Institute of Standards and Technology, and Federal Property Management Standards.

An organization might adopt standards specifying the accepted level of electromagnetic radiation from different classes of hardware, the characteristics of employee photographs used for identification, classes of information requiring encryption when stored, encryption system standards, etc. Policy statements would require or recommend adherence to standards by personnel who design, implement and operate systems. The objective is to ensure good practice in the design, implementation and operation of systems. This is particularly important for information systems because of their inherent complexity and the requirement for interoperability.

Procedures. Procedures are issued to ensure accomplishment of policy objectives. Procedures typically include detailed steps to be followed by users, system operators or others to accomplish a particular task — such as giving a new user access to a system and assigning the appropriate access privileges. Following is an example of a procedural statement to exemplify that instance:

> Only authorized personnel specialists may update fields for weekly attendance, charges to annual leave, employee addresses, telephone numbers or update salary information. Employees may not update their own records.

Documentation and Distribution of Policy, Procedures and Standards. Policy and procedures must be accessible to those to whom they apply. Traditionally, this has implied that policy and procedures must be in printed form. However, with the growing availability of advanced technology like compact disks and intranets, electronic publication becomes increasingly attractive because of the potential time and cost savings.

In some situations, policy and procedures may be sensitive and not appropriate for unlimited distribution. Consequently, it may be necessary to provide for a system to classify the documents and control their distribution.

INFORMATION SYSTEMS SECURITY PROGRAM MANAGEMENT

Risk Management

Risk management is the process whereby risks are assessed systematically and continuously, and appropriate security measures are identified and applied to material risks. In this context, "systematic risk assessment" means that fully qualified people have followed good practice in identifying the material loss exposures and the threats or perils that can trigger the losses. "Security measure" is generally defined as any device, procedure or contractual relationship employed to reduce risk exposures. Examples include insurance coverage, burglar alarm systems and pre-hire screening of candidates for sensitive positions.

The objective of a risk assessment is to generate a quantitative estimate of expected losses, which can be reasonably expected to occur given the risk environment, usually expressed at an annual rate; and material single occurrence losses, which may have a low probability of occurrence but would cause unacceptably high losses. An "appropriate security measure" is one for which there is a good balance between the cost to implement and maintain the security measure and the reduction in expected loss and/or single occurrence loss the security measure is expected to accomplish.

There are two reasons why ISSPs should be based on a careful application of the basic principles of risk management:

1. A systematic and comprehensive risk assessment is required to ensure that all material risk exposures are properly identified, and to permit senior managers to assert that due care has been taken to protect the assets of the organization.
2. Unless security measures are based on a cost-benefit study, there is no assurance that the best use is made of limited resources, a second barrier to assertions of due care. Unless technical staff members have adequate risk assessment information, many important security design decisions — such as data back-up procedures, business resumption plans, and data protection measures — will be based on little more than guesswork.

Risk Assessment Techniques. There are three basic factors that lead to the accurate assessment of a risk. They are listed in descending order of importance:

1. *Potential for loss associated with the functions (such as business interruption losses) and assets (such as damage, theft, liability losses, etc.) of the organization.* Loss potentials are inherent in the character of the mission of an organization, and options to reduce loss potential by modifying operations may be limited.
2. *The rate of occurrence of threat events,* sometimes referred to as the probability of occurrence during a stipulated period — commonly a year. The risk manager can often take action to reduce the occurrence rate of threats without interfering with the organization's mission. For example, facilities can be moved away from hazards or deterrent policies can be adopted.
3. *The vulnerability of the functions and assets to the threats.* Typically, vulnerability is the factor most under the control of the risk manager. Once a risk assessment has identified significant threat-loss

Information Systems Security

potential, the risk manager can consider how to reduce the impact of the threats. For example, the installation of a single burglar alarm system will probably have no effect on the global occurrence rate of burglary attempts, but it will decrease the rate of successful attempts at the protected facility. Similarly, providing a safe to a cashier's office will not reduce the value of the money stored overnight, but it will reduce the theft losses.

The product of these three elements leads to an estimate of expected loss. The product of the last two yields an estimate of single occurrence loss. Note that it is expected loss and single occurrence loss that are significant. The fact that one of the three factors has a material value is not sufficient to create a risk. Consequently, a so-called "vulnerability analysis" is not an adequate substitute for a risk assessment.

While less-experienced risk assessment practitioners may describe numerous, supposedly different risk assessment as "methodologies," all methodologies will produce either the simple checklist procedures and vulnerability analyses, or an assessment of the three basic risk factors.

Threat Occurrence Rate Estimates. Objections to quantitative risk assessments as a risk management tool are often based on the assertion that hard numbers are not available for threat occurrence rates. Because risk assessments deal with future losses, the statement is correct — but irrelevant. Almost all management decisions are based on assumptions about future events. Senior managers understand this and expect that there will be some degree of uncertainty in the assumptions. The risk manager and security professional have an obligation to use due care in the conduct of risk assessments and to use the best available information.

There are a number of ways to estimate the occurrence rate of threats — primarily depending on historic rates, but also on other factors. Threats are not all the same. The following are a few examples that range from the easiest to the most difficult to predict:

1. Keystroke errors result from human factors and are repeatable. Given a defined profile of key operators, quality of operator training, task complexity, and work conditions, the error rate on a new system decreases during the start-up phase until a fairly repeatable level is reached that is dependent upon fundamental and unchanging human characteristics.
2. Hardware failure rates for new hardware devices can be estimated based on prior experience with similar hardware, but protracted use may reveal completely unexpected effects that modify reliability. For example, it has been suggested that when the dimensions of the elements on computer chips get small enough, cosmic ray particles will cause "dropped-bit" errors.

3. Human acts — such as terrorism — do not follow any natural law, therefore preventing a way to develop a high-confidence estimate for the occurrence of a terrorist act at a specific location and/or time. There are a wide range of factors — such as economic conditions, other terrorist acts, declaration of war, law enforcement actions, etc. — that could spur a potential terrorist.

These examples suggest that no single technique will always yield a reliable estimate of the threat occurrence rate. Rather, a suitable combination of historic data, analysis of modifying factors, inference from other similar threats, and fault-tree analysis must be used. A key point is to recognize that not all estimates will be equal in quality; some will be quite dependable while others will be close to guesswork. Thus, the importance of a given estimate will not be known until its expected losses are known. If the expected loss is material, sensitivity analysis will suggest how to treat the threat.

The other two risk assessment elements — loss potential and vulnerability — are easier to estimate reliably because the factors are more precisely defined. In other words, a risk assessment can produce accurate estimates of single occurrence loss. An estimate of the worst-case loss associated with each of an organization's functions and assets will enable the risk manager to identify the potentially fatal risk exposures. They can then be prioritized based solely on loss potential. But risk management resources are always finite, so senior management will need further guidance in making resource allocation decisions.

The Spectrum of Expected Losses. Understanding risk exposures is further strengthened by recognizing that losses appear to extend along a spectrum from those caused by high-frequency/low-impact (H/L) threats such as keystroke errors to low-frequency/high-impact (L/H) threats such as major earthquakes. As a rule, H/L estimates of expected loss will be relatively reliable and will predict with some reliability what will actually happen the following year. As risk exposures lean toward L/H, the expected loss estimates become increasingly problematic.

For example, if a major earthquake threat is estimated to have an occurrence rate of once in 100 years and will do $100 million worth of damage when it occurs, its expected loss is estimated to be $1 million per year. This does not mean we can expect to experience a $1 million loss in each of the next 100 years; but rather, the expected loss estimate is only useful for comparing this infrequent threat with other threats of a similar occurrence rate. What this risk assessment does indicate is what could happen in any one of the next hundred years and if the magnitude of the risk exposure threatens the existence of the organization.

The Spectrum of Risk Management Actions. The previous considerations lead to the following conclusions:

1. Some H/L threat losses at the low end of the loss potential scale may be so low that no cost-beneficial action can be identified, and the losses are accepted as a part of the cost of operations.
2. The organization can take mitigating actions against most H/L threats (for example, electric power failures) based on cost-benefit analyses based high-confidence level estimates of expected loss.
3. Most L/H threats can be prioritized based largely on single occurrence loss but giving some weight to the far less reliable estimates of threat occurrence rate. Remember: the objective of risk management actions is to reduce the single occurrence loss to an acceptable level. For example, insurance with a very high deductible can protect against an L/H threat at relatively low cost compared with the cost of reducing the vulnerability to the threat.

In summary, the risk manager must develop the best possible estimates of risk exposures, recognizing the limitation of L/H threat estimates, and then identify the optimum strategy for dealing with each of the material exposures.

Why Cost-Benefit-Based Risk Management Often Fails. Risk managers sometimes have limited success in trying to implement return-on-investment (ROI)-based security programs. This technique works well with the H/L threats for two reasons:

1. It is easy to generate annualized loss expectency (ALE) estimates upon which senior managers will act. The senior manager who approves an expenditure believes that the risk exists and should be addressed. The technique does not work for the low-probability, high-consequence risks because both factors — credible estimates and management concerns — are likely to be negative. Actions taken after an L/H threat has occurred, when everyone is then in unamimous agreement that the threat was a hazard to the organization, is not a sign of astute management. Despite the difficulties in developing credible risk assessments, it is the duty of the risk manager to identify the material hazards — both H/L and L/H — *before* they occur and to make senior management aware of them.
2. End users commonly have a higher level of concern about risks than information systems managers, but it is the systems managers who make the decisions about security measures. As a rule, a systems manager whose quarterly bonus may depend on meeting performance goals has no difficulty choosing between buying a faster computer and a safer computer. Thus, while a risk manager may have identified

a significant L/H risk before it has occurred, he or she may show an unwillingness to act.

Four Reasons for Adopting a Security Measure. While ROI-based security measures can be identified and implemented for the high and low risks, the L/H risks need different treatment. The risk manager needs to employ a myriad of risk management techniques to manage the spectrum of risks. There are four fundamental tests of the utility of a security measure:

1. The security measure is required by law or regulation. In effect, the governing body has determined that the security measure makes good public policy because it will always meet one of the remaining three tests.
2. The cost of the security measure is trivial, but its benefit is material. For example, if the lock on a little-used door is not usually locked, a procedure should be implemented to ensure that the door stays locked.
3. For an H/L threat, a reliable ROI can be generated to show that the cost of the security measure will be offset by the reduction in future losses it will yield. Simply stated, the security measure has a positive ROI.
4. The security measure addresses an L/H risk that has an intolerable single occurrence loss (SOL). For example, it would be intolerable for a corporation to experience an SOL that exceeded owner equity or net worth. The failure of a prominent merchant bank in 1995 is a tragic example of an organization that failed to address an intolerable SOL exposure to a threat with an uncertain rate of occurrence — human wrongdoing on a grand scale.

Treatment of the L/H risks requires the participation of senior management because judgment, rather than an ROI analysis, is required to decide how safe is safe. The fourth reason suggests the appropriate technique for managing the low–high risks. A brief outline of a procedure for this technique follows.

How to Address Low–High Risks. After the high–low threats have been addressed using an ROI analysis, the risk manager considers all imaginable low–high risks, one by one, and makes an estimate of the SOL, and the rate of occurrence for each. The report of this analysis should describe the confidence level of each estimate of SOL and occurrence rate. The risk manager then arranges the risks in descending order of SOL and presents the list to senior management. Senior management draws a line somewhere on the list and indicates which risks above the line are intolerably high. The risk manager considers each of the unacceptable risks in two ways:

1. Reduction in the magnitude of the single occurrence loss
2. Reduction in the occurrence rate of the threat

Information Systems Security

Reducing the Magnitude of High Single Occurrence Losses. Because most high SOL exposures are associated with low-confidence threat occurrence rate estimates, treating the exposure by reducing the SOL is the more appropriate option. There are several possibilities:

1. *Transfer the risk by obtaining insurance.* The premium will depend on both the maximum insured value (the maximum amount that can be claimed) and the portion of the loss that is deductible. For example, one might obtain insurance against a $100 million SOL with a $10 million deductible. The effect is to convert the intolerable $100 million SOL into a tolerable $10 million SOL at the cost of the insurance policy premium.
2. *Disburse the risk.* Replace a single processing center with an intolerable SOL of $100 million of catastrophic physical damage and service interruption losses with three centers with SOLs of $33 million that are sufficiently isolated from one another to rule out shared disasters. The cost will be the incremental cost of the least cost-efficient operation of three facilities.
3. *Reduce the vulnerability of the facility.* For example, implement an enhanced business resumption plan at some additional cost to speed up recovery off-site from any potential threat. This will reduce the SOL associated with catastrophic service interruption losses to a tolerable level.

Reducing the Occurrence Rate of High Single Occurrence Losses. The risk manager or security professional may also attempt to reduce the occurrence rate of a high SOL exposure. Because of the uncertainty of the estimates of low occurrence rates, this is less satisfactory. Nonetheless, even uncertain occurrence rate estimates can be useful. If two risks have the same SOL but differ by a factor of two in occurrence rate estimates of equal reliability, it is reasonable to assume that the risk with the lower occurrence rate represents a lesser danger to the organization.

There are some rates of occurrence below which risks may be ignored, even if the estimate is low-confidence. It is usually a senior management responsibility to determine the rate. If the risk manager is able to identify a low-cost security measure that reduces the rate of occurrence of a risk to the safe-to-ignore level, senior management may elect to adopt the security measure and ignore the residual risk.

In the remaining cases, the rates of occurrence and the costs of actions to reduce SOL will help senior management to prioritize implementation of the security measures for the exposures that cannot be safely ignored.

INFORMATION SYSTEMS SECURITY AND PLANNING

Information systems specialists often refer to the concept of "system life cycle." This refers to the fact that every information system goes through

ASSET PROTECTION AND SECURITY MANAGEMENT HANDBOOK

five phases during its life. Planning and budgeting are useful in this concept as well as being useful in focusing the allocation of security to systems. The five phases are defined and discussed below.

Initiation

During the initiation phase, the requirement to deploy a system is recognized and system specifications are developed. During this phase, it is important to give recognition to the sensitivity of the data being processed, the criticality of timely processing, and the requirement to protect the system hardware. A risk assessment should be performed for the projected system, based on estimates of its characteristics and its likely risk environment. To the extent possible, security requirements should be anticipated so that the cost estimate includes a proper allowance for security costs. It is unprofessional to develop a system and then decide that providing adequate protection of end users would make the system uneconomical.

There are many different situations in which it becomes important to protect data against unauthorized disclosure. While physical and logical access controls can provide protection, the protection only works when the controls are in operation. Attackers, particularly insiders, may be able to disable controls. Because of these limitations, cryptographic protection is ideal for sensitive data, particularly in situations where other controls may be unreliable. Once data is encrypted, it is protected in proportion to three factors:

1. The strength of the cryptographic technique used
2. The care taken to protect keys
3. The willingness of the intruder to expend resources

Given the ever-decreasing cost of hardware, performance penalties related to encrypting data are shrinking steadily. However, there are other factors to consider. The most important is the new requirement to manage and protect encryption keys. If this is not done carefully, the protection offered may be illusory. Furthermore, it is essential to avoid situations in which data cannot be decrypted because a key has been lost. Quality encryption software includes features that allow special unlocking keys to be shared by several responsible people so that any predefined subset of them can act in unison to unload the data. It would be imprudent to use cryptographic systems that do not include this feature.

If the data is sensitive enough to require cryptographic protection, assured decryption is also a requirement.

Development and Acquisition

Once the system specifications have been approved and funds allocated, the system is designed, the required hardware, software and facilities are purchased, and software developed in-house is programmed. During these stages, specific security requirements should be identified to ensure compliance with existing policy, procedures and standards, and to publish new policy and procedures that result in special characteristics for the new system. The objective is to build in the required security features rather than back-fit them later, after implementation.

Implementation

After initial system testing, the system is installed and placed into operation. All security features should be fully tested as a part of the acceptance testing. Operator and user training, including required security procedures, should be provided during implementation.

Operation and Maintenance

The system is now in production status. Correct operation of the various security controls must be immediately verified. It is quite common for systems to be modified during their operation life to add new features, expanding working capacity, etc. It is important to track such changes to determine if they will trigger material changes to security requirements.

Disposal

At some point, every information system becomes obsolete. An obsolete system may have to be disposed of. Three critical issues are usually involved in this process. The first is the orderly transition to the new system. This process exposes data to loss, or corruption, and may create a one-time opportunity for fraud. The second is the determination of whether there are statutory requirements to retain an archival copy of the stored data at the cutover time. Third is the review of plans for the disposal of the hardware, particularly data storage units.

There have been unfortunate cases in which surplus data storage hardware was sold with readable and sensitive data stored on it. It is important to coordinate with the person responsible for disposal of surplus property to be sure that no data is inadvertently disclosed to others.

OPERATING AND USER CONTROLS

Every information system must interface with human beings. Some of these people operate the system; others use it to perform their duties. Studies and experience have repeatedly shown the vital importance of loyal, honest and qualified employees. While the idea of the outside genius hacker makes a good Hollywood movie, experience suggests that most successful attacks are launched by insiders.

Careful selection and management of personnel with direct access to sensitive information systems are extremely important. In this section we discuss the associated security issues.

ASSET PROTECTION AND SECURITY MANAGEMENT HANDBOOK

Staffing

As an information system unit evolves and applications are implemented, personnel requirements arise and must be satisfied. This leads to the development of job descriptions, work schedules and the selection of individuals to fill the positions. All of these steps have security implications.

Job Descriptions. As each job description is prepared, the information systems security manager needs to review and evaluate its sensitivity. The following factors, arranged in descending order of importance, will generally apply:

1. Direct access to system elements that control access to the system and its data
2. Physical access to system hardware with the ability to make changes
3. Logical access to software with the ability to make changes
4. Physical access to backup data media
5. Normal user access to the system under system controls
6. Physical access to hardcopy system output

These factors serve to identify the relative sensitivity of each job and will consequently influence the factors discussed below.

Work Schedules. When two or more people are in sensitive work areas at all times, they act as a deterrent to wrongdoing. Therefore, work schedules should be analyzed in the context of the sensitivity of the jobs and the physical arrangement of the workspaces. Under some circumstances, remote surveillance — such as CCTV — may compensate for situations in which it is not feasible to enforce a two-person rule.

Another schedule issue involves problems that arise when only one person is qualified to perform a sensitive function. This can cause the same temptation to wrongdoing that working alone does.

Finally, there is ample evidence to support the requirement that all personnel take vacations of not less than two consecutive weeks each year.

Personnel Selection. The sensitivity of various jobs can be evaluated and a reasonable specification set for recruitment.

Personnel Reassignment or Termination

When an individual is reassigned or terminated, his or her physical and logical access authority should be adjusted appropriately and immediately. Established procedures should provide complete and unambiguous guidance for handling reassignments. As previously noted, it is essential to provide automatic links between the personnel system and access control systems so that the latter automatically receives notice of all changes in job status. It is unacceptable to fail to disable a user's ID/password immediately after it is no longer required by the user.

Termination and reassignment procedures should ensure that the following points are covered:

1. The terminated employee returns all documentation, program listings, data storage media, door keys, smart cards, and other property of the organization.
2. The terminated employee receives a formal briefing about the continuing obligation to protect confidential and proprietary information of the organization, and signs an acknowledgment of the briefing.
3. Operating procedures should require systems managers to promptly notify the security director and the personnel manager in the event that a person in a sensitive position does not report timely for work, and cannot be located.

AUDIT TRAILS AND TRANSACTION LOGS

By their very nature, it is easy for information systems to maintain audit trails, transaction logs and the like. These records have several important security benefits:

- Assuming error-free operation, system-generated records are maintained continuously and accurately, unlike human record keeping, which may be inaccurate, incomplete or dishonest.
- The records, if properly designed, can be analyzed in a variety of ways. For example, one can use utility programs to answer questions like:
  — Which staff members were in the computer room and logged in when a particular kind of transaction occurred?
  — Which user-IDs experienced the highest level of failed log-ins, potentially indicative of break-in attempts?
  — Which terminal operators had the highest level of cash refund transactions, possibly indicative of fraud?
- If it appears as though data loss or corruption is occurring, transaction logs may reveal that the cause is software bugs or operator errors, not hardware failures. Problem resolution may depend heavily on the availability of ongoing transaction records.
- A review of operator errors and help desk records may indicate a general failure to understand how a particular transaction should be performed, or the need to provide specific training to a single individual. The knowledge that activities are tracked by detailed records may discourage an employee from attempting a fraud of data theft.

For all these reasons, the information system security manager — with help from the internal audit department and the security director — should ensure that the audit trails and transaction logs for each system will enable that the required information to accomplish each of the above goals be available.

Information systems designers may complain that a given requirement will be difficult to satisfy or cost too much. However, if the security requirements have been based on a carefully performed risk assessment, the security manager can resist such arguments. With each passing year, the cost of hardware decreases, resulting in major increases in performance. Accordingly, the cost to satisfy most audit trail requirements will also continue to decrease.

Audit Trail Integrity

If information systems staff members can disable or destroy audit trails, it may not be possible to detect wrongdoing accurately. Many commercial software systems that include audit trail capabilities allow the customer to control audit features.

For example, it may be possible for the customer to turn off all auditing, thus defeating the whole purpose of the audit trails. Therefore, the information systems security manager must be aware of all available options and reach an agreement with the systems operations manager to determine which audit trails will be maintained.

Subsequent compliance audits should include verification that operations comply with such agreements. At the simplest level, the size of the daily growth of an audit trail file should be relatively stable. Indeed, a marked departure from the norm should trigger an immediate investigation — has the audit trail feature been turned off, or is there some unusual condition that is generating an abnormal number of audit entries?

Block chaining of transaction log records and other techniques can be used, as appropriate, to protect audit trail files against tampering. For example, it may be feasible to isolate physically the hardware used to create such files and limit physical access to audit or security personnel. It is also possible to use write-once media, such as CDR disks, to store the data. To protect against disablement, it can help to cause the system to write a record at regular intervals, such as once every minute. Subsequent auditing could include an automatic check for missing timestamps. Finally, the paper record should not be overlooked as an audit trail technique. It cannot be analyzed automatically, but it is simple.

Operational Use of Audit Trails

Audit trails are of no value if they are never used. Consequently, there should be a plan for how each audit and transaction file will be used. The security analysis of a system will identify the aspects of the system that require regular review and oversight. The system operating procedures

Information Systems Security

should identify these requirements, and identify who is responsible for performing audits, the criteria for evaluating transactions, and reporting procedures if anomalies are discovered.

THE INTERNET

The Internet has a number of very attractive features and, as a result, more and more systems are using the Internet. However, there are five important security considerations: confidentiality, authentication, reliability, response time and hacker attacks. If the use of the Internet is planned, it is important to review these considerations and provide suitable policy and procedures.

Confidentiality and Authentication

The Internet does **not** provide message confidentiality. If a system's transactions are in any sense confidential, it is essential to encrypt all messages. Public key cryptographic software and hardware are widely available, so it is not difficult to purchase an encryption program. But, if users are outside the U.S., it is necessary to take into account the U.S. Government's restrictions on the export of cryptography. Current export regulations ban the export of military-sensitive cryptography — be sure to get expert legal and technical device, and evaluate the potential exposures this limitation may cause. New hardware and software cryptographic systems make it easy to encrypt Internet traffic. Furthermore, public key cryptography solves the key management problems inherent in secret key cryptography.

Because the Internet is a wide open and insecure network, it is important to consider how the system will authenticate users, and users will authenticate the system. The latter is important because there is a risk that someone may attempt to spoof users; for example, to get users to disclose credit card personal identification numbers (PINs).

In situations such as this, cryptography can help. Each message can be encrypted first with the sender's private key and then with the recipient's public key. The recipient reverses the process — decrypt with the recipient's private key and then with the sender's public key. Token-based one-time passwords can also be used to authenticate users. This may sound complicated but remember that it can all be automated, so one should insist on adequate user authentication.

Reliability and Response Time

The Internet consists of a network of networks and functions because of the cooperative interconnections between the networks operated by the individual Internet Service Providers (ISPs). In other words, if an information system and all of its users are connected to the same ISP, then all the system's messages will only pass over that ISP's network. If there is a problem with service, there is only one place to call. It is important to determine if the service agreement provides a specific performance level. If more than one ISP is involved, then there is no guarantee that a given message will ever arrive at its intended destination.

Another point to consider is the ISP's access to other ISPs. The backbone circuits that carry the bulk of the traffic between ISP nodes have a finite capacity. People who surf the Web regularly have doubtlessly noticed how response time degrades during the course of the day — response time is great 7:30 a.m. on the East Coast; but 11:00 a.m., is so slow it will give up and crash.

Using a Value-Added Network

If an information system does not require high reliability and response time from its network, the deficiencies of the Internet may not be important. For example, inter-office e-mail and product information archives will probably function quite satisfactorily on the Internet. On the other hand, if a user sends in a request requiring immediate confirmation, the Internet will represent a threat to service reliability. This should be carefully evaluated.

Accurately estimating service reliability is complicated by the fact that growth factors and ISP investments — both of which will affect future response times — are difficult to predict. However, if the risk assessment indicated that the Internet will not meet performance goals, then it may be wise to use a private, value-added network.

Hacker Attacks

When an information system is connected to the Internet, one is, in effect, inviting the world to access the system. Indeed, the objective of ARPAnet, the progenitor of the Internet, was to allow scientists at one node (computer facility) to execute programs on computers located at another node. Only recently — primarily as a result of the Morris "worm" attack — has attention been directed to controlling remote execution.

Computer Emergency Response Teams (CERTs) were set up to receive and publicize information about security gaps in the operating system software. One can sense the size of the problem by noting that warning messages go out from the CERTs at a rate of one or more a month. This suggests that there are still numerous gaps in the existing software, and there is no reason to feel complacent.

One popular defense is to install a "firewall" host between the in-house network and the Internet. The typical firewall includes software facilities that allow a user to screen both incoming and outgoing messages. One commercial software package allows an organization to monitor Internet usage by its staff and block access to inappropriate sites. This can provide important protection against both wasted staff time and potentially damaging postings by staff members.

Making Wise Use of the Internet

Securing an Internet-based system can be summarized as follows:

1. Unless the transactions are completely benign, use cryptographic protection in both directions. Be sure to get expert technical advice. If the system will have users outside the U.S., get legal advice as well.
2. Be sure to authenticate users reliably before permitting access to confidential data or conducting business.
3. Do not try to use the Internet if network reliability or real-time response is required. Instead, use a value-added network that can meet the performance requirements.
4. Do not expose in-house networks to the Internet unless a suitable "firewall" host has been installed.
5. Establish policy and procedures for Web surfing (to exclude pornography sites) and News Group postings (to exclude flaming).

Selected Bibliography

Caelli, William, Longley, Dennis, and Shain, Michael; *Information Security Handbook;* 1991; Stockton Press, New York.

Carroll, J.M.; *Managing Risk: A Computer-Aided Strategy*; 1984; Butterworth-Heinemann, Woburn, MA.

Dykman, Charlene A. and Davis, Charles K. Editors; *Control Objectives — Controls in an Information Systems Environment: Objectives, Guidelines, and Audit Procedures, 4th ed.*; 1992; The EDP Auditors Foundation, Inc., Carol Stream, IL.

Farmer, Dan and Venema, Wietse; *Improving the Security of Your Site by Breaking into It;* 1993; available from FTP.WIN.TUE.NL.

Fedeli, Alan; Organizing a Corporate Anti-Virus Effort; 1990; *Proceedings of the Third Annual Computer VIRUS Clinic,* Nationwide Computer Corporation.

Fites, P. and Kratz, M.; *Information Systems Security: A Practitioner's Reference;* 1993; Van Nostrand Reinhold, New York.

General Services Administration; F*ederal Information Resources Management Regulations,* specifically 201-2; Washington, D.C.

General Services Administration; *Information Resources Security: What Every Federal Manager Should Know;* Washington, D.C.

Helsing, C., Swanson, M., and Todd, M.; *Management Guide for the Protection of Information Resources;* 1989; National Institute of Standards and Technology, Special Publication 500-170, Gaithersburg, MD.

Holbrook, P. and Reynolds, J. Editors; *Site Security Handbook*; RFC 1244 prepared for the Internet.

Howe, D.; Information System Security Engineering: Cornerstone to the Future; October 15, 1992, Vol. 1, pages 244–251; *Proceedings of the 15th National Information System Security Conference,* Baltimore, MD.

Lobel, J.; *Foiling the System Breakers*; 1986; pages 57–95, McGraw-Hill, New York.

Lunt, T.; Automated Audit Trail Analysis for Intrusion Detection; April 1992; *Computer Audit,* pages 2–8.

ASSET PROTECTION AND SECURITY MANAGEMENT HANDBOOK

National Aeronautics and Space Administration; *Guidelines for Development of Computer Security Awareness and Training (CSAT) Programs;* March 1990; NASA Guide 2410.1, Washington, D.C.

National Institute of Standards and Technology; *Establishing a Computer Security Incident Response Capability;* 1992; Gaithersburg, MD.

National Institute of Standards and Technology; *Guidance on the Legality of Keystroke Monitoring;* March 1993; CSL Bulletin.

O'Neill, M. and Henninge, Jr., F.; *Understanding ADP System and Network Security Considerations and Risk Analysis;* 1992; pages 14–17, ISSA Access.

Office of Management and Budget; *Guidance for Preparation of Security Plans for Federal Computers that Contain Sensitive Information;* 1990, OMB Bulletin 90-08, Washington, D.C.

Organization for Economic Cooperation and Development; *Guidelines for the Security of Information Systems;* 1992; Paris, France.

Owen, R., Jr.; Security Management: Using the Quality Approach; 1992; Vol. 2, pages 584–592, *Proceedings of the 15th National Information System Security Conference,* Baltimore, MD.

Padgett, K.; *Establishing and Operating an Incident Response Team;* 1992; Los Alamos National Laboratory, Los Alamos, NM.

Polk, W. Timothy; *Automated Tools for Testing Information System Vulnerability;* December 1992; Special Publication 800-6, National Institute of Standards and Technology, Gaithersburg, MD.

Schultz, E., Brown, D., and Longstaff, T.; *Responding to Computer Security Incidents: Guidelines for Incident Handling;* 1990; University of California Technical Report UCRL-104689.

Smith, J.; Privacy Policies and Practices: Inside the Organizational Maze; 1993; *Communications of the ACM,* 36(12), 104–120.

Wack, John; *Establishing an Incident Response Capability;* November 1991; Special Publication 800-3, National Institute of Standards and Technology, Gaithersburg, MD.

Wallace, Dolore R. and Fugi, Roger; *Software Verification and Validation: Its Role in Computer Assurance and Its Relationship with Software Product Management Standards;* September 1989; Special Publication 500-165, National Institute of Standards and Technology, Gaithersburg, MD.

Wallace, Dolores R., Ippolito, Laura M., and Kuhn, D. Richard; *High Integrity Software Standards and Guidelines;* 1992; Special Publication 500-204, National Institute of Standards and Technology, Gaithersburg, MD.

Wood, Charles Cresson; *Designing Corporate Information Security Policies;* April 1992; DATAPRO Reports on Information Security.

11
Investigations: General Comments

PUBLIC- AND PRIVATE-SECTOR INVESTIGATIONS

There is a cardinal difference in the purpose of public law enforcement and that of private security. Public-sector organizations exist to serve and protect society in general. Their activities are measured in terms of numbers of arrests and numbers of convictions. The primary purpose of private-sector security organizations is to protect the interests of the employing enterprise. The activities of private-sector organizations are measured in terms of funds expended and funds or assets recovered.

The interests of society as a whole and the interests of the enterprise are not necessarily the same. If criminal activity occurs within the enterprise, the public interests are served by the prosecution and imprisonment of the offender. Likewise, the interests of the private-sector enterprise may be best served by acceptance of restitution without referral to prosecutive authority.

The investigative process should reflect this difference. The public-sector investigator frequently is required to meet a higher standard of proof than that required of the private-sector investigator. While the standards for prosecution (i.e., burden of proof) vary throughout the world, they are generally much heavier than the standards for discipline, including termination of employment. In the private sector, the desired outcome of the case dictates the required burden of proof. If restitution and termination of employment are an acceptable outcome, the organization needs only to make a good-faith investigation and reach a reasonable conclusion.

Early in the private-sector investigation the enterprise should determine the acceptable outcome or outcomes of the case. This determination must consider the legal requirements in the jurisdiction, organized labor contracts in force or pending, public relations and investor relations, and the past practices of the enterprise in similar cases. Legal counsel should always be consulted in making this determination.

Another difference between public- and private-sector investigations: the investigators. Investigators in the public sector tend, even in relatively small organizations, to specialize in specific types of investigations, depending on the agency, department or assignment. Investigators in the private sector tend to be general investigators. Investigators employed by telecommunications companies may be specialists in telecommunications fraud and the banking investigator may specialize in fraud or forgery, but they also will be involved in other types of investigations.

INVESTIGATIONS — IN GENERAL

An *investigation* is a planned and organized determination of facts concerning specific events, occurrences or conditions for a particular purpose. An investigation requires an investigator, a subject of investigation and a purpose.

The investigator must be skilled and prepared. Investigations require common sense; however, it is not possible to conduct a competent investigation merely by being clearheaded and alert. The variety of specialized investigative requirements that arise in a typical organization often make specific demands for talent and technique.

The general investigator, while often demonstrating impressive amounts of specialized knowledge and learning, may not need professional expertise in the specialty under investigation. An investigator does not need expertise in civil engineering to conduct an inquiry into fraudulent construction projects. Findings and conclusions from such a special area may be necessary for guidance, but the investigator does not need the professional skill of an engineer.

An inquiry into construction fraud, however, almost certainly involves observations and assessments of persons and events other than the person or event that caused the investigation. A general investigator must have the skills to observe and talk to all kinds of people and to obtain useful information on any subject. He must also have the ability to observe all manner of objects and events in the context of a special purpose, and to draw useful information from those observations.

A major facet of the investigative process is the collection of information, which is accomplished through communication — the written or spoken word — and by observation. Physical evidence that can be observed, touched or quantitatively measured also plays a role in collecting evidence.

Effective communication is not a natural talent. Training and experience are required in order to extract all the information from a witness. The investigator must be able to empathize with the witness. The ability to listen effectively, formulate and pose the proper questions, and guide the course of the interview are all requisite skills for the investigator. Moreover, a high level of skill is required for effective interrogation in which voluntary admissions and confessions are obtained.

At some point, it may not be possible to communicate with someone who has knowledge of the investigation. If this is the case, the investigator must then utilize the power of observation alone. The experienced investigator develops the ability to determine what is significant in the investigation. In observing physical evidence, the investigator should first look for irregularities — anything out of the norm — and then confirm the expected location and condition of the evidence. Irregularities can be something as simple as a chair out of its normal position. This may have no significance to the investigation, but it must be noted. A finely developed sense of "observation and description" is essential to a competent investigator.

The investigator works in a dynamic environment. People and things change, both in themselves and in relationship to each other. If a person is aware that an investigation is in progress, they may try to deceive or confuse the investigator. Being aware of such obstacles and having the ability to work through or around them are critical to an investigation.

QUALITIES OF AN EFFECTIVE INVESTIGATION

Five attributes characterize an effective and reliable investigation: *objectivity, thoroughness, relevance, accuracy,* and *timeliness.* A skilled investigator can meet these key requirements. Managers who make use of the investigative results ascertain that the investigator fulfilled his job.

Objectivity

The investigator must accept any fact, regardless of its significance to preconceived ideas. Objectivity is achieved by recognizing the investigator's personal prejudices and compensating for, or neutralizing, his effect on the investigation. During an investigation, the investigator usually forms an impression of the probable result. Sometimes, the impression is conscious, in which case it can be regarded as a working hypothesis. Frequently, the impression is not consciously formed but rather accumulates as a fuzzy context. In either case, the professional investigator must ensure that the investigative findings provide the basis for the impression, and not the reverse. Persisting in a version of the facts contrary to, or unsupported by, the actual findings is a frequent mistake of the nonprofessional and a constant danger for the professional. An investigator who cannot sort out and identify personal prejudices about people, places and outlooks is likely to miss the mark.

Using adjectives that connote feeling can prejudice an investigative report. The investigator may slant the report with a personal feeling or position on the matter at hand. Competent investigative reports, on the other hand, often appear dull and colorless because a skilled investigator allows the facts to speak for themselves and does not make suggestions by using adjectives. Nonetheless, when witnesses use adjectives, their exact words, coupled with an accurate description of the interview setting, are useful to the ultimate evaluator in assigning the proper meaning to the information developed.

The professional investigator does not add personal impressions (except when asked for and clearly labeled as such) or modify the expressed impressions of interviewees by using or suppressing adjectives.

Thoroughness

A thorough investigator checks all leads and checks key leads more than once to assure consistency in results. When the statement of an interviewee is critical, the facts should be reviewed several times if at all possible without compromising the investigation. Corroborating important aspects through different sources is a proven means of achieving thoroughness. For example, in one investigation it was important to establish the subject's place of residence ten years earlier. A source had identified the community of residence and the house by street number. A review of the voter registration records of the local board of elections for the year in question indicated that the subject had registered to vote that year and had supplied his residence address, including the apartment number. This information, supplied at a time when the subject had no reason to deceive, corroborated the statement of an informant and was, in itself, extremely convincing.

Relevance

Relevance means that the information developed pertains to the subject of the investigation. A fairly frequent problem is that persons of the same name are confused, either by the informants or by the investigator. Father and son are often confused for each other when they have the same name; mother and daughter likewise.

Another aspect of relevance is cause and effect. Is a developed fact the result of some other fact under investigation, or is it the cause of that other fact? For example, a worker is suspected of stealing company goods. The worker is well-regarded and his record is otherwise good. But the worker's wife has become the victim of a terminal illness. Does the fact of the illness have any relationship to the suspected fact of the theft? Do the medical expenses exceed the worker's ability to pay and make him desperate for added funds? If a relationship can provide a direction for the investigative effort, or working hypothesis, establishing the relationship may materially assist in resolving the entire investigative problem.

Accuracy

The mental processes that collect and sort data from the physical senses often produce errors. The mountain seen in the clear air of Arizona may appear to be half a mile away, but in reality is three miles away. Was the person seen leaving a crime scene short and fat, medium height, running with a limp, wearing a long coat, wearing no coat? Witnesses frequently report conflicting data. Which, if any, are true? Does the fact that there is only one witness, and hence no conflict in testimony, make that witness's statement more, or less, credible?

Sound investigative techniques dictate frequent tests for verification. If data is subject to physical measurement, it must be measured. If an informant is the only source of key data, the informant should be tested at least for consistency in telling the version. All information must be tested for inherent contradictions. (A person claims to have left in an automobile from one place at a certain time and arrived at a destination at a certain later time, but examination of the distance and elapsed time indicates that the person would have traveled at 135 miles per hour to do so.)

Does the interviewee have a reason to lie or color the truth? Reporting as a fact the statement of a person who would have a reason to deceive or conceal, without indicating that such a reason exists, can distort the results of an investigation. Even the possibility of a reason to color the truth affects the credibility of the source of the information.

An opinion frequently offered about pre-employment investigations is that the information provided by personal references is of no value because they are friends and would only say good things about the subject. Actual experience shows that this is often not true. Personal references gratuitously have provided information unfavorable to the person who listed them. (That fact, in itself, should put the investigator on the alert concerning motivation of the interviewee.) Even when people do not consciously say anything uncomplimentary, references can often help indirectly by providing collateral information that is apparently neutral, such as the subject's precise place of residence or employment at a given time. But the fact that a person is a relative or a friend (or enemy) of another person should be considered when evaluating information provided by such a source. The quality or intensity of the relationship may indicate that all information provided by that source must be independently corroborated.

Timeliness

Timeliness is an extension of thoroughness. It requires that the investigation be carried to the latest possible point at which information relevant to the investigation might be found.

Pre-employment investigations frequently lack currency. An applicant may have enjoyed an excellent reputation at all prior places of employment, except the place where he is now working. Ostensibly to avoid upsetting the relationship should the applicant be rejected, an employer may not check the applicant's current performance and will make an unconditional offer of employment. Even if the applicant's record is later checked and the new employee terminated because of unfavorable data, the new employer may be unable to avoid the expenses incurred in adding the employee to staff. Several ways to avoid this predicament will be suggested later. The situation is cited to illustrate the need for currency in investigative data.

Investigative Resources

For small organizations with infrequent investigative needs, the outside agency or contract service is the logical choice. The expense is limited to particular inquiries and is incurred only when an inquiry arises.

In moderate and large-size organizations, justification of a security staff (investigative personnel) is an ongoing activity. Investigative subject matter may not be perceived as such by some senior management persons, but there are a number of areas where accurate fact-finding in complex situations is useful. For example, pre-employment applicant screening, preliminary inquiries into alleged criminal activity, due diligence inquiries and industrial espionage situations are all areas for investigative effort. Every major organization has one or more of these problems. With the added problems of pilferage, embezzlement, fraud and other larcenies, a professionally competent investigative unit would be kept busy in almost any moderate to large-size organization.

Advantages of contract investigations:

- Investigative expenses are incurred only when the inquiry is needed.
- A large contract firm can frequently provide an investigator with experience on a specific type of investigation.

Disadvantages of contract investigations:

- Quality control or work supervision is frequently not controlled by the buyer of the service. The customer states general requirements, sets out the objectives of the investigation and establishes general conditions, after which the conduct of the investigation is left to the contractor.
- A new investigator experiences a "learning curve" in getting accustomed to the company.

Advantages of an internal investigative capability:

- In most locales, the criminal case load is so high that police cannot devote investigative time to cases in which there has not been a formal complaint or at least clear evidence of a crime.
- Many incidents are potentially so sensitive that responsible management would not want any aspect of the inquiry to be beyond its constant control. Not insignificant in this concern is the treatment and disposition of investigative results, documentary and nondocumentary.
- In the United States, under Federal Sentencing Guidelines, an organization found or pleading guilty to a crime, gets favorable consideration if the organization has made its own effort to investigate the circumstances and to correct the conditions that led to the crime.

Disadvantages of an internal investigative capability:

- The costs of maintaining the investigative staff remain relatively constant, regardless of the workload.
- Technical equipment may remain unused for long periods of time.

In a fairly new phenomenon, several large companies have contracted all of their security operations, including investigations, to large contract security firms. The perceived advantages in this arrangement include reduced costs, the availability of highly specialized investigative personnel, standardized training and the legal benefits of investigations conducted by an independent contractor.

Cost Elements

The cost of investigative resources suitable for use in an assets protection program take the form of either *direct labor and benefits expense* when the investigative personnel are hired directly, or of *fees to licensed private agencies* when the work is done on a contract basis.

For employed staff, salaries vary based upon experience before hiring, length of service, and so forth. A 2000 survey sponsored by the American Society for Industrial Security revealed the salary range for *proprietary investigators* to range from $42,000 to $53,300. The survey covered base salaries; however, benefit costs of 35 percent to 40 percent must be added to the salary to ascertain the true cost for the positions. The figures vary significantly when geographic location, type of employer, size of organization, security budget, level of education and length of experience are considered.

The investigative equipment required, such as cameras and other scientific devices, depends on the type of investigative activity involved. For general investigations in a medium-sized organization, the cost might approximate $15,000 to $50,000. The organization performing technical countermeasures surveys may have an additional $100,000 to $150,000 invested.

Incidental costs for travel and clerical support are charged to the investigative element and, in some organizations, a proportional share of overhead costs are allocated to each department or element.

The 2000 survey sponsored by the American Society for Industrial Security revealed the salary range for *contract investigators* as $41,000 to $56,000; however, contract agency services costs are normally billed at a per-hour rate, per-case rate or per-inquiry rate. The per-inquiry rate normally applies to routine or limited types of investigation, generally pre-employment. For background investigations, the charge is per lead. A lead is a single-point inquiry, such as one former employer, one place of residence, and so forth. A background investigation for an applicant, aged early or middle thirties, would probably include an average of two prior employments, one college or technical school, and one other point of inquiry, perhaps a reference or residence.

Sources of Information

The possible sources of information are defined by the type of inquiry being conducted. The extent to which all available sources are recognized and exploited depends on the skill and sophistication of the investigator. The recognition, development and proper exploitation of informants and sources of information are heavily emphasized in all formal training programs involving investigative work. This is one more argument in favor of professionally competent investigative personnel.

A basic maxim of investigations is to *check your own files first*. Some sources of information under the control of the employer are often overlooked in the absence of a formal investigation's function. The most significant sources are those recognized and used because of their specific and perhaps unique relevance to the particular investigation. Possibly on a one-time-only basis, such sources can provide critical data that makes possible the final resolution of the matter at hand.

Table 1 suggests some common internal locations where records concerning property or physical assets may be found. Table 2 indicates common sources of internal data about personnel. Table 3 lists public record sources for information about property and people. These are given by way of illustration; the actual sources are much more numerous. Because of local practice, local law and local custom, the sources of information differ from place to place.

In addition to standard sources, each investigator develops personal sources that can provide certain kinds of information on a repeat basis. All of these sources are organized into a suitably cross-indexed file for the general use by the investigative unit. Those sources that are private or confidential in any special sense can be identified in the file by a symbol or code name. The actual identity can be recorded in a separate place.

In some legal jurisdictions and under appropriate circumstances, investigators and reports of investigations can be legally reached by subpoena or through discovery proceedings. In civil actions against the company, in administrative hearings to which the company may be a party, and in criminal proceedings, the investigator may be compelled to testify concerning the scope, conduct and results of the investigation and the informants utilized. A report of investigation may be demanded and its production compelled by subpoena. Where these legal requirements exist, it is important to note this availability with respect to sensitive sources of information whose compromise is an embarrassment.

Table 1. Some internal sources of information about property and assets.

Department	What information is utilized
Receiving	Date of receipt, quantity received, condition on receipt
Purchasing	Kind, amount, date ordered or received, supplier
Accounts Payable	Amount, source, date billed, cost, date paid or payable
Accounts Receivable	Amount due, date due, items, date shipped, destination
Manufacturing	Amounts, kind, dates on which manufactured, destination
Production Control	Amount, location, kind and condition of raw materials, work-in-process, finished goods
Tax	Kind, location, acquisition date, acquisition cost, depreciated value of capital assets
Accounting, General Ledger	Amount, book value, location of capital assets, expendable supplies
Quality Control	Amounts, kinds, location of finished goods under QC processing
Traffic or Distribution	Amount, kind, value or cost of finished goods shipped, destination, date shipped, carrier
Property Custodian	Kind, amount, location, condition of capital assets in assigned property account
Insurance	Valuations, schedules, descriptions of items on special "floaters," detailed valuations in claims files

Table 2. Some internal sources of information about personnel.

Department	What information is utilized
Human Resources	Application forms, supervisory evaluations, insurance questionnaires, job history, salary record
Insurance	Applications for health, life, or hospital insurance; claims history; names of other carriers of other policies
Payroll	Salary or wage, payroll number, voluntary deductions, bank (from endorsement on canceled checks), liens and garnishments
Medical	Medical history, physical condition and health status (confidentiality and physician–patient privilege make this a sensitive area)
Credit Union	Amount of savings, amount and status of loans, identities of co-makers or guarantors, stated purposes of past loans (federal and state laws govern the disclosure of this information)
Security	Security questionnaires, level and effective date of security clearance, nondisclosure and secrecy agreements, history of violations or incidents, investigative indices (if maintained), auto registration(s)
Accounting (expense reports)	Dates and places of travel, amounts and nature of expenditures

Table 3. Some external or public sources of information.

Department	What information is utilized
County Clerk	Grantor–grantee index for real property, mortgages on real property, conditional sales contracts, military discharge certificates, certificates of incorporation of business in county, certificates of assumed name, dockets for various civil and criminal courts, Uniform Commercial Code security interest filings, assumed and fictitious name filings
Court Clerk	Pleadings and trial records for actions or proceedings in that court, judgment role and docket
Tax assessor	Assessment for specific parcels or pieces of property
Commercial banks	Names, balances and loan history on commercial or regular checking accounts (sometimes on special accounts, as well)
Savings banks, and savings and loan associations	Mortgagors and amounts on outstanding mortgage loans (information on savings accounts is often restricted by state law but may be available)
Credit bureaus and mercantile agencies	File and trade information on buyers and borrowers, character and background information on individuals and firms (available for a fee and governed by Fair Credit Reporting Act)
Police	Arrest and conviction records by name (some departments do not disclose such data; others will to *bona fide* inquirers; some charge a fee)
Motor Vehicle	Ownership and registration of vehicles, license and violation history of operators; varying modes of availability, depending upon state
Newspaper files	Personal data on prominent or newsworthy persons and event data on newsworthy events

Online Investigations

Technological change and competition have substantially reduced the costs for certain types of records checks. Cost constraints and effective use of staff resources dictate that the use of database information sources will increase.

LEGAL GUIDELINES

Investigators conducting investigations in the U.S. need to be aware of the requirements of several federal statutes, including the following:

- Civil Rights Act (42 U.S.C. 200e, *et seq.*)
- National Labor Relations Act (29 U.S.C. 151)
- Freedom of Information Act (5 U.S.C. 522)
- Fair Credit Reporting Act (15 U.S.C.1681, *et seq.*)
- Privacy Act (5 U.S.C. 522a)
- Americans with Disabilities Act (42 U.S.C. 12101, *et seq.*)
- Employee Polygraph Protection Act (29 U.S.C. 2001-2009)

Additionally, a number of states have similar statutes and penal laws regulating or restricting certain resources and techniques of employment candidate investigation. Other legal considerations include:

- Compliance with laws regarding the licensing and conduct of private investigations
- The possibility of civil suits (in some cases, criminal complaints) based on allegations of defamation, false imprisonment, false arrest and various forms of harassment
- The possibility of subpoenas to testify or produce written records of investigation

Local Licensing Statutes

Most jurisdictions require paid investigators to be licensed. Exempt investigators (usually) are those working for a single employer and conducting investigations only for that employer. Certain acts, however, can change that status. For example, if a single-employer investigator exchanges information from his investigation with a counterpart investigator in another company, in some way suggesting reciprocity, that single act may put both investigators — and their employers — in violation of a statute requiring a license to conduct investigations. The limitations depend upon the exact statutory language. The question should be reviewed, with legal counsel, in light of the language of the statute involved. For employers with operations in several jurisdictions, the law of each jurisdiction in which investigative activity is conducted should be reviewed.

Civil and Criminal Suits and Actions

Defamation. An untrue statement made by one person about another, which causes harm or injury to that other in terms of loss of, or reduction in, reputation or esteem in the eyes of others, is a defamatory statement. An oral statement is *slander*; a statement in writing is *libel*. The defamed person has a legal cause of action against the defamer. Unless the defamer can establish that the statement was true, or that he has some privilege, absolute or qualified, he will have to answer in damages. In a limited number of situations (accusations of crime or of conduct that would tend to discredit the defamed person in the exercise of a business, trade, profession or office), the plaintiff needs only to prove that the defamatory statements were made. In all other situations, the defamed person must prove actual damages to establish the defamation.

Dissemination of an investigative report must be carefully controlled and limited to those persons legally able to receive it. The report could contain information that, if untrue, would be libelous. Under certain circumstances, the doctrine of *qualified privilege* affords protection even against such untrue statements. The doctrine holds that when the one making the statement is under some duty to or acts in the interest of another, and the statement is made to that other, and the primary motive for making it is to serve the interests of the other, then even though untrue, it does not establish a basis for a defamation action.

However, if the person making the statement is acting from any provable motive other than serving the interest of his employer or client, or if the untrue statement is communicated to persons other than those whose interests are sought to be protected, the defense of qualified privilege will fail. Thus, gratuitous statements by a former employer to a potential employer, untrue and falling within one of the classes of defamation, could — without further proof of damage — expose the former employer to a suit.

False Imprisonment. If investigators use, threaten or create the reasonable fear that they would use physical force to detain a person being questioned, there might be an action for false imprisonment. Similarly, if in restraining someone there is a physical arrest or statement that the person is under arrest, and if the person submits in the belief that he must, and if the arrest is impermissible, there will be an action for false arrest. If, on the other hand, the person voluntarily agrees to being detained or taken into custody, then he cannot accuse investigators of false imprisonment. Sound practice dictates that a written and witnessed statement be put in the record in all cases where persons are interviewed by investigative personnel who do not have a legal right to detain such persons. In the absence of such a statement or in the face of a refusal to execute one, the next best recourse is clear and repeated statements by the investigators themselves, also on the record, that the interviewee is free to leave at any time. In cases where it may be difficult to prove the voluntary detention or in which its voluntary nature may be attacked, it is best to terminate the interview.

INVESTIGATIVE REPORTS

An investigative report is a written document in which the investigator records the activity in the investigation and the evidence gathered. If this is not the final report of the investigation, it may provide leads for other investigators to pursue. The report also serves as the basis for post-investigation administrative action such as prosecution of disciplinary action. A competent investigator writes a report so that a reader can readily understand what the investigator did, why it was done and the results of the action. Report writing is a crucial part of the investigation. The most diligent and professionally conducted investigation loses its value if the effort is not properly reported.

Types of Reports

The public-sector investigator, the private-sector organization investigator and the private investigator each have different types of reports to file. But, some reports are common to all types of investigations.

Initial Report. The initial report is filed a few days after the investigation is opened. It memorializes the progress of the investigation and details the leads, if any, that remain to be followed. In a simple case, the initial report may be the final or closing report.

Progress Report. An investigation can last for months in the private sector; public-sector cases may remain open and under investigation for years. Progress reports of the case status are submitted at fixed intervals to detail the progress of the investigation and any leads that remain to be followed. In the private sector, the normal interval for progress report submission is 30 days.

Special Report. The special report documents an action other than normal in the course of the investigation. The special report can be a supplement to a progress report, but it must be able to stand alone, separate from the progress report. An example of a special report would be the report of surveillance conducted by a team in the course of an undercover investigation without necessarily involving the undercover operative.

Final Report. A final report is submitted when:

- The investigation is successfully brought to a close
- All investigative leads have been followed without success and further investigative action is deemed to be unproductive
- As directed by the person or office that authorized the opening of the case

Parts of the Report

The format of the investigative report varies widely among organizations. Hard-copy written reports are required in many enterprises; however, the electronic filing of reports to a master file and a centralized database is becoming common. Regardless of the report's format on file, a usable report has certain information.

Administrative. The report must be complete and readily understood without references to other reports. Therefore, it must include the following administrative information:

- The name of the subject of the case
- The case or file number
- The type of case (if not identified by the case or file number)
- The status of the case (open or closed)
- The reporting investigator
- The date of the report

Summary. A summary or synopsis of the report given at the beginning permits a quick assessment by readers. The general rule is that every major point covered by the report requires at least one sentence in the synopsis. Supporting facts are not cited in the synopsis. Conclusions are permissible if they fairly represent the detailed information in the body of the document. For example, if a detailed report of a theft established that John Jones, a night shift porter, admitted in a signed statement that he had taken $25 in petty cash from the desk drawer of Richard Roe in Department 968 at about 9:00 p.m. on May 14, 1997, with the intention of spending the money to purchase a portable radio, the summary or synopsis of that report could read as follows:

John JONES, night porter, payroll #1026, admitted in a signed statement May 20, 1997, having taken $25 from desk of Richard ROE, department #968, at about 9:00 p.m. May 14, 1997, with intention of using it to purchase a portable radio.

The details of the interrogation and any other information relevant to the statement obtained from Jones would then be described. The synopsis immediately identifies to any reader that a confession to a specific crime was obtained and that the victim, the property stolen, the thief, and the date and time of the theft have been established.

Narrative. The narrative segment of the report contains the details of the investigative effort. It provides an easily understood recitation of the investigative process and the facts of the matter. Each step in the investigation should be covered in a separate paragraph. It should be clear, simple and brief. The vocabulary should be easily understood. Technical terms should be avoided and any necessary technical terms should clearly be defined.

Style. Historically, reports are written in the third person. Major governmental investigative agencies and many assets protection departments in major organizations continue to use the third person. This has been the subject of heated discussion among investigators, some of whom think that such reports are awkward and that the use of the first person makes a report easier to write and read.

Among nongovernmental organizations, the use of the first person in investigative reports is becoming the norm. Contract investigative agencies use the first person or the third person, as desired by the client. In a simple case in which a single report suffices, the personal pronoun is easily and fully understandable. In any report, other than when referring to the report writer, pronouns should be judiciously used in order to avoid confusion on the reader's part.

Eugene Ferraro[1] prefers the use of the third person in undercover investigative reports. One of his reasons for the use of the third person is that "if

---

[1] *Undercover Investigations in the Workplace*; Ferraro, Eugene F.; 2000; Butterworth-Heinemann.

the report is written in the first person, it technically cannot be edited by anyone other than the writer until it is converted to the third person." Ferraro, among others, has investigative reports written in the format and the person desired by the client.

The agency or organization for which the investigative report is written usually dictates the writing style. When not otherwise specified, the use of the first person in writing investigative reports is preferred.

Because a report is a recitation of matters that have occurred, the past tense is *always* used.

Objectivity. The investigator must be as objective in writing the investigative report as in performing the investigation. Speculation, hypothesis or opinion on the part of the report writer is not acceptable. The items in the report should be the statements of others or the personal observations of the reporting investigator, and should clearly be identified as such. Should the investigator wish to express an opinion or speculation, these comments should be conveyed in a different report or in a memorandum directed to the investigator's supervisor.

Factual. In writing an investigative report, the investigator must ensure that the information is completely factual. The experienced investigator reviews all of the material to preclude an assumption of facts.

Chronological. The report is written as a chronological record of the investigator's work.

Comprehensive and Relevant. The general rule holds that the investigator does not report selectively but includes everything relevant. This does not imply that the investigator literally reports everything that was done or said, as many leads are fruitless — to set them out at length would be pointless. Practiced judgment and professional experience guide the investigator in his or her recognition of relevancy. Use the following guidelines to help recognize relevancy when writing the report:

- If a complainant or subject has provided a written statement of some facts germane to the inquiry, the written statement should be set out verbatim rather than paraphrased by the investigator. The exception to the rule is a brief summary in a synopsis of the report.
- If a number of people were interviewed, and none of them provided substantial information, they can be identified in a single reference with a notation that none provided relevant information.
- If premises or activities were observed and nothing substantial resulted, a single group reference can be made.

The investigative report should include a complete description of any persons involved in the matter under investigation, to include home and work addresses and contact telephone numbers. All investigative personnel who were involved in the case should be identified by name, title and organization.

Conclusions and Recommendations. Some organizations request that the investigator's conclusions and recommendations be provided as part of the investigative report. The investigator should be a fact-finder. The judicial or administrative actions to be taken should be decided by the appropriate authority in the organization.

Enclosures. All statements, admissions or confessions taken in the course of the investigation should be listed as numbered enclosures to the investigative report. Any audio or videotape made should be listed and enclosed as well.

Report Distribution

The final process in the investigative report is its distribution. Distribution should be restricted to only those with a genuine need to know. The report could contain damaging or sensitive information. The report copies need to be controlled closely, as does the number of file retentions permitted. Finally, any person receiving a copy or retaining a file should have the appropriate security measures in place to protect the material from compromise or loss.

Selected Bibliography

Books

American Society for Industrial Security; *Security Investigations: Basic Guidelines*; 1991; American Society for Industrial Security, Arlington, VA.

Department of the Army; *Law Enforcement Investigations, Army Field Manual*, FM 19-20; Department of the Army; Washington, D.C.

Employment Screening Services; *Guide to Background Investigations;* Employment Screening Services; Tulsa, OK.

Ferraro, Eugene F., CPP, CFE; *Undercover Investigations in the Workplace;* 2000; Butterworth-Heinemann, Woburn, MA.

Nemeth, Charles P.; *Private Security and the Investigative Process*; 1992; Anderson Publishing Co.

Office of Special Investigations; *Investigators' Guide to Sources of Information*; 1997; Office of Special Investigations, U.S. General Accounting Office.

O'Hara, Charles E. and Gregory L. O'Hara; *Fundamentals of Criminal Investigation, 6th ed.*; 1994; Charles C Thomas Publishers, Springfield, IL.

Pankau, Edmund J.; *Check It Out!;* 1990; Cloak & Data Press.

Thomas, Ralph D.; *How to Investigate by Computer*; 1990; Thomas Publications.

Articles

Security Management, American Society for Industrial Security, Alexandria, VA.
    — Cook, Leroy E., CPP; The Truth about Your Sleuth; December 1994.
    — Elzinga, David and David Ray; Ferreting out Fraud; February 1997.

Investigations: General Comments

— Ferraro, Eugene F., CPP; End Game; August 2000.
— Garrett, Glen R.; In-House Investigations in the Information Age; October 1994.
— Harris, Ellen R.; Planning an Investigative Strategy; November 1997.
— Hampson, Thomas R.; Won't Get Fooled Again; July 1996.
— Klump, Carl Stanton; Taking Your Cue from the Clues; September 1997.
— Lander, Ronald, CPP and James E. Roughton; The Security Professional in Cyberspace; January 1996.
— Mendell, Ronald L.; Matching Wits against Bite; May 1999.
— O'Connell,CPP; Is a Ruse the Best Route?; December 1995.
— Pinck, Charles T.; Covering All the Databases; July 1996.
— Sharp, William Arlington; Hot Air or Hot Prospect?; July 1996.
— Steines, John; Analyze This; June 2000.

APPENDIX A
SELECTED INTERNET INVESTIGATIVE RESOURCES

Aircraft and airmen   http://www.avweb.com
Link to Federal Aviation Administration databases

Background, financial, and   http://www.cdb.com
  skip information
  Broad-based public records provider (excellent for beginner database investigators)

Background, financial, and   http://www.irsc.com
  skip information
  Broad-based public records provider (excellent for beginner database investigators)

Biographical information,   http://www.krinfo.com
  newspapers, news

College degrees (Ph.D.)   http://www.dialog.com
  Abstract of the candidate's dissertation at Dissertation Abstracts Online

Internet address finder   http://iaf.net
  Approximately four million Internet addresses

Military locator service   http://www.militarycity.com
  Location of members of the U.S. Military services

Newspapers, trade journals,   http://www.datatimes.com
  business, credit

Patent information   http://www.derwent.com
  Patent filings

Public records resource library   http://www.brbpub.com
  How to access every public filing jurisdiction in the U.S.

Securities and exchange   http://www.sec.gov/edgarhp.htm
  commission
  Financial information and data on officers of publicly traded companies

Social Security Number   http://www.informus.com/ssnlkup.html
   verification
   Verifies the state and approximate year the number was issued

Street maps   http://mapquest.com
   Detailed street map of the area around an address

Telephone listings and Yellow   http://www.dda-inc.com
   Pages
   Telephone Directory Assistance and Yellow Pages

Telephone listings   http://www.switchboard.com
   Listed telephone number and address based on name and city

Vital Records   http://www.medaccess.com/address/vitaltoc.html
   State government addresses to request birth, marriage, divorce and death
   information

Zip Codes   http://www.usps.gov

APPENDIX B

Summary of Consumer Rights as Prescribed by the Federal Trade Commission

The prescribed form for this summary is as a separate document, on paper no smaller than 8-by-11 inches in size, with text no less than 12-point type (8-point for the chart of federal agencies), in bold or capital letters as indicated. The form in this appendix prescribes both the content and the sequence of items in the required summary. A summary may accurately reflect changes in numerical items that change over time (for example, dollar amounts, or phone numbers and addresses of federal agencies), and remain in compliance.

A Summary of Your Rights under the Fair Credit Reporting Act

The federal Fair Credit Reporting Act (FCRA) is designed to promote accuracy, fairness, and privacy of information in the files of every "consumer reporting agency" (CRA). Most CRAs are credit bureaus that gather and sell information about you — such as if you pay your bills on time or have filed bankruptcy — to creditors, employers, landlords, and other businesses. You can find the complete text of the FCRA, 15 U.S.C. 1681-1681u, at the Federal Trade Commission's Web site (http://www.ftc.gov). The FCRA gives you specific rights, as outlined below. You may have additional rights under state law. You may contact a state or local consumer protection agency or a state attorney general to learn those rights.

Investigations: General Comments

1. **You must be told if information in your file has been used against you.** Anyone who uses information from a CRA to take action against you — such as denying an application for credit, insurance, or employment — must tell you, and give you the name, address, and phone number of the CRA that provided the consumer report.
2. **You can find out what is in your file.** At your request, a CRA must give you the information in your file, and a list of everyone who has requested it recently. There is no charge for the report if a person has taken action against you because of information supplied by the CRA, if you request the report within 60 days of receiving notice of the action. You are also entitled to one free report every 12 months upon request if you certify that: (1) you are unemployed and plan to seek employment within 60 days, (2) you are on welfare, and (3) your report is inaccurate due to fraud. Otherwise, a CRA may charge you up to eight dollars.
3. **You can dispute inaccurate information with the CRA.** If you tell a CRA that your file contains inaccurate information, the CRA must investigate the items (usually within 30 days) by presenting to its information source all relevant evidence you submit, unless your dispute is frivolous. The source must review your evidence and report its findings to the CRA. (The source also must advise national CRAs — to which it has provided the data — of any error.) The CRA must give you a written report of the investigation, and a copy of your report if the investigation results in any change. If the CRA's investigation does not resolve the dispute, you may add a brief statement to your file. The CRA must normally include a summary of your statement in future reports. If an item is deleted or a dispute statement is filed, you may ask that anyone who has recently received your report be notified of the change.
4. **Inaccurate information must be corrected or deleted.** A CRA must remove or correct inaccurate or unverified information from its files, usually within 30 days after you dispute it. However, the CRA is not required to remove accurate data from your file unless it is outdated (as described below) or cannot be verified. If your dispute results in any change to your report, the CRA cannot reinsert into your file a disputed item unless the information source verifies its accuracy and completeness. In addition, the CRA must give you a written notice telling you it has reinserted the item. The notice must include the name, address and phone number of the information source.
5. **You can dispute inaccurate items with the source of the information.** If you tell anyone — such as a creditor who reports to a CRA — that you dispute an item, they may not report the information to a CRA without including a notice of your dispute. In addition, once you've notified the source of the error in writing, it may not continue to report the information if it is, in fact, an error.

6. **Outdated information may not be reported.** In most cases, a CRA may not report negative information that is more than seven years old; ten years for bankruptcies.
7. **Access to your file is limited.** A CRA may provide information about you only to people with a need recognized by the FCRA — usually to consider an application with a creditor, insurer, employer, landlord, or other business.
8. **Your consent is required for reports that are provided to employers, or reports that contain medical information.** A CRA may not give out information about you to your employer, or prospective employer, without your written consent. A CRA may not report medical information about you to creditors, insurers, or employers without your permission.
9. **You may choose to exclude your name from CRA lists for unsolicited credit and insurance offers.** Creditors and insurers may use file information as the basis for sending you unsolicited offers of credit or insurance. Such offers must include a toll-free phone number for you to call if you want your name and address removed from future lists. If you call, you must be kept off the lists for two years. If you make the request, complete and return the CRA form provided for this purpose and you can be taken off the lists indefinitely.
10. **You may seek damages from violators.** If a CRA, a user or (in some cases) a provider of CRA data, violates the FCRA, you may sue them in state or federal court.

The FCRA gives several different federal agencies authority to enforce the FCRA.

FOR QUESTIONS OR CONCERNS REGARDING:	CONTACT:
CRAs, creditors and others not listed below	Federal Trade Commission Consumer Response Center — FCRA Washington, D.C. 20580 202-326-3761
National banks, federal branches/agencies of foreign banks (or, if the words "National" or initials "N.A." or "Mail Stop 6-6" appears in or after bank's name)	Office of the Comptroller of the Currency Compliance Management Mail Stop 6-6 Washington, D.C. 20219 800-613-6743
Federal Reserve System member banks (except national banks, and federal branches/agencies of foreign banks)	Federal Reserve Board Division of Consumer & Community Washington, D.C. 20551 202-452-3693

Investigations: General Comments

Savings associations and federally chartered savings banks (or, if the words "Federal" or initials "F.S.B." appear in the federal institution's name)	Office of Thrift Supervision Consumer Programs Washington, D.C. 20552 800-842-6929
Federal credit unions (or, if the words "Federal Credit Union" appear in the institution's name)	National Credit Union Administration 1775 Duke Street Alexandria, VA 22314 703-518-6360
State-chartered banks that are not members of the Federal Reserve System Affairs	Federal Deposit Insurance Corporation Division of Compliance & Consumer Washington, D.C. 20429 800-934-FDIC
Air, surface or rail common carriers regulated by former Civil Aeronautics Board or Interstate	Department of Transportation Commerce Commission Office of Financial Management Washington, D.C. 20590 202-366-1306
Activities subject to the Packers and Stockyards Act of 1921	Department of Agriculture Office of Deputy Administrator — GIPSA Washington, D.C. 20250

12
Security and Protective Lighting

INTRODUCTION

The study of lighting involves many disciplines: lighting science and technology, electrical systems, aesthetic design of fixtures, and socioeconomic considerations such as cost, light trespass and the effect chemicals (such as mercury used in lamps) have on our ecology. In contrast to the technological nature of lighting, the application of lighting to real-life scenarios, in particular for security and safety, requires an appreciation of the subjective reaction of people to different lighting environments. Artificial lighting has developed almost exclusively for the benefit of humans so that they may continue to perform occupations, sports, leisure activities and any other life activity in the absence of the "natural" lighting provided by the Sun. Unlike our distant ancestors, we are less reliant on the Sun and our day may extend well into the night.

Lighting can act as a deterrent to criminal activity. However, lighting comes in many forms — some are more effective than others and some are more expensive than others. This chapter provides a basic understanding of lighting science and its terminology, the features and benefits of different types of lamps, and the effective application of lighting to increase safety and security in the work environment.

LIGHTING AND LIGHTING DEFINITIONS

In this section we will describe how light can be used to better see objects around us and the various properties of artificial light that we need to be aware of when selecting lighting solutions for security and safety problems.

The quantity, or flow of light emitted by a lamp is measured in lumens. For example, a typical household bulb rated at 100 watts may output about 1700 lumens. However, a spotlight or a floodlight may output the quantity of light but the spotlight concentrates its output in a small area, whereas the floodlight disperses the light over a larger area. Illuminance is the concentration of light over a particular area. Illuminance is measured in lux, representing the number of lumens per square meter or footcandles (fc), the number of lumens per square foot. One footcandle is equal to 10.76 lux

Table 1. Natural and visual light levels.

Light level (footcandles)	Natural light source	Visual experience light levels
50,000		Upper limit of visual tolerance
10,000	Direct sunlight	Fresh snow on a clear day
1,000	Full daylight	Average earth on a clear day
100	Overcast day	Average earth on a cloudy day
1	Twilight	White paper 1 ft from standard Candle
0.1	Deep twilight	
0.05		Snow in full moon
0.01	Full moon	
0.005		Average earth in full moon
0.001	Quarter moon	
0.0001	Starlight	Snow in starlight
0.00005		Grass in starlight
0.00001	Overcast night	
0.000001		Absolute limit of seeing

(often approximated to a ratio of 1:10). When evaluating the amount of light needed by a particular CCTV camera (or the eye) to perceive a scene, it is the amount of light shining over the area of the lens iris (camera or eye), or its illuminance, that is critical.

Table 1 provides a measure of light levels that can be gauged from common experience. (Note that the Average Earth light levels are one-half of the natural light source levels – this is because, on average, reflectance of most objects is approximately 50 percent.)

Simply put, reflectance means that when we see an object, our eyes are sensing the light reflected from that object. If there is no light reflected from the object, we do not see it — unless as a silhouette in contrast to its background. If the object is illuminated by other than white light, we will see the object in colors that are not true colors. The color of the surface also has an impact on reflectance; a light surface, such as a parking lot paved in concrete, will have higher reflectance than a dark surface (a parking lot paved in asphalt or black-top). The measure of reflectance of an object is the ratio of the quantity of light (measured in lumens) falling on it to the light being reflected from it, expressed as a percentage. A mirror or any shiny surface will have a high reflectance, while a dull or matte surface will have a lower reflectance. Table 2 provides some measures for the reflectance of some common materials. Note that these are average values and the reflectance value, in particular for man-made objects, will vary depending on the materials and their age.

Security and Protective Lighting

Table 2. Reflectance measurements.

Material		Reflectance %
Asphalt		5
Concrete	(Old)	40
	(New)	25
Red brick		25
Grass		40
Snow		95

Source: Terry McGhee and Charlie Pierce, Lighting the Way to Security, *Security Management,* December 1990.

Corrected Color Temperature (CCT) is a measure of the warmth or coolness of a light. It is measured in degrees Kelvin, which is the Centigrade (Celsius) absolute temperature scale where 0°K is approximately –272°C. To grasp the concept of color temperature it helps to think of a piece of metal being heated in a furnace. When it starts to glow red hot, it is about 2700°K, white hot is at about 4100°K, and blue hot is at about 5000°K — similar to daylight. People often perceive red hot as being warm, and white or blue hot as being cool. The color temperature of a light source has a considerable impact on mood and the ambiance of the surroundings. Table 3 summarizes the color temperatures of various types of lamps and their applications.

Table 3. Color temperature.

Color temperature	Warm 3000°K	Neutral 3500°K	Cool 4100°K	Daylight 5000°K
Associated effects and moods	Friendly Intimate Personal Exclusive	Friendly Inviting Non-threatening	Neat Clean Efficient	Bright Alert Exacting coloration
Applications	Restaurants Hotel lobbies Boutiques Libraries Office areas Retail stores	Public reception areas Showrooms Bookstores Office areas	Conference rooms Classrooms Hospitals Office areas Mass merchandisers	Galleries Museums Jewelry stores Medical exam areas Printing companies
Lamps	Fluorescent Incandescent Halogen	Fluorescent Mercury vapor	Fluorescent Mercury vapor Metal halide	Fluorescent Mercury vapor Metal halide

Note: CCT for low- and high-pressure sodium: 1750°K and 2000°K, respectively.

Table 4. Color rendition index.

Lamp type	Incandescent	Halogen	Fluorescent	Metal halide	Mercury vapor	High-press. sodium	Low-press. sodium
CRI	100	100	75–100	70	50	20	5

Source: Adapted from *Lamp Spcification and Application Guide,* Phillips Lighting Company, January 1999.

Security personnel need the ability to accurately describe color. This is an important aspect in the apprehension and prosecution of criminals who are caught on CCTV displays and recordings. The ability of a lamp to faithfully reproduce the colors seen in an object is known as Color Rendition and is measured as a Color Rendition Index (CRI) on a scale of 0 to 100. A CRI of 70 to 80 is considered good, above 80 is considered excellent, and 100 is considered daylight. Table 4 shows the CRI values of various lamps. Note that the high- and low-pressure sodium and mercury vapor light sources have very low CRI values and should not be used in conjunction with color camera applications or where color identification is critical. For example, under low-pressure sodium light, a green shirt will have a blue hue.

In addition to security operations, high color rendering is important in retail, restaurant and precision manual work. A high CRI also increases visual clarity and has been found to create higher morale and greater productivity. High CRI values in outdoor locations at night make pedestrians feel safer because it allows them to see at a greater distance and have better depth perception.

Brightness and glare are more subjective terms. Brightness is our perception of the amount of light that reaches our eyes. Glare is a term used to describe excessive brightness and it has importance in security applications. Glare is hurtful to the eye and impacts the eye's efficiency; it creates excessive contrast with other objects, makes us turn our eyes away, and generally makes it difficult to see clearly. Glare can be used effectively to deter unauthorized activity at a site perimeter. However, it has an equally negative effect on patrols and on response forces. Additionally, it may cause light trespass onto adjoining properties, including sidewalks and roadways. It is important that light trespass does not cause glare or excessive contrast to drivers and pedestrians, both on your property and adjacent areas. Many communities set limits, through zoning restrictions, on the level of lighting and the amount of light that can spill onto, or trespass, neighboring areas.

LIGHTING SYSTEMS

A lighting system consists of a number of components, all of which are important to the effectiveness of a lighting application. Below is a list of the major components and their function.

- *Lamp* (also known as a light bulb) is the manufactured light source that includes the filament or an arc tube, its glass casing and its electrical connectors. Types of lamps are incandescent, mercury vapor, etc., which describe the type of technologies used to create the light.
- *Luminaire* (also known as *fixture*) is the complete lighting unit, consisting of the lamp, its holder, and the reflectors and diffusers used to distribute and focus the light. Some lamps, such as spots and floods, are designed with integral, shaped reflectors for the focus and distribution of the light. The luminaire will also contain the means of connecting to the power source and — depending on the lamp technology — will include *ballasts* (to generate the correct starting and operating voltage, current and waveform) and *photosensors* (to control switching of lights based on ambient lighting conditions). The selection of luminaire will depend on aesthetics as well as performance characteristics.
- *Mounting hardware* such as a wall bracket or a light pole is used to fix the luminaire at the correct height and location.
- *Electrical power* operates the lamp, ballasts and photocells. Some lamp technologies are sensitive to reduced voltages; in particular, the high-intensity discharge (HID) family of lamps (metal halide, mercury vapor and high-pressure sodium). These lamps require relatively stable voltage levels because they produce light from an arc discharge under high pressure; if the supply voltage is sufficiently reduced, the arc will be extinguished. Restart times are often lengthy (up to 20 minutes). Backup batteries, generators and uninterruptable power supply (UPS) systems need to be considered for the lighting of high security and safety areas, such as vaults, cash registers and paths of emergency egress and assembly.

LIGHTING ECONOMICS

The cost of lighting is a major factor in the decision of the level of lighting that will be installed for security and safety. Some lighting is mandated by code (e.g., fire safety, retail banking, Nuclear Regulatory Commission (NRC) regulated facilities and OSHA). Many times, however, security lighting is an elective cost that must be justified based on identifiable savings or quantifiable reduction in risk.

This section provides some guidance in the cost of operating security lighting. Estimates of the capital costs associated with procurement and installation are best left to a lighting engineer. *The Outdoor Lighting Pattern*

Book (see Bibliography) provides many examples of the equipment, maintenance and energy costs associated with lighting projects for parking structures, office buildings, loading docks, gatehouses and malls.

For a typical lighting installation, the operating cost consists of capital items such as lamps and ballasts, energy, and maintenance. The proportion of these costs is approximately 8 percent capital items, 4 percent maintenance and 88 percent energy. It is obvious that the energy efficiency of the lighting is most important. This is known as a lamp's efficacy and is measured by the lamp's output in lumens, divided by the lamp's power draw in watts. The next highest cost is that of replacement lamps and is a function of the lamp technology and the quality of the lamp. Table 5 shows typical levels of efficacy and lamp life. As a ready guide, there are 8760 hours in a year — a lamp that is on for eight hours per day will burn for 2920 hours per year.

The cost figures[1] shown in the last row are representative of typical costs to provide 16,000 lumens of lighting for eight hours per day for five years (maintenance and labor costs for cleaning and bulb changes, etc. are excluded). Electricity is assumed to cost 10 cents per kilowatt-hour (KWH). While lamp prices remain relatively constant, you can easily modify the five-year electricity costs multiplying the dollar value by the cents per KWH in your area and dividing by 10. For example, the electricity cost for the high-pressure sodium lamp in an area where power costs 15 cents would be $328 × 15/10 = $492.

Maintenance costs include the labor to replace lamps and to clean them. Cleaning cannot be ignored because the lumen output of a lamp will reduce due to dirt accumulating on the fixture over time. In a clean environment, such as a computer room or office area, the percentage of output will reduce by approximately 3 to 4 percent per year and cleaning intervals of three years are recommended. In a very dirty environment, a luminaire could be emitting only 80 percent (a reduction of 20 percent) of its design output after only one year. Because the power consumption remains the same regardless of the amount of dirt accumulated on the luminaire, it makes sense to implement regular cleaning to maintain the designed light output. It should be noted that the performance of most lamps reduces with age and, by the end of their rated life may produce only 80 percent of their designed output even when clean.

Lamps need to be replaced as their useful life is reached, and it is less expensive in labor to perform a planned replacement of all, or a group of, lamps rather than wait until they expire individually and replace them one or two at a time. Planned replacement also ensures that there are no dark areas, even for a short time, caused by individual failures. It makes economic sense to use a suitable multiple of the cleaning cycle as the time to

[1] M.L. McCauley, Lighting Principals, *Security Magazine,* September 1991.

Security and Protective Lighting

Table 5. Lamp efficacy, life and cost.

Lamp type	Incandescent	Halogen	Fluorescent	Metal halide	Mercury vapor	High-press. sodium	Low-press. sodium
Efficacy (lumens per watt)	20	25	60–80	125	65	125	200
Life (hours)	1000–4000	10,000–20,000	10,000–20,000	10,000–24,000	16,000–25,000	16,000–24,000	15,000–25,000
5-Yr lamp	$516		$9	$78	$26	$38	$72
cost elec.	$3039		$438	$433	$720	$328	$187
tot.	$3355		$447	$511	$746	$366	$259

331

re-lamp. For example, if the average useful life of a lamp is six years and cleaning is scheduled every two years, all lamps should be replaced every three cleaning cycles.

The number of luminaires required is a function of the area to be covered, the light levels required, the height of the luminaires and their design, and the type of lighting technology used. To achieve a uniform distribution of light, particularly outdoors, is expensive. Some variation in light levels is considered acceptable and is measured as *uniformity*, the ratio between the average light level and the minimum light level. Typical uniformity ratios would be 1:0.7 for working environments, 4:1 on a pedestrian walkway, and 10:1 on a roadway. Higher uniformity gives better depth perception and a greater perception of security to individuals in the area.

STARTING AND RE-STRIKE

Some lamps require time to re-light if they are switched off intentionally or due to either a full power failure or a brownout. The extended re-lighting time is typical of high-intensity discharge (HID) types of lamps because they rely on an arc to produce light. The lamp tube must cool sufficiently before the arc can be re-struck. In addition, HID lamps (and to a much lesser extent fluorescent lamps) take time on starting from cold to reach their designed light output levels.

These functional limitations of lamps are of concern to the security practitioner. Although lamp switch-on times can be scheduled to allow for their start-up time, a full or partial power failure, however brief, can mean a loss of lighting for a considerable period. Table 6 shows typical starting and re-strike times for the different types of lamps.

Note that new technology and manufacturing methods seek to reduce these times. For example, some HID lamps are available with two tubes — only one is used at a time so that the other remains cool for a quick re-strike.

Table 6. Lamp starting and re-strike times.

Lamp type	Incandescent	Halogen	Fluorescent	Metal halide	Mercury vapor	High-press. sodium	Low-press. sodium
Start time (min)	Instant	Instant	Instant[a]	5–8	5–8	2–5	5–8
Restrike time (min)	Instant	Instant	Instant	10–20	10–20	1–20	0–8

[a] Fluorescent lamps require time (especially in cold weather) to reach full output.

SECURITY LIGHTING APPLICATIONS

The security professional needs to consider lighting in a number of different areas of the facility being secured. The following list provides a sample of such areas, together with lighting recommendations. A useful rule of thumb to use when considering lighting levels is: for pedestrians or normal cameras, the minimum level of reflected light for detection is 0.5 fc, for recognition 1.0 fc, and for identification 2.0 fc.[1]

Perimeter Fencing. Lighting, as well as physical barriers, act as a deterrent to unauthorized intrusion. If perimeter intrusion detection systems are used, the lighting also aids in the use of CCTV systems for alarm assessment and the effectiveness of the response force to delay and/or apprehend the perpetrators. NRC regulations specify 0.2 fc of illumination at perimeter and in the clear area between the two fences. Because the perimeter fence may border on the property of neighbors, light trespass needs to be considered in the design solution.

Site Landscape and Perimeter Approaches. Roadways and pedestrian walkways are lit for both safety and security reasons. Vertical lighting, shining onto the horizontal walkway or roadway, is ideal to identify potholes or objects that may cause tripping. However, when installing lights so that pedestrians can clearly see one another, or for the most effective use of CCTV cameras, some component of the light must be horizontal so as to illuminate vertical surfaces. Site landscapes are particularly difficult and expensive to light, especially if there are trees and shrubs that provide cover to would-be intruders. Ground lighting focused up into the trees and shrubs is most effective in deterring their use as hiding places. Such lighting also provides a high contrast background to detect movement. Typical lighting levels for walkways: 1 to 4 fc for walkways, 0.5 to 2 fc for roadways, 10 fc for entrances and 2 fc for open yards.

Building Facade. Where individual exterior objects cannot be adequately lit, providing a high contrast will give good identification of shape and movement. The floodlighting of a building facade achieves this goal. If the facade has good reflectance, there will also be a measure of horizontal light for a viewer (person or camera) located between the facade and the object to identify the object. Typical lighting levels for security are 0.5 to 2 fc.

Parking Structures. These areas are difficult to light because there are few vertical elements to reflect light or provide contrast to moving objects. In some municipalities, building codes require a bright white horizontal stripe on walls, at waist height, to improve contrast. The lack of ceiling clearance restricts the height of luminaires and requires the fixtures to

---

[1] Terry McGhee, Spotlight on the Night, *Security Management,* March 1988.

spread the light horizontally. This is excellent for lighting vertical surfaces; however, if CCTV cameras are used, the luminaire design should be selected to reduce glare at the camera lens. A horizontal illuminance level of 5 fc with a uniformity ratio of 4:1 provides an adequate level of security.

Open Parking. The height of luminaires is less restricted in open than in covered parking unless local codes and light trespass become factors. The higher light sources tend to provide horizontal illumination. Recommended light levels range from a minimum of 0.2 fc in low-activity general parking and pedestrian areas, to 2 fc in high-activity vehicle areas. Cash collection and vehicular access control areas should be maintained at a minimum of 5 fc.

Loading Docks. Nighttime lighting will depend on off-hours activity. To maintain an adequate level of security for the exterior area without truck parking, 1 fc at the building facade (roll-up doors, stairs, ramps, etc.) and 0.2 fc in open yards is recommended. For nighttime shipping and receiving operations, the illuminance should be increased to 5 fc. Interior dock areas, such as loading bays, should be lit to 15 fc, and unpacking and sorting areas to 20 fc. Packing and dispatch areas are recommended at 30 fc.

Security Control and Monitoring Rooms. Most activities in this area are computer based and should be illuminated to 30 to 50 fc with task areas, such as a console desk, at 50 to 70 fc. Glare from computer and video monitoring screens can be a problem. The positioning of luminaires and the angle of screens are critical in minimizing glare. The type of screens used is also important. Flat screens and those with anti-glare coatings or covers will help to reduce or eliminate glare. If screen monitoring (e.g., alarm and CCTV) is the predominant function, monitoring staff may want to reduce the ambient light levels considerably to minimize glare and increase the contrast of the screens. The security manager should discuss the use of dimmers with the lighting designer.

Guard and Gate Houses. The area surrounding a gate or guard house should be well lit (2 to 5 fc) on the exterior at night. Task lighting on the interior should be high (30 fc) during daytime operations, but should be reduced at night to below exterior levels to permit good visibility of the surroundings and approaching pedestrian and vehicular traffic.

Table 7 is a sampling from *The Outdoor Lighting Pattern Book* (see Bibliography) and summarizes the perceived level of security at different lighting levels for various applications. The book describes practical examples of how lighting can be improved and includes capital and operating costs for each upgrade it details. It should be noted that while in general terms increased lighting increases security, the selection, location and mounting of luminaires (i.e., lighting design) play a vital role.

Table 7. Lighting and security perceptions.

Application	Average horizontal illuminance (fc)	Sense of security (Range 1 = poor; 5 = best)
Pedestrian mall		
Typical	0.43	2
Upgrade	2.00	4
Redesign	3.80	5
Office park		
Typical	0.96	2
Upgrade	1.70	3
Parking structure		
Typical	0.93	2
Upgrade	1.90	3
Redesign 1	3.00	3
Redesign 2	4.10	4
Redesign 3	5.20	5
Loading dock (exterior)		
Typical	0.99	2
Upgrade	0.65	3
Redesign	1.30	4
Guardhouse		
Typical	1.00	1
Upgrade	1.40	3
Redesign	4.30	5
Gatehouse		
Typical	0.46	1
Upgrade	1.00	3
Redesign	2.30	5
Campus green		
Typical	0.33	2
Upgrade	0.61	3
Redesign	1.50	4
Urban school (three-story)		
Typical	0.41	1
Upgrade	0.68	2
Redesign 1	2.70	4
Redesign 2	2.30	4
Rural school (one-story)		
Typical	0.77	1
Upgrade	0.99	3
Redesign	1.20	4

ASSET PROTECTION AND SECURITY MANAGEMENT HANDBOOK

SECURITY LIGHTING AND CLOSED-CIRCUIT VIDEO SYSTEMS

Where CCTV cameras are used to augment security, there are some additional considerations to be taken in the selection and application of lighting, including:

- Color Rendering Index (CRI) for accurate reproduction and identification of colors
- Reflectance of materials, because this is what both the human eye and the camera lens sees
- Directionality of the reflected lighting in the direction that the camera is aimed

Another important factor is the wavelength of the source illumination. The human eye, by definition, sees light in the visible spectrum that has a bandwidth between 400 nanometers (nm) (violet) and 700 nm (red). The electromagnetic spectrum, of which the visible spectrum is only a small part, has a much larger range but human eyes are not sensitive to it. Close to either end of the visible spectrum are the ultraviolet and infrared wavelengths. Both the Sun and artificial lighting sources will produce energy beyond our sensitivity range.

CCTV cameras are generally designed to see what we see, but many have the ability to sense illumination well beyond the visible spectrum into the near-infrared range from 700 to 1100 nm. The use of an infrared (IR) light source in conjunction with a camera incorporating a special sensing element, such as Ex-wave CCD, allows views to be displayed even where there is no visible light. This is useful where zoning restrictions limit the amount of light trespass or where covert surveillance is desired. The use of IR illuminators is limited to monochrome — not color — cameras. The IR luminaire should be co-located with the camera and should be chosen to provide a beam spread consistent with the camera lens setting. For dynamic (pan/tilt/zoom) cameras, the IR source can be mounted on the pan/tilt mechanism to follow the direction that the camera is pointing. The design should ensure that the pan/tilt is rated for the weight of the camera and of the luminaire.

The color temperatures of the various light sources are shown in Table 3. Most cameras data sheets state their performance based on an incandescent tungsten filament 2700°K light source. None of the color cameras generally used for CCTV are effective at the 1700°K range of low-pressure sodium lamps, but newer CCD elements, such as the Hyper HAD, will considerably improve the color rendition of a scene illuminated by high-pressure sodium light (2200°K).

In general, color cameras require approximately twice the light level of a monochrome camera for the same picture quality. In addition, a color camera needs at least 50 percent of its full video signal; otherwise, color registration starts to fade. Black-and-white cameras require only about 20 to 30 percent of full video.

A few other specifications to consider on camera data sheets include:

- Minimum light levels are quoted at 75 percent or 89.9 percent reflectance — as has been discussed in this chapter, the outdoor average is closer to 50 percent.
- Minimum light levels are quoted for specific lens characteristics. For example, a standard color camera may perform at a minimum illumination of 0.25 fc with an f1.2 lens; with an f2.0 lens, the minimum illumination increases to 0.68 fc, an increase of 2.7 times the lighting level. The selection of lens and its quality is important.
- White balance is the automatic adjustment within a camera for the color temperature of the light source. This parameter can range from 2200°K to 7000°K. Check that the range of white balance of the camera that you plan to use is compatible with the existing or designed lighting.

STANDARDS FOR SECURITY LIGHTING LEVELS

The first national standard was issued in 1942 and was modified and sponsored by the Illuminating Engineers Society of North America (IESNA) as ANSI A85.1, American National Standard Practice for Protective Lighting, in 1956. It was reaffirmed in 1970 but has since been withdrawn.

The *IESNA's Lighting Handbook* (2000) contains "Emergency, Safety and Security Lighting." The IESNA also publishes numerous lighting Design Guides and Recommended Practices for applications such as Warehouses (DG-2-92), Parking Facilities (RP-20-98), Automatic Teller Machines (DG-9-97), Walkways and Class 1 Bikeways (DG-5-94) and Exterior Environments (RP-33-99). Other sources of lighting standards are the Department of the Army's Field Manual 19-30 (1979) and the Nuclear Regulatory Commission (NRC) regulations governing licensees who possess special nuclear materials.

These bodies describe significantly different standards for minimum lighting levels, which can cause confusion for security managers, systems designers and architects.

In the interim, the minimum lighting levels are offered in Table 8. They are extracted from a number of sources and are intended for use only as a guide.

Table 8. Guidelines for minimum lighting levels.

Application	Minimum lighting level (IES) standards (fc)	Comments/Other
Perimeter fence	0.50	NRC 0.20
Outer perimeter	0.50–2.00	NRC 0.20 fc; DoAFM 0.15
Open areas	2.00	
Open parking lot	0.20–0.90	IES High Vehicle Activity 2.00 fc
Covered parking structure	5.00	
Pedestrian walkways	0.20	IES 7.50 fc at ATMs
Pedestrian entrances	5.00	DoAFM 2.00 fc
Vehicle entrances	10.00	DoAFM 1.00 fc
Building facade	0.50–2.00	
Gatehouses	30.00	
Loading dock exterior	0.20–5.00	
Loading bays	15.00	
Offices — general	30–50	
Offices — task	50–70	
Interior public areas	10–20	
Retail stores	50.00	
Bank — lobby	20.00	
Bank — teller	50.00	
Bank — ATM	15.00 fc	IES 30 fc on Preparation Counter

Note: IES = Illuminating Engineers Society of North America; NRC = Nuclear Regulatory Commission; DoAFM = Department of the Army Field Manual.

Selected Bibliography

Books

Bernaden, John A. and Neubauer, Richard E.; *The Intelligent Building Sourcebook;* 1988; The Fairmont Press, Inc.

Bintliff, Russell L.; *Complete Manual of Corporate and Industrial Security [The];* 1992; Prentice-Hall, Englewood Cliffs, NJ.

Cumming, Neil; *Security: A Guide to Security System Design and Equipment Selection and Installation, 2nd ed.;* 1992; Butterworth-Heinemann, Newton, MA.

Fennelly, Lawrence J.; *Effective Physical Security;* 1992; Butterworth-Heinemann, Newton, MA.

Fennelly, Lawrence J.; *Handbook of Loss Prevention and Crime Prevention;* 1989; Butterworth-Heinemann, Newton, MA

Gigliotti, Richard J.; *Design for Maximum Protection;* 1984; Butterworth Publishers, Inc., Newton, MA.

Healy, R.J.; *Design for Security;* 1983; John Wiley & Sons, New York.

Higgins, L.R. and Morrow, L.C.; *Maintenance Engineering Handbook, 3rd ed.;* 1977; McGraw-Hill, New York.

Hopf, Peter, Ed.; *Handbook of Building Security Planning and Design;* 1979; McGraw-Hill, New York.

Illuminating Engineers Society; *Lighting Handbook,* 1993; Illuminating Engineers Society, New York.

Kaufman, J.E. and Christensen, J.F.; *IES Lighting Ready Reference,* 2nd ed.; 1990; Illuminating Engineers Society of North America, New York.

Kramer, Joel J., Meguire, Patrick G., and Stewart, Addie; *Security Lighting for Nuclear Weapons Storage Sites: A Literature Review and Bibliography;* 1977; Law Enforcement Standards Laboratory (National Bureau of Standards), Defense Nuclear Agency — Intelligence and Security Directorate, U.S. Government Printing Office, Washington, D.C.

Lindsey, Jack L.; *Applied Illumination Engineering;* 1991; Fairmont Press.

Lyons, Stanley L.; *Lighting for Industry and Security: A Handbook for Providers and Users of Lighting;* 1992; Butterworth-Heinemann, Newton MA.

National Lighting Bureau; *Lighting for Safety and Security;* 1989; National Lighting Bureau, Washington, D.C.

Neidle, Michael; *Emergency and Security Lighting Handbook;* 1988. (A U.K. text distributed in the U.S. by Butterworth-Heinemann, Newton, MA.)

Parking Security Manual and Legal Liability Guide [The]; 1991; Rusting Publications.

Phillips Lighting Company; *Lamp Specification and Application Guide*; 1999; Phillips Lighting Co., Somerset, NJ.

Phillips Lighting Company; *Industrial Lighting Application Guide*; 1997; Phillips Lighting Company, Somerset, NJ.

Physical Security; U.S. Army Field Manual 19-30; March 1979; U.S. Government Printing Office, S/N 0-635-034/1069.

Profiting from Lighting Modernization; 1987; National Lighting Bureau, Washington, D.C.

Reinhold, A. Carlson and DiGiandomenico, Robert A.; *Understanding Building Automation Systems;* 1991; R.S. Means Company, Inc., Kingston, MA.

Russell P. Leslie and Rodgers, Paula A.; *The Outdoor Lighting Pattern Book*; 1996; Lighting Research Center, RPI; McGraw-Hill, New York.

Strobl, Walter; *Crime Prevention through Physical Security;* 1978; Marcel Dekker, Inc.

Thumann, Albert; *Lighting Efficiency Applications, 2nd ed.;* 1991; Fairmont Press.

Tien, James M.; *Street Lighting Projects;* 1977; National Institute of Law Enforcement and Criminal Justice.

U.S. Dept. of Defense; *Design Guidelines for Physical Security of Fixed Land-Based Facilities;* 1987; National Archives and Records Administration.

Various Design Guides and Recommended Practices (e.g., *Recommended Lighting for Walkways and Class 1 Bikeways, Lighting for Automated Teller Machines, Lighting for Exterior Environments*) issued by IESNA, New York.

Periodicals

Security Management; American Society for Industrial Security, Arlington, VA
— Bachner, John P.; The Myths and Realities Behind Security Lighting; August 1990.
— Cassidy, Kevin A., Maurice A. DiPierro, Robert Brandes and Phillip E. Thomas; Watt's Up with Your Security Survey?; August 1989.
— Dubois, Paul A.; The Design and Application of Security Lighting; September 1985.
— Glicksman, Mark; Lighting Requirements for CCTV; January 1981.
— Henry, Phil; Lightening Your Security Dollars; October 1986.
— Jefferson, Bob; Shedding Light on Security Problems; December 1992.
— Johnson, Neal; Bright Spots in Security Planning; October 1986.
— Law, John K.; Lighten Your Liability; August 1989.
— Lewis, Robert A.; Better Security through LPS Lighting; April 1978.

ASSET PROTECTION AND SECURITY MANAGEMENT HANDBOOK

— Lyons, Stanley L.; Lighting Designed for Defense, Part I; June 1982.
— Lyons, Stanley L.; Lighting Designed for Defense: Part II; July 1982.
— McGhee Charlie R. and Terry S. Pierce; Lighting the Way to Security for CCTV and non-CCTV Applications; December 1990.
— McGhee, Charlie R.; Spotlight on the Night; March 1988.
— Nolte, John; Improved Pedestrian Lighting on Campus; May 1977.
— Preserve Security, Conserve Energy; September 1980.
— Save on Lighting without Sacrificing Security; September 1979.
— Tyska, Louis A.; Security Lighting for the Cargo Terminal; July 1976.

Security Technology & Design, Locksmith Publishing, IL.
— Wimmer, Robert A.; CCTV Systems Design: Part 1; August 1999.

Other Resources

National Lighting Bureau: www.nlb.org.

Illuminating Engineers Society of North America: www.iesna.org.

National Council on Qualifications for the Lighting Professional: www.ncqlp.org.

National Association of Lighting Designers: www.iald.org

Philips Lighting Company: www.lighting.philips.com

GE Lighting: www.gestpectrum.com

Sylvania Lighting: www.sylvania.com

13
Crime Prevention through Environmental Design: CPTED

INTRODUCTION

Since the 1970s, the term "Crime Prevention Through Environmental Design" (CPTED,[1] pronounced *sep-ted*) has become the preferred way to describe the following security concept:

> The proper design and effective use of the built environment can lead to a reduction in the fear and incidence of predatory stranger-to-stranger crime, as well as an improvement of the quality of life.[2]

In plain English, Crime Prevention Through Environmental Design is a crime-environment theory based on the proposition that the appropriate design and application of the building and surrounding environment can improve the quality of life by deterring crime and reducing the fear of crime. Security and crime prevention practitioners should have a thorough understanding of CPTED concepts and applications in order to work more effectively with local crime prevention officers, security professionals, building design authorities, architects and design professionals, and others when designing new or renovating existing buildings.

This chapter is intended to provide the reader with the basic information necessary to understand and apply the concepts of CPTED. It is not intended to make the reader an instant expert on crime, especially given that few people have a clear understanding about the true nature of crime and criminal behavior. However, CPTED — at its core — is based on common sense and a heightened sense of awareness of how people are using their space for legitimate and illegitimate criminal purposes.

---

[1] The term CPTED was first used by C. Ray Jeffrey in 1971 in his book *Crime Prevention through Environmental Design*; Sage Publications, Inc.
[2] This definition of CPTED is from the National Crime Prevention Institute and enhanced by Randall Atlas, Ph.D., AIA, CPP.

The rising importance of CPTED in the design and planning process is based upon the belief that crime and loss prevention are inherent to human functions and activities, not just something that police or security people do. What we do — right or wrong — with our human and physical resources produces a lasting legacy. Once the building — concrete, brick, mortar and glass — is set, it becomes infinitely more difficult and expensive to make structural changes that would allow security to function optimally in the building and site.

The study of CPTED has bloomed into a distinct discipline. We limit our discussion in this chapter to theories, concepts and practical applications for the security generalist.

For the security professional, CPTED is a set of management tools focusing on:

- *Physical environments such as a building park office space, apartment, etc.* The physical environment can be manipulated to produce behavioral effects that will reduce the fear and incidence of certain types of criminal acts.
- *Behavior of people in relationship to their physical environment.* Some locations seem to create, promote, or allow criminal activity or unruly behavior while other environments elicit compliant and law-abiding conduct.
- *Redesigning or using existing space more effectively to encourage desirable behaviors and discourage crime and related undesirable conduct.* CPTED practice suggests that crime and loss are by-products of human functions that are not working properly.

CPTED Fundamentals

CPTED involves the design of physical space in the context of the needs of the legitimate users of the space, the normal and expected (or intended) use of the space, and the predictable behavior of both the legitimate users and offenders. In this regard, the proper function must not only match a space that can support it, but the design must assure that the intended behavior has the opportunity to function well and support the control of behavior.

In general, there are three classifications to crime prevention through environmental design:

1. *Mechanical measures*, also referred to as *target hardening*, emphasize hardware and technology systems such as locks, security screens on windows, fencing and gating, key control systems, closed-circuit television (CCTV) and similar physical barriers. Mechanical measures must not be relied upon solely to create a secure environment, but rather be used in context with people and design strategies.

2. *Human and/or organizational measures* focus on teaching individuals and vested groups steps they can take to protect themselves or the space they occupy, at home or work. Organizational methods of CPTED include Block Watches, Neighborhood Watch, security patrols, police officer patrols, concierge stations, designated or capable guardians, and other strategies using people as the basis of security with the ability to observe, report and intervene.
3. *Natural measures* involve designing space to ensure that the overall environment works more effectively for the intended users, while at the same time deterring crime. Natural methods of CPTED use good space planning to reduce user and use conflicts by planning compatible circulation patterns.

Within each of the three CPTED classifications, there are several key concepts that allow CPTED to be implemented:

- *Natural access control*: employing barriers — including doors, fences, shrubbery and other man-made and natural obstacles — to limit access to a building or other defined space. For example, to deter burglars from entering lower-story windows, a choice can be made between planting dense, thorny bushes near the windows and installing locking devices, or installing an alarm system. The decision should rest on the risks associated with that particular facility.
- *Natural surveillance*: increasing visibility by occupants and casual observers (police, others) to increase the detection of trespassers or misconduct within a facility. For instance, if a loading dock is enclosed with a high wooden fence blocking the view of the area, it may invite thieves. Conversely, the use of chain-link fencing that allows an unobstructed view of the area by workers or passers-by would probably discourage thieves.
- *Natural territorial reinforcement/boundary definition*: establishing a sense of ownership by property owners or building occupants to increase vigilance in identifying trespassers. This sends the message that would-be offenders will be identified. One example: the use of small-edging shrubbery along sidewalks in an apartment complex to mark the territory of individual apartments and discourage trespassers from cutting through the area. In addition, the theory holds that people will pay more attention to and defend a particular space or territory from trespass if they feel a form of "psychological ownership" in the area. Thus, it is possible, through real or symbolic markers, to encourage tenants or employees to defend property from incursion.

The concept of *natural* refers to the crime prevention by-product that results from normal and routine use of an environment — such as a building — because the concepts of natural access control and surveillance were designed into the facility from the beginning. In addition to the three classic principles, the two following are also considered:

- *Management and maintenance*: for spaces to look well cared for and crime-free, they must be maintained in the standard of care to industry standards. The "broken window" theory suggests that an abandoned building or car remains unmolested indefinitely; but once the first window is broken, the building or car is quickly vandalized. Maintenance of a building and its physical elements such as lighting, paint, signage, fencing, walkways, and repair of broken items is critical for showing that someone cares and is responsible for the upkeep. Management of properties is essential to ensure maintenance is kept up to the standards of care.
- *Legitimate activity support*: a crime prevention program will only be effective if the legitimate residents engage in the defined, designated, and designed (3D Concept) activities that were intended by the architecture and function of the space or building. Drug and criminal activity thrives in designated spaces because the residents and management do not claim the space and provide no legitimate activities to take place in order to undermine or replace the criminal activities.

By gaining an understanding of the key concepts of natural access control, natural surveillance, territorial reinforcement, management and maintenance functions, and legitimate activity support, a crime prevention planner, security consultant, property manager, architect or community leader can put theory into action and use CPTED to address community disorder, workplace violence, street crime or acts of terrorism. The application of these concepts differentiates CPTED from other traditional target hardening and fortressing techniques. Allowing CPTED concepts into initial consideration of the space configuration and circulation patterns of individuals using the building or site creates considerable efficiency advantages over "retrofitting" space to be secure. In many instances, the use of target hardening without consideration for the built environment has created a fortress effect, leaving residents/users (whether in a multi-family housing property or office building) feeling unsafe.

A final practical note: the target hardening approach by itself is usually not architecturally or aesthetically pleasing and usually results in opposition by architects and others involved in site and design planning matters.

UNDERSTANDING CPTED: THEORY, HISTORY AND PRACTICE

For centuries, historians and researchers have studied the relationship between the environment and behavior. CPTED draws from a multidisciplinary base of knowledge to create its own theoretical framework — including the fields of architecture, urban design and planning, landscape architecture, sociology, psychology, anthropology, geography, human ecology, criminology and criminal justice.

The first widely published studies of crime and the environment were done by a group of University of Chicago sociologists (Park, Burgess, Shaw and McKay). The researchers viewed the social disorganization or lack of community control found in specific inner-city districts as generating high crime rates, and decreasing in concentric circles away from the central business district. In making this case, the University of Chicago sociologists rejected the tenets of early criminological theory that had focused on the characteristics of individuals as causal agents in crime.

After the early works of Burgess, Park, Shaw and McKay, "defensible space" theory was developed by urban planner Jane Jacobs (1961). Using personal observation and anecdote, Jacobs suggested that residential crime could be reduced by orienting buildings toward the street, clearly distinguishing public and private domains and placing outdoor spaces in proximity to intensively used areas. Jacobs's book *The Death and Life of American Cities* gave police and planners the awareness of the value of "eyes on the street" as a crime prevention tool.

The term "crime prevention through environmental design" first appeared in a 1971 book by criminologist and sociologist C. Ray Jeffery. Inspired by Jacobs's work, Jeffrey challenged the old guard of criminology theory to take an interdisciplinary approach to crime prevention. In this work, Jeffrey analyzed the causation of crime from an interdisciplinary approach, drawing from criminal law, sociology, psychology, administration of justice, criminology, penology and other fields. He also drew from relatively new fields at that time — including systems analysis, decision theory, environmentalism, behaviorism and several models of crime control.

In the early 1970s, Oscar Newman also published a study of residential areas and how they contribute to victimization by criminals. The paper was titled "Defensible Space, Crime Prevention through Urban Design." In this work, Newman explored the concepts of human territoriality, natural surveillance and the modification of existing structures to effectively reduce crime. Newman argued that physical construction of a residential environment could elicit from residents behavior that would, itself, contribute in a major way toward their security. The form of buildings and their groupings enables inhabitants to undertake a significant self-policing function.

The primary function of defensible space is to release latent attitudes in the tenants, which allow them to assume behavior necessary to the protection of their rights and property. *Defensible space* is a surrogate term for the range of mechanisms, real and symbolic barriers, strongly defined areas of influence, and improved opportunities for surveillance that combine to bring the environment under the control of its residents. Newman's work became the foundation for what we know today as crime prevention through environmental design.

Defensible space concepts were tested and studied by a Law Enforcement Assistance Administration (LEAA) grant that was awarded to the

Westinghouse Electric Corporation to study four CPTED demonstration projects. These included a school project in Broward County, Florida; a commercial corridor in Portland, Oregon; residential projects in Hartford, Connecticut, and Minneapolis, Minnesota; and a mass transportation center in Washington, D.C.

The Westinghouse CPTED model maintained Newman's territoriality and surveillance themes but attempted to address and expand on the issues of social factors and control that had been overlooked in Newman's work. Westinghouse researchers asserted that residents needed to participate in bringing the necessary physical and operational changes that could serve as crime prevention measures.

As Defensible Space Theory and CPTED swept the nation's law enforcement and architectural communities, the National Crime Prevention Institute (NCPI) was established as a Division of the School of Police Administration at the University of Louisville in 1971. By 1977, the NCPI had trained over 4000 police officers, criminal justice planners, local government officials, private security representatives and individuals representing numerous other organizations. Today, law enforcement-directed crime prevention programs exist at every level of government in the United States and Canada, largely modeled after the approach developed and institutionalized by police in Great Britain. Many believe the work of the NCPI and related organizations has significantly reduced crime in North America and raised awareness to crime prevention by the public at large.

BASIC CRIME PREVENTION ASSUMPTIONS

Applying CPTED requires a knowledge and understanding of basic crime prevention theory and practice. The National Crime Prevention Institute (NCPI) established a number of operating assumptions for crime prevention officers that are relevant to security personnel and others engaged in loss and crime prevention.

These planning and implementation goals are also relevant to CPTED:

- Potential victims and those responsible for their safety must be assisted to take informed actions to reduce their vulnerability to crime.
- The actions potential victims can take to prevent crime are limited by the control they can exert over their environment.
- Focus must be given to the environment of the potential victim rather than that of the potential criminal.
- Crime prevention is a practical versus a moralistic approach to reducing criminal motivation by reducing the opportunities to commit crime.
- Punishment and rehabilitation capabilities of courts and prisons, police apprehension, etc. can increase the risk perceived by criminals and have a significant, but secondary, role in criminal opportunity reduction.

- Law enforcement agencies have a primary role in the reduction of crime by providing crime prevention education, guidance and information to the public, institutions and other community organizations.
- Crime prevention can be both a cause and effect of efforts to revitalize urban and rural communities.
- Crime prevention knowledge is continually developing and is interdisciplinary in nature; thus, there must be a continual analysis of successful practices and emerging technologies and the sharing of this information among practitioners.

Crime prevention strategies must remain flexible and creative to be effective. Success in one situation does not necessarily mean that success can be transferred to another similar set of circumstances without proper consideration to cultural, environmental, and other factors.

CONTEMPORARY THINKING ON CRIME AND CRIMINALS

Security industry research on the effects of environmental design on crime trends — and vice versa — has resulted in new, useful conclusions. These include:

> Although different crimes are affected in different ways by the environment in which they occur, almost every type of "street crime" (crimes "against persons" or "against property" in FBI Uniform Crime Report terminology) is influenced in some way by physical design, layout, or by situational factors such as the presence of a victim or target, the lack of guardianship, or the lack of surveillance possibilities. Theories of crime, such as environmental criminology, focus specifically on analyzing the environmental factors that provide opportunities for crime to occur. For this reason, most theories of crime can also be classified as *opportunity theories*. Environmental criminology, rational choice, situational crime prevention, routine activity, opportunity model, geography of crime and hot spots of crime are all examples of criminological theories that explain factors that provide criminal opportunities.[1]

Studies conducted between the 1970s and 1990s (primarily by the National Institute of Justice in the United States) demonstrated that certain environments tended to encourage informal social gatherings and contacts and raised the fear of crime. These environments include poorly lighted areas, high-rise buildings with inappropriate tenant mix, apartment buildings with large numbers of units that shared one primary entrance and very heavily trafficked streets. Conversely, researchers found that the presence of community centers and well-maintained public parks, etc.

---

[1] Sorensen, Severin L.; Walsh, Ellen M.; and Myhre, Marina. *Crime Prevention through Environmental Design in Public Housing: Resource Manual for Situational Crime Prevention in Public Housing and Community Settings*. Bethesda, MD; SPARTA Consulting Corporation, 1998. (This manual was prepared through a grant from the Community Safety and Conservation Division, U.S. Department of Housing and Urban Development, Washington, D.C.)

increased social interaction, natural surveillance and other informal social controls, thereby reducing both crime and the fear of crime.

According to the *rational choice* approach, criminal behavior occurs when an offender decides to risk breaking the law after considering personal factors (the need for money, cheap thrills, entertainment, revenge) and situational factors (potential police response, availability of target, lighting, surveillance, access to target, skill and tools needed to commit the crime). Before committing a crime, most criminals (excluding drug-stupid impulse crimes, acts of terrorism, and psychopathic criminals) will evaluate the risks of apprehension, the seriousness of expected punishment, the potential value of gain from the crime, and how pressing is the need for immediate criminal gain.

The decision to commit a specific type of crime is thus a matter of personal decision making based upon an evaluation of numerous variables and the information that is available for the decision-making process. Burglary studies have shown that burglars forego a break-in if they perceive that the home is too great a security challenge, that the value or rewards of the goods to be taken are not worth the effort or the target might be protected by guards, police, capable guardians (housekeepers, large dogs, etc.). Reliable evidence[1] suggests that the decision to commit crime, regardless of substance, is structured by the choice of (1) where the crime occurs, (2) the characteristics of the target, and (3) the means and techniques available for the completion of the crime.

In addition to crime-prevention theory, security professionals should also understand contemporary criminological views on how criminals pick their targets and how criminal choice is influenced by the *perception of vulnerability* the target projects.

Target Selection

Studies of professional and occasional criminals have suggested that they choose their targets with a rational decision-making process. Criminals take note of potential targets every day — keys left in cars, open or unlocked residential or commercial establishments, untended homes while on vacation, etc. Studies of burglary indicate that houses located at the end of cul-de-sacs, surrounded by trees, make very tempting targets. Research indicates most street criminals use public transportation or walk so it is more likely they will gravitate to the center of a city, particularly areas more familiar to them that also provide potential targets in easily accessible and open areas.[2]

---

[1] Siegal, Larry; *Criminology, 6th ed.,* 1999; p. 104, West Wadsworth Publishing Co.
[2] Siegal, Larry. *Criminology, 6th ed.*; 1999; page 105 of "Choice Theory," Wadsworth Publishing Co.

Also:

> The environment shapes the factors that contribute to development of criminal opportunities and to the formation of specific patterns of opportunities. Once patterns of opportunities are created, patterns of crime soon follow.... The crime prevention specialist analyzes those opportunities, patterns of opportunities, and patterns of crime to devise and implement appropriate situational and crime specific prevention measures.[1]

Research also indicates that criminal choice is influenced by the *perception* of target availability and vulnerability. Criminals often choose certain neighborhoods for crimes because they are familiar and well traveled, because they appear more open and vulnerable, and because they offer more potential escape routes. Thus, the more suitable and accessible the target, the more likely the crime will occur.

Concept of Capable Guardian

Routine activity theory suggests that the presence of capable guardians may deter crime. Criminals will generally avoid targets or victims who are perceived to be armed, capable of resistance, or potentially dangerous. Criminals will generally stay away from areas they feel are aggressively patrolled by police, security guards, or by nosy neighbors. Likewise, they avoid passive barriers such as alarm systems, fences, locks or related physical barriers.

This avoidance is intuitively logical to the experienced law enforcement or security practitioner. Criminals will look for the easiest path rather than expose themselves to greater risk unless they perceive the risk is justified to override the risk. The concepts of natural surveillance and capable guardians are very powerful tools for reducing the perceived vulnerability a site poses to a potential criminal. CPTED strategies employ the concept of capable guardians within the organizational methods of strategies.

Criminal Choice

Criminals or potential criminals are conditioned by personal factors[2] that may lead them to choose crime. Research also shows that criminals are more likely to desist from crime if they believe:

- Future earnings from criminal activities will be low.
- Other attractive but legal income-generating opportunities are available.

Agnew[3] believes that people more likely to choose a life of crime over conformity to socially acceptable behavior demonstrate the following personality traits:

---

[1] Sorensen et al., p. 7–18.
[2] See Pezzin, Liliana. Criminal Careers, *Journal of Criminal Law and Criminology*, 11, 29–50, 1995.
[3] Agnew, Robert. Determinism, Indeterminism, and Crime: An Empirical Exploration, *Criminology*, 33. 83–109, 1995.

- They lack typical social constraints and perceive freedom of movement.
- They have less self-control and do not fear criminal punishment.
- They are typically facing a serious personal problem that they feel forces them to choose risky behavior (similar to the classic white-collar criminal).

At any given time there are individuals who are capable of criminal behavior. They will take advantage of vulnerable targets, whether they are people, buildings or other facilities, and the perception of vulnerability drives the criminal choice, in terms of which actual target they attack.

Situational Crime Prevention

Situational crime prevention was developed in the late 1970s and early 1980s in Great Britain. Although it was influenced by Jeffrey's work in CPTED and Newman's work in *Defensible Space*, that research only contributed to the expansion of situational crime prevention, not its initial inception. CPTED and Defensible Space theory were more focused on the design of buildings and places, whereas situational crime prevention sought to reduce crime opportunities in all behavioral contexts.

Situational prevention is comprised of opportunity-reducing measures that are directed at very specific forms of crime. It is involved in the management, design or manipulation of the immediate environment in as systematic and permanent a way as possible — so as to increase the effort and risks of crime and reduce the rewards as perceived by a wide range of offenders.

Research in Great Britain caused a shift in the focus of practical crime control policy from attention on the offender and his or her personality or background to the general influences of the surrounding environment that contribute to criminal behavior by creating opportunities that may not otherwise exist. Ronald Clarke's work (cited above) contributed to practical situational crime prevention by developing crime prevention techniques that can generally be applied to almost any situation.

Situational Crime Prevention has applied CPTED in public housing. However, experienced security practitioners can readily apply these techniques to commercial, industrial and governmental facilities. As has been noted:

> Situational crime prevention is the crime prevention approach that utilizes rational choice theory as its theoretical framework, follows a methodology that analyzes the opportunities for a specific crime to occur in a particular situation, and prescribes solutions targeted at removing those criminal opportunities.
>
> Rational choice theory draws on the model of the likely offender who weighs the costs, risks and rewards of committing a specific crime at a particular time and place.... Situational crime prevention measures are effective because they are practical, cost-effective, permanent alteration

Crime Prevention through Environmental Design: CPTED

to the physical environment that are tailored to fit specific types of crime. Four overarching approaches that guide...situational crime prevention techniques are increase effort [needed to commit crime], increasing risks [associated with crime], reduce rewards [of crime], and remove excuses [for illegal behavior by inducing shame or guilt].[1]

Increasing the effort for crime is often accomplished by the following tactics:

1. Target-hardening measures increase the effort by creating physical barriers such as locks, screens, steel doors, fences and shatterproof glass.
2. Access control measures increase the effort by limiting access to the vulnerable areas.
3. Removing or deflecting offenders increases the effort by displacing offenders outside the target area.
4. Controlling the facilitators of crime (limiting access to the tools and devices that criminals use or need to commit a crime, i.e., removing access to cans of spray paint, collect-call-only public telephones, shopping carts, towing abandoned cars, weapon screening policies, etc.).

Increasing the perceived risks associated with crime — such that there is increased risk of the criminal being caught in the act — is accomplished with the following tactics:

1. Entry and exit screening increases risk by monitoring who enters an area and what and who is leaving the property
2. Formal surveillance by CCTV and security guards
3. Surveillance by employees, concierge, parking attendants, security guard stations
4. Natural surveillance with window placement, external lighting, limiting blindspots, cutting hedges

Reducing anticipated rewards is accomplished with the following tactics:

1. *Target removal eliminates the incentive for crime.* A no-cash policy removes the threat of robbery; other target removal strategies include direct deposit checks, removable car radios, cashless transactions.
2. *Identifying the property of value.* Identifying stolen property makes it more difficult for criminals to sell and easier to return to the owner.
3. *Reducing temptation.* Examples include gender neutral listing, rapid repair of vandalism and graffiti.
4. *Denying the benefits of gain.* Plantings on potential graffiti walls, ink explosion kits in bank money bags, computer PIN numbers for credit cards and car radios, rendering them useless if stolen or tampered with.

---

[1] Sorensen et al., p. 7–18.

Removing the excuses of noncompliant behavior is accomplished through:

1. *Rule and boundary setting.* This refers to the rules and regulations that all organizations need to impose on their employees' bad clients. Making rules explicit removes the ambiguity that permits legitimate persons to commit offenses and excuse their crimes with claims of ignorance or misunderstanding).
2. *Stimulating conscience.* Policies that openly declare against shoplifting, speeding, smoking, drug use, littering, etc.
4. *Facilitating compliance.* If the desired behavior or outcome is made easier than the illegal way, most people will choose to comply. Examples include designated trash sites to stop illegal dumping, or public bathrooms to prevent inappropriate bathroom activities, convenient trash bins for litter.

In short, CPTED and other crime prevention approaches, such as situational crime prevention, rely on the assumption that offensible spaces can be improved and transformed from a crime generator to a powerful crime prevention tool. From a routine activity and environmental criminology perspective, certain situations or environments may curb, constrain or limit criminal opportunities. Thus, while certain conditions create criminal opportunities of particular environments, certain environments can prevent crimes from occurring.

Potential Offenders' Perspective

Research has shown that the features of the physical environment can influence the opportunity for crime to occur. The physical surroundings clearly influence the potential offenders' perceptions and evaluation of a potential crime site. Part of this evaluation also includes determining the availability and visibility of natural guardians (residents, passers-by, dogs, etc.) at or in close proximity to the site under consideration. Offenders, when deciding whether or not to commit a crime in a location, generally do so after considering the following questions,[1] assuming a rational offender perspective:

- How easy will it be to enter the area?
- How visible, attractive or vulnerable do the targets appear?
- What are the chances of being seen?
- If seen, will the people in the area do something about it?
- Is there a quick, direct route for leaving the site after the crime is committed?

---

[1] Physical Environment and Crime, National Institute of Justice, January, 1996. For a copy of this report, contact the NIJ at http://ncjrs.aspensys.com:81/catalog.html.

Crime Prevention through Environmental Design: CPTED

Thus, the physical features of a site may influence the choices of potential offenders by altering the chances of detection and by reshaping the public versus private space in question. The main point is, if a potential criminal feels the chances of detection are low or if detected they will be able to exit without being identified or apprehended, the likelihood of crime increases. In effect, if a location lacks a natural guardian, it becomes a more likely target for crime.

Defensible Space

Oscar Newman created defensible space theory when he studied the relationship between particular design features and crime that occurred in public housing developments in New York. The four components of Newman's study were:

1. Defining perceived zones of territorial influence
2. Providing surveillance opportunities for residents and their guests
3. Placing residential structures (public areas and entries) close to safe areas
4. Designing sites and buildings so those occupants are not perceived as being stigmatized as vulnerable

Those sites and buildings that were perceived as most vulnerable and isolated had similar characteristics. These include:

- Unassigned open spaces were unprotected, uncared for, and provided opportunities for residents and outsiders to engage themselves in illegitimate activities.
- An unlimited number of opportunities to penetrate the site with uncontrolled access. The multitude of entry points provided offenders with easy entry and numerous escape routes.
- The lack of territoriality and boundary definition that discouraged legitimate residents from claiming space and taking control of the site. Residents were often unable to recognize strangers from legitimate users.
- Lack of opportunities for natural surveillance and supervision.
- Design conflicts between the incompatible uses and users. Incompatible activities are located next to one another.

Newman used his theory to modify housing developments by implementing some of the most basic elements of CPTED design: high fences, designated paths, and architectural treatment to distinguish private, semi-private, semi-public, and public spaces. Defensible space design should link territoriality and surveillance by creating designs in which the observer feels the area under surveillance is under his sphere of influence and part of his responsibility to prevent crime. The environment of the building should be designed so that the observer can recognize or identify a victim or target. The observer should feel he has a vested interest to intervene and prevent crime from occurring.

Increased legitimate traffic of people and vehicles is a positive experience that is characteristic of a safe place. People who live, work and play in an area will tend to feel a certain ownership and responsibility, and try to protect that area. Proximity to areas with a high volume of legitimate usage encourages the same sense of territoriality, responsibility and effective surveillance.

Newman's work came under criticism for methodological weakness, and academicians viewed Newman's work as architectural — deterministic.[1] Subsequent CPTED demonstration projects in the 1970s by the Westinghouse Corporation were generally unsuccessful as they attempted to extend the defensible space concept to school, commercial and transportation environments in which territorial behavior is much less natural than in the residential context.

Tim Crowe and CPTED

Tim Crowe (1991) further refined the ideas of Oscar Newman. With his experience in the Westinghouse CPTED project during the 1970s, Crowe established a system to categorize CPTED solutions. He organized this CPTED methodology to match the function of the crime area, similar to Newman's layering of space from private to public spaces.

According to Crowe:

> ...in the CPTED approach, a design is proper if it recognizes the designated use of the space; defines the crime problem incidental to and the solution compatible with the designated use; and incorporates the crime prevention strategies that enhance (or at least do not impair) the effective use of the space.[2]

Crowe became director of the National Crime Prevention Institute, as part of the University of Louisville during the mid-1980s. Under his direction, CPTED was presented as a training tool for thousands of police officers who attended the Institute for in-service and basic training.[3]

---

[1] Newman, Oscar; *Architectural Design for Crime Prevention*; Washington, D.C. Law Enforcement Assistance Administration, 1971. See also: Newman, Oscar; *Defensible Space: Crime Prevention through Urban Design*. Macmillan, New York, 1973.
[2] Crowe, Timothy D.; *Crime Prevention through Environmental Design: Applications of Architectural Design and Space Management Concepts*. National Crime Prevention Institute, Butterworth-Heinemann, Boston, MA, 1991.
[3] Atlas, Randall. "Violence in Prison: Architectural Determinism." Dissertation, Florida State University, 1982.

CPTED Survey

The following questions provide an evaluation of the purpose of the space, definition in terms of management and identity and its design as it relates to desired function and behavior management (sometimes referred to as *the three D's*, but expanded here to include other aspects as well):

	Yes	No	N/A
DESIGNATION			
What is the designated purpose of this space?	☐	☐	☐
For what purpose was it originally intended?	☐	☐	☐
How well does the space support its current use or its intended use?	☐	☐	☐
Is there a conflict? If so, how and where?	☐	☐	☐
DEFINITION			
How is the space defined?	☐	☐	☐
Is the ownership of the space clear?	☐	☐	☐
Where are the borders of the space?	☐	☐	☐
Are there social or cultural definitions that affect how the space is being, or will be used?	☐	☐	☐
Are the legal/administrative rules clearly established in policy and effectively enforced?	☐	☐	☐
Are signs present indicating the proper use of the space or defining limits of access?	☐	☐	☐
Are there any conflicts or confusion between purpose and definition of the space?	☐	☐	☐
DESIGN			
How well does the physical design support the intended function?	☐	☐	☐
How well does the physical design support the desired or accepted behaviors?	☐	☐	☐
Does the physical design conflict with or impede the productive use of the space or proper functioning of the intended human activity?	☐	☐	☐
Is there any confusion or conflict in which physical design is intended to control or modify behaviors?	☐	☐	☐
DETERENCE			
Does the presence of security personnel deter illegitimate activity and promote intended behavior?	☐	☐	☐
Does the physical design and layout permit good surveillance and control of access to and from the property?	☐	☐	☐
Does the presence of intended behavior deter or discourage illegal or illegitimate activities?	☐	☐	☐
DETECT			
Is there the ability to control entry onto the property or building?	☐	☐	☐
Is there an assessment process of when an intrusion is legitimate or illegitimate?	☐	☐	☐

ASSET PROTECTION AND SECURITY MANAGEMENT HANDBOOK

	Yes	No	N/A
Is the detection of intrusions accomplished by the physical design, mechanical technology systems or operational manpower?	☐	☐	☐
Is the communication of an intrusion to some person or agency responsible for responding?	☐	☐	☐
DELAY			
Are there passive barriers?	☐	☐	☐
Are there active barriers?	☐	☐	☐
Are there guards or designated responders?	☐	☐	☐
How much time is needed in delay for the property to detect and respond?	☐	☐	☐
RESPONSE			
What are the roles and the post orders of the responder guard?	☐	☐	☐
What equipment is needed to support a complete response?	☐	☐	☐
What are the tactics used to respond quickly and clearly?	☐	☐	☐
What training is given to respond to the appropriate level of threat?	☐	☐	☐
REPORT			
What is the communications network to document intrusions or call for further assistance?	☐	☐	☐
What is the written protocol for incident reports?	☐	☐	☐
How is the documentation organized and stored?	☐	☐	☐
Is the information in sufficient detail and clear?	☐	☐	☐
DISCRIMINATE			
Is there training for staff to discriminate or distinguish legitimate from illegitimate users or threats?	☐	☐	☐
Is the equipment sufficiently sensitive to distinguish false from real threats?	☐	☐	☐
NEUTRALIZE			
Has the threat been sufficiently deterred?	☐	☐	☐
Has the system been reset and tested to prevent complacency or false alarms?	☐	☐	☐
Have the criminals, attackers or threats been controlled, law enforcement contacted, and the scene re-secured?	☐	☐	☐
In the event of fire, smoke or flood, has the threat been neutralized and damage assessed, and the scene secured to prevent contamination or pilferage?	☐	☐	☐

If a conflict or unanswered question is revealed after using the questions above to assess a physical space, a modification should take place. A vulnerable area could be an indication that the space is poorly defined or not properly designated to support or control the intended function, thus increasing the likelihood that crime or the fear of crime may develop. Thus, the challenge is developing an automatic teller machine (ATM) location in a shopping mall location to ensure it is not only functional but also maximizes the personal safety of legitimate users.

Once the questions above have been answered, the space is assessed according to how well it supports *natural access control, natural surveillance* and *territoriality*. These questions are intended to ensure there are no conflicts between the intended space, activity and expected behaviors. For example, if an access control system is difficult to use or experiences frequent outages, employees will often prop doors open to make their routine travel more convenient. In addition to choosing a poor access control system, the original designers also failed to educate users on the importance of maintaining the integrity of the security system.

CONCEPTS OF RISK MANAGEMENT

Anticipating, recognizing and properly appraising and taking action to remove or reduce a risk form the basis of managing risks in a community or organization. Applying the concepts of risk to crime and loss prevention form the definition of Crime/Loss Risk Management, which forms the basis of crime prevention in general and CPTED in particular.

The NCPI defines risk management, in the context of crime/loss prevention, as *the anticipation, recognition, and initiation of a risk and the initiation of some action to remove the risk or reduce the potential loss from it to an acceptable level*. To properly apply any crime or loss prevention techniques or properly assess risks, security practitioners must understand the basic concepts of risk management.

- *Dynamic risk* is defined as any situation that carries the potential for both benefit and cost or loss.
- *Pure risk* is defined as any situation where there is no possibility for any benefit, only for cost or loss.

Risk Management consists of the following steps:

1. *Anticipation*: reviewing existing or planned structures and processes to determine the likelihood or probability of loss, and building corrections in the design, equipment, materials or procedures of existing or proposed facilities and processes to prevent losses.
2. *Recognition*: recognizing opportunities that exist because of the lack of crime/loss prevention techniques into the original design of buildings or procedural operations. The recognition of a crime or loss risk is the first step to remove or reduce a loss opportunity.
3. *Appraisal*: consists of determining four steps:
   a. Probable frequency of commission
   b. Probable severity of loss

c. Possible severity of loss
d. Consequences of the loss to the business

The probable and possible loss factors are of the greatest concern to the business. Smaller losses occurring at frequent intervals may create unacceptable losses, infrequent major losses could endanger the business itself. When all risks have been arranged in order of the probability factors, alternate methods of dealing with those risks can be determined. It is often not beneficial to deal with each risk individually, but to take a logical and systematic approach to problem solving by dealing with the most serious vulnerabilities first.

There are five available alternatives for handling risk:

1. *Risk avoidance.* The first choice to be considered. The possibility of eliminating the existence of criminal opportunity or avoiding the creation of such an opportunity is always the best solution, when additional considerations or factors are not created as a result of this action that would create a greater risk. As an example, removing all the cash from a retail establishment would eliminate the opportunity for stealing the cash — but it would also eliminate the ability to conduct business.
2. *Risk reduction.* When avoiding or eliminating the criminal opportunity conflicts with the ability to conduct business, the next step is the reduction of the opportunity and potential loss to the lowest level consistent with the function of the business. In the example above, the application of risk reduction might result in the business keeping only enough cash on hand for one day's operation.
3. *Risk spreading.* Assets that remain exposed after the application of reduction and avoidance are the subjects of risk spreading. This is the concept that limits loss or potential losses by exposing the perpetrator to the probability of detection and apprehension prior to the consummation of the crime through the application of perimeter lighting, barred windows and intrusion detection systems. The idea here is to reduce the time available to steal assets and escape without apprehension.
4. *Risk transfer.* Transferring risks to other alternatives when those risks have not been reduced to acceptable levels. The two primary methods of accomplishing risk transfer are to insure the assets or raise prices to cover the loss in the event of a criminal act. Generally speaking, when the first three steps have been properly applied, the costs of transferring risks are much lower.
5. *Risk acceptance.* All remaining risks must simply be assumed by the business as a risk of doing business. Included with these accepted losses are deductibles which have been made as part of the insurance coverage.

It is neither cost-effective nor practical to attempt to provide 100 percent protection for any enterprise. The cost of the application of protection can be measured by the sum of the cost of the design and acquisition of the systems, maintenance, and any costs that, as a result of the applications, conflict with the purpose for which the business exists. The risk management alternatives set forth above provide the best measurable methodology for assuring asset protection with flexibility and adaptation in any business situation.

REDUCING CRIME THROUGH PHYSICAL DESIGN

Because the subjects of vulnerability assessment, barriers, locks, alarm systems and related subjects are covered elsewhere in this handbook, we will concentrate on proper design and planning for both new and existing commercial buildings. Planning must be developed in conjunction with community and professional groups who play a key role in new construction or redesign of existing facilities. By understanding how these groups work together, the security practitioner is in the best position to facilitate the proper design features into the facility to prevent future crime and loss opportunities.

Security professionals recognize the importance of early engagement in the planning of new or renovation of existing facilities. Building CPTED into the initial planning is clearly more cost-effective than attempting to add changes after construction has begun. Some communities have ordinances that require the participation of crime prevention officers in this process to ensure that planned facilities are built with proper consideration for crime prevention. Some corporations have policies requiring the same considerations — that facility planning to ensure life safety and crime prevention is considered and added to building plans early in the process.

Introduction to Planning the Building

Security needs for a building must be determined early, as part of the project programming and definition process. Burglary, industrial espionage, shoplifting, riots, vandalism, assault, rape, murder and employee theft are crimes that imperil lives and drive up the cost of doing business. As crime increases, incorporating security into the design and construction in all building types is critical for crime prevention.

Designing without security in mind can lead to lawsuits, injuries, and expensive retrofitting with protection equipment, and the need for additional security personnel. If not properly planned for and installed, that equipment can distort important building design functions, add to security personnel costs and result in exposed unsightly alarm systems or blocked doors and windows.

The Architectural Planning Process

Any building must meet specific functional criteria; and, from the function, the design evolves. A building must permit efficient job performance, meet the needs of the user, and protect the user from safety hazards and criminal acts that affect the production and service delivery of the building's users.

Securing a building that was not originally planned to be secure is expensive. Architects have to sacrifice much more of a building's openness in retrofitting for security than they would if the facility had been designed for security from the outset. Protection personnel and operating expenses are greater than they need to be because of a lack of forethought during the design of the facility. This condition is particularly evident in many of today's buildings, in which modern design and materials have resulted in facilities that are especially vulnerable.

Understanding how a building is designed will provide insight into the architectural process. The following steps illustrate a traditional building construction process:

1. *Programming.* Information supposedly provided by the owner to the architect about the building, its purpose and occupants.
2. *Schematic design.* The architect processes the programming information and develops bubble diagrams reflecting circulation patterns and proximity relationships. The diagrams evolve into single-line drawings of the floor plan, site plan and elevations, as the beginnings of engineering considerations.
3. *Design development.* The architect has presented his or her ideas to the client and made design corrections. The drawings become more sophisticated, and include more engineering considerations such as structural, mechanical, electrical, ventilation, and site planning. Drawings are put into a larger scale, usually 1/4 in.: 1 foot.
4. *Construction documents (or working drawings).* These are the final drawings prepared for construction purposes. All technical data is presented in the drawings and is accompanied by technically written specifications.
5. *Bids for construction and selection of contractor.* The architectural drawings and specifications are put out to bid by qualified contractors who will provide the service at the lowest price.

It should be evident that the stage to first bring up security needs is in the programming phase of design. It is primarily the client's responsibility to define precisely the potential threats to people, information and property, and to determine the level and cost of the protection that will be provided. Many owners, clients and developers may only have a casual awareness of security and of what they need to protect. They may not have the knowledge and experience to develop adequate strategies or security plans.

Crime Prevention through Environmental Design: CPTED

That is why programming for security is very important. Security needs must be determined early. Defining what is needed usually involves a combination of common sense and methodical investigation.

The architect's job is to convert the security requirements identified by the security professional into programmatic directives. The design team uses the program to start the design of the building. The architectural program is one of the most important phases in the whole building process. The program establishes the scope of work, the parameters and initial budgeting for the building.

The program is like the menu in a restaurant, defining what you are going to serve, who you are going to serve, and how much you are going to charge. The architectural program is the menu of the building. This is the point to make a difference with security. From this point forward, security considerations will always require changes in drawing — and additional time and money.

Architects and designers can make the greatest contribution to meeting a project's security objectives. Architects generally make the basic design decisions about circulation, access, building materials, fenestration and many other features that can support or thwart overall security aims.

Building clients and design professionals are not the only ones concerned about security during the design process. Many jurisdictions require security review by the police as part of the building-permit approval process, much the same as with fire safety requirements. Inspectors evaluate the plans for obvious spots where assaults, muggings, break-ins and other crimes of opportunity may exist. Many jurisdictions have security ordinances that require certain lighting levels and secure door and window designs and hardware.

If security is treated as one of the many design requirements, then the implementation and costs for such measures will be no more a burden to the project owners than fire safety features or landscaping requirements. The basic premise of security design is that proper design and effective use of the built environment can lead to a reduction in the incidence and fear of crime and an increase in the quality of life.

The environmental design approach to security recognizes the space's designated or redesignated use — which defines a solution compatible with that use. Good security design enhances the effective use of the space while preventing crime.

The emphasis in security design falls on the design and use of space, a practice that deviates from the traditional target-hardening approach to crime prevention. Traditional target hardening focuses predominantly on denying access to a crime target through physical or artificial barrier techniques such as locks, alarms, fences and gates. The traditional approach tends to overlook opportunities for natural access control and surveillance. Sometimes, the natural and normal uses of the environment can accomplish the effects of mechanical hardening and surveillance.

Security design also involves the effort to integrate the efforts of community citizens and law enforcement officers to prevent crime through the design and use of the built environment. As we have seen, design professionals can use three basic strategies for crime prevention through environmental design: natural access control, natural surveillance, and natural territorial reinforcement. Each of these strategies can be implemented through organized methods (manpower, i.e., police, security guards, receptionists); mechanical methods (technology products, alarms, CCTV, gadgets); and natural methods (site planning, design, landscaping, signage).

Access control is a design concept directed at reducing the opportunity and accessibility for crime. Organized methods of access control include security guard forces. Mechanical strategies include target hardening such as locks and card key systems. Windows may have protective glazing that withstands blows without breaking. Doors and window hardware may have special material and mountings that make them hard to remove or tamper with. Walls, floors or doors may be specially reinforced in high-security areas with materials that are difficult to penetrate. Natural methods of access control make use of spatial definition and circulation patterns.

An example of natural design is the use of security zoning. By dividing space into zones of differing security levels, such as unrestricted, controlled, and restricted, sensitive areas can be more effectively protected. The focus of access control strategies is to deny access to a crime target and create in offenders a perception of risk and detection, delay and response.

Effective Access Control

Effective access control is often the key to many security threats. Access control might be strongly considered in these areas:

- All entrances and exits to the site and building
- Internal access points in restricted or controlled areas
- Environmental and building features used to gain access (trees, ledges, skylights, balconies, windows, tunnels)
- Security screening devices (guard stations, surveillance, identification equipment)

Surveillance strategies are a design concept directed at keeping intruders under observation. Organized surveillance strategies include police and guard patrols. Lighting and CCTV are mechanical strategies for surveillance; natural strategies include windows, low landscaping and raised entrances.

Crime Prevention through Environmental Design: CPTED

Territorial strategies suggest that physical design can create or extend the sphere of territorial influence so that users develop a sense of proprietorship. This sense of territorial influence can alert potential offenders that they do not belong there, that they are at risk of being seen and identified, and that their behavior will not be tolerated or go unreported.

The architect can play a vital role in designing effective natural access control, surveillance, and territorial reinforcement strategies. Security design poses three challenges for architects:

1. *Determining requirements.* Security needs must be determined early in the project's programming and problem definition stage. The design team should analyze the designated purpose of how the space or building will be used. The designated purpose will be clear when designers examine the cultural, legal and physical definitions of what the prescribed, desired and acceptable behaviors are for that space. The space can then be designed to support desired behaviors and the intended function of the space. The design team should inquire about existing policies and practices so that this information will be integrated in the programming process.
2. *Knowing the technology.* Rapid substantial advances in the technology of security systems make keeping up-to-date a challenge. Many projects today, even routine ones, may involve security system specialists as part of the team. As with other areas of specialization, architects must have a basic understanding of security principles. Design professionals must be in a position to evaluate and implement technical security specialists and security equipment manufacturers.
3. *Understanding architectural implications.* Designs must integrate the complicated and sometimes conflicting goals of security and life safety issues as well as other project variables and requirements. Space, function and people must be planned to support the security objectives of detection, delay and response to unwanted or criminal situations.

SITE DEVELOPMENT AND SECURITY ZONING

Whenever possible, security planning should begin during the site selection process. The greatest opportunity for achieving a secure operation begins with locating a site that meets architectural requirements and also provides for security advantages. The security analysis in site planning should begin with an assessment of conditions on-site and off-site, taking into account topography, vegetation, adjacent land uses, circulation patterns, neighborhood crime patterns, police patrol patterns, sight lines, areas for concealment, location of utilities, and existing and proposed lighting. Other key factors for site security planning are off-site pedestrian circulation, vehicular circulation, access points for service vehicles and personnel, employee access and circulation, and visitor access and circulation.

The site analysis represents the first level of security defense planning, which considers the site perimeters and grounds of the facility. Site design measures can include walls, heavy plantings, fences, berms, ditches, lighting, natural topographic separations — or a combination of such elements. Several factors to consider at this stage are:

- What is the physical makeup of the site, and how does it influence security?
- What is the land use surrounding the site?
- What is the type and frequency of criminal activity in the area?

A site that has high security risks may not be automatically disqualified just because of crime if the location is desirable. The owner may choose the site but acknowledge the security threats and vulnerabilities and address them properly through design, technology, manpower and security management.

The second level of security defense planning is the perimeter or exterior of the building. The building shell and its openings represent, after the site perimeter and grounds, the crucial second line of defense against intrusion and forced entry. The area being protected should be thought of as having four sides as well as a top and bottom. The principal points of entry to be considered are the windows, doors, skylights, storm sewers, roof, floor and fire escapes.

Doors and windows are, by nature, among the weakest links of a building and inherently provide poor resistance to penetration. Attention must be paid to the doorframe, latches, locks, hinges, and panic hardware, the surrounding wall and the door leaf. Window considerations for secure design include the type of glazing material, the window frame, the window hardware and the size of the opening.

The building shell itself is a security consideration, because the type of construction will determine the level of security. Most stud walls and metal deck roof assemblies can be compromised with hand tools in less than two minutes. Unreinforced concrete block walls can be broken quickly with a sledgehammer or a car can drive through them. In South Florida recently, two Service Merchandise stores were broken into by cars driving through the front of the stores. The architect's challenge — and the security consultant's task — is to provide security that is attractive and unobtrusive, while providing balanced and effective deterrence to unauthorized access.

The third level of security that the architect should design for is internal space protection and specific internal point security. Sensitive areas within a facility may warrant special protection with security technology, manpower and restricted design circulation. The level of protection may be based on zones, with access to the zones limited to persons with the required level of security clearance.

Crime Prevention through Environmental Design: CPTED

Application of the zoning concept depends on the control of employees, visitors, vendors and others. The idea is to allow them to reach their destinations but prevent them from entering areas where they have no business. Controlling access to each department of a building, where appropriate, screens out undesirable visitors, reduces congestion, and helps employees identify and challenge unauthorized persons.

The zoning design goals are accomplished through the use of the following types of zones: *unrestricted zones, controlled zones* and *restricted zones.* Some areas of a facility should be completely unrestricted to persons entering the area during the hours of designated use. The design of unrestricted zones should encourage persons to conduct their business and leave the facility without entering controlled or restricted zones. Unrestricted zones might include lobbies, reception areas, snack bars, certain personnel and administrative offices, and public meeting rooms.

Controlled zone movement requires a valid purpose for entry. Once admitted to a controlled area, persons may travel from one department to another without severe restriction. Controlled zones might include administrative offices, staff dining rooms, security offices, office working areas and loading docks.

Restricted zones are sensitive areas that are limited to staff assigned to departments within those particular areas. Sections within restricted zones frequently require additional access control. Functions and departments located in restricted zones may include vaults, sensitive records, chemicals and drugs, food preparation, mechanical areas, telephone equipment, electrical equipment, control rooms, laboratories, laundry, sterile supply, special equipment and sensitive work areas.

The security-zoning concept is being used effectively in the designs of hospitals, jails, courthouses, laboratories and industrial plants. Once circulation patterns are successfully resolved through security zoning, physical security systems (mechanical solutions) can be considered.

Security professionals who have studied environmental security design know that the first level of security planning starts with securing the site perimeter and grounds. There are many means available of securing the grounds against trespassing. The most common ways are walls, chain-link fences, moats and other barriers. One way to deter trespassers is to use landscaping.

Landscaping can establish one of the most important action steps against trespassing by establishing a property line. Marking the property boundary is the first step because it actually deters some people who might otherwise walk in and do something.

ASSET PROTECTION AND SECURITY MANAGEMENT HANDBOOK

Privacy versus Security

There is a dilemma when it comes to establishing privacy versus security in project developments. The balance can be difficult and varies from application to application. A low hedge or fence psychologically and physically says what is public and what is private property. A picket fence establishes an edge without obscuring the view or limiting surveillance. If trees are added above the fence, there can be a sense of enclosure but still have the ability to see into the property between the fence and tree canopy.

Block or brick walls offer protection to the hiding thief as well as securing the property owner. Bare walls also invite graffiti. Walls supplemented with landscaping can provide protection and a more effective barrier. Thorny bougainvillea, carissa, wild lime or rather toothy brushes planted in combination with a wall can combine the best of resources.

Individual plants can discourage trespassers when strategically placed. Thorny shrubs could be a safety problem if small children are abundant, and pose a challenge for maintenance crews. Many of the thorny plants come in different sizes to fit the different landscaping needs. Carissa comes in three sizes: emerald blanket, which is a dwarf variety; boxwood blanket, which is an intermediate variety growing up to six feet; and carissa grandiflora, which grows to seven or eight feet.

In a residential application, it is a good idea for the landscaper to provide shrub masses or low-ground coverage that may discourage breaking and entering of windows. Tall, large-leaved plants that could visually protect the intruder should be avoided. Pygmy date palms in front of windows will not block breezes, but their needle-sharp thorns at the base of the palm fronds will slow down anyone climbing through them. Other plants that provide similar coverage are the Jerusalem thorn and cinnecord.

A well-maintained hedge along the building perimeter can discourage people from reaching or crawling through to access a window. Even if a burglar enters through a door and leaves through a window, it will be much more difficult to carry out TVs and computers through bushes, hedges, ferns and other landscaping barriers.

Earth berms are commonly used in landscaping but, if not carefully used, can create visual obstructions. One example of this was a public park that used berms to break up the monotony of the flat site. The result was a total visual obstruction of play areas, used by local gangs, from supervision by roving local police. The berms had to be lowered to no greater than two and a half feet.

Landscaping can be used appropriately to create effective crime prevention measures, or it can create criminal opportunities. The following landscaping and planting considerations are critical for safe design:

- Avoid planting that obscures extensive parts of a main path or recreation area.
- Planting should take into account growth rates and any maintenance requirements and expectations.
- Low-growing plants should be set back one yard (or meter) from the edge of paths or walkways.
- Low-growing shrubs should be maintained not to exceed 32 inches in height.
- Spiny or thorny shrubs should be used in places that could be hiding places, or areas of illegitimate activity, or close to walls where people are desired to be kept away from windows. Thorny plantings may attract garbage and litter and may need a low-perimeter fence to prevent foot traffic or wind-blown debris.
- Hard landscaping should be vandal-resistant and not provide potential missiles, such as loose gravel or stones, or cobbles.
- Landscape features and furniture should not provide the means to gain access to the property, or to see over walls or hedges into rooms or gardens. Street furniture should be designed for short-term use and limit the ability to sleep on or stretch out and make into a bedroom.
- Tree canopies should be trimmed to eight feet in height where appropriate to provide a clear unobstructed line of site, and reduce hiding spots and ambush opportunities.

Lighting for security should be from the tops of trees downward. A security director should be involved in the landscaping and lighting plans for coordination. It is important to realize if the trees are deciduous and shed their leaves, or remain full all year round like pine trees. The type and placement of trees can drastically affect the exterior lighting for full security coverage. A security light that is too bright may reduce the observer's ability to see into the site. Low-level, well-distributed lighting helps reduce night blindness. The type and placement of trees also affects the ability of CCTV to function properly. (For more on security aspects of lighting, see Chapter 12.)

On a blueprint of a site plan, the camera placement may appear to have clear lines of vision. However, when the CCTV plan is overlaid with the landscaping design, there may be numerous blind spots. The height and fullness of the trees must be considered for camera placement.

In summary, the placement of trees and shrubs, and understanding the architecture of plants, can help the security professional make a property more secure.

SECURITY DESIGN CRITERIA FOR PARKING FACILITIES

To achieve environmental security in parking facilities, there must be a balance between design and circulation patterns, surveillance opportunities, and access control: the key principles of CPTED. To develop the proper mix of these elements, the client must identify the threats:

- Parking areas run the risks of crime and accidents.
- Thefts of cars and thefts from vehicles are the primary threats.
- Personal threats include thefts from the person, assault, robbery and rape.
- Vandalism may also be a threat for consideration.
- Safety concerns must also be considered.
- Traffic flow must be clearly shown to discourage collisions or running over pedestrians.
- Awareness of slip and fall accident potential can be planned for.

Considerations:

1. The first and most important point to consider in planning a safe and secure parking area is the layout. Good design will allow for smooth traffic ingress and egress. The spacing of the parking slots and travel lanes can prevent or initiate accidents. Location of entrances and exits is a design factor that can assist in blocking or creating opportunities for outsiders to gain access to the parking area. The necessary movement of persons or vehicles is known as a circulation pattern.
2. Open-area parking lots should consider the parking surface and the impact that it has on maintenance, visibility, reflection of lighting and drainage. Open parking areas will often have landscaping that can provide hiding places and block visibility. Landscaping under Crime Prevention Through Environmental Design (CPTED) guidelines should be intermittent in size and texture. Instead of planting a solid hedge of bushes or trees, a more effective way of achieving environmental security is a combination of low hedges and high-canopy trees. This combination allows unobstructed vision and no hiding places for criminals, while providing the required greenery on the site. The rule of thumb is hedges lower that $2\frac{1}{2}$ feet and tree bottoms higher than eight feet.
3. Enclosed parking structures should consider the location and visibility of the stairways and elevators. Many parking structures have the sides of the parking garage covered to hide the ugliness of cars. However, with a priority given to surveillance, the design would allow open building fronts with heavy cables as the wall system. The cables have been used to prevent cars from falling over the edge. Cable systems have been used extensively in parking garages for over a decade. The benefit of open facades for garage structures are the visibility and surveillance from the ground to the cars, and increased capability of hearing calls for assistance.

4. Enclosed parking structures must also consider the circulation of traffic, wall and ceiling finish color, and the use of CCTV and alarm systems. The most desired traffic flow is one-way movement. If the garage is part of a high-rise with structural columns coming through, paint the columns a bright and different color than the walls or floor surface. Columns may even have bumper guards to prevent scraping. Clear graphics are needed for direction to exits, how to get assistance, and for pedestrian movement to elevators and stairs. It is advisable to allow for as much natural surveillance as possible using natural, organizational, and mechanical means. The use of open building fronts provides a natural surveillance tool. Garages should be patrolled by guards or staff to prevent and respond organizationally to incidents. Mechanical surveillance tools include CCTV and sound sensors, which can detect screams or breaking glass.
5. Cash collection in parking structures is an important security design consideration. Cash can be handled manually at kiosks or by automatic systems. The cashier, however, can provide an important link in providing surveillance during operation hours. Automatic systems should be located where they are visible to other employees in order to reduce the opportunity for vandalism or burglary.
6. Lighting levels for parking lots have been an area of intense controversy. The Illuminating Engineering Society has established recommended standards that have self-parking areas at 1.0 footcandle and attendant parking at 2.0 footcandles. Lighting should be evenly distributed, nonglaring, and have long-life bulbs. It is important to be aware that different types of bulbs have varied effects on color. For example, sodium vapor bulbs eliminate the reds and yellows; most colors appear to be dark or blue. This has an impact on CCTV or witnesses describing an assaulter's jacket color, or the color of a car cruising by suspiciously. It is desirable to provide a bulb with full-spectrum lighting. Lighting fixtures that are subject to vandalism should use polycarbonate, break-resistant covers. Wiring should be in conduit underground to prevent tampering. The height of the fixtures should be carefully thought out to prevent glare to users and security personnel. Lighting can be an important link in a parking building's security design.
7. The owners of parking structures also have a legal responsibility to provide a safe and secure environment for the users and invited guests. Pedestrian access is one of the most commonly overlooked design features of parking lots and structures. The most common thought about parking garages and lots is to provide a space that "works" for moving the cars in an orderly and efficient way. In reality, the cars are providing a means for people to arrive at a destination. This priority is important to remember.

8. Pedestrian access involves safety and security design planning. For open parking lots, a key design consideration is full handicap accessibility. Accessibility includes dedicated handicap spaces, ramps, stair design, elevator location and design, railings, floor surfaces, pedestrian crossovers, and dedicated pedestrian paths. A primary design rule for designing parking areas is to avoid, whenever possible, a pedestrian crossing the path of a car. With double-sided lots, this may be unavoidable; however, the design can create a "safe" passageway for pedestrians and handicapped persons to move along a clear path until they come to a marked crosswalk, which serves as a caution for drivers.
9. Speed bumps and humps have provided a means of slowing down cars and trucks. They have also provided a means to damage cars, provide tripping hazards to pedestrians, and the source of numerous personal injury lawsuits. There are many natural (design, construction), organizational (guards), and mechanical (signs, graphics, texture) means to warn pedestrians and drivers of each other. The same principles and design features that allow good visibility to prevent accidents will also be helpful in preventing assaults, rapes and robberies.
10. Graffiti management is an important consideration, as this represents a territorial ritual-type marking of gangs or vandals. Graffiti is a form of vandalism and should not be ignored. If a wall surface is a frequent target, either paint the surface with graffiti-resistant epoxy paint for easy removal, or increase lighting and surveillance to catch perpetrators. Graffiti should be covered as soon as possible, to prevent further vandalism and creating "territorial" messages of not caring. Graffiti and vandalism can sometimes be employee- or union-related. One post office in Florida going through contract negotiations had a rash of tire slashings, window breakage, and graffiti-related incidents directed against administrators' cars. When the contract was negotiated, the criminal acts ceased. During labor disputes, it might be advisable to increase security personnel in the parking, loading, and entryways.
11. Surface car parks should be designed to be overlooked from the road and occupied buildings.
12. Provide pedestrian routes that are clearly identified within a surface car park.
13. Support pillars in enclosed car garages should be as few and as slim as possible to minimize dangers from blindspots and ambush.
14. Where possible, provide direct access at each level to the building served in an enclosed garage.
15. Consider mixed-use occupancies within a multi-level garage to encourage legitimate traffic flow 24 hours a day.

16. Exits and direction signs should be frequent and clearly visible.
17. The quality of finish and materials used should be as high-grade as possible.
18. The underside of the structure or ceiling should be painted white for maximum reflective value and refraction of lighting.
19. Glazing should be used when possible to allow views in and out of concealed areas.
20. Natural lighting should be used as extensively as possible in multi-story garages.
21. Artificial lighting should be consistent and very bright, with as few shadows as possible. The lighting should illuminate parking areas and circulation paths.
22. Exterior doors to the garage should egress only and not allow entry from the street into the garage. Entry access should only occur where there is an attendant.

Maintenance of parking lots and garages is a final consideration for security and safety concerns. A building may be designed to operate very efficiently and look good. However, if the building is not given the necessary maintenance, it will deteriorate quickly. The same principle applies to most building environments and parking areas.

- Maintenance is a function of value engineering and life-cycle costing. Many of the design features that could provide better safety and security usually have a dollar cost involved. The challenge is convincing the client that the cost for an open building front, perimeter fencing, continuous site lighting, controlled egress and ingress, CCTV, graphics and signage, vandal-resistant materials and paint, security personnel, handicap accessibility and a maintenance budget is in the long-term best interest of the client through liability protection and longer building life.
- Maintenance is the commitment by the owner, for example, to replace light bulbs, fix fencing that is damaged, fix potholes and cracks, and paint over graffiti. If quality materials are specified in the design stage, the products will have a long life. If products and materials are abused, the facility will fall into disrepair quickly. Maintenance is one of the first budget items to get cut in tough times, and has the greatest impact in keeping operating/capital costs low for the future.

Parking lots and garages appear on the outside as simple structures. However, a look inside reveals that car parking areas are a careful compromise between man and machine. Criminals know that parking areas have a history of being dark, abandoned, and that they often provide a wealth of criminal opportunities. Parking areas and garages can use CPTED features to increase environmental security with surveillance, access control, and territorial reinforcement. The interface of design, security patrol and technology provides the means to achieve these CPTED goals.

DESIGN CONSIDERATIONS FOR INDUSTRIAL BUILDINGS

When designing a building, an architect has to consider a number of conflicting interests; designing out crime is just one of those. The physical environment contributes to the risk of a building, or its contents, being attacked. Inappropriate design or choice of materials may provide easier targets for the criminal.

Listed below are several points and areas that require special security treatment and should be considered by the architect when planning security design features for industrial buildings. It is very common for industrial buildings to be designed and erected without any consideration for security. Crime Prevention Through Environmental Design (CPTED) considerations might include:

1. Clearly define incoming and outgoing traffic.
2. Clearly define the perimeter boundaries with landscaping, fences, walls, etc.
3. Separate public versus service vehicle entry.
4. Provide clear and unobstructed pedestrian access.
5. Keep openings in the building periphery to a minimum. Lobbies and entrances should be clearly defined and provide a transition from the security perimeter of the plant or production area.
6. In industrial plants and production areas, openings in the building perimeter that are larger that 96 square inches and lower than 18 feet from ground level should be reinforced and provided with additional security protection. Glazing openings larger than five inches can allow someone to crawl through. Therefore, conventional windows must be secured with polycarbonate glazing, window laminates, screens, or other devices.
7. Exterior doors used as emergency exits should be monitored/alarmed by plant security. Doors located in remote areas should be supervised by CCTV cameras and anti-intrusion alarms.
8. Service doors on building exteriors should lead directly to the service department so that outside employee foot traffic is restricted within the property. Service doors should be located in an area that can be under direct employee supervision or remote CCTV supervision.
9. As much distance as possible to avoid contamination, collusion, and pilferage opportunities should physically separate shipping and receiving areas. Shipping and receiving doors should be planned so there are no space gaps between the trailers and the loading docks. Operation of the dock area should be constructed on the inside of

the building rather than outside where the dock materials are exposed.
10. Shipping and receiving dock areas should provide for driver waiting areas with restrooms to prevent unauthorized traffic through the building or material storage areas. Restrooms must be designed to meet the NFPA Life Safety Code requirements for handicapped accessibility.
11. A trash removal system should be designed to permit custodial staff direct access to compactors or incinerators without leaving the building.
12. R&D proprietary and classified areas should be designed to be out of the normal operational circulation paths.
13. Employee entrances should be planned so they are located directly off the employee parking lots. The doors should be sized to be large enough to accommodate the traffic flow and permit supervision by staff for pilferage control.
14. Designated areas for clocking-in should be near the employee entrance and separated by barriers for controlled ingress and screening of IDs by security staff.
15. Personnel hiring offices and areas for related employment use should be located near the periphery to reduce exposure risks to the building by unknown individuals being interviewed.
16. Some industrial buildings have company stores which sell products to employees. These areas should have an outside customer entrance, or be located close to an employee exit.
17. Multiple-story buildings serviced by elevators should be designed to separate freight and personnel elevators. Separation of functions will reduce exposure of freight to theft and pilferage.
18. Finished product warehousing areas should be physically separated from operational areas. Doors into warehousing should be alarmed with anti-intrusion devices and possibly card readers for accountability.
19. Tool rooms, stockrooms, and storage areas within a building should be designed with a ceiling enclosure when the room is lower than the roof of the remainder of the building.
20. If a perimeter door in working areas must be left open for ventilation, a substitute door can be designed to be of a chain-link material to permit ventilation, visibility, and maintain floor security.

Industrial facilities are an important building type and security must be considered as an integral part of the design. Industrial buildings are subject to the high risk of crimes such as employee theft, burglary, robbery of cash assets, commercial espionage, vandalism and arson. Using CPTED processes, industrial buildings can be designed to reduce the opportunity of these high-risk crimes.

ASSET PROTECTION AND SECURITY MANAGEMENT HANDBOOK

DESIGN CONSIDERATIONS FOR OFFICE BUILDINGS

The renovation, addition, or new construction of office buildings may require the security professional and owner to interface with the design professional in new and challenging ways. The security professional may be an employee of the business and be responsible for many sectors of security and safety within that business. The architect or design professional will need many aspects of information from the owner client and security professional to develop the architectural program and design an efficient and secure building. The person who can provide critical information to the architect on security needs and procedures is typically the security director. If there exists no security director, then a trained security professional should be hired to provide that knowledge and assistance to the company and architect.

In order to provide the information in a format that the architect can work with effectively, the security professional should identify what corporate assets are vital to protect. The three most common assets to businesses are:

1. People
2. Information
3. Property

Asset to Be Protected: People

Of course, the resource of *people* is the first and most valuable asset to be protected and elaborated on for developing security criteria for the architect. With any of the three assets, the critical questions asked in a needs assessment are:

1. Who are the users? (visitors, staff, service crew, sales)
2. What can the users do in the building? (tasks, recreation, work)
3. Why are the particular users there? (official business, guests)
4. When do the users get there and leave? (time, shift, patterns)
5. Where can users go in the building? (horizontal, vertical)
6. How can the users get there? (access methods, circulation)

The security professional will need to be clear on the implications of each of the answers to these questions. It is recommended that a task summary can be prepared to give to the architect (Table 1).

The scenario development of asking the six key questions applies the same to a vice-president of a company or a janitorial cleaning service. The security professional will then determine the security implications and the design implications.

Taking the example of the janitorial service, the *security implications* might be:

Crime Prevention through Environmental Design: CPTED

Table 1. Task summary.

Who	Why	What	When	Where	How
Vice-president	Company business	Administration manage	8 a.m.–6 p.m., M–F	All areas total access	Staff elevator
Janitor	Clean offices, vacuum	Clean/garbage pick-up	1 a.m.–4 a.m., M–F	Lobby floors	Guard lets in, has keys to special service offices

- Control of after-hour access
- Verification of cleaning employee status
- Security manpower to sign in and supervise entry and exit
- Key control

These security concerns could then translate into *design implications* such as:

- A sign-in desk for the service trades
- Design of access control system to allow staff to control entry and log in movement
- Placement of garbage dumpsters
- Location of service elevator
- Location of service doors
- Alarm systems for offices and control room ties in and deactivation

These examples are just a small sample of the issues and concerns that need to be addressed by the architect based on information that the security professional has developed.

The security professional must ask the right questions to develop security criteria. The architectural program or problem-seeking stage should incorporate the information developed from answering the six questions. Later, the information will be passed on to the problem-solution stage of architecture: the schematic drawings, design development drawings, and construction documents.

In protecting the asset *information*, the critical questions that can be asked as part of the need assessment are:

- Who has access to the information (staff, management, mailroom)?
- What is the information being protected (data, trade secrets, personnel records, blueprints, computer programs)?
- Why is the information worth protecting (What is the physical, operational, and dollar cost you are willing to incur)?

- When is the information accessible or vulnerable?
- Where is the information available or vulnerable?
- How can the information legitimately and illegitimately be acquired or compromised?

When the security professional is clear on the answers to these questions, a description of the threats and proposed solutions is presented to the architect. An example of what a security professional might present the architect is shown below.

Asset to Be Protected: Information

- *Who.* The president of the company and top management have unrestricted access to all records. The personnel record supervisor only has access to job reviews and drug tests results. Mail clerks screen mail and make copies of memos. Operation managers are responsible for control of shipping and receiving. Stock persons have access to storerooms, computer disks, archives.
- *What.* Assets of information might include personnel files, sensitive memos, trade secrets, computer software, financial records, quarterly statements, formulas, documents, marketing plans, client information, etc.
- *Why.* Personnel and financial records must be protected from outside intrusion and used for promotion or discharge. Computer software, records, data, contains all of the programs and information that is proprietary, classified, or sensitive. Data is protected from competitor espionage, for audits, and decision making. Owner must be prepared to provide physical protection of records, fire protection, backup protection, with strict access and accountability.
- *When.* Personnel records are available for review upon request Monday through Friday, 8 a.m. to 5 p.m. Storage rooms are available during working hours. Shipping and receiving 7 a.m. to noon, Monday through Friday. Mail and copying are available during normal working hours. Computer rooms are operating 24 hours a day. Service delivery is Saturdays and Mondays. Most vulnerable times are during shifts, after hours from threat of burglary, and cleaning crews at night.
- *Where.* Information is typically stored on most management personnel desks within their computers. Data storage is on computer disks located within computer room. Classified and sensitive archival documents are in vault. Vulnerable areas are computer room, loading docks, storage rooms, vault, file cabinets, top management offices, and personal computers on desktops.
- *How.* Office information is most vulnerable to compromise by internal threats by employees stealing memos, computer info, through their unobserved availability and absence of screening and access control.

Crime Prevention through Environmental Design: CPTED

Outside threats are from burglars breaking in for equipment, and collusion from staff with service people and night cleaning staff.

Once the security professional has discussed the threats and vulnerabilities with the owner/client, then counter-strategies can be developed. Architectural, technological and organizational (security manpower) responses can then be examined for practicality and cost.

Architectural design changes that could reflect the security professional's concern for protection of information could be as follows:

- Limit the number of exterior penetrations to a minimum. Doors should be controlled and monitored for accountability. Architecturally define location of main entrance for visitors and staff. Design a service entrance that is under supervision and secure. Storage rooms can be monitored and placed where a supervisor can oversee movement.
- Design a reception desk or counter that screens visitors, vendors, and outsiders. The counter or reception desk should be designed to view all entry doors, and elevators if provided. The reception area establishes the layering of public versus private entry into the building.
- Provide clear demarcation of VIP areas with layering of access to these zones.
- Design the computer room for strict access control, protected utility lines, high-security glazing for easy supervision and visibility, and centered building location.
- Computers can be secured and protected in workstations with anchor pads.
- The access and egress of employees must be controlled. Controlled and supervised employee egress will permit screening of packages, briefcases, and purses. Staff locker area should be well lit and located in an area supervised to prevent theft and pilferage.
- Elevators should be designed to open up to the supervised core area. Special floors or VIP offices may require special elevator access control programming or dedicated elevators.
- Service delivery areas should have a separate or clear roadway system that does not conflict with employee or visitor travel. The loading dock should be designed with ground loops and intercom to notify security staff when a truck is in the loading area during hours when personnel are not directly supervising it.
- The mailroom should be located within a clear and unobstructed line of travel from loading or mail delivery area. The mailroom should be a secure room with monitoring of the door to provide controlled access and accountability. If security of interoffice mail is critical, pneumatic tubes can be used for delivery of letters without human intervention.
- Placement of the vault and fire safes and record files will depend on the frequency of use. The placement and location of these functions

can be as layered or open as defined by the client. Supermarkets place the vault in the front of the store for visibility, while other stores place the vault in a hidden, undisclosed area.

Asset to Be Protected: Property

To examine the asset of *property*, the same process of asking the six questions, determining the security criteria, the architectural criteria, and scenario development would apply. No asset is too small to take through this process. Those companies that go the extra yard in asset identification and scenario development will realize more profits and gain market advantage. The market advantage of designing out shoplifting, pilferage, espionage, assaults, terrorism, and employee theft will result in a better bottom line for the company, lower prices to the consumer, and more profits for the owner/client.

Crime Prevention Through Environmental Design (or CPTED) uses a number of architectural, technological, and operational innovations to design in security. The possibilities are fairly limitless, subject only to your creativity.

The greatest temptation is to jump to a shopping list of technology and design solutions. In practice, the answers are not as important as the questions. Each building has a unique function, operation, and combination of materials and methods of construction. If the security professional uses the threat/asset vulnerability analysis to develop a needs assessment for the architect, the correct solutions will emerge. The architect can best respond to the security professional when both participate fully, together, in the early stages.

To achieve environmental security, the designers and users must have balanced development, adequate support systems, predominant land use, and territoriality. On an individual building level, the owners may not have control over the neighborhood streets; surrounding activities such as stadiums, bars, parks, waste dumps, etc.; or control over land-use conflicts, competition for use of roads, public services, or police protection.

There is seldom just one element out of scale, so a building can have many environmental conflicts that provide opportunities for would-be offenders. Each conflict can precipitate a pattern of crime. Crime Prevention Through Environmental Design (CPTED) and defensible space principles can be offered to the planners and architects as a means of preventing or reducing crime opportunities.

Offices and Office Buildings. Offices and office buildings are vulnerable to walk-in thefts, burglary, theft by deception and fraud, vandalism, loss of information, and employee theft. With these crime risks identified, the owner and security director should identify the major areas to be considered

Crime Prevention through Environmental Design: CPTED

for security design: site security, building security and internal security needs.

1. The first point to consider is the location of the site. What are the zoning and building code limitation and restrictions for the site and surrounding area? Existing and proposed landscaping should be examined for security application.
2. External areas need to be considered for security design. Car parks, garages, and parking lots need to be carefully designed. Entrances and exits, paths and roads need to be carefully thought out for circulation conflicts and security issues. Fences, gates and site lighting should be identified and prioritized. CCTV should be thought out once the circulation patterns are planned. Decisions must be made for the delivery areas and waste disposal services. Scenario development, or role playing, should be made for all service delivery situations to the building.
3. The office building must consider primary and secondary access points. Scenarios must be developed for how the owner or client wants the employees, visitors and service personnel to gain entry. Fire exits and life safety code requirements need to be considered early on so as not undermine the security features. Loading bays should be identified and designed for secure shipping and receiving. Security needs for basement areas and mechanical plant rooms need to be considered. Careful planning should go into external stairways, roof access, doors and windows.
4. Internal points of security to be considered are the lobby entrances, secondary entrances, reception area, cash office areas, computer areas, electrical/telephone service areas, executive areas, canteens, location of staff restrooms, security central control, and point protection of vault rooms or special equipment.
5. The point where most visitors and public enter a building is a lobby entrance. The architect uses a lobby entrance of a building to create a landmark point for establishing to all that you have arrived and that this is the entry point. Usually richer, higher-grade materials are used in the lobby to create an image and ambiance of success, stability and power.
6. To complement this atmosphere is a checkpoint usually known as a reception desk. Through this reception desk pass the many groups of people who gain entry to the building. From CEOs to janitorial staff, all pass through this checkpoint.
7. To create a secure working environment, the lobby entrance and reception desk create the first layer in the building perimeter security system. The receptionist serves the important function of identifying everyone who enters the building or office and establishing a legitimate purpose for their being there. Having a person checking

identity and purpose of visitors is often preferred to having an automatic credential reading system. Many visitors do not have automated credentials and must be screened personally.

8. The reception desk must be positioned with good surveillance of entranceways and persons entering the building or office. The desk can be located in a way to prevent access to all areas leading to office or restricted areas. The reception desk should be positioned to be able to intercept persons before reaching elevators or stairs.
9. The design of most reception desks is semi-circular or oval to give maximum working surface and visual flexibility. Because the receptionist will usually be seated, it is common for the seating platform to be raised 12 to 18 inches to permit unobstructed visibility by the receptionist. Human factor considerations are important in the design of counters. Most reception counters are 42 to 48 inches high to allow placing your elbow on the desktop. The normal height of a desk is 30 to 32 inches from the floor. However, at this height, the receptionist is looked down upon rather than at an equal height.
10. Psychologically, a receptionist is more likely to successfully challenge a visitor if eye contact is parallel and the receptionist does not have to raise his/her voice. Therefore, visitors should be funneled to the desk and not access restricted areas without having to pass close to the desk. It is common for a locked door or gate entry system to control passage of visitors.
11. Receptionists may also serve other distracting functions besides the security function of screening people. They may also be answering phones, controlling door entry, screening mail, or serving as a drop-off counter for packages and deliveries. Protection of company assets depends on the receptionist being able to conduct her screening function as unimpeded as possible.
12. If a reception desk contains CCTV equipment, switchers, VCRs and other electronic equipment, the counter must be designed to allow concealment of equipment. It must also allow tilting of monitors for proper human factor viewing angles, and allow ventilation for equipment. Conduit considerations must be planned for in the design of the building to avoid expensive after-the-fact renovations.
13. One feature that is often overlooked at reception desks is emergency assistance call buttons. With this duress device, the receptionist can summon help if a visitor or employee becomes a problem. Backup from security is important to reduce the opportunity of a physical attack on the receptionist. The design of the counter can slow an attack. Bank teller counters are designed wide to prevent the quick reaching over and grabbing of money or papers. The reception desk is designed high to prevent easily jumping over it.

14. The design of receptionist desks may serve high-rise, low-rise buildings, single- or multi-tenant operations. The receptionist serves as the point-person for a layered security system. The lobby and reception point can be designed for aesthetics and restrictive movement. As always, the first step is the threat analysis to determine what goals, directives and threats need to be considered. Input from management, employees and the security consultant need to be expressed to the architect. Through this clear communication, the function of access control can be natural, flowing and unobtrusive.
15. Access control and surveillance systems should be designed as part of the building design and architectural programming phase, not after the fact. Stairs, elevators and corridors should be examined for security requirements. Key systems should be carefully addressed to accommodate growth, change and flexibility.
16. Pedestrian access should be direct from the road to the front of the building.
17. Buildings should be oriented to allow views into the site.
18. Doors and windows may need extra security considerations, especially on the ground floor.
19. Limit the entrances into the building to as few as possible. There may be additional exit only doors, but they should not allow ground-level entrance.

One of the most important design features to be considered for internal security is planning for conduits. If a dedicated security conduit is planned for in the beginning, it will be of very little inconvenience and expense. Conduit should be run horizontally and vertically in mechanical cases and sized to accommodate future growth and servicing of wires. Lines may need to be shielded, depending on the communication systems being used.

In providing for the security of office buildings against crime, the security professional can identify the risks and plan for the security and welfare of the people, information and property.

SPECIAL CONSIDERATIONS REGARDING U.S. FEDERAL BUILDINGS

The General Services Administration (GSA) Security Standards

The bombing of the Murrah Federal Office Building in Oklahoma City gave birth to a federal effort to develop security standards that would apply to all federal facilities and an Interagency Security Committee has recommended their adoption as a government-wide standard. During the testing of the standards, a number of state governments also reviewed the standards and applied them to several new construction projects. Consult local and state authorities for their specific applications.

ASSET PROTECTION AND SECURITY MANAGEMENT HANDBOOK

The process of risk assessment and security design is especially relevant in the architecture of schools, hospitals, airports, office buildings, multi-family apartment buildings, etc. Recently, buildings have been targeted for bombing by terrorists because of their "architectural vulnerability." This vulnerability will be addressed by methods described in this section.

The GSA Security Standards encourages a Defensible Space/Crime Prevention Through Environmental Design (CPTED) approach to clearly defining and screening the flow of persons and vehicles through layering from public to private spaces. Edges and boundaries of the properties should clearly define the desired circulation patterns and movements. The screening and funneling of persons through screening techniques is an effort to screen legitimate users of the building from illegitimate users who might look for opportunities to commit crime, workplace violence or acts of terrorism.

The result of approximately one year of work by the GSA panel is a set of criteria covering four levels of protection for every aspect of security addressed by the U.S. Marshal's report. The U.S. Marshal's report made a large number of recommendations for both operational and equipment improvements. The GSA Security Standards addresses the functional requirements and desired application of security glazing, bomb-resistant design and construction, landscaping and planting designs, site lighting, and natural and mechanical surveillance opportunities (good sight lines, no blind spots, window placement, proper applications of CCTV). These recommendations were further subdivided according to whether they should be implemented for various levels of security (e.g., a level-one facility might not require an entry control system, while a level-four facility would require electronic controls with CCTV assessment). Those requirements of the report that affect facility design and engineering are presented here in four general categories of corrective action used in the report.

The following should be addressed by the architect and engineering team for renovations or new construction on any federal building, and is also recommended for state and local buildings:

1. Perimeter and exterior security:
   — Parking area and parking controls
   — CCTV monitoring
   — Lighting, to include emergency backup
   — Physical barriers
2. Entry security:
   — Intrusion detection system
   — Upgrade to current life safety standards
   — Screen mail, persons, packages
   — Entry control with CCTV and electric door strikes
   — High-security locks

3. Interior security:
   — Employee ID, visitor control
   — Control access to utilities
   — Provide emergency power to critical systems
   — Evaluate location of day care centers
4. Security planning:
   — Evaluate locations of tenant agencies as concerns security needs and risk
   — Install mylar film on exterior windows
   — Review/establish blast standards for current projects and new construction
   — Develop a design standard for blast resistance and street setback for new construction

The criteria take a balanced approach to security, considering cost-effectiveness, acknowledging acceptance of some risk, and recognizing that federal buildings should be not bunker or fortress-like, but open, accessible, attractive and representative of the democratic spirit of the country. Prudent, rather than excessive, security measures are appropriate in facilities owned by and serving the public.

Application of GSA Security Standards to All Building Types

Whatever the building or its use, security and crime prevention should be design criteria, similar to fire safety, accessibility and structural integrity. Any piece of architecture should establish a hierarchy of space that goes from open access by the public, to semi-public, to semi-private, to private spaces. Any areas or spaces that are unassigned to a specific purpose or capable guardian should be avoided as it becomes "no man's land" and not claimed, protected or defended by any individual or group. Traffic patterns of pedestrians and vehicles into sites and buildings should be carefully thought out and controlled for the desired goal. The design of any building should maximize the potential for natural observation by the legitimate building users.

Key defensive architectural site design considerations for bomb resistance:

1. Establish a secured perimeter around the building that is as far from the building as feasible. Setbacks of 100 feet are desired.
2. Design artistically pleasing concrete barriers as flower planters or works of art and position them near curbing at a distance from the building, with less than four feet of spacing between them to block vehicular passage.
3. Build new buildings in a simple geometric rectangular layout to minimize the "defraction effect" when blast waves bounce off U-shaped or L-shaped buildings causing additional damage.

4. Drastically reduce or totally eliminate ornamentation on buildings that can easily break away, causing further damage to building occupants or pedestrians at street level. All external cladding should be made of light-weight materials that will minimize damage if they become flying objects following an explosion (hurricane or related weather disaster).
5. Eliminate potential hiding places near the facility.
6. Provide an unobstructed view around the facility site or place the facility within view of other occupied facilities.
7. Locate assets stored on site, but outside the facility, within view of occupied rooms of the facility.
8. Minimize the signage or indication of assets on the property.
9. Provide a 100-foot minimum facility separation from the facility boundary, if possible.
10. Eliminate lines of approach perpendicular to the building.
11. Minimize the number of vehicle access points.
12. Eliminate or strictly control parking beneath facilities.
13. Locate parking as far from the building as practical (yet address ADA spaces and proximity) and place parking within view of occupied rooms or facilities.
14. Illuminate building exterior and exterior sites where assets are located.
15. Secure access to power/heat plants, gas mains, water supplies, electrical and phone service.

Crimes are committed because they are easy to commit. A person sees an easy opportunity and so they do it, regardless of the legality or consequences. Increasing the effort needed to commit a crime eliminates casual criminals. Target hardening is one method of increasing the effort using the increased use of fencing, landscaping and plantings, and curbs.

Another technique of CPTED is natural access control, which includes installing symbolic and real barriers, designing paths, walkways and roads so that unwanted and unauthorized users are prevented from entering vulnerable areas. Barriers may include limiting entrance to specific individuals, places or times; security vestibules; parking lot barriers; entry phones; visitor check-in booths; guard stations; vehicle control systems; and biometric screening for access control.

GRAPHICS AND SIGNAGE FOR CRIME PREVENTION AND ENVIRONMENTAL SECURITY

When users of an environment or building occupy a space, there are messages that are given by the environment of what the designated use of that space was designed for. The use of graphics and signage is one way of giving messages to the user.

Graphics refer to symbols that pictorially portray an image or convey a message. An example is the symbol of a man at a men's toilet. Signage refers to conveying a message with letters or words. One of the major purposes of security signage is to put the user of that space on notice; that is, shifting the load of responsibility back to the user. The expression "Let the buyer beware" is becoming translated by the courts to be "Let the user beware." In order for the building and or the owner/manager to partially shift the load of responsibility, the building must clearly state what the expectations or ground rules are.

Some of the ground rules that we are accustomed to seeing are:

- Do Not Walk On The Grass
- Enter At Own Risk
- Lock Your Valuables
- No Trespassing
- Don't Even Think Of Crime

Just putting up a sign does not relieve the building owner of liability. However, the building can put the users on notice of what to expect and how to behave. A common example is parking garages. Good signage and graphics tell the users where the entrance and exits are; location of speed bumps; posted speed limits; direction of traffic; to lock all valuables; head-in parking only; management not responsible for losses; this lot is under CCTV surveillance; location of fire exits and alarms; location of panic buttons and intercoms for assistance.

Security signage and graphics have architectural design criteria, systems considerations, and procedural design criteria. The architectural design criteria start with the architect or graphics consultant. Some considerations are:

- What is the size of the letters?
- What is the type style of the letters?
- At what distance are graphics to be read?
- What kind of illumination is needed to support signage?
- Where is the location of signage?
- Who is sign intended for?

For a sign to be clearly read by a person with 20/20 vision at a distance of 50 feet, the letters would need to be six inches in height. If the signage is graphics or symbols, it should be at least 15 inches in height. The type style or font is an important consideration for clarity in reading. Letter styles with fancy serifs (such as Gothic) are difficult to read at distances. A font style popular with architects is Helvetica. Lighting levels should be at least 20 footcandles and positioned to avoid glare on the signage.

Systems considerations for graphics and signage include a consistent, uniform and well-distributed graphics package. Just as fire exits must be illuminated and displayed at all stairways, security signage should be systematically displayed at all critical areas.

Procedural considerations develop the process of what the signage is to say, whom the signage is directed to, and where it should be located. Examples of signage clarifying procedures include having employees wear ID badges for clearance, letting guests of a restaurant know of a level change, or putting shoppers on notice of shoplifting surveillance.

The role of graphics and signage in the security and crime prevention arena is to make the users clearly aware of designated uses and behaviors in an environment. If the users or invitees of the property do not follow the ground rules, then the burden of responsibility shifts, and they can be challenged as to their intent. Without the notice given by signage, people's actions are subject to personal interpretation and are difficult to challenge. Early involvement of the architect with the security manager is the best step for creating a secure environment with the use of signage and graphics.

SUMMARY

Situational crime prevention consists of a set of opportunity-reducing measures directed at the potential offender: increase the effort, increase the risks, reduce the rewards, and remove the excuses for criminal behavior. CPTED differs slightly, with its focus on altering the physical environment to reduce criminal opportunities. The major difference between these two crime-prevention methods is the scope and depth of devising and applying crime-prevention measures. Situational crime prevention falls within the theoretical framework of criminal opportunity theories, such as rational choice, routine activities, and environmental criminology.[1]

CPTED draws on the multidisciplinary theoretical background from the social and physical sciences that serve as the basis for CPTED's environmental alterations. Newman's work on defensible space and Crowe's first-generation work in CPTED have paved the way for second- and third-generation CPTED that incorporates elements of behavioral psychology and sociology of human behavior with the architectural modifications needed to make a safe environment.

While Situational Crime Prevention and CPTED differ in terms of their theoretical base, they can be used together and even complement each other. CPTED and Situational Crime Prevention are valuable tools for security directors and law enforcement, especially POP (problem oriented policing), the SARA model and community-oriented policing.

It is important to distinguish that the CPTED is not always enough to stop crime.[2] If CPTED measures are employed alone, they can sometimes

---

[1] Sorenson, Severein. appendix to *HUD CPTED Training Manual.* SPARTA Consulting Corp., Bethesda, MD, 1999.

create more problems than they solve in the community, neighborhood or project in which they are implemented. Certain CPTED or security measures may create or exacerbate tension between groups in the community because certain people or groups may not feel they are receiving the correct crime-prevention measures. Second, persistent or motivated offenders or youth may dedicate time and unlimited energy to figuring out how to overcome the CPTED measures, resulting in corrections that end up being fortress-like target hardening. Finally, CPTED measures do not address the social and economic problems of the community, neighborhood, society or building project.

The solution is to integrate a CPTED program with additional initiatives, and collaborate building processes to make the community or neighborhood whole (remember: the goal of CPTED is to reduce the incidence and fear of crime and improve the quality of life!).

Selected Bibliography

Atlas, Randall; The Other Side of CPTED, *Security Management,* March 1991.

Clarke, R.V.; Situational Crime Prevention: Its Theoretical Basis and Practical Scope, *Crime and Justice: An Annual Review of Research;* Edited by M. Tonry and N. Morris; vol. 4, p. 225–256, The University of Chicago Press, Chicago.

Crowe, T.D.; *Crime Prevention through Environmental Design: Applications of Architectural Design and Space Management Concepts;* 1991; Butterworth-Heinemann.

Jeffrey, C. Ray; *Crime Prevention through Environmental Design;* 1971; Sage Publications, Inc.

Newman, Oscar; *Defensible Space Crime Prevention through Urban Design*; 1973; Macmillan Publishing Co., Inc.

Newman, Oscar and Franck, Karen; *Factors Influencing Crime and Instability in Urban Housing Developments;* 1980; U.S. Government Printing Office, Washington, D.C.

Wilson, James Q. and Kelling, George; Broken Windows; *Atlantic Monthly,* 211, 29–38, 1982.

[2] ibid.

14
United States Criminal Law

INTRODUCTION

When establishing and maintaining an assets protection program, security professionals must know their jurisdiction's legal requirements where the program functions. Otherwise, the program designed to protect the assets of the enterprise may fail and cause a significant loss of those assets. Security professionals must have a working knowledge of the legal system and its interrelationships in order to apply the law properly in matters of security.

FEDERAL AND STATE CONSTITUTIONS

The U.S. Constitution is the basic document for U.S. law. It defines the federal government, its branches and powers. Individual state governments remain separate from the federal government. The U.S. Constitution is the foundation on which states and their citizens base their definitions of the rights and duties of the government and those of the people. The individual states have their own respective constitutions that establish the rights and duties of its citizens and state governments.

The U.S. Constitution grants the power to make laws to the legislative branch. State constitutions contain similar provisions, granting powers to the counterpart departments of those governments. Each constitution may define certain actions as criminal. (For example, Article III, Section 3 of the U.S. Constitution defines treason.) Except for these limited instances, the power to declare what constitutes a crime is part of the general legislative power granted to the U.S. Congress under the U.S. Constitution and to the state legislatures under their respective state constitutions. By exercising this power, the body of criminal law is created. These statutes are referred to as *criminal codes* or *crimes codes*.

STATUTORY LAW

An action of a sovereign legislative branch becomes a law when it is approved by the executive branch in the manner required by the constitution. Each law, or statute, is combined with others passed before and after it into the body of statutory law. Laws passed by cities, towns, and villages, however, are not generally referred to as statutes because the local level of government is not sovereign. Thus, these enactments become ordinances or local laws.

Statutory law is generally comprised of criminal laws and noncriminal or civil laws. Frequently, however, acts or omissions are defined as criminal even if they are not specifically included in the criminal sections of any statutory code. These crimes are nonetheless crimes and must be included when assessing the criminal laws. Examples of these types of crimes are related to vehicle and traffic laws of several states. In these laws, a number of offenses — such as driving while under the influence of drugs or alcohol or leaving the scene of an accident without reporting it to the police — are defined as crimes.

DEFINITION AND CLASSIFICATION OF CRIMES

Generally, a crime is anything the statute defines as a crime. More specifically, a *crime* is an act or omission prohibited by law for which a penalty can be imposed.

Not every act or omission prohibited by the law is a crime, nor is every fine or forfeiture necessarily a criminal punishment. The ultimate guide as to what constitutes criminal conduct is the statutory language that describes the prohibited conduct. The language either (1) defines the conduct specifically as a crime, or (2) establishes fine and/or imprisonment penalties that can only be imposed for crimes.

Under both federal and state laws, the first place to search for the definition of crimes is in the criminal statutes or codes.

Federal Criminal Law

The main body of federal criminal law is codified in Title 18 of the United States Code, one of 50 titles comprising the United States Code. Reference to a particular provision includes the title number, the abbreviation of the code and the section number. For example, the federal kidnapping statute is found in Section 1201 of Title 18 of the United States Code and is cited as 18 U.S.C. §1201.

Federal crimes are also created in other titles in the United States Code. For example:

- 15 U.S.C. 1644, Fraudulent Use of Credit Cards
- 21 U.S.C. 801, *et seq.*, Drug Abuse and Control
- 26 U.S.C. 5861, *et seq.*, Firearms
- 26 U.S.C. 7201, *et seq.*, Tax Matters
- 31 U.S.C. 5322, Financial Transaction Reports
- 41 U.S.C. 51, *et seq.*, U.S. Contractor Kickbacks
- 46 U.S.C. 1903, Maritime Drug Enforcement
- 50 U.S.C. 1801, Foreign Intelligence Surveillance Act

Definition of Federal Crimes

Section 3559 of Title 18 classifies all offenses defined by any federal statute according to the maximum authorized term of imprisonment. This scheme produces five classes of felonies, three classes of misdemeanors and one class of infractions, as follows:

Crime	Maximum authorized imprisonment
Class A Felony	Death or life imprisonment
Class B Felony	25 years or more
Class C Felony	10 to 25 years
Class D Felony	5 to 10 years
Class E Felony	1 to 5 years
Class A Misdemeanor	6 months to 1 year
Class B Misdemeanor	30 days to 6 months
Class C Misdemeanor	5 to 30 days
Infraction	5 days or less, or no authorized imprisonment

Definition of State Crimes

Specific definitions of crimes vary from state to state; however, the same general test — the period of possible imprisonment — remains a common theme. An example is the Penal Law of New York. The following definitions are found in Article 10:

- *Crime*: A misdemeanor or a felony.
- *Misdemeanor*: An offense, other than traffic violations, for which a sentence to a term of imprisonment in excess of 15 days may be imposed. The sentence to a term of imprisonment cannot be in excess of one year.
- *Felony*: An offense for which a sentence to a term of imprisonment in excess of one year may be imposed.
- *Offense*: Conduct punishable by a sentence to a term of imprisonment or to a fine as provided by a law, order, rule or regulation.

The distinction between felonies (more serious crimes) and misdemeanors (less serious crimes) has great significance. Not only are the penalties significantly different, but the extent to which police officers and private citizens — including assets protection professionals — may lawfully apprehend, prevent or control criminals depends upon whether the crime is a felony or a misdemeanor.

The Essential Character of a Crime

Criminal laws are based on a basic concept: prohibited conduct is a wrong against the general public, not merely a wrong against a particular person. For example, if one man strikes another with a blunt instrument — without provocation or justification — this is clearly a wrong to the struck person. However, this isolated strike is not the root of criminal law; rather, the general *concept* that such an act is a threat to public welfare provides the basis for laws.

The circumstances of the blow, the weapon used and the extent of the injuries determine the extent of the crime (e.g., assault, assault with a deadly weapon, attempted murder, manslaughter, murder, etc.). These circumstances must be examined in relation to the specific victim and the specific aggressor. Nonetheless, an act is deemed criminal when it is a threat to the general public welfare.

Obviously, the victim of the crime is the state's focus (or the people's concern) because the victim sustains the personal injuries. But the victim must look toward civil law, not criminal law, to be compensated for his injuries, no matter how serious.

Another important aspect frequently overlooked by business executives is the idea that crimes threaten the public welfare. Because a crime is a threat against the public, the isolated victim does not have the exclusive prerogative to determine whether a criminal is prosecuted. If a business is the victim of a crime, our justice system imposes an obligation on the proprietors or managers of that business to assist public law enforcement authorities in the prosecution of the crime. This requires, at the least, that facts are truthfully communicated clearly to the police or the prosecutor or other appropriate law enforcement representatives.

The obligation to report crime is not so absolute as to involve criminal liability on people who do not report it.[1] However, criminal laws fail when those with knowledge of crimes do not inform law enforcement authorities. Treating crimes as though they affect only the parties involved — and not the whole community — undermines the intent of criminal laws. Corporate entities should avoid situations where management decides not to report criminal activity. Such decisions weaken the overall protection offered by criminal laws. An effective security professional implements management decisions that regard the purpose of the law.

Criminal Intent

In general, an act or omission is not criminal unless the person committing the act is aware of what he is doing and intends to commit the act that the law specifically forbids (or fails to do what the law commands). The

---

[1] Title 18 U.S.C. 4, "Misprison of a felony" reads, in part: Whoever having knowledge of the actual commission of a felony cognizable by a court of the United States, conceals and does not as soon as possible make known the same to some judge or other person in civil or military authority under the United States, shall be fined under this article or imprisoned not more than three years or both. However, numerous federal decisions have held that some affirmative act of concealment is required and that the mere failure to make known would not be sufficient. (*Neal v. U.S.* 102 F 2d 643; *U.S. v. Aarons* 718 F 2d 188; *U.S. v. Thomas* 469 F 2d 145 (Cert. Denied, 410 U.S. 957); *U.S. v. Joiner*, 429 F 2d 489.)

term *mens rea* (guilty mind) describes this state of mind or wrongful purpose required by criminal laws. It does not mean that the person committing the act must know that the act or omission *is* a crime (in other words, he need not be aware of the criminal statute). It does require, however, that the act prohibited or required by the criminal statute be one that the accused intends to perform or omit.

An exception to this general requirement: when the criminal law defines *criminal negligence* (as in criminally negligent homicide or injury resulting from criminal negligence). In such cases, a person or entity must determine what a reasonable person would have foreseen as a substantial and unjustifiable risk or specific result. For example, a man picks up a pistol without determining whether it is loaded, points it at another person and pulls the trigger several times. If the weapon fires and kills or injures another person, the person firing is criminally negligent.

Establishing Guilt for Crime

In general, responsibility for a crime is established in a systematic way. A criminal prosecutor determines that there is sufficient evidence to request a grand jury to issue an *indictment* (an accusation against a person). Prosecutor's evidence may take the form of a complaint from a victim or witness, an investigation by the police, an admission or confession by the alleged criminal, physical evidence (including forensic studies), or any combination of these.

However, the initial determination of whether to proceed after the facts have been collected is the prosecutor's responsibility. In federal matters, this is the U.S. Attorney or Assistant U.S. Attorney for the particular location. In state actions, it may be the Attorney General or Assistant Attorney General, a District Attorney, a county attorney or a special prosecutor appointed under state law for the purpose of prosecuting specified crimes. While the police recommendation carries great weight with most prosecutors, the prosecutor ultimately decides whether the evidence is sufficient to proceed with prosecution. Assets protection professionals who deal with a high volume of criminal activity often cultivate close connections with public prosecutors. In these situations, the professional often goes to great lengths to collect and analyze any evidence of wrongdoing. He must ensure that investigators follow all appropriate standards.

Forensic studies and investigations are significantly more acceptable and reliable today. Therefore, security professionals must properly preserve the physical evidence of a crime. The prosecutor closely examines whether the physical evidence was disturbed in any fashion (by assets protection personnel or others); whether it was properly preserved, collected, prepared and tested; and whether the chain of custody was properly documented to dispel any allegations of evidence tampering.

Formal Charge

The accused is formally advised of the charge against him. This formal charge can be in the form of an *indictment* or an *information*.

If the prosecutor requests the grand jury to return an indictment, witnesses are heard and evidence is introduced to the grand jury. The grand jury determines whether there is sufficient evidence to establish that a crime has been committed and that the person named in the indictment committed it. The indictment is basically an accusation, and it is issued for three main reasons:

1. To comply with federal and state constitutional requirements that crimes be prosecuted by way of grand jury indictment
2. To inform the defendant that he is accused of a crime
3. To establish a recital of the ultimate facts of the crime so that the courts can determine the sufficiency of the charge

Some states do not use the grand jury system. The prosecutor reviews the available evidence to determine whether or not a crime has been committed and whether or not the accused committed it. After that determination, the prosecutor issues an information accusing the person of the crime.

The procedure for minor crimes and offenses is usually much more simple than an indictment. Whatever the process, and irrespective of whether it is a state or federal proceeding, an accused defendant always has access to the courts to review and determine the propriety of the accusation he or she faces.

Arraignment

After a grand jury returns an indictment, the person or persons named are taken into custody to appear before the appropriate court. This is when they are informed of the charge and their rights with respect to the charge. Sometimes, a defendant is permitted to enter a plea at the time of arraignment. More often, the plea comes later and the arraignment merely informs the accused of the crimes and determines his or her *status* until the next step. That status can either be confinement or release, which involves release on one's own recognizance (by showing that the accused understands the charge and agrees to appear when ordered) or release on bail.

Bail is a security (usually in the form of money or its equivalent) to assure the later appearance of the defendant and to compel him or her to remain within the jurisdiction of the court. Courts and U.S. magistrates may consider a defendant's potential danger to the community. Bail may be refused if the government establishes that no conditions or restrictions can be imposed to ensure public safety. And, if a person awaiting trial is rearrested while on bail or recognizance, he or she can be confined without bail. Bail may also be refused on the grounds that no amount assures a later appearance. The government often denies bail in narcotics and organized crime prosecutions.

Bail procedures under various state laws generally require courts or magistrates to:

- Release on personal recognizance
- Release on bail
- Remand to the custody of the sheriff or other law enforcement officer. Crimes for which capital punishment or a life sentence may be imposed are non-bailable in some states (and under the Uniform Criminal Extradition Act, which applies to foreign nationals accused of serious crimes)

Trial

After an accused is indicted and arraigned, and if the indictment is not dismissed for legal insufficiency, a plea — his answer to the charges — is entered. If the plea is "not guilty," a criminal trial ensues in which the fact of guilt must be established by the prosecution "beyond a reasonable doubt." In major crimes requiring accusation by indictment, the accused has a right to a trial by jury. This right may be waived in some states (as long as the crime charged does not involve a potential death sentence) and the trial carried out before a judge only. In either case, the court, whether judge or jury, must find the accused guilty beyond a reasonable doubt.

There is no absolute definition of *beyond a reasonable doubt*. It often means "more than merely substantial" and requires "clear and convincing evidence." Such doubt would cause a prudent person to hesitate before acting in matters of importance to himself. This requirement is particularly significant when contrasted with the requirement of proof in a civil case. In a civil case, prosecutors must prove guilt by a "preponderance of the evidence" (in other words, that the evidence points more to fault than to innocence). So, a defendant might be acquitted in a criminal trial but lose in a civil damage action for assault based upon essentially the same facts and evidence, because the burden of proof in a criminal matter is more stringent. An obvious illustration of this is the experience of O.J. Simpson. He was acquitted of criminal charges of murdering his ex-wife but lost a civil case involving the same facts — but on a wrongful death charge.

Sentence

If convicted after trial, and if the conviction is not set aside for legal insufficiency or other reasons, the accused is sentenced. This area of the law is quite complex and varies considerably from state to state. In general, the maximum and minimum sentences for specific crimes are prescribed by statute. Within those limits, the sentencing judge has discretion, depending on the specific state or jurisdiction. A sentence can consist of a period of confinement, a fine, a period of supervised freedom (probation), or a combination of these. A sentence may be executed or suspended. If suspended, the actual punishment is not meted out to the convicted person. However, the convicted person remains subject to the court for the period of the sentence, which may be imposed later if the conditions of the suspension are not met.

For federal crimes, much of the individual discretion of the sentencing judge was removed in the 1980s when the Federal Sentencing Guidelines were passed. These guidelines apply to both individuals and organizations convicted of federal offenses. The purpose of the guidelines is:

- To guarantee that offenders serve close to the actual sentences imposed
- To allow minimal sentence reductions for good behavior
- To provide adequate guidelines to structure and constrain judicial discretion to assure more uniform treatment
- To introduce rights to appellate review of sentences where none existed previously

These guidelines establish stringent sentencing parameters, which require the imposition of specified sentences for designated federal crimes — unless the sentencing judge deems otherwise. The guidelines ensure fairness of sentencing.

The Federal Organizational Sentencing Guidelines are of particular interest to the assets protection professional. The guidelines stiffen the penalties imposed on corporations when their employees violate federal criminal statutes. They apply to antitrust, securities, tax, bribery, the Employee Retirement Income Security Act (ERISA), fraud, money laundering and environmental violations. And, while the guidelines substantially increase the penalties for businesses that do not make any effort to deter, detect and report crime, the guidelines significantly decrease the penalties for those businesses that do.

The deterrence aspects of the guidelines provide that every company make restitution to any party injured by criminal conduct and pay a non-tax-deductible fine. The fine for a criminal violation that results in a $20 million gain for the company can result in a fine ranging from $1 million to $80 million. The amount of the fine is determined by the application of a table of multipliers based on aggravating and mitigating factors to arrive at a *culpability score*.

A compliance program designed to deter and detect criminal conduct can result in a significant reduction in the culpability score and the fine. An effective compliance program must meet seven requirements:

1. The company establishes compliance standards that are reasonably capable of preventing criminal conduct.
2. High-level management oversees the standards.
3. The standards are communicated to the employees and training in compliance issues is offered.
4. The company tests the system by monitoring, auditing and utilizing other systems designed to detect criminal conduct.
5. The company exercises due care to ensure that discretionary authority is not delegated to individuals with a propensity to engage in crime.
6. The compliance standards are enforced through appropriate disciplinary procedures that include provisions that individuals be disciplined for failing to detect or report an offense.
7. After an offense is detected, all reasonable steps are taken to prevent a future similar offense.

Another statute important to the assets protection professional, the Foreign Corrupt Practices Act (FCPA), provides criminal penalties for "controlling persons" in corporations under certain conditions.

The FCPA (15 U.S.C. Section 78dd1) applies to any company that has a class of securities registered pursuant to Section 12 of the Securities Exchange Act of 1934 and any company that is required to file reports pursuant to Section 15 (d) of that Act. One segment of the FCPA makes it a criminal offense to offer a bribe to a foreign official in order to obtain or retain business. The segment of the FCPA that is most pertinent to security professionals requires that the company devise and maintain a system of internal accounting controls sufficient to provide reasonable assurances that the following four objectives are met:

1. Transactions are executed in accordance with management's specific or general authorization.
2. Transactions are recorded as necessary to:
   a. Permit preparation of financial statements in conformity with generally accepted accounting principles or any other criteria applicable to such statements; and
   b. Maintain accountability for assets.
3. Access to assets is permitted only in accordance with management's general or specific authorization.
4. The recorded accountability for assets is compared to the existing assets at reasonable intervals and action is taken with respect to any differences.

The penalties for failure to maintain these internal controls include a fine of not more than $10,000, imprisonment for not more than five years, or both. These internal control requirements are not solely within the purview of the accounting department. The assets protection organization makes a significant contribution to controlling employee access to assets.

In January 1998, the Organization for Economic Cooperation and Development (OECD) adopted a "Convention on Combating Bribery of Foreign Public Officials in International Business Transactions." The OCED consists of 29 member nations, and an additional five non-member nations (Argentina, Brazil, Bulgaria, Chile and the Slovak Republic) who also ratified this approach. The convention requires all signatory countries to enact legislation similar to the requirements of the FCPA in the U.S. A corporation is required to adhere to the provisions of the FCPA and meet the tenets set forth by each specific country where it does business. These requirements subject the corporation to potentially multiple prosecutions in the event that a bribe to a government official is discovered.

Confinement

There are two ways to avoid confinement for conviction of a crime or to reduce the period of such confinement. One is *probation*, or the release of convicted persons under certain conditions that allow regulation of their behavior for a given period of time. The sentencing judge sets the conditions and grants the probation following a criminal conviction but before confinement commences. The other, *parole*, is the release of a person who has served part of a sentence. In state systems, parole is granted by an independent agency, typically a parole board, and is based upon the convicted person's behavior while in confinement. The conditions that govern a paroled person's behavior are set by statute or regulation of the parole board. Violation of those conditions can result in return to confinement for the remaining period of the original sentence. Under the Federal Sentencing Guidelines, there is no parole for federal crimes.

CASE OR DECISIONAL LAW

The courts ensure that the statutes do not exceed the bounds set by the Constitution and the courts resolve ambiguous or doubtful areas. In a larceny case, for example, the prosecutor may introduce a statement made by the accused or physical evidence seized by the police in the course of their investigation. The defense may allege that the evidence is inadmissible because it was obtained in violation of the constitutionally guaranteed rights of the accused.

Those preliminary questions (which do not bear on whether the accused is guilty of the crime but, rather, on the way the evidence was obtained) are often raised by a *motion*, or a request to the court for a ruling. The court then discerns if the evidence is admissible.

To determine whether the evidence is admissible, a court often has to state precisely how and to what extent the constitutional safeguards granted by federal and state constitutions apply to the case. A court may decide whether the law "on its face" could reasonably be applied in such a way as to exceed constitutional limitations. When a court finds the law capable of exceeding constitutional limitations, it will rule the law unconstitutional. In other cases, a court may find the law appropriate but that its application in a particular case violates constitutional safeguards. If this is the case, the case is dismissed or an earlier judgment is reversed.

In other cases, a court is called upon to fill in the doubtful areas — to declare whether a law covers a particular act or omission. This involves interpreting the law, or determining — in the light of a particular case, with its own facts — what the legislature intends the statute to mean. Such decisions clarify "doubtful law" and declare its proper application in new factual contexts. When such decisions have been sustained through the appellate process, they become "the law" as much as the words of the statute. Subsequent decisions apply the law in the same way in situations with substantially similar facts. By this process, described as *stare decisis*, or to stand by precedents, a competent court's authoritative determination of the law's meaning makes future application more predictable.

Federal and State Constitutions

In the normal course of a state criminal trial, the questions presented involve analysis and application of state law and the state constitution. The federal Constitution may also be involved if it is alleged that some act or omission contravened the Constitution's guaranteed rights and immunities. In this regard, it is important to note that the Fourteenth Amendment to the U.S. Constitution states, in part:

> No State shall make or enforce any law which shall abridge the privileges or immunities of citizens of the United States; nor shall any State deprive any person of life, liberty or property without due process of law; nor deny to any person within its jurisdiction the equal protection of the laws.

Courts have held this to mean that the privileges and immunities guaranteed to U.S. citizens in the first 10 amendments are, by the language of the Fourteenth Amendment, guaranteed to citizens of the United States in matters arising in state courts.

This provision is readily understandable in that citizens of a state are at the same time citizens of the United States. In state proceedings of a criminal nature, the U.S. Constitution assures that states do not deprive citizens of their granted rights and immunities.

RELEVANCE TO ASSET PROTECTION

The following outline of the U.S. system of criminal justice provides a foundation for the relationship between criminal law and asset protection.

1. Required elements of crimes
2. Required conduct by the security or asset protection organization in criminal matters
3. Distinctions between crimes and other conduct

If a person's activities result in a loss or value reduction of an entity's assets, and if such activities involve criminal conduct, the entity's security function is engaged. Security must safeguard the threatened assets and avoid interference with or damage to the police or prosecutor's position.

Although there are hundreds of different specific crimes, there are relatively few categories of crimes relevant to assets protection programs. The common categories include:

- Crimes based upon unauthorized entry or presence in a given place
- Crimes based upon theft or larceny
- Crimes based upon force or threats of force against people
- Crimes based upon damage or threats of damage against property

Crimes Based upon Unauthorized Entry or Presence

In general, *burglary* consists of unlawfully entering or remaining within a building with the intent to commit some crime therein. A theft can occur during a burglary, but it is not an essential element of burglary. Varying circumstances change the degree or severity of the burglary; for example, if the building is a dwelling, if the unlawful entry is at night, if a dangerous weapon is used or possessed or if physical injury is involved.

The essential elements, however, are *the unlawful entry or remaining* and *the intent to commit some crime*. An accused who can rebut either of these two elements is not guilty of burglary (but may be guilty of some lesser offense). One who rebuts both elements is probably not guilty of any crime involving unauthorized entry or presence.

A person who is found in an unauthorized place does not necessitate a charge of burglary. To establish that a crime has been committed, however, it is necessary to first prove that the accused knew or should have known that he did not have authority to be in that locale. Use of force to enter, while not required to prove the crime, can help prove this. Next, the intent to commit some crime in connection with the unlawful presence or entry must be proven. Cases in which the unlawful presence can be proven but not the criminal intent typically involve crimes of criminal trespass or breaking and entering — less serious offenses.

To the assets protection professional, the immediate significance of the burglary elements is this: *places where all or certain classes of persons are prohibited from entering must be secured and marked such that people prohibited are aware of the prohibition.* For example, if stockrooms or other interior spaces in an office building are prohibited to the public (but the

United States Criminal Law

public can be in the facility), then a notice of prohibition must be unambiguous and clearly displayed.

A good protection program uses physical safeguards — including locks, barriers and alarms — to prevent or detect unauthorized entry. For example, if an individual gains entry to a locked space by forcibly breaking the lock or the door, one can infer that the individual knew he was prohibited from entering. At the other extreme, if an individual enters through an unlocked or defective security door, charging that person with unlawful entry or burglary gets difficult.

If an entire building is closed to the public, and the only persons authorized to be in such a facility are employees and non-employees with a business purpose, then the presence of a non-employee without a business purpose after normal business hours warrants a charge of burglary or criminal trespass.

The main points to keep in mind with regard to crimes involving an unauthorized presence or entry are that:

- The entrance to a prohibited area must be clearly marked in some way
- The persons prohibited from entering must be made aware of this

Precisely which entry or presence constitutes a crime (or a burglary) is determined by reference to the relevant statutory and case law of that state. Further, if the situation involves an unlawful entry into federal facilities, there may be a federal crime. See Chapters 103 and 113 of Title 18 of the U.S. Code for more on this topic.

Crimes Based upon Theft or Larceny

Crimes involving theft or larceny include larceny grand and petit, embezzlement, abstraction, fraud, extortion and obtaining by false promise. The elements of larceny include the wrongful taking, obtaining or withholding of property belonging to another with the intent to deprive the owner of the use and benefit of such property or to appropriate the property to the taker or some third person.

In certain situations, the wrongful taking or obtaining can occur in conjunction with other facts that form the basis for a different and more serious crime. *Robbery* is the taking of property through the use of force or threat of force. *Larceny*, or the unlawful taking of property, can be accompanied by threats of injury or property damage or by the abduction of another person to be held for ransom. These raise the crime of larceny to a more serious crime of extortion or kidnapping. (The threat or use of force is described in greater detail later, as a separate category of crime.)

Note that the elements of any larceny include *taking property of another.* Obviously, an essential element in proving larceny is establishing the true ownership of the property. This is a separate problem from establishing the specific identity of the property allegedly taken.

If an employee is accused of stealing tools belonging to his employer, it must be proven that the employee unlawfully took, obtained or withheld the tools; and it must also be proven that the tools were owned by the company or, at the very least, that the company had some superior right to possess the tools. The problems of "which" property and "whose" property often get resolved together. If tools are involved, the identification of those tools by company name and the proven unlawful taking, obtaining or withholding of them by an employee establishes the required elements.

Having items that contain some identification marking reduces the problem of proving a larceny charge. To this end, it is important to identify tangible assets and keep adequate records for when a question of ownership arises.

For larger or more expensive items, a serial number (often affixed by the manufacturer) may identify it. Documentation must accompany the equipment. For items not serialized by the producer or manufacturer, a distinctive numbering or lettering system should be devised. The number or symbol should be affixed to the asset permanently by etching, indelible markings or a tightly bonding label. Placing this type of symbol in a place not usually inspected by individuals unfamiliar with the asset can help prevent any attempts to remove or deface it. Again, proper documentation is essential.

Another important element of larceny is the intent of the taker. Unless the accused confesses or makes a statement to a witness about his intent, it must to be inferred from conduct. This is one reason why conduct should be unambiguous.

In retail establishments, for example, it is customary not to apprehend alleged shoplifters until they have actually left the premises with the stolen property. This is because *the departure without payment or declaration* indicates an intent to deprive or appropriate. If a suspect is apprehended while still inside the store, his defense could be that he intended to pay before leaving the store, even though he had left a particular sales area. However, if this conduct is accompanied by other questionable behavior, such as stealthy movement, furtive observations and the use of shoplifting techniques to conceal the property, larceny might be proven even if apprehension took place inside the store. Absent such conduct or of exiting the premises, it might be difficult to prove larcenous intent beyond a reasonable doubt.

Crimes Based upon Force or Threats of Force against Persons

The third set of crimes are among the most serious in federal and state penal codes. Among the crimes in this category are murder, manslaughter, kidnapping, maiming, rape, sexual abuse, assault, unlawful imprisonment

United States Criminal Law

and robbery. In addition to these crimes that specifically include an element of force, other crimes can be made more serious when force is used and a person is endangered. Examples include arson, larceny by extortion or criminal negligence.

The basic elements of crimes of force against a person are:

- The use of force or threat of force
- The actual injury or intimidation of the victim

As with any crime, the accused must be shown to have acted knowingly and with the intent to do the specific act prohibited. This intent may be presumed in crimes of negligence but must be proven specifically in the other crimes. This means that any defense tending to rebut the criminal intent by showing another purpose, such as protecting or repossessing one's own property or by showing justification for the intentional use (such as defense of self or another, assisting a police officer at his command, etc.) is relevant. As every crime must be proven beyond a reasonable doubt, credible evidence of such noncriminal purpose or intent may be enough to secure an acquittal.

Inherent to crimes of force or threatened force is the concept of *justification* — for example, the use of force for some purpose approved by the law. For security professionals, this often is a crucial issue, because circumstances may arise where it is possible to use force against individuals. What kind and how much force gets determined on a case-by-case basis, so it is essential to have a general awareness of lawful limits on the use of force.

Permissible Use of Force

Reasonably necessary force — the minimum amount needed to accomplish the permitted purpose — is generally allowed in the following circumstances:

- To defend yourself or others
- To restrain others you believe are about to commit suicide or do themselves serious harm
- To correct a minor — with the authority to do so (e.g., parent or legal guardian)
- By a police officer, a person directed by a police officer to assist him or her, or a private citizen to arrest a criminal or prevent one from escaping — with the authority to do so (e.g., police officer or individual directed by a law enforcement official)

The permissible use of force varies from jurisdiction to jurisdiction, and local and state law *must* be consulted. Generally, fatal force — force resulting or likely to result in death — can only be used in:

- Response to fear of one's own life (where debilitating the offender is not possible)

    or

- Prevention of a crime or in apprehension of a criminal when a deadly weapon is employed

In *Tennessee v. Garner*, the U.S. Supreme Court ruled that a Tennessee statute, which permitted the use of fatal force to capture a felon who was not a serious threat to safety, was unconstitutional.[1]

In some jurisdictions, the law requires that the unlawful attack or threat of attack be actual, while in others a "reasonable belief" that such an attack is occurring or threatened is enough to justify the use of force. Also, when using force in defense of another, some jurisdictions require that the defended person actually be authorized to use force to defend himself or herself. Here, the defender acts at his or her own peril.

An example: A security officer witnesses an altercation in a company parking lot where one person is about to strike another with a weapon. The security officer comes to the defense of the apparent victim, but he later discovers that the *apparent* victim is a mugger who first attacked the person preparing to use the weapon. In some states, the security officer is unable to excuse his use of force, because the mugger — the person whose protection was sought — had no right to use force. In other states, the "reasonable belief" of the security officer is a sufficient defense.

The permissible amount or degree of force also depends upon local law. Some jurisdictions allow individuals to use the amount of force "reasonably believed" necessary. Other jurisdictions require that individuals use only an amount of force that is necessary to prevent the attack, apprehend the criminal or defend the premises or property.

When force is required and the question of what constitutes enough force comes up after the event, the "reasonable belief" is not the only consideration. An individual may not use force if he is the initial aggressor or provoked another individual to use or threaten force. An exception to this rule: when the initial aggressor has clearly withdrawn from the situation and the other person (the initial victim) becomes the aggressor.

With regard to the use of force in defense of premises, the general rule is that an individual in lawful occupancy or a responsible individual in charge of premises may use an amount of force reasonably necessary (but not fatal force) in preventing or terminating a perceived criminal trespass. This can be tricky, especially when perceptions are involved.

---

[1] *Tennessee v. Garner*, 53 L.W. 4410, decided March 27, 1985.

Criminal trespassers are people who intentionally enter or remain on private property. If a trespass is disputed, for example, a security officer discovers strangers in a locked office building after hours, but the strangers allege that they were attempting to visit an occupant, the officer must prove that he "reasonably believed" the others to be trespassers before he can use force. So, the situation would require, at the least, that the strangers be ordered to leave and that they stand their ground or refuse to go.

If the security officer has other evidence that establishes a "reasonable belief," then the strangers' mere assertion that they are not trespassers is not enough to prevent the use of "reasonably necessary" force. Moreover, if the security officer elects to apprehend the strangers for some other crime that they may have committed or attempted, then the use of force is based on that ground and not on the ground of terminating a criminal trespass.

In the case of apprehension, however, it may be necessary (depending upon the local law) not only to show reasonable belief that a crime has been committed and that force was necessary, but that a crime did, in fact, occur.

The foregoing considerations enforce the importance of having a security program that establishes the bases for reasonable belief by those who suspect that persons have committed or attempted crime. *Locks, alarms, warning notices and other physical resources thus acquire a twofold relevance: first as actual deterrents and second as a basis for appropriately invoking criminal sanctions against aggressors by security personnel acting in good faith.*

Crimes Based upon Damage or Threat of Damage to Property

Crimes involving damage to property constitute the final general category of crimes commonly encountered in an assets protection program. These include arson, vandalism and criminal mischief; extortion; bombings and threats of bombing; tampering; reckless endangerment; sabotage; rioting; and insurrection.

Property crimes become a more serious violation when the force used or threatened also threatens individuals. The seriousness of a crime is related to the use of dangerous weapons and the value of the property.

In cases of extortion and bomb threats, it is extremely common for the criminal to use interstate wire communications or the U.S. Postal Service to communicate the threat or demand. Refer to Titles 18 U.S.C. 844(e) and 876 for material that explains the appropriate response to mailed and telephoned threats of this type. Note that mailing a kidnap or extortion threat or demand from a foreign country to the U.S. constitutes a U.S. felony crime under the provisions of 18 U.S.C. 877.

IMPORTANT PROCEDURAL CONSIDERATIONS

Constitutional privileges and immunities are guaranteed to citizens under both state and federal constitutions. The federal Constitution assures that the states must, at the very least, afford the federal safeguards to all persons involved in state criminal proceedings. Some state-guaranteed protections are more stringent than the federal ones; therefore, any entity developing an assets protection program should check the local jurisdiction's law for compliance with federal, state and local protections.

A critical distinction must be made between a citizen who is dealing with the government and a citizen who is dealing with another private citizen. Constitutional safeguards protect the citizen against the government — but not the citizen against other private citizens. If a police officer or other representative of the government engages in conduct that amounts to a violation of due process of law, the aggrieved citizens (and in some cases non-citizens) can invoke the full protection of the Constitution in order to end or invalidate any criminal proceedings that result. In precisely the same circumstances, however, if a private citizen — such as the security staff of a private enterprise — engages in such conduct, the aggrieved person has no constitutional immunities.

If a private citizen violates due process, then the conduct may amount to a crime under either federal or state law, or a "tort" (a private wrong). In this situation, damages or other civil relief is available. (Torts are discussed in Chapter 15 dealing with civil law. For the remainder of this discussion, we will consider those special situations where the question of constitutional immunity may arise.)

Arrests

The term "arrest, in criminal procedures, is defined as *the taking into custody of a person to answer to a criminal offense*.[1] Elements of an arrest include:

- The intention to take the person into custody of the law
- Through actual or constructive seizure or detention
- With the understanding of the arrestee that he or she is arrested

Because security officers may at any time be required to detain someone, they must be familiar with the law regarding arrest, search and seizure. Some of the more important general aspects of these are noted here.

An arrest can be made:

- Pursuant to federal or state law
- With a warrant and without a warrant
- By police, peace officers and private citizens

---

[1] 18 U.S.C. 203.

United States Criminal Law

Federal or State Law. The U.S. criminal code specifically authorizes named federal and local officials to make arrests for federal crimes. State laws authorize arrests for offenses against state criminal laws. Whether an arrest for a federal crime can be made by a state official or even a private citizen depends upon the statutory or common law of the state where the arrest is made. Some states follow the common law rule — the general practice sanctioned by case law in states that do not have statutes specifically dealing with this type of arrest.

In states that have adopted statutory definitions of arrest and provisions for crimes and circumstances under which an arrest may be made, the statutory provision governs. If the statutory provision allows for federal crimes, then such arrests may be made. If it prohibits such arrests or excludes them, then they may not lawfully be made pursuant to state law.

Many crimes in violation of the federal law are also crimes in violation of state law. In these cases, state law applies if the federal crime is committed within the jurisdiction of the state.

A number of crimes — such as customs violations — are uniquely federal, and legitimacy of arrests are reviewed under the rule just described. In such cases, a complete review of local and/or state law is the only reliable basis for determining a lawful course of conduct.

With or Without a Warrant. A *warrant* is a judicial process, issued upon probable cause, authorizing or commanding an act. An *arrest warrant* authorizes the taking into custody of the named person. A *search warrant* authorizes the search of the named place under the conditions imposed. Warrants are normally issued only to law enforcement or judicial officers for execution. In most assets protection situations, unless the security personnel are deputized as law enforcement officers, they do not get involved in arrests under a warrant. If the security personnel are deputized law enforcement officers, then whether they can execute a warrant depends upon the terms of their appointments. (The deputation question is discussed in greater detail later.)

An arrest without a warrant can be made either by a police officer or a private person. The conditions for each are controlled by state law. In general, police officers may arrest an individual without a warrant when they have reasonable cause to believe that the person committed an offense in their presence. They may also arrest an individual for any crime, whether committed in their presence or not, when they have reasonable cause to believe the person has committed the offense. Because "offense" may include petty offenses as well as crimes (generally misdemeanors and felonies), police officers have broad latitude with regard to warrantless arrests. They need only satisfy the requirement for *reasonable cause*. This means that a police officer is not liable — even if no crime was committed — or if the arrested person did not commit it.

When a private person makes an arrest, it is called a *citizen's arrest*. The authority of a private person to make an arrest is generally limited to:

- Any crime committed in the presence of the arresting person

  or

- A felony, even if not in that person's presence

In certain states, "reasonable cause" may be enough to arrest for a felony offense. There is an extremely important distinction between the powers of a private person and those of a police officer with regard to an arrest. If a mistake is made as to the person apprehended, the private person who errs in causing the arrest has no excuse. "Reasonable cause" is generally not a permissible defense. An arrested individual could file a civil action for damages.

In addition, the law commands a private person to take the arrested individual "without unnecessary or unreasonable delay" before a court, judicial officer or police officer. Failure to make an arrest legally exposes the arresting private person to civil damages and — if they used force or threat of force to accomplish the arrest — possible criminal charges as well.

The security officer must have authority to make the arrest, and the person to be arrested must be made aware of that fact. If the security officer has no right to make the arrest — such as when no crime has been committed or the wrong person has been apprehended — the security officer's actions may constitute false arrest or assault. If the officer kills a person, such action may render the officer guilty of manslaughter or murder. Note: A person who is unlawfully arrested can resist with all reasonable force.

Security officers or employees who hold a valid police officer appointment and who make an arrest without a warrant (pursuant to the terms and under the authority of that appointment) are protected as police officers. That is, they are permitted to rely upon reasonable cause. A security employee who does not possess such an appointment is treated as a private person.

Although this suggests that police officer appointments are desirable, the separate problem of constitutional due process, which is created by status as a police officer or government representative, must also be considered. (The implications of those due process requirements are further explored in the subsequent discussion of interviews and interrogations.)

By a Police Officer or Private Person. Constitutional rights are available to a citizen aggrieved by the actions of the government. A police officer is typically the government representative who becomes involved in such situations. If, therefore, a police officer makes an unreasonable search or illegal seizure, or conducts an interrogation in violation of due process, the results — things seized or admissions and confessions obtained — can be suppressed and made unavailable for prosecution. Any evidence derived as a result of the proscribed action is deemed inadmissible

United States Criminal Law

in a legal action. In effect, the constitutional impropriety of the police officer can defeat the prosecution.

If a private person engages in the constitutionally proscribed conduct, however, the same result does not necessarily follow. The evidence or admissions obtained may be admissible. This can be true even if the private person is guilty of a crime or is liable in civil damages for the way he or she conducted the search, seizure or interrogation.

The legality of an arrest has a direct bearing on the later prosecution. If security officers claim police officer status for the purpose of protecting their arrest activities, they will not be able to disclaim it for purposes of an interview or interrogation. Once the "government representative" or "agent of the state" status has been asserted in a particular case for one purpose, it remains in the case for all purposes.

Interviews and Interrogations

The criminal law uniformly requires that any statement made by persons against their own interest (and meant to be used against them in criminal proceedings) must be *voluntary* — that is, not the result of threats, intimidation, coercion or inducements. This is true irrespective of whether the statements were made to a police officer or a private person.

In addition to the requirement that admissions and confessions be voluntary, the landmark *Miranda* decision imposed additional, significant restraints on police and government representatives.[1] Following the *Miranda* case, officers who take an individual into custody must inform the individual that:

- He need not make any statement
- Any statement he does make may be used against him in court
- He has the right to counsel
- If he cannot afford counsel, one will be provided by the court
- He need make no further statement or answer any further question after requesting counsel until counsel has been provided

Individuals in police custody are usually more than witnesses, but are not necessarily suspects in a crime. They are generally not at liberty to leave the place of interview or interrogation. Custody can occur without a formal arrest and in areas other than a police station.

Although these additional constraints affect police and government agents, *they do not apply to private persons.* Case law holds these requirements inapplicable to the private person, including the private security officer.[2] Therefore, if suspects are interrogated by security personnel who

---
[1] *Miranda v. Arizona*, 384 U.S. 486, 86 S. Ct. 1602, 162 L. Ed. 2nd 694 (1966).
[2] *U.S. v. Casteel*, 476F 2d 152 (KS 1973); *U.S. v. Antonelli*, 434F 2d 335 (NY 1970); *People v. Jones*, 301 N.E. 2d 85 (IL 1973).

are not police officers, the law only requires that their admissions or confessions are voluntary — that is, made without coercion, without fear of punishment or promise of reward.

When the security officer or investigator is also a police officer, however, a different problem emerges. Dependent upon the facts, the private interrogator may act as an instrument of the state — if the court finds coordination or complicity between the security officer and the police. Even when the interrogator is not a police officer but acts in aid of one, or the interrogation takes place within earshot of a police officer, the prohibitions may become relevant if the facts support that the interrogator was an agent or instrument of the state.

A prudent security professional acts cautiously in this area. If a situation calls for an interrogation under the *Miranda* requirements, either because the interrogator has police status or acts in support of police officers (or because the interrogation takes place within earshot of police), a *Miranda* warning should be given.

Searches and Seizures

The Fourth Amendment to the U.S. Constitution (and its extension to the states by the Fourteenth Amendment) prohibits unreasonable searches and seizures. Case law has defined this to mean searches:

- Without a warrant when a warrant could have been obtained
- For items not covered by the warrant
- In locations not included within the warrant
- Warrantless searches, otherwise permissible, that have gone too far

For example, a warrantless search incidental to an arrest is authorized if it does not extend beyond the immediate area where the accused may reach to get a weapon or other evidence.

As with the Fifth Amendment extension established in *Miranda,* the Fourth Amendment applies only to government agents and representatives. Any search by a private person, not made at the direction or in support of police or government agents, is not governed by the Fourth Amendment. Therefore, material seized is admissible in a criminal proceeding, even if a crime or tort was committed in the seizure.

Note, however, that the considerations of crime and tort committed in the course of a search may be far more important than the admissibility of evidence seized. If a security officer or investigator is liable for imprisonment and an employer is liable for serious financial loss in a civil damage action, it may be a Pyrrhic victory that the suspect was convicted.

Typical cases presented in a commercial setting involve searches of employee lockers and desks, and inspections or searches of individuals entering or leaving a facility. Such searches can occur on a consensual basis (i.e., the individual agrees to the search either at the time or in advance as a condition of employment or continued employment).

A company rule, built into company policy, would establish an adequate basis for such searches — with two exceptions. First, a consent to a search in advance can always be revoked. In such a case, the company would consider whether to proceed with the search anyway, take disciplinary action against the revoking employee or both.

If the search were of a desk or locker — ultimately the property of the company — revoking the employee's right to give consent is not valuable. However, if an individual is searched and consent is revoked, the use of force to conduct the search may be both a tort and a crime, although the noncriminal intent of the searcher might be sufficient to void the criminal charge. If the employee is suspected of concealing evidence of a crime, the employer (and the private security person involved) has three alternative courses:

1. Arrest the employee on the charge of the crime committed. This is a citizen's arrest (assuming the security officer does not act as a deputy or law enforcement officer) without a warrant. The charge may have to be supported by proof that the employee committed the crime. In this case, some authorities permit a search of the person to arrest, even when the arrest and subsequent search are conducted by private persons. In other jurisdictions, the right to make a search incidental to arrest is denied when the arrest is by a citizen without a warrant. If a search is conducted in these jurisdictions, evidence seized is admissible in court, but the force needed to complete the search might constitute a crime or a tort.
2. Permit the employee to leave but file a criminal complaint with the police, based upon the evidence available. This would then transfer the problem to the authorities who, if they were willing to act in these circumstances, would proceed by warrant.
3. Take disciplinary action against the employee in the context of his or her employment. This would not affect the criminal case if one later develops.

In doubtful circumstances, some combination of alternatives 2 and 3 is wiser than making a citizen's arrest, with or without the search.

The second exception to the company search rule involves a company's collective bargaining contract in which employee discipline is subject to grievance or arbitration. For now, it is important to note that in these circumstances an independent arbitrator determines if the search is:

1. Permitted under the contract
2. Reasonable

3. Fairly applied
4. On sufficient notice

Independent arbitration also determines whether the employee discipline for an alleged infraction is just.

This does not add to or detract from the criminality or tortuousness, if any, of the employer's conduct in searching. It would, however, present an entirely new and additional set of considerations. An arbitrator might find discipline after an involuntary search to be "tainted" and might find for the employee on some general basis of fairness. Such a finding is binding upon the employer.

Entrapment

Entrapment is an affirmative defense available under both federal and state law to a person charged with a criminal offense. In essence, *entrapment* is the inducement by a law enforcement officer of another person, not otherwise disposed to do so, to commit a criminal offense for the purpose of prosecuting that person. In federal law, the doctrine has been developed by case decisions and is a common-law doctrine.

Entrapment cannot be the result of a private person's conduct. It must be committed by a law enforcement officer.

Some states adopt the rule under common law; others adopt it by statute. The common law entrapment rule generally includes only law enforcement officers. The statutory rule in states enacting statutes extends the defense and makes it available against private persons if they are acting in concert with or in support of police.

Conduct not constituting entrapment under common law might be considered a criminal act, sufficient to support charges of *criminal solicitation* — procuring another to commit a crime — or *criminal facilitation* — rendering aid to another with the knowledge that it is in aid of the commission of an offense. The mere act of giving another the opportunity to commit an offense is neither facilitation nor solicitation, nor is it entrapment under current common law.

SPECIFIC CRIMINAL STATUTES OF SECURITY INTEREST

The Economic Espionage Act

The U.S. Congress enacted the Economic Espionage Act in 1996 to combat foreign economic espionage and provide criminal penalties for theft of trade secrets by a foreign power.[1] The act also makes domestic theft of trade secrets a federal crime, whether or not a foreign government is involved.

[1] 18 U.S.C. 1831–1839.

The act defines the term "trade secret" to mean all forms and types of financial, business, scientific, technical, economic or engineering information, including patterns, plans, compilations, program devices, formulas, designs, prototypes, methods, techniques, processes, procedures, programs, or codes; whether tangible or intangible; and whether or how stored, compiled or memorialized physically, electronically, graphically, photographically or in writing if:

- The owner thereof has taken reasonable measures to keep such information secret; *and*
- The information derives independent economic value, actual or potential, from not being generally known to, and not being readily ascertainable through proper means by, the public; *and*
- The term "owner," with respect to a trade secret, means the person or entity in whom or in which rightful legal or equitable title to, or license in, the trade secret is reposed.

The penalties for trade secret theft are severe. Foreign economic espionage is punishable by a personal fine up to $500,000, imprisonment for up to 15 years, or both. An organization can be fined up to $10 million. The penalties for domestic trade secret theft include personal fines and imprisonment up to 19 years, or both. An organization involved in domestic theft can be fined up to $5 million.

The act provides for confidentiality of the information involved as cases are investigated and brought to trial.

Eavesdropping Statutes

Eavesdropping, in a broad context, means any unauthorized listening, whether done physically or by means of equipment that is electronic or otherwise.

It is important to have a basic knowledge of the legalities of electronic eavesdropping in order to ensure proper investigative activities. From another perspective, because the basic precept of security is the prevention of loss, the assets protection professional must be guided by common sense and existing statutes.

The largest segment of the laws regarding electronic surveillance applies to the government's monitoring of citizens. The laws list the conditions under which monitoring is allowable, procedures for obtaining court orders and the rules of surveillance conduct, etc., but very little law addresses the issue of citizens monitoring one another. Loopholes in the laws and conflicting court decisions regarding the interception of communications complicate the issue.

Pertinent Federal Law

1. Title III of the Omnibus Crime Control and Safe Streets Act (18 U.S.C. 2510, *et seq.*):
   — Authorizes law enforcement use of electronic surveillance
   — Safeguards wire and oral communications
   — Prohibits private-sector possession/use of electronic surveillance equipment
   — Creates acceptable uniform circumstances for electronic surveillance
   — Sets constitutionally acceptable procedures for government surveillance
2. The Electronic Communications Privacy Act (ECPA) (18 U.S.C. 2510):
   — Extends Title III protection to cellular telephones, fiber optic transmissions, teleconferencing, voice mail, electronic mail, encrypted transmissions and most pagers
   — Strengthens Title III criminal and civil penalties
   — Provides for court-ordered roving interceptions
3. Mobile Tracking Devices (18 U.S.C. 3117):
   — Extends the validity of a court order for a tracking device to all jurisdictions
4. Pen Register and Trap and Trace Devices (18 U.S.C. 3121–3126):
   — Limits private use to communications providers and consensual situations
5. Foreign Intelligence Surveillance Act (50 U.S.C. 1801–1811):
   — Allows government surveillance in the interest of national security
6. Communications Assistance for Law Enforcement Act (18 U.S.C. 2522):
   — Requires a telecommunications carrier to assist a law enforcement agency in court-authorized interceptions of communications

Summary of Federal Law

The federal law describes the circumstances under which communication interception can be authorized and conducted, and by whom. It requires a U.S. court to authorize federal communications interceptions, after application by the U.S. Attorney General or a designee. At the state level, the federal law forbids interception of defined communications without a state statute. The state statute must provide that any interception be addressed to the appropriate state court by a state attorney general or designee, and conform to both the state and the federal statutory requirements. The law permits civil actions by aggrieved people seeking injunctive relief and financial damages.

The law permits interception of any communication causing interference to lawfully operated stations or consumer electronic equipment, to the extent necessary to identify the source of the interference. Also permitted are receptions of communications by other lawful users on the same frequency, as long as the communication is not scrambled or encrypted.

Additionally, the law addresses electronic message delivery systems — such as e-mail and other systems that receive and temporarily store or process wire or electronic communications. It is unlawful to access, without authorization, a facility through which electronic communications service is provided. It is also unlawful to exceed the limits of an authorization for such access and thereby to obtain, alter or prevent authorized access to any wire or electronic communication while it is in electronic storage.

The federal law prohibits the following intentional acts:

- Interception or attempt to intercept any wire, oral or electronic communication
- Use or attempt to use any electronic, mechanical or other device to intercept oral communications
- Disclosure or attempt to disclose the contents of any wire, oral or electronic communication, knowing the information was obtained in violation of the act
- Use of or attempt to use the contents of any illegally intercepted wire, oral or electronic communication
- Manufacture, distribution, possession or advertising of a device that is primarily useful for the surreptitious interception of communications

Take note that the prohibition is for devices that are *primarily useful for the purpose of surreptitious interception*. However, spy toys are often sold for other ventures. Wireless microphones, for example, are used to sing over the radio or monitor a baby's room. Contact microphones (used for listening through walls) are used to track down rodents' nests. Microcassette and voice-activated tape recorders have dozens of applications. Hidden telephone transmitters are used to broadcast the children's phone call to a radio near a family member's sick bed.

The federal law does not prohibit interceptions:

- By a communications company or the Federal Communications Commission (FCC) in the normal course of business
- By a party to the communication or with the consent of a party to it, unless such interception is in furtherance of a crime or tortuous act under U.S. or any state laws
- That are authorized under the Foreign Intelligence Surveillance Act
- Of electronic communications that are readily accessible to the public

This last provision permits interception of radio communications made to the general public; radio communications by any government, private land mobile or public safety communications system; and transmissions on CB or general mobile service frequencies or by any marine or aeronautical communications system.

State Laws

State laws generally follow the federal law. A state law may be more restrictive than the federal law *but is never less restrictive*. Approximately 32 states have enacted their own eavesdropping laws. Most use the federal model as a foundation and add restrictions. Hawaii, Louisiana, Ohio and Pennsylvania statutes are considerably different. For example, federal law allows communications interception when one party to the communication consents. Many states' laws follow this law. However, some states do not allow interception unless all parties agree. Employers who record conversations with their employees may be within their rights in one state while committing a felony in a neighboring state. New Jersey — one-party consent — and Pennsylvania — two-party consent — are examples of this. The federal law applies in states without their own specific statutes.

Laws evolve with court decisions, and states can hold opposite opinions about the same electronic eavesdropping questions. Contradictory interpretations of the eavesdropping laws can be confusing. Keep a copy of applicable state laws on file, update them regularly and obtain current legal advice on these issues. Above all, *never rely on a law to keep communications private*.

Number of Government Interceptions

The restrictions on interceptions by government agencies at all levels are rigid. Despite the restrictions, interceptions in the U.S. and other countries have steadily increased. These notable increases notwithstanding, the individual or organization that is not involved in serious criminal activity does not need to be concerned with authorized interceptions by a government agency. For such entities, the illegal intruder poses the greatest danger.

DECEPTION DETECTION INSTRUMENTS

Federal Polygraph Legislation

With some exceptions, the Employee Polygraph Protection Act of 1988 (EPPA) prohibits any private employer engaged in or affecting interstate commerce, or producing goods for interstate commerce, from requiring or requesting any employee or prospective employee to take or submit to any lie detector test, or from using the results of any lie detector test. The complete text of the act is codified at 29 U.S.C. 2001, *et seq.* The implementing Department of Labor rules are codified at 29 C.F.R. 801, *et seq.* Refer to the U.S. Code and the text of the rules themselves for detailed information.

United States Criminal Law

The EPPA does not preempt state laws or the provisions of any collective bargaining agreements that prohibit lie detector tests or are more restrictive than the federal law in regard to lie detectors.

Paper and pencil or oral honesty tests are not included in the coverage of the polygraph act.

The EPPA extends to all employees of covered employers, regardless of citizenship status, and to foreign corporations operating in the U.S.

Broad Interpretations of the EPPA

The 7th Circuit U.S. Court of Appeals stretched the EPPA to its outer bounds when it held that an employer violated the EPPA by requesting a tape recording of the employee's voice.[1] The court in *Veazey v. Communications and Cable of Chicago, Inc.* opined that a tape recording used in conjunction with either a polygraph, deceptograph, voice stress analyzer, psychological stress evaluator or any device that renders a "diagnostic opinion" regarding honesty or dishonesty, is considered a "lie detector" for purposes of the EPPA.

Definitions

> *Lie detector.* A polygraph, deceptograph, voice stress analyzer, psychological stress evaluator or similar device, whether mechanical or electrical, that is used or whose results are used to reach an opinion as to the honesty or dishonesty of an individual. The distinction among devices is important, because in later sections which exempt certain private-sector employers or situations from coverage of the act, the exemption is applied only to the polygraph and not to any other form of lie detector.
>
> *Polygraph.* An instrument which, as a minimum, continuously, visually, permanently and simultaneously records changes in cardiovascular (blood pressure), respiratory (breathing) and electrodermal (skin electrical property) patterns. Single-feature devices or even multiple-feature devices that do not meet this criterion are not treated as polygraphs (although they would remain under the general term "lie detector" if they are used to support diagnostic opinions regarding honesty).

Prohibitions. Unless exempted as listed below, no employer subject to the EPPA may:

---

[1] *Veazey v. Communications and Cable of Chicago, Inc.*; 194 3d 850 (7th Cir. 1999).

1. Require, request, suggest or cause any employee or prospective employee to take or submit to *any lie detector* (*note:* not just polygraph) test
2. Use, accept, refer to, or inquire about the results of any lie detector test of any employee or prospective employee:
3. Discharge, discipline, discriminate against, or deny or threaten to deny employment or promotion to:
    a. Any employee or prospective employee who refuses, declines or fails to take a lie detector test
    b. Discriminate against any employee or prospective employee on the basis of the results of any lie detector test
4. Commit or threaten to commit any of the foregoing acts against any employee or prospective employee because such person has filed any complaint or instituted any proceeding under the chapter, testified in any such proceeding, or exercised any rights under the chapter personally or on behalf of any other person

Covered employers must prominently post a notice prepared by the Secretary of Labor notifying employees of pertinent provisions of the chapter.

An employer who cooperates with police in their use of polygraph tests of employees does not violate the act as long as the cooperation is passive and the employer does not participate in the testing or reimburse police for testing.

The simulated use of a polygraph by an employer, which leads an individual to believe an actual test is being conducted, is a violation of the act.

Exemptions.

Government and National Security Exemptions. The government at all levels — federal, state and local — is exempt from coverage of the EPPA. The federal government may administer lie detector tests to several categories of experts, contractors and consultants (or their employees) to the Departments of Defense and Energy and to the CIA, DIA, NSA and FBI in the performance of intelligence or counterintelligence functions.

Ongoing Investigations Exemption. This limited exemption establishes the conditions under which tests are permitted in connection with actual losses. An employer, otherwise prohibited from testing by the act, may administer tests if *all* of the following conditions are met:

- The test is limited to the polygraph.
- The test is in connection with an ongoing investigation of economic loss or injury to the employer's business, such as theft, embezzlement, misappropriation, industrial espionage or sabotage.
- The employee tested had access to the property involved in the loss.

- The employer has a reasonable suspicion that the tested employee was involved.
- The employer provides a written statement to the persons tested, before administration of the test, which:
  — Identifies the matter being investigated and the basis for testing particular employees
  — Is signed by a person other than the polygraphist, authorized to bind the employer
  — Is retained by the employer for at least three years
  — Contains an identification of the specific loss or injury, and a statement that the employee tested had access, and a statement describing the employer's reasonable suspicion that the employee was involved

The ongoing investigation exemption does not apply if the employee is discriminated against on the basis of his polygraph chart or his refusal to take the test. Evidence of reasonable suspicion, needed to administer the polygraph test, may also support employment action.

An employer may not use this exemption for continuous or random testing. There must be a specific incident or activity. For example, an inventory shortage is not enough to support a polygraph exam. If additional information is obtained, giving rise to a reasonable suspicion that an employee is the culprit, then an exam would be permitted. The misappropriation of confidential or trade secret information is cited as a specific incident that would constitute direct economic loss to the employer.

Indirect losses by an employer include the use of the employer's business to commit a crime, such as check kiting or money laundering. The mere occurrence of a criminal act on employee premises, such as a drug sale in the parking lot, is not enough. Losses from unintentional or otherwise lawful conduct (e.g., losses from vehicle or workplace accidents or routine cash register shortages) is also not enough to permit polygraph exams.

Although the act does not prohibit the use of medical tests to determine the presence of alcohol or controlled substances, polygraph exams cannot be used for that purpose, even if such a substance contributed to an employer loss.

Security Services Exemption. This exemption to commercial security services in the private sector permits testing by private employers if *all* the following conditions exist:
- The employer's primary business purpose consists of providing armored car, security alarm or other uniformed or plainclothes security personnel.

- The employer's function includes the protection of:
  — Facilities, materials or operations having a significant impact on U.S. national security or the health or safety of any state (to include electric or nuclear power and public water supply facilities, and radioactive or toxic materials and public transportation, all to be particularly described in regulations to be issued), *or*
  — Currency, negotiable instruments, precious commodities or instruments, or proprietary information.
- The test is conducted with respect to a prospective employee who will be employed directly in the described functions.
- The test is a *polygraph* test (i.e., not any other lie detector).

This exemption does not apply if the refusal to take a test or the analysis of a polygraph test chart is used as the sole basis for an adverse employment action against the employee or prospective employee.

For screening purposes, polygraph tests may only be given to prospective employees under this exemption. Qualified employers may use polygraph tests on incumbent employees under the incident investigations exemption.

For this exemption to apply, at least 50 percent of a business' revenue must come from the type of security services mentioned in the act. A firm that provides its own security service but is primarily engaged in other activity does not qualify.

When applying the statute's requirement that protected facilities have a significant impact on the U.S. or a state or subdivision, the facilities may be either private or government, but their importance to national or state welfare cannot be minor. An employer whose business is not specifically mentioned in 29 U.S.C. 2006(e) may petition the administrator of the Wage and Hour Division for an interpretation. But the employer must do this *before* administering any polygraph tests.

The rules define the term "proprietary information" used in the statute as meaning trade secret type data.

Applicants "employed to protect" the enumerated types of assets or activities must hold positions such that they would have at least an opportunity to cause or participate in a breach of security. Prospects for custodial or maintenance type jobs, not involving the sensitive type locations or assets, are not covered.

Drug Security Exemption. This exemption applies to testing by any employer manufacturing, distributing or dispensing controlled substances in any of the first four schedules of the Controlled Substances Act. It applies if *all* the following conditions exist:

- The test is a *polygraph* test.
- When conducted with respect to a prospective employee, that employee has direct access to the manufacture, storage, distribution or sale of the controlled substance.
- With respect to current employees, the test is given in connection with an ongoing investigation of criminal or other misconduct involving loss affecting the controlled substance, and the tested employee had access to the person or property that is the subject of the investigation.

The exemption applies only to employers licensed by the DEA to manufacture, distribute or dispense a controlled substance. As it applies only to employers registered with the DEA, it does not apply to truck drivers and warehouse personnel whose possession is in the normal course of their business or employment and whose employers are not DEA-registered. To test prospective employees under this exemption, they must be under consideration for a job in which the employee has an opportunity to divert controlled substances. To test incumbent employees, there need only be access to a person or to property that is the subject of an ongoing investigation. Direct access to a controlled substance is not required; random or opportunistic access is enough.

An example: employees in a supermarket that has a pharmacy. Personnel assigned to the pharmacy have *direct* access to controlled substances, whereas personnel whose duties do not involve handling controlled substances, but require occasional entry into the pharmacy, have access. Other supermarket personnel whose duties do not require or permit entry into the pharmacy do not have access.

Again, this exemption does not apply if the refusal to take a test or the analysis of a polygraph test chart is used as the sole basis for an adverse employment action against the employee or prospective employee.

Restrictions on Exemptions. An otherwise exempt employer who discharges or disciplines an employee after an investigative polygraph test must have, in addition to the test results, independent evidence that the employee had access, that there was reasonable suspicion pointing to that employee, and/or that the employee made admissions before, during or after the exam.

An employer who takes adverse employment action after a polygraph test or in the face of an employee's refusal to be tested must have an additional reason. Such reasons could include conventional background data from prior employment, education and the like, or statements made by the employee or prospect before, during or after the test.

Note that even in the exemptions listed above, the tests are limited to the polygraph.

Rights of the Examinee. The ongoing investigation, security services and drug security exemptions do not apply unless *all* the following conditions are met:

1. The examinee can terminate the test at any time.
2. Degrading or needlessly intrusive questions are not asked.
3. No question is asked concerning:
   — Religious beliefs or affiliations
   — Opinions or beliefs on racial matters
   — Political beliefs or affiliations
   — Sexual behavior
   — Labor union beliefs, affiliations or lawful activities
4. No test is conducted if there is sufficient written medical evidence of a condition or treatment that might cause abnormal responses.
5. Prior to the test the examinee is given written notice of the date and place and of the right to consult with counsel or an employee representative.
6. Prior to the test, the examinee is informed in writing of:
   — The nature of the test and the instrument involved
   — Whether the test area contains a two-way mirror or camera or other such device
   — Whether any other device, including one to record or monitor the test, is used
   — That the employer or employee (with mutual knowledge) may record the test
7. Prior to the test, the examinee signs a written notice:
   — That the test cannot be required as a condition of employment
   — That any statement made during the test may constitute additional evidence supporting adverse employment action
   — Of the limitations imposed by the act
   — Of the examinee's rights if the test is not done in accordance with the act
   — Of the employer's legal rights, including the right to disclose to the government information from the test involving admission of criminal conduct
8. Prior to the test, the examinee is allowed to review all questions to be asked during the test and is informed of the right to terminate the test at any time.
9. During the test, the examiner does not ask any question relevant during the test that was not presented in writing for review prior to the test.
10. After the test but prior to any adverse employment action, the employer:
    — Conducts further interviews of the applicant on the basis of test results

— Provides the examinee with a written copy of any opinion or conclusion from the test and a copy of the questions asked and the chart responses
11. The test shall be at least 90 minutes long and the polygraph operator shall not conduct more than five such tests on the test day.

Qualifications of Examiners. The exemptions discussed above do not apply unless the polygraph examiner:

1. Possesses a valid polygraph license if required in the state
2. Maintains a minimum $50,000 bond or equivalent professional liability insurance
3. Renders any opinion or conclusions in writing and solely on the basis of an analysis of the charts
4. Does not include any information other than admissions, case facts and interpretation of the charts relevant to the purpose and stated objectives of the test, or any recommendation concerning employment of the examinee
5. Maintains all charts and other test-related records for three years after the test

Disclosure of Information. The examinee may disclose to anyone information developed during the polygraph test. The examiner may only disclose: (1) to the examinee or person designated in writing by the examinee; or (2) to the employer who requested the test, to any court, government agency, arbitrator or mediator in accordance with due process of law, pursuant to an order from a court of competent jurisdiction.

An employer (other than the government or consultants, experts or contractors to the government) who requests the test may disclose in the same fashion as the examiner or to a government agency (without a court order) but only so much of the information as is an admission of criminal conduct.

Enforcement. Civil penalties up to $10,000 for violation of any provisions of the chapter are permitted, as are actions for injunctions by the Secretary of Labor in U.S. District Courts. Any employee or prospective employee affected by a violation of the chapter may bring any action in any federal or state court of competent jurisdiction, for any legal or equitable relief required, including but not limited to employment, reinstatement, promotion and back wages or lost benefits, plus court costs and attorneys' fees. This section also prohibits waiver of any rights under the chapter unless done as part of a written settlement agreed to and signed by the parties to any pending action or complaint under the chapter. (Note: any

ASSET PROTECTION AND SECURITY MANAGEMENT HANDBOOK

waiver obtained prior to a test or after a test but prior to the filing of a complaint is not effective.)

Admissibility of Polygraph Results in Evidence

Admissibility of the Lie Detector. Prior to 1993, admissibility of evidence was governed by the general acceptance test, which held that the admissibility of expert scientific evidence depends on its acceptance by the scientific community. The general acceptance test has for the most part been replaced by the *Daubert* decision and the Federal Rules of Evidence 702 (FRE 702).[1] The admissibility of expert scientific evidence is analyzed by the methodology used by the expert. Moreover, the *Daubert* analysis pertains only to cases submitted before the federal court system. However, the Supreme Court in *Daubert* opined that when seeking the admissibility of evidence, such as the lie detector, the trial judge may consider five nonexclusive factors:

1. Whether the technique or theory can be or has been tested
2. Whether the technique or theory has been subject to peer review and publication
3. The known or potential rate of error of the technique or theory
4. The existence and maintenance of standards and controls
5. The degree to which the technique or theory has been generally accepted within the scientific community

Further, the Supreme Court recognized that FRE 702 may also be a crucial factor in determining admissibility of expert scientific evidence. Under FRE 702, the trial judge must ensure that the expert's testimony is "scientific knowledge" capable of "assisting the trier of the fact." Once the trial judge determines that the proposed testimony meets this standard of assisting the jury, the judge may then admit the lie detector examination.

State Laws. The current rules on admissibility of polygraph evidence vary among the states. Some hold it inadmissible on any basis. Some hold it admissible with a proper foundation. (That means that the nature and scientific acceptability of the polygraph is demonstrated to the court through proper testimony before the polygraph evidence itself is introduced.) Some hold it admissible on stipulation of the parties. (A *stipulation* is a writing signed by both parties or their counsels in which an agreement as to facts or the admissibility of some evidence is stated. It can also be an oral agreement between the parties made in open court under the oversight of the presiding judge.) Some states have not articulated a clear rule but have decided cases in which polygraph evidence is a collateral issue.

Federal Jurisdiction. The federal circuit courts of appeals generally allow trial courts to decide on admissibility of polygraph evidence. But

---

[1] *Daubert v. Merrell Dow Pharmaceuticals, Inc.*; 509 U.S. 579 (1993).

they are not uniform in this position. The U.S. Supreme Court has in the past declined to hear any polygraph case.

The National Labor Relations Board. The National Labor Relations Board has rejected union arguments that the polygraph constitutes an unfair labor practice. The labor law only protects against dismissals or discrimination because of union membership or activities, or other collective activities; it does not prohibit the use of the polygraph to uncover employee dishonesty.

The Military. The use of polygraph evidence in courts-martial is prohibited by the Manual for Courts Martial. Polygraph results, however, play a significant role in pretrial hearings. The results of polygraph examinations may be given consideration by the convening authority when the results of a court martial are reviewed. The sentence may be reduced or reversed based on the polygraph results. Military appellate courts do not consider polygraph results.

Labor Arbitrators. Generally speaking, labor arbitrators have excluded polygraph evidence and ruled against attempts to punish or dismiss employees for refusal to submit to testing, or for negative results obtained under suspicious circumstances, or for situations in which guilt has not been established by other sources.

Arbitrators have permitted the results of a polygraph test to be used as evidence, on the theory that an employee who consents to an examination agrees that the results aid in validating or invalidating charges. Some arbitrators have admitted examination results into proceedings but have placed minimal or no reliance upon them.

A few decisions rejecting the use of test results have indicated, however, that had the bargaining contract provided for such tests, the outcome would have been different. In one case, six plant guards were discharged for failure to take polygraph examinations following the theft of televisions. The union contract stated that the guards were to cooperate in the investigation of theft or other security matters. The polygraph technique was considered by the arbitrator to be one method of investigation; he held that the failure to submit to it constituted insubordination, since the right to refuse had been waived in the contract.

Voice Stress Analyzer

The use of the voice stress analyzer has been prohibited in the private workplace setting for firms regulated under the Employee Polygraph Protection Act of 1988 (EPPA). The exemptions to the EPPA, which do permit such firms to use the polygraph in incident investigations, *do not permit use of any device but the polygraph.* The stress analyzer is, therefore, not available to interstate commerce employers for any employment-related purpose nor by interstate employers in the controlled substance and security fields. Use of the voice stress analyzer in the private sector for purposes other than employment screening or incident investigations is not regulated under the federal act.

Besides the federal prohibition, a number of states enforce local statutes prohibiting the stress analyzer. Such laws that apply to purely intrastate employers are not subject to the federal act. In the case of state laws, it may be any use of the stress analyzer that is prohibited, not just use in the employment context. (For example, the California penal code, Section 637.3, forbids any person to use any system that records or examines the voiceprints or voice stress patterns of another person to determine the truth or falsity of that person without express, prior written consent from such person.) Also, states that do not regulate the polygraph in employment situations (e.g., New York, except for a limited prohibition against Consumer Reporting Agencies keeping reports of polygraph or other lie detector results in file) or that permit the polygraph but regulate its use (e.g., Wisconsin), may prohibit the stress analyzer. A larger number of states, which, in express terms, only prohibit use of the polygraph, do use catch-all language such as "polygraph, lie detector or similar test or examination" or define lie detector or lie detector test so as to include the polygraph and any other device, mechanism or instrument whose purpose is to verify truth or render a diagnostic opinion concerning honesty.

Notwithstanding the federal and state prohibitory statutes, there remain many areas where the use of the stress analyzer is still available. In interstate commerce and in states prohibiting it only in the employment context, the stress analyzer is still available in litigation preparation, sales/purchase situations and various forms of personal communication. As the federal and state acts govern the use of polygraphs and stress analyzers, it is likely those who prohibit both the polygraph and the stress analyzer in the private sector are the biggest users of both kinds of devices. Despite record statements dealing with the unreliability of these devices as the reason for prohibition, the real reason seems to be political or sociological.

CONCLUSION

By understanding the United States' legal framework for criminal laws, the security professional can best protect the organization, its employees and its assets. The assets professional can ultimately assist law enforcement personnel via a working knowledge of the laws, their function and limits.

Selected Bibliography

Books

Ansley, Norman and Garwood, Maria; *The Accuracy and Utility of Polygraph Testing*; 1984; U.S. Dept. of Defense, Washington, D.C.

Bilak, A.J., Klotter, John C. and Federal, R. Keegan; *Legal Aspects of Private Security*; 1981; Criminal Justice Studies, Anderson Publishing Co., Cincinnati, OH.

Bossard, Andre; *Transnational Crime and Criminal Law*; 1990; Office of International Criminal Justice, Univ. of Illinois, Chicago, IL.

Brickley, Kathleen F.; *Corporate Criminal Liability, 2nd ed.*; 1992; Clark Boardman Callaghan, Deerfield, IL.

Federal Criminal Code and Rules; 1991; West Publishing Co., St. Paul, MN.

George, B. James, Jr.; *Contemporary Federal Criminal Practice*; 1992; Aspen Publishers.

George, B. James, Jr.; *The Comprehensive Crime Control Act of 1984*; 1986; Aspen Publishers.

Federal, R. Keegan; *Private Security Case Law Reporter*; Federal Press & Stratford Publications, Inc., Atlanta, GA, a monthly case law reporter.

Federal Labor Laws, 16th ed.; 1994; West Publishing Co., Inc., Minneapolis, MN.

Larson, Lex K.; *Employment Screening*, 1994; Matthew Bender & Co., Albany, NY.

Ringel, William E. and Franklin, Justin D.; *Searches & Seizures, Arrests and Confessions, 2nd ed.*; 1991; Clark Boardman Callaghan, Deerfield, IL.

Periodicals

American Polygraph Association Publications, Suite 408, Osborne Office Center, Chattanooga, TN.
- Ansley, Norman; *Quick Reference Guide to Polygraph Admissibility, Licensing Laws and Limiting Laws, 10th ed.*
- Ansley, Norman and Janet Pumphrey; *Justice and the Polygraph*; 1985.

15
The Civil Law

DEFINITION

Civil law in the United States is that vast body of statutory and common law that deals with private rights and remedies. Although the state may be a party in civil law matters, the principal impact is to establish and adjudicate rights as between or among private persons, both natural and corporate.

The term "civil law," as used in the United States (and in other common-law countries), has a somewhat different meaning than when it is used elsewhere, primarily in Europe. Civil law in Europe generally refers to the organized system of codified law which began with the Roman Empire under Justinian and continued under his successors. This body of law, more correctly referred to as the "civil code," is in many ways quite different from Anglo-American common law and includes both penal or criminal elements, as well as noncriminal. In the United States, the state of Louisiana retains a large portion of the French civil code — a heritage from the period when it was a French possession. Similarly, the Commonwealth of Puerto Rico incorporates some aspects of the Spanish civil code in its local law.

The remainder of the discussion on civil law will deal with civil law as it is known in the United States. In any special context in which the European civil codes are meant, they will be so identified.

MAJOR BRANCHES

The distinction made in the preceding chapter between *statutory* and *common* or case law must be kept in mind. The asset protection professional will find large areas of responsibilities governed by statutory provisions, both federal and state, and will also find that, on a daily basis, decisions and actions are affected in a major way by the civil common law, especially the civil law of torts. For clarity in this treatment, we consider the two branches separately, although it must be noted that a very large number of transactions and situations are quite thoroughly mixed — that is, they involve principles of both statutory and common law. In fact, it is probable that no practical problem to confront the security professional will ever be a simple question of contract or tort, statute or common law, but will touch on several if not all of the branches and categories.

STATUTORY LAW

Federal Statutory Law

Federal statute law is comprised of the 50 titles of the United States Code (USC). Title 18 deals with criminal matters. The other 49 titles are primarily civil. They deal with a whole range of federal government activity from General Provisions, the President, and the Congress (Titles 1, 2 and 3) through Commerce and Trade, Conservation and Copyrights (Titles 15, 16 and 17), to Transportation and War and National Defense (Titles 49 and 50).

State Statutory Law

Civil law on the state level is varied and diversified because of the differences in history, political complexion, and areas of economic activity among the states. There is a far greater diversity on the civil side of state statute law than on the criminal side because the number of subjects dealt with in civil law is so much greater.

It will generally be found that those areas of civil law that are the most developed and that contain a large volume of legislation will be the areas that most nearly describe or encompass the state's economic center. In the plains states, agriculture will be a central subject. In the western states, animal husbandry, livestock, land and water use will be prominent. In the mineral-rich states, minerals law will be fully developed; and in the industrial states, those areas of law dealing with manufacture and commerce predominate. This is not to say that all areas of civil law are not found to some measure in each state's statutes, but only that emphasis or detail in development is generally a good clue to that state's sources of economic wealth.

There is also a division of interest among the states, and between each of them and the federal government, with regard to the regulation of matters of interest to each level of government. It is a general principle that, when the federal government has authority to legislate in a given area, such law is exclusive and the states may not pass their own laws. An illustration is the area of national defense. No state may pass laws dealing with national defense, because that subject is reserved exclusively for the federal government. However, each state may pass laws dealing with its own defense (thus the many local laws dealing with state guards), and it frequently becomes a fine point to distinguish where state sovereignty begins and ends.

There is a second principle under which possible conflict between the two levels of government is resolved. It provides that, where the federal Constitution permits the federal government to legislate but does not deny the states that right, then both may act, each to regulate its own proper sphere. Should the federal government legislate in such a way as to make subsequent legislation by the states in the same area a source of conflict, the principle of "pre-emption" is invoked, under which the exclusive right to legislate reposes in the federal government. The final arbiter of conflicts of laws such as these is the judiciary, and the ultimate decision-making body resolving constitutional problems presented by the clash of federal and state laws is the U.S. Supreme Court.[1]

Important Areas of Statutory Law. Although the range of state civil statutory law will be as broad as there are subjects requiring legislation, some sections or subjects are of special importance to the asset protection specialist. The provisions may be different from state to state; but if there is any statute law at all on the subject, it will be significant for a security or asset protection program. Some of these areas are *licensing of private investigators;* (guards and security services); *labor law* (in which safety and personnel practices in commerce and industry are regulated); *personal property law* (which may contain provisions on the handling and disposition of lost or found property); *civil rights law, business corporation or general business law;* and, for each enterprise, the specific area of law that regulates or is appropriate to its special identity, such as *hospital or health law* for health institutions, *education law* for schools, etc.

Irrespective of what form the enterprise takes, whether it is government or private, a corporation, partnership or single proprietor, it will probably be affected by many provisions in all areas of the statutory law. From a security point of view, however, the special areas indicated will contain a great deal of relevant material. As was suggested with regard to the criminal law, frequent reviews with company counsel are necessary for the security and asset protection manager, to assure that the security program is consistent with the law in the particular state.

It should be noted that even if the security manager or director is an attorney, the reviews are still required. Law, despite what may seem to many to be a central motif of conservatism and delay, is very dynamic and in constant change. It requires continuing application to all its subject matter to remain competent in understanding its effects. That is the task of counsel and not of the asset protection specialist.

Administrative Law. Because federal and state executive agencies and independent authorities exist to administer provisions of basic statutes, additional legal precedent and further layers of regulations made under statutory authority come into existence. For example, the Interstate Commerce Commission (ICC) on the federal level is given broad responsibility

---

[1] The U.S. Constitution does not explicitly confer upon the courts the power to review acts of Congress (as it does the acts of state legislatures). However, the principle of judicial review of the acts of Congress was established in Chief Justice John Marshall's opinion in the famous case of *Marbury v. Madison*, 1 Cr 137 (1803).

for enforcement and administration of the basic federal statutes dealing with the regulation of interstate and foreign commerce. A congressional enactment created the ICC[1] (and all other federal agencies and departments not specifically established by the federal constitution) and is regarded as the founding or "enabling" statute. Usually it contains only the broadest substantive provisions, chiefly describing the structure and powers of the agency it creates, and leaves specific regulation of the central subject matter to the rules and decisions of the agency. A similar approach is followed on the state level.

What results is an executive agency with powers very much like those of a court (called quasi-judiciary), which also has the power to make rules and regulations, much as a congress or legislature (called quasi-legislative). This hybrid then (1) makes rules and regulations that affect citizens, corporate and otherwise; (2) cites citizens for violations of such rules; and (3) holds hearings or adjudications in which the guilt of the charges is determined and penalties assessed.

It is probable that, in matters of civil statutory law involving business enterprises, particularly when the protection of assets and security operations are affected, it will be an administrative agency with which the enterprise deals. For example, if matters of state labor law are involved, it will probably be an industrial commission or board of standards (safety rules and some personnel practices), a labor relations board or agency (in matters of collective bargaining), or an employment practices agency (in matters of job-related employer conduct.) With regard to civil rights law, it will probably be a state or local commission against discrimination. In matters of licensing, it will be a licensing agency or executive department of the state government. In short, it is highly probable that the asset protection program and the enterprise, in general, will have more contacts with independent agencies or the executive department in matters of state civil statutory law than it will with the courts.

In this regard it is most important to note that the courts really play quite a limited role when an agency exists to make and enforce broad rules. That role is generally limited to assuring that the agency does not act in an arbitrary or capricious manner, that it does not exceed the authority given it under the enabling statute, and that there is at least some evidence to support its expert conclusions. It is most infrequent that a court will upset an agency decision by simply substituting the court's judgment for the agency's on the same basic facts. The doctrine of "administrative expertise" is relied upon in such cases, and the courts will usually hold that the legislative body that created the agency determined that it was the agency's judgment, not the court's, that was to control in matters properly before the agency.

[1] An Act to Regulate Commerce, February 4, 1887, 24 Stat. 379, (49 U.S.C. 1-22)

The Civil Law

The net result is that if an independent agency ruling goes against the enterprise's interests, the likelihood that it will be reversed or modified in a later court proceeding is slight, provided that the agency did act reasonably and did have the statutory authority to act in the first place.

CIVIL COMMON LAW

The other major branch or division of the civil law is civil *common* law. It is the collection of decisions by courts at various levels of government dealing with conflicts and disputes among and between citizens and other private persons. Although it is literally true that there is common law on both the federal and state levels, there is not the clear distinction here that one finds in the area of *civil statute law*. The reason is that the kinds of situations and conflicts arising between persons have existed for very long periods of time and are usually not specifically related to which level of government ultimately resolves the conflict in a court decision.

For example, if one person assaults another, or breaches a contract with another, or defames another by slanderous words or libelous writings, the wrong done is measured by standards more related to the history of the conduct than to whether it is a federal or state court hearing the matter. As a consequence, the civil common law or "case law" has grown up from very early beginnings in the English courts and has been carried forward in America, chiefly in the state courts of this country. By definition, these are "common law" or nonstatutory matters, so there is no question of different or conflicting provisions of state and federal statute — there are no statutes.

If and when federal courts do hear disputes involving common law (because for one reason or another the parties are not completely within the exclusive jurisdiction of a single state, or because the incident or conflict arises in such a way that only federal courts have jurisdiction), the common law principles applied will be the same as would be applied if the matter were heard in a state court in the same location. So, if a federal district court in, say, Arkansas hears a common law dispute, it will apply the same common law principles to resolve it as would an Arkansas state court.[1] An exception to this doctrine exists in those other rare cases in which there is no common law precedent in the state common law or there is no state jurisdiction at all (as, for example, in the District of Columbia). In these cases, the federal courts can look to any source they deem appropriate and, indeed, may add to the common law by enunciating new principles to resolve novel situations for which there is no precedent anywhere.[2]

The chief effect of this difference between statutory and common law is that the common law conflicts involved will usually be resolved in much the same way, irrespective of whether it is in a state or a federal court. If there

---
[1] *Erie v. Tompkins*, 304 U.S. 64 (1938).
[2] *Standard Accident Insurance Co. v. Roberts*, 132 F 2d 794 (1942).

is such similarity, one might wonder why it would make any difference at all which court was chosen. The answer is that it often makes a critical difference, but not because of the basic dispute. Rather, the procedural rules are different in federal courts from those in state courts. Depending upon the exact facts and the positions of the parties, one or another party might find it of great advantage to be in one court rather than the other. For example, in matters of "discovery" (i.e., requiring by subpoena or otherwise the production by one party of certain evidence deemed useful to the other party), the scope and methods permitted in federal and state courts differ widely.[1] It will often be because of procedural advantage that a party will seek to move a common law dispute to a federal court.

If the federal statutory law does give a federal court the authority to hear a certain law dispute, based upon the nature and relationship of the parties, and if that relationship exists (a question of fact for the federal court), and if one or the other party seeks to bring or transfer the action to the federal court, that is where it will be tried. If the case were originally brought in a state court and if, despite the federal jurisdiction, neither party sought to move it to the federal court, it would remain in the state court for decision.

Major Areas of Civil Common Law

In a greatly oversimplified way we can divide the civil common law into two major branches: the first is contract common law and the second is tort common law. The vast majority of common law disputes will fall into one of these branches. The contract branch deals with matters arising out of agreements, express or implied, between persons. The tort branch deals with alleged wrongs, intentional or negligent, done by one party to another. There is a middle area in which an alleged wrong (for example, inducing a breach of contract, or fraud in inducing another to make a contract) actually deals with an existing contract. However, the questions proper to each are quite distinct, as the following discussions should make clear.

Contract Law. A *contract* may be defined as "an agreement between two or more persons which creates an obligation to do or not do a particular thing."[2] Contracts may be express or implied, written or oral. They may involve a single act or omission, or multiple acts or omissions. They may be between natural persons, corporations, and partnerships, or between any or all of these parties and agencies of government. Brief descriptions of the foregoing terms will be helpful for a clear understanding of what a contract is and when one has been made.

---

[1] Section V, Rule 26, *et seq.* of the Federal Rules of Civil Procedure establishes the way discovery is conducted in the U.S. District Courts. State Civil Practice Acts set forth discovery requirements for state courts.
[2] *Black's Law Dictionary*, 5th ed.

Express Contract. An *express contract* is one whose terms and conditions have been stated in words. Thus, a statement by a vendor of security supplies that he promises to sell and deliver a specific model identification camera at a price of $100 on a certain date to you, and your promise to buy that camera and take delivery on that date, would be an express contract between you and the vendor for the sale and delivery of the named camera at the stated price.

Implied Contract. An *implied contract*[1] is one whose terms and conditions have not been stated in words but are added or supplied on the theory that the parties really intended such terms and conditions. A contract may be implied in law or implied in fact. In the first case, the law will imply an agreement, or more precisely an obligation, on the part of one who has obtained a benefit at the expense of another to do some act (such as to make a payment), or to refrain from doing something (such as to refrain from using or enjoying items received without a request, but under circumstances making it clear that if used or enjoyed, some compensation would be paid the one furnishing the items). This kind of implied contract really has nothing to do with the intention of the parties to enter into an agreement, but more with the equity which requires a person not to enrich himself at the expense of another. It is sometimes referred to as *quasi-contract.*

A contract implied in fact is based upon the conduct of the parties evidencing the intention to agree, even though formal words of agreement are absent. For example, if a customer enters a store, inquires about the price of an item and then instructs the sales clerk to send that item to the customer's residence, there is an implied contract that, if sent, the customer will pay the quoted price. Note: the merchant did not promise to send it, nor did the customer promise to buy. But the conduct is so clear that the agreement to buy and pay for if sent, and the agreement to send as ordered, will be implied.

A contract will not be implied in fact if some critical term is unstated. If, for example, a contract guard agency promises to furnish guard service and an enterprise promises to pay for such service, nothing being said about how many guards or when the service is to be provided, there will not be an implied contract because vital terms — quantity and time of performance — are unstated. On the other hand, if a guard agency promises to provide a specific number of guards at stated times, and the enterprise promises to pay for those services but no price is stated, it will be implied that the reasonable value of the services rendered was agreed to be paid.

---

[1] The Uniform Commercial Code (UCC), which has been adopted in all states (partially in Louisiana), tends to make enforceable contracts in situations in which the common law would not, as long as the intentions of the parties are clear. The UCC, as adopted in each state, should be considered in any contract situation to which it might apply. These situations typically involve commercial transactions.

This can be quite interesting because "price" and "reasonable value" are not the same thing.

Continuing the example of the guard agency, assume that the "price" usually charged was $9.00 per guard-hour. However, in this case, price was not included in the agreement (which, by the way, might have been oral or written). The services are rendered and the agency submits its bill, calculated at $9.00 per guard-hour. The enterprise refuses payment, alleging no contract because no "price" was agreed to. If the agency sues, as it must to obtain satisfaction in such a case, the court will undertake to determine what the "reasonable value" of the services rendered was. That is a question of fact, and relevant considerations would be the agency costs, the typical profit made by that agency on similar contracts elsewhere, and the typical or average price charged by other agencies for similar services. "Reasonable value," using those criteria, might prove to be $8.25 per guard-hour. In that case, the agency would collect at the rate of $8.25 per hour, the implied "reasonable value," and not at $9.00 per hour, the actual "price." The contract is real because the parties did intend that guard services should be rendered and accepted. What is implied is the value. As price was omitted in the agreement, reasonable value will be implied.

Using the same example in a rather extreme situation, assume that after sales presentations by the agency, the enterprise said, "We can use guards," but no numbers, dates, times or any other terms were agreed. If the agency then sent a notice that beginning on a certain date a given number of personnel would be assigned at a stated price per hour, and on that date such personnel did arrive and the enterprise allowed them to function, there would be a contract implied in law. The difference from the contract implied in fact is that in the contract implied in fact there was an expression of intent to furnish and accept guard services. In the contract implied in law there was an ambiguous statement by the enterprise, followed by performance by the agency which was accepted by the enterprise. At that point the law, concerned that the enterprise not unjustly enrich itself, will imply the agreement because the enterprise should either have prevented the service from being rendered or should pay the expected price for it. In the contract implied in fact, the unstated price will be converted to "reasonable value" because of the clear intention that the services should be rendered.

Some Precautions. It is obvious that most business dealings are not — or at least should not be — conducted in ways so vague and unclear that recourse will be required to theories of implied contract. But many business dealings do result in contracts, albeit not always of the precise kind the parties would have wished. Some simple precautions are therefore in order.

The Civil Law

1. *Avoid oral arrangements and rely on written documentation whenever possible.* Certain kinds of agreements, such as those not to be completed within one year, or those to make good the debt of another, or those touching on real property, will not be enforced unless in writing. Laws in most states, referred to as "statutes of frauds," specifically require those kinds of agreements to be in writing because of the seriousness of consequence and the ease with which fraudulent practices could occur when unusual, involved or important contracts of the kind treated by the statute could be established on the mere recollection of witnesses to oral statements.
2. *When an agreement has been reduced to writing, it will generally not be permitted to be changed on the basis of oral statements.* Again, the rule is to assure that truth and accuracy are observed and that an agreement, important enough to be made in writing, should not be varied by mere oral statements. This rule would operate even if the parties both intended to modify or change the original agreement by a later oral agreement. The intention of the parties will only be permitted to be shown by a written instrument.[1]
3. *The subject matter of a contract, oral or written, must be lawful or the alleged contract will not be enforced.* For example, if an enterprise agreed with an investigative service that such service was to perform investigations to determine the labor union affiliations of applicants for employment, the contract would be unenforceable almost everywhere because it would violate the public policy of the federal government and most state governments that such inquiries not be conducted because they restrain or interfere with the workers' right to freedom of collective bargaining association. (In addition, such an agreement might very well constitute violations of both statutory civil and criminal law, federal and state, on the part of both the enterprise and the service.)

Warranties. *Warranties are statements by persons that things done or said by them, or products or services rendered by them, are actually as they are described or said to be.* The warranty generally becomes an obligation enforceable against the warrantor (the one making the statement) by any person who relied upon the statement or used the product or services, and whom the warrantor knew or should have known would do so. Typical of warranties are those contained on products purchased at retail. The manufacturer or supplier, or both, agree that, for a stated period, the product

---

[1] But note that unless the written agreement *expressly* stated that it was the complete agreement between the parties, oral evidence might be admissible to show *additional terms* not inconsistent with or repudiating the existing written terms. Such additional terms would be admissible under the "parole evidence rule" (*Cf.* UCC, Section 2-202).

will perform as described and that if, without fault by the buyer or user, it should fail to perform, it will be repaired at no cost to the buyer or user.

A warranty is a very special kind of promise or statement because if the thing warranted is not as it is represented, then the warrantor may be responsible in money damages to the person who relied on the warranty, to the extent that such a person was injured or suffered any physical, economic or legal detriment.

The warranty (often popularly referred to as a guaranty which, in fact, is something quite different) is, in effect, a promise that the buyer or user can rely on the statements made by the warrantor. Purchase or use of the product or service is an acceptance by the user of the warranty promise and constitutes a new contract, separate from the purchase contract or use contract but related to it. The measure of damage or injury in the purchase contract will, at most, be the total price or reasonable value of the things or services involved. However, the same things, as the basis for a warranty contract, could produce a measure of damages tens or even hundreds of times greater.

For example, an asset protection manager purchases fire-fighting equipment (portable extinguishers, say) and the vendor warrants that the extinguishers will discharge a certain amount of extinguishing agent at a certain rate, if used in accordance with the instructions. In reliance on that warranty, the extinguishers are placed throughout the enterprise. A small fire of the type for which they are appropriate occurs and the extinguishers are used. They all fail to perform, and the fire rapidly gets out of control and results in very large destruction. If the user can establish that: (1) he used the extinguishers as instructed; (2) he also took other reasonable precautions against fire; (3) when the small fire occurred, it would have been controlled if the extinguishers had operated properly; and (4) if the user also shows that he did everything reasonable under the circumstances to control the fire but, nevertheless, the fire spread out of control, then the manufacturer or vendor of the extinguishers, or both, may be liable in damages for several hundred thousand dollars, even though the purchase price of the extinguishers may only have been several hundred dollars.[1]

This phase of contract law, namely the warranty contract, is ultimately involved with the area of product liability and is of major current interest to the whole business community. In the security and assets protection area, major questions of warranty obligation are raised by the agreements to purchase and use of such things as alarm services and devices, weapons, investigative and guard services, courier, and safe deposit service and facilities.

---

[1] The fire loss would be as a consequence of the failure of the extinguishers and would result in "consequent damages." Most product warranties today specifically exclude consequent damages and would limit recovery to the cost of the extinguishers.

Limitations of Liability. To protect themselves against overwhelming liabilities and to ensure continued availability of insurance, security product and service vendors usually rely upon some specific language in the contract, service agreement, or purchase memorandum to limit their liability. For example, in the typical central-station alarm contract will be found a provision like the following.

> "It is understood that the contractor [alarm company] is not an insurer, that insurance, if any, shall be obtained by the subscriber [the user of the alarm service] and that the amounts payable to the contractor hereunder [the cost of the alarm services] are based upon the value of the services and the scope of liability as herein set forth and are unrelated to the value of the subscriber's property or the property of others located in subscriber's premises. The contractor makes no guaranty or warranty, including any implied warranty of merchantability or fitness, that the system or service supplied will avert or prevent occurrences or the consequences therefrom, which the system or services is designed to detect. The subscriber does not desire this contract to provide for full liability of the contractor and agrees that the contractor shall be exempt from liability for loss or damage due directly or indirectly to occurrences, or consequences therefrom, which the service is designed to detect or avert. The subscriber further agrees that, if the contractor should be found liable for loss or damage due to a failure of service or equipment in any respect, its liability shall be limited to a sum equal to 10 percent of the annual service charge or $250, whichever is the greater, as the exclusive remedy, and that the provisions of this paragraph shall apply if loss or damage, irrespective of cause or origin, results directly or indirectly to person or property from performance or nonperformance of obligation imposed by this contract or from negligence, active or otherwise, of the contractor, its agents or employees."

Applying that kind of limitation of liability language to a possible real case would produce the following situation. A bank contracts with a central-station alarm company to install burglar alarms in its vaults. The company agrees to install them in such a way as to comply with Underwriters Laboratories (UL) and American Society for Testing & Materials (ASTM) standards. In fact, the equipment supplied does not meet the standards, and the workmen installing it are slipshod in their task and do not make the proper wiring connections. The contractor does not inspect his workmen, and the job is finished. The next night a burglary occurs; the alarm fails to operate, and $1 million is stolen from the bank vault. The cost of the alarm installation was agreed upon between the two parties at $10,500 and the annual service charge at $3500.

The bank (or more likely its insurance carrier) sues the alarm company and proves the following: (1) the installation did not meet the agreed standards and the components were not those agreed to be furnished; (2) the burglary would have been discovered if the alarm system had functioned properly; (3) had the burglary been discovered, there would have been police and bank security personnel on the scene within three minutes, not enough time for the burglars to have entered the vault and removed the cash; (4) the alarm did not function properly; (5) the alarm did not function because of the manner of installation and the type of components; (6) the burglary was successful; and (7) the loss is $1 million.

At the trial, the alarm company introduces the contract and the clause just quoted. Result: judgment against the alarm company in favor of the bank. But the amount of judgment would be only $350 (10 percent of the annual service charge, that being more than $250).[1]

If there had been no such clause, the alarm company could very well have been liable for $1 million because of its breach of express contract to meet U/L and ASTM specifications, and because of its breach of an implied warranty that the service sold was what it was said to be and was fit for the purpose for which intended by the purchaser (subscriber).[2]

Agency

The question of *agency* — of whether one person is acting for or on behalf of another — is a most important practical question in business generally and for asset protection matters. Some typical situations will indicate why.

A guard employed by the enterprise is assigned to an entrance. A person seeks admittance but for some reason does not satisfy the guard as to a right to be admitted. A quarrel ensues. Words go to shoves; and finally the guard strikes the visitor, knocking him to the ground. The visitor suffers a serious injury and sues the enterprise, alleging that the injuries caused by the fall resulted from the shove from the guard and that the guard was acting for the enterprise, or at least that the enterprise was responsible for his actions. Does the visitor recover damages?

Change the facts so that the guard works for a contract agency but the visitor still sues the enterprise. Does he recover damages?

Change the facts further. The guard works for an agency, the visitor sues the agency and the agency sues the enterprise. Will the visitor recover against the agency? Will the agency recover against the enterprise?

---

[1] But if the bank had sued the alarm company on the theory of negligence rather than breach of warranty (a negligence action is a tort action, a breach of warranty is contract) and had proved not merely simple negligence but wanton or gross negligence, public policy in most states would have disallowed the limitation of liability clause and allowed a recovery of the full $1 million. (See later discussion of negligence.)

[2] But note that if the exculpatory language is obscure or written so as to confuse the subscriber, the courts may allow the question of whether it may be relied upon to go to the jury (*A&Z Appliances v. Electric Burglar Alarm Co.*, 455 N.Y.S. 2d 674, 1982).

The Civil Law

Another situation: Your investigator, in conducting an investigation of an employment applicant, speaks to several neighbors. Using what he later describes as a "testing technique," he suggests to the neighbors that the applicant is an alcoholic, ostensibly to see if they agree or deny. They do neither, but instead tell other neighbors that the applicant is an alcoholic, according to what they heard from your investigator. The applicant, in fact, is not an alcoholic. He learns of the talk about him among his neighbors and calls on your enterprise, where he meets you (the security manager) to complain about the false and defamatory statements made by your investigator. You reply that it is important to be sure all applicants are carefully screened because your enterprise handles very sensitive research work and, besides, has a great deal of extremely valuable equipment easily available in the labs. You add that skillful investigators often use ploys like the one your investigator used to establish the real facts. You point out that your investigator did establish to his own satisfaction that the applicant was not an alcoholic or even a heavy drinker by the very use of the device and that, therefore, the real value of the approach is evident. Unsatisfied, the applicant leaves and later sues you and the investigator for slander. Can he recover against either? Against both?

Before the liability questions posed in the last few paragraphs are answered, let's consider how the representative status of someone, his being an agent, is determined.

How Agency Is Determined. There are many kinds of agency and many ways in which one person can act for another. A trustee, for example, acts in the interest of another. An employee acts in the interest of the employer. An executor acts in the interest of the estate of the deceased. However, not all these relationships have the same legal consequence. A key distinction is to be made between the person who acts in his own right (the trustee or executor) but on behalf or in the interests of another, and the person whose authority to act (the employee) in matters of concern to the employer is derived entirely from the employer and in which the employee/agent is acting as a substitute for or extension of the employer/principal. It is these situations that are of concern in this discussion.

Such principal/agent relationships can be created in several ways. One way is by express agreement in which the principal (employer) tells the agent (employee) to perform specific tasks or duties or to act within a general area in carrying out the employer's instructions, This is the typical employment situation, whether or not the hiring involves a contract or the more typical "employment at will."[1]

---

[1] A hiring "at will" is one in which the employer may terminate the employment at any time for any or no reason, save that it may not be for a reason prohibited by law (such as racial discrimination). The common law of the states varies on what, if any, exceptions to that "at will" doctrine may be recognized.

Another way in which the relationship can be established is if the principal, although not initially authorizing the other to act as agent, adopts the action and ratifies or approves it. For example, a courier service has bid for a contract with your firm to transport cash and valuables. One day, a driver for the courier comes upon a street accident in which one of your regular employee drivers has wrecked the truck while carrying a sum of money. The courier, recognizing the truck as yours, arranges with the driver to take the cash shipment on to its destination to protect it against loss while your own driver remains at the scene of the accident. The delivery is made and the courier company reports the event to you. You express thanks and offer to pay the usual fee for such a delivery. Although you did not initially request the courier to act as your agent, when you learned that he had, you adopted or approved his action, thus making him your agent for the purposes of that action.

Another agency relationship will exist or, more exactly, the courts will presume it to exist under a situation in which a person with "apparent authority" to act for you does so. "Apparent authority" means that, while you have not really appointed the agent or ratified any previous actions, you are in a position to know the agent is acting as such and do not disclaim the actions, or you put a person into the position in which that person appears to be acting as your agent.

Example: You give your contract guard instructions when visitors arrive not to accept custody of any of their belongings or allow them to check them. A visitor arrives with a package. He tells the guard that it is quite bulky and inconvenient, and that he would like to leave it with the guard during his visit so as not to be inconvenienced. He notes that it is quite valuable and he asks that it be put in a safe place, out of sight. The guard accepts it, places it in a coat closet and leaves the reception desk for some reason. During the absence, a thief enters, removes a number of items and the contents of the closet, including the visitor's package. The visitor discovers the loss when leaving, declares the package to have contained very valuable material and later sues your company.

Although you gave the contract guard specific instructions not to accept packages, the visitor had no way of knowing that. Moreover, the guard was your representative for the very purpose of receiving and assisting visitors. When the guard agreed to accept the package, it was reasonable for the visitor to conclude he was authorized to do so — he acted with "apparent authority." If the visitor can prove the guard was negligent, and acted without due care and diligence, as a direct result of which the theft occurred, then he has a very good chance of recovering against your company. The agent (the contract guard) had apparent authority and the agent's negligence (assuming it is proved) can be imputed or charged to the principal, because it occurred in the course of the very duties in which the agent was acting with the apparent authority. True, the guard was an actual employee of the contract agency, not your firm, but he was acting as the agent of your firm. We will see later how a client firm can protect itself against liability for the acts of a contractor employee.

The Significance of an Agency. If the relationship can be established by (1) express appointment, (2) ratification of actions taken, and (3) permitting one with apparent authority to act, what are the consequences to the principal?

The major consequence is that, if the agent acts in a wrongful way, the law may "impute" or charge that action to the principal or employer. Primarily, "wrongful" is held to mean negligently wrongful rather than intentionally wrongful; that is, the agent does not exercise due care or diligence in what he does on behalf of the principal. However, in situations typical in security work, if the area of activity of the agent is one involving inherently dangerous features (as would be the use of guards with deadly weapons), then the principal may be responsible for even the willful misdeeds of the agent if they were directly connected with the purpose for which the agent was retained — either because the agent's action is foreseeable and "imputed" to the employer, or because the employer himself did not act prudently in selecting or allowing that kind of agent to perform the misdeeds.

Vicarious Liability. The imputation of an employee's negligence to the employer is described as "vicarious liability," liability for the acts of another without personal fault of the one liable. The significance of vicarious liability is that, while the agent who was negligent may not be liquid enough to permit substantial recovery against him through judgments, the principal probably will be. Hence, suit will probably be brought against both the agent and the principal, but certainly against the principal. So, if a guard earning $20,000 a year and having no accumulated savings acts in a negligent way (or even willful, as noted above), as a result of which a third person is injured and can prove damages of $500,000, the employer (guilty of no personal fault at all) may pay the judgment.

The Earlier Questions. With this discussion as a background, let's go back to the earlier questions about an employer's responsibility for the actions of agents.

Question 1. The first involved the company-employed guard who shoved a visitor. Could the visitor recover against the company? Probably. The guard was a servant or employee; was within the scope of employment; and the conduct, if not willful, was certainly without due care. The amount of the recovery is a question of fact for the trier of the facts and will be determined by many things, including medical expense, loss of earnings, pain, and probability of long duration of injuries.

Question 2. Changing the facts to make the guard a contract agency employee would normally bring a new principle into the situation — the principle that one is not responsible for the acts of an independent contractor. However, there are many exceptions to this rule. Among them: that the principal requires the task to be done on his land (owned or leased); that he provides specific instructions on how the task is to be done; and that the task involves inherently dangerous aspects. When an act of an independent contractor involves one or more of these exceptions, the principal may still be vicariously liable. The cited case could be argued to involve all of those exceptions and there is a very good likelihood that the injured visitor will recover against the company.

Question 3. In the last version of those facts, the visitor will recover against the employer of the guard (the alleged independent contractor) because, while the guard can be argued not to be the employee of the company using the guard service, he is clearly the employee of the guard agency. On normal principles of agency, then, the firm employing the guard will be liable for the negligent acts.[1] The agency, however, will not generally recover against the company under most states' rules. The company was guilty of no active negligence of its own and, at most, would be vicariously liable (as the guard company itself is) to the injured party only.

However, there is a different rule in some states and the matter is not absolutely clear-cut. In the typical guard agency situation, there would probably be some language in the contract between the agency and the company dealing with this problem. The most typical would be an "indemnity" or hold-harmless provision by which the agency agrees to indemnify or hold the company harmless from any damages arising out of the performance by the agency of its contracted tasks. However, if there were no provision, and depending upon the locale of the incident, there might be a recovery of part of the judgment (a proportionate share) by the agency from the company under a doctrine called "contribution."

The doctrine of contribution holds that where several have been jointly negligent, and recovery by an injured party was against only one, that one is entitled to a proportionate contribution by the others. *The point here is that the matter of liability, vicarious and otherwise, of a company for the acts of its contract agencies should be clearly resolved in the contract between them.*

Question 4. In the case of the investigator, upon learning of his defamatory statement, you ratified it; you defended the conduct and adopted its results. Although the act of the investigator in "testing" informants on the applicant's drinking was intentional and not negligent, it was in furtherance

---

[1] In this case, the principal is that of "respondeat superior," or let the master answer. This principal holds the employer responsible for the negligent acts of the employee which occur in the normal course of the employment.

The Civil Law

of your general program of applicant screening. The law generally holds a principal liable even for the willful or intentional wrongful acts of the agent under such circumstances, unless a clear case of disclaimer and other suitable precaution to prevent the action in the first place can be proved. (A specific training program for the investigator would be such a precaution.) Your ratification after the fact would almost certainly make you liable if the applicant could prove some damage. As the investigator was the one primarily at fault, the applicant can recover against him too.

TORTS IN GENERAL

The preceding discussion of agency illustrated ways in which the principal can be liable for the acts of agents. We have illustrated such acts by both the intentional and negligent acts of the agent. Both kinds of acts, when they cause injuries to another, are included in another major branch of the civil common law, namely the law of torts.

A tort is a willful or negligent wrong done to one person by another. Unlike contract injuries, it does not require any agreement between the parties and, in cases of negligence, may not depend upon the intentions of the parties. The law of torts will have a major impact on protection of assets programs because in every encounter between the security organization and other persons, inside and outside the enterprise, there is always present the possibility that a wrong will be done.

Willful Torts

The willful tort is one in which the actor intends the consequences of the act or intends to do the act that results in the injury. If an investigator deliberately and knowingly makes a false and damaging statement about the subject of the investigation, that is a *tort of slander* — deliberate false and defamatory spoken words. If a guard, without proper cause, takes a person into physical custody and prevents or intimidates him from leaving, that is the *intentional tort of false imprisonment.* If a security firefighter, driving a fire vehicle without using warning lights, bell or siren, drives in a reckless manner, there being no circumstance or urgent situation requiring it, and in so doing strikes and injures a pedestrian, that is the *tort of negligence.* The first two are willful because the guard and investigator intended to do what they did. The firefighter did not intend to strike a pedestrian but drove in a careless manner. Negligence is not a willful tort and will be discussed later.

Specific Willful Torts. The following are actions that the common law has defined as torts or civil wrongs and for which there will be liability in damages to the extent the injured party can establish and prove those damages:[1]

---

[1] See, generally, *Black's Law Dictionary,* 5th ed.

- *Battery:* the actual use of force against another; involves physical touching.
- *Assault:* the putting of another in fear that force will be used against him or her; does not involve physical contact.[1]
- *False imprisonment:* the deprivation of another's liberty or freedom; may involve actual physical restraint and may involve intimidation that physical force will be used if an escape is attempted.
- *Conversion:* wrongful appropriation of the personal property of another to the use of the taker, or the exercise of dominion by the converter over the personal property of another in a way inconsistent with the rightful owner's or possessor's interest.
- *Fraud or misrepresentation*: use of a trick device false scheme, or other deception that causes another to suffer loss because of reliance on the one committing the fraud.
- *Nuisance:* behavior that causes or results in noisome, annoying, unwholesome or destructive conditions, or produces substantial interference of the right of another in the use or enjoyment of property.
- *Defamation:* Includes both oral (slanderous) and written (libelous) statements that are not true and are damaging to another. The truth of a statement is generally an adequate defense to an action of defamation. Even when the damaging statement is false, a defense of privilege may often be made, in which the special relationship between the party making the false statement and the one to whom made will allow even a false statement without liability, provided there is no actual malice or ill-will by the one making the statement. In the earlier example of the investigator describing an applicant as an alcoholic, if the false statement had been made only to the employer, and if no malice by the investigators could be shown, qualified privilege would have been available as a defense to the slander action. Because the statements were made to third persons and strangers, the defense was not available.
- *Invasion of privacy:* occurs when, without justification or proper cause, there is (a) intrusion into the secret affairs of another, (b) disclosure of such affairs, (c) the placing of another in a false public light, or (d) the appropriation of some private or secret aspect of another for the commercial use or gain of the appropriator. This tort will be the typical charge of a citizen who claims to have been unlawfully searched, or claims property to have been unlawfully inspected, or claims private conversations to have been eavesdropped upon. Note that the information or secret affair must be just that, not already something public. The intrusion or disclosure must be a kind that an ordinary, reasonable man would find objectionable, and whatever the form of invasion, there is no justification for it.

[1] Assault required the victim to be *aware of the threat* of force. A menacing gesture toward a blind person would not be assault (although it might be if directed at a sighted person).

In security situations, for example, in which employees are required to open parcels and packages for inspection, or where lockers are searched, the question of invasion of privacy might arise. However, if the searches or inspections were consented to or were made conditions of employment, or in cases where the employee was not given sole and exclusive right of possession (as to a desk or locker), there would not be a sound basis for alleging the tort. Also, in cases where a search or inspection discloses a crime (larceny, for example), the claim of invasion of privacy will probably not stand. (However, under criminal law, an unreasonable search, even if evidence of a crime is found, will not be permitted and such evidence will be suppressed in a prosecution.

Negligence. Our earlier illustrations of agency relationships involved samples of negligence sufficient to make clear what it is. It is the failure to use reasonable care and due diligence under the particular circumstances, as a result of which another is injured or suffers some damage. Negligence does not require an intent, even an intent to be negligent. Rather, it is the absence of an attitude or intent — that to be duly careful — that characterizes it.

Gross Negligence. Negligence that is so gross or reckless as to be tantamount to acting with total disregard for the consequences of the action will sometimes be held to be similar to an intentional wrong. Therefore, gross and wanton negligence may lead to heavier liability on the part of the negligent person. Such heavier penalty, called an *exemplary* or *punitive* award of damages, is often also found in the intentional tort cases, and consists of a multiplication or extension of the actual damages suffered by an injured or aggrieved person. Exemplary damages are awarded as a special deterrent to such conduct, and because intentionally wrongful or grossly negligent conduct is more blameworthy than merely negligent conduct.

THE AREA OF CIVIL RIGHTS

This is properly an area involving statutory law rather than common law. However, it is of special and growing importance and has been reserved for treatment at the end of this chapter, with the thought that the preceding discussions of both statute and common civil law will facilitate the understanding of civil rights laws.

Civil Rights at Common Law

Unless a case could be made that a recognized tort was involved, discrimination based upon race, color, religion, sex, national origin or handicap was not actionable at common law. There was no legal remedy if the conduct fell short of being tortuous.

The constitutional safeguards provided by the federal and state bills of rights only protected the citizen against the government, not against a fellow citizen. There was, in short, virtually no definable civil rights against another citizen.

Civil Rights under Statute

Statutes passed immediately following the Civil War did establish specific rights of the then recently emancipated slaves, notably the same rights to hold property, sue, make and enforce contracts, and enjoy equal benefits of law as white citizens, and to be subject only to the same legal penalties as white citizens.

Even these civil rights statutes did not deal in detail with the problem of discrimination by one citizen against another, except to the extent that such discrimination eventuated in the denial or attempted denial of substantive rights other than in matters of employment.

Various states passed anti-discrimination statutes over the years, in which practices tending to discriminate against persons in the course of seeking or holding employment because of race, religion, national origin, sex, age, and labor union affiliations and actions were made unlawful, usually as "unfair employment practices." There remained no overall federal law, however, until the passage of the Civil Rights Act of 1964.

The Civil Rights Act of 1964 (42 U.S.C. 200e). Establishing for the first time a national standard, this act prohibits discrimination, failure or refusal to hire, discharge, limitation, segregation, or classification in any way adverse to an employee or employment applicant on the basis of race, color, religion, sex or national origin. Originally applicable to businesses and not to government itself, the Civil Rights Act was amended in 1972 and most recently in 1991,[1] and is now applicable to any employer with 15 or more employees whose business affects interstate commerce, to the federal government, and to state and local governments. Title VII of the act is the section containing the prohibition against discrimination. This federal statute, together with the Age Discrimination in Employment Act of 1967[2] (no discrimination against workers or applicants over 40 years of age) and the Equal Pay Act of 1963 (same work, same pay irrespective of sex) make up a formidable federal legal arsenal to suppress discrimination in employment. The substance of what is prohibited will be discussed a bit further on.

State Anti-discrimination Statutes. In addition to the federal laws noted above, the states have their own laws in the area. Not all states have the same provisions, but most deal in some way with discrimination

---

[1] P.L. 102-166 (105 Stat. 1071) effective 11/21/91.
[2] As amended through 1991.

The Civil Law

because of race, religion and national origin. Prohibition in state law of discrimination on the grounds of sex or age is less general.

State laws will be applicable, within the state, to intrastate activities not touched by the federal laws. In addition, in a state with a state anti-discrimination law, an aggrieved person may not bring a complaint under the federal civil rights law until the state law has been used and the state agency has had at least 60 days to act. When the charge is brought under the federal civil cights law, it results in an investigation by the Equal Employment Opportunity Commission (EEOC). If the EEOC dismisses the complaint, fails to effect a conciliation or other resolution, or fails to act within 180 days of receipt of the complaint, the aggrieved person can bring the complaint to the U.S. District Court.

The Test for Discrimination. It is not simply an express refusal or rejection on the proscribed grounds that will be censured under the Civil Rights Act. In an early decision of the U.S. Supreme Court (*Griggs v. Duke Power Company,* 91 S.Ct. 849), the principle was enunciated that any practice that tends to discriminate against a racial group and that cannot be shown to be job related is prohibited. In that case, it was a general requirement for high school diplomas. However, the doctrine of job relatedness, approved by the U.S. Supreme Court in *Griggs*, has undergone continuing development; and now any employment practice, screening technique, or selection criterion that operates adversely against minority racial groups (as measured by the actual percentage of such minorities processed and hired, or promoted, or retained compared to like percentages of the racial majorities) will be held to be unlawful.

An illustration of that principle is found in the most noteworthy civil rights case to date from the security point of view. This case was *Gregory v. Litton* (472 F2d 631), in which the use of arrest record information as a rejection criterion was disallowed. The reasoning was that proportionately more blacks than whites are arrested; that an arrest is not equivalent to a conviction; and that, if arrest records were allowed to be used to reject employment applicants, the practice would tend to operate against blacks because they outnumbered whites on a proportionate basis in terms of arrests.

The *Gregory* decision has been followed by others, some of which have held that even a conviction in some cases may not be used to reject, because such use would tend to operate unfavorably against minorities.[1] Although this argument has even been applied to felonies, it has been held that when the conviction can be related to the job of the candidate, it will not be held to be discriminatory.[2]

---

[1] *Green v. Missouri Pacific Railroad,* 523 F22 1290.
[2] *Carter v. Gallagher,* 452 F2d 315 (1971); *Richarson v. Hotel Corporation of America,* 332 F Supp 519; and *Avant v. South Central Bell Telephone Co.,* 716 F 2d 1083.

The Trend in Civil Rights

It appears that, increasingly, the agencies and courts will look with disfavor upon any practice that tends to produce a disproportionately unfavorable result among racial minorities and that has not been shown to be *job related*. The asset professional must pay careful attention to certain security practices, such as pre-employment and post-employment investigation, whether for general suitability or in light of actual or suspected offenses. No investigative technique that can be shown to produce disproportionately unfavorable results for racial minority groups or against a particular sex, and which has not been demonstrated to be related, will likely survive.

The traditional arbitrary requirements of height, sex, physical appearance and muscular skills that for long periods were used to screen applicants for jobs such as police officer (or industrial guard), firefighter and similar occupations have already been attacked and fallen, where there was no showing that the specific physical requirement was related to the job to be performed.

Said another way, if a job can be shown to require specific physical or intellectual abilities, as lifting a stated weight to a given height, or running a stated distance in a given time, or reading and understanding English language communications at a certain level of literacy, then the job requirements should be couched in language related to the demonstrated need and not in general form. Further, the whole development of civil rights law in the anti-discrimination area suggests that requirements heretofore considered essential may, upon deeper examination, be shown to be unnecessary or unrelated to the job and, if discriminatory, may be rejected.

Discrimination Based on Disability

This is the area of most recent extension of civil rights protection. The governing U.S. laws are the Rehabilitation Act of 1973 and the Americans with Disabilities Act of 1990.

Selected Bibliography

Books

American Society for Industrial Security; *Civil Liability: Current Issues;* American Society for Industrial Security, Telephone/Telecommunications Standing Committee, 9/25/1986.

Bilek, Arthur J., Klotter, John C. and Federal, R. Keegan; *Legal Aspects of Private Security;* 1981; Anderson Publishing Co., Cincinnati, OH.

Bottom, Norman R., Jr.; *Security Loss Control Negligence;* 1985; Hanrow Press, Columbia, MD.

Branch, James A., Jr.; *Negligent Hiring Practice Manual;* 1988; John Wiley & Sons, New York.

Employment Practices Guide; Commerce Clearing House, Inc., Chicago, IL. (A biweekly subscription service.)

Federal, R. Keegan, Jr. and Fogleman, Jennifer L.; *Avoiding Liability in Premises Security;* 1989; Strafford Publications, Inc.

The Civil Law

Federal, R. Keegan, Ed.; *Private Security Case Law Reporter;* Strafford Publications, Inc., Atlanta, GA. (A monthly case law reporter.)

Green, Ronald M. and Reibstein, Richard J.; *Negligent Hiring, Fraud, Defamation, and Other Emerging Areas of Employer Liability;* 1988; Bureau of National Affairs, Washington, D.C.

Hall, Gerald; *The Failure to Warn Handbook;* 1986; Hanrow Press, Columbia, MD.

Inbau, Fred E., Aspin, Marvin E. and Spiotto, James E.; *Protective Security Law;* 1983; Butterworths Publishing Co., Stoneham, MA.

Kuhlman, Richard S.; *Safe Places?: Security Planning and Litigation;* 1989; Michie.

McGoey, Chris E.; *Security, Adequate ... Or Not? The Complete Guide to Premises Liability Litigation;* 1990; Aegis Books.

Nemeth, Charles P.; *Private Security and the Law;* 1989; Anderson Publishing Co., Cincinnati, OH.

Page, Joseph A.; *The Law of Premises Liability, 2nd ed.;* 1988; Anderson Publishing Co., Cincinnati, OH.

Pepe, Stephen P. and Dunham, Scott H.; *Avoiding and Defending Wrongful Discharge Claims;* 1987; Callaghan.

Prosser, William L. and Keeton, W. Page; *Law of Torts, 5th ed.;* 1984; West Publishing Co., Inc., St. Paul, MN.

Roberson, Cliff; *Staying out of Court: A Manager's Guide to Employment Law;* 1985; Lexington Books.

Schultz, Donald O. and Service, J. Gregory; *Security Litigations and Related Matters;* 1982; Charles C Thomas Publishers, Springfield, IL.

Sherman, Eva F., Ed.; *Security Law Newsletter;* Crime Control Research Corp., Washington, D.C. (A monthly case law reporter.)

Smith, Robert; 1984–1985 Compilation of State and Federal Privacy Laws, *The Privacy Journal;* Washington, D.C., 1984.

Spires, Jeremiah J.; *Doing Business in the United States;* Matthew Bender & Co., Inc., Albany, NY (especially Vol. I, chaps. 1–4).

Tarantino, John A. and Dombroff, Mark A.; *Premises Security: Law and Practice;* 1009; 1990; John Wiley & Sons, New York.

Articles

Security Management, American Society for Industrial Security, Arlington, VA (monthly magazine).
— Bates, Norman David; Reducing Liability's Toll; October 1988.
— Bates, Norman David; Litigation: A Loss to Prevent; April 1988
— Bates, Norman David; Understanding the Liability of Negligent Hiring; July 1990.
— Bequai, August; What Can You Ask? (How to stay within the law when checking backgrounds); November 1991.
— Canton, Lucien G.; Limiting Liability Exposure — Have We Gone Too Far?; January 1990.
— Chamberlain, Jeffrey; Don't Take the Fall; July 1990.
— Decker, Kurt H.; The Rights and Wrongs of Screening; January 1990.
— Dunn, Patrick A.; Your Rights to References; July 1991.
— Edwards, James Loren; Changes in Liability Laws; November 1986.
— Jackson, Lawrence A.; Using Force Wisely; May 1992.
— Meadows, Robert J.; The Likelihood of Liability; July 1991.
— Meadows, Robert J.; How Liable Are You?; January 1990.
— Service, Gregory J.; Let the Master Answer; May 1987.
— Service, Gregory J.; Negligent Hiring: A Liability Trap; January 1988.
— Wiatrowski, Michael D.; Are You Liable?; July 1986.

16
Security as a Management Function

INTRODUCTION

A fundamental change in security, accelerating over the past 20 years, recognizes that the protection of assets is an important *management* function and not merely a housekeeping chore or minor administrative responsibility. That change has been critical to the professionalism in the security field because it has created opportunities for personal growth and attracted highly qualified personnel.

The earlier paradigm for security was borrowed largely from military and paramilitary models. It equated the protection function with military or civilian law enforcement. The emphasis was largely upon physical safeguarding, through the use of guard personnel, and investigations. The security unit was often operated in an authoritarian fashion and was often regarded with disfavor or outright hostility by many other workers. Information about security activities was sometimes needlessly restricted and an atmosphere of distrust permitted to develop. In many earlier programs, there was little constructive cooperation between security and other management areas, and insufficient attention was given to increasing productivity by reducing costs and employing appropriate technology.

Today, however, management is demanding that modern techniques be utilized. More and more, the concept of *loss prevention or avoidance* is being encouraged, and the value of the systems approach (discussed in Chapter 1) recognized as methods to be utilized in developing and managing an effective assets protection program. To be successful in this new environment, the protection professional must utilize current technology and be able to relate security directly to the basic objectives of the enterprise.

DEVELOPING THE ORGANIZATION

Who Is the Customer?

Peter Drucker, an international authority and writer on management,[1] suggests that "Who is the customer?" is the first and most crucial question

---

[1] Drucker, Peter F.; *Management Tasks, Responsibilities, Practices*; Harper and Row, New York; 1974, p. 80.

to be asked in defining business purpose and mission. It is essential that the purpose and mission of the protection activity be known before an organization structure is adopted, and it is important that this question be answered as a first order of business. The answer may appear obvious for an asset protection organization. However, the way some protection organizations have been organized and operate suggests otherwise.

For instance, a topic of popular periodic discussion among security executives is how to "sell" protection to management. At security seminars, the subject is frequently included on the program agenda. Articles discussing the problem periodically appear in security publications but there are few really useful suggestions. The reason is probably a wrong focus on security. What those discussing the problem are often trying to sell is not protection, but programs whose costs are difficult to defend when compared with demonstrated results.

Instead of attempting to justify the programs being administered, it would be better to ask the question suggested by Drucker: "Who is the customer?" It quickly becomes apparent that management is not the only customer, and that there is a need to identify and serve the others as well.

DEFINITION OF RESPONSIBILITIES

Many enterprises include all functions relating to the protection of assets in a single organization. Traditionally recognized security functions, such as guards and investigations, are joined with safety, risk and insurance management, fire protection, and auditing.

Three valuable benefits can result from such an arrangement.

1. There will be a better opportunity to use the systems approach (discussed in Chapter 1) to ensure that the entire spectrum of protection is covered and that countermeasures have been designed to neutralize risks to a maximum extent.
2. It will usually be possible to utilize personnel more efficiently so there should be less duplication of efforts and lower costs. For example, if guard and fire responsibilities are not in the same organization, there will be a tendency to have guards and firefighters perform overlapping or duplicate tasks.
3. It should be possible to hire highly qualified asset protection management personnel because the responsibilities, job content and growth opportunities will attract them.

An example of poor results from improper organization is the enterprise that fragments the protection responsibilities into a number of different units. Some enterprises have the guard operation and lock program in the plant engineering activity, the fire department reporting to the plant manager, individuals responsible for government security in the contract administration area, and responsibilities for safety in the personnel or industrial relations organization. Under such an arrangement, each single activity may not only be less effective than it could be, but the entire area of asset protection may be degraded because no single knowledgeable person is coordinating the overall program. Costs will usually be higher because of the duplication of effort that is almost guaranteed to result.

Another pitfall to avoid is copying a structure adopted by another enterprise. Despite an appearance of effectiveness, many of the problems already discussed might exist in such an organization but not be apparent. Each protection organization should be designed to meet the particular needs of its own enterprise. A useful way to see this task is from a "zero base" viewpoint. If there were no security function or organization, how could one be built from scratch to serve *this* enterprise optimally?

When a protection activity must be established or upgraded, it will often be found that there is no one in the enterprise sufficiently expert to determine the functions that should be included. Some organizations have solved this problem by retaining a qualified consultant to analyze the problems, methods of operation and the requirements of the enterprise, and then to recommend the functions to be included in the protection activity.

Some organizations have also utilized the consultant to recruit a qualified professional to manage the protection activity after it has been established. Other organizations have hired a professional protection executive with a successful record in another enterprise. In such an arrangement, the protection professional not only organizes the protection program, but normally manages it after it has been set up.

PROGRAM IMPLEMENTATION

Top Management Responsibility

A basic requirement for any protection program is that the top officials show interest. Top management must support the protection program completely on a continuing basis, and must be willing to take actions to ensure that individuals at all levels are cooperating.

Indications of top-level support can be transmitted in policy statements and published procedures. Such material will normally outline the program requirements, the attitude the organization is adopting concerning protection, the role that everyone must play in the program, and the responsibilities and functions being delegated to the protection organization.

An important consideration is setting limitations on the authority of the protection organization. The old Prussian idea of a citizen's rights — "Everything not expressly ordered is forbidden" — does not work and is abhorrent in a democratic culture. But without defining some limitations, supervisors and members of the protection organization may take actions that usurp the prerogatives of other operating personnel.

Most situations requiring limitations on the actions of protection personnel can be anticipated. Plans can be made and procedures established to involve the appropriate line supervision in the decision-making process. Two examples are the handling of bomb threats, with the related question of evacuation, and the arrest and prosecution of an employee. Both decisions of should be made by appropriate line management, with protection personnel supplying information and making informed recommendations.

In the bomb threat case, the definition of responsibility should clearly call out the line manager, who should make an evacuation decision and also provide for exceptions and conditions under which some other identified member of management might make the decision.

With reference to the arrest and the prosecution situation, the protection organization's authority should be defined and the required management reviews spelled out. If this is not done, a situation might develop like that which occurred on a college campus and resulted in great criticism of the protection organization and the responsible protection executive.

In the college incident, patrolling members of the protection organization made several reports indicating that marijuana was being smoked each night by students in one of the campus dormitory rooms. The protection executive in charge reported the incident to the appropriate college administrator. But one night, a protection supervisor decided to take it upon himself to correct the situation because it had been several days since the initial report was made and he thought no action was being taken. He called the local police and had them break in and arrest a room full of students smoking marijuana. He also filed complaints against each of the students involved.

The school officials disagreed violently with the action taken, because they felt the problem had not been solved but only aggravated. The administrators had not ignored the problem, as the protection supervisor thought, but instead were in the process of arriving at a realistic solution administratively and had no intention of involving outsiders.

The local news media publicized the incident widely. The school newspaper gave the occurrence prominent coverage and was most critical of the protection organization and the top protection executive because of the tactics utilized. The result: The protection organization lost a great deal of credibility with both students and school officials, and the effectiveness of the organization was severely damaged. The incident might have been prevented if the supervisors in the organization had had the limit of their authority explained to them.

Security as a Management Function

A restriction on authority should not be regarded by members of the protection organization as a reflection on their judgment or importance to the enterprise. It should be understood that limitations are also imposed for their own protection. Such restraints are not confined to the protection organization. Every individual in an enterprise must work within the framework of restrictions. Even a chief executive officer is subject to limitations placed upon him by the board of directors and corporate bylaws.

A fact sometimes overlooked is that a protection organization should generally act in a staff or service capacity to line supervisors. Assumption by members of the protection organization of authority that rightly belongs to operating line supervision may result in criticism and loss of credibility for the protection organization.

Involvement of Others

Anyone with whom the protection organization has a relationship should be considered when an asset protection program is being planned or implemented. Employees outside the protection unit can be of great assistance, and their ongoing participation can make a significant contribution to success, if they are properly motivated.

In a protection program, a prime objective should be to motivate every employee to become part of the protection team. Each employee should be encouraged to assume responsibility for the protection of enterprise assets as an essential element of his or her own job. Supervisors at all levels should be required to ensure that all employees under their cognizance are assuming such responsibility and performing as required.

This concept of assigning responsibility to employees is not unique to protection. Management writers now stress that employees not only want, but expect to assume responsibility because they seek a sense of achievement. Drucker[1] stresses the fact that the psychological and social position of workers in recent years has changed. They are now better educated and better paid. What he describes as the knowledge worker — an individual more skilled and intelligent because of automation, etc. — has emerged as a large segment of the workforce. New human relations techniques now emphasize worker participation in all decisions affecting them and their work environment.

There has been a proliferation of writings and studies on the achievement and the motivation of workers in recent years. Most management experts now seem to agree that all employees, to varying degrees, seek positive accomplishments and will take pride in their work if properly motivated. Further, it is agreed that the majority are trustworthy, dependable and responsible.

[1] *Op. cit.*, p. 179.

COMMUNICATIONS

The subject of communications has probably been given more attention in recent years than any other area of management. There has been a constant effort to improve communications in every enterprise, but the results are not always what were expected. Frequently, a communication gap can be observed within an enterprise, as well as between an enterprise and outside groups despite the communication efforts being made.

Effective communication methods are central to the success of any asset protection program. One of the mistakes often made is that communication is regarded as one-way. Instructions are sent out to employees and supervisors in the form of policies, procedures and directives, but no attempt is made to obtain feedback. Feedback from individuals at all levels in the enterprise is one effective technique that can be utilized to test the system.

Methods of obtaining feedback should be included in program design. Two groups within the enterprise should be considered when a feedback plan is devised. One group is composed of employees of the protection organization, the other of all other employees. Feedback from both groups is important and may take many forms. And it does not have to be formal, such as a system of structured written reports, although this may be one method. Probably a more effective technique would be to utilize discussions and interviews with employees and supervisors.[1]

A provision for listening and reacting to feedback is also important. This may seem obvious but if it is not included in the plan, it may be found that a large amount of information is being collected but nothing is being done with it. Also, those who have provided information or suggestions should be informed of actions or corrections that have been taken as a result of it.

If the communication techniques involving feedback are followed, the participation and cooperation of employees outside the protection organization will be stimulated. The protection program should also be easier to administer because revisions and changes can be made to correct deficiencies or gaps defined by those supplying information. As in any communication system, irrelevant information will also be obtained, but this can easily be sorted out and discarded. The morale and efficiency of those in the protection organization should be improved because they will feel they are a key element in the program and will take a personal interest in it.

STAFFING THE PROTECTION ORGANIZATION

Selection of the top professional to design, implement and manage an asset program is a key element in its success. Knowledge and the ability of

---

[1] The currently popular *focus group* or *focus panel* is another form of feedback. It utilizes a selected sample of persons affected by a policy or practice to examine the probable impact of implementation in a nonconfrontational setting.

the executive to apply modern management techniques and methods are essential. The executive must be familiar with protection problems and techniques but the main focus should be the implementation of the systems approach and the management of the system. The protection head will be required to deal with problems involving investigations, guards, fire protection and physical security, but this does not mean that a majority of time and effort should be devoted to such individual problems. A complex, sophisticated protection program will be required to neutralize the many risks faced by the contemporary enterprise, and a person with a broad range of management talents will be required to lead such a program.

One test for the selection of protection staff personnel is their degree of participation in professional organizations — in particular, the American Society for Industrial Security (ASIS). This is the leading professional organization in the security area with over 25,000 members worldwide.

An important professional activity that the ASIS has been sponsoring since 1977 is the Certified Protection Professional (CPP) program. Those qualifying as Certified Protection Professionals must meet certain education and experience requirements and achieve a passing grade on a written examination. Increasingly, organizations recognize the value of the CPP designation and have identified in security staff job descriptions that designation as a desirable qualification.

A variety of professional training programs are also offered by the ASIS for the purpose of improving the professionalism of members and others working in the protection field. Such training includes workshops on specialized subjects, management-oriented courses and an annual seminar. Current schedules of ASIS training programs are published each month in the POA *Bulletin*, and complete details are available from the ASIS. Because of the current recognition that security is an important management function, an applicant for a responsible protection position who is not able to demonstrate a professional interest in the field might not be a successful contender.

At one time, it was a common practice to select an individual from government, military, or public law enforcement to head a protection organization. Sometimes, such persons could not apply the broad range of techniques necessary to implement and manage a complete, modern protection program but had a tendency to focus the efforts of the security organization on areas in which they had their own prior experience. So much effort and attention was devoted to these areas that the enterprise did not have a well-rounded program because many risk areas were overlooked or neglected. While prior experience in law enforcement or government security is very useful, it is not enough to ensure optimal performance in private-sector security.

Compensation

The salary and benefits that go with a position will depend to a great extent on the functional responsibilities assigned to the protection organization. The more challenging the position and the more it pays, the better qualified the candidates for the position.

In recent years, more and more enterprises have upgraded or reorganized their protection organizations. Security professionals with management potential have been obtaining experience as middle managers in large protection organizations or as managers of smaller activities, such as divisions or plants. Those individuals now constitute a growing pool of talent from which senior-level positions are being filled.

Compensation will vary, depending on geographical location and other factors; but in general, it should be expected that the range for a highly qualified executive for a smaller organization will be between $45,000 and $75,000 annually, while large organizations should be prepared to pay from $80,000 to over $125,000 a year.

After the appropriate benefit package has been established for the top manager, the amount of compensation for the rest of the security staff can be established. Ranges and paid rates will be developed based on standard salary and wage administration practices. But it is important to establish a wide enough range for professional positions that require a high degree of skill but do not always lead to rapid promotion to maintain an incentive for qualified incumbents. In other words, promotion should not be the only avenue to increased compensation for security professionals who are making a measurable contribution to mission. Investigators come to mind as a good example. If investigators consistently recover diverted assets, identify undesirable employment applicants and expose serious loss vulnerabilities, they should have access to a wide salary range or incentive compensation, or both.

Reporting Level

The reporting level of the top protection executive is also an important performance factor. There is no rule requiring that security report to or through any particular type of senior management. It has worked in industrial relations, legal, administrative and even operations lines. What is important is that the reporting level be high enough so that security activity, which may be seen as a threat by some intermediate managers, not be prematurely or improperly terminated or redirected.

It is the sensitivity and potential importance of security work to enterprise well-being that requires it to be under the direction of a senior official. The personal chemistries and culture in any given enterprise are more important to a successful security operation than conformance to standard organization theory.[1]

PROGRAM MANAGEMENT

Planning

Planning is indispensable for a successful program. It has been defined as deciding in advance who does what, and how. Planning bridges the gap from where we are to where we want to go, and makes it possible for things to happen that would not otherwise occur.

> "Plans are nothing; planning is everything"
>
> — Eisenhower
>
> "If you don't know where you're going, it doesn't matter what road you take to get there"
>
> — Cordiner, GE

Protection organization managers who do not plan will always be reacting to events that have already occurred or will be attempting to solve problems that might otherwise have been avoided. The first planning step should be to determine overall goals and objectives. As much information about the affairs of the organization as possible should be obtained. This is a continuing process, as objectives may change or be revised.

The normal, structured supervisory communication chain cannot always be depended upon for this type of information. The senior executive to whom the protection manager reports may forget to provide important information or may not realize that certain data would have an effect on the protection operation. Key protection personnel must constantly be alert for needed information. For example, information is received that a new plant is being considered, or that a new product may be released in the future, or that a manufacturing process is being changed and a precious metal is being incorporated in the process. All of these situations would require some planning action by the protection organization. As soon as information of this type is received, the cognizant staff or operating official who would know what is being planned should be contacted so that the necessary details can be obtained and action taken.

The protection staff members should not adopt a head-in-the-sand attitude. Obtaining information in almost every organization is a problem — not because individuals are reluctant to give it out or because it is not available, but because people are too busy or preoccupied to communicate it.

---

[1] See, for example, Security: A Concept and a Management Technique, *Fortune* magazine, September 1974, p.47; Security: The Essential Corporate Asset, *The Wall Street Journal,* August 10, 1978, special supplement on security; Corporate Security: Top Management Mandate, *Dun's Review,* January 1980, p. 94.

ASSET PROTECTION AND SECURITY MANAGEMENT HANDBOOK

The protection executive who does not recognize this problem may be operating in the dark, not knowing what is going on in the enterprise and not being able to make adequate protection plans.

Through planning, including information gathering, the energies and resources of the protection organization can be focused on the correct results: avoidance or control of losses. To obtain those results, it is necessary that an action program be implemented with concrete work assignments. Definite goals must be established with deadlines and clear accountability for results. The organization should always be working today to avoid future problems. The organization that is devoting full time to today's problems clearly indicates that there has been no planning but that it is definitely needed.

> Plans are not abstractions, dreams, or good intentions. They should be practical commitments to obtain results so that future problems can be avoided. Planning must also be flexible to cope with the unpredictable or unexpected event.

Any plan that no longer appears to serve a useful purpose should be abandoned. To accomplish this, it is necessary that plans be regularly and systematically reviewed. There may be a tendency in an organization to re-double efforts because there has been a lack of results when, instead, a plan or project should be abandoned because it no longer has any value to the enterprise.

The fact that individuals have a tendency to procrastinate should also be recognized. An employee responsible for implementing a project may be given a deadline date sometime in the future and be expected to perform certain tasks over the period between now and then. Without a timely review of progress, it may be found that he or she only started working on the day the project was due, or the day before.

Individuals should be familiar with plans in which they have a role. Those responsible for accomplishing certain objectives should clearly understand what is demanded of them and that they will be expected to obtain the results called for, absent mitigating circumstances.

Plans of the protection organization must always be related to the overall objectives and plans of the enterprise. Cost-effectiveness must be a consideration in achieving an objective. To suggest a project that would cost thousands of dollars need not result in disapproval, even in a period of austerity, if favorable savings or return can be shown. On the other hand, to suggest an expenditure of one dollar to save 99 cents is bad planning and poor management.

Training

Professionals in the protection organization can no longer limit their knowledge to security-related topics. Management techniques and methods must be known and utilized in a contemporary protection program. Protection professionals must also be familiar with other technologies. One obvious example is data processing. Other high-risk areas involving advanced technology may be revealed during a vulnerability analysis.

Excellent courses are now available in colleges and universities, providing security specialization in a general, academic context. Approximately 200 colleges and universities in the United States and Canada offer security courses. The training offered by the American Society for Industrial Security has already been mentioned. A number of professional journals in the protection field are now available, and many textbooks dealing with modern protection techniques have been published in recent years. The Selected Bibliographies to the chapters of this handbook identify some of them.

Training programs organized within the enterprise and within the protection organization can be used to good advantage. But no single training technique will be adequate to ensure that staff members are professionally trained. A variety of techniques will be required.

Delegation

Delegation of authority and responsibility from the operating head of the enterprise to the protection organization should be implemented through the issuance of policy. Delegation of responsibility and authority within the protection activity itself is particularly important because of the fact that the organization must operate around the clock, seven days a week. If both authority and responsibility are not explicitly delegated, a bottleneck may develop, and necessary actions and decisions delayed. Lack of delegation has been observed in some protection organizations as a serious limitation on their effectiveness.

A serious professional responsible for managing a protection operation should learn and heed the ten rules of management suggested in Table 1.

Relationships: Internal and External

The need for the protection manager and staff to work closely with the top operating officials of the enterprise is obvious and has been mentioned earlier. The need to work closely and to have good relationships with personnel of other staff and operating activities must not be overlooked. Developing and keeping such relationships is a continuous process. For example, the finance staff members are of particular importance because almost every action the protection staff takes will have an impact on the finances of the enterprise. Before any plans that involve expenditures of funds are submitted to the top operating officers, the implications should be discussed with appropriate financial staff members to obtain their reactions and advice.

Table 1. Management rules that should be applied by executives in the protection organization.

1. Definite and clear-cut responsibilities should be assigned to each executive.
2. Responsibility should always be coupled with corresponding authority.
3. No change should be made in the scope or responsibilities of a position without a definite understanding to that effect on the part of all persons concerned.
4. No executive or employee, occupying a single position in the organization, should be subject to definite orders from more than one source.
5. Orders should never be given to subordinates over the head of a responsible executive. Rather than do this, management should supplant the officer in question.
6. Criticisms of subordinates should, whenever possible, be made privately; and in no case should subordinates be criticized in the presence of executives or employees of equal or lower rank.
7. No dispute or difference between executives or employees as to authority or responsibilities should be considered too trivial for prompt and careful adjudication.
8. Promotions, wage changes and disciplinary action should always be approved by the executive immediately superior to the one directly responsible.
9. No executive or employee should ever be required, or expected, to be at the same time an assistant to, and critic of, another.
10. Any executive whose work is subject to regular inspection should, whenever practicable, be given the assistance and facilities necessary to enable an independent check of the quality of the work.

External relationships are also important. Examples of some are other enterprises, government and law enforcement agencies, and professional organizations. The protection staff members should not wait until a problem with an outside organization or activity arises to develop a relationship. In most areas, various organizations hold meetings of those having mutual interests, meetings at which common problems and interests are discussed. Meetings of this type will often involve a luncheon or dinner and perhaps a registration fee for attendance. Attendance at such a meeting should not be regarded as a mere social event but as an essential measure to develop necessary relationships.

Many organizations have found that external relationships can be developed and improved by inviting outside representatives to visit the facility. By organizing a tour or a briefing focused on the activities of the organization, and by providing a luncheon or dinner for the visitors, useful discussions regarding mutual problems can be carried on in a friendly, relaxed atmosphere.

Selected Bibliography

There is a voluminous amount of management literature available and it is difficult to select a reading list that every reader might regard as the best

Security as a Management Function

of the available material. Those included in this selected list will provide material for a start. For convenience, the list has been divided into general categories.

Books

Protection Management:

Cole, Richard B.; *Protection Management and Crime Prevention;* 1974; W.H. Anderson, Cincinnati, OH.

Compensation in the Security/Loss Prevention Field, 6th ed.; 1990; Abbott, Langer & Assoc., Crete, IL.

Dalton, Dennis R.; *Security Management: Business Strategies for Success;* 1995; Butterworth-Heinemann.

Healy, Richard J. and Walsh, Timothy J.; *Principals of Security Management;* 1981; Professional Publications, New Rochelle, NY.

Higgins, Clay; *Applied Security Management;* 1991; Charles C Thomas Publishers, Springfield, IL.

Post, Richard S. and Kingsbury, Arthur A.; *Security Administration, An Introduction to Protective Services, 4th ed.;* 1990; Charles C Thomas, Springfield, IL.

The Security Manager's Handbook; 1990; Bureau of Business Practices, Prentice-Hall, Waterford, CT.

Ursic, Henry S. and Pagano, Leroy E.; *Security Management Systems;* 1974; Charles C Thomas, Springfield, IL.

Accounting and Finance:

Goodman, Sam R. and Reece, James S., Eds.; *Controllers Handbook;* 1978; Dow Jones-Irwin, Homewood, IL.

Horngren, C.; *Cost Accounting: A Managerial Emphasis;* 1972; Prentice-Hall, Englewood Cliffs, NJ.

Pyle, W.W. and White, J.A.; *Fundamental Accounting Principles;* 1972; Dow Jones-Irwin, Homewood, IL.

Rachlin, Robert; *Return on Investment;* 1976; Marr Publications, New York.

Weston, J. Fred and Breghorn, Eugene F.; *Managerial Finance;* 1972; Holt, Rinehart, and Winston, New York.

General Management:

Band, William A.; *Touchstones: Ten New Ideas Revolutionizing Business;* 1994; Wiley, New York.

Bittel, Lester R. and Ramsey, Jackson E., Eds.; *Handbook for Professional Managers;* 1985; McGraw-Hill, New York.

Dale, Ernest; *Management Theory and Practice, 3rd ed.;* 1973; McGraw-Hill, Hightstown, NJ.

Drucker, Peter F.; *Managing for Results;* 1964; Harper & Row, New York.

Drucker, Peter F.; *Management: Tasks, Responsibilities, Practices;* 1974; Harper & Row, New York.

Drucker, Peter F.; *The Practice of Management;* 1954; Harper & Row, New York.

Ewing, David W.; *Do It My Way or You're Fired!: Employee Rights and the Changing Role of Management Prerogatives;* 1983; John Wiley & Sons, New York.

Fulton, Roger V.; *Common Sense Supervision: A Handbook for Success as a Supervisor;* 1988; Knight Management Corp.

Henderson, George; *Cultural Diversity in the Workplace: Issues and Strategies;* 1994; Quorum Books.

Herman, Roger E.; *Keeping Good People: Strategies for Solving the Dilemma;* 1990; Oakhill Press.

Hrebiniak, Lawrence G.; *The We-Force in Management: How to Build and Sustain Cooperation;* 1994; Lexington Books.

Knouse, Stephen B.; *The Reward and Recognition Process in Total Quality Management;* 1995; ASQC Quality Press, Milwaukee, WI.

Koontz, Harold and O'Donnell, Cyril; *Principles of Management;* 1972; McGraw-Hill, New York.

Korman, Abraham K.; *Human Dilemmas in Work Organizations: Strategies for Resolution;* 1994; Guilford Press.

Kotter, John P.; *The Leadership Factor;* 1988; Free Press.

McGill, Michael E. and Slocum, John W., Jr.; *The Smarter Organization: How to Build a Business that Learns;* 1994; Wiley, New York.

McGregor, Douglas; *The Human Side of Enterprise;* 1958; McGraw-Hill, New York.

McGregor, Douglas; *The Professional Manager;* 1967; McGraw-Hill, New York.

Rae, Leslie; *How to Measure Training Effectiveness;* 1986; Nichols Publishing Co.

Roberts, Harry V. and Sergesketter, Bernard F.; *Quality Is Personal: A Foundation for Total Quality Management;* 1993; Free Press, New York.

Shapero, Albert; *Managing Professional People: Understanding Creative Performance;* 1985; Free Press, New York.

Shearer, Clive; *Practical Continuous Improvement for Professional Services;* 1994; ASQC Quality Press, Milwaukee, WI.

Snyder, Neil H., Dowd, James J., Jr., and Morse, Dianne; *Vision, Values and Courage: Leadership for Quality Management;* 1994; Free Press, Milwaukee, WI.

Thompson, Brad Lee; *The New Manager's Handbook;* 1995; Irwin Professional Publishing.

Tjosvold, Dean and Mary M.; *The Emerging Leader: Ways to a Stronger Team;* 1993; Lexington Books.

Organization:

Argyris, Chris; *Organization and Innovation;* 1963; Yale University Press, New Haven, CT.

Bennis, W.G.; *Changing Organizations;* 1966; McGraw-Hill, New York.

Guth, William; *Organizational Strategy: Analysis, Commitment Implementation;* 1974; Irwin, Homewood, IL.

Sayles, Leonard R. and Chandler, Margaret K.; *Managing Large Systems: Organizations for the Future;* 1971; Harper and Row, New York.

Periodicals

Security Management magazine; American Society for Industrial Security, Arlington, VA.
— Band, William A.; Making Peace with Change; March 1995.
— Bronstein, Howard; Steering Teams through Troubled Waters; May 1995.
— Burley-Allen, Madelyn; Conducting Reasonable Reprimands; November 1995.
— DeSalvo, Gerald; Maintaining Quality through Management Reviews; August 1994.
— Heck, Gary L.; Managing by Example; June 1993.
— Henderson, George; Traveling the Path to Diversity; July 1995.
— Plante, William J.; The Art of Planning; March 1993.

— Smith, Jim L.; Understanding the Nature of Leadership; January 1994.
— Somerson, Ira S.; The Next Generation; January 1995.
— Veich, Anthony M. and Head, Thomas; Management's Neglected Tool; September 1993.

17
Ethics in the Security Profession

INTRODUCTION

This chapter defines the concept of professional ethics and discusses how ethical concepts can and should be applied to the asset protection field. It does this by:

- Examining the basic claims made for the field by its practitioners
- Considering specific situations and the implications for the individual professional
- Exploring the development of professional ethics in the security field and suggesting some extensions of current principles

In addition, this chapter provides an overview of the context and application of professional ethics in general, with specific examples of how such concepts can be applied to the asset protection practitioner.

WHAT ARE PROFESSIONAL ETHICS?

Professional ethics are those rules of conduct by which members of a profession regulate their conduct among themselves and with all other persons with whom they deal in their professional capacities. Such rules can be considered a code of professional responsibility. They exist in addition to the precepts of the basic ethical or moral code that the society at large observes. They also exist in addition to the requirements of the civil and criminal law. *Professional ethics are statements describing proper behavior for persons engaged in highly specialized activities that are not sufficiently regulated by general morality or the law.*

The Need for Professional Ethics

Why are general moral values and the legal system not enough to regulate professional conduct? Some answers:

- General moral codes operate in an individual's conscience and do not prevent actions by persons lacking this conscience.
- Criminal and civil laws, which have enforcement capability, cannot deal with all the situations that arise in the course of professional conduct.

- Actions of professionals are beyond the ability or capability of the public to evaluate; they involve or depend upon skills and knowledge that the public does not generally share and hence cannot properly assess.

Because the public cannot critically examine those actions, which are neither regulated nor monitored by law, special rules of conduct are necessary. Otherwise, unchecked actions by professionals can result in significant harm to people.

Professional Responsibility Matches Professional Recognition

When a group of specialists whose actions affect the public insists on recognition for the special skills and knowledge of its members — when it refers to itself as "professional" — it is also describing itself as requiring special rules of conduct. If such a group is truly professional, then it possesses skills and knowledge not possessed by the community at large and it acts in matters that have the potential to significantly harm innocent persons who must deal with members of the profession. There is implicit a claim that such skills are to be rewarded, that the expertise displayed by the professional demands material or other compensation in equal measure. But the implicit demand for reward and the insistence upon recognition must be coupled with a manifest willingness to behave responsibly or the public is threatened, not served. The more a group insists upon professional recognition, the more it must display responsible behavior. It must articulate the principles to regulate that behavior. Such an organized and systematic statement of principles represents the code of ethics for that profession.

THE SECURITY PROFESSION

In regard to insistence upon professional recognition, security and assets protection do not differ from other fields. The periodical literature in the security field contains repeated references to professionalism, by which the writers mean highly competent performance in a field requiring special knowledge and skills. Security practitioners, by laying claim to professional status, assume the obligation of professional regulation. This requires a method for generating the rules of conduct. This means that those persons claiming professional status must establish the statement of principles by which they will be regulated and must design a practical vehicle for applying it to themselves, individually and as a group. More is required than individual goodwill.

THE PROFESSIONAL SOCIETY

The traditional way to achieve publication of a code of professional ethics has been for the sponsoring group, the professional society, to see the

Ethics in the Security Profession

code as a condition for continued membership in the society. In some cases, the professional code of ethics is given the force of law. Attorneys, for example, if found in violation of the Code of Professional Responsibility adopted by the American Bar Association and the various state bar groups, face very severe penalties including, as the ultimate sanction, disbarment by the courts. Likewise, the state and county medical societies can institute proceedings to censure physicians guilty of unprofessional conduct. These proceedings can lead to revocation of the medical license by licensing authorities.

The usual means for enforcing the professional code is the grievance and hearing — a trial by professional peers. It is often pointed to as a sign of laxness when established professions express few professional censures over long periods of time.

Without a professional society — a peer group qualified to express the behavioral standards — there is no way to generate a code of professional responsibility. Without a professional code, conduct not expressly prohibited by the law is regulated merely by an individual's conscience.

The security field has had a peer group since 1955. The American Society for Industrial Security (ASIS) has a membership of 25,000 practitioners. In 1957, the ASIS first adopted a code of professional ethics. Modifications were made in that code, and it remained the primary statement of principles in the field until June 27, 1980.[1] Every member of the ASIS, as a condition of acceptance into membership, agreed to:

> "... be governed by (the Society's) constitution and bylaws; abide by its code of ethics; and promote the objectives of the Society as long as my membership or affiliation remains in effect."

Unlike the traditional learned professions, the security profession does not yet have direct recourse to the law to enforce its rules of conduct,[2] nor is it a universal requirement that persons in the security field even join the society. But, because the American Society for Industrial Security is the oldest and, by far, largest such group, and because it has made adherence to its code of ethics a requirement for almost 50 years, it is the most important source of professional standards in the security field. It is of interest to examine the historical development of that code, as first stated in the pre-1980 formulation. Thus, the remainder of this chapter comments on the initial code.

---

[1] On that date the ASIS published a completely revised Code of Ethics that was adopted by ASIS.
[2] While it is true that a number of states have passed statutory schemes for regulating private security, it is those states, directly, and not any professional group which initiate and prosecute penalty proceedings under such schemes.

ASSET PROTECTION AND SECURITY MANAGEMENT HANDBOOK

THE CODE OF ETHICS OF THE AMERICAN SOCIETY FOR INDUSTRIAL SECURITY

The earlier code, quoted below, is taken verbatim from the Society Directory of Membership, 1964–1965 edition.

As members of this Society we share a singular responsibility for maintaining inviolate the integrity and trust of the security profession. In discharging this responsibility, therefore, we mutually pledge that:

I. *We will endeavor, under God, to perform our professional duties in accordance with the highest moral principles.*

II. *We will direct our concerted efforts toward the support, protection, and defense of liberty and justice for all.*

III. *We will work vigilantly and unceasingly to thwart the activities of individuals or groups who seek to change or destroy the democratic government processes by force or violence or any other unlawful means.*

IV. *We will strive to strengthen our Governments by the securing of facilities and the conserving of resources.*

V. *We will be faithful and diligent in discharging the duties entrusted to us, protecting the property and interests of employers and safeguarding the lives and well-being of employees.*

VI. *We will observe strictly the precepts of truth, accuracy and prudence.*

VII. *We will respect and protect confidential and privileged information.*

VIII. *We will promote programs designed to raise standards, improve efficiency, and increase the effectiveness of security.*

IX. *We will work together toward the achievement of the professional objectives of the Society.*

X. *We will strive to work with and assist one another.*

Official Commentary on the Early ASIS Code of Ethics

On January 11, 1966, the Board of Directors of ASIS approved, and in April 1966 published, an amendment to the ASIS bylaws that established in the bylaws of Article VIII, a new committee entitled "Grievance Committee." The Board also adopted rules of professional conduct at the same time. Comment will be made later on the Grievance Committee. Immediately below is the language used by the ASIS Board in creating the rules of professional conduct. From that date until June 1980, the rules constituted the only official comment by the ASIS on its code of ethics, and they had to be considered when assessing the full impact of the code as it was then.

THE PRACTICAL APPLICATION OF PROFESSIONAL ETHICS

The preamble to the official commentary on the ASIS code of ethics stressed that no code can particularize all the duties and obligations of the professional security specialist. In the practical area of daily decisions, this

Ethics in the Security Profession

Rules of Professional Conduct

No code or set of rules can be framed which will particularize all the duties and obligations of the professional security specialist in the varying phases of his responsibility, or in all the relationships of his professional life. The following rules of professional conduct, implementing the Code of Ethics, are adopted by the American Society for Industrial Security as a general guide. The enumeration of particular duties and obligations should not be construed as a denial of the existence of others, equally imperative, though not specifically mentioned.

I. *We will endeavor, under God, to perform our professional duties in accordance with the highest moral principles.*

   A. *It is the duty of a member not only to his employer but also to the individuals over whom he has responsibility to be punctual and thorough in discharging his security responsibilities.*

   B. *It is the duty of a member to conduct his business and discharge his responsibility with the utmost candor and fairness to all concerned. It is unprofessional and dishonorable to deal other than candidly with the facts and the analysis and interpretation of those facts and in the recommendation of action to be taken pertaining to any individuals.*

II. *We will direct our concerted efforts toward the support, protection, and defense of the United States of America.*

[Ed.: Note that a subsequent amendment of the basic Code changed the last five words of this provision to those quoted on the preceding section. No commentary was ever developed under either version.]

III. *We will labor vigilantly and unceasingly to thwart the activities of individuals or groups who seek to change or destroy our form of government by unconstitutional means.*

[Ed.: Note that a later amendment to the basic Code changed the language of this article to that quoted in the preceding section. No commentary was ever developed under either version.]

IV. *We will strive to strengthen the nation by securing and conserving its industrial facilities.*

[Ed.: Note that here, again, a later amendment to the basic Code changed this article slightly to the form quoted in the preceding section. A commentary had been developed under the earlier version and it follows next.]

   A. *It is the duty of a member to present clearly the consequences to be expected from courses of action proposed, in which relevant, professional industrial security counsel is overruled by non-technical authority.*

V. *We will be faithful and diligent in discharging the duties entrusted to us, protecting the property and interests of employers and safeguarding the lives and well-being of employees.*

   A. *It is the duty of a member to act in professional matters for each employer or client as a faithful agent or trustee. He will act with fairness and justice between employers or clients and when dealing with third parties.*

   B. *It is the duty of a member to guard against conditions that are dangerous or threatening to character and reputation, life, limb or property in work for which industrial security is responsible and, if not responsible, will call such condition to the attention of those who are responsible.*

   C. *It is the duty of a member to engage or advise his employer or client to engage, and cooperate with other experts and specialists whenever the employer's or client's best interests are served by such service.*

D. It is the duty of a member to accept no compensation, financial or otherwise, from more than one interested party for the same service, or for services pertaining to the same work, without the consent of all interested parties.
E. It is the duty of a member to accept no commissions or allowances, directly or indirectly, from contractors or other parties whose equipment, supplies or services he may recommend to his employer or client.
F. It is the duty of a member to promptly disclose to his employer or client any other business interest which may compete with or affect the business of the employer or client. He will not allow an interest in any business to affect his professional judgment regarding industrial security work for which he may be employed or on which he may be called to perform.

VI. We will observe strictly the precepts of truth, accuracy and prudence.
A. It is the duty of a member not to display, promote, advertise or publicize work or accomplishments in the field of industrial security for reasons of personal gain or satisfaction, unless, after a full disclosure of intent, he has obtained the approval of his principal, or the employer for whom the work was originally performed and, further, it is the duty of the security officer to avoid all conduct or practice likely to discredit, or to do injury to the dignity and status of the industrial security profession.
B. It is the duty of a member to diligently examine all pertinent facets of every matter within his responsibility bearing on industrial security and to objectively place before the proper constituted authority the pertinent information and, where appropriate, his judgment and recommendation and decision without, even in the slightest degree, expression of prejudice, opinion or influence.
C. It is the duty of a member to ascertain prior to any disclosure that there is a justifiable need to disclose information pertaining to the suitability, reputation, integrity, and loyalty of any individual and that the person to whom the information is to be disclosed has a bona fide right to the information and that no such information shall be disseminated unless the need and right exist.

[Ed.: It is noted that the January 1966 commentary did not mention Article VII dealing with the confidential and privileged information. This must be assumed to have been an oversight.]

VIII. We will promote programs designed to raise standards, improve efficiency, and increase the effectiveness of security.
A. It is the duty of a member to do everything consistent with propriety and other principles to protect the image and reputation of the industrial security profession collectively and specifically from misrepresentation and misunderstanding.
B. It is the duty of a member to take care that credit for significant accomplishments in industrial security work is given to those to whom credit is properly due.
C. It is the duty of a member to uphold the principle of appropriate and adequate compensation for those engaged in industrial security work, including those in subordinate capacities, as being in the public interest.
D. It is the duty of a member to endeavor to provide opportunity for the professional development and advancement of personnel he employs or supervises.
E. A member will not directly or indirectly injure the professional reputation, prospects or practice of colleagues or associates. However, if it is considered that a colleague is guilty of unethical, illegal, or unfair practice, he will present the information to the proper authority for action.
F. It is the duty of a member to exercise due restraint in criticizing a colleague's work in public, recognizing the fact that professional societies and publications provide the proper forum for technical discussions and criticisms.

G. No member will become associated in responsibility for work with colleagues who do not conform to ethical practices.

IX. We will work together toward the achievement of the professional objectives of the Society.

A. Members should expose without fear or favor before the appropriate individuals and bodies, including the Board of Directors of this Society, corrupt or dishonest conduct in the profession and should undertake without reservation to present knowledge of such conduct to the appropriate body. The member should aid in protecting the Society against admission to membership of candidates unfit or unqualified because of deficiency in character, training or education. The member should strive at all times to uphold the honor and to maintain the dignity of the profession and to improve its administration.

B. It is the obligation of members to extend the knowledge and effectiveness of the industrial security profession, by the interchange of information among other members where such interchange will advance the profession or aid in the protection of appropriate interests, by contributing to the objectives of educational institutions, professional societies, and organizations whose objectives further the interests of industrial security, and through training and study achieving the degree of excellence commensurate with the obligations and responsibilities which he undertakes to discharge.

[Ed.: Note that at the time of the development of this official commentary there was no Article X to the basic code. That was added by a later action of the ASIS Board of Directors.]

---

statement means that, although a specific rule may not exist, each professional will be guided at least by a general principle. A narrow or legalist view of ethics would hold that, unless an activity were prohibited expressly by the code, it would be acceptable. But the basic aim of professional ethics is to imbue the professional with an attitude that results in the opposite position, an attitude that restrains action when the results of that action might be improper, or might merely appear improper.

Another approach to identifying the general principle that is the source of specific ethical requirements can be found in Peter Drucker's work on management.[1] In Chapter 28, entitled "The Ethics of Responsibility," the author writes:

> No professional, be he doctor, lawyer, or manager, can promise that he will indeed do good for his client. All he can do is try. But he can promise that he will not knowingly do harm. And the client, in turn, must be able to trust the professional not knowingly to do him harm. Otherwise he cannot trust him at all...not knowingly to do harm is the basic rule of professional ethics, the basic rule of an ethics of public responsibility.[2]

---

[1] Drucker, Peter F.; *Management, Tasks-Responsibilities-Practices;* 1974; Harper & Row, New York.

[2] Drucker, Peter F.; *Management, Tasks-Responsibilities-Practices;* 1974, Harper & Row, New York, NY.

The avoidance of knowingly doing harm is also a general principle that can be relied upon by any professional as his ultimate guidance. When applied with the other general principle, avoiding the appearance of impropriety, the result will go a long way toward a high standard of professional behavior, even without specific rules. What is required for the application of these basic principles, as well as for the application of the detailed rules, is honesty with oneself and a purpose of obeying, not avoiding, the ethical requirements. No purely ethical consideration will restrain a person of bad will or extreme selfishness. This is the reason for the objective penalties, for censure, suspension from practice and, ultimately, for dismissal from the profession. However, the facts that point to a professional's failure to conscientiously apply the ethical rule in the first place also support objective penalties for that failure.

The Former ASIS Code as a Practical Guide

With the basic determination neither to do harm intentionally nor to engage in professional conduct that appears to be improper, what useful guidance did the security professional find in the early Code of Ethics of the American Society for Industrial Security and in the Rules of Professional Conduct promulgated under that Code?

A consideration of the Code and Rules against some typical situations that regularly arise in the security profession may indicate how helpful the Code was to a professional who wished to act with propriety. We will consider each of the former Code Articles and relevant Rules in this light.

Article I. Explicitly, this article placed the system of professional ethics within the broader context of general ethics and morality. The professional, in addition to acting in accordance with the special rules, had to act in accordance with morality of the culture.

Rule A. Under the original Article I, this rule contained the requirement to be thorough and punctual in discharging responsibilities. In this context, punctual implied not merely being "on time" but being "timely" — doing what needs to be done at the time it needs to be done. Acting punctually in this sense means acting before the rights or positions of persons who had been adversely affected by unnecessary delay.

An example: A security professional is conducting or directing an investigation of an applicant for employment. In the course of the investigation, some ambiguous information is developed that, under one possible interpretation, is unfavorable to the applicant. Further investigation is required to resolve the doubt. There is great pressure to fill the particular position for which the applicant is a candidate, and there are other candidates. The security professional has at least two options:

1. Complete the investigation expeditiously, at whatever personal inconvenience that involves.
2. Allow another candidate to be chosen, thus permitting the doubt to remain unresolved.

On these facts, it is the ethical responsibility of the professional to complete the investigation or at least to extend it until it is clear a real doubt existed about the candidate — and not unresolved ambiguous data. Moreover, there is an ethical obligation to do that additional work while the candidate in question is still in contention. Note: the candidate might not have any legal right to such further consideration. An employer can refuse to hire for any reason that is not legally discriminatory. The obligation to complete would spring from the ethical requirement of the professional to be thorough and punctual.

Rule B. This rule contained the requirement that candor and fairness characterize professional conduct. Candor is defined as "openness; frankness; a disposition to treat subjects with fairness; freedom from prejudice or disguise; sincerity."[1] To deal candidly, therefore, one must avoid attempts at deliberate deception and at causing or permitting another to gain an incorrect impression, that is, to misunderstand or misinterpret vague or equivocal language. To be candid means to take pains to be sure the truth, as you know the truth, is what is communicated to another. But there are times when the security professional is expected to protect information, to conceal and avoid its communication. Does this not create a conflict?

The force of the rule applied to situations in which the professional is under a duty to communicate, not to those in which there is a duty to maintain silence. Using the earlier example of the background investigation, the requirement for candor can be illustrated.

If, in the course of the investigation, at the point where the unresolved data had been developed, the employer or whoever in the organization had the hiring responsibility asked the security professional for an interim assessment of the candidate, it is unethical to report the doubt as though it exists after thorough investigation. The unresolved nature of the matter and the need for further investigation to resolve it before considering it unfavorable to the candidate must be made clear by the security professional. There is a duty to speak in this situation, hence the ethical requirement for candor in the matter.

Fairness, the other requirement of Rule B, means having the quality of being open, frank, honest, just or equitable.[2] It denotes a transaction in

---
[1] *Webster's 20th Century Dictionary of the English Language, 2nd ed.;* Simon and Schuster, New York, 1983.
[2] *Ibid.*

which there has been no trickery, artifice or unequal advantage. Again, as in the given example, it would be unfair to report as unfavorable, information that was really only in doubt because the one reported upon would not know of the report and would not be in a position to correct its error or resolve the doubt.

The example chosen should be understood correctly. It does not suggest that it would be improper or unfair or illegal for the prospective employer to eliminate the candidate, even before resolving the doubt. Whether to do that is a question resolved under the employer's overall policies and with due regard to legal requirements against various forms of discrimination. What the example illustrates is that it is unethical for a security professional to permit that result because the employer believed there was unfavorable data rather than mere doubt that might be resolved with further effort.

Article II. The preamble to the U.S. Constitution promises U.S. citizens such protections as liberty and justice. Article II of the original ASIS Code of Ethics used similar language, indicating that the Code sought to emphasize the substantive benefits derived by persons living under a benign system of government. These are also the same benefits that are enumerated each time the pledge of allegiance is recited. This article obligated the security professionals, as a group, to support, protect and defend those benefits. The ethical significance of the article lay in the "concerted efforts." This required specific activity by all the members of the Society, and it implied, therefore, that such efforts be organized and led in some visible way by the profession through its organic identity, the professional society. For the individual professional, it required active, personal participation in those "concerted efforts."

Article III. Under both versions of the Code of Ethics, Article III obliged the security professional to take an active and continuing role in neutralizing the activities of persons seeking to change the democratic form of government by the proscribed means. This would seem to require more than mere philosophical opposition to such persons. It called for vigilant and unceasing work, that is, objective, external effort. At the level of practical action, this article of the Code obliged the security professional to engage in personal efforts, within the orbit of assigned responsibilities, to identify persons making such threats and to counter the threats personally.

The great danger in too zealously applying this article is that vigilance becomes vigilantism. But the earlier general principle, that one will not knowingly do harm, could be relied upon to prevent precipitous action.

Article IV. This article summarized the special function of the security professional: to secure or protect facilities and to conserve or prudently manage resources. Why was there a need to restate this obvious proposition in a Code of Ethics? Because inattention to the substantive requirements of a security assignment, sloppy work, general incompetence and failure to discharge obligations are as much threats to the profession as to the individual employer or client. Yet, without a canon requiring competence or at least measurable efforts toward it, there is no criterion for judging the professional in this area. Even if an employer does not move against palpably inadequate performance, this article provides a basis for judgment by professional peers. A failure to make an honest effort at competence is sanctioned.

Furthermore, the Society had chapters in foreign countries and a growing contingent of citizens of foreign countries as members. The ethical requirements had to be framed in a way fitting and acceptable to all the members.

Rule A. This rule required the professional to clearly inform his principal of the security consequences of a decision to disregard or modify security recommendations. The most typical application is the elimination of security resources for budgetary reasons. To discharge the obligation, the security professional needed to be in a position to evaluate the real impact of failure to provide resources. The security threat or risk must have been properly defined and the consequences of its occurrence adequately assessed, whether as dollars of cost or other disadvantages. Finally, there must be a rational method for estimating the increase in the risk assumed as a result of eliminating the recommended security resource. This rule placed a burden upon the professional to be as quantitatively precise as possible because, without such precision, it would not be possible to explain the consequences of overruling security advice.

The rule also envisaged the situation in which a specific recommendation (for example, to take criminal prosecutive action, or to invoke some penalty against an offender) is overruled.

Article V. *Rule A.* This rule made the security professional a fiduciary to the principal. As such, his duty was to take all lawful and available means to safeguard the principal's interests. Furthermore, when representing the principal in third-party negotiations, the professional was required to be fair and just. The duty of highest care was owed to the principal. However, in discharging that duty, the security professional must not overreach, deliberately deceive, take improper advantage or in any way abrogate the rights of others.

Rule B. This rule required the professional to conduct activities in such a way as to minimize physical and moral dangers and, when not directly responsible for work that might involve such dangers, to point them out to the one who was responsible. A practical example of the application of this rule involves the use of deadly weapons. The professional had an ethical obligation under this rule to weigh with great care all the factors in a particular situation in which the use of deadly weapons was considered and to minimize the dangers by the ultimate action or recommendation. This is not to say that either position — the use or non-use of deadly weapons — is necessarily the correct position in all cases or in any given case. It is to say, however, that minimizing physical and moral danger is a required element of the final decision.

Rule C. This might be referred to as the "consulting opinion" rule. It required the professional to counsel the principal to obtain additional or other expert guidance in the security field when it was in the principal's interest to do so. It also required the professional to cooperate with other such experts.

An example: The principal changes the method of operations, product or services, or even the locale. Such changes might introduce risks and hazards never before experienced and not within the field of personal experience of the security professional. In such a case there is an ethical obligation to determine whether another source of expert counsel is better qualified to advise the principal, to identify such a source and to urge the use of that source. The use of outside experts does not necessarily mean added expense. Professional and trade associations might be in a position to render such assistance, or even someone in the principal's own organization might have the expertise. The thrust of the ethical requirement of Rule C was that the security professional not resist seeking outside expertise but, rather, upon recognizing the need for it, take the initiative and recommend it.

Rule D. As there were no advisory opinions interpreting this rule, it is difficult to see its anticipated application. There comes immediately to mind the situation in which an independent security professional of some kind (investigator or forensic expert, for example) is asked by several parties to conduct an investigation or render an opinion of the same facts. In such a case, the parties might be allied in interest, adverse in interest or unrelated in interest as to the outcome. While the impropriety of working simultaneously for parties adverse in interest is clear, it is not clear that it is improper in the other two situations.

If the rule was addressed to the idea of unjust compensation, that is, being paid twice for the same service, it would seem to imply that there can be only one value or that a service rendered separately to several parties can only be compensated by one if all consent. The obligation seems to have been to make a disclosure to all parties for whom the service was to be rendered, irrespective of their relationships and, absent the consent of all, not to accept compensation from more than one. It would also seem a requirement to consider that the same service to parties adverse in interest should not be rendered under any circumstances.

Rule E. This rule was aimed at the prevention of corruption. If one accepts compensation from a supplier and then recommends that supplier's services or products, the possibilities exist:

1. That the services or products are inferior to others that might have been recommended instead
2. That the services or products were unnecessary, either completely or to the extent to which they were recommended

There does not appear to be any permissible middle ground in which the security professional makes an honest recommendation and still accepts compensation from the advantaged supplier. To permit that position would be to restrict the capability to judge wrongdoing or dishonest conduct exclusively to the professional. An objective test is necessary. Moreover, under the general rule to avoid even the appearance of impropriety, the ethical professional will take special pains to avoid this situation.

Rule F. This rule applied to situations where the security professional, during free time, accepted employment with someone other than the principal. Although such employment might not be expressly prohibited by the principal, and although the other employment might not be directly related to the principal's interests, the very fact that time and energy were required in the other endeavor could reasonably be expected to "affect the business of the employer." The ethical requirement is to disclose other employment.

More serious is the situation in which the professional had some tangible interest in a business or outside activity and could gain an advantage with the principal because of it. A good example is the situation in which a security professional owned or was financially interested in a company from which some security product or service was purchased by the principal. Another is financial interest by a security professional in some outside venture which could use some resource or property of the principal. In any such case, the professional was ethically obligated to disclose such interest and to disaffiliate from any in which it was reasonable to assume that, despite the disclosure, professional judgment on behalf of the principal might be affected.

When the financial interest was restricted to stock ownership in a publicly traded company and such ownership is not at all effective in controlling the company, it was usually considered sufficient if the disclosure of ownership is made. However, the rule did not provide this degree of guidance. In such a case, the professional had to seek guidance or choose the surely blameless course. The method of seeking guidance will be discussed later in this chapter.

Article VI. *Rule A.* This rule obligated a professional not to publicize work on behalf of a principal, even in professional journals and for purposes of professional development, without consent of the principal for whom the work was done. This is because the "personal gain or satisfaction" would or could be derived from the mere publication of such work, if credited to the professional. The rule would seem not to apply to publication of work if the identity of the principal for whom it was done could be effectively concealed without in any way committing a palpable fraud or deception on the persons to whom the publication was directed. Read in conjunction with Rule A under Article V, the net effect was to require the professional to obtain consent from the principal both because of this specific rule and because of the overall fiduciary responsibility of the professional.

Rule B. This rule required two things. First, that a conscientious review be made of all matters before the security professional and a judgment, recommendation or decision rendered on such matters to the proper constituted authority, where required. Second, it required that no expression of prejudice, opinion or influence be included in the judgment, recommendation or decision.

The second requirement was easier to deal with. Clearly, if a matter required a professional opinion to be rendered, the rule could not mean not to render it. It meant not to include any opinion other than that which is the good-conscience conclusion drawn by the professional. Prejudice or influence, again, cannot mean all influence. A professional opinion is rendered on the premise that it probably will influence; otherwise, there is no point to the opinion. The rule must be held to have meant that the professional would not seek to influence or express an opinion not fully consistent with the content and plain meaning of his professional conclusion on the matter before him. In the case of prejudice, the rule also obliged the professional not to permit prejudice (i.e., a previously formed opinion or bias of the mind) to interfere with objective analysis of the actual facts. The conclusion drawn, in other words, should be drawn from the facts and not from prejudice.

The first part of the rule was a bit more obscure. For example, if a security professional in the course of assigned duties discovered that a crime had been committed, did the rule require him to report that crime to the police or prosecutor having jurisdiction? The police would be the "proper constituted authority" for the normal investigation of the crime and the prosecutor for its prosecution. But the law does not require a person with knowledge of a crime to report it to the police. It requires only that a person not hinder an official investigation of a crime. Such interference constitutes the separate crime of misprision.

Does one interpret the Rule of Professional Conduct to oblige the security professional to report mere knowledge of a crime? A more reasonable interpretation of the rule would be that the security professional, should judgment indicate an adequate basis for not reporting a particular crime to the public authorities, include in communication with the principal on the matter, a reference to the fact that it was not so reported and why. There does not appear to be any professional objective or public good to be gained from requiring the security professional to do more than the law requires of any citizen. Indeed, there are situations in which not reporting a crime would more clearly serve the ends of justice and the objectives of the security program. One such case is where the only person who constitutes an adequate complainant does not desire to institute a prosecution.

On the other side of this discussion about reporting to "proper constituted authority," the appropriate conduct must be weighed when the security professional sincerely believes, after careful review and analysis of the facts, that a report to some authority other than the principal is required, but the principal objects. This poses the classical problem faced by any professional when there is a conflict between the public good and the private good of the client. The acceptable resolution could be as follows. If the crime (or other incident producing the same kind of dilemma) would not result in a further crime, or in a gross injustice, or in the loss or diminution of any particular person's rights or harm to his or her person or property (as distinguished from the general harm to the public at large from any crime), and if the objection of the principal does not itself spring from criminal or unlawful motives but from a desire to protect a position or interest, the professional could regard fiduciary duty under Article V, Rule A, as obliging protection of the lawful position of the principal.

A rather common application of this interpretation is the situation in which an employee is discovered to have stolen from the employer/principal and even confesses guilt in a properly drawn statement. Although the decision not to prosecute should not be taken lightly or taken without due consideration of the real obligation of all citizens to assist in the active enforcement of the laws, there is room for another choice in this situation. If, after serious analysis, the employer, who is the victim, elects not to prosecute the employee, the security professional is ethically bound to assist in carrying out the decision. The professional is also bound, under Article IV, Rule A, to advise the principal of the probable effect of non-prosecution, and bound, under Article V, to assure the most competent investigation of the suspect employee, and, under Article I, one fair to the suspect employee.

Rule C. This rule looked to the protection of personal and private information about persons while in the hands of security professionals as a result of their professional activities or in connection with their professional responsibilities. Typical examples of such information are the results of pre-employment and post-employment background investigations; reports or other documents dealing with incident or criminal inquiries; personnel or industrial relations actions, decisions or deliberations involving security; supervisory comment or evaluations, etc. The disclosure of such information may only be made ethically to persons with both a need for it and a *bona fide* right to it. In practical application, the need may also determine the right. A worker's direct supervisor, for example, would have a need for information about the worker's off-the-job activity that could have impact on work. An excessive or habitual use of intoxicants or other drugs is an example of such information. Both to protect the employer and other workers against mistake or error and to assist the affected worker in rehabilitating, the supervisor would have to know about the probable problem. However, in the same situation, co-workers, personal acquaintances, and even supervisory or management personnel not specifically concerned with that worker's performance or output would not need the information.

The problem can be acute in a situation in which a security professional in Company A (about to hire or thinking of hiring applicant Smith) asks the security professional counterpart in Company B (which formerly employed Smith) about Smith's suitability, competence and performance. If Smith had had a problem with alcohol while at Company B but had successfully solved it and had left honorably and with a good record, there would be an ethical objection to the Company B security professional telling the Company A professional about the earlier problem. If, on the other hand, employee Smith had been discharged for failure to resolve the problem and for unacceptable performance or behavior as a result of it, that information, subject to the general policy of Company B on disclosing information about former employees, would be legitimately disclosed to Company A. In an effort to make an informed employment decision, Company A would need to know that applicant Smith had not maintained a satisfactory record with Company B because of an uncontrolled problem of alcohol abuse.

If the inquiry from Company A were not from a person known to the security professional at Company B to be responsible, or if Company A had indicated it would not treat such information with care, using it to help resolve the employment question but not further disclosing it to the discomfiture or harm of applicant Smith, the Company B professional would be ethically obliged not to disclose the data.

The central point of the rule is summarized by stating that a security professional with private information about a person does not have a general right to use that information to the disadvantage of that person, despite the unfavorable nature of the information. Rather, the opposite is the case. The professional may use that information only when honestly satisfied that the disclosee has a *bona fide* right and need for it. This is a particularly important area. A self-righteous security professional could do extraordinary harm to individuals and to the profession by improper disclosures. Indeed, this very danger is at the root of much public concern about the collection of personal data by both public authorities and private security organizations. This rule made clear that the security profession does not approve such disclosures unless they meet the twin criteria of need and right to know.

Article VII. As this article was not commented upon at all in the Rules, there was only the basic guidance of the article. It might be useful to distinguish between "privileged" and "confidential" information because, although the professional is ethically bound to respect and protect both, they are different.

Confidentiality of *privileged information* is assured by operation of law. Communications between husband and wife, doctor and patient, lawyer and client, minister and penitent are among the examples of privileged communications.[1] The law says that, without the consent of the one making a communication, in the context of these relationships, the one receiving the communication cannot be compelled by law to disclose it. Practically, this means that the one receiving the disclosure will not be compelled or permitted to disclose it further without the consent of the one first making it. Although a wife, for example, is willing to and may even actually make seriously damaging disclosures of privileged communications to her from her husband, the law will not allow them to be used in any judicial tribunal to the disadvantage of the husband. The concept of legally privileged communications extends only to compulsory testimony in a judicial proceeding.

A *confidential communication* is any communication that is so designated by the one making it and that is made under circumstances reasonably indicating the intent of that person that to make the information confidential. So, for a person to say to a large group at a cocktail party or public meeting that he is making a confidential disclosure would not result in a confidential disclosure because of the circumstances. Also, one person cannot bind another to secrecy without the agreement of the other unless there is already a relationship of special trust between them.

The security professional, as we have noted from Article V, Rule A, is a fiduciary of the principal. Any lawful disclosure from the principal to the security professional, in the context of his professional responsibilities,

---

[1] Additional relationships are sometimes designated under the various state civil practice and criminal procedure acts. The law of the particular state should be consulted.

which the principal designates as confidential would bind the professional to respect it as such. However, other persons cannot automatically bind by mere disclosure. A security professional who is the recipient of such a disclosure, and has not agreed to be bound by secrecy, is not bound under the law and should not be under the Code of Ethics. However, if the security professional expressly or impliedly agrees to be bound, as by receiving a disclosure made in confidence without indicating he would not be bound, the former Code obliged him thereafter to respect the confidence. The professional might be compelled to testify in a legal proceeding (if it is not a legally privileged communication) and might be obliged by a higher duty to the principal to disclose the confidence. However, absent a sufficient cause for such disclosure, he would have been obliged under the Code not to disclose the information received in confidence.

Article VIII. *Rule A.* This rule required the security professional to make reasonable efforts to explain the profession to outside groups asking for information, to correct misinformation or misunderstandings that the professional knew or had reason to believe existed and had some unique opportunity to act.

This is an active duty. It is simply not enough *not* to engage in discreditable behavior. The professional is obliged to seize the initiative, when it is available and apparent, to correct misunderstandings or misinterpretations or misrepresentations that could result in damage or harm to the reputation of the profession. At the least, this suggested an active duty to disclaim or caution about others in the profession patently misrepresenting it or themselves or their role in it.

Rule B. This is a self-evident proposition. It condemned taking credit for someone else's work (or allowing third persons to incorrectly attribute credit for it) as unethical. Not every effort by one in the profession is coupled with an understanding that its results will be credited, by name, to the one making it. As in all professions, it is common in this profession, in business in general and in the world at large for the collective work product of a group to be regarded as the joint product of that group without any special attribution. Staff work of all kinds is accomplished this way. What the rule sought to prevent was the active arrogation of special praise for significant, unique or especially meritorious work done by another and reflecting that other's special skill or diligence.

Rule C. This required the professional to urge the proper economic balance between security work and compensation. That balance is appropriate as between the professional and subordinates, and between security professionals or security personnel as a group and other classes or groups. It does not suggest rates or amounts. These vary obviously from time to time, region to region and case to case. It does require that some just proportion exist between the work done and the reward paid, and it required the professional to uphold that need for a just relationship.

Rule D. At a minimum, this rule required the professional to share skills and knowledge with subordinates and to act as a model and a source for them in their professional development. To the extent possible, the professional was also obliged to provide developmental opportunities for staff, to assist actively in their consideration for opportunities to do more responsible work, to contribute in a more important way and, as a corollary, to become entitled thereby to material and other rewards.

An implication of the rule is that the professional provides or ensures the training necessary to acquire the higher skills.

Rule E. Every person must be sure not to allow critical comments about another to amount to defamation. The security professional must observe this same caution — but the rule required more. It required that nothing be done, directly or indirectly, secretly by device or subterfuge, to injure the prospects or standing of other security professionals. Anonymous criticism of an associate is unethical. Serious complaints of unprofessional conduct by another, however, must be brought to the proper authority for disposition. In the case of ASIS at that time, this would have been the Ethical Standards Committee.

Rule F. This is a slightly different development of the obligation than in the preceding rule. This rule required that, if there was a difference of opinion or approach or even of principle that did not involve any question as to the integrity or propriety of behavior of the professional with whom the difference exists, critical commentary within the profession was preferable to public criticism, if that consensus might be achieved on the proper approach. However, should the criticizing professional have been convinced there was a danger of imminent, serious harm to others because of the position of the professional criticized, there would be a more urgent duty under Article IX, Rule A (discussed later), to take action. In such a case, bringing formal charges before a professional society alone might not be adequate to prevent the anticipated harm or danger. In that case, action with some other body or even government agency is required. What was not appropriate under this rule was *public* criticism of one professional by another on professional grounds.

Rule G. This type of rule was critical to the success of a program of professional ethics. It required that non-complying members of the profession be denied the professional aid of other members. It acted as the companion to professional censure. Unlike censure, however, which operates directly upon the offending member, this rule required the other members to disassociate professionally. It is professionally unethical to associate with one who is professionally unethical.

Article IX. *Rule A.* This rule required each member of the profession who subscribed to the Code, and certainly for every member of ASIS, to be vigilant against corruption and dishonesty and to denounce it when encountered. In a less dramatic, but ultimately more effective way, each member was bound to protect the Society against deficiencies of character, training or education. As stated, this applied only to the Society and would not be applicable to one entering the profession without also joining the Society. To the extent it was applied to Society members, it would oblige all who recommend, endorse or otherwise play a role in bringing persons into the Society, to assure themselves that the proposed candidate met all stated requirements of membership.

Rule B. While it applied no quantitative measure to any single professional's expected participation in professional activities or output in professional journals, this rule did require participation in some way. It is apparent that this rule would not have lent itself to enforcement through grievance and hearing. It is more an exhortation toward ideal professional conduct. However, the regard of one's peers is one of the most effective motivators. Total inactivity on the professional level should be noted and, if nothing more formal, there should be direct encouragement by other professionals in the personal circle of acquaintances to become more interested and responsive.

Article X. As was observed earlier, this article did not exist at the time the Rules were adopted and there was no official commentary upon it. By its plain language, however, it required that, subject to all the other articles and specific rules, each professional assist professional associates when asked or when assistance would be material. The objective was mutual support, as in formal and informal consultations, to the extent that errors and bad judgments harmful to the profession-at-large be avoided.

Selected Bibliography

Books

Berenbeim, Ronald E.; *Corporate Ethics;* 1987; Conference Board.

Codes of Ethics for Private Security Management, etc.; 1976; Private Security Advisory Council to the Law Enforcement Assistance Administration.

Codes of Professional Responsibility, 3rd ed.; 1994; Bureau of National Affairs.

Ethics in American Business: A Special Report; 1988; Touche Ross & Co.

Ethics in Practice: Managing the Moral Corporation; 1989; Harvard Business School Press.

Goodell, Rebecca; *Ethics in American Business: Policies, Programs and Perceptions;* 1994; Ethics Resource Center.

Korman, Abraham K.; *Human Dilemmas in Work Organizations: Strategies for Resolution;* 1994; Guilford Press.

Piper, Thomas, Parks, Mary Gentile, and Daloz, Sharon; *Can Ethics Be Taught?;* 1993; Harvard Business School Press.

Pollack-Byrne, Jocelyn; *Ethics in Crime and Justice: Dilemmas and Decisions;* 1989; Brooks/Cole Publishing Co.

Shea, Gordon F.; *Practical Ethics;* 1988; American Management Association, AMA Membership Publications Division.

Periodicals

Security Management; American Society for Industrial Security, Arlington, VA.
— Albanese, Jay S.; When the Company Is the Culprit; September 1984.
— Berenbeim, Ronald E.; Defining Corporate Ethics; September 1988.
— Berenbeim, Ronald E.; Ethics Codes and Educational Programs; October 1988.
— Besecker, Kenneth H.; The Tensile Test of Professional Ethics; September 1986.
— Carter, Roy.; A Security Role in Corporate Morality; June 1985.
— Foster, Alfred L.; What Ever Happened to Right and Wrong?; November 1989.
— Hill, Ivan; Common Sense and Everyday Ethics; July 1981.
— Kingsbury, Arthur A.; Ethics; November 1974.
— Miller, Michael H. and Baker, Steven J.; The Stormy World of Business Ethics; January 1987.
— Raelin, Joseph A.; Professional and Business Ethics: Bridging the Gap; March 1990.
— Rockwell, Richard D.; Ethics: Is Peer Pressure the Answer?; April 1991.
— Simonsen, Clifford E.; What Value Do Ethics Have in the Corporate World?; September 1992.

18
Detecting Deception in Interviews and Interrogations

INTRODUCTION

There are two basic ways to evaluate the accuracy of information in any given investigative situation: the analysis and comparison of factual evidence or information, and the behavioral assessment of the person who is the source of the information. Every investigator who questions a person about procedures that were followed, the sequence of events on a given day, the reasons why an action was executed in a particular manner, etc., evaluates the behavior displayed by that person and draws conclusions from it as to that person's truthfulness or deception. These conclusions are usually reached by a comparison of the information provided against a subconscious assessment of the behavior displayed by the source.

The purpose of this chapter is to identify specifically those behavioral characteristics that can be consciously observed and evaluated for possible indications of truth or deception, thereby increasing the accuracy of behavior assessments. The verbal and nonverbal behavior displayed by a person during questioning may provide very valuable and accurate indications of truthfulness or deception. In the following discussion we will describe some of the behavioral characteristics of each group.

DIFFERENT TYPES OF RESPONSES

Verbal responses include both spoken words and gestures that serve as word substitutes, such as nodding of the head to indicate *yes* or a side-to-side head motion to indicate *no*. Also within the category of verbal responses are such vocal characteristics as tone, speed, pitch and clarity.

The careful listener is aware not only of the significance of a verbal response but also of the timing, words, and emphasis associated with the response. Fundamental to the psychology of verbal behavior is that the normally socialized individual does not enjoy lying; deception leads to a conflict that results in anxiety and stress. A suspect who offers an evasive answer or an objection in response to a direct question does so because of an attempt to avoid the internal anxiety associated with outright denial.

Nonverbal responses include body movements and position changes, gestures, facial expressions, and eye contact. Nonverbal behavior is internally motivated to reduce anxiety. Whether through distraction (such as shifts in body posture, bringing a hand to the face, or crossing the arms) or through displacement behavior (such as picking the lint off one's clothing, pacing, or repetitious fast movement), *all nonverbal behavior that accompanies a deceptive response emanates from a guilty suspect's efforts to relieve anxiety.*

SOME PRELIMINARY CAUTIONS

Before beginning a discussion of these behaviors, it is very important to keep in mind the following cautions:

1. There is no single word or nonverbal behavior that automatically means in all cases that a person is lying or telling the truth. Each behavior characteristic displayed must be considered in the context of the environment and intensity of the setting, and in comparison to the subject's normal behavioral patterns.
2. The assessment of a subject's truthfulness should be based upon the overall behavioral pattern displayed, and not upon any single observation.
3. Behavioral indications should be evaluated on the basis of when they occur (timing) and how often they occur (consistency). To be reliable indicators of truth or deception, behavioral changes should occur immediately in response to a question, or simultaneously with the subject's answer.
4. Evaluation of behavior symptoms should take into consideration the subject's intelligence, sense of social responsibility, and degree of maturity. As a general rule, the more reliable behavior symptoms will be displayed by persons who are socially responsible — the ones who have more at stake in the outcome of a case, for example, family, job or reputation. Also, the more mature person will display more reliable behavior symptoms. On the other hand, extreme caution must be used in the evaluation of behavior symptoms of persons who are emotionally or psychologically unstable.
5. It is important to remember that some behavioral characteristics, which will be described further on in this chapter as indicative of deception, may be displayed by a subject who is actually telling the truth, but in whom fear, anxiety, anger, mistrust or some other emotion is causing the misleading behavioral display.

VERBAL RESPONSES

Generally, a truthful person answers questions in a direct, straightforward, spontaneous and sincere manner, particularly if the question is simple and unambiguous. Conversely, a deceptive person may delay response or repeat the question before giving an answer. Often, the delay or repetition of the question is a stalling tactic used by the deceptive person to contrive a false answer. Some deceptive subjects may answer questions too quickly, sometimes before the question is completed. Subjects who hesitate in answering a question by saying, "Let me see now," prior to saying "No," may be trying to borrow time to deliberate on how to lie effectively, or to remember previous statements and to camouflage reactions with pretended serious thought. The truthful person does not have to ponder an answer. Truthful subjects have only one answer for any given question, and it will be substantially the same answer regardless of any repetition of the inquiry. Contrary to the directness of the truthful person's verbal response, the deceptive person may give an evasive answer such as, "I was home all day," or "I don't even know the combination," when asked if he stole money from a safe.

A lying subject will sometimes speak in an irrational manner or use fragmented or incomplete sentences, such as, "It's important that ..." or "If you think ..." or "I ...I hope that you ...".

A deceiver may also develop a memory failure when confronted with a probing question and may respond with a half-lie such as "I don't remember" or "As far as I know," or "I don't recall," or may try to bolster an answer with such phrases as, "To be perfectly honest with you," or "To be quite frank." More sophisticated liars may use the same types of evasions but they usually plan beforehand so that their answers include a protective verbal coating, such as "At this point in time," "If I recall correctly," "It is my understanding," "If my memory serves me right," or "I may be mistaken, but ...". By these tactics, lying subjects seek to establish an escape hatch rather than risk an outright lie. Some lying subjects may exhibit an unreasonably good or selective memory, even as to irrelevant details. The end result, however, will be so patently implausible as to reveal the attempted deception.

Truthful subjects tend to use harsh, realistic words such as steal, rape, kill, rob, or stab, while deceptive subjects usually avoid such language in order to assuage their guilty feeling. A person who uses an insincere facade of religion or oaths to support an answer is, in many instances, not telling the truth. Typical examples of expressions used by lying subjects who try to make their statements believable are, "I swear to God, sir," or "I'll swear on a stack of Bibles," or "With God as my witness." Some may even go so far as to state, "On my poor mother's grave, sir." A subject who uses religion as a defense, such as "I couldn't do something like that, sir. I am a (naming a religious affiliation)," is usually not telling the truth.

Truthful persons not only respond directly but also speak with relative clarity. Some liars, however, tend to mumble or talk so softly that they cannot be heard clearly, while others may speak at a rapid pace or may display erratic changes in the tone or pitch of their voice. Similarly, a verbal response coupled with nervous laughter or a wisecrack is a common attempt to camouflage deception.

Deceptive subjects are more likely to challenge minute details of factual information on a case, as in "They said this thing happened at 1:30 and I didn't come back until 1:45." Deceptive subjects tend to offer excuses or justifications to support their claims of innocence and may give very specific denials: "I did not take that $12,437.18." The truthful subject will generally offer much more general denials: "I did not steal that $12,000 or whatever it is. I didn't steal a penny of it."

Verbal Profiles

The verbal behavior characteristics of a person who is telling the truth differs from that of one who is withholding relevant information.

- The truthful person:
  — Makes general, sweeping denials
  — Offers unqualified, direct, and spontaneous answers
  — Exhibits a reasonable memory
  — Responds to questions in a rational manner with a distinct and clear tone of voice
- The deceptive person:
  — Offers very specific denials
  — Avoids realistic words
  — Gives delayed, evasive or vague answers
  — Exhibits an unusually poor, selective or remarkable memory
  — Qualifies answers or uses religion or oaths to support statements
  — Speaks in an irrational manner, fragmented sentences, and in a mumbled or subdued manner

NONVERBAL RESPONSES

Nonverbal behavior is responsible for more than half of the information and meaning of a message communicated in a conversation.

While the verbal statements a person makes are usually carefully thought out and certainly under the person's conscious control, most people do not pay the same careful attention to their physical movements and gestures. As a result, the true meaning of a person's statement, in many cases, may be discerned only by considering the verbal content in conjunction with the nonverbal behavior that accompanies it. For example, if you ask whether person A was involved in a particular act (such as an embezzlement) and A responds in a firm voice by saying, "Absolutely not. I had nothing to do with that" while leaning forward in the chair, in an open posture and maintaining steady eye contact, the entire message conveyed is one of sincerity and directness. But if you ask person B the same question, and the response is in a weak tone of voice but with the same words, and person B shifts positions in the chair, drops eye contact to the floor, crosses arms and legs into a closed posture, and leans back in the chair while completing the answer, an entirely different message is conveyed — one of insincerity and lack of candor. Most people would recognize this difference but would be unable to verbalize the basis for distinguishing the *good* answer from the *bad*. However, there are very specific and observable nonverbal behaviors that can be consciously evaluated for possible indications of deception.

Activities Suggesting Deception

Physical activities of the deceptive person may be categorized into the following general types:

1. *Significant posture change.* This would include changes such as quick and sudden movements of the upper and lower body, or perhaps even leaving the room while being questioned.
2. *Grooming gestures and cosmetic adjustments.* Such gestures would include rubbing and wringing the hands, stroking the back of the head, touching the nose, earlobes, or lips, picking or chewing fingernails, shuffling, tapping, swinging, or arching the feet, rearranging clothing or jewelry, dusting, picking lint or pulling threads on the clothing, adjusting or cleaning glasses, and straightening or stroking the hair.
3. *Supportive gestures.* Among these are placing a hand over the mouth or eyes when speaking, crossing arms or legs, hiding the hands or feet, holding the forehead with a hand, or placing the hands under or between the legs.

When a suspect repeatedly combines any of the foregoing nonverbal reactions with verbal responses, there is a strong indication that the verbal responses may not be truthful.

Comparative Postures

A comparison of the general posture displayed by a truthful and deceptive person may be described as follows:

- A truthful person will:
  — Sit upright but not rigid
  — Position himself or herself in front of the questioner
  — Lean forward toward the questioner when making a point
  — Appear relaxed and casual
- A deceptive person will:
  — Slouch or lean back in a chair
  — Sit unnaturally rigid and stiff

- Sit off to the side and not directly in front of the questioner
- Pull elbows close to the side, arms folded and locked in front, with legs crossed
- Exhibit rapid and erratic posture changes

Eye Contact

One of the most important transmitters of nonverbal behavior symptoms is the degree of eye contact maintained by the suspect with the questioner. Deceptive people generally do not look directly at the questioner; they look down at the floor, over to the side, or up at the ceiling. Anxiety is relieved if their eyes are focused somewhere else other than on the questioner. It is easier to lie while looking at the ceiling or floor. Consequently, deceivers either try to avoid eye contact by making compensatory movements, or else overreact by staring in a challenging manner.

Truthful people, on the other hand, are not defensive in their looks or actions and can easily maintain eye contact with the questioner. Their speech is fluid and straight to the point; they do not move excessively during the questioning and refrain from fidgeting when responding. Truthful persons remain relaxed and display confidence even though apprehensive. They show no concern about the credibility of their answers. They are attentive and their casual manner is natural.

Evidence is the cornerstone of any investigative decision. The point of origin for all evidence is people. An investigator's ability to elicit full and complete information from others, as well as the ability to assess the truth of that information, will have an impact on the direction of the investigation.

An investigator with knowledge of these behavior symptoms and the ability to analyze them can be far more effective in distinguishing fact from fiction. This skill can be a valuable weapon in determining whether or not the truth was told.

THE BEHAVIOR ANALYSIS INTERVIEW

The *Behavior Analysis Interview* (BAI) was first developed about 40 years ago by John E. Reid, founder of John E. Reid & Associates, Inc. For several years, its underlying concepts have been used as an alternative to polygraph examinations to assist employers in internal investigations. Since passage of the federal Employee Polygraph Protection Act in 1988, the Behavior Analysis Interview has become a standard investigatory procedure for many companies.

New research verifies the accuracy of the interview technique as a highly effective investigatory tool. One study, for example, targeted a sample of 160 employee theft investigations and compared results from the

Behavior Analysis Interview with polygraph results. No statistical difference was found between the two procedures.[1]

The polygraph technique, for example, produced useful results in 89 percent of the investigations that were analyzed, while the Behavioral Analysis Interview produced useful results in 94 percent of them, giving the latter a slight edge.

What Is a Behavior Analysis Interview?

The Behavior Analysis Interview (BAI) is the systematic evaluation of an employee's verbal and nonverbal behavior during the course of a structured interview. During the BAI, the subject is asked two types of interview questions: *investigative* and *behavior provoking*. Investigative questions are designed to elicit factual information to such inquiries as the who, what, when, where, why and how of the incident.

As the suspect responds to each question and provides a version of events, the investigator should be carefully evaluating not only the content of the responses, but also the verbal and nonverbal behavior symptoms displayed, to help assess the credibility and truthfulness of the answers as described above.

To enhance the effective evaluation of a subject's truthfulness during the interview process, as well as to gain important insight into thought process, the investigator should intermix behavior-provoking questions with traditional investigative questions. The combination makes up the core of the BAI.

Behavior-Provoking Questions. Behavior-provoking questions asked during a BAI were designed to draw out specific verbal responses or behavior that can be utilized to distinguish between a truthful person and one who is lying. Theoretical models were developed and statistically tested and validated for the predicted differences in the type of responses given by truthful and deceptive subjects. More than 30 behavior-provoking questions have been developed and utilized during BAIs.[2] Five of these questions are presented here to illustrate some of the differences in message characteristics.

The following questions are asked in the context of an investigation into credit cards stolen from a mail room. Each question is followed by examples of response types normally offered by truthful and deceptive subjects.

1. *The purpose question:* What is your understanding of the purpose of this interview?

---

[1] Jayne, 1989.
[2] Differentiation of Truthful and Deceptive Criminal Suspects in Behavior Analysis Interviews, Horvath, Jayne, and Buckley; *Journal of Forensic Sciences,* May 1994.

The truthful response provides an accurate description of events. The subject may use descriptive language such as steal and may mention numbers of cards stolen and/or victims' names, if known. The deceptive subject's response is a vague and nonspecific description of events. He/she may use nondescriptive language (an incident, something happened, etc.), or use qualifiers such as "apparently," "evidently" or "may have." He/she does not mention any details about the number of stolen cards or the victims' names.

2. *The "you" question:* Over the past several weeks we have had a number of credit cards disappear from the bank, and specifically, the mail room. If *you* had anything to do with stealing these missing credit cards, *you* should tell me now.

    A direct and unequivocal brief denial — for example, "No, I didn't steal any credit cards" — characterizes the truthful response. It may use broad, all-encompassing language: "Absolutely not! I haven't stolen anything from here." The deceptive response is a longer and unemotional denial — for example, "I do not know anything about this" (an evasive response), or "I didn't even know credit cards were missing," or an objection, "Why would I risk my job by doing something like that?"

3. *The knowledge question:* Do you know for sure who did steal any of the missing credit cards?

    Truthful subjects often volunteer suspicion: "Not for sure, but I have some ideas." They may express concern or anger: "I wish I did know, but I just don't have any idea." The deceptive subject gives a brief, unemotional denial: "No, I do not." The subject does not offer spontaneous thoughts or feelings.

4. *The suspicion question:* Who, do you suspect, may have stolen these missing credit cards?

    The truthful subject gives the question careful thought and, when offering a suspicion, can substantiate the basis for that suspicion. A deceptive response is: "I don't have any idea," without giving the question any careful thought. Deceivers may name improbable suspects, such as people without opportunity or access.

5. *The vouch question:* Is there anyone with whom you work who you feel is above suspicion and would not do anything like this?

    The truthful subject will give the question thought and typically eliminate possible suspects. The deceptive one, however, will not vouch for others so as not to narrow the field of suspects. Doing so could increase the chance of exposure.

By incorporating these types of behavior-provoking questions into the interview process, in conjunction with the investigative questions, the investigator will develop a significantly greater insight into a subject's probable truthfulness or deception. The investigator will be much more confident in eliminating people from suspicion, as well as when initiating an interrogation of the suspected guilty person.[1]

THE REID NINE STEPS OF INTERROGATION

An *interview* is a nonaccusatory conversation in which, through questions and answers, the interviewer tries to develop investigative and behavioral information that will test the veracity of statements made by a suspect, victim or witness. An *interrogation* is an accusatory procedure designed to elicit an acknowledgment that the subject did not tell the truth during an initial statement, whether that subject is a suspect who originally denied involvement or a victim who fabricated the nature of the alleged offense.

Interrogation of a suspect should occur only after a nonaccusatory interview and when you are reasonably certain of the suspect's involvement in the issue under investigation.

The Positive Confrontation

Most interrogators enter the room with a file summarizing the investigation results. After an exchange of greetings, the interrogator confronts the suspect with an accusation of guilt. This type of accusation is made only when the suspect's guilt seems very clear. Otherwise, the statement should be less direct. Following the confrontation, the interrogator pauses to evaluate the suspect's reaction to the statement, then repeats the initial statement of involvement. At this time, the investigation file is placed aside, and the interrogator sits down directly opposite the suspect and makes a transition to a sympathetic and understanding person.

Theme Development. The next step is to present moral justification for the suspect's criminal behavior. One way of doing this is to place moral blame for an illegal activity on another person or an outside set of circumstances. This appeals to a basic aspect of human nature. Most people tend to minimize responsibility for their actions by placing blame on someone or something else. In a credit card fraud case, for example, one can suggest that the suspect was not paid enough by the employer or that someone left the card where it was an open temptation. Other moral justifications include unusual family expenses, desperate circumstances, a friend came up with the idea, retribution for an argument, or drug/alcohol dependence.

The moral justification should be presented in a sympathetic and understanding way. An interest in working with the suspect to resolve the problem breaks the ice. Voice the justification in a monologue, not giving the suspect an opportunity to speak until ready to admit guilt.

---

[1] For a complete list of the behavior-provoking questions used in the BAI, see *Criminal Interrogations and Confessions,* by Inbau, Reid and Buckley, 3rd edition, 1986, Williams & Wilkins, Baltimore, MD.

Handling Denials. The more often the suspect denies guilt, the more difficult it becomes to admit guilt later. Therefore, the interrogator should interject a blocking statement whenever the suspect enters an "I didn't do it" plea. By keeping fast and hard to theme development, you weaken the guilty suspect's denials. Many guilty people will change from a defensive position to an offensive one, offering objections. The innocent suspect generally will not ask to make a statement but will, instead, without any display of etiquette, promptly and unequivocally maintain innocence. An innocent suspect never moves past this denial stage and remains steadfast in the assertion of innocence.

Overcoming Objections. Most suspects' objection statements can be categorized in two general groups: *trait objections* (e.g., "I wasn't brought up that way" or "A person who would do something like that is really stupid") and *factual objections* (e.g., "I don't even have the safe combination" or "I didn't even know him" or "I don't need the money"). Statements from either group are feeble explanations, even when they may be partly true. In any event, you should not argue with the suspect over the statement, or show surprise or irritation. Such a reaction discourages the suspect, who then perceives that the statement made was wrong, or at least ineffective. If you overcome the objections, a suspect often withdraws into a shell and focuses on impending punishment.

Keeping a Suspect's Attention. Following the objection stage, the guilty suspect often becomes pensive, apathetic and quiet. It is most important during this stage to ensure that the suspect listens attentively to the theme (psychological justification for the suspect's behavior) and does not concentrate on punishment (which would serve to reinforce a resolve to deny the crime). To do this, draw nearer to the suspect. This closer proximity often regains attention, and the suspect will watch and listen to you more intently. Verbally, you begin to channel the theme down to the probable alternative components.

Handling a Suspect's Passive Mood. At this stage, some suspects may cry, which often expresses remorse. Many other suspects do not cry but express their emotional state by assuming a defeatist posture — slumped head and shoulders, relaxed legs and a vacant stare. To facilitate the impending admission of guilt, intensify the theme presentation and concentrate on the psychological justification for the unlawful act. Gestures of sympathy, such as a hand on the suspect's shoulder, aid truth-telling.

Presenting an Alternative Question. The alternative question is one in which you present two incriminatory choices concerning some aspects of the incident or crime. Elements of the alternative are developed as logical extensions of the theme. If the theme focuses on contrasting behavior that is impulsive or spur-of-the-moment with planned or premeditated acts, the alternative question is, "Did you plan this thing or did it just happen on the spur of the moment?" Either choice is an admission of guilt. The alternative question should be based on an assumption of guilt. It *should not* be something to the effect of, "Did you do this or didn't you?" A poorly phrased question invites denial. A suspect who accepts one alternative has made a first admission of guilt. The task, then, is to develop this admission into an acceptable confession.

Having the Suspect Relate Details. Once the alternative question has been answered, you respond with a statement of reinforcement. Essentially, this is a statement that acknowledges the suspect's admission of guilt. Your objective is to obtain a brief oral review of the basic sequence of events, while obtaining sufficient detail to corroborate the suspect's guilt.

Questions asked at this time should be brief, concise and clear, calling only for limited verbal responses from the suspect. It is premature to make such a broad statement as, "Well, just tell me everything that happened." Further, questions should be open-ended and devoid of emotionally charged words. Once you have obtained a brief verbal statement about the crime sequence, you should ask detailed questions to obtain information that can be corroborated by subsequent investigation. After this full verbal statement is complete, it may be necessary to return to the suspect's choice of alternatives, or to some other suspect statement, to establish the actual purpose and intent at the time of the crime.

Converting an Oral Confession. After advising the suspect, you should leave the room, ostensibly to check on something. You then return with a witness who may be introduced as someone who has been involved in the investigation. Repeat the essential details of the suspect's confession, after which the witness asks a few confirming questions. Now is the time to convert an oral confession into a written one. One of four formats can be used:

1. A statement written by the suspect;
2. A statement written by you, and read and signed by the suspect;
3. A statement taken down by a secretary or stenographer and transcribed into a typed document for the suspect to read and sign; or
4. A tape-recorded or video-recorded statement.

Keep in mind that the statement of guilt must be readable and understandable by someone who is not familiar with what the suspect has done. Leading questions should be avoided, the confessor's own language used, and full corroboration established. Any errors, changes or crossed-out words should be initialed with an "OK" written in the margin by the suspect. The statement should reflect that the suspect was treated properly, that no threats or promises were made, and that the statement was freely given by the suspect. A suspect who has completed reading the written statement is instructed to "write your name here," while you point to the place for signature. Avoid asking, "sign here" because "sign" connotes too much legalism. The suspect signs each page of the statement in front of you and the witness, and then you both can sign as well.

Obtaining the written confession at the end of the interrogation is not the capstone. Every effort should be made to verify the statement and to obtain the supporting evidence necessary for trial.

Selected Bibliography

Association of Certified Fraud Examiners; *Beyond the Numbers;* 1994; 50-minute videotape, Association of Certified Fraud Examiners.

Buckwalter, Art; *Interviews and Interrogations;* 1983; Butterworths Publishing Co., Stoneham, MA.

Fisher, Ronald P. and Geiselman, R.E.; *Memory-Enhancing Techniques for Investigative Interviewing;* 1992; Charles C Thomas, Springfield, IL.

French, Scott R. and Van Houten, Paul; *Never Say Lie;* 1987; Paladin Press, Boulder, CO.

Inbau, Fred E., Reid, John E., and Buckley, Joseph P.; *Criminal Interrogation and Confession, 3rd ed.;* 1986; Williams & Wilkins, Baltimore, MD.

Link, Frederick C. and Foster, D. Glenn; *The Kinesic Interview Technique;* Interrotec Associates.

MacHovec, Frank J.; *Interview and Interrogation: A Scientific Approach;* 1989; Charles C Thomas, Springfield, IL.

McDonald, Patrick; *Make 'em Talk: Principles of Military Interrogation;* 1993; Paladin Press, Boulder, CO.

Morgan, Raymond C.; *Interviewing Techniques in the Detection of Deception;* 1986; Idaho Assessment Center.

Rabon, Don; *Interviewing and Interrogation;* 1992; Carolina Academic Press.

Royal, Robert E. and Schutt, Steven R.; *The Gentle Art of Interviewing and Interrogation;* 1976; Prentice-Hall, Englewood Cliffs, NJ.

Rudacille, Wendell C.; *Identifying Lies in Disguise;* 1994; self-published.

Yeschke, Charles L.; *Interviewing: A Forensic Guide to Interrogation;* 1993; and *Interviewing: An Introduction to Interrogation;* 1987; Charles C Thomas, Springfield, IL.

Zulawski, David E. and Wicklander, Douglas E.; *Practical Aspects of Interview and Interrogation;* 1993; CRC Press, Boca Raton, FL.

Periodicals

Buckley, Joseph, P. and Mullenix, Philip A.; The Use of Behavior Symptoms in the Search for the Truth, *Prosecutor,* 19(1), 1985.

Buckley, Joseph P.; How Do I Know if They Told Me the Truth? Internal Audit Advisor, March–April 1986; The Behavioral Profile of a Liar, *NEWS,* International Association of Credit Card Investigators, Vol. 118, 1Q 1991.

Security Management magazine; American Society for Industrial Security, Arlington, VA.
 — Buckley, David M.; Dealing with Artful Dodgers; April 1993.
 — Buckley, Joseph P.; The Nine Steps of Interrogation; May 1983.

- Buckley, Joseph Paul, III and Jayne, Brian C.; Criminal Interrogation Techniques on Trial, October 1992; and Read Between the Lines; June 1987.
- Force, H.R.; Interrogations; September 1972.
- Hinerman, Joseph W.; Self-Incriminatory Statements; January 1973.
- Marshall, Keith D.; Unmasking the Truth; January 1985.
- Penley, William J.; Interviews Do Not Always Lead to the Truth; November 1979.
- Royal, Robert F. and Schutt, Steven R.; The Art of Interviewing and Interrogating; February 1978.
- Scanning Words for True Confessions; August 1992.
- Wygant, James R.; The Language of Truth; September 1986.

19
A Plan for Threat Management

OVERVIEW

In a North American context, workplace violence has evolved into a problem that involves all segments of society and the "workplace" now includes even schools at all levels. Elementary school students have been found carrying knives and handguns, and incidents of high school homicides unfortunately occur all too often. The increase in workplace violence is a mirror image of a changing society. In some segments of the media, particularly in movies and on television, violence is portrayed as an acceptable response to personal problems.

The media tends to focus on the spectacular incidents of lethal violence, but we seldom hear of the violence that results in injury rather than death. Data from National Crime Victimization Studies indicate that U.S. residents experienced more than 2 million violent incidents each year while working or on duty.[1] Of those incidents, 1000 were homicides while 1.5 million were simple assaults. Homicide was the second leading cause of death in the workplace between 1992 and 1996 (second to auto accidents). Workplace homicides accounted for about one of every six fatal occupational injuries during this time period.

Homicide in the workplace has always been a concern; but a more disturbing trend, mass murder by individuals associated in some way with the workplace, is the current focus of concern. For example, a disgruntled former employee returns to the workplace and takes out his frustrations by shooting several of his former colleagues. These killers — employees, spouses or other companions, students, customers or clients, and suppliers to the organization — generally have some connection to individuals associated with the organization. Their actions can devastate an organization for years after the violent event.

Even when these individuals do not kill, they can and often do cause other problems. Homicides, assaults, threats and harassment in the workplace will probably increase in frequency because the contributing factors identified for this problem will not abate. These factors include disintegration

[1] *Workplace Violence, 1992–96*; Bureau of Statistics, U.S. Department of Justice; July 1998.

of family, church and community on individual behavior; the process of employer restructuring, downsizing and realignments; the growing number of untreated mentally ill, both within and outside the workforce; and the relentless media coverage of incidents of workplace violence that may influence others to act in a similar fashion. (Often, individuals will act out either in response to actual or perceived wrongs or gain media attention they probably would not otherwise receive.)

The sad reality is that many organizations have a lax attitude toward workplace violence even though threats in the workplace are increasing.

THE CONCEPT OF THREAT MANAGEMENT

Threat management is an interdepartmental and interdisciplinary process that involves:

- Pre-employment screening
- Access control and other physical security measures
- A fully disseminated written policy statement and reporting procedure
- Formation of an Incident Management Team (IMT)
- Guidelines for threat and incident management

Any security program, at any level of application, is meant first to divert someone from committing an unsafe or harmful act and, only if diversion is unsuccessful, to delay the undesirable act until trained individuals can respond. Security programs work on the assumption that an appropriate response by properly trained personnel will occur, if needed. For threats of workplace violence, this means that response should be made at a predetermined threshold point by properly trained personnel, armed when necessary. In some cases, those responding may be law enforcement personnel but in many others properly qualified private security personnel may be the only available resource.

The solution to any given incident of workplace violence demands that we understand the current emotional and mental state of the offender and properly intercede before that person acts on his fears, anger or mental disorder and commits a violent act. Early awareness of the problem allows thorough assessment and successful intervention. Companies need to develop a comprehensive threat management system that requires central reporting of threats, ensures their thorough assessment and provides for a coordinated response by necessary organizational and community support groups.

The Focus of a Threat Management Program

Every employer in the United States has an obligation to provide a safe workplace under federal law[1] and often under state laws as well. This obligation does not distinguish between internal and external sources of danger.

[1] Occupational Safety and Health Act, 29 U.S.C. 654(a)(1).

A Plan for Threat Management

If an employer has reasonable cause to believe that someone may commit an act of violence on the premises or against an employee, the employer has an obligation to provide protection. It does not matter who the offender is — an employee or spouse of an employee, or a contractor, vendor, client, guest or third party. The employer must provide protection against that person's reasonably foreseeable violent actions.

The principal focus of a Threat Management Program will involve incidents of:

- Verbal or written threats
- Assaults
- Acts of sabotage or vandalism
- Homicide
- Other threatening actions, such as the display of weapons at work

Harassment, discrimination and other unacceptable but initially nonviolent workplace behavior must also be considered as possible precursors to violence. A series of escalating incidents of unacceptable behavior on the part of a single person should be considered as significant. A Threat Management Program can also help control liability exposure and damage to productivity and workplace morale.

Liability is a principal source of concern about workplace violence. Suits continue to grow in number with plaintiff judgments averaging more than $1 million per case. But equal or sometimes greater economic cost results from loss of morale and productivity. Absenteeism, sick leave, work slowdowns, management and worker distraction, and general disruption associated with a violent incident can be very expensive. The costs for treating injuries must also be noted.

The Threat Management Program may have limited outside support and resources available to help it meet its objectives, and an organization must be ready to contend with the following problems in developing it:

- Limited law enforcement resources
- Limited legal experience in the process of workplace violence management
- A limited number of credible experts in the psychology of workplace violence
- A limited number of security firms capable of providing the broad range of responses necessary

LIABILITY AND LEGAL CONSIDERATIONS

In addition to being required to provide a safe workplace under federal and many state laws,[1] U.S. enterprises will also be affected by tort and

---

[1] For example, California Labor Code 6400 and 6401.7.

employment law in claims arising out of workplace violence. These claims could allege negligent hiring, negligent retention, failure to warn, violations of the Civil Rights Act, discrimination, defamation, slander, invasion of privacy, harassment and violations of the American with Disabilities (ADA) and Rehabilitation Acts. However, if an individual threatens to hurt persons at a work site and is assessed as being mentally unstable, it does not follow that such behavior will be protected under the ADA.

Workplace violence might also involve federal and state laws that criminalize threats; stalking; harassing phone calls; trespassing; violating a restraining or protective order; possessing, brandishing or exhibiting dangerous weapons; assault, battery; assault with a deadly weapon; rape; robbery; kidnapping; homicide; and attempts to commit these crimes.

It is especially important that the company understand how it or its employees can obtain protective orders against individuals who threaten harm. In some jurisdictions, these orders can only be obtained by natural persons. But the law is beginning to recognize that business entities can also be the victims of threats and harassment. Some people question the value of a "piece of paper" as protection against a real threat of violence. Experience has shown that in the majority of cases in which protective orders have been violated and individuals hurt, the orders were obtained much too late in the process to be effective.

In one high-profile case, Laura Black, the object of a former co-worker's anger during a tragic workplace violence incident, delayed for two years obtaining a restraining order against him after he was fired from his job for harassing her. She now believes that if she had obtained the restraining order earlier, it might have prevented the tragedy.[1]

THE PSYCHOLOGICAL DYNAMIC OF WORKPLACE VIOLENCE

What is known about incidents of workplace violence that have not involved robbery is that they typically are not caused by individuals who "snap" one day and decide to act violently. These incidents are caused by persons who have progressed through a series of emotional and behavioral stages before becoming violent. They have come to believe that violence is the only way to solve their problem. They are emotionally driven to act, may be mentally unbalanced and may be under the influence of drugs or alcohol at the time of the incident. Offenders who have survived an incident often say that, if someone had been able to listen, understand and work with them, they would not have acted violently.

This psychological dynamic means that the most effective means for resolution requires:

---

[1] TV interview of Laura Black; KPIX TV; February 1993, San Francisco, CA.

A Plan for Threat Management

- Early detection of a disturbed individual
- Assessment of that person's current mental and emotional level on a scale of violent behavior
- A plan to forestall violence through a specific combination of communications, organizational and community resources, and the legal system

In general, the scale of violent behavior starts with disgruntlement, then progresses to nonspecific verbal intimidation, nonspecific verbal threats, specific verbal threats, written threats, physical violence against property, physical violence against people without the use of weapons, and finally, physical violence against people with weapons.

An individual may move back and forth across the scale, skipping steps or creating new ones, escalating or de-escalating behavior. But each movement back up the scale will involve behavior that is increasingly more serious. The entire process leading to an act of physical violence will normally occur within one year of a precipitating incident, but it can take longer. The process can also occur within as short a time span as a week, given the right conditions.

Emotionally driven offenders view the world from their own perspective and use their own logic. One must understand that perspective and logic and then provide acceptable alternatives to violence. This does not mean that the organization "gives them what they want." Instead, within established guidelines, the organization constructs mutually agreeable alternatives that deflect the offender from the enterprise and its employees. Merely terminating people who pose a threat, by itself, will not resolve the problem and may actually precipitate violent behavior.

Psychological and behavioral assessment requires obtaining as much information as possible about the threatening individual. Particular attention should be paid to any past history of stressful events (death, divorce, job loss, financial pressure, etc.) and reactions to them. Researchers in this area agree that the best predictor of future behavior is past behavior. The more we know about the offender's emotional history, history of physical violence, reactions to stress and current stressors, the better the current assessment.

PRE-EMPLOYMENT SCREENING

Pre-employment screening, a vital facet of the security program in a modern organization, must include screening for workplace violence prevention. History does indeed repeat itself and the best predictor of future violent behavior is past violent behavior.

Factors to be considered would include past violent behavior, criminal history, substance abuse and reasons for leaving prior employment. The pre-employment procedures should be reviewed in light of changes to the Fair Credit Reporting Act (FCRA). (See Chapter 11 for more information on restrictions imposed on certain investigative techniques by the FCRA.)

PHYSICAL SECURITY

The practicality of the use of different physical security measures will vary with the type of facility and the physical configuration of the property. Physical security measures to be considered include access control, employee and visitor identification, interior and exterior lighting, closed-circuit television, and the physical configuration of furniture and equipment to provide escape routes.

Access Control

The strict access control implemented in a research and development facility would be impractical in a retail store. There are, however, areas in virtually every facility to which access can and should be controlled. Access control measures that are implemented for basic asset protection will, in many cases, be suitable for the prevention of workplace violence. Entry to administrative and executive offices should be controlled by a receptionist or by card access. Movement from lobby areas to other sections of the building should be similarly controlled. Card access is preferable to key locks or combination locks in that the card of a terminated or suspended employee can be immediately invalidated.

The number of possible access points to the facility should be restricted to the minimum consistent with efficient operations. (Refer to Chapter 7 for a more detailed discussion of access control.)

Employee and Visitor Identification. Identification cards should be issued to employees. Many facilities issue photo identification cards and require that they be displayed at all times when the employee is on the premises. A single card can be used for identification and access control. Employees should be required to immediately report the loss of a card. (See Chapter 7 for more on identification cards.)

The validity of access for each visitor should be determined prior to admission to the facility. Visitor passes should be issued to all visitors, including contractors, and should be displayed at all times while on the premises. Many facilities use a type of pass that self-invalidates after a given period of time, usually one day.

Lighting

Interior and exterior lighting should be evaluated for adequacy. Parking lots and garages require particular attention. (Chapter 12 includes details for interior and exterior lighting.)

A Plan for Threat Management

Closed-Circuit Television (CCTV)

Closed-circuit television (CCTV) can be a deterrent to improper activity, especially when a potential offender is aware that the system is in operation. Signs should be posted to that effect. CCTV can be particularly useful in evaluating a situation in an area such as a lobby, parking lot or garage. The lobby receptionist and similar personnel should have panic buttons to alert security to a problem. CCTV recorders capture all images from the CCTV cameras. The recordings can be used for later verification if there is a problem. (For more information on the use of CCTV systems, refer to Chapters 6, 12 and 13.)

Furniture and Equipment Configuration

The physical configuration of furniture and equipment should be examined to ensure that the optimum escape routes are available for occupants of the building. This examination will contribute to fire safety as well as allow rapid egress in a violence situation.

POLICY STATEMENT AND REPORTING PROCEDURE

Some organizations choose to implement a workplace violence program without a formal written policy statement. In these organizations, information about the program is disseminated via training meetings, posters and newsletters. Note that the absence of a formal written policy does not preclude disciplinary action by management when unacceptable behavior occurs.

Most organizations elect to formulate and disseminate a formal written workplace violence policy. Employees throughout the organization are advised of the policy through meetings and other internal communications means. The document should clearly indicate that the policy of the organization is to promote a safe environment for all persons on property under the control of the organization.

The written policy should be brief. Implementation instructions and the responsibilities of elements of the organization should be detailed in memoranda or other organizational communications.

One objective of the policy is to encourage employees to report incidents. These reports may well provide early identification of a potentially violent person. The use of the term "zero tolerance" may appear to indicate inflexibility in dealing with problem situations. This can discourage incident reporting and early intervention in potentially violent situations. The victim wants the behavior stopped, but does not want the offender to be terminated from employment with the organization. Defining terms such as harassment, violence and threat can also discourage employees from reporting situations that they believe may not fall within the definitions of

ASSET PROTECTION AND SECURITY MANAGEMENT HANDBOOK

the terms. Definitions can also cause legal difficulties in disciplinary actions and appeals.

Legal counsel should be consulted prior to issuing the workplace violence policy. A model policy is provided in Appendix A to this chapter.

THE INCIDENT MANAGEMENT TEAM (IMT) AND SUPPORTING RESOURCES

The Incident Management Team (see Table 1) for incidents of threats or violence should include, at a minimum:

- A senior management representative
- A senior human resource manager
- A senior security manager
- A legal representative familiar with labor and employment law and litigation

Should the company have multiple locations, this team can be broken down into Core and Divisional members. Core members provide an extended experience and resource base for the assessment and management of all incidents. Divisional team members provide specific local incident knowledge, authority and insight. Members of the consulting team may be added as deemed necessary. Any operational support team member may serve in an advisory capacity to the IMT during the development of certain portions of the incident plan, or may carry out instructions from the IMT.

The IMT should be authorized to commit whatever company assets and personnel are necessary to resolve the incident. Delays caused by a requirement to get decisions from others on employment actions, deployment of personnel or expenditures could seriously slow the process and significantly increase the risk of an unsuccessful resolution.

A study of 21 randomly selected Fortune 500 companies[1] found that labor participation appears to enhance the threat assessment team's effectiveness in unionized work sites.

Union participation should be invited early in the workplace violence prevention process. As the elected representative of bargaining unit employees, the union is legally entitled to negotiate many conditions of employment. The fact that some of the issues relating to workplace violence may be outside the duty to bargain does not preclude discussion and consultation with the union.

Union endorsement can well be a critical consideration in acceptance and participation of a workplace violence program by represented employees. In a policy statement on workplace violence, a major union stated that

---

[1] See Appendix C to this chapter for a flowchart of a standard incident assessment and resolution process.

Table 1. Incident Management Team (IMT) and resources.

Core Incident Management Team members (one of whom needs to be a senior management representative):
    Senior Human Resources representative
    Security representative
    Legal counsel
Divisional Incident Management Team members
    Divisional senior management representative
    Manager of victim or offender's department, if applicable
Outside consulting team[a]
    Licensed psychological or psychiatric professional
    Additional legal support
IMT Operational Support Team members
    Employee Assistance Program (EAP) representative
    Public Affairs/Corporate Communications representative
    Records and Benefits representative
    Personnel liaison
    Health Services representative
    Facility Services representative
    On-site contract security representative
    Labor union representative

[a] See Appendix B to this chapter.

"Workplace violence programs or threat assessment teams that do not have union-designated representatives will have little credibility with employees, tend to blame non-management workers for problems, and will inevitably fail to effectively address the problem of workplace violence."[1]

THE INCIDENT MANAGEMENT PROCESS[2]

Notification of a Potential or Actual Problem

The workplace violence policy should require employees to report any violent, threatening, harassing, intimidating or other disruptive behavior that they observe or become aware of to a Designated Management Representative (DMR), regardless of the relationship between the offender and the victim.

The DMR then takes the steps necessary to verify the information, makes an initial assessment and documents any decision involving further action. The DMR will also enter the information in a database for future retrieval and trend analysis.

---

[1] See Appendix A to this chapter for a model policy on workplace violence.
[2] See Appendix C to this chapter for a listing of the types of resources that could be checked.

To speed communication and the assessment process, the DMR should be a member of the Core IMT. Even in decentralized companies, the DMR and Core IMT positions should initially be set up at the corporate or central level to ensure maximum use of trained personnel, allow rapid expansion of the experience base of the company in this area, and maintain a centralized reporting structure for multi-jurisdiction incident tracking.

When a threat policy requires threats to be reported to the employee's immediate supervisor or manager rather than a separate DMR, experience indicates that important events leading up to a major incident will go unreported, creating an unnecessary level of risk. This seems to occur because co-workers or others either do not want to cause trouble for the individual making the threat by talking to a supervisor or manager directly, or do not want to take any action that will jeopardize themselves. This avoidance behavior is so common in situations of threats or potential violence that in most cases, when an offender has finally been psychologically assessed and found to be an immediate danger to self or others, fellow employees come forward with several previously unreported incidents of verbal or physical threats made by the individual, indicating that the individual had for some time been exploring violence as an option.

Having an objective person in the company to whom threats can be reported confidentially makes their timely reporting much more likely. Early intervention enhances the opportunity to redirect the offender into a nonviolent mode of expression.

ASSESSMENT PHASE

The Assessment Phase continues through the process but initially consists of the original report of the incident, additional information gathering, assessment by the IMT, and then review and monitoring of the individual.

Initial Information Collection by the DMR

Initial Contact. When the initial contact is made, a case file is opened and detailed information concerning the offender, victim or victims, and witnesses is documented and recorded. It should include the date, time, location and type of actual or perceived threat or observed behavior. It is extremely important that the details of the event and chronology are precise and exactly worded.

After the initial report has been received, the DMR should begin assessment by reviewing the information provided and comparing it to the company's assessment guidelines.

The DMR may determine that additional interviews are warranted. Should those interviews involve victims, witnesses, or other informants who are or have been employees of the company, their personnel files should be

A Plan for Threat Management

reviewed prior to interviewing them. This may provide insight into their personalities, attitudes, work performance, prejudices and connections to the offender.

Additional Interviews

Decision to Interview in Person or by Phone. Interviews of the victim(s) and witness(es), if any, are crucial. The purposes of an interview are:

- To learn exact details of the event that led to notification
- To allow the DMR or interviewer to understand the emotional, psychological and situational context and chronology of the event or events that led to this report, the background and perspective of the victim or witness
- To help the victims or witnesses to take back control of their emotional life

With all these goals in mind, a decision is needed as to whether the initial interview should be done by phone or in person. In person is preferable in most cases because it provides maximum sensory input to the interviewer during the process. But considerations of time, distance, scheduling problems and personal interactions may make the phone a necessary alternative. Voice mail, e-mail or other nondirect contact media should be used only as a last resort.

Selection of the Interview Site. For in-person interviews, the interview site should not be one normally used by the victims, witnesses or offender. It should be located in an area providing enough pedestrian traffic that someone coming to the interview room will not be obvious, but not in such a densely populated area that many people will know that a stream of individuals is coming and going from the room. A standard conference room of medium size is suitable if it meets the other criteria. An unoccupied office can be used as well, but is not optimal because offices are normally smaller and may cause the interviewee to become anxious.

These interviews can also be conducted in hotel rooms or other locations offsite. This has been done in some extreme circumstances, but it has been found that the level of uneasiness engendered in the victim(s) or witness(es), and the logistical and other problems caused, almost always outweigh any advantage gained.

Decision to Secure the Interview Site. The type of threats made or behavior exhibited may be intense enough to require protection for the interviewer and the victim or witness against possible harm during the interview. This is most probable where the offender is likely to learn of the interviews and is capable of disrupting them. Security personnel should be placed next door or nearby the interview site and should be able to observe

ASSET PROTECTION AND SECURITY MANAGEMENT HANDBOOK

all avenues of approach while remaining out of the way and out of direct sight. Security should establish a method for nonverbal communication between the interviewer and themselves. This will allow the interviewer to summon security, should it become necessary, or alert them to certain activities inside the interview room. The security team should also be prepared to intercept and divert any unauthorized person attempting to enter the interview room.

Development of an Offender and Incident Chronology. The DMR and subsequent interviewers should create a log that reflects the total contact the offender has had with the company and its personnel. Included in this log should be detailed chronologies of all events, statements and actions that are part of the incident.

The complete time log is valuable because it provides a method of understanding the incident or incidents in the greater context of the offender's life. It may make it clearer how and why the individual is acting or reacting.

Analysis of Initial Information. After the initial interviews and log development, the DMR or the IMT should conduct a complete case review. All information should be weighed against the violence scale and a decision reached on whether only to monitor the offender's behavior for additional cues or to continue gathering information for further assessment. Available security options should also be determined at this point.

Extensive Background Investigation of the Offender

Should a decision be made to gather more information, it will come from the following sources:

- Interviews of individuals who have yet to be contacted
- Public records, including certain law enforcement records
- Information from internal company documents, such as personnel records, that have not already been reviewed

There are two guiding principles to help determine which records to research and which individuals to interview. The first is comfort level. Enough additional information has to be gathered to make the necessary decisions. The second is preparing a legal defense. Enough information has to be gathered so that the IMT can successfully demonstrate that it acted reasonably. Information must be gathered swiftly (normally within 24 to 72 hours) and with the awareness that it may not be possible to contact a source again within the time allotted.

Location of Any Prior Relevant Data. *Relevant data* is any information that can provide insight into the individual and his or her past pattern in

A Plan for Threat Management

dealing with life events. This would include past violent behavior; training in the use of weapons (which might include military service and training); criminal activity; substance abuse; past and current personal turbulence (death, divorce, birth, poor finances, accident, injury, loss of employment, lawsuits, natural disasters, etc.); and reactions to any of these. (See Chapter 11 regarding restrictions imposed on certain investigative techniques by the Fair Credit Reporting act.)

Check other states and counties for adult residence and employment. This should be considered in situations in which significant relevant information might be present for any year or place of residence of adult life. Juvenile records are normally sealed and will not be available to the investigator.

Consider checking the background of the offender's spouse. The past behaviors, attitudes and life events of a spouse have provided significant insight into the current outlook of the offender in many cases. In several cases, although the offender did not own any weapons, the spouse did, and the offender had access to them.

Information Sources

1. *Employment application.* Relevant information includes date of application; full name; other names used; Social Security number; previous employers (including locations, job descriptions and reasons for leaving); driver's license number, if available; past addresses; and emergency contacts.

   This information should be compared with any newly acquired information to find conflicting dates of birth or Social Security numbers, and significant gaps in employment. In addition, the information concerning residence and work addresses will be used to identify jurisdictions in which public records need to be checked.
2. *Employment evaluations.* A review of previous employment evaluations can provide good insight into current performance, attitude and expectations. Especially significant are remarks from the offender disputing portions of any evaluation.
3. *Disciplinary actions.* A review of disciplinary actions can provide insight into reaction to authority or discipline. (Consider whether the individual's response is to improve behavior or defend it.) Also, disciplinary actions coming at a more accelerated pace can point to a deteriorating attitude or state of mind, the causes of which may be responsible for, or adding to, the current behavior of concern.
4. *Medical information.* In serious cases, information identifying current treating physicians, psychiatrists, psychologists and other providers of health services may facilitate contact with those providers to ascertain the offender's current mental or physical condition, use of medication, and stability. Employee safety and privacy need to be

weighed when considering whether to review these records and initiate contact. Some medical personnel will notify the patient of any contact requesting information about condition or treatment.

5. *Co-worker interview(s).* Special care is needed when interviewing co-workers. Co-workers are in position to reveal their knowledge of the incident and the progress of the evaluation to the offender or victims. This is not desirable. The best strategy, should information from co-workers be considered important, is to interview them immediately prior to interviewing the offender, and to impress upon them the need for strict confidentiality. Where co-workers believe that the offender is truly dangerous, they may feel compelled to notify him or her of the interview in an attempt to prove their loyalty or friendship and avoid the physical violence they believe the offender may perpetrate. These same considerations apply to family members or relatives considered for interviews.

Law Enforcement Liaison. At some point, assistance from law enforcement may be needed. This can include access to criminal history and state-wide weapons registration information. But unless police involvement is managed carefully, it can complicate an already-difficult situation.

In an actually violent situation, the goals of law enforcement and the company are very closely aligned — the protection of employees. The job of company personnel is to get law enforcement and other public emergency service personnel to the scene as quickly as possible and provide whatever assistance they require to restore workplace safety. In a potentially violent situation, law enforcement and company objectives may not be as closely aligned. Before an incident arises, communications and a relationship of mutual support should be worked out with local law enforcement. It should be remembered that once information is provided to law enforcement officials, they may act as they see fit rather than doing what the enterprise might think is in its own best interest.

Decision to Interview the Offender

It is always recommended that trained personnel capable of assessing the potential for violence conduct the interview of the offender, regardless of the offender's affiliation with the company. This interview serves several critical purposes:

1. It provides an opportunity for the trained individual to communicate directly with the offender and glean exactly what he or she is thinking, thus permitting direct assessment of the offender's state of mind.
2. It allows the personnel member to explore a variety of possible ways the situation might be resolved and to determine how the offender might react if the outcome was not in his or her favor.

A Plan for Threat Management

3. It allows assessment personnel to suggest ways for the offender to move away from violence and accomplish his or her objectives in another way.
4. It provides a direct, defensible opportunity to offer legal warnings and establish boundaries.
5. It may help provide a defense in employment-related actions and legal claims against accusations that the matter was never discussed with the individual, prior to some precipitating action being taken.

When the offender is an employee, contractor, temporary worker, customer or other affiliated individual, this interview should be fairly easy. Interviews with a spouse, ex-employee or other individual not directly connected with the enterprise may be more difficult.

It is preferable that the interview take place on property owned and controlled by the company, as this allows for control of the site. But some interviews may only be accomplished at the offender's home or work site, and plans should allow for such a contingency.

A plan should be developed for the interim action that will occur at the end of the interview so that the offender will leave with an understanding of what steps may be taken next. For an employee, temporary employee, contractor or other affiliated person, a range of interim options is available. These may include any or all of the following:

- Suspension, with or without pay, pending resolution
- A request that the individual refrain from coming to any company sites, pending a final decision
- Permission for the individual to go back to his or her normal routine, pending further contact
- A request not to return to work without a completed "fitness for duty" report by a designated health-care provider

Information on the option chosen would normally be communicated by a company employee who may need to be introduced into the interview room at the end of the interview. Should the offender be asked to leave the site, this company employee would provide the name and phone number of a company representative to be the exclusive contact during the interim period. The offender should be told not to return to the work site without specific approval from the designated contact person.

For a person not affiliated with the firm, the company normally makes a request that the individual not return to company property until further notice. A company contact name and telephone number are also provided.

It must be remembered that one individual can never be compelled to talk to any other individual, so the ability to do this assessment interview may hinge on the skill of the interviewer in persuading the offender to participate.

Securing the Interview Site and Assessment Personnel

Site Selection. As mentioned previously, the interview site should be one not normally observed or used by a victim or witnesses and should allow for "next-room" access by security personnel. It should be located in an area that will not unduly alert the offender to the purpose of the interview and be isolated enough to minimize concerns of physical, emotional and psychological injury or trauma should a violent incident occur. A standard conference room of small to medium size is normally adequate.

Site Preparation. This requires rearranging the furniture and fixtures inside the interview room to accommodate the unique nature of this interview. Minimal furnishings will allow more free space for security personnel to move in should there be a violent episode during the interview.

It usually means that objects easily converted to weapons are removed and security personnel position furniture to allow for easy access through the door. The seat for the offender is placed nearest the door for quick physical control by security, if necessary. The seats of the interviewers are placed in such a way that it allows them to move back and away from the offender and out of the line of action of security personnel entering the room.

Site Security. The same arrangements for security personnel and nonverbal communications should be followed as described earlier in the section headed "Initial Information Collection by the DMR."

Hostage Contingency Plan. Despite careful planning, a situation could arise in which the interviewee takes one or more of the interviewers hostage by actual use or credible threat of force. This might involve a concealed weapon. Plans to contain and control such an event must be included in the preparation for the interview. Arranging for the offender to report to the interview site immediately upon notice of the interview, without first going back to a desk or locker area, or having the person who gives notice of the interview actually accompany the offender to the site, can reduce the likelihood that a weapon will be obtained.

Training of Interview Participants. The interview team (usually two individuals) should be trained in the use of the nonverbal communication system, the possible responses by the security personnel, and what they should do when those occur. Prior to each interview, regardless of the number of times the interview and security teams have participated in interviews of this type, all of these areas should be reviewed to refresh the knowledge of the participants in the established procedures and responses.

Summary Assessment and Plan for Further Action

Immediately after the offender interview is held, the IMT is normally reconvened for full incident review in light of the content of the interview

A Plan for Threat Management

with the offender. At this time, all remaining situation variations and options are considered, decision trees agreed upon and plans made to implement the options chosen. At a minimum, the various options that need to be evaluated are:

- Further medical or psychological evaluation
- Demotion
- Reassignment
- Suspension
- Termination
- Obtaining a restraining order
- Pursuit of criminal charges

One or a combination of these options may be decided upon and plans then made to implement them.

Plan in Event of Termination

Should the decision be made to terminate the employment of an offender and there be a concern that the individual may become violent, it may not be necessary to accomplish termination in a face-to-face interview onsite. Termination notice by certified or registered mail would eliminate the security concerns of a termination interview and, if properly planned, could accomplish the same controlled result.

But under most circumstances, a face-to-face termination interview is desirable and in those instances detailed planning is necessary. If the employee is still working on site, an interview needs to be requested with minimum notice to the employee. If the employee is offsite, due to suspension or for other reasons, some notice will be necessary to schedule the meeting.

For reasons mentioned earlier, the meeting should take place on company-owned or -controlled property. Some other considerations for this meeting are as follows.

Company Personnel Selected for Interview. Two individuals should be in the room during this meeting to diffuse the focus and anger of the interviewee. One person is normally from Human Resources (or the equivalent) and the other is from the individual's unit or department. The direct supervisor need not be involved in terminations, as this will prolong the meeting by having the offender attempt again to explain his or her position. A more senior person in the department, who does not have daily contact with the offender, may be the most appropriate.

As the meeting may become confrontational, the selection of these two people should be based primarily on their emotional equilibrium and proven ability to handle confrontations. No other consideration is more important in the selection of the individuals for this type of interview.

Site Selection and Preparation. These requirements are the same as those for the offender interview detailed previously.

Time of the Interview. The time should be chosen so that the interview can be planned to conclude when the rest of the personnel in the building are either fully engaged or are few in number. Lunchtime or shift changes should be avoided, even if this means having the offender work some overtime to allow for isolation.

Planning Communications with the Offender. Special consideration needs to be given to the content and delivery of all communications with the offender. Scripting the interview seems to provide the best way of making certain that all the essential information is communicated, the meeting moves along at a pace that keeps it within the suggested 10–20 minute range, and that the individuals conducting the interview avoid opening up old grievances. Interviewers should also be shown how to take back control of the meeting, should it be lost. Special attention should be paid to the following parts of this process:

1. *The call to the interview.* This call should be made directly to the individual and not communicated by answering machine, voice mail or letter. This action will preclude the individual from guessing the intent of the interview and avoiding contact or acting inappropriately while the company is still uncertain whether he or she knows about the interview. Answers to questions concerning the reason for the interview and whether it involves termination should be prepared.
2. *Written documents for presentation.* Certainly the main focus of these documents should be the information that needs to be communicated to satisfy the legal requirements of the termination. But special effort should be made to adjust the "tone" of the letter in an attempt to minimize a hostile or violent reaction.
3. *Security arrangements.* Nonverbal communications, intervention by security and a hostage contingency plan should be assured, as described earlier for the initial offender interview.
4. *The close of the interview.* The offender should be provided with the name and phone number of a company person to contact concerning any future questions (benefits, etc.) and should be requested not to contact anyone else at the company concerning the termination. There also should be an instruction not to return to the property without specific approval from the contact person.

Plan for Exit of Offender from Company Property. The plan for removal of an openly hostile, threatening or violent offender from the site should be the same as that developed during the initial offender interview. In addition, consideration should be given in the termination interview of whether the offender will be accompanied by an escort or will be allowed to leave the premises on his/her own but with loose surveillance. An escort from the interview room, if appropriately introduced, can be a very good way to maintain contact in order to judge the offender's current state of mind. Conversely, an individual who observes security personnel trailing him/her around the company site may be more likely to display hostile feelings.

It is not recommended that the offender be allowed to return to the work area or locker prior to leaving the premises. This lessens the likelihood of workplace disruption and reduces the opportunity to obtain weapons. The person can be asked to leave and told that personal possessions will be boxed, inventoried and delivered by courier. This also provides an opportunity to assess the offender in the future, when delivering the possessions. Delivery can also provide the opportunity to serve a restraining order, if necessary, and judge the reaction of the offender to this document. The courier service in these cases should be highly trained security personnel who can make a reliable field assessment of the individual and also meet the legal requirements for the proof of service of the restraining order.

Extended Security and Incident Monitoring

Sizing Up the Threat. Two items need to be considered after an offender has been terminated or ordered to leave the premises. The first is the possibility that the offender will not honor the request to remain away from the property and will make an attempt to return. Should return be considered likely to disrupt the workplace, security should be heightened.

The second item is the level of needed security. This must cover the likelihood that the individual will arrive with a weapon. If evaluation indicates that there is some need for increased security but that probability of a weapon is low, then the increased security must be able to respond promptly. If there is a significant probability that the individual will return with a weapon, then increased security should be able to identify and meet the person prior to entry into a company building.

Establishment of the Reaction Response Plan. This plan should provide a procedure for the regular security force and other employees to report a "sighting" of the offender on or near the property. The plan should specify the various levels of response by security personnel, depending on whether they meet the offender inside or outside the building, whether or not the offender is hostile, is openly armed or has used a weapon on enterprise property in the past. Any planned intervention should start with the least confrontation and escalate only if necessary up to the possible use of weapons.

Protective Team's Responsibility. Based on the threat assessment, different protective roles will be assigned to normal and any special additional security elements, both armed and unarmed. Unarmed security personnel should be in position to observe and report any attempt to enter the property, with enough lead time to allow special personnel, armed if necessary, to meet the individual outside the building.

Control and oversight of all security personnel should be under one manager. If there is a security professional on site, that person can handle direction of the regular security force and the special incident response plan. If not, a responsible member of the management staff must be expressly designated to be responsible for the response plan.

Establishment of Continuing Communications

Contact between Offender and the Company. A method of communication between the offender and the company is needed and is usually developed during the investigation or at suspension or termination proceedings. It should take the form of a formal written or documented verbal request, acknowledged by the threatening employee or a representative, not to contact anyone in the company except a designated individual. The designated individual will usually be a human resources specialist who has been trained in handling difficult employees and has been instructed to communicate all contact with the offender to the DMR or IMT.

If the offender is not an employee of the company, it may still be appropriate under certain circumstances to limit contact to only one person authorized to speak for the company. In those circumstances, this contact individual could be any employee of the company, possibly one responsible for the area or function that is the focus of the offender's anger. Whoever is selected must have the emotional and psychological fortitude to handle these contacts well, even though they will become burdensome over time.

Offender Contacts with Other Employees of the Company. As part of the communication process, other company employees who might have contact with the offender should be asked to report the substance and tone of such contact to the DMR. The continuous flow of information about contacts with the offender is essential for understanding the offender's changing perception of the situation and the resulting potential for violence.

Communication within the Protective Team. Communications procedures must allow for radio communication between regular and any special security elements. Security should have an exclusive radio frequency. But in those situations where regular security must share radio frequencies with other users, cellular telephones can be assigned to the special security group for the period of heightened alert.

Public Emergency Services Personnel. Communication should be assured between any public emergency service personnel (fire, police, paramedics, etc.) and the regular security force. This could be as simple as handing the responding units a radio that works on the facility security frequency or assigning them a security force member for liaison, or as complex as having programmable radios on site with frequencies to match those of the incoming agencies. The simpler the approach, the better the solution. In situations involving special security personnel, the interaction with responding public emergency service personnel should still be the responsibility of the regular security force.

Plan for Situation Reassessment

Monitoring the ongoing actions of the offender and periodic reassessment of the situation are essential in resolving the incident. People who might have continuing contacts with the offender must be taught how to handle them and to report the results to the DMR. The IMT should conduct periodic reassessments, either based on significant changes in the nature of the offender's contacts or on agreed time intervals, until the incident is judged to be over. This process could take up to a year — longer in some cases — to resolve.

Physical surveillance of the offender should not be employed without careful consideration. The reasons normally given to place the offender under surveillance are:

- To identify possible co-conspirators and allies
- To allow protective personnel to know the offender's whereabouts so that they can be aware of any attempt to initiate a violent act

There are some serious concerns about surveillance, however. The first is the cost in manpower and dollars of an adequate surveillance — a minimum of two cars and four personnel assigned 24 hours per day are normally necessary. The second and more important consideration is that surveillance exposes the company to increased liability if the surveillance triggers a violent event. An individual who may commit violence in the workplace often has some paranoid and/or delusional thoughts. The sudden recognition that he or she is under surveillance may so seriously agitate the individual as to cause an incident that might not otherwise occur. Finally, surveillance in most cases is not necessary because the responsibility of the company is to protect individuals while at work and the implementation of an adequate protective plan will allow response time should the offender enter company property.

Phased Withdrawal of Protective Personnel

There should be gradual withdrawal of special or extra security personnel, based on the assessment of the potential for violence. The nature and intensity of ongoing contacts with the offender will dictate the withdrawal of security. More frequent contacts and increasing intensity will require sustained or increased security, while less frequent contacts and decreasing intensity will allow reduced security. Consideration must be given to decreasing security in a way that allows the protected personnel to readjust to a "regular" work environment. Too quick withdrawal of special protective personnel has caused productivity disruptions that outweighed the cost of continuing the protection.

And, of course, communication with protected personnel is essential to facilitate the transition from a climate of special protection to a more normal level of security.

Selected Bibliography

Combating Workplace Violence: Guidelines for Employers and Law Enforcement; 1997; International Association of Chiefs of Police, Washington, D.C.

*Dealing with Workplace Violence: A Guide for Agency Planners;*1998; U.S. Office of Personnel Management, Washington, D.C.

Early Warning, Timely Response — A Guide to Safe Schools; 1998; U.S. Department of Education, Washington, D.C., http://www.ed.gov/offices/OSERS/OSEP/earlywrn.html.

Guidelines for Preventing Workplace Violence for Health Care and Social Service Workers; 1996; Occupational Safety and Health Administration, U.S. Department of Labor, Washington, D.C., http://www/osha.gov/oshpubs/.

Preventing Workplace Violence; 1998; American Federation of State, County and Municipal Employees, Washington, D.C.

Violence and Mental Illness; 1998; American Psychiatric Association, Washington, D.C., http://www.psych.org/.

Violence in the Workplace: Risk Factors and Prevention Strategies; 1996; National Institute for Occupational Safety and Health, Washington, D.C., http://www.cdc.gov/niosh/homocide.html.

Workplace Violence, 1992–96; 1998; Bureau of Statistics, U.S. Department of Justice, Washington, D.C.

Periodicals

Security Management; American Society for Industrial Security; Alexandria, VA.
  — Albrecht, Steven; The Public Challenge of Private Problems; May 1996.
  — Arnheim, Louise A.; Mastering Security Amid Merger Mania; February 1999.
  — Caldwell, George E., CPP; Workplace Crime and Violence Mirrors a Troubled Society; September 1997.
  — Carpenter, John J.; Trial by Fire; May 1998.
  — Gargan, Joseph P.; Stop Stalkers before They Strike; February 1994.
  — Hermann, Martin B.; When Strikes Turn Violent; March 1995.
  — Janes, Timothy T., CPP; Anatomy of a Successful Intervention; April 1996.
  — Johnson, Dennis L.; A Team Approach to Threat Assessment; September 1994.
  — Johnson, Dennis L., Kiehlbauch, John B., and Kinney, Joseph A.; Break the Cycle of Violence; February 1994.
  — Koch, Noel; Will Workplace Violence Broaden Corporate Liability?; August 1995
  — Lindsey, Dennis; Of Sound Mind? Evaluating the Workforce; September 1994.
  — Lynch, Michael O.; An Analysis of Incident Response Teams; October 1998.
  — Mattman, Jurg W.; What's Growing in the Corporate Culture?; November 1995.
  — Michelman, Bonnie S., CPP, Robb, Nancy P., and Coviello, Leah Marie; A Comprehensive Approach to Workplace Violence; July 1998.

— Post, Jerrold M.; More than a Figure of Speech; December 1996.
— School Safety at a Premium; March 1999.
— Sollars, Robert D.; The Taming of the Workplace; March 1996.
— Waxman, Harvey S.; Putting Workplace Violence in Perspective; September 1995.

Security Technology & Design; Locksmith Publishing, Park Ridge, IL
— Hamit, Francis; Cyberstalking: Harassment Goes Online; April 1999.
— Walton, J. Branch; Violence in the Workplace is Not the Exception Anymore; February 1997.

Security Products, Stevens Communications Inc., Dallas, TX.
— McIndoe, John; School Security, Making the Grade; June 1999.

Other Resources

Department of Justice, National Criminal Justice Reference Service
   http://www.ncjrs.org

National Institute for Occupational Safety and Health
   http://www.cdc.gov/niosh/homepage.html

Occupational Safety and Health Administration
   http://www.osha.gov

Partnerships Against Violence
   http://www.pavnet.org

U.S. Department of Education
   http://www.ed.gov

U.S. Office of Personnel Management
   http://www.opm.gov

APPENDIX A
MODEL POLICY FOR WORKPLACE THREATS AND VIOLENCE

Nothing is more important to [ORGANIZATION] than the safety and security of its personnel. Violence, threats, harassment, intimidation and other disruptive behavior against employees, visitors, guests or other individuals by anyone on [ORGANIZATION] controlled property will not be tolerated.

All reports of incidents of such behavior will be taken seriously and will be dealt with appropriately. The behavior can include oral or written statements, gestures or expressions that communicate a direct or indirect threat of physical harm. Individuals who commit such acts may be removed from [ORGANIZATION] premises and may be required to remain off-premises pending the completion of an investigation of the incident. Should an investigation substantiate that violations of this policy have occurred, [ORGANIZATION] will initiate a decisive and appropriate response. This response may include, but is not limited to, suspension and/or termination of any business relationship, reassignment of job duties, suspension or termination of employment, and/or seeking arrest and prosecution of the person or persons involved.

ASSET PROTECTION AND SECURITY MANAGEMENT HANDBOOK

In carrying out all [ORGANIZATION] policies, it is essential that all personnel understand that no existing [ORGANIZATION] policy, practice or procedure should be interpreted to prohibit decisions designed to prevent a threat from being carried out, a violent act from occurring or a life-threatening situation from developing.

All [ORGANIZATION] personnel are responsible for notifying the management representative designated below of any violence, threats, harassment, intimidation or other disruptive behavior when that behavior is job related or might be carried out on a company controlled site, or is connected to company employment. Employees are responsible for making this report regardless of the nature of the relationship between the individual who initiated the inappropriate behavior and the person or persons who were the focus of the behavior.

The [ORGANIZATION] obligation to provide a safe workplace and protect employees from threats to their safety cannot be effectively accomplished unless [ORGANIZATION] is informed about individuals who have been ordered by the courts, or other legally constituted entities, to remain away from [ORGANIZATION] company locations. All individuals who apply for or obtain a protective or restraining order which lists company locations as protected areas, are required to provide to the designated management representative: (1) a copy of the petition and declarations used to seek the order, (2) a copy of any temporary protective or restraining order which is granted, and (3) a copy of any protective or restraining order which is made permanent. [ORGANIZATION] understands the sensitivity of the information requested and has developed confidentiality procedures which recognize the privacy of the reporting employee(s).

The designated management representative is:

Name:

Position:

Telephone:

E-mail:

Office Mail:

APPENDIX B
MINIMUM QUALIFICATIONS FOR OUTSIDE CONSULTING TEAM MEMBERS

1. *Security and Investigations Professional:*
   a. Appropriately licensed and insured
   b. Proven ability to provide in-depth multi-state or multi-jurisdictional background investigations in a 24- to 72-hour turnaround

c. Past experience in providing threat analysis and assessment in a workplace-related context
   d. Prior experience in providing and supervising armed and appropriately trained protective personnel
   e. Proven ability to work with multi-disciplinary teams on protection-related issues
   f. Proven ability to interface effectively with law enforcement on threat and violence-related issues
2. *Licensed Psychological or Psychiatric Professional:*
   a. Appropriately licensed at a Ph.D. or M.D. level, and insured
   b. Past experience in providing threat analysis and assessment in a work-related context
   c. Substantial experience in interaction with violent individuals
   d. Experience in trauma management
   e. Experience in treating workplace-related stress, productivity, morale and substance abuse issues
   f. Proven ability to work with multidisciplinary teams in a work-related context
   g. Experience in the involuntary commitment of individuals who are assessed to be a danger to themselves and/or others
   h. Experience in working with law enforcement
3. *Additional Legal Support:*
   a. Admitted to the state bar and insured
   b. Extensive experience in labor law-related issues concerning employment and employee rights
   c. Substantial experience in defending companies in employment-related cases
   d. Substantial experience in seeking and obtaining restraining and/or protective orders

APPENDIX C
NORMAL INCIDENT ASSESSMENT/RESOLUTION PROCESS

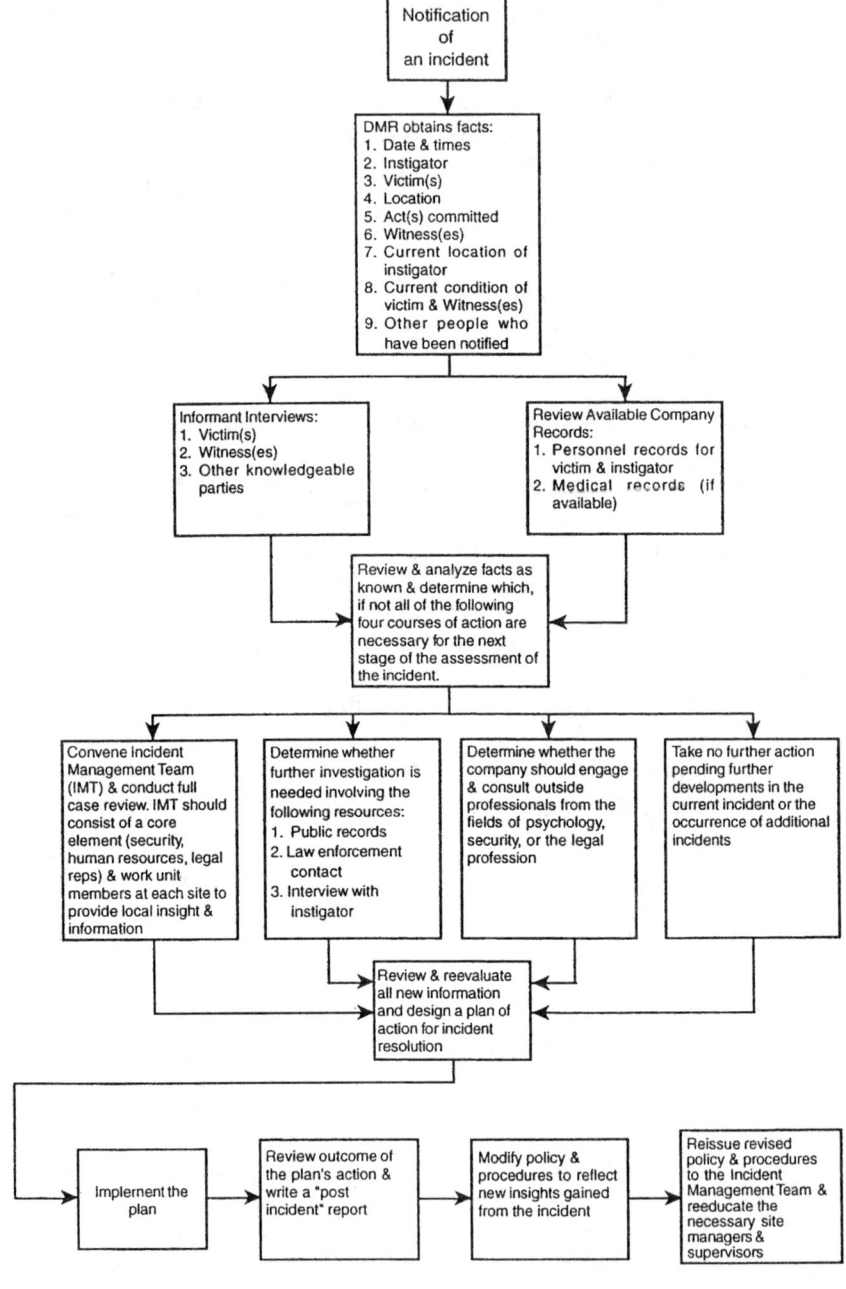

Index

A

Absenteeism, 507
Academic bodies, UL standards and, 113
Access control, 187–210
  authorized access control, 190–193
    access control sub-system, 191
    equipment requirements, 192–193
    large systems, 190–191
    operational requirements, 191–192
  basic access control objectives, 187
  coded card technology, 193–198
    barium ferrite, 194
    biometric technology, 195–196
    dielectric readers, 196
    embossing readers, 196
    hollerith readers, 196
    magnetic stripe cards, 193
    optical character readers, 196–197
    proximity/contact readers, 194–195
    radio frequency readers, 195
    resonant circuits, 195
    smart card, 197–198
    watermark magnetics, 193–194
    Wiegand wire, 194
  distributed intelligence systems, 198
  granting/denying entry, 187–190
    exit control, 188–190
    locks, 187–188
  natural, 357, 384
  special access features and applications, 198–205
    anti-passback, 198–199
    dressing rooms at performing art centers, 205
    elevator control, 203–204
    gatehouse, 200–201
    hotels and motels, 205
    janitor's privileges, 204
    mantrap, 199–200
    monitoring prisoners, 205
    office equipment, 204
    personal equipment at work, 204
    personal safety, 205
    sally port, 200
    tools and inventory, 204
    two-man rule, 199
  vehicle parking garages, 201–203
  weapons and contraband screening, 205–209
    explosives detectors, 209
    organizations associated with smart cards, 210
    physical configuration, 206
    screening policies and procedures, 206–207
    x-ray inspection, 208–209
Acoustic glass break sensors, 122
Acoustic sensors, 121
Activity log, automatic, 254
ADA, *see* Americans with Disabilities Act
Administrative expertise, doctrine of, 432
Admission of guilt, 501
Age Discrimination in Employment Act of 1967, 448
Agency, 440
Air conditioning breakdown, protection of information systems in event of, 284
Air transport industry, screening of baggage in, 205
Alarm(s), 405
  emergency, 202
  local, advantages and disadvantages of, 154
  positive feature to, 154
  termination(s)
    central station, 154
    combination, 158
    fire department, 156
    local, 153
    methods of, 153
    proprietary, 157, 159
  transmission, 131
Alarm sensors, 111–151
  categories of sensors, 116–132
    alarm transmission and control panels, 131
    audio sensors, 128–129
    capacitance sensors, 128
    dual-technology sensors, 123
    electromechanical sensors, 123–126
    glass break sensors, 120–123
    microwave sensors, 127–128

531

other sensors, 130–131
passive infrared sensors, 116–120
photoelectric sensors, 129
shock and vibration sensors, 128
ultrasonic sensors, 126–127
federal specification components for interior alarm systems, 140–151
sensor applications, 111–116
    ASTM standards, 114–115
    emerging technology, 138
    fixed-temperature sensors, 135–136
    other standards and specifications, 115–116
    rate-of-rise sensors, 136
    sensors for fire detection, 132–139
    sensor types and selection, 134–135
    smoke or combustion product sensors, 136–137
    stages of fire, 133–134
    UL standards, 113–114
    water flow indicators, 137–138
Alarm systems, federal specification components for interior, 140–151
    applicable documents, 141–142
    American Society for Testing and Materials, 142
    government publications, 141–142
    notes, 150–151
    intended use, 150
    ordering data, 150–151
    qualification, 150
    preparation for delivery, 149–150
    civil agency marking, 150
    preservation, packaging, packing, and marking, 149–150
    quality assurance provisions, 148–149
    components and material inspection, 148
    inspection for acceptance, 148–149
    inspection of preparation for delivery, 149
    inspection responsibility, 148
    qualification, 149
    requirements, 142–148
    access control units, 146
    annunciator units, 144–145
    circuit supervision units, 145–146
    detectors, 143–144
    electromagnetic radiation interference, 148
    electronic components, 143
    equipment enclosures, 143
    general, 142–143
    identification markings, 147
    lightning protection, 148
    parts and materials, 143
    primary power requirements, 146–147
    spare parts, 148
    technical manuals and operator instructions, 147
    workmanship, 147–148
    scope and classification, 140–141
    classification, 140–141
    scope, 140
ALE, see Annualized Loss Expectancy
All-metal door, 64
American Bar Association, 471
American National Red Cross, 226, 227
American Society for Industrial Security (ASIS), 459, 463, 471
    Code of Ethics, 472, 478, 479
    Rules of Professional Conduct, 473–475, 476, 483
American Society for Testing and Materials (ASTM), 114, 439
Americans with Disabilities Act (ADA), 98, 195, 508, 207, 230, 450
American Standard for Computer Information Interchange (ASCII), 248
Annualized Loss Expectancy (ALE), 275, 276, 291
Anti-discrimination, 450
Anti-passback, 198
Antisocial behavior, 4
Antitrust, Federal Sentencing Guidelines for, 396
Apparent authority, 442
Application-specific integrated circuit (ASIC), 118
Armed attack, 213
Arrest(s)
    citizen's, 411
    definition of, 406
    warrant, 407
    warrantless, 407
Arson, 213, 373, 403
Artificial intelligence, 171
ASCII, see American Standard for Computer Information Interchange
ASIC, see Application-specific integrated circuit
ASIS, see American Society for Industrial Security
Assault(s), 361, 392, 508
    cost of doing business driven up by, 359

Index

preventing, 370
workplace, 505
Asset(s)
  corporate, access to vital, 56
  cost of lost, 31
  definition of, 2
  information, protection of, 375, 376
  internal sources of information about, 311
  protection, relationship between criminal law and, 399
  recoveries, 46
  vulnerability, 192, 288
Assets protection, 1–17
  basic considerations, 4–8
    communicating of plan, 8
    countermeasures planning, 4–5
    management support, 5–8
    statutory and regulatory requirements, 8
  countermeasures, 9–13
    hardware, 10–11
    people, 9–10
    software, 11–13
  definition of, 2–4
  department, database fields, 25
  management function, 1–2
  practice, violation of, 13
  procedures, 9
  professionals, 391
  self-inspection and protection of assets, 15–17
  systems approach, 8–9
  system test, 13–14
ASTM, *see* American Society for Testing and Materials
ATM, *see* Automatic teller machine
Attack(s)
  detection of systematic, 281
  hacker, 300
  Morris worm, 300
Audio sensors, 128
Audit(s)
  compliance, 298
  trail(s), 297
    circumventing of, 282
    integrity, 298
    operational use of, 298
Authentication server, 273
Automatic dialers, 157
Automatic teller machine (ATM), 257, 337
Awareness presentations, 12
Awning windows, 65

B

Background investigations, 484
Backscatter technology, 208
Backup computers, 218
BAI, *see* Behavior Analysis Interview
Balanced pressure sensor, 130
Ballasts, 329
Banking, requirement to success of, 195
Bank vaults, 222
Barricade/hostage situation, 213, 214, 220
Barrier(s), *see also* Structural barriers
  categories, 56
  definition, 55
  highway median, 76
  hydraulic impact, 77
  light vehicle penetration of, 76
  vehicle, 75, 76
Barrium ferrite, 194
Batch processing mainframe systems, 258
Battery, 446, 508
Behavioral indications, evaluation of, 492
Behavior Analysis Interview (BAI), 496, 497
Behavior assessments, accuracy of, 491
Behavior-provoking questions, 497
Biased switches, 125
Biometric devices, 195
Biometric readers, 190
Biometric systems, 167
Black-and-white cameras, 337
Blast
  damage, 73, 74
  relative resistance to, 74
  wave, phases of, 73
Block Watches, 343
Bomb
  incident, 213, 214, 230
  kinds of damage produced by, 73
  protection, 70
  squad, 219
  threat, 4, 456
Breaking strike, 103
Break-ins, 361
Bribery, 21, 396
Brightness, 328
Brisant explosives, 74
Broken window theory, 344
BRPs, *see* Business resumption plans
Building(s)
  codes, local, 70
  construction process, 360
  high-rise, vulnerability of roof in, 61
  openings, 62
  weakest links of, 364

533

Building surfaces, 57–60
  ceilings, 60
  concrete structures, 58
  design criteria for, 70
  evaluation of, 60
  exterior walls, 57
  floors, 58
  interior walls, 58–60
  roofs, 57
Burden of proof, 303
Burglary
  cost of doing business driven up by, 359
  discovered, 440
Buried detector, 130
Burn victims, 227
Business(es)
  enterprise, hazards faced by, 2
  law, 431
  most common assets to, 374
  resumption plans (BRPs), 282
  risk, 20

C

California penal code, 426
Camera(s)
  black-and-white, 337
  CCTV, amount of light needed by, 326
  color, 336
  tagging of, 204
Candor, definition of, 477
Canine, detection reliability of, 209
Capable guardian, concept of, 349
Capacitance sensors, 128
Capital costs, 47
Card
  access, recorded information on, 198
  reader systems, 190, 191–192
Cardiopulmonary resuscitation (CPR), 227
Casement windows, 65
Cash
  register shortages, 419
  reserves, 31
Catastrophic problems, 3, 4
CCTV, see Closed-circuit television
CDR disks, 298
CD-ROM, 252
Cellular telephone, 131, 222
Central processing unit (CPU), 248
  instruction set, 250
  memory size, 251
Central station
  alarm termination, 154
  methods of receiving signals, 155

  service, radio transmissions to, 155
Certified Protection Professional (CPP)
  program, 459
CERTs, see Computer Emergency Response
  Teams
CFT, see Corrected Color Temperature
Change key, operation of, 87
Check kiting, 419
Chemical sensors, 131
Child care centers, 216
Chip
  fabrication plant, 251
  number of transistors on, 251
Circuit systems, 173
Citizen's arrest, 411
Citizen's rights, old Prussian idea of, 455
Civil actions, 5, 311
Civil code, 429
Civil damage action, financial loss in, 410
Civil disorders, 213
Civil disturbance, 20, 21
Civil law, 429–450
  civil common law, 433–445
    agency, 440–445
    major areas of civil common law,
      434–440
  civil rights, 447–450
    civil rights at common law, 447–448
    civil rights under statute, 448–449
    discrimination based on disability,
      450
    trend in civil rights, 450
  definition, 429
  major branches, 429
  statutory law, 430–433
    federal statutory law, 430
    state statutory law, 430–433
  torts, 445–447
    negligence, 474
    willful torts, 445–447
Civil rights
  law, 431
  trend in, 450
Civil Rights Act of 1964, 448
Civil statute law, 433
Clones, 257
Closed-circuit television (CCTV), 10, 130,
  296, 342, 371
  access control installation, 162
  assessment, 382
  camera(s)
    activation of when PIR is triggered,
      118
    amount of light needed by, 326

Index

control methods, 161
installation, 190
placement of, 200, 203
use of to identify perpetrator, 106
use of to monitor movement, 109
function, placement of trees and, 367
monitoring, 382
personnel reductions and, 161
recorder, 163
surveillance, 44, 385
switcher, 171
tape recordings, 191
use of as deterrent to improper activity, 511
CMT, *see* Crisis management team
Coded card technology, 193–198
dielectric readers, 196
embossing readers, 196
hollerith readers, 196
optical character readers, 196–197
smart card, 197–198
Code of Ethics, ASIS, 472, 478, 479
Color Rendition Index (CRI), 328, 336
Columbine shooting incident, 224
Combination lock(s)
dial-type, 86
electronic dial-type, 89
number of tumblers in, 88
theoretical maximum number of combinations, 88
Combustion product sensors, 136
Commercial espionage, 373
Communication(s)
chain, structured supervisory, 461
effective, 304
gap, 458
interception of, 414
legally privileged, 485
links, interruption of, 211
Company, *see also* Organization
assets, protection of, 380
newsletter, 12
Compartmentation, 56
Compensation, unjust, 480
Competitive intelligence, 20
Compliance
audits, 298
program, requirements, 7
standards, 8
Computer(s)
abuse, 4
backup, 218
desktop, 268
digital, characteristics of, 248

Emergency Response Teams (CERTs), 300
hardware
fragility of, 270
multiprocessing, 253
installation, fire detection subsystem in, 41
Internet-compatible, 265
laptop, 258
mainframe, 255
operators, programmers, sharing of passwords by, 282
peripherals, 255
personal, 256
room, control of physical access to, 270
system
designers, optimism of, 254
failure, 213
Computing, stored program, 249
Concerted efforts, 478
Concierge
stations, 343
surveillance by, 351
Concrete
block(s)
barriers, 67
shapes and sizes of, 71
wall, 58, 73
highway median barrier, 76
structures, vulnerability of, 58
Confession
oral, 501
written, 502
Confidential communication, 485
Conflicts of interest, 4, 20, 21
Consequent cost, 31
Construction fraud, 304
Consulting opinion rule, 480
Consumer
organizations, UL standards and, 113
reporting agency (CRA), 320, 321, 322
Contact microphones, 415
Contingency plans, types of, 214
Continuity of operations plan (COOP), 214, 222
Continuous power, 173, 175, 176
Contraband screening, 205
Contract(s)
custodial staff, turnover in, 26
express, 435
guard, 442
implied, 435
investigations
advantages of, 308

535

disadvantages of, 308
investigators, 309
law, 434
organized labor, 303
security service personnel, 10
subject matter of, 437
warranty, 438
Contractors, access to information by, 1
Contribution, doctrine of, 444
Controlled Substances Act, 420
Controlled zones, 365
Controlling persons, criminal penalties for, 6
Conventional risk, 20
Conversion, 446
COOP, *see* Continuity of operations plan
Corporate assets, access to vital, 56
Corporate security staff, return on expenditures of, 47
Corrected Color Temperature (CCT), 327
Corruption, prevention of, 481
Cost(s)
    abatement, 32
    avoidance, 42, 43
    capital, 47
    consequent, 31
    -effective, definition of, 279
    insurance, 43
    justification, 30
    -of-loss formula, 32
    lost income, 31
    security, quantified, 47
    of security program (CSP), 47
    temporary substitute, components of, 31
    types of, 30
Counterintelligence, covert penetration of a target in, 55
Countermeasures, 9–13
    criteria
        approximate cost, 39
        degree of reliability, 39
        delay, 39
        validity, 39
    hardware, 10–11
    people, 9–10
    planning, 4
    software, 11–13
Court decisions, laws evolving with, 416
Courts-martial, use of polygraph evidence in, 425
Covert surveillance, 336
C-4 plastic explosive, 209
CPP program, *see* Certified Protection Professional program
CPR, *see* Cardiopulmonary resuscitation
CPTED, *see* Crime Prevention Through Environmental Design
CPU, *see* Central processing unit
CRA, *see* Consumer reporting agency
Crash bar, 106
Credit bureaus, 320
CRI, *see* Color Rendition Index
Crime(s), 20, 21, 391
    classification of, 390
    codes, 389
    controlling facilitators of, 351
    decision to commit, 348
    -environment theory, 341
    federal, definition of, 391
    incentive for, 351
    obligation to report, 392
    organized, 23
    patterns, neighborhood, 363
    prevention
        education, 347
        knowledge, 347
        theory, 348
        tool, 345
    situational, 347, 350
    state, definition of, 391
    true nature of, 341
    white-collar, 350
Crime Prevention Through Environmental Design (CPTED), 341–387
    basic crime prevention assumptions, 346–347
    concepts of risk management, 357–359
    considerations regarding U.S. federal buildings, 381–384
        application of GSA security standards to all building types, 383–384
        General Services Administration security standards, 381–383
    contemporary thinking on crime and criminals, 347–357
        concept of capable guardian, 349
        CPTED survey, 355–357
        criminal choice, 349–350
        defensible space, 353–354
        potential offenders' perspective, 352–353
        situational crime prevention, 350–352
        target selection, 348–349
        Tim Crowe and CPTED, 354
    design considerations for industrial buildings, 372–373
    design considerations for office buildings, 374–381
        protection of information, 376–378

protection of people, 374–376
protection of property, 378–381
fundamentals, 342–344
graphics and signage for crime prevention and environmental security, 384–386
reducing crime through physical design, 359–363
architectural planning process, 360–362
effective access control, 362–363
planning of building, 359
security design criteria for parking facilities, 367–372
site development and security zoning, 363–367
theory, history and practice, 344–346
Criminal codes, 389
Criminal complaint, goal of, 5
Criminal facilitation, 412
Criminal intent, 392
Criminal law, United States, 389–427
case or decisional law, 398–399
deception detection instruments, 416–426
admissibility of polygraph results in evidence, 424–425
broad interpretations of EPPA, 417–424
federal polygraph legislation, 416–417
voice stress analyzer, 425–426
definition and classification of crimes, 390–398
arraignment, 394–395
confinement, 398
criminal intent, 392–393
definition of federal crimes, 391
definition of state crimes, 391
essential character of crime, 391–392
establishing guilt for crime, 393
federal criminal law, 390
formal charge, 394
sentence, 395–398
trial, 395
federal and state constitutions, 389
important procedural considerations, 406–412
arrests, 406–409
entrapment, 412
interviews and interrogations, 409–410
searches and seizures, 410–412

relevance to asset protection, 399–405
crimes based upon damage or threat of damage to property, 405
crimes based upon force or threats of force against persons, 402–403
crimes based upon theft or larceny, 401–402
crimes based upon unauthorized entry or presence, 400–401
permissible use of force, 403–405
specific criminal statutes of security interest, 412–416
eavesdropping statutes, 413, 414
Economic Espionage Act, 412–413
number of government interceptions, 416
state laws, 416
summary of federal law, 414–416
statutory law, 389–390
Criminal negligence, 393, 403
Criminal solicitation, 412
Crisis Communications Creed, 225
Crisis management
objectives of, 212
team (CMT), 219, 220
Criticality
approaches to, 34
ratings
fatal, 33
moderately serious, 33
relatively unimportant, 33
seriousness unknown, 33
symbols assigned to, 34
very serious, 33
Cryptography
government restrictions on exporting of, 299
military-sensitive, 299
CSP, *see* Costs of security program
Culpability score, 7, 396
Custodial staff, turnover in contract, 26
Customs violations, 407
Cylinder locks, 90, 98

D

Damage, blast, 73, 74
Damaging statement, 446
Data
backup, 271, 272
entry clerks, 253, 254
loss, 297
performance penalties related to encrypting, 294

537

relevant, definition of, 516
security, 269
storage hardware, 253, 295
-tampering attack, 270
Database
reporting software, 25
sabotage, 271
Daubert v. Merrell Dow Pharmaceuticals, Inc., 424
Deadbolt, 100
electric, 101, 102
vulnerability of to attack by force, 92
Deadlocking latch, vulnerability of to attack by force, 92
Deadly weapons, use of, 480
Death, wrongful, 395
Deception in interviews and interrogations, detection of, 491–503
behavior analysis interview, 496–499
nonverbal responses, 494–496
activities suggesting deception, 495
comparative postures, 495–496
eye contact, 496
preliminary cautions, 492
Reid nine steps of interrogation, 499–502
converting oral confession, 501–502
handling denials, handling details, 500
handling suspect's passive mood, handling suspect's passive mood, 500
having suspect relate details, 501
keeping suspect's attention, keeping suspect's attention, 500
overcoming objections, overcoming objections, 500
presenting alternative question, presenting alternative question, 500–501
theme development, 499
types of responses, 491–492
verbal responses, 492–494
Deceptograph, 417
Declaration of war, 290
Decryption, 294
Defamation, 314
Defamatory statements, 441
Defense Investigative Service training manual, 89
Defensible space, 345, 346, 353, 378
Delayed egress locking system, 106
Department of Defense (DoD), 115
Designated Management Representative (DMR), 513

Desktop computers, 268
Detector(s)
buried, 130
explosives, 209
flame, 134
foil, 123
loop, 201
metal, 206, 207
screen, 125
smoke, 132
wire, 125
Diagnostic opinion, 417
Dial-type combination locks, 86
Dielectric readers, 196
Digital computers, characteristics, 248
Digital data, encoding of, 247
Digital photo badging, 167
Digital systems, estimating cost of, 165
Direct costs, 30
Disaster
control organization, 241, 242, 243
recovery, items to consider in planning for, 236–237
scene, photographic coverage of for insurance purposes, 226
Discrimination, 507Discovery proceedings, 311
Discriminator logic, 126
Dishonesty, 3, 481
judgment of, 481
losses resulting from, 12
Disk drive files, backups, 255
Distributed intelligence systems, 198
Distributed processing systems, 267, 268
DMR, *see* Designated Management Representative
DoD, *see* Department of Defense
Dog, detection reliability of, 209
Door
all-metal, 64
hinge pin removal, 64
industrial pedestrian, penetration times for standard, 63
locks, 97
openers, activation of when PIR is triggered, 118
preparation, cylinder and mortise locks with typical, 98
vault, time lock on, 61
Doppler effect, 126
Double-door booth control, 168
Double-hung windows, 65
Doubtful law, 399
Dropped-bit errors, 289

Index

DSS, *see* ERDA Division of Safeguards and Security
Dual-technology sensors, 123
Due process, violation of, 405
Dumb terminals, 260, 264
Duress code, 131
Dynamic risk, definition of, 357
Dynamite, 74

E

Earthquake, 4, 212, 213, 290
EAS, *see* Electronic article surveillance
Eavesdropping, 413
Economic Espionage Act, 412
ECPA, *see* Electronic Communications Privacy Act
EDP, *see* Electronic data processing
Education law, 431
EEOC, *see* Equal Employment Opportunity Commission
Electric deadbolt, 101, 102
Electric latch, 101, 102
Electric lockset, 104, 105
Electric strike, 102, 103
Electrified locking mechanisms, types of, 100
Electromagnetic interference (EMI), 131
Electromagnetic lock, 106, 108, 109, 189
Electromechanical sensors, 123
Electronic article surveillance (EAS), 204
Electronic Communications Privacy Act (ECPA), 414
Electronic data processing (EDP), 247
Electronic dial-type combination lock, 89
Electronic message delivery systems, 415
Electronic sensors, integration of, 158
Electronic surveillance, laws regarding, 413
Electronic touchpads, 187
Elevator control, use of coded cards for, 203
Embezzlement, 269, 418
Embossing readers, 196
Emergency
  alarms, 202
  medical services (EMS), 227
  normalcy after, 212
  power, 172
  response agencies, 224
  situations, potential, 5
  succession provisions, 221
Emergency planning, 211–246
  advance planning, 211–217
    components of emergency plan, 217
    development of plan, 215–216
  objectives of emergency planning and crisis management, 212
  planning formats, 214–215
  planning process, 216
  special planning needs, 216–217
  stages of incident, 212
  types of contingency plans, 214
  types of threats and contingencies, 213
  after plan is written, 234–237
    keeping plan up-to-date, 235–236
    training, drills and exercises, 234–235
  alert and warning system, 230
  company disaster control program
    policy, 240–244
    general, 240–242
    procedure, 243–244
  emergency evacuation, 230–231
  emergency medical services, 227–228
  emergency shutdown and restoration, 231–233
  external liaison and coordination, 223–225
  family/victim support, 226–227
  first step, 211
  other considerations, 234
  planning issues and considerations, 217–234
    command/management and control, 219–223
    planning assumptions, 218–219
    priorities, 217–218
  public affairs/media relations, 225–226
  resources and logistics equipment and services, 244–246
    equipment to consider, 244–245
    services to consider, 245–246
  security and fire protection, 228–229
  transportation, 233–234
Emhart high-security cylinder, 84
EMI, *see* Electromagnetic interference
Emotional problems, 4
Employee(s)
  accused, 402
  arbitrary controls and, 11
  arrest and prosecution of, 456
  background investigations of, 26
  disciplinary action against, 411
  discussion sessions, 232
  equipment, tagging of, 204
  identification cards, 510
  interviews with, 458
  joint venture, 1
  methods used to inform, 12

539

morale, 29
offender contact with other, 524
parking lots, 373
polygraph tests given to prospective, 420
suggestions, 13
surveillance by, 351
terminated, 297
theft, 359, 373
union, 220
Employee Polygraph Protection Act of 1988 (EPPA), 416, 425
　broad interpretations of, 417
　disclosure of information, 423
　enforcement, 423
　exemptions, 418
　prohibitions, 417
　qualifications of examiners, 423
　rights of examinee, 422
Employee Retirement Income Security Act (ERISA), 396
EMS, see Emergency medical services
Encryption
　smart card, 198
　software, 294
　system standards, 287
Entrapment, 412
Environmental criminology, 347, 386
Environmental violations, 7, 396
EPPA, see Employee Polygraph Protection Act of 1988
Equal Employment Opportunity Commission (EEOC), 449
Equal Pay Act of 1963, 448
ERDA Division of Safeguards and Security (DSS), 115
Erie v. Tompkins, 433
ERISA, see Employee Retirement Income Security Act
Espionage
　commercial, 373
　industrial, 20, 359
Ethics in security profession, 469–489
　code of ethics of American Society for Industrial Security, 472
　definition of professional ethics, 469–470
　need for professional ethics, 469–470
　professional responsibility matches professional recognition, 470
　practical application of professional ethics, 472–488
　professional society, 470–472
　security profession, 470
European civil law, 429

Evacuation drills, 234
Evidence
　admissibility of polygraph results in, 424
　point of origin for, 495
　polygraph, 425
　preponderance of, 395
Excel, 257
Exemplary award of damages, 447
Exercise planning issues, 236
Exit
　control, 188
　hardware, 106, 107, 189
Explosion, 12, 74, 213
Explosive(s)
　brisant, 74
　detection, 131, 209
　intensity of, 74
　plastic, 209
Express contract, 435
Extortion, 403
Ex-wave CCD, 336
Eye contact, 492, 496

F

FAA, see Federal Aviation Administration
Face scanner, 195
Facial expressions, 492
Facial recognition, 167
Facility vulnerability, 293
Factory Mutual (FM) requirements, 157
Factual objections, 500
Fail safe locking mechanism, 101
Fail secure lock, 101
Fair Credit Reporting Act (FCRA), 8, 320–322, 510
Fairness, definition of, 477
False alarms, 111, 121
False imprisonment, 314, 445, 446
FBI
　headquarters, windows at, 66
　Uniform Crime Report, 347
FCC, see Federal Communications Commission
FCPA, see Foreign Corrupt Practices Act
FCRA, see Fair Credit Reporting Act
Federal Aviation Administration (FAA), 206
Federal Communications Commission (FCC), 415
Federal crimes, definition of, 391
Federal Emergency Management Agency (FEMA), 226
Federal Organizational Sentencing Guidelines, 7

Index

Federal Rules of Evidence 702, 424
Federal Sentencing Guidelines, 396, 398
Federal Trade Commission, 320
Feedback, methods of obtaining, 458
Felony, 391, 408
FEMA, *see* Federal Emergency Management Agency
File server
    data, access to, 262
    messages broadcast on, 264
Final report, 315
Fingerprints, 167, 190, 195
Finished goods inventory, theft from, 37
Fire(s), 213
    code issues, 170
    department alarm termination, 156
    detection, 41, 132
    exits, 379
    flame stage, 134
    heat stage, 134
    incipient stage, 134
    loss, 438
    occurrence, probability of, 27
    protection of information systems in event of, 284
    safety applications, vapor detection for, 138
    sensors, factors to consider when selecting, 135
    smoldering stage, 134
    stages of, 133, 134
    terms, glossary of, 182–185
Firewall, typical, 300
Fitness for duty report, 519
Fixed-temperature sensors, 135
Flame detectors, 134
Flaming, 301
Flood, 213
    major, 212
    protection of information systems in event of, 284
Floors, 57, 58
Floppy diskettes, 257
FM requirements, *see* Factory Mutual requirements
Foil detector, 123
Foreign Corrupt Practices Act (FCPA), 6, 397
FPCA, *see* Foreign Corrupt Practices Act
Fraud, 4, 249, 285, 446
    construction, 304
    Federal Sentencing Guidelines for, 396
    targets for, 269
French civil code, 429
Fresnel lens, 117
Fuel leak, 213
Future behavior, best predictor of, 509
Fuzzy logic, 171

G

Gambling, 4
GANs, *see* Global area networks
Garages, CCTV cameras placed in, 203
Gatehouse, construction of, 200
Gate post design, 72
General Services Administration (GSA), 115, 149, 381, 382, 383
Glare, 328
Glass break
    sensors, 120, 121
    technology, devices combining PIR with, 123
Global area networks (GANs), 163
Government
    agencies, interagency support agreements of, 225
    UL standards and, 113
Graffiti, 370
Grand jury, indictment returned by, 394
Graphic image, encoding of, 248
Graphic user interfaces (GUIs), 257
Gregory v. Litton, 449
Griggs v. Duke Power Company, 449
Ground rules, examples of, 385
GSA, *see* General Services Administration
Guard(s), 190
    average cost of one, 160
    company, 10
    contract, 442
Guilt, admission of, 501
GUIs, *see* Graphic user interfaces

H

Hacker attacks, 300
Hand geometry, 167, 190
Harassing phone calls, 508
Harassment, workplace, 505
Hard drives, 260
Hardware
    data storage, 295
    failure rates, 289
    removal of computing, 283
    theft of, 270
Hazard material (HAZMAT), 230
    incident, 213
    plan, 231
    response plan, 214

HAZMAT, *see* Hazard material
Health law, 431
Heating and ventilation controls, activation of when PIR is triggered, 118
Help desk
  functions, 282, 283
  logging of activity by, 283
HID, *see* High-intensity discharge
High-frequency/low-impact (H/L) threat, 290, 291
High-intensity discharge (HID), 329, 332
High–low threats, 292
High-rise buildings
  master systems, 97
  vulnerability of roof in, 61
High-security cylinder
  Emhart, 84
  Medeco, 84
Highway median barrier, concrete, 76
Hijacked truck, 46
H/L threat, *see* High-frequency/low-impact threat
Hollerith readers, 196
Homicide, 505, 507, 508
Horizontal sliding windows, 65
Hostage contingency plan, 520
Human problems, 3
Human relations techniques, 457
Human resources
  database, 164
  manager, 284
Human threats, 213
Hurricane, 212, 213, 384
HVAC monitoring, 191
Hydraulic impact barriers, 77
Hyper HAD, 336

I

IC, *see* Integrated circuit
ICC, *see* Interstate Commerce Commission
Identification verification, types of, 190
IESNA, *see* Illuminating Engineers Society of North America
IFPs, *see* Intelligent field panels
Illuminance, measurement of, 325
Illuminating Engineers Society of North America (IESNA), 337, 369
Implied contract, 435
Imprisonment, false, 314
IMT, *see* Incident Management Team
Incident
  assessment/resolution process, 530
  chronology, 516

Management Team (IMT), 506, 512
monitoring, 523
stages of, 212
tracking, multi-jurisdiction, 514
Indictment, 394
Indirect costs, 30
Industrial buildings, design considerations for, 373
Industrial disaster, 20, 21
Industrial enterprise, hazards faced by, 2
Industrial espionage, 20, 359, 418
Industrial pedestrian door, penetration times for standard, 63
Industrial revolution, 2
Information
  gathering, 462
  proprietary, 420
  public sources of, 312
  sources, 517–518
    co-worker interview, 518
    disciplinary actions, 517
    employment application, 517
    employment evaluations, 517
    medical information, 517–518
  systems (IS), 247
    early, 259
    hardware for, 260
    multi-tier, scalability, 267
    obsolete, 295
    operations, 252
    parts of, 252
  systems security program (ISSP), 279
    management, aspects of, 280
    statements, kinds of, 286
  Technology (IT), 247
  theft of, 269
  ways to evaluate, 491
Information systems security, 279–302
  audit trails and transaction logs, 297-297–299
    audit trail integrity, 298
    operational use of audit trails, 298–299
  classes of computers, 255–258
    laptop computers, 258
    mainframe computers, 255–256
    minicomputers, 256
    personal computers, 256–258
  definition of information systems security, 269
  encoding digital data, 247–248
  evolution of information system risks, 270–273
    batch system risks, 270–271

Index

distributed systems, 273
Internet risks, 272
local and wide area network risks, 272
online information systems risks, 271
evolution of information systems, 258–268
   batch processing mainframe systems, 258–260
   distributed, three-tier information systems, 267–268
   Internet, 265–267
   local area networks, 262–264
   online information processing systems, 260–262
   wide area networks, 264–265
functional definition of information systems security, 274–276
impact of large-scale integration, 251–252
importance of information systems security, 269–270
information systems security policies, procedures and standards, 285–287
   documentation and distribution, 287
   procedures, 287
   standards, 286–287
Internet, 299–301
   confidentiality and authentication, 299
   hacker attacks, 300–301
   making wise use of, 301
   reliability and response time, 299–300
   using value-added network, 300
management of information systems security, 273–274
operating and user controls, 295–297
   personnel reassignment or termination, 296–297
   staffing, 296
processing digital data, 248–249
program management, 287–293
   how to address low–high risks, 292
   reasons for adopting security measure, 292
   reducing magnitude of high single occurrence losses, 293
   risk assessment techniques, 288–289
   spectrum of expected losses, 290
   spectrum of risk management actions, 291
   threat occurrence rate estimates, 289–290
   why cost-benefit-based risk management often fails, 291–292
   reducing occurrence rate of high single occurrence losses, 293
roles and responsibilities, 279–285
   information systems operational management, 281–283
   program management, 280–281
   senior management, 280
   supporting functions, 283–285
   users, 285
security and planning, 293–295
   development and acquisition, 294–295
   disposal, 295
   implementation, 295
   initiation, 294
   operation and maintenance, 295
typical central processing unit, 249–251
typical information system, 252–255
   activity monitoring, 254–255
   application programs, 253
   computer and network hardware, 253
   computer system software, 253
   operating procedures, 253–254
   operating staff, 253
   physical facilities, 253
   user training, 254
Infrared (IR)
   energy, 116, 118
   light source, 336
Initial report, 315
Injury prevention, 218
Input
   devices, examples of, 166
   /output ports, 250
Inspection authorities, UL standards and, 113
Insurance
   cost of, 43
   coverage, availability of for losses, 32
   industry, UL standards and, 113
   management, 454
   transfer of risk by obtaining, 293
Insured losses, 24
Integrated circuit (IC), 197
Integrated systems, 153
Intel Corporation, 257
Intellectual property, 2, 4
Intelligence, covert penetration of a target in, 55
Intelligent detection devices, 132

543

Intelligent devices, 133
Intelligent field panels (IFPs), 163
Intentional tort of false imprisonment, 445
Interagency Security Committee, 381
Internal investigative capability
    advantages of, 308
    disadvantages of, 309
Internet
    attractive features of, 299
    investigative resources, 319–320
    risks, 272
    Service Providers (ISPs), 265, 299
        investments, 300
        ISP access to other, 300
Interoffice mail, security of, 377
Interrogation, Reid nine steps of, 499
Interstate Commerce Commission (ICC), 431, 432
Interview
    company personnel selected for, 521
    participants, training of, 520
    site, securing of, 515
    technique, accuracy of, 496
Intimidation, 403
Intruder
    detection of, 154
    potential, 55
Intrusion
    alarms, 44, 168
    decoder, 249
    detection systems, 11, 112, 333, 382
Invasion of privacy, 446
Inventory
    theft, effect of security program on, 44
    variance, 46
Investigations, general comments, 303–323
    Internet investigative resources, 319–320
    investigative reports, 314–318
        parts of report, 315–318
        report distribution, 318
        types of reports, 314–315
    legal guidelines, 312–314
        civil and criminal suits and actions, 313–314
        local licensing statutes, 313
    public- and private-sector investigations, 303–304
    qualities of effective investigation, 305–312
        accuracy, 306–307
        cost elements, 309–310
        investigative resources, 308–309
        objectivity, 305–305
        online investigations, 312
        relevance, 306
        sources of information, 310–312
        thoroughness, 306
        timeliness, 307–308
    summary of rights under Fair Credit Reporting Act, 320–322
    summary of rights as prescribed by Federal Trade Commission, 320
Investigators
    contract, 309
    local licensing statutes for, 313
    proprietary, 309
Ionization sensor, 138
IR, *see* Infrared
IS, *see* Information systems
ISPs, *see* Internet Service Providers
ISSP, *see* Information systems security program
Issue-specific policy, 286
IT, *see* Information Technology

J

Jalousie windows, 65
Jewelry vaults, commercial, 157
Jingle keys, 94
Joint venture employees, access to information by, 1
Justification, example of, 403

K

Keys
    jingle, 94
    try, 94
Keystroke errors, 289
Keyway, picking of tumblers through, 93
Kickbacks, 21
Kidnapping, 508
Knowledge
    question, 498
    worker, 457

L

Labor
    arbitrators, 425
    disputes, 370
Lamp
    efficacy, 331
    starting and re-strike times, 332
    technology, 329
Landscaping
    CPTED guidelines for, 368

Index

trespassing and, 365
use of to create crime prevention measures, 366
LANs, *see* Local area networks
Laptop computers, 258
Larceny, 400, 401
Large Scale Integration (LSI), 251
Latch, electric, 101, 102
Latchbolt, 100
Law(s)
  business, 431
  civil rights, 431
  civil statute, 433
  contract, 434
  doubtful, 399
  education, 431
  enforcement
    liaison, 518
    protection organization headed by individual from, 459
    requirement to success of, 195
  federal criminal, 390
  health, 431
  loopholes in, 413
  personal property, 431
  state, 416
Law Enforcement Assistance Administration (LEAA), 345
LCD, *see* Liquid crystal
LEAA, *see* Law Enforcement Assistance Administration
LEDs, *see* Light-emitting diodes
Legally privileged communications, 485
Lever
  lock, 81, 90
  tumblers, 82
Leverage, principle of, 38
L/H threat, *see* Low-frequency/high-impact threat
Liability
  limitations of, 439
  vicarious, 443
Liars, sophisticated, 493
Libel, 313
Lie detector, 417, 420
Life-cycle costing, 371
Life safety code requirements, 379
Light
  -emitting diodes (LEDs), 207, 252
  levels, 326
  source, infrared, 336
Lighting
  ground, 333
  installations, 330
  levels, guidelines for minimum, 338
  loading docks, 334
  parking structures, 333
  security perceptions and, 335
Liquid crystal (LCD), 133
Loading docks, lighting of, 334
Local alarm(s)
  advantages and disadvantages of, 154
  termination, 153
Local area networks (LANs), 133, 163, 262
  file server, installation of, 264
  linking of low-traffic, 264
  risks associated with, 272
  security weakness, 263
  workstations, user programs on, 263
Local building codes, 70
Lock(s), 405
  classes of, 79
  combination
    dial-type, 86
    electronic dial-type, 89
    number of tumblers in, 88
    theoretical maximum number of combinations, 88
  cylinder, 90, 98
  door, 97
  electromagnetic, 106, 108, 109 189
  fail secure, 101
  high-security, 382
  lever, 81, 90
  mechanical, 79
    fail safe, 100
    rearrangement of, 94
  mortise, 98, 99
  pin tumbler, 81, 83
    cylinder, 85
    enhancing security in, 84
    innovations in security, 94
    master keying, 90
    with multiple tumbler axes, 86
  push-button, 187, 205
  rotation of existing, 95
  Schlage mortise, 98
  shear, 108, 109
  stairtower, 103, 104
  wafer
    master keying, 90
    tumbler, 84
  warded, 80
Locking concepts, 79–110
  basic lock grouping, 79–89
    dial-type combination locks, 86–89
    electronic dial-type combination lock, 89

545

lever lock, 81
   pin tumbler lock, 81–84
   wafer tumbler lock, 84–86
   warded lock, 80–81
electrified locking mechanisms, 100–109
   electric deadbolt, 101
   electric latch, 101–102
   electric lockset, 104–106
   electric strike, 102–103
   electromagnetic lock, 106–109
   exit device, 106
master keying mechanical locks, 89–91
   lever lock, 90
   pin tumbler lock, 90–91
   wafer lock, 90
security vulnerabilities of mechanical locks, 92–100
   attack by force, 92
   door locks, 97–100
   rearranging mechanical locks, 94–97
   surreptitious attack, 93–94
Lockset
   electric, 104, 105
   storeroom function, 98
Loop detector, 201
Loss
   avoidance formulas, most valuable application of, 45
   control
      cost avoidance in, 43
      optimizing of, 218
   impact, measurement of, 29
   insured, 24
   occurrence of on weekends, 61
   potentials, inherent, 288
   prediction of, 45
   prevention, 5, 453
   spectrum of expected, 290
   total, calculated, 44
Loss event(s)
   criticality, 19, 29–34
      concept, 29–30
      cost abatement, 32
      cost-of-loss formula, 32–33
      criticality ratings, 33–34
      kinds of costs, 30–32
      rating symbols, 34
   historical information about, 24
   occurrence of, 38
      measurement of, 21probability, 19
      physical environment factors, 23
      political environment factors, 23
      social environment factors, 23
   profile, 19

Lotus 1-2-3, 257
Low explosives, 74
Low-frequency/high-impact (L/H) threat, 290, 291
LSI, see Large Scale Integration
Luminaire, 329
Lying, 491

M

Machine tools, damage to, 232
Macroeconomics, 1
Magnetic ink character readers (MICR), 196
Magnetic locks, 108
Magnetic stripe cards, 193
Magnetic switch(es), 124, 190
   options, 124
   parts, 125
Magnetic tapes, storage of data on, 259
Mail
   interoffice, security of, 377
   screening of using x-ray machines, 206
Mainframe computers, 255, 258
Main memory, 249
Management Information Systems (MIS), 247
Mantrap, 167, 168, 199
Manufacturing costs, 20
Marijuana, 456
Market
   demand, 20
   share, 1
Mass casualty situation, 228
Master key
   applications, lever tumblers and, 82
   operation of, 87
Master keying, 81
   defense of, 89
   lever lock,
   pin tumbler
      cylinder, 91
      lock, 90
   wafer lock,
Master system(s)
   high-rise office building, 97
   taking lock off, 95
Mechanical locks, 79
   rearrangement of, 94
   security vulnerabilities of, 92
Mechanical surveillance tools, 369
Mechanical switches, 124
Medeco high-security cylinder, 84
Memory
   CPU, 251

failure, deceiver development of, 493
main, 249
programmable, 197
selective, 493
Metal detectors
pass through rate of, 207
types of, 206
MICR, *see* Magnetic ink character readers
Microphones
contact, 415
wireless, 415
Microsoft NT, 262
Microwave sensors, 127
Military law enforcement, protection function equated with, 453
Military munitions, high-explosive, 74
Military-sensitive cryptography, 299
Minicomputers, 256
Miranda v. Arizona, 409, 410
MIS, *see* Management Information Systems
Misdemeanor, 391
Misinformation, correction of, 486
Misrepresentation, 446
Missiles, wall thickness required to protect against, 75
Money laundering, 7, 396, 419
Moral codes, 469
Moral justifications, 499
Morris worm attack, 300
Mortise lock, 98, 99
MS-DOS, 253
Muggings, 361
Multiprocessing computer hardware, 253
Multi-tier information systems, scalability, 267
Murder
attempted, 392
cost of doing business driven up by, 359
Murrah Federal Office Building, bombing of, 381
Mutual aid association, 225

N

National Burglar and Fire Alarm Association (NBFAA), 111
National Crime Prevention Institute (NCPI), 346
National Crime Victimization Studies, 505
National Fire Protection Association (NFPA), 115, 229, 240
National Industrial Security Program Operating Manual (NISPOM), 240
National Labor Relations Board, 425
Natural access control, 357, 384
Natural catastrophes, 3, 20, 21
Natural disasters, 12
Natural guardians, visibility of, 352
Natural light levels, 326
Natural surveillance, 343, 353, 357
Natural threats, 213
NBFAA, *see* National Burglar and Fire Alarm Association
NCPI, *see* National Crime Prevention Institute
Negligence, 445, 447
Neighborhood
crime patterns, 363
Watch, 343
Network
abuse, 4
Access Points, 267
hardware, fragility of, 270
interface card (NIC), 262
operating systems (NOS), 262
reliability, 301
value-added, 300
New Jersey Bounce, 76
News Group posting, 301
NFPA, *see* National Fire Protection Association
NIC, *see* Network interface card
NISPOM, *see* National Industrial Security Program Operating Manual
Nitroglycerin, 74
Noncompliant behavior, excuses of, 352
NOS, *see* Network operating systems
Novell NetWare, 262
NRC, *see* Nuclear Regulatory Commission
Nuclear Regulatory Commission (NRC), 8, 329, 333, 337

O

Objections
factual, 500
trait, 500
Occupant emergency plan (OEP), 214
OCR, *see* Optical character readers
OECD, *see* Organization for Economic Cooperation and Development
OEP, *see* Occupant emergency plan
Offenders, emotionally driven, 509
Offense, 391
Office buildings, design considerations for, 374
Off-the-shelf software packages, 171

O.J. Simpson, 395
Oklahoma City bombing, 381
OMC, *see* Optical Memory Card
Online information processing systems, 260, 261
Operating system (OS), 260
    common, 253
    network, 262
Optical character readers (OCR), 196–197
Optical fiber circuits, 201
Optical Memory Card (OMC), 197
Optical passage, 188
Oral confession, 501
Organization(s)
    attacks on, 270
    bomb incident plan, 231
    countermeasure adopted by, 5
    emergency success lists in, 221
    example of poor results from improper, 454
    hazards faced by, 3
    HAZMAT plan, 231
    mission of, 288
    planning, 211
    policy of for protection of information systems, 280
    priorities, 217
    protection
        management rules, 464
        staffing of, 458
    risk managers of for-profit, 284
    security breach, 276
    theory, 461
    welfare, requirement to success of, 195
Organization for Economic Cooperation and Development (OECD), 7, 398
Organized crime, 23
Organized labor contracts, 303
OS, *see* Operating system
OSHA, 329
Output devices, examples of, 166

P

Panic bar, 106
Parking structures
    cash collection in, 369
    CCTV cameras placed in, 203
    lighting of, 333
    security design criteria for, 367
Parole, 398
Passive barriers, 349
Passive infrared (PIR)
    design, 117

detection patterns, 120
devices combining glass break technology with, 123
motion detectors, 202
quad element pyros, 119
sensors, 116
Password(s)
    encryption, 281
    failure to disable, 281
    token-based one-time, 299
Patrol personnel, supervision of, 160
PCs, *see* Personal computers
Pedestrian passageway, 188
Penal Law, New York, 391
Penetration
    probability, determination of predictable, 192
    types of, 55
Perimeter intrusion detection systems, 333
Personal computers (PCs), 163, 204, 256
    business use of, 257
    clones, 257
Personal gain, 482
Personal grudge, 21
Personal identification number (PIN), 161, 165, 197, 299
Personal property law, 431
Personal references, 307
Personnel
    common sources of internal data about, 310, 311
    control, 165
    doorways, 62
    patrol, 160
    protection, supervision of, 170
    reassignment, 296
    reductions, closed-circuit TV and, 161
    selection, 296
    termination, 296
Photoelectric cell, 129
Photoelectric devices, extremes of weather affecting, 129
Photosensors, 329
Physical barriers, categories, 56
Picture windows, 65
Pilferage, 22
PIN, *see* Personal identification number
Pin tumbler(s)
    cylinder(s)
        force used on, 92
        lock, 85, 96
        master keying of, 91
    lock(s), 81, 83
        enhancing security in, 84

master keying, 90
   security, innovations in, 94
   manipulation, techniques for defeating, 93
   operations, modification of conventional, 93
   parts of, 83
PIR, *see* Passive infrared
Planning liaison, 223
Plastic explosive, C-4, 209
Points of Presence (POP), 265–266
Police
   patrol patterns, 363
   relations, 23
Policy
   definition of, 285
   documentation of, 287
   issue-specific, 286
   program, 286
   system-specific, 286
Polygraph, 417
   evidence, 425
   license, 423
   results, 424
   simulated use of, 418
   technique, accuracy of, 497
   test, 420, 421
POP, *see* Points of Presence
Positive confrontation, 499
Post-disaster restoration, 241, 244
Post-employment background investigations, 484
Power
   continuous, 173, 175, 176
   emergency, 172
   outage, 213
   standby, 172, 174, 176
   supplies, monitoring of status of, 176
   transfer devices, 105
Pre-alarms, 132
Pre-employment
   background investigations, 484
   investigations, 13, 307
   screening, 506, 509
Prejudice, 482
   freedom from, 477
   identification of personal, 305
Preponderance of evidence, guilt by, 395
Pressure mates, 125
Privacy
   invasion of, 446
   security versus, 366
Private investigators, licensing of, 431

Private security programs, parallel development of law enforcement and, 2
Privileged information, confidentiality of, 485
Probability
   data matrix, 54
   ratings
      highly probable, 27, 29
      improbable, 28, 29
      moderately probable, 27, 29
      numerical statements, 34
      probability unknown, 28, 29
      virtually certain, 27, 29
Probation, 398
Problem(s)
   catastrophic, 3, 4
   emotional, 4
   human, 3
   total, comprehensive solution to, 8
Procedures, documentation of, 287
Professional censure, 487
Professional code, means for enforcing, 471
Professional conduct, ASIS rules of, 473–475
Professional ethics
   aim of, 475
   definition of, 469
   need for, 469
Professional regulation, obligation of, 470
Program instruction bytes, storage of, 249
Progress report, 315
Projected windows, 65
Proper constituted authority
   police as, 482
   reporting to, 483
Property
   crimes against, 21
   crimes based upon damage to, 405
   greatest destroyer of, 228
   internal sources of information about, 311
Proprietary alarm termination, 159
Proprietary information, 2, 420
Proprietary investigators, 309
Prosecution, standards for, 303
Protection
   activity, establishment of, 455
   of assets field, required skills sets in, 3
   executive, reporting level of top, 460
   of life, principles applied, 217–218
   organization
      management rules, 464
      staffing of, 458
   personnel, supervision of, 170

549

Protective lighting, *see* Security and
  protective lighting
Proximity/contact readers, 194
Psychological deterrent, 154
Psychological evaluation, 521
Psychological ownership, 343
Psychological stress evaluator, 417
Public emergency services personnel, 524
Public housing, CPTED in, 350
Public key cryptography, 299
Punched card readers, 258
Punitive award of damages, 447
Pure risk
  definition of, 357
  loss events, 20, 21
Purpose question, 497
Push-button locks, 187, 205

Q

Qualified privilege, doctrine of, 313
Quasi-judiciary powers, 432
Question
  knowledge, 498
  purpose, 497
  suspicion, 498
  vouch, 498
  you, 498

R

Radio frequency interference (RFI), 118
Random access storage devices, 260
Rape, 359, 370, 508
Rate-of-rise sensors, 136
Rational choice, 348
Real-time processing, 271
Real-time systems, exposure of to
  catastrophic failure, 273
Reasonable belief, 404, 405
Reasonable cause, 407, 408
Reasonable value, 436
Reception desks, overlooked feature of, 380
Reduced instruction set chip, 251
Reflectance, measure of, 326, 327
Rehabilitation Act of 1973, 450
Relevant data, definition of, 516
Remote surveillance, 296
Report
  distribution, 318
  final, 315
  initial, 315
  parts of, 315
  progress, 315

special, 315
Responses, types of, 491
Restoration procedures, 232
Restraining order, violation of, 508
Restricted-access software, 90
Restricted zones, 365
Retinal patterns, 190, 195
Retinal scans, 167
Return on expenditures (ROE), 46, 47
Revenge, acts of, 21
RFI, *see* Radio frequency interference
Rioting, 4, 21, 359
Risk(s)
  acceptance, 358
  alternatives for handling, 358
  assessment techniques, 288
  avoidance, 358
  business, 20
  conventional, 20
  disbursement, 293
  dynamic, definition of, 357
  high–low, 292
  management
    functions of, 42
    loss prevention and, 32
    steps, 357
  pure
    definition of, 357
    events, 20
  ranking of, 35
  reduction, 358
  segregation of, 28
  spreading, 358
  threat logic pattern, 36
  transfer, 358
Robbery, 370, 401, 508
ROE, *see* Return on expenditures
Roofs, vulnerability of, 57
Rules of Professional Conduct, ASIS,
  473–475, 476, 483

S

Sabotage, 4, 21, 507
  occurrence of, 38
  software, 271
Safe deposit service, 438
Salami swindle, 269
Sally port, operational requirements for, 200
Sandia Laboratories, 115
San Francisco earthquake, 4
Sargent Maximum Security System, 84
Satellite telephone, 222
Scatterplot, vulnerability/criticality, 34, 35

Schlage mortise lock, 98
School campuses, card functions required of, 203
SCIF, *see* Sensitive Compartmented Intelligence Facility
Screen detectors, 125
Search warrant, 407
Security
  breaches, investigation of suspected, 283
  costs, quantified, 47
  countermeasure(s)
    financial consequences, 45
    planning of, 20
  deliberations involving, 484
  design, challenges of, 363
  economic justification of, 42
  exercises, 235
  failures, cost impact of, 285
  intercom, 202
  justification, avoidance approach for, 43
  loss events, predicting probability of, 22
  management, unprofessional, 274
  manpower, 377
  measure, definition of, 287
  officers
    inspection duties of, 14
    uniformed, 13
  perceptions, lighting and, 335
  privacy versus, 366
  professionals, credibility of, 29
  program, objective of, 274
  resourcing, optimum, 40
  sensors, categories of, 113
  service personnel, contract, 10
  staff, compensation for, 460
  system(s), *see also* System considerations
    automated, 163
    costs, 165
    levels of reliability in, 41
  terms, glossary of, 177–182
  window film, 66
Security as management function, 453–467
  communications, 458
  definition of responsibilities, 454–455
  development of organization, 453–454
  program implementation, 455–458
    involvement of others, 457
    top management responsibility, 455–457
  program management, 461–464
    delegation, 463
    internal and external relationships, 463–464
    planning, 461–462
    training, 462–463
  staffing of protection organization, 458–461
    compensation, 460
    reporting level, 460–461
Security and protective lighting, 325–340
  lighting economics, 329–332
  lighting and lighting definitions, 325–328
  lighting systems, 329
  security lighting applications, 333–335
    building facade, 333
    guard and gate houses, 334
    loading docks, 334
    open parking, 334
    parking structures, 333–334
    perimeter fencing, 333
    security control and monitoring rooms, 334
    site landscape and perimeter approaches, 333
  security lighting and closed-circuit video systems, 336–337
  standards for security lighting levels, 337–338
  starting and re-strike, 332
Security vulnerability, 19–54
  alternative approaches to criticality, 34–36
  basic matrix, 54
  basic security survey, 48–53
    controls, 53
    fire and disaster, 52
    geography and climate, 48–49
    indemnity, 53
    internal activity, 51
    physical safeguards, 52
    size and configuration, 49–50
    social and political environment, 50–41
  defining problem, 19
  economic justification of security, 42–48
    asset recoveries, 46
    cost avoidance in loss control, 43–45
    measuring return on expenditures, 46–48
  loss event criticality, 29–34
    cost abatement, 32
    cost-of-loss formula, 32–33
    criticality concept, 29–30
    criticality ratings, 33–34

551

kinds of costs to be considered, 30–32
rating symbols, 34
loss event probability or frequency, 21–28
   application of probability factors analyses, 25–26
   checklists, 26
   historical experience, 24–25
   probability factors, 23
   probability ratings, 27–28
   rating symbols, 28
   risk matrix, 26–27
loss event profile, 19–21
network design, 38
problem solving, 38–41
   countermeasures, 38–40
   keeping system current, 41–42
   risk management, 42
   systems evaluation technique, 40–41
solution preparation, 36–38
   leverage, 37–38
   threat analysis, 36–37
statement of in monetary terms, 29
Seismic shock frequencies, 120
Selective memory, 493
Self-insurance, 24
Sensitive Compartmented Intelligence Facility (SCIF), 61
Sensor(s)
   acoustic, 121, 122
   application and evaluation of, 112
   audio, 128
   balanced pressure, 130
   capacitance, 128
   categories of, 113, 116
   chemical, 131
   combinations of, 131, 132
   combustion product, 136
   dual-technology, 123
   electromechanical, 123
   electronic, integration of, 158
   fire, factors to consider when selecting, 135
   fixed-temperature, 135
   glass break, 120, 121
   ionization, 138
   microwave, 127
   monitoring of, 170
   passive infrared, 116
   photoelectric, 129
   rate-of-rise, 136
   selection, 134
   shock, 122

   ultrasonic, 126, 127
   vibration, 128
   water flow, 139
Server
   authentication, 273
   file
      access to data on, 262
      LAN, 264
      messages broadcast on, 264
Severe weather, 213
Sexual harassment, 4
Shear lock, 108, 109
Shock sensors, 122
Shoplifters, apprehending alleged, 402
Shoplifting
   cost of doing business driven up by, 359
   surveillance, 386
Shoulder-surfing, 167
Sick leave, 507
Signaling line circuit (SLC), 133
Signature analysis, 167
Single occurrence loss (SOL), 275, 276, 292, 293
Situational crime prevention, 347, 350
Slander, 313, 445
SLC, see Signaling line circuit
Slip and fall accident potential, 368
Small Business Administration, 62
Smart card, 197–198
   encryption, 198
   programmable memory, 197
Smart detection devices, 132
Smart telephones, 229
Smart terminals, 263
Smoke detector, 132
Software
   development of custom, 171
   encryption, 294
   houses, 253
   off-the-shelf, 171
   restricted-access, 90
   sabotage, 271
   system, 281
SOL, see Single occurrence loss
Source illumination, wavelength of, 336
Special report, 315
Speed bumps, 370
Spreadsheet programs, 257
Stairtower lock, 103, 104
Stalking, 508
Standard Accident Insurance Co. v. Roberts, 433
Standards, documentation of, 287
Standby power, 172, 174, 176

Index

State
　crimes, definition of, 391
　law, 389
　sovereignty, 430
Statute violation, 313
Stealth, barrier penetrated by, 55
Stipulation, definition of, 424
Stockholder's suit, 6
Stored program computing, 249
Storeroom function lockset, 98
Street crime, 344, 347
Strength-of-field readers, 193
Strike, electric, 102, 103
Structural barriers, 55–77
　bomb protection, 70–75
　building openings, 62–70
　　concrete block barriers, 67–70
　　doorways, 62–64
　　other openings, 66–67
　　windows, 65–66
　building surfaces, 57–60
　　ceilings, 60
　　concrete structures, 58
　　exterior walls, 57
　　floors, 58
　　interior walls, 58–60
　　roofs, 57
　categories, 56–57
　evaluation of building surfaces, 60–61
　vehicle barriers, 75–77
Subpoena, 311, 434
Substance abuse, 3
Sun, natural lighting provided by, 325
Surveillance
　CCTV, 385
　concerns about, 525
　covert, 336
　electronic, 413
　natural, 343, 353, 357
　remote, 296
　shoplifting, 386
　strategies, organized, 362
　tools, mechanical, 369
Suspicion question, 498
Suspicious events, investigation of, 280
Switch(es)
　biased, 125
　magnetic, 124, 190
　　options, 124
　　parts, 125
　mechanical, 124
System(s), *see also* Information systems
　biometric, 167
　controllers, 131, 132
　digital, estimating cost of, 165
　elements, examples of, 164, 166
　evaluation technique, 40–41
　life cycle, 293
　outages, 269
　programmers, sharing of passwords by, 282
　software, 281
　-specific policy, 286
Systems considerations, 153–185
　alarm termination, 153–158
　　central station termination, 154–156
　　direct police or fire department termination, 156–157
　　local alarm termination, 153–154
　　proprietary termination, 157–158
　　termination combinations, 158
　automated security system, 163–172
　　centrally controlled systems, 163–164
　　control center, 164, 172
　　costs, 165
　　other security system tasks, 170–171
　　personnel control, 165–170
　　programming of system, 171
　　system expansion and flexibility, 172
　　systems computer applications, 164
　cost reduction and protection improvement, 158–162
　　closed-circuit TV and personnel reductions, 161–162
　　patrol reduction, 160–161
　　protection enhancement, 160
　emergency power, 172–176
　　continuous power, 173–176
　　standby power, 172–173
　glossary of fire terms, 182–185
　glossary of security terms, 177–181
　systems design, 158

T

T&A control, *see* Time and attendance control
Tailgating, 168
Tape-recorded statement, 501
Tape recorders, voice-activated, 415
Target
　availability, perception of, 349
　hardening, 342, 351, 362
Telecommunications failure plan, 214, 217
Telephone
　cellular, 131, 222
　circuits, protection of, 253

553

entry systems, 187, 188
satellite, 222
Temporary substitute cost, components of, 31
Temporary workers, access to information by, 1
Tennessee v. Garner, 404
Termination notice, 521
Territorial influence, perceived zones of, 353
Territorial messages, 370
Terrorism, 21, 290, 344
Terrorist(s)
   activity, 213
   bomb, 70
Theft
   crimes based upon, 400
   finished goods inventory, 37
   inventory, effect of security program on, 44
   occurrence of, 38
Thermostat, 135
Third-party negotiations, 479
Threat(s)
   accidental, 213
   assessment, 512, 523
   bomb, 4, 456
   earthquake, 290
   high-frequency/low-impact, 290
   high–low, 292
   human, 213
   laws criminalizing, 508
   low-frequency/high-impact, 290
   model, 36, 37, 38
   natural, 213
   occurrence rate estimates, 289
   types of, 213
   verbal, 507
   vulnerability of assets to, 288
   workplace, 505
   written, 507
Threat management, plan for, 505–530
   assessment phase, 514–526
      additional interviews, 515–516
      decision to interview offender, 518–519
      establishment of continuing communications, 524–525
      extensive background investigation of offender, 516–518
      extended security and incident monitoring, 523–524
      initial information collection by DMR, 514–515
      phased withdrawal of protective personnel, 525–526
      plan in event of termination, 521–523
      plan for situation reassessment, 525
      securing interview site and assessment personnel, 520
      summary assessment and plan for further action, 520–521
   concept of threat management, 506–507
   incident management process, 513–514
   incident management team and supporting resources, 512–513
   liability and legal considerations, 507–508
   minimum qualifications for outside consulting team members, 528–529
      additional legal support, 529
      licensed psychological or psychiatric professional, 529
      security and investigations professional, 528–529
   model policy for workplace threats and violence, 527–528
   normal incident assessment/resolution process, 530
   overview, 505–506
   physical security, 510–511
      access control, 510
      closed-circuit television, 511
      furniture and equipment configuration, 511
      lighting, 510
   policy statement and reporting procedure, 511–512
   pre-employment screening, 509–510
   psychological dynamic of workplace violence, 508–509
Thunderstorm, 213
Time and attendance (T&A) control, 171
Time-delayed egress door, 189
TNT, 74
Token-based one-time passwords, 299
Tornado, 213
Tort(s), 405, 429
   definition of, 445
   intentional, 445
   of negligence, 445
   of slander, 445
   willful, 445
Total loss, calculated, 44
Total problem, comprehensive solution to, 8
Touch card, 194
Touchpads, 187

Index

Trade associations, 480
Trade secret, definition of, 413
Traffic analysis, 168
Training exercises, 234, 235
Trait objections, 500
Transaction logs, 297
Trespassing, 365, 508
Try keys, 94
Tumblers, picking of through keyway, 93
Turnstiles, 169, 188
Two-man rule, 199

U

UL, *see* Underwriters Laboratories
Ultrasonic detector, range of, 126
Ultrasonic sensors, 126, 127
Unauthorized entry, crimes based upon, 400
Undercover investigative reports, 316
Underwriters Laboratories (UL), 113, 157, 189, 439
Uniform Criminal Extradition Act, 395
Uniformed security officers, 13
    approval, required, 114
    standards, 114
Uninterruptible power supply (UPS), 173, 329
United States Code (USC), 430
United States criminal law, *see* Criminal law, United States
UNIX, 253
Unjust compensation, 480
Unrestricted zones, 365
UPS, *see* Uninterruptible power supply
U.S. Attorney General, 414
USC, *see* United States Code
U.S. Congress, 412
U.S. Constitution, 389, 410, 478
U.S. Department of Defense, 197
User ID, failure to disable, 281
U.S. Government, restrictions on exporting of cryptography, 299
U.S. law, basic document for, 389
U.S. Postal Service, 405

V

Value-added network, 300
Vandalism, 507
    cost of doing business driven up by, 359
    form of, 370
    threat of, 368
Vandal-resistant materials, 371
Vapor trace analyzers, 131

Vault(s)
    door, time lock on, 61
    fire-resistant barriers for, 67
Veazey v. Communications and Cable of Chicago, Inc., 417
Vehicle
    barriers, 75, 76
    doorways, 62
    parking garages, 201
Verbal threat, 507
Very Early Smoke Detection Apparatus (VESDA), 138
VESDA, *see* Very Early Smoke Detection Apparatus
Vibration sensors, 128
Vicarious liability, 443
Victim
    apparent, 404
    intimidation of, 403
Video compression, 162
Video-recorded statement, 501
Video recorders, activation of when PIR is triggered, 118
Violence
    precursors to, 507
    workplace, 525
Violent offender, plan for removal of, 522
Visi-Calc, 257
Visual light levels, 326
Vital records, examples of, 224
Voiceprints, 167, 195
Voice stress analyzer, 417, 425, 426
Volcano, 213
Vouch question, 498
Vulnerability
    analysis, 9, 289
    assessment, 25, 28
    eliminating of common, 37
    perception of, 348
    prime, 36

W

Wafer tumbler cylinder, 87
Walk-through drills, 234
Wall(s)
    design criteria, concrete block, 73
    relative time required to penetrate, 59
    types of foundations used in construction of, 70
    vulnerability of, 57
WAN, *see* Wide area network
War, 20, 290
Warded lock, 80

555

Warning notices, 405
Warrant
   arrest, 407
   search, 407
Warranties, 437, 438
Warrantless arrests, 407
Water
   flow indicators, 135, 137
   outage, 213
Watermark magnetics, 193
Weapons
   brandishing dangerous, 508
   deadly, 480
   screening, 205
Weather disaster, 384
Web surfing, 301
Weigand cards, 194
Welfare organizations, requirement to success of, 195
Westinghouse CPTED model, 346, 354
White-collar crime, 350
Wide area network (WAN), 163, 264, 272
Willful torts, 445
Window(s), 253
   awning, 65
   casement, 65
   classes of, 65
   design of, 65
   double-hung, 65
   glass, ways of installing, 66
   horizontal sliding, 65
   jalousie, 65
   penetration times, comparative, 68–69
   picture, 65
   projected, 65
Wireless microphones, 415
Wire strain gauges, 125
Witnesses, conflicting data reported by, 306
Workers, motivation of, 457

Workplace
   accidents, 3
   assaults, 505
   harassment, 505
   homicide, 505
   obligation to provide safe, 528
   threats, 505
   violence, 12, 21, 525
      prevention of, 42
      program, union endorsement of, 512
      psychological dynamic of, 508
      /trauma plan, 214
      use of CPTED to address acts of, 344
Work slowdowns, 507
Worm attack, Morris, 300
Wrist proximity badges, 205
Write-once media, 298
Written confession, 502
Written threat, 507
Wrongdoing, evidence of, 393
Wrongful death charge, 395

X

X-ray machines, 208
   screening of baggage by, 205
   screening of mail by, 206

Y

You question, 498

Z

Zero tolerance, 511
Zones
   controlled, 365
   design goals, 365
   restricted, 365
   sensors grouped in, 111\